CRISIS IN
AMERICAN INSTITUTIONS

CRISIS IN
AMERICAN INSTITUTIONS

Third Edition

JEROME H. SKOLNICK
University of California
Berkeley

ELLIOTT CURRIE
University of California
Berkeley

LITTLE, BROWN AND COMPANY
Boston • Toronto

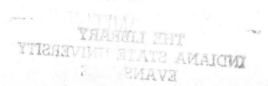

C̶I̶   MAR.   5 1979

PREFACE

Once again, in revising our last edition of *Crisis in American Institutions*, we have ended by producing what is practically a new book. Although the problems of American society are persistent and enduring, the amount of good writing about them varies widely — fortunately, it generally increases over time. In this revision we have tried to do two related things: to develop several new chapters dealing with areas of social life that are only now beginning to be investigated intensively, and to keep up with the most recent work in those areas we've already covered.

Accordingly, we've added chapters on the environment and the workplace, and expanded our chapter on welfare into a more comprehensive one on social services in general, including child care, housing, and problems of the aged. New chapters on capitalism and imperialism place our primary focus on the basic contours of the American economy, replacing our earlier chapter on corporate power with entirely new selections. And in two other areas — education and criminal justice — we have scaled down our coverage to make room for other issues. The result, we feel, is a more balanced and deeper analysis of American institutions. In addition, we have added new selections, and removed old ones, in every chapter. Again, over two-thirds of the selections are new to this edition.

We are always grateful to the authors whose articles we have selected. Each edition has offered us an opportunity to survey the literature on America and its social problems, and we increasingly find more good new material than size constraints permit reprinting. Once again, the Center for the Study of Law and Society, University of California, Berkeley, provided space, secretarial assistance, and a supportive environment. We are especially indebted to Wendy Rakocy who furnished some orderliness to what often threatened to be a chaotic enterprise. The two earlier editions of this book have been commented upon by numerous students and teachers. We are extremely grateful for such interest and we look forward to its continuation.

Jerome H. Skolnick
Elliott Currie

CONTENTS

SYSTEMIC PROBLEMS

INSTITUTIONS IN CRISIS

As a response to the social movements of the sixties, the United States has
developed an elaborate and wide-ranging system of political surveillance.

The most costly crimes — those committed by large corporations — are the
least punished.

Rhetoric about "treatment" of criminals masks the growing arbitrary
power of prison officials.

CRISIS IN
AMERICAN INSTITUTIONS

INTRODUCTION: APPROACHES TO SOCIAL PROBLEMS

Inflation. Unemployment. Energy crises. Soaring food prices. Bankrupt cities. Political corruption and business bribery as routine news items. As we move from 1970 toward 1980 it is no longer a secret that the American system is not working the way we were taught it should. When we first put this book together, in the late sixties, most people who wrote about "social problems" still thought of the United States as a society whose basic economic and political problems had been solved. It is hard to find anyone today who seriously believes that — even among professional social scientists. Opinion polls show that most Americans are increasingly dissatisfied and cynical about the major institutions that affect their lives. The important question is no longer *whether* American institutions are in crisis, but *why* — and what can be done about it.

The new mood among writers, in fact, is one of deep pessimism. Theorists are no longer trying to pretend that there are no real problems; instead, they are seeking the causes in "human nature" or people's genetic structure or the "population bomb." In the face of the deepening crisis of the seventies, many people — both the "experts" and the public — are losing faith in the possibilities of human cooperation, social equality, and personal fulfillment.

The new pessimism is, in fact, a direct outgrowth of the earlier exaggerated optimism. Both result from the traditional failure of American social science to confront directly the deeper, structural sources of American social problems. For the most part, social problems analysts have served to excuse and support the existing patterns of power and privilege in the United States — buoying them with a false optimism in good times, and deflecting concern onto our own (presumably in-

1

adequate) natures in harder times. The development of the field of "social problems" illustrates this process vividly.

DEFECTIVES AND DELINQUENTS

The earliest writers on social problems in this country were straightforward moralists, staunch supporters of the virtues of thrift, hard work, sexual purity, and personal discipline. Writing at the end of the nineteenth century, they sought ways of maintaining the values of an earlier, whiter, more Protestant, and more stable America in the face of the new challenges of industrialization, urbanization, and immigration.[1]

This early social science usually concentrated on the problems of what one nineteenth century textbook described as the "defective, dependent, and delinquent classes."[2] The causes of social problems were located in the physical constitution or the moral "character" of the poor, the criminal, the insane, and other "unfortunates." For these theorists, the solution to nineteenth century social problems lay in developing means of transforming the character of these "defective" classes, in the hope of equipping them better to succeed within a competitive, hierarchical society whose basic assumptions were never questioned. Social reformers working from these theories created, in the last part of the nineteenth and the first part of the twentieth centuries, much of the modern apparatus of "social control" in the United States: reformatories, modern prisons, and institutions for the mentally ill, and the beginnings of the modern welfare system.

THE RISE OF "VALUE-FREE" SOCIAL PROBLEMS

During the first decades of this century this straightforward moralism was increasingly discarded in favor of a more subtle, ostensibly "neutral" approach to writing about social problems. By the 1930s, the idea that the social sciences were — or could be — purely "objective" or "value-free" had come to be widely accepted. From this point until the present, social problems theory has been characterized by a tortuous attempt to prove that theories and policies which serve to support the status quo are actually scientific judgements arrived at objectively. In this view, social scientists do not try to impose their own values on others in deciding what kinds of things will be defined and dealt with as social problems. Instead, the "scientific" student of social problems simply accepts "society's" definition of what is a problem and what is not. This approach is apparent in these statements, taken from major textbooks, on what constitutes a social problem:

Any difficulty of misbehavior of a fairly large number of persons which we wish to remove or correct.[3]

What people think they are.[4]

Whenever people begin to say, isn't it awful! Why don't they do something about it?[5]

Conditions which affect sizable proportions of the population, which are out of harmony with the values of a significant segment of the population, and which people feel can be improved or eliminated.[6]

Any substantial discrepancy between socially shared standards and actual conditions of social life.[7]

These definitions share the common idea that social problems are popularly defined. No condition is a problem unless a certain number of people in a society say it is. Since we are merely taking, as our starting point, the definitions of the problem that "other people," "society," or "significant segments of the population" provide, we are no longer in the position of moralizing about objective conditions.

The basic flaw in this happy scheme is that it does not make clear *which* segments of the population to consult when defining problems, or how to decide between conflicting ideas about what is problematic and what is not. In the real world, societies are divided along class, racial, sexual, and other lines; often there is significant disagreement across those lines on social problems. The sociologist who proposes to follow "people's" definitions of social problems in fact generally adopts one of several competing ideologies of social problems. In practice the ideology thus adopted has usually been not too different from that of the "unscientific" social problems writers of the nineteenth century.

These points are not new; they were raised as early as 1936 in an unusually perceptive paper called "Social Problems and the Mores," by the sociologist Willard Waller. Waller noted, for example, that discussions of poverty in the social problems literature of the 1930s were shaped by the unquestioning acceptance of the ideology of competitive capitalism:

A simpleton would suggest that the remedy for poverty in the midst of plenty is to redistribute income. We reject this solution at once because it would interfere with the institution of private property, would destroy the incentive for thrift and hard work and disjoint the entire economic system.[8]

Waller's question is fundamental: what has been left out in a writer's choice of things he considered as problems? What features of society are going to be taken for granted as the framework *within* which problems will be defined and resolved? In this case, of course, the taken-for-granted framework is the principle of private property and individual competition. In general, Waller argued, "social problems are not solved because people do not want to solve them";[9] they *are* problems mainly because of people's unwillingness to alter the basic conditions from which they sprang. Thus:

. . . venereal disease becomes a social problem in that it arises from our family institutions and also in that the medical means which could be used to prevent it, which would unquestionably be fairly effective, cannot be employed for fear of altering the mores of chastity.[10]

For Waller the definition of *social problems* was, in the broadest sense, a "political" issue involving the opposed ideologies of conflicting groups. To Waller the important ideological conflict in the 1930s was that between the *humanitarian mores* — the values of the do-gooder and reformer — and the *organizational mores* — the "mores upon which the social order is founded, the mores of private property and individualism, the mores of the monogamous family, Christianity, and nationalism."[11]

Waller's points still ring true. In more recent treatments of social problems, the basic mores are rarely so explicitly acknowledged, but otherwise not much has changed. Most social problems writers in the United States still tacitly accept the basic structure of American society, and restrict their treatment of social problems to maladjustments *within* that structure.

Social Problems in the 1950s: Gradualism and Anticommunism

This is not to say that the literature on social problems since the 1930s is all the same. Books on social problems, not surprisingly, tend to reflect the preoccupations of the time when they were written. Those conceived in the 1950s, for example, reflect social and political concerns that now seem bizarre. The shadow of McCarthyism and the general national hysteria over the "Communist menace" pervade this literature. Consider the discussion of "civil liberties and subversion" in Paul B. Horton's and Gerald R. Leslie's textbook, *The Sociology of Social Problems.*[12] Horton and Leslie see the "American heritage of liberty" being attacked from both left and right, from both "monolithic communism" and overzealous attempts to defend "our" way of life from it. Their position is resolutely liberal and centrist. They claim a scientific objectivity; yet, they are quite capable of moral condemnation of people whose politics are "extreme," whether right or left:

Most extremists are deviants. Most extremists show a fanatical preoccupation with their cause, a suspicious distrust of other people in general, a disinterest in normal pursuits, recreations, and small talk, and a strong tendency to divide other people into enemies and allies.[13]

The preference for "normal pursuits," even "small talk," over social criticism and action was common in an age noted for its silent generation, but it is hardly "scientific." Among the other presumably objective features of the book are the authors' eight "rational proposals for preserving liberty and security," including these:

An adequate national defense is, needless to say, necessary in a world where an international revolutionary movement is joined to an aggressive major power. This is a military problem, not a sociological problem, and is not discussed here.

Counterespionage is essential. Highly trained professional agencies such as the FBI and the Central Intelligence Agency can do this efficiently and without endangering personal liberties of citizens. If headline-hunting congressmen, Legion officials, or other amateurs turn G-men, they merely scare off any real spies and destroy the counterespionage efforts of the professionals.[14]

The military and intelligence services themselves are not considered as problems relevant for social science. Questions about the operation of these agencies are viewed as internal and technical, military rather than sociological, issues.

In a section, "Questions and Projects," the authors ask: "How have conservatives or reactionaries sometimes given unintentional assistance to the Communists? How have liberals sometimes given unintentional assistance to the Communists?"[15]

In the introduction to their book, Horton and Leslie consider the possibilities of social change and the proper role of social scientists in promoting it. They carefully adopt a middle ground between conservatives to whom social problems are primarily problems of individual character and "extremists" hoping for sudden or radical changes in social structure. They argue that the resolution of social problems "nearly always involves sweeping institutional changes"; but also that such changes are "costly" and "difficult," and that therefore:

. . . it is unrealistic to expect that these problems will be solved easily or quickly. . . . Basic solutions of social problems will come slowly, if at all. Meanwhile, however, considerable amelioration or "improvement" may be possible.[16]

Social change, according to these authors, must be gradual and realistic; it must also be guided by experts. The authors insist that their own role, and that of social experts in general, is merely to show the public how to get what they already value. But in this role it is folly for the "layman" to question the expert. Horton and Leslie write that: "When experts are *agreed* upon the futility of one policy or the soundness of another, it is sheer stupidity for the layman to disagree."[17]

An elitist, cold-war liberalism and gradualism, a fear of extremism and of an international Communist conspiracy — all these are presented not as moral and political positions but as fundamental social scientific truths. The sturdy enterpreneurial and Protestant values described in Waller's paper of the 1930s give way, in Horton and Leslie's book of the 1950s, to a general preference for moderation, anticommunism, and "normal pursuits."

THE 1960s: AFFLUENCE AND OPTIMISM

A different imagery dominates the social problems literature of the next decade. Robert K. Merton's and Robert M. Nisbet's *Contemporary Social Problems*[18] is a product of the beginning of the 1960s, the period of the "New Frontier," which saw a significant shift, at least on the surface, in the focus of social concern. People were becoming aware of an "underdeveloped" world abroad and a "disadvantaged" world at home, both unhappily excluded from the benefits of an age of general "affluence" and well-being. New agencies of social improvement were created at home and abroad. A critique of old-style welfare efforts began to develop, along with the notion of "helping people help themselves," whether in Latin America, Harlem, or Appalachia. The idea of inclusion, of participation, in the American way of life became predominant. From a slightly different vantage, the idea emerged as development or modernization. The social problems of the 1960s were to be solved by extending the technological and intellectual resources of established American institutions into excluded, deprived, or underdeveloped places and groups. An intervention-minded government combined with an energetic social science on a scale unprecedented in this country.

In this period — very brief, as it turned out — social problems were often seen as problems of being *left out* of the American mainstream: "left behind," as the people of Appalachia were described; "traditional," like the Mexican-Americans; or "underdeveloped," like most Africans, Asians, and Latin Americans. In social problems theory, these ideas were manifested in a conservative ideology that celebrated American society as a whole, coupled with a liberal critique of the conditions hindering the extension of the American way to all.

One variant of this view is given in Nisbet's introduction to *Contemporary Social Problems*. For Nisbet social facts become problematic when they "represent interruptions in the expected or desired scheme of things; violations of the right or the proper, as a society defines these qualities; dislocations in the social patterns and relationships that a society cherishes."[19]

Nisbet's assessment of the American situation is in keeping with the exaggerated optimism of the early 1960s:

In America today we live in what is often called an affluent society. It is a society characterized by imposing command of physical resources, high standards of private consumption, effective maintenance of public order and security, freedom from most of the uncertainties of life that plagued our ancestors, and relatively high levels of humanitarianism. There are also, of course, squalid slums, both urban and rural; occasional epidemics of disease; sudden eruptions of violence or bigotry, even in the most civilized of communities; people for whom the struggle for food and shelter yet remains obsessing and precarious. Thus, we are not free of social problems, and some of them seem to grow almost in direct proportion to our affluence.[20]

Nisbet is aware that America has not yet solved all its problems; indeed, that some seem to come with the generally glittering package that is America in the twentieth century. Yet, the problems are viewed as peripheral, as occasional eruptions in the squalid backwaters of society where modern institutions have not fully penetrated.

Like earlier theorists, Nisbet sharply separates the role of the scientific student of social problems from that of other concerned people. The social scientist, as a scientist, should not engage in moral exhortation or political action, but should concentrate on understanding. At the same time, the scientist is:

. . . as interested as the next citizen in making the protection of society his first responsibility, in seeing society reach higher levels of moral decency, and, when necessary, in promoting such legal actions as are necessary in the short run for protection or decency.[21]

Here the scientific stance masks a preference for vaguely defined values — "societal protection" and "moral decency" — which in turn determine what will be selected as social problems. In this instance, problems are selected according to whether they offend the values of social stability — that is, values associated with the conservative tradition in social thought.

Thus, problems are repeatedly equated with "dislocations and deviations";[22] they are problems of "dissensus," as if consensus might not also be a problem. Indeed, the entire book is divided into two sections, one of which deals with "deviant behavior" and the other with "social disorganization." The articles in the text are not all of a piece. A paper by Robert S. Weiss and David Riesman on the problems of work takes a different view on what constitutes a problem; the authors declare that "social forms which tend toward the suppression or frustration of meaning and purpose in life are inferior forms, whether or not they tend toward disorganization."[23] But several papers simply accept the purposes of existing institutions and define problems in terms of combatting disorganization *within* those institutions. Perhaps the clearest illustration of this tendency appears in an essay by Morris Janowitz dealing with problems of the military establishment:

It is self-evident that the military establishment, the armed forces, and their administrative organizations have become and will remain important institutions of United States society. The distinctive forms of military organization must be analyzed in order to understand the typical sources of personal and social disorganization found in military life.[24]

The existence of a large military establishment is defined as outside the critical concern of the sociologist. The focus is not on the effect of the military or national or international life, but on the problems of maladjustment within the military apparatus. The increasing scope of military activities is noted but simply accepted as a fact of modern life:

The armed forces have also become involved in a wide variety of logistical, research, and training activities. In the current international scene, they must take on many politico-military duties, including military assistance of allied powers. . . .[25]

The implication is that the militarization of American society is not itself a problem for social analysis. Instead, the important problems of the military system, for Janowitz, are the individual and organizational problems connected with the need to maintain constant readiness under cold-war conditions.

The acceptance of the place of the military in American society leads to the enlistment of the resources of social science in the service of military ends. Thus, in discussing changes in the requirements of military discipline Janowitz notes that, in the 1960s, instead of employing "shock technique" to assimilate the recruit into the military, the problem had become how to foster "positive incentives and group loyalties through a team concept."[26] Janowitz doesn't ask *what* the recruit is being assimilated *into*. The effect of primary-group relations on morale under cold-war conditions is extensively discussed, but the cold war itself is not.

Robert Merton's epilogue to *Contemporary Social Problems,* called "Social Problems and Sociological Theory," represents a major attempt to give theoretical definition to the "field" of social problems. Merton distinguishes between "ordinary" conceptions of social problems and the "technical sense in which the sociologist employs the term."[27] He considers the "first and basic ingredient of a social problem" to be "any substantial discrepancy betweeen socially shared standards and actual conditions of social life."[28] Merton is well aware that different interests are present in society and therefore that definitions of social problems are likely to be contested — "one group's problem will be another group's asset" — and more specifically that "those occupying strategic positions of authority and power of course carry more weight than others in deciding social policy and so, among other things, in identifying for the rest what are to be taken as significant departures from social standards."[29]

According to Merton, however, this diversity of perspectives does not mean that sociologists must succumb to relativism or abandon their position as scientific students of society's problems. The way out of the dilemma is to distinguish between "manifest" and "latent" social problems — the latter are problems also "at odds with the values of the group" but not recognized as such. The task of the sociologist is to uncover the "latent" problems or unrecognized consequences of existing institutions and policies; in this way, "sociological inquiry does make men increasingly accountable for the outcome of their collective and institutionalized actions."[30]

The demand that social science make people accountable for their actions is a healthy departure from the false relativism of some earlier theorists. But the distinction between manifest and latent problems does not do what Merton claims for it: it does not make the choice of problems a technical or neutral one. Actually, Merton's approach is best seen as providing a rationale for evaluating and criticizing particular policies and structures within a presumably consensual society whose basic values and institutions are not seen as problematic.

We can easily agree with Merton that "to confine the study of social problems to only those circumstances that are expressly defined as problems in the society is arbitrarily to discard a complement of conditions that are also dysfunctional to values held by people in that society."[31] But what about those values themselves? Shouldn't they be examined and, if necessary, criticized? It seems obvious to us, for example, that it is part of the sociologist's task to study and criticize the values held by people in German society during the Nazi era, or by slaveholders in the antebellum American South, rather than to confine ourselves to studying those conditions that might be "dysfunctional" in terms of those values. To do otherwise amounts to an acceptance by default; the social scientist becomes an expert at handling problems within the confines of an assumed consensus on basic social goals and values.

The division of social problems into the two categories of *deviant behavior* and *social disorganization* reflects this acceptance, for both categories are defined as "disruptions" of an existing social order and do not question the adequacy of that social order itself. Thus:

Whereas social disorganization refers to faults in the arrangement and working of social statuses and roles, deviant behavior refers to conduct that departs significantly from the norms set for people in their social statuses.[32]

It is not, as some critics have suggested, that this kind of analysis suggests that whatever is, is right. But it does imply that whatever *disturbs* the existing social system is the primary problem.

The sociologists's "expert" judgment, of course, may conflict with what people themselves feel to be their problems, and if so, according to Merton, the expert should prevail. Merton argues that:

We cannot take for granted a reasonably correct public imagery of social problems; of their scale, distribution, causation, consequences and persistence or change. . . . Popular perceptions are no safe guide to the magnitude of a social problem.[33]

The corollary, presumably, is that the sociologist's imagery of social problems is at least "reasonably correct," even, perhaps, where segments of the public strongly object to having their problems defined, or redefined, for them. We seem back again to the same condescending attitude toward the public expressed by Horton and Leslie and other sociologists of the 1950s.

This kind of attitude wasn't, of course, confined to writers on social problems. It was a major theme in the social thought and government policy of the sixties, a decade characterized by an increasing detachment of governmental action from public knowledge and accountability — as exemplified in the growth of a vast intelligence apparatus, the repeated attempts to overthrow popularly elected governments overseas, and the whole conduct of the Vietnam War. This process was often excused on the ground that political decisions involved technical judgments that were out of the reach of ordinary people.

The conception of social problems as technical rather than moral and political issues was explicit in Merton's and Nisbet's text. Thus, Merton suggests that "the kind of problem that is dominated by social disorganization results from instrumental and technical flaws in the social system. The system comes to operate less efficiently than it realistically might. . . ."[34]

If the problems are technical ones, of course, then it is reasonable to view social scientists as technicians and to regard their intervention into social life as free from partisan

interest. It is this, apparently, that renders the social scientist
a responsible citizen rather than a "mere" social critic or
ideologue:

Under the philosophy intrinsic to the distinction between manifest
and latent social problems, the social scientist neither abdicates his
intellectual and professional responsibilities nor usurps the position
of sitting in judgment on his fellow men.[35]

It is apparent, however, that this kind of "philosophy" lends
itself all too easily to an alignment of expertise and profes-
sionalism with dominant values and interests masquerading as
societal consensus. This is apparent in the choice of topics
offered in most textbooks. Merton and Nisbet — whose widely
used textbook has gone through several editions — character-
istically deal with mental disorders, crime and delinquency,
drug use, alcoholism, suicide, sexual behavior, the population
crisis, race relations, family disorganization, work and automation, poverty, community disorganization, violence, and
youth and politics. The book does not deal with (to take some
examples from our own table of contents) corporate power,
imperialism, sexism, the schools, health care, the justice system and so on. The pattern of these differences is obvious:
Merton and Nisbet focus most heavily on those who have for
one reason or another failed to "make it" within the American
system — delinquents, criminals, the mentally ill, drug users
— and on disorganization *within* established institutions. Even
where individual authors in their book attempt to analyze
the system itself, the effort is usually relegated to a peripheral
or merely symbolic place.

In spite of its claim to political neutrality, the social science
of the 1960s typically focused on the symptoms of social ills,
rather than their sources; criminals, rather than the laws; the
mentally ill, rather than the quality of life; the culture of the
poor, rather than the crimes of the rich; the "pathology" of
students, rather than the crisis of education. What "socially
shared standards" dictate this choice of emphasis? In the introduction to a newer edition of *Contemporary Social Problems*, Professor Nisbet tries to answer this question. "It may
well be asked," he writes, "why these problems have been
chosen by the editors," rather than others, which "for some
persons at least might be regarded as even more pressing to
national policy."

The answer is that this is a textbook in sociology. Sociology is a
special science characterized by concepts and conclusions, which

are based on analysis and research, yielding in turn perspectives on society and its central problems. For many decades now, sociologists have worked carefully and patiently on these problems. In other words this book is concerned not only with the presentation of major social problems but with the scientific concepts and procedures by which these problems have been, and continue to be, studied.[36]

Nisbet seems to be explaining that these problems were selected by the editors because sociologists have studied them and not others in the past. Such an argument is hardly persuasive.

THE SEVENTIES: DEEPENING CRISIS AND DECLINE OF OPTIMISM

The social problems literature of the sixties — and the official policies that paralleled it — assumed that the problems of American society could be solved by piecemeal measures. If people could be given enough training, there would be no unemployment and no "social dynamite" in the ghettoes. If criminals and drug addicts could be "rehabilitated," there would be no more crime and social disintegration. This approach, like those before it, although giving considerable lip service to the idea that "society" was to blame for social problems, ultimately laid the burden of change on individuals. And when in the seventies things began to get worse instead of better, many social scientists could only conclude that there was something fundamentally wrong with people.

The new, gloomy social science of the seventies rediscovered, and made respectable, some of the old theories of degeneracy and defectiveness. Writers like William Shockley and Arthur Jensen resurrected long-discredited hereditary theories of racial inferiority to "explain" why blacks still were not succeeding in America, in spite of all that had been done for them in the 1960s. Other theorists concluded that the reason there was still considerable poverty in the United States was that poor people either really *liked* living in slums or were sunk in a "culture of the lower class" that prevented them from thinking ahead, accumulating savings, or staying on the job.[37] The persistence of crime and urban violence was increasingly held to be the result of a "subculture of violence" among the black poor (as opposed, say, to mainstream white culture, which presumably eschewed violence and aggression) or, in even more pessimistic fashion, was attributed to the "innate" aggressiveness of the human species or to chemical imbalances in the brain. In a real sense, conventional social science in the United States had come full circle, shedding even the limited optimism and social activism of the sixties to focus once again on the "defective" classes and the remedy of containment through punishment.

Fortunately, though, the new pessimism is not the whole story. On the other side, the deepening crisis of the seventies accelerated the development of more critical approaches to social issues. When we first wrote this introduction in 1969, we commented that there were virtually no serious studies of the American business system, or of the police, courts, military, and other key institutions, particularly those operating in secret under the clouds of national security. Today, this statement, happily, could not be made. A new school of economists is effectively challenging the conventional images of the affluent economy; an extensive and almost entirely new literature on imperialism has emerged; and the amount of serious critical writing on the health care system, the workplace, the human services and other governmental institutions is much greater than we anticipated a few years ago.

It is out of this emerging body of critical work that we have taken our selections for this reader. As in earlier editions, the selections represent a diversity of opinions, styles, and perspectives, but all within a common general framework: a critical, democratic approach to social institutions that sees them as changeable and accountable, and that emphasizes human potential and the possibility of meaningful social change. Our emphasis is on the economic and political structures that are shaped by the imperatives of profit and power — not on the supposed flaws of the people victimized by these structures.

Within this admittedly very broad perspective, there is room for much controversy over particular theories of social structure and strategies of institutional change as well as particular definitions of human and social priorities. The editors of this book rarely agree with each other on more than the most basic themes. Both of us would describe ourselves as to the left of center politically; both of us have been participants in many of the movements for social change of the 1960s and early 1970s. But as the recent history of those movements makes clear, this isn't a very clear guide to anyone's specific intellectual and political views.

We find ourselves in a continuing debate over many of the issues covered in this book — for example, the importance of imperialism to the American economy, the relation between the schools and the dominant economic interests in the United States, and many others — as well as over the more general question of whether American social problems should be seen as problems of capitalism in particular, or as problems common to industrial societies of any economic base. But we think this tension is fruitful, and we have tried to reflect it in our selection of readings, which represent a fairly wide spectrum of political opinion and of theoretical perspective.

The plan of the book remains basically the same as in earlier editions, but there are important additions and deletions. In the first part, Systemic Problems, we consider basic processes within the American system that affect the way all other institutions work — the power of corporations, the scope of imperialism, the patterns of class, racial and sexual inequality. For this edition, we have increased our coverage of the corporate economy by completely revising our earlier chapter on Corporate Power and by adding a new chapter on Imperialism. We have dropped the chapter on Militarism, preferring to deal with that issue within the more general one of the domestic and international operation of the United States economy. We have added a chapter on environmental destruction — something we wanted to do before, but were unable to because of a lack of good material on the relation between environmental problems and the larger social and economic system.

The second part, Institutions in Crisis, considers several key institutions in the light of these basic processes. There are important changes here, too. We have added a chapter on the problems of the workplace, and expanded the chapter on Welfare into a larger and more comprehensive one on Social Services — including housing, child care, and the problems of aging. And we have condensed our earlier chapters on The Schools and Higher Learning into one on Education, and our chapters on Police and Criminal Law into one on Justice. In this way, we are able to deal with more areas of current concern, and in a more concise and balanced fashion.

We see this book as an introductory work, useful for beginning courses in sociology, social problems, or political science. Its purpose is to raise issues, to provide students with the beginnings of a critical approach to the society they live in and will hopefully help change. It provides few definitive

answers and it leaves unresolved many basic theoretical and
practical questions about the sources and solutions of the
American crisis. But its purpose will be accomplished if it
helps lead students to begin their own process of confronting
those questions.

REFERENCES

1. C. Wright Mills, "The Professional Ideology of the Social
Pathologists," in Irving L. Horowitz, ed., *Power, Politics, and
People: The Collected Essays of C. Wright Mills* (New York:
Ballantine, 1963).

2. Charles Richmond Henderson, *An Introduction to the Study
of Defective, Dependent and Delinquent Classes* (Boston: Heath,
1906).

3. Lawrence K. Frank, "Social Problems," *American Journal of
Sociology*, 30 (January 1925), p. 463.

4. Richard C. Fuller and Richard R. Myers, "The Natural
History of a Social Problem," *American Sociological Review*, 6
(June 1941), p. 320.

5. Paul B. Horton and Gerald R. Leslie, *The Sociology of Social
Problems* (New York: Appleton-Century-Crofts, 1955), p 6.

6. Arnold M. Rose, "Theory for the Study of Social Problems,"
Social Problems, 4 (January 1957), p. 190.

7. Robert K. Merton and Robert M. Nisbet, *Contemporary Social
Problems* (New York: Harcourt, Brace and World, 1961), p. 702.

8. Willard Waller, "Social Problems and the Mores," *American
Sociological Review*, 1 (December 1936), p. 926.

9. *Ibid.*, p. 928.

10. *Ibid.*, p. 927.

11. *Ibid.*, p. 924.

12. Horton and Leslie, *Sociology*. We refer here to the original
edition in order to place the book in its historical context.

13. *Ibid.*, p. 517.

14. *Ibid.*, p. 520.

15. *Ibid.*, p. 523.

16. *Ibid.*, p. 12.

17. *Ibid.*, p. 19.

18. Merton and Nisbet, *Contemporary Social Problems*. Here,
too, we refer to the first edition in order to consider the book in
historical perspective. The general theoretical perspective in the
book has changed little if at all, as we will note later: there have
been some substantive changes, however—for example, the chapter
by Janowitz has been dropped, and new chapters added.

19. Robert A. Nisbet, "The Study of Social Problems," in *ibid.*,
p. 4.

20. *Ibid.*, p. 5. The reader might compare C. Wright Mills' notion, developed during the same period, that the United States should be seen as an "overdeveloped" society: see Irving L. Horowitz, "Introduction," in Horowitz, *Power, Politics, and People*, p. 8.

21. Nisbet, "The Study of Social Problems," p. 9.

22. *Ibid.*, p. 12.

23. Robert S. Weiss and David Riesman, "Social Problems and Disorganization in the World of Work," in Merton and Nisbet, *Contemporary Social Problems*, p. 464.

24. Morris Janowitz, "The Military Establishment: Organization and Disorganization," in Merton and Nisbet, *Contemporary Social Problems*, p. 515.

25. *Ibid.*, p. 516.

26. *Ibid.*, pp. 533–534.

27. Robert K. Merton, "Social Problems and Sociological Theory," in Merton and Nisbet, *Contemporary Social Problems*, p. 701.

28. *Ibid.*, p. 702.

29. *Ibid.*, p. 706.

30. *Ibid.*, p. 710.

31. *Ibid.*, p. 711.

32. *Ibid.*, p. 723.

33. *Ibid.*, pp. 712–713.

34. *Ibid.*, p. 723.

35. *Ibid.*, p. 712.

36. Robert M. Nisbet, "The Study of Social Problems," in *ibid.*, p. 2.

37. For Jensen's perspective and some criticisms of it, see *Harvard Educational Review*, May 1968; for another influential work in this vein, see Edward Banfield, *The Unheavenly City* (Boston: Little, Brown and Co., 1968).

SYSTEMIC PROBLEMS

CAPITALISM I

The myth of American capitalism is individual free enterprise; its accompanying imagery envisions a solitary, hard-working, efficient, thrifty entrepreneur competing with others to seek his fortune. The economic reality of America is what Ralph Nader has called "corporate collectivism," more familiarly known as "big business." "Engine Charlie" Wilson, a former head of General Motors who served as secretary of defense in the Eisenhower administration, once remarked — to the embarrassment of the president: "What's good for General Motors is good for America." Mr. Wilson's remark may have proved indiscreet, but it reflected a powerful point of view, which many could accept as the essential reality and driving force of the American nation–state.

General Motors is, first of all, a *corporation,* that is, a form of legal organization allowing a business to use the capital of a number of persons called shareholders. The modern, large corporation has three elements: the shareholders, a board of directors, and the officers of the board of directors who are usually responsible solely to the board. The officers — or management — actually run the corporation. For many years students of corporations have observed that the owners of the corporation — the shareholders — have very little control over its policies. In the modern industrial corporation, control is exercised by a virtually omnipotent management. Bayless Manning remarks:

In 1932, Berle and Means vivisected the modern corporation. They found a virtually omnipotent management and an impotent shareholdership. A quarter-century of unparalleled corporate law reform intervenes. In 1958, Livingston surveyed the lot of the shareholder in a reformed world — a world of SEC regulation, extensive disclosure requirements, elaborate proxy machinery, Security Exchange self-discipline, Corporate Good Citizenship, Peoples Capitalism, Corporate Democracy. His findings? A virtually omnipotent management and impotent shareholdership.[1]

The industrial wealth of the United States is concentrated in the hands of several hundred corporations, and within those corporations a relatively small number of persons occupying positions as officers make major policy decisions regarding the industrial expansion of the United States. More than a decade ago, A. A. Berle was able to write:

The economic power of these corporations is enormous. Today approximately 50 percent of American manufacturing — that is everything other than finance and transportation — is held by about 150 corporations reckoned, at least, by asset values. If finance and transportation are included, the total increases. If a rather larger group is taken, the statistics would probably show that about two-thirds of the economically productive assets of the United States, excluding agriculture, are owned by a group of not more than 500 corporations. This is actual asset ownership. . . . But in terms of power, without regard to asset positions, not only do 500 corporations control two-thirds of the nonfarm economy but . . . a still smaller group has the ultimate decision-making power. This is, I think, the highest concentration of economic power in recorded history. Since the United States carries on not quite half of the manufacturing production of the entire world today, these 500 groupings — each with its own little dominating pyramid within it — represent a concentration of power over economics which makes the medieval feudal system look like a Sunday-School party. In sheer economic power this has gone far beyond anything we have yet seen.[2]

Corporate concentration is encouraged by and dependent upon the key institution of modern capitalism, the commercial bank. A commercial bank, as David Leinsdorf and Donald Etra point out in their study of the largest one in the United States, the Federal National City Bank ("Citibank"), sells money at a profit; but it sells it at different prices to different customers. The *prime rate* is the price charged to the "best" customers, those major corporations with whom, as this study shows, major banks are integrally tied through their own patterns of concentration, values, and interlocking directorates. Thus, although national and multinational corporations are clearly distinguishable from banks, as the heart is an organ distinguishable from the brain, the well-being of one is dependent upon the health of the other. American capitalism, in turn, is dependent on both operating institutions, the corporation and the commercial bank.

The body of American capitalism lately has not been altogether well. Its circulatory system — technology — has been operating with increasingly less efficiency. Power supplies, transportation, and communication systems are generally agreed to comprise the essentials of a modern industrial society. In America, cities and regions suffer from power shortages, communication breakdowns, inadequate and sometimes inoperative transportation systems. Seymour Melman's selection discusses the decline in American industrial efficiency and the reasons for it, particularly its relationship to the sustenance of a military economy.

Although corporations are usually thought of as manufacturers of durable goods and services — motors, business machines, communications — one of the major areas of corporate concentration is food: its growth, processing, packaging, transport, and retail sales. Daniel Zwerdling, in "The Food Monopolies," discusses the evidence for believing that inflated food prices are encouraged and managed by the giants of the food industry.

Corporate concentration is one of the factors cited by David M. Gordon to explain the severity of America's mid-1970s economic recession. Yet, Gordon does not interpret this economic decline as unusual, except for its severity. His major argument is this: capitalism requires recession as a way of constraining the demands of organized labor, which rise during periods of prosperity. Corporations command the resources to ride out recessions. Wage earners do not. In this, Gordon perceives a measure of inequity, and, in the analyses of establishment economists, a measure of obfuscation and false optimism over the equitable possibilities of United States capitalism.

REFERENCES

1. Bayless Manning, quoted in Melvin Aron Eisenberg, "The Legal Roles of Shareholders and Management in Modern Corporate Decision-Making," *California Law Review*, Vol. 57, No. 1 (January 1969), pp. 23–24.
2. A. A. Berle, "Economic Power and the Free Society," in Andrew Hacker, ed., *The Corporation Take-Over* (New York: Harper and Row, 1964), pp. 101–102.

1. CITIBANK

David Leinsdorf
and Donald Etra

A commercial bank is a merchant of money. It accumulates money from people, corporations, and governments and lends it to people, corporations, and governments. The difference between the cost of attracting funds and the price charged for lending is the bank's profit. The key to the banks' profitability is growth. Although bank profit *margins* have declined dramatically in recent years, banks have expanded their operations fast enough to offset the lower rate of profit earned on each dollar of gross revenue. This growth has been achieved — even during the recession of 1970 — for a variety of reasons.

One reason is the fact that banks have exclusive control over 75% of America's money supply. The principle economic function of commercial banks is to operate the nation's payments mechanism, i.e., to hold demand (checking) deposits and honor checks drawn against them. No other institutions have the right to receive such deposits which, in the United States, are the equivalent of currency and coin and constitute 75% of the nation's money supply. As the Federal Reserve Board increases the money supply to meet the needs of our ever-expanding economy, commercial banks are guaranteed a minimum rate of growth.

The power to make loans with these deposits gives banks another exceptional prerogative — the capacity to create money. An example will show how this process works.

Banks must set aside part of their deposits as legal reserves at the district Federal Reserve banks. Legal reserves are designed to ensure that banks have enough funds to honor checks presented for payment, and to provide the Federal Reserve Board with a means of regulating the amount of money that member banks can create. Presently, 17.5% of demand deposits must go into reserves.[1] For the sake of simplicity, however, the following description of how banks create money assumes a 20% demand deposit reserve requirement.

Suppose that someone deposits $1,000 in newly printed currency in a Citibank checking account. Given our hypothetical 20% reserve requirement, FNCB puts $200 of the $1,000 deposit into its reserve account at the Federal Reserve Bank of New York. Suppose that FNCB makes an $800 vacation loan with the balance, which the borrower uses to pay his travel agent. If the travel agent deposits the $800 in an account at Chase Manhattan Bank, the original $1,000 has expanded to $1,800 in demand deposits — the man who sold the bond has $1,000 at FNCB which he can withdraw at any time and the travel agent can do the same with his $800 at Chase.

Chase, too, will put 20% of the deposit, or $160, into its reserve account, but can lend out the remaining $640 to its customers. If Chase lends the $640 to a customer who pays the money to a used car dealer who has a Chemical Bank account, the bank deposits flowing from the original $1,000 now total $2,440 — $1,000 at FNCB, $800 at Chase, and $640 at Chemical. As the process continues, the bank following Chemical will add four-fifths of $640 to the banking system's demand deposits and so on until finally, the original $1,000 deposited at FNCB will have expanded to $5,000 of demand deposits in the banking system.

Another factor behind the growth of the banking industry is the fact that banks have expanded into new fields of activity from which they have traditionally been excluded. With the Comptroller of the Currency leading the way with novel reinterpretations of long-standing laws and FNCB initiating a veritable stampede by banks to diversify through the creation of one-bank holding companies, banks have obtained new freedom to compete with nonbank corporations.

Another reason for the growth of banks — and this applies primarily to the largest banks — is the fact that the top priority of the billion-dollar banks is meeting the needs of the fastest growing companies in America's economy, the giant national and multinational corporations. As FNCB and the other money-market banks apply their best talent, the largest part of their funds, and their new technology to handling the global financial transactions of large corporations, they ensure that, as an increasing share of America's productive resources come under the control of fewer and fewer giant corporations, the large banks that serve those corporations will achieve similar growth for themselves. Consequently the concentration of America's productive resources is reflected in a corresponding concentration in the banking industry. Although there are more than 13,000 commercial banks in the United States, 100 banks hold half of all deposits and ten banks hold one-quarter. The three largest banks have 13% of all deposits and Citibank alone has 4% — $1 out of every $25.

The corporate merger boom has been another means of promoting FNCB's growth. Citibank has acted as a marriage broker by maintaining a list of acquisition-minded companies for its customers. It has waived covenants in bank loan agreements that would otherwise prohibit acquisitions and it has financed acquisitions by customers with a virtual rubber stamp. Citibank thus applies itself with many of the most aggressive conglomerate companies in the economy, and the bank and its corporate customers each nurture the growth of the other.

The merger movement has had important ramifications on competition in the banking industry and on local economic development. Small, local banks are precluded from competing for local deposits; when a national company buys a local business, the acquired company's bank deposits are typically transferred to the acquiring company's money-market banks. This removes funds from the local economy and fosters economic colonialism.

Although the central role of commercial banks in our economy imbues bank activities with the character of a "public trust," there have been virtually no attempts to study banks in terms of how they serve their individual, corporate, and government customers, what they do with their depositors' money, how they affect the communities in which they operate, how they deal with their employees, and how they affect economic priorities. This report is a first step toward developing the information needed to make an informed evaluation of how commercial banks affect people. We have concentrated on one bank in order to develop as much concrete, specific information as possible on the framework within which priorities are formulated and far-reaching decisions are made and implemented.

FNCB was chosen as the subject of our study for a variety of reasons. It is the largest bank in New York City, which is the most important money market in the world. With 25% more branches than Chase Manhattan, the second largest bank in New York, it is the city's largest consumer bank, atracting more individual deposits and extending more consumer credit than any other New York City bank. Citibank is also very innovative in developing new deposit gathering and financing devices. It was the first New York City bank to lend money to consumers, the first to open overseas branches, the first to form a one-bank holding company, and the first to develop the important negotiable certificate of deposit, thus offering corporations, wealthy individuals, and other large investors with a short-term investment alternative to U.S. Treasury Bills. In all of these developments, other banks followed Citibank's lead. Thus, by studying FNCB, it is possible to better understand the direction in which the banking industry is moving.

Forbes magazine calls banking America's fastest growing industry and Citibank the fastest growing of the 20 largest banks. Citibank's growth has been staggering. Deposits have doubled in seven years, loans and assets in six years, profits in nine years, and employees in ten years. Although California's Bank of America is larger than Citibank, Bank of

America has it easier because it can branch and gather up deposits all over one of America's largest, fastest growing states. Citibank's domestic operations, on the other hand, have been confined to New York City and two suburban counties. Consequently, Citibank has had to rely more on innovation and aggressiveness to offset the inherent comparative advantage that California's unrestricted branching laws give to Bank of America.[2]

Although Bank of America ($28 billion in assets) is somewhat larger than Citibank ($26 billion), Citibank is very large nonetheless. Only AT&T, Prudential Life, and Metropolitan Life have more assets. In addition to the $26 billion of assets owned by FNCB, the bank's trust department manages another $14 billion in assets for pension funds, personal trusts, investment advisory accounts, and estates and has exclusive investment discretion over almost half of these assets.

As might be expected, the information gathered by the task force indicates that Citibank is a microcosm, albeit a large one, of the contradictions and distortions, the strengths and weaknesses found throughout the American business community. Citibank's hiring and promotion practices provide a good case in point. Until a few years ago, when the tight New York City labor market induced Citibank to reexamine its hiring policies, it adhered to needlessly high employment standards. Although most jobs at Citibank require few or easily taught skills, the bank required applicants to have a high-school diploma, thereby excluding thousands of people from jobs for which they were otherwise qualified. Blacks and other poorly educated minorities were especially likely to be excluded.

Although Citibank was forced to relax its hiring standards to replace the 5,000–6,000 employees who leave each year and to support the bank's high growth rate, the opportunities for blacks, women, Jews, and other groups to move into positions of responsibility are still very limited. This is largely because there are more promotable employees than responsible positions, giving Citibank the opportunity to pick and choose, and locking thousands of employees into dull jobs for which they are overqualified and underpaid. Consequently, employee alienation and turnover are extremely high, undermining management's capacity to retain control over its rapidly expanding activities.

Widespread employee dissatisfaction takes its toll on the bank's customers — especially the individual customers of the retail branch network. Service in Citibank's branches is inadequate. Customers have to wait even when the branch is not busy. Operating policies are implemented haphazardly, resulting in wide variations from branch to branch in the quality of customer service. Customers are confused about the operation and cost of services and branch officers fail, with distressing frequency, to enlighten customers and end the confusion. Lending criteria are frequently ignored, resulting in extensions of credit to tens of thousands of people who cannot afford to meet their monthly payments.

Despite Citibank's failure to service its present volume of retail business adequately, FNCB has had great success expanding the range of its services, the number of its branches, and its share of the market. Deceptive advertising, descriptive brochures that don't describe, and volume-oriented employee incentive programs are all used to maximize growth without regard to the human toll. And the human toll is substantial.

One result of Citibank's slovenly but ever-expanding operation is that the bank is New York City's number one plaintiff. In 1969, FNCB sued $10,000 people (increasing to 15,000 in 1970), more than five times as many lawsuits as any other bank. Adjusted for the volume of consumer credit outstanding, Citibank's rate of suit is more than double that of any other bank. Ninety-five per cent of the judgments are default judgments and impose an additional 25% in attorney fees, court costs, and interest charges on the average judgment debtor (70% of whom earn less than $6,000 a year). Furthermore, Citibank's practice of calling and threatening to call the debtor's employer exploits the fact that many employers illegally fire employees rather than deduct 10% of the judgment debtor's wages pursuant to a garnishment order. As a result, many debtors must refinance the debt by taking out a new loan in order to avoid being fired. Another component of FNCB's collection operation is widespread "sewer service," i.e., the practice by which process servers fail to serve the summons and complaint properly, preventing the defendant from finding out about the lawsuit against him and insuring a high default judgment rate.

In sharp contrast to its aggressive posture in the retail banking market, FNCB virtually ignores the credit-starved residential mortgage market, aggravating New York City's housing crisis. Though in 1970 FNCB held nearly $2 billion of peoples' savings deposits, the bank's residential mortgage loan portfolio was only one-fourth as large. Yet savings deposits are long-term, stable funds that are ideally suited to long-term residential mortgage lending. Citibank's refusal to provide the funds needed to preserve, rehabilitate, and construct housing underscores the bank's obliviousness to the needs of the community from which it draws its deposits. The branch network thus operates like a system of receptacles where people deposit their money to be siphoned off into the bank's "central pool" and made available to the giant corporations. Meanwhile, the people who provide the funds must suffer deteriorating housing conditions because FNCB and other banks have virtually unfettered discretion to lend the peoples' money where they want. Citibank's retail branch operation, therefore, is like a regressive tax, taking money from those who can least afford to lose it and giving it to those who need it the least.

Though Citibank gathers up billions of dollars from individuals and then ignores the critical shortage of long-term residential mortgage money, it is not so oblivious to corporate needs. With a board of direc-

tors composed almost exclusively of top executives from its large corporate customers, Citibank's sensitivity to corporate wants contrasts
sharply with its contempt for human needs. In 1970, FNCB was interlocked with 40 of the 300 largest industrial corporations in the United
States, including 7 of the top 10, plus 6 of the 15 largest life-insurance
companies, 2 of the 4 largest retailers, and the 2 largest utilities.

But interlocking directorates constitute just one factor behind Citibank's obeisance to corporate wants. More important is the bank's fetish
with preserving and strengthening in every possible manner the total
account relationship between the bank and its corporate customers. Because corporations have numerous alternative sources of credit both
within and without the banking system and because the deposit balances of
individual corporations are so substantial, corporations have the leverage
to obtain a vast array of services in exchange for their deposits, a volume
of credit that far exceeds the amount of corporate deposits, and favorable credit terms.

As a result, financially hard-pressed corporations in America obtain
huge amounts of credit at the "prime rate," the lowest corporate lending
rate that is purportedly reserved for only the most creditworthy companies. Citibank is not the only bank to behave in this manner. Indeed,
the typical loan to a giant corporation is made through a multibank lending syndicate in which most or all of the large New York City banks
participate, with interest rates fixed by agreement instead of competitive
forces.

Citibank's aggressive development of its relationships with national
and multinational corporations contrasts sharply with its niggardly involvement in fostering local economic development by minority business
enterprises. Although the bank pays lip service to the policy of promoting
minority economic development, its small-business investment company avoids small neighborhood businesses of the type that could significantly increase grass-roots entrepreneurship, preferring to invest in
million-dollar enterprises that have high growth potential. Similarly, the
bank has a passive approach to making economic development loans in
the ghettos of New York, waiting for borrowers to seek out the bank instead of drumming up business. It has also failed to require its loan officers to apply their expertise to counseling minority enterprises.

The financial crisis that plagues New York City has been aggravated
by FNCB and the other large banks. Preferential bank income taxes cost
New York City $10 million a year in lost revenues. The fact that the
banks have provided the city with relatively few services in exchange for
hundreds of millions of dollars of interest-free demand deposits has cost
New York City many millions of dollars in excess costs each year ($8
million in 1969 alone). And the banks' abandonment of the municipal
bond market, especially in times of tight money, has weakened the mar-

ket for municipal securities, adding millions of dollars a year to New York City's borrowing costs.

At the same time that FNCB has been receiving preferential tax treatment, earning exorbitant profits on New York City's accounts and adding to New York City's borrowing costs, Citibank has wielded considerable influence over public spending decisions through its membership on public bodies and private civic associations. FNCB was represented on a commission appointed by Governor Rockefeller that recommended a $65 million giveaway to purchase the bankrupt Long Island Railroad from a major FNCB debtor. FNCB is a member of the Downtown Lower Manhattan Association, the financial community's local planning board, that initiated the Port of New York Authority's giant World Trade Center, the largest office building in the world. As lead bank for the Port Authority, FNCB played a central role in the financial arrangements for the World Trade Center. Having participated in the creation of the World Trade Center, FNCB uses its membership on the Metropolitan Transit Authority to accelerate the construction, at taxpayers' expense, of new subway facilities to handle the World Trade Center's additional burden on New York's already crowded transit facilities.

Citibank also performs governmental functions for New York City, such as processing New York City's personal income-tax returns. Although the contract with the city prohibits the bank from using the information extracted from the income-tax returns for any private purpose, Citibank retains copies of the computer tapes and city officials admit that they have no way of ensuring that the bank does not utilize the information for its own credit files. At a time when massive, computerized data banks are proliferating, compiling secret dossiers on all citizens, this Citibank practice raises the possibility of further invasions of citizens' rights to privacy.

Citibank not only provides commercial services to individuals, corporations, and municipalities, it also provides trust services. Citibanks manages $14 billion in its trust department, most of which is in personal estates and trusts, and corporate and municipal pension funds. While almost complete yet unwarranted secrecy surrounds the trust activities of banks, the public has been, of late, becoming increasingly aware of the conflicts that arise when a commercial bank also provides trust services. Some of the conflicts are blatant: a trust department can invest a pension fund in a company deeply indebted to the commercial side of the bank. Some of the conflicts are more subtle: a trust department can deliberately keep a portion of a trust fund uninvested and leave the uninvested cash in demand deposits with the commercial bank. The presence and potential for such conflicts demand that the public ask whether trust departments have any place as part of a commercial bank.

Because commercial banking is imbued with a "public trust," banking has always been a regulated industry. Permission to open a bank or new branches has always required government approval and a showing of community need. Branching has been restricted, in part, to preserve local control over local funds and to ensure that citizens' deposits remain available for reinvestment in the local economy. The freedom of banks to engage in nonbanking activities has been circumscribed severely to prevent banks from using their access to interest-free demand deposits to gain unfair competitive advantage over nonbank competitors and to avoid conflicts of interest that could arise from bank diversification.

But the bank regulatory agencies have failed to monitor banks to ensure that community needs are met, and have steadily relaxed the traditional restrictions on bank expansion into new activities and territories. The Comptroller of the Currency, who is responsible for regulating national banks, has been particularly responsive to the banks' desire for greater freedom to expand. Branch applications are routinely approved despite findings by the Comptroller's own examiners that the community to be served already has enough banks. Contrary to the statutory requirement that the Comptroller observe state branching laws in acting on branch applications by national banks, the Comptroller has allowed national banks to open branches where state banks could not. Regulations and rulings were rewritten to permit banks to carry on some of their operations through subsidiaries and to allow banks to expand into travel agency services, including automobile rentals and trip insurance, warehousing, data processing, leasing of personal property, mutual funds, messenger services, and the selling of insurance. Bank mergers, too, were approved almost with a rubber stamp.

The Comptroller's *laissez-faire* approach to bank regulation affected the Federal Reserve Board, which regulates state-chartered banks that are members of the Federal Reserve System. As it became increasingly apparent that national banks were obtaining unique advantages despite the long-standing statutory policy of putting national and state banks on a competitively equal footing, Chase Manhattan Bank, the largest state bank in the country, and more than 160 other state banks converted to national charters during the 1960s. The Fed, as the Federal Reserve Board is called, under pressure from state member banks to restore competitive equality, followed the Comptroller's lead and permitted state banks to engage in many of the activities permitted by the Comptroller, leading one Fed member to characterize bank regulation as "competition in laxity."

This permissiveness also prevails in the examinations that the regulatory agencies are supposed to make of bank operations. This is especially true of the Comptroller's examination of the largest banks, which are examined less frequently than the law requires and with a disproportionately small amount of examination resources. Although Bank of America,

Citibank, and Chase have one-fifth of all national bank assets, the Comptroller allocates a total of only 3% of his examination resources to them, because he has so much confidence in their solvency. The Comptroller gives little or no attention to many other important areas that bear on compliance with the law by the giant banks.

Citibank also has a high degree of autonomy from Fed monetary policy. In 1969 and early 1970, FNCB continued expanding its loan portfolio despite Fed monetary policy designed to slow down the economy and inflation by restricting bank credit growth. Citibank did this by borrowing billions of dollars in the unregulated international Eurodollar market and from its one-bank holding company which raised funds in the unregulated commercial paper market. As a result of these activities by FNCB and other large banks, it took longer than anticipated for the economy to respond to the Fed's credit restraint policies. Furthermore, the impact of credit restraint was distributed unevenly throughout the economy because the large banks, with vast overseas branch networks and holding companies, could continue to finance their customers' expansion plans while smaller banks were required to restrict their loans.

The latest, and potentially most far-reaching, development in the area of bank regulation has been the development of one-bank holding companies. In order to escape some of the restrictions on bank activities, FNCB created a corporation to own the bank. Because Citicorp, as the holding company is called, is not itself a bank — it just owns a bank — it can engage in many activities prohibited to banks. When Citicorp tried to take over a large insurance company, it became apparent that bank holding companies could change the entire structure of the American economy. After two years of legislative battling, Congress, at the end of 1970, passed legislation requiring bank holding companies to obtain approval from the Federal Reserve Board before acquiring or creating new subsidiaries. The statutory formula, however, gives the Fed a large amount of discretion to determine what activities are closely related to banking.

Though nominally independent, bank holding companies are, in fact, mere extensions of the banks they own. They share the same directors, managers, offices, technological resources, customers and, most important of all, they generate their funds by virtue of their affiliations with banks. Accordingly, bank holding companies have competitive advantages that independent, nonbank competitors cannot match, making it safe to predict that if the Fed allows substantial expansion into new fields, the long-range consequence will be to introduce the rapidly-diminishing diversity and countervailing economic powers in our economy.

The fundamental issue facing the American banking system is whether the people and government will reassert the concept that banking is a "public trust" to be operated as objectively, independently, and free from conflicts of interest as possible. If banks and their government regulators continue to make growth and profits a higher priority than ensuring an equitable distribution of financial resources across all sectors of the economy, then it is safe to predict that the distortions that pervade America's economy today — such as the dearth of money to finance the preservation, rehabilitation, and expansion of the nation's housing, the higher cost of borrowing by state and municipalities to construct needed public facilities, the increasing concentration of our economic resources, the inability of local communities to influence local economic decisions, and the powerlessness of millions of consumers to transcend the anonymity of an account number — will grow worse, not better, in the coming years.

REFERENCES

1. The actual demand deposit reserve requirements are 17% on deposits under $5 million, and 17.5% on deposits over $5 million.
2. The New York State legislature recently amended New York's branching laws to allow statewide branching, starting January 1, 1976. This will permit the large New York City banks to expand their share of the market further.

2. THE WAY THINGS [DON'T] WORK

Seymour Melman

While President Nixon was hailing the manned lunar landing in August 1969 as "the greatest week since the Creation," a rather different technological drama was enacted in America's largest city. Millions of New Yorkers were suffering the effects of breakdowns in basic industrial services. Firms that could no longer be reached by phone placed ads in the newspapers to announce that they were still in business. The telephone service, normally taken for granted, seemed to be falling apart as ordinary local and long distance calling became annoyingly difficult. At the same time the gradually-deteriorating commuter railroads into New York City reached a new low in unacceptable performance with collisions, casualties, train cancellations and delays.

Even more disastrous for normal function in modern urban life were the successive breakdowns in electric power generating plants of Consolidated Edison during the August heatwaves, leaving buildings without air conditioning, elevator services or proper illumination.

Economists and engineers commonly agree that competent power supplies, transportation and communication comprise the infrastructure of a modern industrial system. That is to say, in the presence of these services, competently performed, it is readily possible to design all manner of modern industry. In the absence of such services a country is understood to be "underdeveloped." And so it came to pass by the summer of 1969 that the conditions of economic underdevelopment were manifested in New York.

Only a few years ago a technological debacle of this kind would have been unthinkable in the United States. For as long as any person can remember, Americans have regarded the state of their industrial technology as one aspect of American society and economy that was beyond criticism. Here, beyond any doubt, were the world's greatest achievements in applying mass production on a large scale. American industry, its management, research, production methods and product design had been held up as a model to all the world. However, the events of August 1969 in New York City are but one fragment of a larger process of deterioration of American industrial efficiency.

INDUSTRY AFTER INDUSTRY

On July 1971 the *New York Times* reported an unusual development in the automobile industry:

While this is the best auto sales year in the nation's history, with sales expected to approach 10 million cars, unemployment in Michigan is approaching 10% of the work force and is at 16% in Detroit. Never before has there been a combination of a strong auto year and a high unemployment in the nation's leading automobile production state. One major reason is that one of seven new cars sold comes from Europe or Japan, while another 700,000 are being imported this year from Canada for sale in the United States.

Here is an unprecedented combination of financial success for the major automobile firms and high unemployment rates in their industrial home-base. Apparently it has become increasingly profitable for the major American auto producers to invest fresh capital abroad and import foreign-made products under their own label into the United States.

The U.S. auto industry has been, without question, the home-base of modern mass-production technology, where ideas of standardization, the assembly line and mass-production as conventionally understood were initiated and put into wide practice. According to *Business Week,* car models and options during the 1960s proliferated such that the Chrysler Corporation alone increased the number of parts in use from 12,000 to 23,000 within the decade. This is a tribute to the multiplication of design complexity, the failure to apply standardization techniques and modular design and the elaboration of model change for stylistic or allied merchandising purposes. By the 1960s the U.S. auto industry had become a classic example of failure to utilize many aspects of modern production engineering. And there are other failures.

In 1970 the Federal Communications Commission, making its first national survey of telephone service, compiled voluminous evidence that, while the New York City phone system was judged to be the worst in the country, and getting worse, the condition there was not unique. Reports from 20 large cities serviced by the Bell Telephone System indicated that failure to satisfy the industry's own service standards was the rule, not the exception, in principal metropolitan centers of the United States.

By 1971 a national energy crisis was clearly in evidence, showing signs of being durable and likely to become rather more intensive. The same problems of crisis extend to fuel supply in the form of natural gas. Optimistic assumptions about the availability of natural gas, which surely lay behind the construction of interstate gas lines and the conversion of gas-using units to natural gas, were unreasonable estimates based on faulty knowledge.

In the late 1960s work began on the Bay Area Rapid Transit System in San Francisco. But because public rail transportation had been neglected for decades it was discovered that the most sophisticated developments — wheelless, linear-electric powered, air-cushioned vehicles capable of traveling 250 miles per hour — were available only from France or Japan. Moreover, when the civil engineering work for the BART system was put out for bids, very few contractors were interested. It seems that BART management had not "reckoned with the fact that many of these firms were committed up to their eyeballs on construction work in Vietnam and were not eager to take on additional work." By late 1971 the BART Transit System for San Francisco was in trouble. Prototype models, which had been built for a system scheduled to be in operation by 1968, crashed late in 1971. And the price of the system zoomed from $792 million to $1,400 million, representing the kind of "cost growth" which is customary in military economy. It is surely not accidental that the Rohr Company, which made its reputation in the aerospace and related industries, was the prime contractor. (The Rohr Company, incidentally, was also the subcontractor to Lockheed for the engine pylons which cracked on the giant C-5A transport.)

During 1969 new railroad equipment was delivered to the Long Island

and to the Penn Central Railroad. According to the *New York Times,* August 6, 1969,

The Long Island Railroad accepts 94 new cars and finds mechanical defects in all 94. . . . . Because of breakdowns, it takes a standby fleet of 10 replacement cars to keep an average of 18 cars moving on the New York to Washington Metroliner. Two of the new Metroliner cars must be scrapped for spare parts. Twenty additional cars are delivered more than 6 months behind schedule and they also have serious defects.

"It seems nobody knows how to make a passenger car anymore," complains one railroad executive.

Dr. Robert Nelson, Chief of the Federal Government Office of High Speech Ground Transportation said of the rail supply industry: "The industry simply does not have the massive manpower and technical resources that, for example, the aerospace industry has. The profits in railway supply equipment have been depressed for some years and bright young engineers have not been going into it."

The steel industry of the United States has become a major center of industrial depletion with about 18% of the domestic market being serviced from abroad. About 80% of the Japanese steel industry makes use of the basic oxygen process whereas only about 50% of the U.S. industry is so equipped. The U.S. industry's managements have failed to do research and development on a scale necessary to offset cost differentials between U.S. and foreign countries. The consequence is that costs in the U.S. steel industry have risen to a level making imported steel saleable at from $20 to $40 per ton less than domestic steel.

Profit margins are also a factor. The non-U.S. steel-makers have been prepared to operate at substantially lower than American profit rates. A report by the Iron and Steel Institute shows that in 1968 in the U.S. steel industry net income as a percent of revenues averaged 5.3% while figures for identified firms in Japan were as follows: Yawata, 3.0%; Fuji, 3.3%; Kawasaki, 2.8%. Similar comparisons obtain for the relation of U.S. steel firm profits to those of Belgium, France, West Germany and Italy. The higher U.S. profit applied to the price has made U.S. steel essentially noncompetitive, which helps to explain why the steel structure of the World Trade Center, constructed at the foot of Manhattan, was shipped from Japan — and not from any U.S. steel source.

The case of civilian electronics is perhaps the most striking example of industrial depletion in the United States. The design and manufacture of small radio receivers and most TV sets has dropped sharply. And civilian electronics firms, with close ties to the burgeoning military–space electronics field, have managed to avoid technological options which could help make U.S.-based production economically viable.

On September 19, 1971, the *New York Times* reported that Mr. Robert

A. Schieber, Vice President of Operations for the RCA Corporation's consumer electronics division, announced that RCA had developed for television sets a circuit module printed on ceramic wafers. Mr. Barton Kreuzer, an Executive Vice President of RCA, predicted that, if the adaptation of the devices went smoothly, "it could make us competitive once again to the point where we could bring back at least a good part of the industry to the United States." He further stated that by late 1971 through the use of ceramic modules, "we should be competitive with Oriental costs and next year we ought to be able to beat them."

In order to realize this potential, however, it would have been necessary to standardize circuit design, thus making it economic to operate the manufacturing facilities required for mass-producing the modules. These modules have the further capability of being readily manipulated by mechanical means. But the American firms have refused thus far to undertake the standardization process.

In August 1973 the *New York Times* reported that the U.S. was turning to French suppliers for modern railroad equipment. Amtrak imported the first of a series of French-built turbo trains.

Why did the United States have to turn to France for a turbo train? [Amtrak official] Mr. Day explained that the American and Canadian turbos built by United Aircraft have had so many mechanical difficulties that the New York–Boston turbo run is no longer an extra-fare charge. And the French trains, costing about $2.7 million, are cheaper, he said. But Amtrak hopes to stir up further competition among builders.

One of the main difficulties is the condition of American tracks. Jean Fleche, chief test engineer for the research department of the French National Railways, said that he had operated the RTGs at better than 160 miles an hour. But one official noted that 70 is the top allowable speed now between Chicago and St. Louis.

In industry after industry requiring quality engineering there has been a manifest falling-off of the U.S. position. Miniature ball bearings are an important component of many precision devices. By 1971 over half of the U.S. requirement of miniature ball bearings was supplied by imports, mainly from Japan.

MISPLACED CONFIDENCE

After the Second World War, industry in the United States developed strong leads in certain "high-technology" fields. These industries included computers, commercial jet aircraft, nuclear power and the design of semiconductors. These classes of products benefited directly from the force-feeding of areas of U.S. technology that were of special interest to the military. Indeed, the U.S. lead in these fields led to fears in Western

Europe and elsewhere of a "technology gap" between the U.S. and Western Europe. This fear did not endure long as European and Japanese industrialists began to reap the benefit of their sustained concentration on civilian research. In January 1972 *Business Week* reported that:

Foreign steelmakers . . . were . . . installing new processes, such as the basic oxygen furnace, on a wider scale than American steelmen. And even in the early 1960s, U.S. heavy machinery builders such as the makers of turbine generators were running into intense foreign competition on design as well as on price. . . . These days some of Europe's older high-technology industries, such as chemicals and electrical equipment, are selling more and more of their products and licensing more and more of their technology to U.S. companies. . . . Extra high voltage transmission, a more efficient way of conducting electric power for long distances, was pioneered in the U.S. by ASEA, the Swedish electrical equipment maker. When Colt Industries sought to rescue its faltering program for developing big diesel engines, it had to turn to Austrian consultants for help. . . . The American construction industry is just beginning to use "systems building" techniques that are already widely applied in Europe.

The aircraft industry is a notable example of the new international competition. In France and in Japan airframe and aircraft engine builders are developing designs that are sharply competitive with U.S.-made products. Mr. Alan E. Puckett, Executive Vice-President of Hughes Aircraft Company, says, "Our R&D money just isn't keeping pace."

The DC-3 was one of the most successful commercial aircraft of all time. Its special operating characteristics of slow landing speed, short take-off requirement, rugged operating characteristics, continued to be valued more than 35 years after the plan was initially introduced. In the mid-1960s the Federal Aviation Agency announced a contest for the design of a successor plane to the DC-3 (which I reported in my book, *Our Depleted Society*, 1965). No American aircraft-producer entered the design contest — not even the Douglas firm which had been the designer and fabricator of the DC-3. However, a few years later, at the international air show in Hanover, Germany, the Soviet aviation industry presented a short haul passenger jet that aspired to the workhorse virtues of the venerable DC-3. This plane was three-engined, seating 34 passengers, and was offered at the obvious bargain price of $770,000 per plane, or about ⅓ the price of a small airliner made in the west.

Until 1971 federal officials believed that, come what may, American strength in the "high-technology" industries would more than overcome noncompetitiveness in traditionally "labor-intensive" industries. Therefore when a weakening position showed up in the areas of presumed strength, alarm bells sounded in the federal establishment. The scale and quality of U.S. industrial research was reviewed on July 27, 1971, by Maurice H. Stans, then Secretary of Commerce, when he appeared before the House Committee on Science and Astronautics.

Though the U.S. still maintains a much higher level of R&D expenditures than any individual country in the world, it is becoming evident that other countries, notably Western Germany and Japan, are placing a much higher relative emphasis on civilian R&D. In 1968, the U.S. spent $13 billion for civilian R&D. Equivalent figures for Japan and West Germany amount to $3 and $4 billion, respectively. These individual expenditures represented 1.5% of U.S. GNP, versus 2.6% of German GNP and 2.0% of Japan's. If the capitalized value of purchased foreign technology is computed and added to these figures, the U.S. level stays the same but both German and Japanese levels jump to $5 billion annually.

While the dollar level of our R&D exceeds the sum of West German and Japanese expenditures, there are two factors that qualify this apparent conclusion. One is that wage costs in those countries are much lower, with the result that they can purchase more R&D per dollar invested. Secondly, and perhaps more importantly, it takes a greater R&D effort, at much greater cost, for the leading country to find innovations to stay ahead.

This was the first time since 1893 that a deficit had appeared in U.S. trade with other nations. And there were predictions of more to come. So the government announced a series of moves to improve civilian technology. William Magruder was moved from NASA, where he was in charge of the supersonic transport program, to the White House and asked to plan civilian technology programs. A task force from the President's Office of Science and Technology was set up to encourage the transfer of federally-generated technology to state and local governments. Research and development pooling among smaller companies was to be promoted, and patent policies were to be altered in order to encourage private use of government-owned patents. Furthermore, the government indicated that it was planning to make money available to start new high-technology enterprises, and a bill was submitted to the Congress in 1972 for this purpose. Also, a series of investigations were started to discover ways of inducing business firms and others to develop and utilize new technology. But the administration had soon recovered from its panic.

QUESTIONABLE SOLUTIONS

The Department of Defense came through with a major plan for enlarging world sales of armaments from the United States, increasing such exports from $925 million in 1970 to $3,800 million per year in 1973. Negotiations were undertaken with the U.S.S.R. for large sales of agricultural produce, and the administration proceeded to deal vigorously with the Japanese to slow down the rate of Japanese penetration into U.S. markets and accelerate the export of U.S. goods.

However, increased export of U.S.-produced grains to Japan, Western Europe and the U.S.S.R. has led to sharp reductions in American stocks

Table 1   Federal 1974 Budget

Note: Public expenditure tradeoffs are a major connection between war economy and quality of life, and the link is visible in a set of choices made by the Nixon Administration for 1974. Here is a list of proposed cuts in civilian items contrasted with increased money recommended by the Administration for military and related projects.

Civilian Economy Cuts	($ million)	($ million)	Military Economy Increases
CUT in grants for basic water and sewer facilities under HUD Community Development Program	7.3	6.9	INCREASE for MK 48 Torpedo
CUT in construction loans and grants for higher education	18.0	15.3	INCREASE for E-3A Airborne Warning & Control System
CUT in education for the handicapped under HEW Office of Education	23.9	22.9	INCREASE for SAM-D Missile
CUT in library resources under HEW Office of Education	33.9	29.0	INCREASE for B-1 Bomber
CUT in federally supported hospital and health facility construction	36.0	39.5	INCREASE for manned space flight research and development under NASA
CUT in operations, research, and facilities of the Environmental Protection Agency	75.4	73.9	INCREASE for NASA
CUT in Indian programs under Minority Assistance Programs (to broaden opportunities for economic participation and self-determination)	82.2	94.3	INCREASE for A-X Tactical Attack Aircraft
CUT in federally aided health training and education	86.0	92.0	INCREASE in Air Force research, development, text, and evaluation
CUT in child nutrition for elementary and secondary education	200.0	194.2	REQUEST for SAM-D Missile

CUT in manpower reve- nue sharing under DoL Manpower Administra- tion	252.0	239.9	INCREASE for F-15 Tactical Fighter Air- craft (77 planes)
CUT in emergency em- ployment assistance under DoL Manpower Administration	519.7	546.3	REQUEST for S-3A Vik- ing Anti-Submarine Warfare Aircraft
CUT in elementary and secondary education	1,500.0	1,200.0	REQUEST for one Tri- dent Submarine

Sources: *The Budget of the United States Government, Fiscal Year 1974*, U.S. Government Printing Office, Washington, D.C.; *Special Analyses, Budget of the United States Government, Fiscal Year 1974*, U.S. Government Printing Office, Washington, D.C.; *Program Acquisition Costs by Weapon System, Department of Defense Budget for Fiscal Year 1974*, Department of Defense, Washington, D.C.

and significant price increases in grains and in grain-dependent products for domestic markets. Thus, the prices of all grades of meat products in the United States increased dramatically during 1972–73 as a response to the increased cost of feeding and fattening cattle. In the short run, it is true that armaments sales abroad will restore a more favorable balance of trade, but it will also ensure a high-capacity utilization of military–industry facilities in the U.S. with all its depleting consequences.

Every year since 1961 the Secretary of Defense has presented to the Congress a report on the military security position of the United States. The content of these reports has been wide-ranging, from military–technical subjects and the balance of payments, to various efforts by the Pentagon to participate in the War on Poverty. In none of these elaborate statements is there so much as a hint that the Pentagon's enterprise might have a negative effect on the domestic security of the American people due to the drain on capital, manpower and the preemption of social attention. There is also a year-round effort by the military and civilian officers of the Pentagon to justify the operation of the military directorate as an all-around boon to American economy and society.

The assumption that sustained war economy brings economic and allied well-being encounters a cruel contrast in the shape of what is foregone in the United States in health care, housing, education, and minimum nutrition. These are all recognized areas of public responsibility partly because the consequences of deficiencies in these realms have blighting effects on the entire society.

The idea that quality of life could be a public responsibility gained support from a sizable minority in the United States during the 1960s. However political leaders, intellectuals and the general populace did not concur. The quality of life was to remain mainly a personal and private responsibility, while grudgingly subsidized from the public purse. The rule here was subsidy-minimization. The ideological consensus obscured the actual connection between priority to military economy and deficient health care, decay of the central cities, and the general failure to carry out economic and social development for the industrialized parts of American society.

Item: From 1970 on the federal government undertook across-the-board reduction in sponsoring scientific research of every sort. In particular major reductions or total elimination was ordered for educational support of new biologists, chemists, physicists, and every other science. Thereby the directorate of war economy withdrew investment in the future of the United States as a productive society.

Item: By 1970 the actual demand for new doctors in the United States was 50% greater than the 8,500 new M.D.'s receiving their degree in that year.

Item: In New York City the municipal hospitals had 4,480 nurses on their staff, but needed 1,400 more to meet reasonable standards.

Item: The National Academy of Sciences in September 1972 found that emergency medical services represented "one of the weakest links in delivery of health care in the nation," and that thousands of lives are lost through lack of systematic application of established principles of emergency care.

Item: The American population as a whole is described as a nation of "nutritional illiterates," and among the poor, one out of four have been found to be anemic to the degree requiring medical care. Among children of migrant workers malnutrition is found as severe as that once seen in Biafra during the civil war and siege of the 1960s.

Item: California, the capital state of military industry, has been importing 70% of its physicians, 75% of its registered nurses and 60% of its pharmacists, thereby draining the medical resources of the donor states.

Item: In 1970, studies of adult literacy show that "half the nation's adults may lack the literacy necessary to master such day-to-day reading matter as driving manuals, newspapers and job applications."

Item: From 1970 to 1973 there was an epidemic of reductions in school budgets, teaching personnel and educational programs throughout the country. The length of the school year was reduced in a series of large cities.

This unexpected turn of events fits neither with the ideological consensus about the U.S. economy, nor with the urgency for being Number One that pervades American culture. To Americans, the idea of being Number One means not merely having surpassed military and industrial power, but also a high and rising level of material well-being for the population as a whole. Being superior in both guns and butter has been part of the

American self-image — guns were even supposed to help make butter. One of the core contradictions in American life has been between this ideology and economic reality. For as it has turned out, guns have inevitably taken away from butter.

3. THE FOOD MONOPOLIES
Daniel Zwerdling

As the American food crisis got worse and worse — by September the average grocery bill had increased 35 per cent in just two years — food industry magnates and officials of the U.S. Department of Agriculture began pointing accusatory fingers at that old and unpredictable villain, the weather. Newspaper clippings before me read like a farmer's almanac: back in August [1974], according to the Associated Press, USDA said retail food prices would increase in the second half of 1974 instead of declining "as predicted" because "summer droughts decreased harvest prospects." Two months later USDA told us we had unexpectedly lost "a powerful hedge against rising food prices" because the corn crop had succumbed to early frosts. Then, at a news conference in late November, the president of the national supermarket lobby announced that supermarket prices were high "for the simplest of reasons": supply had fallen lower than demand because "the 1974 American grain crop was a distinct disappointment."

It was almost tempting to join USDA and the food industry in this fantasy — to imagine that the United States, with all its dazzling military, industrial, and agricultural might, could be rendered helpless by so cosmically pure a force as a frost alighting one crisp September morning on the corn stalks surrounding Dubuque. It is not that changes in the weather have no effect on crop production and prices — certainly they do. But there were far more troubling and deep-rooted causes of the American food crisis than the USDA barometer could register:

Clue Number One — Profiteering: While food prices were pushing millions of Americans toward serious financial sacrifice and even poverty, the giants in the food industrial complex were crying all the way to the bank. Safeway Stores, Inc. boosted its profits by 51 per cent during the first nine months of 1974 (compared to the first nine months of 1973), while Kroger increased its profits by 94 per cent, and Colonial by a respectable 37 per cent. A little further down the food chain, Del Monte, the nation's largest producer of canned fruits and vegetables, increased profits by 43 per cent; Pillsbury reported a 32 per cent jump in profits, and A. E. Staley, which makes soybean-based meat substitutes, did well with an 89 per cent boost in profits. The manufacturers who make the food containers, American Can and Continental Can, increased profits by 52 per cent and 35 per cent, respectively. And while you cursed (or cried) at the meat counter, Iowa Beef Processors, the largest beef packer in the nation, managed to contend with consumer beef boycotts and major internal strikes and still produce profit increases of 50 per cent, following profit jumps the previous two years of 73 per cent and 99 per cent.

Clue Number Two — Corporate Empires: At Safeway's latest count, this $7 billion food empire owned more than 2,400 supermarkets, 109 manufacturing and processing plants, sixteen produce packaging plants, sixteen bakeries, nineteen milk and sixteen ice cream plants, four soft drink bottlers, three meat processors, three coffee roasting plants, a soap and peanut butter and salad oil factory, plus a fleet of 2,100 tractor-trailers shuttling among Safeway's sixty distributor warehouses (not to forget Safeway's half-interest in twenty-five Holly Farms fast fried-chicken outlets in the Southeast, and others scheduled for the Middle West).

Safeway's corporate strategies are formulated by the board of directors, titans of industry who also help control such corporations as the Bank of California, General Electric, Wells Fargo Bank (reportedly a big investor in California grape syndicates), Shell Oil, Pacific Gas and Electric, Caterpillar Tractor, and Southern Pacific Co. (the largest private agricultural landowner in California). Safeway also interlocks with the $1.6 billion Owens-Illinois Manufacturers — one of America's largest suppliers of shipping cartons, plastic, and glass packaging — and the multi-faceted AMFAC, which besides being the largest producer of raw cane sugar in Hawaii, has spread tentacles into food processing, mortgage banking, land management, and food sales to holtel restaurants and resorts.

Clue Number Three — Controlling Markets: While the price of lettuce was hopping from twenty-nine cents to forty-nine cents to fifty-nine cents a head, the United Brands conglomerate was pursuing its dreams of taking over large segments of key agricultural markets. As a Federal Trade Commission staff report revealed, United Brands (formerly United Fruit) bought out at least six major lettuce and celery growers and shippers in 1968 and 1969. Its goals: to seize a "non-preemptable position as leader in fresh and semiprocessed salad products," according to company officials, and then to boost the price of lettuce a hefty seventy to ninety cents per carton. United Brands already has control over 50 per cent of the

United States banana market, A&W International (of root beer drive-in fame), Baskin-Robbins ice cream parlors, and John Morrell & Co. (one of four gigantic meat packers, which together sell most of the processed meats in America).

Knowing that United Brands is trying to seize control of the salad industry does not explain price fluctuations in lettuce and celery over the past six months. And learning that Safeway owns bakeries and an edible oils refinery does not tell precisely why the price of a half-dozen glazed doughnuts jumped from thirty-eight cents last year to sixty-eight cents today. No one seems able to account for the precise factors that have caused such explosive price spurts. The economists I have interviewed, on Senate committees, at USDA, at the Federal Trade Commission, all argue their own favorite combinations of devalued dollars, increased demand overseas, soaring fuel costs, and, of course, the weather. One FTC economist had just finished a classic textbook lesson on supply and demand when I asked him if any of his colleagues had a different theory. "Sure," he told me cheerfully, "why don't you call ———?" He gave me the name of an economist next door.

But focusing most of our attention on these recent and volatile price spurts and the mercurial conditions which cause them makes as little sense as blaming the flu for causing fever in a patient whose body is ravaged by cancer. They obscure the most crucial and pervasive inflationary force, which more than any other is inexorably pushing food prices higher and will continue pushing them higher still long after the dollar has regained its value and the weather has returned to normal. Giant corporations and conglomerates are maneuvering into control over vast markets in the food industrial complex. While USDA was preoccupied with analyzing price fluctuations from week to week — chicken at sixty-nine cents a pound one week, down to fifty-nine cents the next — corporations were exerting their control over just thirteen food lines to inflate prices permanently by $2.1 *billion*, according to a 1972 FTC staff study. And there are about forty-five food lines — major types of foods — in the market.

A quick look at food industry profit figures shows that some of the most powerful corporations have clearly been taking advantage of outside inflationary pressures to mask profit gouging. "Profit gouging?" a leading FTC food economist mused. "I wouldn't use that phrase. I'd prefer to say 'profit maximization.'" But whatever you want to call it, consumers have seen it before. In 1974 the energy conglomerates said there were emergency shortages of heating oil and gasoline, remember, and fuel prices soared; then, as Congressional investigations revealed that the oil companies had actually *cut back* refinery production, the companies reported they had boosted their profits by as much as 83 per cent (Shell) and a phenomenal 174 per cent (Pennzoil) during the first nine months of 1974.

In a similar vein, beef farmers slaughtered hundreds of calves because they said that at the price they were getting from processors they could not afford the feed costs, only to discover that Missouri Beef Packers, one of the nation's leading meat producers, boosted its profits by 60 per cent after having doubled them the year before. While energy conglomerates begged to strip-mine Montana so they could supply Americans with desperately needed fuel — and then started shipping some of the Montana coal to Japan — food conglomerates blamed rising food prices on grain shortages, and then exported a record $20 billion worth of food overseas, two and a half times as much as 1972 exports. Those exports were not destined for starving people, but for foreign importers willing to pay the price.

Some food corporations have obviously gained enough control over the market to manipulate suppliers and prices at will. "These firms are always going to perform in their own best interest," says Russell Parker, assistant to the director of FTC's Bureau of Economics. "The situation [of growing corporate concentration in the food industry] is getting worse, and it will continue to get worse in the future." While high prices now may drop a bit, rise a bit, then drop a bit again, he says, "the food corporations are setting the stage for permanently higher prices in the future."

All the trends in the food industry mimic trends in the energy industry. Compared to the seven energy conglomerates which control most of America's fuel, the food industry seems far less concentrated — fifty food processors control more than 60 per cent of all processing profits. But when you examine corporate concentration in individual food lines and in local retail markets — where concentration really counts — much of the food industry is revealed as even more tightly controlled than energy.

Many economists agree that when four corporations exercise control over 50 per cent of any market, they have created what monopoly expert William Shepherd calls a "tight oligopoly" (see his *Market Power and Economic Welfare*). According to this definition, tight oligopolies have already seized control of the breakfast cereals industry (where four firms control 90 per cent of sales), the bread and prepared flour industry (four firms control 75 percent of sales), the baking industry (65 per cent), the fluid milk industry (60 per cent), the dairy products industry (70 per cent), and processed meats (56 per cent). Four corporations sell 65 per cent of the sugar, four account for 80 per cent of the canned goods, and just one company (Campbell's, of course) produces 90 per cent of the soups. A little closer to the farm, a tight oligopoly controls more than 70 per cent of the farm machinery industry, inflating farm equipment costs by about $250 million in 1972, according to the FTC.

And while huge corporations have not yet taken control over most of the farmlands, they have taken control over most of the nation's farmers. So, according to researchers at the University of Illinois, farmers sell more than half of their fresh vegetables under contract to agribusiness corporations, almost all their vegetables for processing, most citrus fruits, most poultry, and virtually all of their beet and cane sugar.

When the food finally arrives at the supermarkets, the oligopolies are still in control. In most of the nation's 200 largest metropolitan areas, according to the FTC, just two or three or four chains control the majority of grocery sales.

When I began research for this article, I wanted to find statistics which could explain precisely how many cents in last week's grocery bill we could blame on these food oligopolies. The FTC estimates $2.1 billion in overcharges in just thirteen food lines; Ralph Nader maintains that a secret FTC staff report shows that if the oligopolies were broken up, food prices would drop by 25 per cent. But no one seems to have more specific data. "The brutal reality is we don't know how corporations are manipulating prices and profits in individual food lines," an FTC official told me. The Congressional Joint Economic Committee recently subpoenaed supermarket records, and the FTC has been trying to pry some figures out of major food manufacturers' books. "We've been getting one hell of a lot of resistance from all quarters, except consumers," the FTC official complains.

But we can get some glimpses inside the food industrial complex which suggests how the giant corporations are exerting their enormous power to take over markets and drive up prices. United Brands frankly told the Federal Government that it wants to achieve with salad and lettuce what it has already achieved with bananas – control enough of the market (50 per cent in the case of bananas) so the corporation can set new prices higher than consumers have paid in the past. Tenneco, which controls major pesticide, farm machinery, and packaging corporations, has also taken over Heggblade-Margoleas, the largest fresh fruits and vegetables marketer in the nation – expressly, according to a corporate vice president, to do with fresh produce "what Del Monte has done with canned foods." That means to market produce under the Tenneco Sun Giant label and – if Tenneco follows the Del Monte strategy – to sell less produce for more money than most other brands.

Or, consider how powerful chains manipulate prices in the supermarkets. The supermarket industry in Washington, D.C., is more concentrated than in any city in the nation. The Giant Food stores and Safeway stores ringing the Justice Department and Federal Trade Commission – which are responsible for breaking up monopolies – control almost 60 per cent of all metropolitan area grocery sales, according to FTC reports.

In 1967 a competitive little supermarket chain called Shop Rite announced it intended to penetrate the Washington market. So, according to FTC files never before released, Giant and Safeway hired an industrial espionage firm to investigate Shop Rite's marketing practices in other cities and then map a hard-hitting offensive. Giant and Safeway followed the firm's advice and slashed prices at selected supermarkets *only* in those neighborhoods where Shop Rite stores were scheduled to open. The Shop Rite attempt failed, and Giant and Safeway prices went back up.

Again in August 1970, a new competitor called Memco (Lucky Stores) announced plans to penetrate the Washington market. But this time the FTC staff had started an antitrust investigation of Giant, Safeway, and two other leading chains. Perhaps because they feared Federal indictments, Giant and Safeway failed to hit hard at Memco — and the chain opened a few successful stores. Giant and Safeway did compete by introducing chain-wide discounting, which actually dropped prices lower than the national average.

But that is not the end of the story. When the FTC suddenly announced in August 1973 that it was dropping its antitrust investigation, prices at Giant and Safeway immediately began to climb. By September 1974, Giant and Safeway had boosted their Washington prices a spectacular 3.5 per cent *higher* than supermarkets across the rest of the country. In the supermarket business, that 3.5 per cent excess is a whopping amount. Coincidence? An official at the FTC told me that the chances of Giant and Safeway boosting prices that much because of justifiable economic reasons are "about one in a million."

Now consider the pricing power a food corporation gains through vertical integration. Until 1961, the Southland Corp. was a profitable ice manufacturer; now it is one of the most remarkable food empires in the United States. You help it grow every time you shop at one of its 4,800 retail stores: your neighborhood, high-priced 7-Eleven's, the New York area's Gristede's and Charles & Co. gourmet food shops. Bradshaw supermarkets, the Barricini candy chain, plus 1,000 supermarkets and food stores in the British Isles which Southland controls through huge interests in Wright's Biscuits, Ltd.

Southland has designed its empire so that its retail stores serve as captive outlets for other profitable ventures under the same corporate roof. Southland stocks most of the dairy products in its stores from its thirty major dairies (which sell milk under the Embassy, Oak Farms, Cooper Farms, Briggs, and other labels). Southland fabricates its dairy products and candies using chemical additives purchased from Southland's own chemical manufacturing plants. The corporation ships its own products in its recently acquired trucking fleets, and it promotes them with advertising campaigns devised by its own advertising subsidiary. All these ventures — dairies, chemical plants, truck fleets, and advertising agencies — sell their own goods and services to Southland's competitors as well.

Southland's potential market and pricing powers are enormous. The

FTC has already charged, in early 1973, that Southland's chemical division was making reciprocal deals with some of its "competitors"; Southland executives made it clear that if other corporations wanted Southland's business, they had better buy Southland chemicals. Southland agreed to an FTC consent order forbidding such reciprocal deals. Have other companies in the powerful Southland conglomerate been making similar arrangements? FTC investigators are reportedly examining some of the corporation's dairy practices. In any case, while farmers were dumping thousands of gallons of raw milk into Los Angeles sewers last year in protest against prices offered them by processors, the Southland Corp., dairies and all, boosted its first nine months' profits by a comfortable 30 per cent.

The forward march of powerful conglomerates into the food industrial complex exerts a new influence on food prices which tends to throw traditional USDA price indicators out of kilter. As financial institutions and industrial conglomerates take over more and more of the food industry, the production and pricing of food will become less and less related to traditional factors — like the weather — which regulated food prices and increasingly dependent on conglomerate wheelings and dealings which have nothing to do with food itself. Aetna Life and Casualty becomes a partner with the massive Kaiser Aluminum conglomerate in purchasing large land holdings and crops. *The Los Angeles Times* and the Oppenheimer Fund sink millions into ranches and cattle. ITT makes Wonder Bread and Smithfield hams, and Ling-Temco-Vought makes Wilson meats (which, together with United Brands-Morrell, Greyhound-Armour, and Swift control the U.S. meat products industry). Unilever makes Lipton's tea and Imperial margarine. The examples, which the Agri-business Accountability Project in Washington, D.C., has so widely and valuably publicized, go on and on.

When a major food corporation becomes just one more listing on a conglomerate's cash-flow chart, food production becomes subject to a brand new kind of economics. When United Brands started taking over producers in the lettuce and celery industry, its InterHarvest division lost $8.3 million — but no matter, because it "was saved by a massive transfusion of funds from the parent," according to the FTC. As the FTC went on to say, no other lettuce grower or shipper could take an "$8 million drubbing." The significance here is not that InterHarvest lost money at first, but that its lettuce economic strategies were less related to conditions in the lettuce fields than to economic conditions in other United Brands subsidiaries.

We may be suffering this perversion of food industry economics right now, when we buy sugar. A year ago five pounds of sugar cost eighty-eight cents in the supermarket. Today the same bag costs up to $3. Economists have various theories for the astronomical increase: worldwide demand exceeds supply, rich Arab nations are buying lots of the stuff, speculators are hoarding and driving prices upward. The major sugar producers in America are making a killing. Amstar increased its profits about two and a half times in the first nine months of 1974. Great Western Sugar increased its profits too — but how does one explain how Great Western increased its profits by *2,000 per cent?*

The answers lie in the corporate books of the Great Western United conglomerate, which owns, among other interests, Great Western Sugar, the nationwide Shakey's Pizza chain, a ranch, and three new-town developments in California, Colorado, and New Mexico. While Great Western's real estate holdings are enormously valuable — its California City sits on a small portion of *119,000 acres* between Los Angeles and Bakersfield — the returns from these holdings are poor. And over the past few years Great Western United Corporation has been sinking into a crisis. It has missed paying dividends.

The Colorado City Water and Sanitation District says the Great Western conglomerate's new town in Colorado cannot get enough water, scaring potential investors away. The Environmental Protection Agency is badgering Great Western to clean up waste water in refineries spread across four states. The Justice Department may indict the conglomerate's sugar company for price-fixing. The former chief executive officer has sued the corporation for allegedly defrauding its stockholders. So, in the midst of this crisis, Great Western United was planning during most of 1973 to sell its sugar company to get a quick infusion of desperately needed cash.

But suddenly, all this has changed. In a large advertisement in *The New York Times* financial section in November, Great Western United claimed it is making up overdue payments, paying back dividend arrears, forgetting plans to sell the sugar company, and urging stockholders to turn down an attractive offer by the Hunt billionaires, the powerful oil family, to take over 51 per cent of its stock. Everything at Great Western United looks rosy. Why? Credit its good fortune, the conglomerate says, to the "favorable impact of developments" — namely, that Great Western Sugar has been reaping phenomenally high profits from white gold.

One can only speculate: did Great Western Sugar soak consumers to help pull its parent conglomerate out of desperate financial straits? It is conceivable that when consumers took Great Western Sugar through the supermarket checkout line, they were paying the price — an outrageous price — to help bolster a sagging real estate venture called California City.

Trends in Safeway, United Brands, Southland, Great Western United, and other conglomerates offer only the faintest sketch of the enormously complex picture of the food industrial complex. It is an unsatisfying sketch, with few details, few firm statistics to go on. The way Government economists grope in vain for some credible explanations of the food price crisis measures just how completely large corporations have taken control of this most vital resource — food, which sustains life — and transformed the most basic facts of supply and pricing into private corporate secrets.

The Consumer Federation of America will bring consumer groups and farmers together this month to discuss possible action they can take to fight high food prices. By bringing these two exploited groups together, the conference will platform a valuable educational service. But consumers and farmers, no matter how united, have little hope of even denting nationwide food prices. They can fight such corporate tools as Federal and state marketing orders, which require farmers to allow a certain percentage of peaches, potatoes, and other fruits and vegetables to rot in the fields (and, consequently, to limit supply and "stabilize" prices). They can fight the Internal Revenue Service's farming tax shelters, which encourage syndicates of corporations and wealthy individuals to invest in farming ventures merely to reap huge tax benefits. The U.S. Treasury estimates it loses about $900 million in taxes this way every year.

But really fighting the food price structure means fighting the food industry; and fighting the food industry means tackling the most powerful corporations in America. To food industry experts I interviewed, both in government and in consumer groups, the future looks bleak. "I believe this is just about the last chance we've got to fight back, before the takeover of the food industry by conglomerates is complete," says Jim Hightower, director of the Agribusiness Accountability Project. From his office in the Federal Trade Commission, Russell Parker shakes his head. "I am not optimistic," he says, "about the future of the food industry." Down the street, the president of the National Association of Food Chains, Clarence Adamy, sounds more jubilant. "The supermarkets' profits have been too low for too long," he says cheerfully. "This year we did better. But our profits are still not big enough."

It all depends, I suppose, on whether you are paying or cashing in.

4. RECESSION IS CAPITALISM
AS USUAL

David M. Gordon

Capitalism . . . is not intelligent, it is not beautiful, it is not just, it is not virtuous — and it doesn't deliver the goods. — JOHN MAYNARD KEYNES, 1933.

I don't know too much about economics. I do know we're in trouble.
— SENATOR MIKE MANSFIELD, 1975.

San Francisco, Christmas, 1974. More than 5,000 of the nation's professional economists had gathered for their annual convention. The atmosphere was hardly festive. The economy had been unraveling. Economists had neither predicted its problems nor prescribed their solutions. They had been caught, as several wits had quipped, "with their parameters down."

Minnesota's Walter Heller, as outgoing president of the American Economic Association, gave the closing address of the convention. Heller had been a leading public advocate of the "New Economics" in the nineteen-sixties, helping promote the investiture of the secular priests. "We have . . . harnessed the existing economics . . . to the purpose of prosperity, stability, and growth," he wrote in 1966, putting economists "at the President's elbow." Would he now publicly moderate his claims, perhaps admitting that the priests had been defrocked?

Undaunted, Heller asked, "What's Right With Economics?" "I intend to accentuate the positive," he began. "As economists, we have many sins, none deadly, to confess. But these are far outweighed by the virtues, all quite lively, that we can legitimately profess."

And so it goes. Smiling through the egg on their faces, the established American economists are still keeping the faith. But there is another group of American economists, a smaller, less visible and less prestigious group. We call ourselves "radical political economists." Whatever our forum, we try to make a few basic and different points.

In our view, the current economic crisis flows from corporate and Government efforts to make working people in this country pay the costs of the collapse and reconstruction of the American corporate empire. The crisis is beginning to push the American economic system toward some basic institutional changes. As those changes develop, we shall all be forced to ask whose interests they will serve and whose they will subvert.

I want to try to elaborate that view with some care here.[1] Before we can raise our red flags, we must first weave and dye the cloth. Like the economic problems we analyze, the texture of the fabric is intricate.

Mainstream economists are locked in debate over the date of the downturn and the indicators of continued deterioration or recovery. But the current crisis cannot be measured by any one indicator. Its severity is revealed by a combination of developments, reinforcing one another over the past several years.

Unemployment. The measured rates, while the highest since 1941, provide only a partial count of the jobless. The Government officially records more than eight million as "unemployed." At least another five million want and need full-time jobs but cannot find them. The Government overlooks those potential workers, either because they have grudgingly accepted part-time jobs or because, as "discouraged workers," they are no longer actively seeking work. Added together, the "official" and "unofficial" jobless now total nearly 15 per cent of the labor force.

Inflation. While the rate is slowing, prices still soar by earlier standards. It now costs $1.58 to buy what cost $1.00 in 1967. We have suffered over the past eight years the longest period of sustained inflation in this country since the first tabulated aggregate price statistics in 1820.

Income. Unemployment and inflation have combined to erode workers' purchasing power. By February, 1975, the average American working family could buy less with its weekly earnings than it could in 1964. Workers' real incomes (adjusted for inflation) have declined as rapidly over the past 18 months as they did at the beginning of the Great Depression.

Production. Declining consumer demand and rising wholesale prices have together staged an industrial blood-letting. The index of industrial production fell by almost 10 per cent in the first quarter of 1975, the most rapid drop since monthly data were first reported in 1947.

Credit. Both corporations and families have been racing desperately to forestall hard times by borrowing. The credit structure gets shakier and shakier. By 1974, banks had lent a higher percentage of total deposits than before the Great Depression, the highest since before the collapse of 1893.

Trade. Economic events spread like ripples through the world economy. By the middle of 1973, the business cycles of the advanced industrial countries had become synchronized for the first time since World War II. As countries seek protection from the crisis, foreign trade contracts. That only makes the problem worse, for declining exports accelerate the drop in income almost everywhere.

While politics is not "determined" by economics, economic instability is likely to breed political instability. Like marathon dancers stumbling toward their hundredth hour, Western governments have been fainting from exhaustion. There have been major changes of administration during the past three years in the United States, Japan and 14 of the 16 capitalist countries in Western Europe. Only Spain, waiting for Franco to die, and Austria have escaped the trend.

The current crisis caught almost everyone by surprise. With economists as guides, we were apparently traveling the Yellow Brick Road. The primary postulate of the "New Economics," as Yale's James Tobin put it last year, was "that government policy could and should keep the economy close to a path of steady real growth." Instability, like the Wicked Witch of the West, would dissolve.

However appealing, that analysis was superficial. Employment, output and prices are derivative variables in capitalist economies. Capitalism is based on production for *profit*, not for employment. Corporations count their earnings, not the jobs they create. Corporations accumulate profits by getting workers to produce more in value than they earn in wages. Economic growth is conditioned by conflict between the corporate "werewolf hunger" for profits, as Marx called it, and workers' resistance to the relatively lower wages, hierarchical command structures and degrading working conditions that the hunger requires.

Probing beneath the surface harmonies of full employment, we begin to see that economic stability cannot endure in capitalist economies. The American economy has roller-coastered over at least 16 business cycles in the past 100 years. It turns out that continuous growth, however productive of jobs, is bad for profits. And, as Charles Wilson of General Motors might have put it, what's bad for profits is bad for the country.

Continuous prosperity eventually threatens profits through the market mechanism. Individual capitalists — profit junkies on prosperity highs — invest feverishly during a boom. Sooner or later, they begin to exhaust the reserve supplies of workers. The labor market tightens. This over-investment has two shattering consequences for corporations. Wages begin to rise rapidly, cutting into profits. And workers take advantage of their scarcity by resisting the "werewolf hunger" more militantly and more effectively; workers' productivity slows, directly undercutting capitalist control of the production process.

In a market economy, corporations have only two recourses. They must restore competition in the labor market in order to ease labor scarcity and undercut labor strength. And they must find new ways to make more efficient use of their workers. When booms persist, they can accomplish neither. Prosperity protects workers from the competition of the unemployed and cushions relatively inefficient enterprises.

In a market economy, therefore, periodic recessions are indispensable for profits. With a rise in unemployment, labor "discipline" improves. As output falls, the razor of market competition trims worker power and pares away inefficient operations. Recessions restore the basis for capital accumulation. "By momentary suspension of labor and annihilation of a great portion of capital," Marx wrote 125 years ago, production for profit can resume.

That analysis helps explain the recent eruption of crisis. A quick review of the past decade through that lens reveals the underlying patterns.

By 1966, the economy had been growing steadily for almost five years and was due for a cooling bath. The Government could not afford to admit the costs of the war in Vietnam by raising taxes. The restorative functions of recession were postponed. The boom continued until early 1969.

Corporations began to pay the price of postponement as profits suffered their classic decline. The ratio of profits to wages fell nearly by half between 1965 and 1969. With labor markets tight, worker militancy grew. Productivity growth slowed to one-quarter its rate of increase during the first half of the boom.

Corporations, in classic response, speeded up the pace of production. Industrial accidents increased by more than a quarter in less than six years. Angered by the speed-up, workers struck more frequently. By 1970, work-time lost through strikes had risen to three and one-half times its 1963 level. The notorious wildcat strike at the G.M. Vega plant in Lordstown, Ohio, dramatized this resistance. The company had increased the speed of the assembly line the preceding year from 60 cars per hour to more than 100. "The more the company pressured them," a local union leader observed, "the less work they turned out."

By the time President Nixon took office in 1969, the signs of trouble were unmistakable. "Many manufacturing executives [had] openly complained in recent years." The Wall Street Journal observed, "that too much control had passed from management to labor." Nixon knew the remedy. He slammed on the fiscal and monetary brakes. The recession of 1969–70 followed.

But time was short. Because the boom had continued so long, it would take several years for the recession to exercise its fully restorative powers. Nixon was afraid to campaign for President with millions out of work. Corporate profits had fallen to such low levels by 1969 that few businesses could easily countenance the prospect of a sustained recession.

So the Administration, in late 1970, stepped on the accelerator again. Almost immediately, the speedometer indicated that the economy was racing too fast. Prices were climbing. Huge labor contract settlements, as high as 15 per cent, chilled corporate spines. Most important, profits fell in 1970 to their lowest share of national income since World War I.

The Administration had few options. It had shrunk from waiting out a sustained recession. Untempered boom could prove disastrous for profits. Continually rising prices would also poison the balance of payments, whose trade deficits were deteriorating every month. "Caught in this trap," as *Business Week* editorialized at the time, "there is only one thing the Administration can do." Nixon established his New Economic Policy as a compromise. Stimulative measures would continue, but a wage–price freeze, it was hoped, would contain the fires the short-lived recession had failed to cool.

The President assured the public, of course, that controls were designed to protect us all from the ravages of inflation. In fact, their purpose was quite different. Workers had to be disciplined so that profits could recover. Arnold Weber, freeze administrator under Nixon, admitted candidly in a recent interview with Clayton Fritchey that business "had been leaning" on the Administration "to do something about wages." "The idea of the freeze and Phase II was to zap labor and we did."

To some extent, the controls worked. Profits recovered momentarily. Workers' militancy was constrained. But the controls did not restore economic stability. Indeed, they largely compounded prevailing distortions by freezing them. When Phase IV guidelines were finally lifted in early 1974, the explosion was felt around the world. Prices skyrocketed. Workers struggled to recover their wage losses and strike activity surged.

By 1974, we were still suffering the consequences of the postponement of recession in the mid-nineteen-sixties. No substitute had yet been found for the normal functions of recession. The economy was like a car on an icy road. Once the skid began, each steering correction simply seemed to exaggerate it. Now we were careening off the pavement.

This brief history helps explain why some kind of crisis was destined. It does not explain why the crunch has been so jarring. There are three additional, equally fundamental reasons why the current crisis is the worst since the Depression.

Concentration. Large corporations have gained increasing control over wealth, markets and supplies in the United States. The largest 100 corporations now control half of all industrial assets. The effects seem obvious.

When demand is high, prices rise more rapidly in a concentrated than in a competitive economy because powerful corporations can repress the rate of increase in supply. When demand falls, inflation is much less likely to slow down because concentration dampens price-cutting competition. This simple phenomenon helps explain the recent combination of simultaneously rapid inflation and high unemployment. Corporations in protected markets often respond to slack demand by *raising* their prices in order to protect their revenues. The auto companies' recent rebates, for instance, gave back only part of the price increases that had been put into effect at earlier stages of the downturn.

A second effect is just as important. The size of the modern corporation complicates some of the traditional cleansing effects of the recession. When large corporations confront the downturn, they can often afford to keep their inefficient operations afloat. Often they can't tell the inefficient from the productive. Because the postwar prosperity lasted so long, a more than usually stringent recession will be required to restore American corporations, flabby from 20 years on the winter banquet circuit, to something like their normal spring-training trim. Yet their size magnifies the hazards of stringent recession. If a small firm folds, fewer than 100 workers may lose their jobs; if a giant corporation tumbles, as many as 100,000 employees may hit the streets. "The huge U.S. corporations have become such important centers of jobs and incomes," *Business Week* concludes, "that [the Government must] protect . . . the great corporations instead of letting the economy make deflationary adjustments."

International instability. American corporations emerged from World War II with international hegemony. They rapidly dominated world business, helping stabilize the world economy. The dollar cemented trade relations. Imperialist rivalries moderated. But the age of Pax Americana has come to an end. The world economy will never be the same. Three developments have combined to erode international economic stability.

First, Western European and Japanese corporations have begun to flex their muscles. The big kid on the block has some rivals. International economic competition has intensified.

Second, the political dominance that supported American economic supremacy has also eroded. Following the interventions in Greece, Iran, Guatemala, Lebanon and the Dominican Republic, Vietnam was supposed to have added another victory bead to the imperialist necklace. The American defeat in Vietnam, the fall of Cambodia and the Arab challenge all dramatize the decline of American power.

Third, American corporations, like their European and Japanese rivals, have gone multinational. And growing multinationals begin to escape the Government leverage that is necessary for Keynesian anticyclical strategies. With scattered resources, they can quickly shift either real investment or liquid capital to avoid tax increases or Government controls. The more rapid these movements, the more quickly the economic ripples spread.

This international instability has contributed to the current crisis in many ways. International competition compounded the profit squeeze on United States corporations in the late nineteen-sixties. The collapse of American supremacy exacerbated balance-of-payments deficits; this in turn narrowed the Government's options in dealing with the crisis. Multinational growth helped bring business cycles among the advanced countries into a single worldwide cycle; that congruence has been amplifying the recent collapse. Finally, at the highest level, the collapse of American hegemony has contributed to the chaos of the present situation. The "enforcer" has lost its power. "For the world economy to be stabilized," Charles P. Kindleberger of the Massachusetts Institute of Technology has written, "there has to be a stabilizer."

Economic growth under capitalism is like an expanding balloon with a leak. We have to keep blowing to avoid deflation. As we huff and puff, the leak may itself widen. If we blow it up too fast, the balloon may burst. Growth itself may collapse.

Why do capitalist economies have leaks? Profits provide the clue.

On one side, capitalists may seek to earn higher profits by depressing their workers' relative wages. When many act in the same way, they run the risk that workers may not be able to purchase commodities available on the market. Unable to sell those products, producers must eventually cut back on production. *Unless* they can discover new markets with new customers.

On another side, corporations may expand production too rapidly, creating labor shortages, paying overtime, bidding up wages. As wages rise, they may compensate by replacing workers with machines, hoping to reduce their costs. But this response may backfire in the end. Individual employers earn profits only on the basis of "value added" within their own enterprises, profiting from the margin between the value their workers produce and the wages their workers earn. Machines can't add value because the individual producers must pay some other capitalist, the one who made the machine, the full worth of that machine. (If a machine contributed more over its lifetime than it cost, other producers would rush to join the parade, bidding up the machine's price.) The only purchase on which the producers may earn some extra money is the purchase of the workers' labor time. The fewer workers the employers hire, therefore, the narrower the base for profit accumulation. As they replace workers by machines, the rate of profit may fall. *Unless* they can find some ways of increasing the productivity of their declining numbers of workers fast enough.

Unless, unless! Those "ifs" pose continuing risks for individual corporations and, in the aggregate, for the entire economy. The risks seemed remote for a time after World War II. New markets had opened up in Europe and Japan. The Depression and the war had created conditions in which corporations could replace their inefficient operations. But the expansion of those markets slowed. And unions began to struggle for a bigger share of those "productivity gains." On an average, profits as a percentage of national income declined during the nineteen-fifties by more than a quarter. The leaks were beginning to appear. Corporations and the Government began huffing and puffing to keep the balloon inflated.

One source of extra air was the Government. The effective tax rate on corporate profits fell from 45.8 per cent of corporate net income in 1961 to 26.9 per cent in 1970. Oil depletion allowances, accelerated depreciation, investment tax credits — all those provisions amounted to Government welfare programs for corporate profits.

Another source of inflation has had potentially more dangerous consequences. Corporations have been borrowing money frenetically, hoping to stay ahead of the profit squeeze. Corporate bank loans as a percentage of corporate product have doubled in just 14 years, rising from 13.8 cents in 1960 to 25.2 per cent in 1974. Banks have been straining to meet the demand. Less than one-seventh of total bank deposits are now covered by available bank reserves, down from a reserve ratio of more than one-third in 1960. As banks have raced to lend money, they have had to borrow themselves. Banks' short-term borrowings rose from 4.5 per cent of their total loans to customers in 1960 to 48.5 per cent in 1974.

All those numbers add up to one simple and frightening picture. American economic growth has been constructed for the past 15 years like a house of credit cards. If the tremors increase, the house of credit cards may collapse.

All this indicates that the current crisis has deep roots. But according to the media, Government officials and mainstream economists, a few accidents are to blame for almost all our problems. Lousy weather cut into food supplies. Greedy Arab oil sheiks hiked petroleum prices. "We've had the food shock, the oil shock, Watergate and its malaise," moans Harvard's Otto Eckstein, ". . . wholly unforeseen shocks that upset all our economic forecasts in the last couple of years."

Blaming fundamental economic problems on "unforeseen shocks" deflects our attention from the economic system itself. Accidents may have helped trigger some recent complications, but they did not cause the crisis. First and simply, the economy was already in crisis before the weather failures of 1972 and the Arab oil price hikes of 1973. Second, the weather and the Arabs do not explain why the food and energy "shortages" had such a wide impact. That second argument requires elaboration.

Food prices began to rise precipitously in 1972. It appeared that bad weather and Soviet buyers had caused those increases by cutting into supplies. In fact, supplies had been artificially limited since World War II. American grain dealers had been gaining control over world grain production for more than two decades. They sought more and more to tighten supplies in order to increase their leverage over both domestic and world prices. Government policies supported their efforts. Arable acreage was withheld from production in the United States. Export subsidies and the threat that the Government would "dump" surplus commodities on the world market kept world prices artificially low; since most developing countries have accrued heavy debts to the rich countries and must pursue foreign earnings relentlessly, low world grain prices have maintained pressures on those countries to garner foreign exchange by specializing in cash crops for export, like cocoa, coffee, tin or rubber, and have discouraged them from allocating their resources to the expansion of domestic grain production. (During the nineteen-thirties, Third World countries exported more grain than North America; now they import roughly four times what they used to export.) World year-end grain reserves had fallen from 25 per cent of annual consumption in 1961 to just under 15 per cent in 1971. With world supplies down, world grain prices were more than usually vulnerable to the sudden drops in annual production that occurred because of bad weather in late 1972 and 1973.

Similarly, the sheiks have been made the scapegoats for the inflation of fuel prices. Almost everyone except the oil corporations and the Government is now willing to admit that there was no real energy shortage during the winter of 1973–74. American oil corporations took advantage of Middle Eastern events to justify domestic price increases. The companies had actually created most of the shortages themselves, holding surplus oil in overseas refineries and offshore tankers long enough to establish the effect. Oil started flowing again a month before the Arabs lifted their own embargo.

This analysis suggests that the current crisis has flowed from the internal character and dynamics of our modern capitalist economy. Capitalism requires periodic recessions to restore profits and discipline labor; we finally got ours — worse because later. Corporate concentration, an inescapable development under capitalism, has accentuated the depth of recession required to fulfill those restorative functions. The dissolution of American hegemony, whose benefits many North Americans enjoyed for 25 years, has thrown the world capitalist economy into a period of intense international instability. Desperate corporate attempts to postpone their days of reckoning are proving counterproductive, as our bloated debt economy stumbles toward an entirely conceivable collapse.

Business leaders and the business press appreciate the magnitude of the crisis. Business Week has recently editorialized: "It is inevitable that the U.S. economy will grow more slowly. . . . Some people will obviously have to do with less. . . . The basic health of the U.S. is based on the basic health of its corporations and banks. . . . Yet it will be a hard pill for many Americans to swallow — the idea of doing with less so that big business can have more. It will be particularly hard to swallow because it is quite obvious that if big business are the most visible victims of what ails the Debt Economy, they are also in large measure the cause of it. . . ."

How will business try to ease the pill down our throats? Only two clear options now present themselves. One looks backward. The other augurs a new era.

The Ford Administration only appears to be indecisive. In public, both Nixon and Ford have offered tolerable economic imitations of Herbert Hoover. One notes the litany, in Arthur Schlesinger's words, "of pep talks, slogans, incantations, voluntarism, 'natural forces,' and random measures of manifest inadequacy." But public appearances aside, the Ford Administration has made a clear choice. Dominated by the advice of free marketeers like Alan Greenspan and William Simon, the Administration is staging the Invisible Hand's Last Stand. They believe that the basis for corporate profits can only be restored if labor's strength is broken and inefficient operations are eliminated. If the market's razor has been dulled, sharpen it!

The Administration made its choice in 1973. Production bottlenecks were about to force the discontinuation of wage-price guidelines. Worse yet, 1974 promised a period of intense collective bargaining, with the contracts of millions of American workers expiring. The time had come for a direct challenge to labor militancy.

The Administration moved quickly. Government spending was cut sharply in the middle of 1973. The monetary screws were tightened a little later. The brakes were screeching.

The present plunge began, as a result, as a politically induced recession. In a fact sheet accompanying Ford's economic address last fall, the White House regretted that "twice within the past decade, in 1967 and in 1971–72, we let an opportunity to regain price stability slip through our grasp." They have vowed not to repeat the mistake.

Many economic observers now acknowledge the Administration's private intentions. "If you turn the present recession upside down and read on the bottom," Nobel Prize Laureate Paul Samuelson said, "it will say 'Made in Washington.'" Pierre Rinfret, a leading economic consultant to the business world, calls the program "benign neglect — there is no program and it has been done on purpose. Greenspan wants to let the economy take a deep bath to correct inflation."

From the corporate perspective, of course, the strategy is working. Real wages have fallen sharply. Workers seem subdued, with the incidence of strike activity down. As one American labor official explained, "Layoffs take the steam out of members. . . . They take away the urge to strike." But the Administration's "cold bath" strategy is too risky to last long. The economy is teetering closer to the brink than Ford and his free marketeers realized. The Administration is in "the position of the sorcerer's apprentice," Harvard's Nobel Prize Laureate Wassily Leontief observes. "They took steps to produce unemployment, and now they can't stop it."

The second risk is that many Americans might be pushed toward open political rebellion. More and more people recognize the recession's political roots. Job marches in Washington have begun and will surely spread. Union anger is mounting. Congress is restless. The "free market" solution can "work" economically if it is applied long enough. It cannot work politically because, as depression approaches, political instability carries radical potential. Even gritty Harry Truman turned squeamish at the thought of deep recessions. As he commented in 1950 about the nineteen-thirties, "There was real danger that the American people might turn to some other system. If we are to win the struggle between freedom and

Communism, we must be sure that we never let such a depression happen again."

If the "free market" strategy cannot work, only one other option seems to remain: "state planning." What steps might conceivably lead to adoption of that alternative?

The first stage would necessarily involve new governmental fiscal and monetary stimulus to pull out of the recession. If the Government gives the economy a big booster shot soon — well beyond the recent $22-billion tax cut — we may be able to avert a major depression and resume economic growth. But, as in 1971, we will continue to experience growth with rapid inflation and unremitting instability.

Anticipating those strains, many now expect relatively permanent wage-price controls. Like ordinary stimulus, however, wage-price controls will be insufficient to restore stability to the economy. Some firms will have their prices frozen at relatively high levels and will find it profitable to produce as much as possible. Others, for whatever reason, will find their prices frozen at lower levels and will cut back on production. However adept the administrators, bottlenecks, shortages and distortions can quickly emerge.

"Suppress the Invisible Hand for long," as Harvard's Stephen Marglin has put it, "and it must be replaced by the Visible Hand." If we cannot avoid the problems of controls by doing without controls, then we can probably overcome those problems by moving beyond controls — by adding direct Government management of allocation and investment. If shortages develop, the Government can direct that production be expanded in that sector. (Such directives, aimed at oil refining capacity, would certainly have tempered the energy "shortages.") If some firms are slipping into bankruptcy but are engaged in "essential" production, the Government can provide investment and credit for a salvage operation. That kind of Government management digs beneath wages and prices to supervision of the physical quantities of commodities produced for and exchanged in the market. And this would mean, in Richard Goodwin's words, "rudimentary Government planning for the entire economy."

Free marketeers blanch at such thoughts, of course, and the whole language of "state planning" sounds dissonant to many American ears. Does this prospect smack too much of a "socialist" America to have a chance of adoption?

Perhaps not. Unregenerate capitalists have begun to call for such planning. Their public discussion has focused around a resurrection of the New Deal's Reconstruction Finance Corporation. Advocated by Henry Ford II, Rohatyn and others, a new R.F.C. would channel investment funds toward sectors and firms whose own funds were too tight to finance necessary expansion. The R.F.C. advocates have no illusions that such reforms will be temporary. "There can be no denying," Rohatyn writes, "that such an organization . . . can be perceived as a first step toward state planning of the economy. . . . What many will call state planning would, to the average family, be no more than prudent budgeting."

The corporate community has begun to believe that more intensive state intervention is necessary to protect its very existence. State planning, from this perspective, becomes the mechanism by which business gets the rest of America to "swallow the pill" of material sacrifice. As Government capital begins to flow toward shaky corporations, taxpayers will be compelled to support private corporations that cannot make it on their own. (Penn Central, Rolls Royce and Lockheed writ large!) Forbes magazine characterized Rohatyn's proposal candidly: "As a boardroom philosopher once remarked: "Socialize the losses and keep the profits private!' "

Some labor leaders and liberals have also called for state planning. One group, called the Initiative Committee for National Economic Planning, is co-chaired by the United Automobile Workers' Leonard Woodcock and Harvard's Wassily Leontief. Its members range from J. K. Galbraith, who has finally declared himself a socialist, to World Bank President Robert McNamara and Robert Roosa of Brown Bros., Harriman, who most certainly have not.

State planning, in fact, seems sure to come. When it arrives, it will politicize all those hard economic choices whose consequences are normally hidden by the Invisible Hand. In a new era of declining American power, planners will continually have to balance the reduction of business profits against the reduction of our own living standards. And every time they reach a decision, the rest of us will be asking: Who made that decision in whose interests?

Many radical economists entered graduate school in the nineteen-sixties. If our professors ever deigned to mention Marx at all, they typically dismissed him, in Samuelson's words, as a "minor post-Ricardian." Growing more and more critical through our political experiences and our studies of the economy, most of us eventually decided that the Marxian perspective provided a more penetrating view of the world than conventional analyses. While we are still "first fired, last hired" in economic departments around the country, we have begun to claim some professional turf. As the economy continues to deteriorate and mainstream economists have not yet come up with a cure, more and more people have begun to listen to other kinds of explanations.

And many are beginning to ask about different kinds of solutions. It may be that a quick move toward state planning will save us from depression. Many will once again praise the resilience and flexibility of our system. We shall sigh obligatory relief. Such a wonderful "mixed economy"!

But it will still be capitalism. Corporations will still dominate state planning policies, arguing credibly, as Nixon himself put it, that "all Americans will benefit from more profits." As long as profits remain private, the profit addicts will still pursue their prosperity trips, pushing us feverishly toward recurrent instability. As long as profitability dominates corporate decisions about resource allocation, we shall continue to endure the wastefulness of our past and future ecological blight. As long as our livelihoods are tied directly to private property ownership, we shall continue to suffer or avert our gaze from egregious poverty and inequality. As long as corporations claim absolute authority during the working time of their employes, we shall continue to wither from and/or struggle against the boredom, degradation and submissiveness of our working lives.

For those of us who are seeking to move beyond that economic system, two main issues will emerge in the coming years.

First, the evolution of state planning will provide a central challenge. Most Americans will have to organize defensively at the national level simply to protect our interests against those of the corporations. As that national movement develops, can we move beyond? Can we liberate ourselves from capitalist instabilities by securing an even and balanced growth in output, with income and job security for all? Can we sever our dependence on some of the excrescences of our present economy — energy-wasting, fire-trapping skyscrapers and fuming private cars — and move toward more useful and collective patterns of social living?

Equally important for many radicals, I think, is the issue of greater control over our working and political lives. Capitalism has historically promoted hierarchical and authoritarian working relations. State planning will directly involve the Government in the organization of production. Will this involvement, combined with the abolition of private property, provide the basis for the transition toward a society in which everyone is free from the bonds of subsistence and shares equally in his/her material and social relations? Even if meeting the consumption needs of the working majority, a state planning system could tend quickly toward the kind of centralized economy manifest in the Soviet Union, featuring tight discipline over the labor process. Many of us place high priority on reversing historical tendencies toward such hierarchical control of work. As state planning develops in this country, we shall be forced to defend ourselves more and more vigorously against centralized control over the pace and character of our jobs and communities. As we develop local institutions of resistance and collective support, can we forge decentralized planning systems that would combine local autonomy with the requirements of collective planning?

As we grapple with those issues, we begin to perceive the real possibilities of their resolution.

Taking advantage of our technological sophistication, our affluence, and our individual capacities, we could clearly begin to break down hierarchies within enterprises and reduce the specialization of many jobs. Involved in more participatory work relations and more varied jobs, Americans might find more motivation for energetic work in their work's intrinsic satisfactions, requiring fewer material rewards. Becoming more active in decisions about production, many might develop a much more collective consciousness about the needs of their communities and the impact on social life of different kinds of commodities. Investment and allocation decisions could consequently begin to reflect other criteria than their "profitability."

The possibilities proliferate. Emboldened, we dare more and more openly to struggle for a socialist America, a society promoting both rational planning and democratic control of our working and political lives. Arguing the possibility of that transition, none of us can yet provide a "model" of the specific social relations that might eventually unfold, so some call us "utopian" for dreaming about the future. We think it is the mainstream economists who are "utopian" for dreaming that our present economic system could possibly work.

REFERENCES

1. Most radical economists, including myself, belong to the 2,500-member Union for Radical Political Economics. The views expressed here are my own and do not necessarily reflect the views of U.R.P.E. as an organization.

II IMPERIALISM

Throughout its history, American capitalism has shown a tendency to expand beyond its national boundaries. In the nineteenth century, this meant westward expansion into lands and territories held by Native Americans and Mexicans. In the twentieth century, it has meant increasing American penetration of the economies and political structures of the Third World and, in recent years especially, of Europe and Canada as well. During the nineteenth century, this expansionary movement was justified by the concept of *manifest destiny* — the theory that the United States had the right, even the duty, to intervene in more "backward" countries because of our supposedly higher degree of "civilization." In the twentieth century, as Richard Barnet and Ronald Muller show, American expansion overseas has been excused, and its effects obscured, by an ideology of "development"; the new forms of economic, political, and military intervention mounted by the United States after World War II were said to be in the interest of helping the "underdeveloped" world to reach the level of social and economic well-being that we had.

As Barnet and Muller show in the selection from their book *Global Reach*, the truth has been very different. The net effect of American corporate intervention in the nations of Latin America, Africa, and Asia has been to maintain their impoverishment, not to "develop" them to the level of the advanced industrial countries. Investment by multinational corporations does bring some new wealth to poor countries, but it takes out more than it puts in; and the wealth it does bring remains concentrated in the hands of a small and privileged elite.

The rise of the multinational corporations, and the emergence of the United States as the dominant imperial power in the world, can be seen most dramatically in the period since World War II. But as Robert Heilbroner points out in "None of Your Business," the tendency toward expansion is inherent in modern capitalism and has been clearly evident throughout the twentieth century. Heilbroner's point is not that the new explosion of multinational enterprise is unimportant, but that it represents a continuation of the fundamental processes of monopoly capitalism, not a new phenomenon peculiar to the recent past.

From the beginning, United States expansion into other countries has been backed by military force and clandestine operations designed to make the rest of the world safe for American corporate interests. After World War II, as United States overseas expansion reached its peak, the level of this military and "intelligence" activity reached unprecedented heights. One of the most important aspects of this was the growth of a complex and wide-ranging secret intelligence apparatus, in which the Central Intelligence Agency (CIA) has played the most important role. David Wise's selection gives an overview of the covert operations of the CIA since its founding in the late 1940s, showing how the agency grew over the years into an increasingly effective instrument for subverting other governments in the interest of American corporate power.

5. ENGINES OF DEVELOPMENT?

Richard J. Barnet
and Ronald Müller

1

The closest thing to a universal goal in the contemporary world is development, the twentieth-century embellishment of the myth of progress. Modern-day religion, philosophy, and psychiatry are absorbed with the challenge of individual development, the struggle of human beings to realize their full potential. For poor countries the word means escape from backwardness and foreign domination. For rich societies the word symbolizes heightened possibilities, the achievement of the affluent society, then its transcendence, a process culminating in a postindustrial world from which scarcity has been banished. The 1960's were hailed as the "Decade of Development," and the Cold War, which reached its peak during those years, was fought in the name of development. The issue was whether the "Free World model" or the "Communist model" would prevail. Rich, poor, capitalist or Communist, everyone is for development.

Much of the popularity of the term can be attributed to the fact that it can mean anything one chooses. In U.S. economic reports and state papers during the 1960's, development had a particular meaning. A developing society was one in which per capita income and gross national product were increasing. If a poor country in which each person was earning an average of $80 a year should pursue policies that would increase per capita income to, say, $100 within three years, that country was developing, indeed, at a spectacular rate. Similarly, if the sum total of goods and services exchanged within the society — i.e., the gross national product — should increase, that too was a test of development. By these criteria a few countries around the world developed rather dramatically during the 1960's. Mexico, for example, went from a per capita income of $488 in 1960 to $717 a year in 1972. Brazil boasted an annual growth in GNP of more than 9 percent a year. According to the prevailing theories of the 1960's, societies that showed such economic growth were at the "takeoff" stage in development. Their increasing levels of economic activity would generate the savings needed to buy their tickets of admission to the twentieth century — roads, schools, hospitals, etc. — and an industrial capacity that would make their children comfortable.

By the end of the Decade of Development, however, despite dramatic economic growth in a few poor countries, it had become abundantly clear that the gap between rich and poor throughout the world was widening. A succession of studies by the U.N. and other international agencies established the statistics of global poverty: For 40 percent to 60 percent of the world's population the Decade of Development brought rising unemployment, decreases in purchasing power, and thus lower consumption. In a World Bank survey of income-distribution patterns in poor countries around the world, Irma Adelman and Cynthia Taft Morris found that the development track of the 1960's shows a "striking" increase in incomes, in both absolute and relative terms, for the richest 5 percent while the share of the poorest 40 percent shrinks. While according to such gross economic indicators as GNP the countries are developing, millions in the bottom 40 percent of the population actually have less food, worse clothing, and poorer housing than their parents had. As

Brazil's President Emilio Médici once put it, "Brazil is doing well but the people are not."

Particularly in those countries which experienced "economic miracles," the pattern was increasing affluence for a slowly expanding but small minority and increasing misery for a rapidly swelling majority. Concentration of income in Mexico, for example, has increased significantly during the "Mexican miracle." In the early 1950's, the richest 20 percent of the population had ten times the income of the poorest 20 percent. By the mid-1960's the rich had increased their share to seventeen times what the bottom 20 percent received. A 1969 United Nations study reports that in the Mexico City area the richest 20 percent of the population lived on 62.5 percent of the area's income while the poorest 20 percent attempted survival on 1.3 percent of the income. During the Decade of Development, according to U.S. Government estimates, the share in the "Brazilian miracle" for the 40 million people at the bottom dropped from 10.6 percent to 8.1 percent. The richest 5 percent have increased their share of the national income from 27.8 percent to 36.8 percent. (A 1970 U.N. study estimates that the share of the richest 5 percent is one-half of the national income.) In September 1972, Robert McNamara, president of the World Bank, reported on what the continuation of prevailing development policies, with their modest annual growth rates and their income-concentration effects, would mean by the end of the century. "Projected to the end of the century — only a generation away — that means the people of the developed countries will be enjoying per capita incomes, in 1972 prices, of over $8000 a year, while those masses of the poor (who by that time will total over two and one-quarter billion) will on average receive less than $200 per capita, and some 800 million of these will receive less than $100."

Most of the world lives in countries with a per capita income of less than $200, and it is these countries which have shown an increase in per capita income of no more than 1.7 percent a year. But even in the Brazils and Mexicos, as we have seen, income concentration has meant that the benefits of the miracles do not flow to the poor. It is an elementary but often forgotten bit of statistical truth that every million dollars Mr. Rockefeller receives increases the per capita income of every Mississippi tenant farmer. Increases in national income, Mr. McNamara points out, "will not benefit the poor unless they reach the poor."

When the global corporations proclaim themselves engines of development, we can judge their claims only if we know what development track they are on. A mechanical definition of development based on growth rates is obscene in a world in which most people go to sleep hungry. A development model like Brazil's, in which the stock market booms and two-thirds of the population is condemned to an early death by poverty, hunger, and disease, is a caricature of progress. If a development model is to have any real meaning in a world in which most people are struggling just to stay alive, it must, as the development theorist Dudley Seers has pointed out, provide solutions to the most critical, interrelated social problems of the late twentieth century: poverty, unemployment, and inequality. (A development strategy that does not cope with these problems must assume either escalating mass misery on a scale that cannot even be imagined or the mysterious disappearance of the world's poor.) The evidence of the 1960's is now in. It is an unhappy fact that the development track pursued by the global corporations in those years contributed more to the exacerbation of world poverty, world unemployment, and world inequality than to their solution.

In the light of the conventional development wisdom of the 1960's, these appear to be irresponsible charges. After all, global corporations do spread goods, capital, and technology around the globe. They do contribute to a rise in overall economic activity. They do employ hundreds of thousands of workers around the world, often paying more than the prevailing wage. Most poor countries appear to be so eager to entice global corporations to their territory, so eager in fact to create a good "investment climate" for them, that they are generous with tax concessions and other advantages. If corporations were really spreading poverty, unemployment, and inequality, why would they be welcomed?

The negative impact of the global corporation in the deterioration of living standards, employment rates, and economic justice around the world has occurred despite the fact that many corporate officials would like it to be otherwise and believe that it can be. The unfortunate role of the global corporation in maintaining and increasing poverty around the world is due primarily to the dismal reality that global corporations and poor countries have different, indeed conflicting, interests, priorities, and needs. This is a reality that many officials of underdeveloped countries, lacking alternative development strategies, prefer not to face.

The primary interest of the global corporation is worldwide profit maximization. As we shall see, it is often advantageous for the global balance sheet to divert income from poor countries. As anxious to be "good corporate citizens" as they are, the World Managers are the first to proclaim their primary allegiance to the shareholders. Global corporations, as they themselves like to say, are neither charities nor welfare organizations, although some devote modest resources to good works. (The Ford Motor Company, for example, is building schools in Mexico, asking only that the name FORD appear prominently over the door.) The claims of the global corporation rest instead on a theory of the marketplace which says in effect that by enriching themselves they enrich the whole world. In this chapter we shall examine the evidence that shows why it has not been so.

2

The central strategy of the global corporation is the creation of a global economic environment that will ensure stability, expansion, and high profits for the planetary enterprise. The implementation of that strategy depends upon the control of the three basic components of corporate power: finance capital, technology, and marketplace ideology. The record of the past dozen years suggests clearly that the global corporation has used these components of power, as one might expect, to promote its growth and profitability. But it is these very strategies which have had an adverse effect on distribution of income and on employment levels in underdeveloped countries around the world.

Let us look first at the financial policies of global corporations in poor countries. Perhaps the strongest argument in favor of the global corporations' claim to be engines of development is that they are a source of needed capital for backward countries. Particularly at a time when government aid programs are drying up, the foreign corporation, it is argued, is a crucial source of the finance capital that poor countries need to supplement local savings and to obtain foreign exchange. (Capital accumulation is of course a prerequisite for economic growth. If it cannot be raised abroad, so the argument goes, then it must be squeezed out of the hides of workers. In short, foreign private capital is the best available instrument for avoiding the Stalinist model of industrialization through forced labor.)

The claim that global corporations are major suppliers of foreign capital to poor countries turns out to be more metaphor than reality. The practice of global corporations in Latin America, as Fernando Fajnzylber has shown in his exhaustive study for the United Nations, has been largely to use scarce local capital for their local operations rather than to bring capital from either the United States or Europe. Individual investors and banks in poor countries for understandable business reasons normally prefer to lend money to Sears, Roebuck or General Motors than to some local entrepreneur without the worldwide credit resources of the planetary giants. Thus during the years 1957–1965, as Fajnzylber shows, U.S.-based global corporations financed 83 percent of their Latin American investment locally, either from reinvested earnings or from local Latin American savings. Only about 17 percent of U.S. investment during the period, therefore, represented a transfer of capital from rich countries to poor. A variety of studies, including those of the Argentine economist Aldo Ferrer and the Chilean government under the Frei regime, confirm the same trend: from 1960 to 1970 about 78 percent of the manufacturing operations of U.S.-based global corporations in Latin America were financed out of local capital. What these figures show is

that global corporations are not in fact major suppliers of finance capital
to poor countries.

True, in the manufacturing sector 38 percent of the financial resources
being used by U.S. global-corporation subsidiaries in Latin America
comes from reinvested earnings, which accountants classify as foreign
capital. But this classification misses the real economic meaning of what
has happened. These reinvested earnings were to a great extent generated by local resources. While they can be thought of as additions to
local savings, they may well not be available for the urgent development
needs of the country, since they are controlled by the global corporations
and used for their purposes. A primary purpose is to take such earnings
out of the country as fast as possible. Between 1960 and 1968, according
to Fajnzylber's U.N. study, U.S.-based global corporations reported taking on the average 79 percent of their net profits out of Latin America.
It makes good business sense to try for a quick return on a modest
investment in countries which, like the Latin American republics, are
considered relatively unstable. In contrast, the same corporations operating in the developed economies of Western Europe are much readier to
leave their profits in the country. But of course the poor countries are
precisely the ones that most need to keep the earnings for their development. This is but one example where sound business judgment and the
needs of poor countries conflict.

Between 1965 and 1968, 52 percent of all profits of U.S. subsidiaries
operating in Latin America in manufacturing — the most dynamic sector
of the hemisphere's economy — were repatriated to the United States.
This means that for every dollar of net profit earned by a global-
corporation subsidiary, 52 cents left the country, even though 78 percent
of the investment funds used to generate that dollar of profit came from
local sources. If we look at the mining, petroleum, and smelting industries, the capital outflow resulting from the operations of global corporations is even worse. Each dollar of net profit is based on an investment
that was 83 percent financed from local savings; yet only 21 percent of
the profit remains in the local economy.

These aggregate statistics are confirmed by reports of individual companies. A retired executive of one of the three largest multinational banks
recalls for us that in the late 1950's and early 1960's his bank always tried
to use about 95 percent local savings sources for its local loans and no
more than 5 percent of its dollar holdings. A vice-president of another
U.S.-based global bank told us how profitable it is for his bank to lend
what is substantially Latin American capital to U.S.-based global companies. "I should not really tell you this," he confided, "but while we earn
around 13 to 14 percent on our U.S. operations, we can easily count on
a 33-percent rate of return on our business conducted in Latin America."

However, these profitable practices, far from representing an import of capital, actually decrease the availability of local capital for locally owned industry. (Global corporations preempt financing because, as 1970 Chilean Government studies show, they can borrow about twice as much on their inventories and capital assets as can locally owned industries.) At the same time, scarce financing is retailed to the general public in the form of consumer debt at exorbitant interest. (In Colombia a prominent economist has estimated that the actual interest rate charged by Sears, including hidden charges, is in excess of 30 percent a year.)

The adverse financial impact of the global corporation in Latin America has to do not only with the source of its investment but with its character. A principal argument for foreign investment is that it supplies new capital through which the superior management skills of global corporations can be channeled into new productive facilities. (The World Managers sometimes argue that they can use local capital much more efficiently for the development of the country than can local entrepreneurs.) But again the record suggests otherwise. A study by the Harvard Business School of the 187 largest U.S.-based global corporations which account for some 70 percent of all U.S. in Latin America shows that in the years 1958–1967 U.S. firms used a substantial part of their investment to buy up local firms. (About 46 percent of all manufacturing operations established in the period were takeovers of existing domestic industry.) Again, it is sound business judgment to buy an already operating plant rather than take the risk of building a new one, but changing ownership does not increase productive facilities needed for development.

What was called the American Challenge in Europe a few years ago is a fait accompli in Latin America. Local industry, particularly the most dynamic sectors, is more and more in the hands of American-based global corporations. To those who criticize the takeover of local industry in poor countries the World Managers have two answers. The first is that the global corporations make a greater contribution to development than local entrepreneurs. The companies are more efficient, can marshal more resources, and develop more advanced technology. Some even argue that they are "better citizens" of the countries where they operate than local businessmen. They have more scruples about paying bribes. If they repatriate earnings to stockholders in the United States, is that not better than repatriating them to a numbered bank account in Switzerland, a practice of some local businessmen who like to use nationalistic rhetoric to fight foreign takeovers but who have no interest in the nation except as a source of personal profit? Whatever truth there may be to all of this, it hardly justifies foreign takeover of industry in poor countries. There are more alternatives open to developing countries than domination by foreign firms or exploitation by native entrepreneurs.

The second reply of the World Managers to the charge of "economic imperialism" heard in Latin America and other underdeveloped regions might be termed the "it's a tough world" argument. Where, they ask, are poor countries going to get the capital and the technology to develop if not from global companies? Yes, they acknowledge, it might be better for the countries if they owned their own industry, knew how to run it, and had their own money to develop it, but they don't. They can't expect us just to give the money and technology. The stockholders wouldn't permit it. Therefore the social benefits from our investment, marginal as they may be in some cases, constitute the only development poor countries can realistically expect.

However, the "you can't get the money without us" argument turns out to be an exaggeration. Life is hard for poor countries, but not that hard. The fact is that the companies, as we have seen, bring in relatively little of their own money. The capital that global companies raise locally could also be available to local firms or to the government for development projects. Peter Gabriel, dean of the Boston University Business School, estimates that even reasonably tough tax policies in Latin America would produce considerable capital for significant development advances. Then too, other sources of outside capital exist. In 1972 Brazil floated a bond issue of $140 million, which was more than the capital contribution sent from the United States to all U.S. global-corporation manufacturing subsidiaries in all of Latin America during that year. Japan's phenomenal postwar development, it must be remembered, was based largely on the exclusion of foreign investment. Noting the experience of the Communist countries in obtaining foreign capital and technology without turning over their basic industries to foreigners, poor countries are taking a harder look at the traditional arguments of the foreign investor. (What this is likely to mean for both the poor countries and the global corporations is the subject of the next chapter.)

Another standard argument in chamber-of-commerce speeches around the world is that global corporations help solve the balance-of-payments problems of poor countries. One characteristic shared by poor countries is a lack of foreign exchange. The reason, of course, is that the more undeveloped a country is the less likely it is to make things that foreigners want. The only way to get dollars or pounds or marks needed to buy capital goods or consumer luxuries from the United States, Britain, or Germany is to make, mine, or grow something that these countries need or want. During the last decade the underdeveloped countries' share of world exports has declined precipitously. This has been due to the dramatic increase in trading among the developed countries (most of it stimulated by global corporations) and to the loss of markets and decline in price for certain agricultural products, such as hemp, for which synthetic substitutes have been found. In Latin America during the Decade of Development the value of exports declined as the price of imports rose. Compounding the balance-of-payments problem was a steep rise in foreign debt. By the mid-1960's service on foreign debt exceeded the value of new loans, and by the end of the 1960's Latin America's external debt has doubled.

The World Managers argue that it is precisely these unhappy facts of life which make the contribution of the global corporations so important. But again the figures are unsettling. There is no doubt that U.S.-based global corporations account for a significant portion of Latin America's total trade. In 1968 U.S.-based companies were responsible for 40 percent of all manufacturing exports from the region and more than one-third of the region's imports from the United States. More than half of all U.S. exports take the form of exports from U.S. parents to their subsidiaries overseas. This means, of course, that the claim of the global corporations that they have a crucial impact on the balance-of-payments situation of Latin America is absolutely correct.

The issue is the nature of the impact. Whether exports benefit a poor economy depends critically on the price. It does not help the foreign-exchange problem of a poor country to export goods at a bargain. When global companies buy from and sell to their own subsidiaries, they establish prices that often have little connection to the market price. Indeed, when the corporate headquarters is acting as both buyer and seller, the very concept of the market has lost its significance. The literature on how to run global corporations is filled with advice on how to set prices on intracompany transfers to maximize the global profits of the parent corporation. Such "transfer prices," as they are called, deviate from the market price for good business reasons. For example, if an automobile manufacturer with operations in many countries wishes to export from a manufacturing subsidiary it owns in one country to a distributing company it owns in another country, it is often advantageous for tax reasons to direct the exporting subsidiary to undervalue its exports. One common reason for this is that the taxes in the manufacturing country may be higher than the taxes in the importing country. Thus the artificial price charged on the export minimizes total taxes for the world corporation and increases its global profits, but the result in the manufacturing country is that it loses foreign exchange (not to mention tax revenues) it would have received had there been an arm's-length transaction between independent buyers and sellers. Another technique even more attractive to the world headquarters is to ship underpriced exports or overpriced imports to a tax-free port such as the Bahamas (known in the business literature as a tax haven) and then reexport the goods at their normal market value or even an inflated price to another subsidiary in the country where they are to be sold. This modern version of the 18th-century "triangular trade," in which cotton, rum, and slaves shuttling between the Caribbean and New England created an American upper class, offers the same sort of profitable flexibility for the global corporation. In an econometric study prepared as part of the research for this book it was found that 75 percent of U.S.-based global corporations in Latin America which are engaged in export conduct all such transactions with other subsidiaries of the same parent, under circumstances in which price can be controlled because the company is trading with itself. The study also shows that despite their claim to expand exports for poor countries, global companies in Latin America were outperformed by local companies in exports outside Latin America, and within Latin America (with the exception of Argentina, Brazil and Mexico) did no better than local firms. U.S. global companies, the econometric analysis reveals, consistently underprice their exports, charging on the average 40 percent less than prices charged by local firms.

At the same time, where it is to their overall advantage global corporations wildly overvalue their imports. Constantine Vaitsos has completed a detailed study of import overpricing in Colombia. By comparing prices charged by a large number of subsidiaries of global companies in the pharmaceutical, rubber, chemical, and electronics industries with world market prices, he found the following average overpricing: in the pharmaceutical firms 155 percent, in the rubber industry 40 percent, and in the electronics industry a range from 16 percent to 60 percent. When he compared the import price of certain popular drugs produced by U.S.-based global companies with the price charged in the United States, he found that the Colombian prices for the tranquilizers Valium and Librium were, respectively, 82 and 65 times higher than the established international market price. The price charged for the antibiotic tetracycline was almost ten times the U.S. price.

These special prices for poor countries, which are not limited to the drug industry, are of course passed on to local consumers — in a country with a per capita income of $300 a year. Transistors go for eleven times their U.S. price in Colombia, Vaitsos reports. A certain TV amplifier is sold for two and one-half times its U.S. equivalent. In Chile, according to Andean Common Market studies, overpricing ranges from 30 percent to more than 700 percent. According to the studies of Pedroleón Díaz, overpricing in Peru ranges from 50 percent to 300 percent and in Ecuador from 75 percent to 200 percent. U.N. studies reveal the same practices in other parts of the world, including Iran, the Philippines, and Pakistan.

In addition to the standard practice of overpricing imports are cruder practices which divert foreign exchange and tax revenues from poor countries. In Columbia, one of the leading government economists told us, foreign firms not infrequently collect the 15 percent subsidy the governments pays on all exports on the basis of empty crates shipped to Panama. The head of a subsidiary of a European-based global corporation showed us boxes of pharmaceuticals that had just passed local customs in a Latin American country which contained 30 percent of their declared contents although the subsidiary had paid for full crates (at a price, incidentally, twenty-five times the world market price). Vaitsos estimates that overpricing in the drug industry alone in 1968 cost Colombia $20 million in losses of foreign exchange and $10 million in tax revenues.

There are several other advantages to the company in addition to tax avoidance in manipulating import and export prices. Minimizing local profits is often an essential public relations strategy. Moreover, in countries which impose a percentage limitation on the repatriation of profits, overpricing imports and underpricing exports are good ways to repatriate more profits than the local government allows. All of this makes good business sense, but its impact on the economy of poor countries is cruel. It means exorbitant consumer prices for such necessities as lifesaving drugs and a loss of tax revenues and foreign exchange. It is one more example of the basic conflict in outlook, interest, and goals between the global corporation and countries trying to solve the problems of poverty, unemployment, and inequality. As Harry G. Johnson, professor of economics at the London School and the University of Chicago, puts it, the purpose of the global corporation "is not to transform the economy by exploiting its potentialities — especially its human potentialities — for development, but to exploit the existing situation to its own profit by utilization of the knowledge it already possesses, at a minimum cost of adaptation and adjustment to itself."

The various profit-maximizing strategies of the global corporations give us a glimpse of the true profits earned by the companies in poor countries. Thanks to the magic of modern accounting, these bear little relation to the figures that the companies report either to the local government or to the U.S. Treasury. To get a true picture of the annual return on investment that a U.S.-based global corporation derives from its subsidiary in, say, a Latin American country, it is necessary to include in the calculation overpricing of imports and underpricing of exports as well as reported profits, royalties, and fees repatriated to the global headquarters. This total can then be divided into the declared net worth of the subsidiary. Vaitsos performed this exercise for fifteen wholly owned drug subsidiaries of U.S.- and European-based global corporations. He found the effective annual rate of return ranged from a low of 38.1 percent to a high of 962.1 percent with an average of 79.1 percent. Yet that year these firms' average declared profits submitted to the Colombian tax authorities was 6.7 percent. In the rubber industry the effective profit rate on the average was 43 percent; the declared profit rate, 16 percent. Vaitsos' investigations are corroborated by other studies which conclude that during the Decade of Development the *minimum* rate of return of U.S.-based manufacturing corporations in Latin America could not have been much below 40 percent. But even these estimates understate the actual profits being generated. For example, neither the work of Vaitsos nor that summarized by the Rand Corporation could take account of the underpricing of exports or the fact that the subsidiary's declared net worth is usually considered overvalued. Another and equally revealing approach has been taken by economists at the University of Lund, Sweden. In an analysis of 64 mining operations of U.S. companies in Peru between 1967 and 1969, they found that while the companies reported to the local government total profits of 60 million dollars, the declarations to the U.S. government on the identical operations showed profits of 102 million dollars. In 1966 the Peruvian Parliament established an investigatory commission to study the double accounting methods of the U.S.–controlled Southern Peru Copper Corporation. For the years 1960–1965, the investigation found that Southern Peru had reported net profits to the Peruvian government of 69 million dollars, whereas to the U.S. Securities and Exchange Commission the corporation had filed net profits of some 135 million dollars.

These are some of the reasons which led Princeton economist Shane Hunt in the Rand Report to conclude that the "calculation of country-specific profit rates . . . presents a statistical challenge that the U.S. Department of Commerce has failed to meet, at least up to the present." A Colombian economist, Dario Abab, has pointed out the meaninglessness of officially declared profits by noting that between 1960 and 1968 the average *reported* rate of return for global corporations in all manufacturing sectors of the country was 6.4 percent. He found it "difficult to accept" that these global corporations would continue to enter Colombia at this rate of reported profitability while national firms were showing higher return and the interest rate in financial markets was running between 16 and 20 percent. Abad's remarks are reflected in those of an assistant to the president of a large U.S.-based global corporation operating in Latin America who told us it was "no problem" to maintain real rates of return from 50 percent to 400 percent a year. "Calculations in general use in Latin America," Sol Linowitz points out, "estimate an average of $235 million annually in new direct investment during the past decade (omitting reinvested earnings) against $1 billion per year [reported] profit repatriation." These statistics, he notes sadly, are "accepted at face value by many Latins" despite the fact that they "overlook other benefits in export earnings and import savings" from these investments. An analysis of the widespread practice of transfer pricing, however, makes it clear that these "benefits" are accruing elsewhere than in the poor countries and thus make the capital outflow from Latin America even worse than these statistics suggest. The Guatemalan economist Gert Rosenthal, calculating the "financial contribution" of global corporations to the Central American Common Market countries, has found that while net capital inflows increased in the years 1960–1971 by 344 percent, out-flows rose 982 percent.

High profit rates, on rare occasions when they are admitted by global corporations, are defended as justifiable compensation for the heavy risks of operating in countries where coups, kidnappings, and earthquakes are everyday occurrences. These risks seem manageable, however. In the last ten years, with the exception of Cuba and Allende Chile, no U.S. manu-facturing subsidiary has been nationalized by a Latin American govern-ment. Global companies have on the whole tended to benefit from military coups such as those that Brazil and Bolivia have experienced in recent years. In any event, one can afford a string of disasters if he is able to recover anywhere from 47 cents to $4 a year on every dollar he invests. To be sure, in a profit system it is unsporting to begrudge in-vestors high profits. But the system has yet to evolve to the point at which everybody profits. One man's profit usually means another man's loss. The profits of the global corporations derived from poor countries, it must be said, are made at the expense of the people of those countries. The proposition that developed and undeveloped countries will get rich together through the expansion of global corporations is, at best, exactly half true.

6. NONE OF YOUR BUSINESS

Robert L. Heilbroner

The term "multinational corporation" has become familiar only recently. Writing in these pages just five years ago, I felt obliged to explain that the multinations were not merely giant corporations that did a world-wide export business, but giants whose manufacturing or servicing facil-ities were located around the globe, so that Pepsi-Cola, to take an example, could be bought in Mexico or the Philippines (or another 100-odd countries) not because the drink was turned out in America and then shipped abroad, but because it was produced and bottled in the country where it was consumed.

In recent years, largely as a consequence of the oil crisis, the word "multi-national" has become standard newspaper usage, so that we now understand that Exxon or ITT are not just "American" companies, but maintain a network of refineries, factories, warehouses, service establishments, laboratories, training centers, and retail establishments spread across the continents. What we do not perhaps yet understand sufficiently is that the multinationalization of business is not just an American but an international phenomenon, so that when we fill up the tank at a Shell station or buy Valium at a pharmacy we are purchasing commodities produced in the United States by companies of non-American nationality.

Nevertheless, it is one thing to talk knowingly about the multinationals, and another to grasp the significance of their operations. Are they, as Richard Barnet and Ronald Müller write in *Global Reich* [Simon and Schuster], "the most powerful human organization[s] yet devised for colonizing the future"? Do they challenge the nation-state as a main force for shaping the destinies of billions of men and women? Will their penetration into the underdeveloped world condemn these areas to perpetual backwardness — or can they serve as the conduits of technology and capital without which the underdeveloped nations will be condemned to eternal poverty?

It is not easy to answer these questions, for the impact of the multinationals remains in many ways obscure and perplexing. Or perhaps I should say that *I* find their impact difficult to appraise. Many other observers do not. . . .

Why are the multinationals so difficult to discuss? The first reason is that we know so appallingly little about them. How large are they? How big are their sales? How vast their profits? We really do not know.

Take, for example, the basic question of the value of the direct foreign investment — the plant and equipment, not the portfolios — owned by American enterprises. Our knowledge of the extent of this direct investment largely rests on a Commerce Department survey conducted in 1966. This survey collected data on 3,400 parent companies and 23,000 foreign affiliates. But efforts to enlarge and update that survey, now sadly out of date, have been systematically impeded. A government questionnaire sent to 500 companies in 1970 elicited only 298 responses. A more recent effort to discover some of the missing facts was severely truncated by the opposition of a committee of government representatives to questions that would invade the "privacy" of corporate life.

Hence some of the most important information required to assess the place of the multinationals in the world economy remains fragmentary or incomplete. We do not accurately know their capital outlays, their research and development expenditures, their foreign-based employment, the trade relationships between parent corporations and affiliates, or their full stockholdings in local companies. Let me add that if American data are inadequate, the statistical information obtained by other nations on their multinational enterprises is far worse. Many of the multinationals maintain two sets of books, one for the tax collector, another for themselves, and most European countries do not even have the staffs to compile the inaccurate statistics available from the "official" (i.e., tax-collector) books.

So we begin in a shadowy land of dubious facts. According to these facts (based largely on projections from the 1966 survey) the book value of American foreign direct investment was $78 billion in 1970 and is likely well over $100 billion today. In round numbers this compares with total assets (*including* foreign assets) of a little over $500 billion for the top 1,000 industrial corporations in America in 1973: we have no idea what the corresponding figures would be for, let us say, Sweden or the Netherlands or Switzerland.[1]

We have still less reliable data when we try to estimate the sales of U.S. manufacturing affiliates abroad. The estimates we use are based mainly on guesses about how much output each dollar of investment is likely to generate. Working on this basis, the Commerce Department places the value of overseas production − *not*, remember, exports from the United States, but "American" goods produced abroad − at $90 billion in 1970. Assuming that sales abroad have been growing in accordance with past trends, this would put the value of American foreign production today at perhaps $125 billion. Again by way of comparison, total sales (domestic plus foreign) of the top 1,000 manufacturing companies are something over $600 billion, as of 1973.

This seems clear enough. At a first glance we can locate a second "American" economy, scattered around the globe (although mainly concentrated in the European industrial market and the Near East oil market), which is about a quarter as big as the "home" economy.

First glances are, however, notoriously unreliable. For example, the value of American assets abroad includes $22 billion of assets in the petroleum industry, as of 1970. The marketable value of that portion of those assets represented by oil reserves is now much larger than in 1970 − or is it much *smaller*, because the oil now "belongs" to the nations under whose sands it lies in a much more decisive fashion than in 1970? Another example: what about the banks that play so critical a role in supporting the growth of overseas enterprise? Any appraisal of the extent of multinationalism should take into account the fact that foreign deposits in the nine biggest US banks have risen from less than 30 percent of their total deposits in the late 1960s to over 66 percent today, and that the total number of foreign locations for the twenty largest US banks rose from 211 to 627 over the same period. But this information also escapes the standard measurement of the extent of multinational wealth.

So we begin with uncertainty about the true size of the multinational sphere. But we do know, with a fair degree of certainty, that the sphere is expanding very rapidly. Industrial sales abroad, to judge by the fragmentary data we possess, have been growing twice as fast as sales at home. So has the flow of capital into new investments abroad — in 1957 American companies invested about ten cents abroad for every dollar of investment at home; today (at least until the recent depression) they are investing twenty-five cents. Total profits earned on operations abroad have risen from 25 percent of total profits at home in 1966 to 40 percent in 1970.

Furthermore, European and Japanese multinational firms are also accelerating their rate of growth. On the basis of past trends, these non-American multinationals are probably expanding even faster than U.S. firms. According to the estimates of Karl P. Savant of the University of Pennsylvania, about a quarter of world marketable output was attributable to the multinationals in 1968 and this share will rise to a third by the end of the 1970s and to over 50 percent by the last decade of this century.

Are we then in a new era of capitalism? These scattered figures — most of them, I emphasize again, based on partial or even erroneous data — seem to indicate that some great sea change is underway. But here is where the picture becomes even more obscure and confusing. Consider, to begin with, the following thumbnail description of the multinational economy whose salient features we have been examining:

1. The concentration of production and capital has developed to such a high degree that it has created monopolies that play a decisive role in international economic life.

2. Bank capital has merged with industrial capital to create a financial "oligarchy."

3. The export of capital, as distinguished from the export of commodities, has become of crucial importance.

4. International cartels, or oligopolistic combines, have effectively divided up the world.

This description, . . . surely covers many of the salient features of the multinational phenomenon. The trouble is that it was written (with a few emendations by myself) by Lenin in 1917. This surely suggests that the phenomenon is not as new as we tend to think — or rather, that whatever is "new" about it cannot be discovered in the mere presence of great sums of capital invested by the enterprises of one country in the territory of another country.

Add to that the following disconcerting fact. According to the calculations of Myra Wilkins, in *The Maturing of Multinational Enterprise* [Harvard University Press], the value of total US foreign investment in 1970 amounted to about 8 percent of United States GNP. In 1929, long before the great multinational "acceleration" took place, it was 7 percent. In 1914 it was also 7 percent. Although the geographic location of investment has changed — out of the agricultural and mining belts into the industrial markets of the world — and although the type of investment has altered accordingly — away from plantations into factories — the global magnitudes remain surprisingly constant.

Of course one is tempted to say that the shift into "high technology" industry has hugely increased the economic leverage of this foreign investment. Has it? One could also argue that in an era of impending constraints on growth and technology, and increasing importance of food and raw materials, this very shift has also reduced their potential for economic power.

Can one, in the midst of so much confusion, make some sense of the multinational presence? With much trepidation, I shall try.

We must begin by recognizing that the fundamental process behind the rise of the multinational corporation is growth, the urge for expansion that is the daemon of capitalism itself. Why is growth so central, so insatiable? In part the answer must be sought in the "animal spirits," as Keynes called them, of capitalist entrepreneurs whose self-esteem and self-valuation are deeply intertwined with the sheer size of the wealth they own or control.

But growth is also a defensive reaction. Companies seek to grow in order to preserve their place in the sun, to prevent competitors from crowding them out. Hence the struggle for market shares has always been a central aspect of the capitalist system, lending color to the robber baron age, taking on a more restrained but no less intense form in the age of the modern "socially responsible" firm.

A number of economists, primary among them Alfred Chandler,[2] have described the dynamics of the typical stages of business expansion, from the small owner-operated factory to the managerially directed multiproduct, multiplant "big business." Only recently, however, have we begun to describe the sequence of events that drives a firm to make the decisive leap across national boundaries, with all the headaches and problems that such a venture entails — foreign governments to deal with, foreign languages to speak, foreign currencies to worry about. As Myra

Wilkins points out, any number of stimuli may finally tempt an expanding company to make the leap. It may have begun to penetrate a foreign market with exports, and then may decide to locate a production facility abroad in order to avoid a tariff that impedes its exports. It may locate a manufacturing branch abroad to forestall — or to match — a similar step by one of its rivals. It may seek the advantages of manufacturing abroad because wages are cheaper — Hong Kong is the great example of this — although Dr. Wilkins believes that lower wages have not been a major stimulus for most overseas expansion.[3]

This phenomenon of expansion, with its aggressive and defensive roots, emphasizes an extremely important aspect of what we call "multinationalization," which is that all the multinationl companies are in fact *national* companies that have extended their operations abroad. They are not, as their spokesmen sometimes claim, companies that have lost their nationality. Two giant companies — Shell and Unilever — have in fact mixed nationalities on their boards of directors, and IBM never wearies of boasting that Jacques Maisonrouge, president of the IBM World Trade Corporation, is French. But I can see little evidence that IBM is not an "American" company, notwithstanding; and no evidence that any other of the giant multinationals cannot be so unambiguously identified as having a distinct nationality.

This puts into considerable doubt a thesis that runs through much of the literature on the multinationls. When Richard Barnet and Ronald Müller write in *Global Reach* about the multinationals as the great colonizers of the future, they swallow whole the declarations of a few companies that they have risen above the parochial views of mere nationalism. Yet even Barnet and Müller speak of the advent of true multinationals, responsible to no one but themselves, as a possibility rather than an actuality. So, too, although Myra Wilkins sketches out a sequence of multinational organizations evolving from a "monocentric" to a "polycentric" form, in which the planets disengage themselves from the parent sun and wander about the economic universe on their own, she is hard-pressed to cite a case of the latter. (She suggests that ITT could properly have been called such a "true" multinational as early as the 1920s or 1930s, but recent events in Chile make one wonder how much ITT today is "above" the considerations of national identity.)

Thus I think we must view the world of very large, expansive national enterprises, extending their operations abroad, as a change in degree, not kind, from the world of very large expansive enterprises still contained within national borders. I realize that this suggestion challenges the central thesis of the books I have read, above all the one by Barnet and Müller. Nevertheless, I think skepticism is in order when we ask whether

the multinationals signal a radically new development in world capitalism.

Here it is useful to review the basic characteristics of monopoly capitalism. An economy dominated by the kinds of expansive organizations
I have described sooner or later encounters extreme difficulties of economic coordination. We do not know if a world of atomistic enterprises
would run as smoothly as the theory of pure competition suggests, and
we never shall know. We do know that an economy dominated by giant
firms encounters serious problems in dovetailing its private operations so
as to provide substantially full employment, maintain a stable level of
prices, and produce the full array of goods and services needed by the
population. In every capitalist nation this has led to what is euphemis-
tically called a "mixed" economy — an economy in which the world of
business is restrained, guided, subsidized, protected, buttressed by a
growing array of public instruments and agencies. Governments, for all
their ideological skirmishes with business, have always been the silent
partners of business; indeed, as Adam Smith was explicit in declaring,
private property would not exist a minute without government.

In what way does the multinational change this basic picture? I must
confess that I do not think it changes it at all. I am aware, of course, of
the much discussed erosion of "sovereignty" caused by the ability of the
multinationals to locate their plants in this country or that one, or to
transfer their profits from one nation to another by means of arbitrary
pricing. But is this significantly different from the failure of nation–states
to exercise control over companies *within* their national boundaries?
What effectiveness does the United States have, for example, in directing
the location of the investment of General Motors inside the United States,
or for that matter in affecting the design of its products, its employment
policies, etc.? What difference does it make to our national sovereignty if
Valium or chocolate bars are made by a Swiss rather than a US firm?

Of course, there are some differences, mainly having to do with the
flows of funds across our national borders. But in the absence of the
flows generated by the multinationals — the export of capital out of the
US, the import of profits back — there would be the flows of funds generated by normal exports and imports, equally capable of working international monetary mischief, equally difficult to control.

The situation is somewhat different with regard to the underdeveloped
countries. Foreign corporations play a powerful and sometimes pernicious
role in determining the pace and pattern of the economic advance of
these nations. They often support technologies and social structures that
are inimical to the rounded development of the backward areas — for
example in shoring up corrupt and privileged classes and in encouraging

some countries to concentrate agricultural production on exports rather than on badly needed food for local consumption. The technology they introduce is as often as not deforming rather than transforming for these countries, as Barnet and Müller show in vivid detail; the profits they earn are often extremely high.

But is this a *new* condition of affairs? Myra Wilkins reviews for us the company towns and plantation enclaves of an earlier era, in every way as deforming (and as profitable) as the operations of the multinationals today. It was, after all, under the drive of foreign capital that such countries as Brazil and Honduras and Rhodesia first became adjuncts of the modern industrial system, each producing a single commodity for the world market. If there is any remarkable change to be noted, it seems to be the long overdue assertion of political independence on the part of these one-time economic colonies, and their attempts to impose much stricter forms of supervision over the foreign bodies embedded so firmly and dangerously in their midst. Indeed, where is the process of the subordination of private international economic power to local political control more evident than in the places where the multinationals are most visible — the oil-producing regions of the world?

In suggesting that the role of the multinationals may be exaggerated, I do not wave away the charge that these companies exercise vast influence, both overtly and covertly. I only maintain that this is an odd rather than a new state of affairs.

What remains, then, of the multinational phenomenon? Certainly some new and very important problems have been introduced. The problem of the trade unions, facing companies that can offset the growth of labor strength in one nation by transferring production to another nation, is one.[4] The ability to juggle profits by arbitrary pricing is another. The prospect of a dangerous coalition of world-wide national corporate power with world-wide national political power is a third: witness the case of Chile,[5] and the covert operations we hear about in other Latin American countries.

Yet with regard to the proposition that the multinationals represent a wholly new phase of capitalism I have become increasingly doubtful. Throughout the capitalist world the trend toward bigness and unwieldiness is evident, and the difficulties of managing national economies are front page news. This is driving all industrialized nations, whatever their ideologies, toward a system of centralized planning: socialism, a cynic might say, has become the next stage of capitalism. But I cannot view the international scope of economic power as constituting a special feature of this "socialism."

Suppose that every multinational corporation, whatever its national base, suddenly had its foreign affiliates lopped off and awarded as prizes to the management of domestic enterprise — that, for example, GM lost its plants in Germany to Volkswagen, or that Olivetti-owned factories in the US were transferred to Pitney-Bowes. In some of the underdeveloped countries such a shift would be regarded as a windfall — and it would indeed be one for those nations where the benefits of ownership could be widely distributed and not simply taken over by small groups which are already too rich and powerful. (Where are such countries?) But would the problems of capitalism as a social order radically change? Would the management of unemployment, inflation, pollution, energy, workers' alienation, corruption, or any other of the evils of our time be greatly lessened or worsened? That capitalism will have to make far-reaching adjustments to keep the lid on things. I do not for a moment doubt; but that capitalism has entered a new stage, in which corporations will fundamentally change the intrinsic problems of the system by extending the international reach of their operations, is an assertion that I do not believe has yet been convincingly demonstrated.

REFERENCES

1. There is some scattered data in Levinson's book [*Capitalism, Inflation, and the Multinationals*, New York, Macmillan, 1974.], p. 94f., including the extraordinary fact that Holland, with a population of only 13 million, has three companies (Shell, Unilever, Philips) that are among the largest in the world.

2. *Strategy and Structure* ([Cambridge:] MIT, 1962).

3. In my own view, one important explanation of the recent surge of multi-nationalization is the development of technologies of travel and information that makes it possible for executives to visit distant plants, or to communicate with overseas subordinates, with as little trouble as with underlings on one US coast or another.

4. A problem much debated is whether the multinationals export jobs. This is a difficult question to answer, since foreign multinationals coming into the United States create jobs. In any event, is the problem altogether different from the loss of jobs that results from automation, or from the movement of a textile firm from New England to the South?

5. One aspect of the multinationals that has received too little attention is the growth of networks of corporate intelligence that may be put to political use. See Richard Eels, "Do the Multinational Corporations Stand Guilty as Charged?," *Business and Society Review*, Autumn, 1974, p. 86, and Charles Levinson, *A Concrete Trade Union Response to the Multinational Company*, ICF Secretariat: 58, rue Moillebeau, Geneva, 1974, p. 70.

7. CLOAK AND DAGGER OPERATIONS:
AN OVERVIEW

David Wise

Citizens who telephone the Central Intelligence Agency (CIA) at Langley, Virginia, asking for a description of the Agency's activities receive a handsome blue-covered booklet bearing the CIA seal — a baleful eagle atop a shield emblazoned with a sixteen point star.

The booklet however, is less than a sixteenth of an inch thick and contains only eleven pages. The citizen reading it is told that the CIA produces estimates and "intelligence reports" to assure that the President receives information on foreign policy and national defense that is "complete, accurate, and timely." The booklet also gives the CIA's zip code, which is Washington, D.C. 20505. Nowhere in the booklet is it mentioned that the CIA conducts secret political operations around the globe, ranging from payments to foreign political figures and attempts to influence elections abroad to overthrowing governments — in which the target national leaders are sometimes killed — and full-scale para-military invasions. Nowhere does the booklet mention that the CIA operates its own air force, and, at times, its own army and navy.

These covert political operations have gotten the CIA in trouble, focused public attention upon its activities and led to demands for reform. Such activities have also raised fundamental questions about the role of a secret intelligence agency in a democracy, and, specifically, whether the requirements of American national security justify clandestine intervention in the internal affairs of other countries.

More recently, the Watergate scandal has dramatically demonstrated the dangers posed by secret intelligence agencies when their personnel, resources and methods are employed in the American political process.

For many years the CIA has been operating domestically, in ways never contemplated by the Congress. That fact may not have been understood by the public at large until it was revealed that the CIA had provided E. Howard Hunt, Jr., its former clandestine operative, with equipment used in the break-in of the office of Daniel Ellsberg's psychiatrist, and that the CIA had prepared two psychiatric profiles of Ellsberg. In addition, most of the burglars who broke into Democratic National Headquarters at Watergrate had CIA backgrounds, and one, Eugenio Rolando

From *The CIA File* by Robert Borosage and John Marks. Copyright © 1975 by Transaction, Inc.; copyright © 1976 by The Center for National Security Studies. Reprinted by permission of Grossman Publishers.

Martinez was, at the time of the break-in, still on the CIA payroll at a retainer of $100 a month. Thus, Watergate, to an extent, represented the application of covert intelligence techniques to American politics: President Nixon created his own secret police force — the plumbers and their apprentices — to conduct covert operations against domestic "enemies," real and imagined. He resigned; the problem remains.

THE LEGAL BASIS

Some definitions are necessary before discussing the legal basis of covert operations. Intelligence is information, gathered either secretly or openly. Clearly, information about military, strategic, political and economic conditions in other countries, and about the background and intentions of the leaders of those countries, may be of great value to the President and other leaders in making decisions and formulating policy. Intelligence is collected from electronic ears stationed around the globe, from reconnaissance satellites overhead, from newspapers, journals and other open sources, and by traditional espionage. Some of the means of acquisition of intelligence are highly sophisticated and themselves secret. From CIA stations abroad, by cable and courier, tons of information flow into CIA headquarters at Langley every day. Once in house, it is sifted and analyzed, or it would be of little use to policymakers.

In addition to analyzing, summarizing and evaluating the information collected, the CIA also has an estimating function. On the basis of what it knows, the CIA attempts to predict to the President the likely course of future events in other countries. The intelligence process, then, consists essentially of collecting, evaluating and estimating. It is basically passive, in that it is a process designed to *reflect* events and conditions, and to draw conclusions and logical deductions on the basis of the information collected.

Covert political action; on the other hand, seeks to manipulate events, to *cause* them to happen. The clandestine operators of the CIA are engaged not merely in reporting events, but in attempting to shape them.

The organization of the Central Intelligence Agency reflects this basic split. Beneath the Director of Central Intelligence and the Deputy Director of Central Intelligence are two principal divisions: the Directorate of Intelligence headed by a Deputy Director, and a Directorate of Operations, headed by a Deputy Director.

The Directorate of Intelligence engages in overt collection, analysis and estimating. The Directorate of Operations, or Clandestine Services, engages in covert collection and secret political operations. (Until 1973, it was known as the Directorate of Plans.) This is the so-called "dirty tricks" branch of the CIA.

The Central Intelligence Agency was in a very real sense a result of the Japanese attack on Pearl Harbor. Until World War II, the United States had no centralized intelligence machinery. During the war, on June 13, 1942, President Roosevelt established the Office of Strategic Services (OSS) under General William J. Donovan. The OSS gathered intelligence, but it also engaged in political operations and paramilitary operations, dropping agents by parachute behind enemy lines in Europe and Asia. Thus, the pattern was established under OSS of an intelligence agency that both collected information and engaged in covert operations. In the autumn of 1944, at Roosevelt's request, Donovan submitted a secret memo to the White House urging the creation of a permanent United States intelligence agency.

The plan was put aside, and on September 20, 1945, President Truman issued an order disbanding the OSS. But the wartime experience had created momentum for a centralized intelligence agency. In January, 1946, Truman established a National Intelligence Authority under a Central Intelligence Group, the forerunner of the CIA. Then Congress created the CIA, in the National Security Act of 1947. Officially, the Agency came into being on the eighteenth of September of that year. The same legislation established the National Security Council (NSC).

CIA Duties

The duties of the CIA are set forth in the act in Section 102 (d) which states:

For the purpose of coordinating the intelligence activities of the several Government departments and agencies in the interest of national security, it shall be the duty of the Agency, under the direction of the National Security Council —

(1) to advise the National Security Council in matters concerning such intelligence activities of the Government departments and agencies as relate to national security;

(2) to make recommendations to the National Security Council for the co-ordination of such intelligence activities of the departments and agencies of the Government as relate to the national security;

(3) to correlate and evaluate intelligence relating to the national security, and provide for the appropriate dissemination of such intelligence within the Government using where appropriate existing agencies and facilities: *Provided,* That the Agency shall have no police, subpoena, law-enforcement powers, or internal-security functions: *Provided further,* That the departments and other agencies of the Government shall continue to collect, evaluate, correlate and disseminate departmental intelligence: *And provided further,* That the Director

of Central Intelligence shall be responsible for protecting intelligence sources and methods from unauthorized disclosure;

(4) to perform, for the benefit of the existing intelligence agencies, such additional services of common concern as the National Security Council determines can be more efficiently accomplished centrally;

(5) to perform such other functions and duties related to intelligence affecting the national security as the National Security Council may from time to time direct.

There is no specific mention in the law of overthrowing governments or other cloak and dagger operations, but the CIA has carried out these activities under the "other functions" clause contained in subparagraph five. It is not apparent from the legislative history of the 1947 act establishing the CIA that Congress expected that the CIA would engage in covert political operations. Congress did express concern that the CIA not engage in domestic operations, and subsequent experience has proved these fears justified.

The House report on the legislation states that the CIA was created in order that the NSC "in its deliberations and advice to the President, may have available adequate information." The CIA, the report added, "will furnish such information." Certainly, the executive branch officials testifying about the proposed legislation did not talk about overthrowing governments.

One small hint of what was to come was contained in a memo submitted to Congress by Allen Dulles in 1947. He said the CIA should have "exclusive jurisdiction to carry out secret intelligence operations." And, while some individual members of Congress may have realized that covert political operations would continue in peacetime, certainly the majority of the members of Congress reading the House report on the legislation, or the Senate hearings, would not have reached this conclusion. Almost from the start, however, the CIA was in fact involved in covert political operations, which the clandestine operators of the CIA prefer to call "special operations."

In 1948, the Truman Administration was alarmed by the Communist takeover in Czechoslovakia and nervous over the possibility of a Communist victory in the Italian elections. Secretary of Defense James Forrestal wished to move to counter Communist strength in Italy. It was felt this would require a massive infusion of money. But the wealthy industrialists around Milan feared reprisals if the Communists won and were reluctant to contribute funds. So members of the Eastern establishment literally passed the hat at the Brook Club in New York.

SECRET DOCUMENT

There was no CIA mechanism to deal with the problem — the Plans Directorate was not created until January 4, 1951. As a result, in the summer of 1948, the NSC issued a secret document, NSC 10/2, authorizing special operations, providing they were secret and small enough to be "plausibly deniable" by the government. The same document created an operating agency under the euphemistic title of Office of Policy Coordination (OPC). Former OSS agent Frank G. Wisner was brought in to direct this office, which operated within the CIA, but under the joint authority as well of the Department of State and the Department of Defense. In 1950 General Walter Bedell Smith, then director of the CIA, managed to eliminate control by these outside agencies and placed Wisner's group entirely under the CIA.

Meanwhile, a separate Office of Special Operations (OSO) handled covert intelligence gathering for the CIA. OSO and OPC were merged in January, 1951 (while Smith was still Director of the CIA) into the new Directorate of Plans.

In 1949, the Central Intelligence Agency Act was passed exempting CIA from all statutes requiring the disclosure of the "functions, names, official titles, salaries, or numbers of personnel employed by the Agency." It gave the Director of Central Intelligence unprecedented power to spend money "without regard to the provisions of law and regulations relating to the expenditure of government funds." The 1949 Act permitted "such expenditures to be accounted for solely on the certificate of the director."

A series of highly classified National Security Council Intelligence Directives have been issued since 1948, permitting the CIA to carry out special operations. The directives are known as NSCIDs; within the intelligence community they are called "Nonskids." In addition, the Director of Central Intelligence issues directives called DCIDs. Under the authority of the NSCIDs, these apparently can be issued by the Director of Central Intelligence without further clearance by the NSC. These directives and other Presidential and CIA documents together form what is sometimes referred to as the "secret charter" of the CIA.

Thus, a secret agency engages in secret operations that carry the risk of war, under secret directives unavailable to the press, the public or most members of the Congress. Indeed, until the Watergate revelations of 1973, Congress was not curious about this "secret charter." In July of 1973, however, Senator Stuart Symington did question William Colby about NSCIDs at hearings of the Senate Armed Services Committee on the nomination of Colby to be Director of the CIA.

Symington: We understand some . . . directives to the intelligence community are included in classified documents called National Security Council Intelligence Directives, NSCIDs. Would you describe in general the subject matter of these Directives; and, if you believe they should remain classified, would you tell the committee why you think so?

Colby: These Directives are the application of the [other functions] provision of the law that I cited, Mr. Chairman. . . . They include some general directives which describe the functions of the different members of the intelligence community and there is certain sensitive information in those. Those are National Security Council documents, Mr. Chairman, and I do not have the authority for the declassification since they originate with the National Security Council.

MECHANISM OF CONTROL

Before discussing the machinery for the control of covert operations, the nature of those operations should be more precisely defined. Perhaps the best definition was provided by Richard M. Bissell, the CIA's deputy director for Plans between 1958 and February, 1962, in which capacity he ran covert operations for the Agency. Bissell was one of the fathers of the U-2 reconnaissance aircraft and the principal planner of the Bay of Pigs invasion. The minutes of a private discussion on intelligence sponsored by the Council on Foreign Relations in 1968 summarizes Bissell's view:

Covert operations should, for some purposes, be divided into two classifications: (1) *intelligence collection*, primarily espionage, or the obtaining of intelligence by covert means; and (2) *covert action*, attempting to influence the internal affairs of other nations — sometimes called "intervention" — by covert means.

In the Council on Foreign Relations meeting. Bissell went on to list the dimensions of covert action. He said:

The scope of covert action could include: (1) political advice or counsel; (2) subsidies to an individual; (3) financial support and "technical assistance" to political parties; (4) support of private organizations, including labor unions, business firms, cooperatives, etc.; (5) covert propaganda; (6) "private" training of individuals and exchange of persons; (7) economic operations; and (8) paramilitary for political action operations designed to overthrow or to support a regime (like the Bay of Pigs and the programs in Laos). These operations can be classified in various ways: by the degree and type of secrecy required by their legality, and, perhaps, by their benign or hostile character.

The distinction contained in Bissell's point eight is important. Special operations may be designed either to place pressure upon, overthrow a government, or to maintain it in power. The "Special Group," the interagency government committee customarily cited by intelligence officials as the principal mechanism for the control of covert operations, was nonexistent for the first several years of the CIA's life. Not until late in the first Eisenhower Administration was the Special Group established. Before that, covert operations were discussed at the "OCB luncheon group." The participants were members of the now defunct Operations Coordinating Board, who were drawn from various departments of the government dealing with foreign affairs. During this period, apparently, intervention in the internal affairs of other countries was a subject for casual discussion by an informal group over lunch.

The Special Group was also known during the Eisenhower years as the "54/12 Group" and has been periodically renamed; during the Johnson years it was known as the 303 Committee — after a room number in the Executive Office Building — and during the Nixon Administration, it acquired the name "40 Committee." The 40 Committee is reportedly a designation taken from the serial number of the NSC document defining its membership and responsibilities. In 1974, the members of the 40 Committee were the President's Assistant for National Security, the Deputy Secretary of Defense, the Undersecretary of State for Political Affairs, the Director of the Central Intelligence Agency and the Chairman of the Joint Chiefs of Staff.

POLITICAL ESPIONAGE

Since we are told that we must rely on the wisdom and judgment of these high officials, and that every covert operation undertaken by the CIA anywhere around the globe is approved at this high level, it is not entirely comforting to note that during the period that John N. Mitchell served as Attorney General he was added to the ranks of the 40 Committee. As a member of the committee, Mitchell listened to CIA plans for cloak and dagger operations designed to influence the political affairs of other nations. Possibly he became so accustomed to this atmosphere that he was willing to listen to G. Gordon Liddy's plans for domestic political espionage. For it was while Mitchell was Attorney General and a member of the 40 Committee that he permitted discussions in his office of bugging the opposition political party, of financing floating bordellos to suborn Democratic politicians, and of a plan to kidnap domestic dissidents and spirit them to Mexico in order to avoid any problems during the Republican National Convention.

It is perhaps tiresome to point out that we are a government of laws not men, but in citing the 40 Committee as proof of control over covert operations, we are really relying on a group of men who operate entirely in secret and can, in the final analysis, approve almost anything. No more mysterious group exists within the government than the 40 Committee. Its operations are so secret that, in an appearance before the Senate Armed Services Committee, CIA Director Colby was even reluctant to identify the chairman. Finally, Colby relented and named Henry Kissinger as chairman as the Assistant to the President for National Security Affairs.

Because of the cocoon of secrecy enveloping the operations of the 40 Committee, it is very difficult to assess the extent to which the committee exercises effective control over special operations. For example, executive branch officials consistently refused to explain the actions of the 40 Committee investigating the role of the CIA and the International Telephone & Telegraph Company (ITT) in Chile during 1970–71. The Subcommittee on Multinational Corporations, headed by Senator Frank Church, Democrat, of Idaho, conducted the 1972 investigation of charges that ITT and the CIA were involved in a plot to prevent the 1970 election of leftist President Salvador Allende of Chile. The record of this tangled story of CIA intervention in Chile is replete with contradictions. In 1973, Richard Helms was questioned about the CIA role by Senator Symington during hearings on Helms' nomination to be ambassador to Iran and on CIA international and domestic activities. This exchange took place:

Symington: Did you try in the Central Intelligence Agency to overthrow the Government of Chile?
Helms: No, sir.
Symington: Did you have any money passed to the opponents of Allende?
Helms: No, sir.

However, John A. McCone, former Director of the CIA and a Director of ITT, testified to the Church subcommittee that Helms had told him that, while the 40 Committee had decided against any major action designed to prevent Allende's election, some "minimal effort" would be mounted which "could be managed within the flexibility of their own [CIA] budget," without seeking additional appropriated funds.

In 1974, however, CIA Director Colby testified in secret to Congress that the CIA had been authorized to spend $8 million in Chile between 1970 and 1973 to "destabilize" the Allende government. Colby testified that the CIA's operations in Chile were approved by the 40 Committee. He said that, of the total, the committee had authorized $350,000 to be spent in an unsuccessful effort to bribe members of the Chilean Congress to stop Allende's election.

The ITT–CIA story is a complex one, but it is clear from the record of the Senate subcommittee that the Agency's clandestine directorate was in constant touch with ITT (which had substantial investments in Chile) about ways to block Allende from becoming President. McCone suggested to Helms that CIA originate discussions with ITT, and Helms had William V. Broe, Chief of the Western Hemisphere Division of the Clandestine Services, contact Harold S. Geneen, the Chairman of ITT. Later, McCone testified, Geneen told McCone "that he was prepared to put up as much as $1 million in support of any plan" to oppose Allende. McCone testified that Helms had informed him that the 40 Committee had discussed the situation in Chile in June of 1970 and decided that the

CIA would do nothing of consequence to intervene in the September 4 election. On that date, Allende received the most votes, but no candidate had a majority; as a result, the election was thrown into the Chilean Congress, which was to decide the outcome on October 24, 1970.

ACCELERATED CHAOS

During this critical six-week period, Washington apparently became much more receptive to plans to block Allende's election in the Congress. Charles Meyer, Assistant Secretary of State for Inter-American Affairs, testified that soon after the election, the 40 Committee met again to discuss United States policy toward Chile. Meyer declined to tell the Church subcommittee what took place at this meeting of the 40 Committee or what instructions were given to the United States ambassador to Chile. It is known, however, that on September 29, at the direction of Helms, Broe met Edward Gerrity, a top ITT executive, in New York and proposed a plan to accelerate economic chaos in Chile in order to weaken Allende's position.

While the role of the 40 Committee in the Chilean affair remains obscure, it is clear that the committee could not possibly have exercised control over everything that occurred. For example, the initial discussion between Broe and Geneen was not the result of any instruction by the 40 Committee, but of the direct approach by McCone to Helms. Patently, the "old-boy" network was involved here. A former Director of the CIA, the man who had appointed Helms as the Agency's top covert operator, simply telephoned his old colleagues. Since McCone was also Director of ITT, the interests of CIA and the multinational corporation neatly dovetailed.

If the 40 Committee did approve intensified contact between CIA and ITT just prior to the runoff election in the Chilean Congress, then the 40 Committee was merely seizing upon a channel of communication that it never opened in the first place. One may ask whether the 40 Committee, in this instance, was in the position of the tail wagging the dog. In any event, the administration was unwilling to describe the role of the 40 Committee to a duly constituted subcommittee of the Senate of the United States. Thus, we were asked to take on faith the assurance that secret operations conducted under secret directives are adequately controlled by a secret committee that makes its decisions in secret. Moreover, in the manner of the fox placed in charge of the chicken coop, the Director of Central Intelligence is a member of the 40 Committee.

Covert operations are a tempting shortcut to the achievement of policy goals. The covert operators can naturally be expected to make the best possible case to the 40 Committee. One official familiar with the operations of the committee has been quoted as saying: "They were like a bunch of schoolboys. They would listen and their eyes would bug out. I always used to say that I could get $5 million out of the 40 Committee for a covert operation faster than I could get money for a typewriter out of the ordinary bureaucracy."

Senator William Proxmire, who has studied the intelligence community, has stated:

In practice, it appears that the 40 Committee mainly approves activities co-ordinated at lower levels. If a promising operation can be coordinated at a working level where the concept originates, it often rises through the intelligence community with little critical challenge until it arrives at the 40 Committee. There, because it has been reviewed by the "experts," it is frequently approved.

Since the President is not a member of the 40 Committee, its existence permits the claim that covert operations are controlled at a high level in government. On the other hand, the existence of the committee permits the President to disclaim personal knowledge of a covert operation if it should fail and prove embarrassing.

It seems reasonable to speculate that certain covert operations are considered so sensitive that the CIA will not bring them to the attention of the 40 Committee. One former high official of the CIA told this writer, "There are some things that you don't tell Congress; some things you don't even tell the President."

Once a covert operation is underway, it may move in directions that cannot be controlled by a committee in Washington, however distinguished its members. A case in point might be the circumstances surrounding the assassination of dictator Rafael L. Trujillo of the Dominican Republic. In 1959, Henry Dearborn, then a foreign service officer, arrived in the Dominican Republic as charge d'affairs. When the United States broke off diplomatic relations with Trujillo in August of that year, Dearborn remained on as Counsel General and the senior United States official in the Dominican Republic. "For the last year my job was to know what was going on," Dearborn said in an interview with this writer. "I had very good connections with the underground. I did know what was going on." The group planning the assassination of Trujillo during this period did so "knowing that the United States wasn't going to be unhappy if he was 'bumped off'," according to Dearborn. "I did not know when it was going to happen, but I had a feeling that it was going to happen, and so reported it [to Washington]."

Dearborn denied any direct knowledge of CIA encouragement of the plotters. Asked whether he gave encouragement to the anti-Trujillo group, he replied: "Our attitude — they didn't have to ask us about that, the mere fact that we were in contact with them reflected that."

At the time of the Bay of Pigs invasion in mid-April of 1961, Henry Dearborn said, "Washington's attitude abruptly reversed." Until then, Dearborn had received "only an interested reception in Washington of imminent plans to move against Trujillo. Up to that time we did not object to their plot. After the Bay of Pigs, I did tell them of the dismay in Washington, that the attitude had changed. But we didn't control them, so it didn't change their plans." Dearborn said the State Department "did instruct me to urge them [the underground]" not to take action against Trujillo. It was too late; Trujillo was assassinated in May, 1961.

In addition to the 40 Committee, there are two other possible or potential mechanisms of control of covert operations: the President's Foreign Intelligence Advisory Board (FIAB) and the Shadowy CIA oversight committees in the House and Senate. But the available evidence does not indicate that either the FIAB or the congressional committees control these operations. The FIAB was originally established by Eisenhower in 1956 as a result of a recommendation of the Hoover Commission. It was permitted to lapse and then revived by President Kennedy with its present name in 1961. Under President Nixon, the board was headed by retired Admiral George W. Anderson, Jr. The eleven-member board consists of prominent businessmen, scientists and others outside the government. While the board has, from time to time, investigated intelligence failures and made recommendations for organizational changes within the intelligence community, it does not approve covert operations in advance. The board is something of an anomaly in that it consists of private citizens privileged to know the innermost secrets of United States intelligence agencies that are denied to the public at large.

WATCHDOG COMMITTEES

Four subcommittees of the House and Senate are supposed to serve as "watchdog" committees over United States intelligence agencies. They are the subcommittees of the Armed Services and Appropriations Committees in the Senate and in the House. These committees give the appearance of control over CIA without the reality. For the most part, they consist of senior members of Congress, many of whom are friendly to CIA. The attitude of members of these committees toward covert operations may have been summed up best by former Senator Leverett Saltonstall of Massachusetts. To Saltonstall, the problem was that "we might obtain information which I personally would rather not have. . . ."

Covert operations may be viewed most clearly against the background of the Cold War that provided their justification in the eyes of the policymakers. For two decades, Americans were warned of the perils of a monolithic international Communism; to preserve the Free World it was deemed necessary, in the words of Allen Dulles, to "fight fire with fire." The external enemy was the rationale for the establishment of a vast secret intelligence bureaucracy, its operations subject to none of the usual checks and balances that the American system imposes on more plebeian government agencies.

THE CHANGING WORLD

What might have seemed logical and necessary in an era of Cold War does not seem justified today. The world has changed; the Communist "monolith" has become fragmented, the superpowers seek detente, but covert political action goes on.

Yet it is difficult to discover any moral or legal basis for such operations, and they are, at best, of doubtful constitutionality. Morally, no one appointed the United States to intervene in the internal affairs of other nations. Such operations violate the charter of the United Nations. And one can imagine the reaction in this country if a foreign intelligence service launched an invasion of the United States in Florida, poured millions of dollars into the country to support a Presidential candidate or congressional candidates in order to influence the outcome of an American election, or attempted a coup to overthrow the President. A world groping for peace cannot afford secret wars.

Legally, the argument that the "other functions" clause can justify large-scale covert operations is extremely tenuous. There is no indication that Congress intended the "other functions" provision to justify such operations, and if Congress did, the language of the statute would be overly broad. Moreover, covert operations — at least those involving para-military action or the overthrow of governments — would appear almost by definition to be unconstitutional. The Constitution vests the war power in the Congress, and operations on this scale are clearly the equivalent of undeclared war. Yet they are undertaken by executive action alone; Congress and the public, which Congress represents, have no opportunity to debate or approve such operations in advance.

The President has a constitutional responsibility to protect national security, but this does not extend to waging undeclared wars. If there is no moral legal or constitutional basis for covert political operations, it may be argued that there remains a practical basis — that such operations are pragmatically necessary to protect American security. There is, however, a fatal flaw in such an argument.

A democracy rests on the consent of the governed, and the governed are not permitted to give their consent to covert political actions because of their very nature. Moreover, when secret political operations are exposed, the government lies to protect them, by denying responsibility. The price has proved too high in terms of public confidence in the system of government. It does not work. The road to Watergate was paved with government lying, often to protect covert political operations. The result was the greatest crisis in the American political system since the Civil War, the impeachment vote by the House Committee on the Judiciary and, for the first time in almost 200 years, the resignation of a President while in office. The standard of "plausible deniability" has no place in the American constitutional system. For in plain language, it means that the government can act as it pleases if it can get away with lying about its actions to the electorate.

The damaging effect of covert operations on the American political system is the crucial and overriding consideration. But even from a practical standpoint, covert operations often have had the opposite effect of that intended. The Bay of Pigs strengthened Castro's position and weakened President Kennedy's. The governments of Iran and Guatemala were overthrown, but the reputation of the United States in Africa, South America and Asia has been tainted precisely because of such covert operations. As a result, the United States has sometimes been blamed for activities for which the CIA has not been responsible.

The inescapable conclusion is that the United States should cease covert political operations. Congress, which has been struggling to regain its war powers from the President, should assert its right to end secret political intervention and secret wars as well. Congressional and national debate and legislation to accomplish these ends are required. The "other functions" clause should be rewritten specifically to exclude covert political operations. Congress should improve its control over the CIA and the intelligence community generally, and establish a joint committee or more broadly based committees in the House and Senate for this purpose.

The Watergate crisis was a dramatic illustration of where the covert mentality can lead us when applied to American domestic politics. Watergate also proved something about the resiliency of the American system, for the impeachment proceeding and the resignation of Richard Nixon in one sense marked the drawing of a line by the people: thus far — but no further. America showed that it was not ready for totalitarianism. The impeachment vote and Nixon's resignation represented a cleansing of the American political process domestically. The people and the Congress can and should assert themselves just as powerfully in the field of foreign wars in Laos or Cambodia, no more Bays of Pigs. American foreign policy can be carried out openly, without covert manipulation in the affairs of other nations.

The fact that other nations may engage in covert political action is not sufficient justification for the United States to do so; for if we adopt the methods of our adversaries, we will become indistinguishable from them. In time, covert operations will change the character of the institutions they seek to preserve. Covert operations may be dangerous to other nations, but ultimately they impose the greatest danger to ourselves.

III INEQUALITY

Poverty is periodically rediscovered in America. The latest rediscovery took place around the beginning of the 1960s and culminated in the War on Poverty. The discovery came just when many people had gotten used to celebrating the rapidly approaching end of income disparities in the United States and other Western capitalist democracies. The belief in diminishing economic inequality served as a major element in a more general argument, which saw these countries as having solved the basic political problems of industrialization; any remaining conflicts could be dealt with by what one writer called "piecemeal technology." [1]

The American poor undoubtedly recognized that this celebration was premature. The poor, however, had little voice in public affairs. The fact of continuing poverty had to be "rediscovered" by others to become a matter of national concern. Two conceptions of the meaning and causes of poverty soon emerged. Both, in general, agreed on the dimensions of the problem; both agreed on the necessity for some kind of social action to ameliorate it. Beyond this, the agreement ended.

According to one view, poverty demonstrated the failure of American institutions to reach certain segments of the population. Nonetheless, America was still to be considered an affluent society and a paragon of the relatively smooth social and economic development that might become the pattern for less fortunate nations to follow. Poverty meant that there were underdeveloped areas of the United States that had to be brought up to par with the rest of the country. This could be accomplished through a combination of popular goodwill and governmental action. The envisioned governmental action generally involved relatively minor adjustments on the level of social and economic structure, and substantial intervention into the culture and habits of poor people. These priorities stemmed from a general satisfaction with the American economy as a whole, coupled with a distaste for the immorality, waste, and suffering felt to characterize the poor.

According to the second view, poverty was one aspect of a system of maldistribution of income, wealth, and power. This system was a central fact of American society: it had changed little for many decades and showed few signs of changing in the future. In this view, extensive poverty and great wealth were closely related parts of a whole. Speculations about the cultural deficiencies of the poor masked a refusal to confront the basic inequity of the American economy itself. A significant attack on poverty would require fundamental changes in the economy as a whole.

The sections in this chapter lend support to the second view. Edward S. Herman shows the inadequacy of the commonly accepted idea that there has been a "revolutionary" equalization in income in the United States and the world as a whole. On the contrary, Herman argues, income disparities are becoming *greater*, both within individual countries and between the rich countries and the poor ones (as suggested by Barnet and Müller in chapter II). In the United States, Herman shows, income gains of working people made before World War II are now being steadily eroded as a result of a conscious, deliberate "counterrevolution" by the Nixon and Ford administrations. One lesson from this is that the persistence of income inequalities is neither inevitable nor accidental, but reflects the political dominance of business interests in American society.

One of the key ways in which that political dominance is expressed is through the tax system. In capitalist societies the "progressive" income tax is usually considered the great equalizer — the agency through which a society based on private profit softens the inequalities it creates. As Philip Stern shows, however, the tax system is rigged. Through a bewildering variety of loopholes and special conditions, the richest people in America get what amounts to a vast and costly welfare program all their own. The welfare program for the rich is many times more generous than the better-known one for the poor, and it costs us far more — both in terms of dollars wasted and of vital social services neglected.

Paul Jacobs' selection gives us a graphic analysis of the way the system operates at the other end of the income ladder. A whole specialized economic system — the "poverty market" — works to ensure that the poor pay more and receive less. Jacobs shows compellingly that middle-class people enjoy a number of subtle and rarely recognized economic advantages, which make all the difference between security and insecurity, well-being and anxiety. Poverty is a self-perpetuating system. Economic life is very different for the poor, and much more difficult — something often ignored by those social scientists who explain poverty as the result of "lower class culture" or lack of motivation.

One of the key themes in the argument that the United States was fast becoming an affluent, conflict-free society was the idea that the blue-collar working class was rapidly disappearing or, at least, becoming more and more indistinguishable from the great American middle class. As Andrew Levison's selection shows, this was largely a myth. Blue-collar workers are still the largest single sector of the population in the United States; most of them still live uncomfortably close to the poverty line; and most of them suffer from job insecurity and the constant threat of unemployment — especially if they are minorities or women. Full employment, in Levison's view, is the best solution for the problems of the blue-collar worker; but Levison does not confront the problem, raised by David Gordon in chapter I, of whether full employment is even possible in the modern capitalist economy.

REFERENCES

1. An important book in this tradition is Daniel Bell's *The End of Ideology: On the Exhaustion of Political Ideas in the Fifties* (New York: Free Press, 1962).

8. THE INCOME 'COUNTER-REVOLUTION'

Edward S. Herman

WHO GETS WHAT IN DOLLARS AND CENTS

According to Arthur F. Burns, writing in 1951, the "transformation in the distribution of our national income . . . may already be counted as one of the great social revolutions of history." This view was echoed in *Fortune* and other vehicles of conventional opinion, and it has been widely accepted in the intellectual community from the Truman era to the present. The "revolution" was deduced from a relative decline in the share of income going to the top 1 and 5 percent of income-receiving units in the U.S. between 1929 and 1945, a decline which also led to great expectations for New Deal type reformism in further reducing inequality. Belief in a continuation of the revolution was also based on the greater inequality observed in poor countries, which brought forth Rostowian-type stage theories in which growth would lead to affluence and equality as part of a "natural" process applicable throughout the world of free markets.

These optimistic doctrines and pronouncements had an important political and ideological function in the Cold War environment of the post-1945 era. They pointed to capitalism and "free world" membership as an assured source of income and distributional improvement, and thus as the proper route for peoples who might otherwise be tempted by radical alternatives. In Rostow's system, and in orthodox trade theory, "aid" and private international capital flows would serve as supplements helping to bring about sustained growth in the underdeveloped countries and "factor price equalization" as between rich and poor lands. A continuing income revolution was thus envisaged both for the U.S. and its friends and clients.

Both the political and economic analyses underlying these perspectives were superficial, and their narrow empirical base has crumbled under the impact of a quarter century of experience. This article focuses on some of the recent evidence on changes in income distribution, both between and within countries, and some neglected factors which may have contributed to the results. The latter suggest that in our era of rapid economic

From *Commonweal* (January 3, 1975). Reprinted by permission of Commonweal Publishing Co., Inc.

growth, inflation, increasing political conservatism, and the spread of the military junta in the Tihrd World (frequently under U.S. sponsorship), income distribution has become more unequal to a degree that makes it reasonable to characterize the past three decades as an era of "income counter-revolution."

Measurement of income inequality is fraught with difficulties, both conceptual and because of data limitations. Even in the U.S., where relatively extensive and dependable information is collected on incomes, there are serious deficiencies in available data. Much of it is gathered in connection with IRS tax collections, in which case incomes leaking through tax loopholes are often excluded by the definition of taxable income. Thus, unrealized capital gains and interest on tax-exempt bonds do not show up in these data; and incomes transformed into expense accounts do not appear as income. The Census Bureau also collects sample data on earnings, but again, unrealized capital gains and expense accounts are not "earnings."

In assessing trends based on official statistics it is important to recognize that tax "avoidance" (legal) and "evasion" (illegal) are not only a prerogative mainly of the upper-income classes, but are functionally related to both time and the level of tax rates. That is, as time elapses tax lawyers, wealthy individuals, and business firms devise new ways of reducing tax liabilities, and the higher the tax rates the greater the incentives to escape taxation. "Attrition" of the tax system may also result from deliberate legislative creation of loopholes, frequently done on the ground that the solution to one inequitable privilege is the granting of an equalizer to some other insistent party. Attrition is reflected, for example, in the fact that the effective tax rate paid by commercial banks declined from 38.3 percent to 16.8 percent between 1961 and 1972. Another illustration is the tax status of Americans working overseas, who have been exempt from U.S. taxes on the first $20,000 of income for the first three years of working abroad, after which the exemption rises to $25,000. It was recently disclosed that overseas Americans have also been able to escape British income taxation, because they have been held liable only for taxes on income received *in* Britain. The threat of Labor government elimination of this windfall has revealed that many Americans and their employers have arranged for salaries to be paid into U.S. banking accounts — by which means incomes are not received in Britain — with the employees borrowing money from U.S. banks if necessary to finance living expenses. This tax dodge is illustrative of a flexibility in working the crevices of the tax system that is not available to the lower 90 percent of income-receiving units.

Another difficulty in assessing income distribution trends is conceptual.

Even if the share of income going to the lowest 20 percent is constant, or even falling, their absolute levels of income may rise if aggregate income is increasing. Thus, even if inequality in the literal sense remains constant, or even increases, it is at least debatable whether the welfare of the poor may not still be improving. With stable or increasing inequality, for example, there may be a decline in the number of individuals or families who fail to meet some minimum living standard — who fall below a "poverty line" — and are thus said to constitute a social ill and problem on the basis of some concept of need. This "social welfare" approach to income distribution, however, at least as it has been applied in the U.S., has been based on a rather arbitrary and low minimum required budget, which allows little or no room for leisure, minor luxury, and status-sustaining expenditures that are essential to a sense of well-being in a consumerist society. This arbitrary line tends to be biased downward for class reasons, including a simple desire on the part of the affluent to minimize payments for the needy (often based on poverty line definitions). If "social necessities" rise with increasing consumption opportunities, poverty lines will have a downward bias for this reason as well. Poverty line budgets also rest on the assumption that people at the lower end of the income scale have the time, energy, motivation, resources and information to shop with high efficiency. This assumption is contrary to well-known facts.

Finally, if satisfaction is a function of relative position as well as absolute income, then people in the lower-income brackets may be "worse off" (less satisfied, more alienated) even with rising absolute income. That is, the gap may have widened between income received and income required to supply strongly felt wants (based on what the affluent now consume, a matter rapidly communicated by salesmanship to all potential buyers). As absolute income rises certain basic physical needs and comforts can more readily be met, but even in a rich society like the U.S. vast numbers have sub-standard housing, inadequate medical care, and even nutritional deficiencies. This is a result of both the structure of income and our excessive reliance on the market for its disposition. The market has long failed to perform satisfactorily in supplying cheap basic necessities such as housing and primary medical care. Homes are rarely produced in the U.S. on a mass production basis to meet low income needs, and the poor can only afford hand-me-downs in various stages of decay. Medical services are provided almost exclusively by highly trained, certified, and expensive practitioners, so that the poor obtain such services only sporadically and *after* the onset of illness. The great social costs of inadequate preventive medical care and poor, overcrowded lower-income housing, with cumulative deterioration and ghettoization of large urban enclaves, and major health and morale effects on happiness and work efficiency, are not taken into accounts by private enterprise. They are what economists call "externalities," much discussed but treated as "exceptions" to market beneficence and underrated in importance.

Obviously, where there are large numbers on the margin of subsistence or comfort, the capture of even a proportionate share of rising income by the upper income brackets is contrary to general welfare interests, even if absolute incomes of the poor are increasing. This implies not only that larger absolute increases in income go to the more affluent but that relative inequalities remain intact. Insofar as equality is a goal in itself, and a condition for a less competitive, less growth-oriented society, stable income shares under conditions of substantial inequality mean at best holding the line, not moving closer to a major end.

The "one world" of Second World War euphoria has obviously not materialized. Among the many ways of looking at the fractured world of our day, one that has become commonplace is the division between the "rich," "developed" nations and the "poor," "under" or "less developed" countries (LDCs) of the "Third World." Contrary to the expectations of many, this division has sharpened since 1945 as the rich countries have, on average, grown faster in per capita incomes than the poor lands. (The expectation of a shrinking differential was based in part on the belief that Western technology could work productivity miracles in the now "aware" Third World, a belief which reflected a failure to grasp the nature and intractability of the institutional obstacles to development widely prevalent in the LDCs.)

Gunnar Myrdal wrote in 1968 that "it is abundantly clear that the discrepancy between the economic well-being of the haves and the have-nots, so far as South Asia is concerned, is rapidly widening." Data extending beyond Asia on rates of growth of real per capita income for the period 1950–1971 indicate that the rich countries of the "free world" continue to grow somewhat faster than the poor. Given the enormous initial income discrepancies between rich and poor, this means that the absolute income gains in the rich countries are huge, and steadily widening, relative to those in the poor countries: the 3.6 percent rate of per capita real gain for the developed countries, 1960–1971, applied to the 1959 per capita U.S. figure of $2,830, represents a per person increment of $102 a year; the 3.1 percent rate for LDCs, applied to India's base of about $80, represents an increment of $2.48. It will be noted that the U.S. per person *increment* exceeds the original *total* per capita income figure for India.

There is little basis for optimism that increasing world inequality will be reversed in the near future. It is true that oil profits have bolstered the position of some relatively underdeveloped countries, such as Iran, Saudi Arabia and Indonesia, but others have suffered in the same process.

Among them oil importers like India and Pakistan have been unable even to sustain their unsatisfactory growth rates of earlier years and show signs of stagnation and even retrogression. The worldwide rise in the price of food and other raw materials has had a mixed impact on poor countries, depending on their structure of imports and exports, but on balance it has been unfavorable. And its damaging effects have been greatest on the poorest (India, Pakistan, Sub-Saharan Africa), often suffering from elemental hunger and dependent on a shrinking external largesse.

A few of the totalitarian free enterprise LDCs such as Brazil, Iran, Indonesia and South Korea have grown rapidly in recent years, but by a process combining the turning over of a large part of development to external interests and ignoring or deliberately depressing the condition of the underlying population. (The income distribution effects of this phenomenon are discussed in the next section.) The military plays a large role in these societies and absorbs a large fraction of aid plus increments to social output. The recent huge arms sale arranged by the Pentagon with Iran, a country with a 70 percent illiteracy rate, involving $2.5 billion in advanced planes, helicopters and missiles, is a reminder of the sobering fact that arms purchases in the Third World are growing twice as rapidly as its overall economic growth. This not only involves huge direct waste that these countries cannot afford, it also has an obvious socio-political component, helping to keep the lid on any internal challenges to the rule of traditional elites. As U.S. direct intervention recedes, in response to the impact of Vietnam, the capacity of neo-colonial elites to protect themselves from their own people must be enlarged accordingly.

In sum, as a recent study by Irving Kravis notes, there is a "growing polarization of income levels in the world," with three-fifths of the human race having per capita incomes of $310 or less a year and the gap between rich and poor nations increasing. "The inescapable conclusion," says Kravis, "is that the benefits of economic progress have been confined to a minority of the world's population." And by and large the trade-investment-aid package offered by the West has provided neither adequate growth nor minimally humane social orders among Free World LDCs.

Not only has growth been slow on the average among the poor countries, income distribution within them has tended to become more unequal. In their recent invaluable study of this subject, *Economic Growth and Social Equity in Developing Countries,* Irma Adelman and Cynthia Taft Morris state in their preface that "The results of our analyses came as a shock to us . . . we had shared the prevailing view that economic growth was economically beneficial to most nations. We had also not greatly questioned the relevance today of the historical association of successful economic growth with the spread of parliamentary democracy. Our results proved to be at variance with our preconceptions." On the basis of an elaborate analysis of data for 43 LDCs, they found that,

The position of the poorest 60 percent typically worsens, both relatively and absolutely, when an initial spurt of narrowly based dualistic growth is imposed on an agrarian subsistence economy. . . . The gains of the top 5 percent are particularly great in very low income countries where a sharply dualistic structure is associated with political and economic domination by traditional or expatriate elites.

The idea of temporary regression in mass welfare at some stage in the growth process had been suggested earlier by Kuznets and others on the basis of Western historical evidence. But recent developments have been based on special factors of the modern era and may not be a passing abnormality or transitional phase of the growth process. A number of these special factors arise from the extreme division of today's world into rich and poor countries and the ready communication and unequal power relations among them. One factor is the extent to which the aggressive development and marketing of new consumer goods by rich countries to local poor country elites results in a perverse "international demonstration effect," which absorbs in autos, gasoline, roads, gadgets, and luxury housing resources that might otherwise contribute to basic development. These elites "need" any growth dividend to meet a rising international consumption standard, so that with sufficient force at their command they may capture all surpluses and even depress further the real incomes of the masses (frequently via inflation in a context of downward pressures on many wages).

As just implied, a second factor is the ability and willingness of these elites to use force to assure their privileged command over income. Where they are actually threatened with income redistribution downward via democratic processes, the termination of democracy in favor of "order" and "austerity" is a foregone conclusion (*vide* Brazil, Uruguay, and even more conspicuously, Chile). And the threats to domination by privileged elites tend to be greater today than in the early years of Western capitalist development, again partly because of the duality between rich and poor countries and the spread of ideas and knowledge of the possibilities of a better life for both rich and poor alike (although by radically different processes).

Another special factor in the modern era has been the efforts of the rich countries to shape the postcolonial developments in the Third World, not according to their own image, as in the common cliché, but according to their interest. This has meant interventionist efforts to create and sustain a neo-colonial elite. As the greatest world power after 1945, the

U.S. has been the leader in this process. Despite a mass of rhetoric claiming devotion to democracy and self-determination, the clear essence of U.S. policy has been the unremitting support of counter-revolution in this age of Third World upheaval. A community of interest has united Third World elites and the leaders of the U.S., resulting in a huge influx of military and intelligence "aid" into the LDCs, occasional violent intrusions (Vietnam, the Dominican Republic), and a steady general support for conservative, increasingly military-dominated regimes.

The building up of a large neo-colonial military force, linked to the U.S. by training and material aid, has had as its main purpose the provision of an "insurance policy" against internal social revolution. The community of interest rests on the need of Third World elites for external support, given their lack of any mass domestic constituency; and, on the U.S. side, the interest of the leadership both in the "open door" for its expanding economy and dependable political allies. Bankers Trust, as well as the Pentagon, is "bullish on Brazil" under junta auspices (quoting a recent widely placed ad by the bank) — its open door is wide, its support of U.S. leadership is reliable, and its use of torture and stifling of a democratic order does not bother either Bankers Trust or the military. Nor are they unduly troubled by the fact that the Brazilian income distribution has worsened markedly under the junta, the relative share of the richest 5 percent increasing from 29 percent in 1960 to 38 percent in 1970, the real income of the poorest 40 percent falling absolutely.

The Dominican Republic provides an even clearer case study of the regressive impact of U.S. policy on the distribution of income and wealth in poor countries subject to dominant U.S. influence. In that client state hunger is rampant, with much of the potentially rich agricultural land unused or misused, and with fewer than 1 percent of the farmers owning 47.5 percent of the land, many of the rest operating under semi-feudal tenure conditions. A *Wall Street Journal* report (Sept. 9, 1971) cites one foreign economic expert as saying that "Per capita income is about the same as before 1965, but it's less equitably distributed." The invasion of 1965, however, preserved a large U.S. investment stake, and tax subsidies and low wages have encouraged a considerable further influx. Low wages are assured by stagnation plus U.S. supported terror. Even the *Wall Street Journal* noted that "the [U.S.] embassy has done nothing publicly to dissociate itself from the terror. The U.S. continues to provide substantial aid, including training, equipment and arms to the Dominican police and army." And the *Journal* also described the more specific ways in which repression affects the class distribution of income:

When a union attempted to organize construction workers at a foreign-owned ferronickel mill project last year, Mr. Balaguer sent in the army to help straighten things out. While the soldiers kept order, the contractor fired 32 allegedly leftist leaders. . . . The strike was broken in eight days.

The *Wall Street Journal* also reported the use of army troops in the Dominican Republic to evict peasants from land needed for the construction of a plush foreign-owned vacation resort in which George Meany, among others, had an interest; which may have added something personal to Meany's well-known acquiescence in the crushing of free unionism in America's client states.

Adelman and Morris found socio-political factors to be of great importance in explaining cross-country differences in income distribution; in case after case, "the more firmly entrenched the expatriate financial, commercial and technical elite, the greater the concentration of income in the hands of the top 5 percent . . . ;" and "broad-based economic growth provides a way to achieve redistribution only where accompanied by social and educational development as well as substantial broadening of political participation."

In brief, then, income distribution has tended to worsen in the poor countries of the Free World because rapid growth has generated wealth that has been used not to improve the condition of the masses but to serve the growing consumption needs of a neo-colonial elite. The preservation of their position has required a costly diversion of resources into the military (the "insurance policy") and a subordination of development and welfare needs to the consumption-oriented demands of U.S. open-door entrants and affluent domestic consumers. Lon Nol, Thieu, Park, Balaguer, Suharto, Marcos, etc., all have in common institutionalized venality, terrorization of the masses, and service to the needs of "the expatriate financial, commercial, and technical elites" specified by Adelman and Morris as tied in closely with a worsening income distribution. The Nixon Doctrine formalized a support of such regimes, which was, however, in practical effect well before Nixon and is being continued under the Ford Administration.

The distribution of income in the United States is highly unequal, and has changed little in this respect since the end of World War II. As may be seen in the accompanying Table, the bottom fifth of families in 1972 had only 5.4 percent, the top 20 percent had 41.4 percent, and the highest 5 percent had 15.9 percent of money income. These figures refer to a narrowly defined pre-tax money income, however, which includes welfare payments but excludes (among other things) realized or unrealized capital gains and the impact of taxes on income shares. The last two columns of the Table show how important some of these differences may be in influencing the degree of inequality. They are taken from a recent study by Pechman and Okner, who use data for the year 1966 to make a great many of the corrections necessary for a fuller picture of pre-tax income. Incorporating wage supplements, capital gains, the value of the services of owner-occupied homes, and indirect business taxes, they

Table 1   *Money Income Shares in the United States Adjusted and Unadjusted, for Selected Years Since World War II*

	1947[1]	1972[1]	1966[2]	1966 Adjusted[2]
	%	%	%	%
Lowest Fifth	5.1	5.4	4.3	3.7
Second Fifth	11.8	11.9	11.3	9.9
Third Fifth	16.7	17.5	17.3	16.1
Fourth Fifth	23.2	23.9	24.5	22.6
Highest Fifth	43.3	41.4	42.6	47.9
Top 5%	17.5	15.9	16.0	22.1

Sources: (1) U.S. Bureau of Census, Current Population Reports, "Money Income in 1972 of Families and Persons in the United States," 1973, p. 45.

Sources: (2) Joseph A. Pechman and Benjamin Okner, *Who Bears the Tax Burden?*, Brookings, 1974, p. 46. These computations were made from a 1967 Survey of Economic Opportunity and other sample data for 1966.

found that these adjustments not only raised average income by almost 60 percent, but had "a dramatic effect on the distribution of income." It reduced the share of the poorest fifth by 0.6 percent and increased that of the upper fifth by 5.3 percentage points. The Pechman–Okner adjusted data show a significantly greater degree of inequality than the commonly used Census money income figures.

The Table also suggests that the U.S. distribution of income has remained approximately constant since World War II. Between 1947 and 1972, the share of the top 5 percent of families declined from 17.5 percent to 15.9 percent or by 1.6 percentage points. In 1947 the lowest fifth of families received 5.1 percent of money income, the highest 43.3 percent, slightly more unequal than in 1972. But given the post-1947 increase in, and use of, loopholes – the system of "creeping preferences" – and the rise of more regressive state and local taxes, it is probable that the slight equalization of pre-tax money income would be at least offset by appropriate adjustments. As a transformation in income shares, therefore, the "revolution" was over by the time it was discovered. The rather modest 1929–1945 transformation, furthermore, was essentially a redistribution from the very top to the middle-income classes, with the relative position of the bottom fifth unchanged.

With roughly constant shares since 1947, real incomes of the lowest fifth have risen in proportion to the total, and numbers below the poverty line have diminished. The 1974 *Economic Report of the President* focuses on the fact that the number of persons below the line has declined from 39.5 million in 1959 to only 24.5 million in 1972, or from 22 percent to "only" 12 percent of the population. If poverty line definitions are biased downward, however, if relative incomes are important determinants of welfare, and if equality is an ideal that carries weight and has social consequences in its own right, then very limited satisfaction can be derived from trends in poverty line numbers.

Given roughly constant shares, the gap between rich and poor in the U.S. has actually risen substantially. The median (middle) income of the top fifth of families (in 1969 dollars) was $10,565 higher than that of the bottom fifth in 1947; it was $19,071 higher in 1969 and has since crossed the $20,000 mark. Thus the huge growth dividend of recent decades has been used to reinforce and increase inequality. As in Brazil, Indonesia and South Vietnam, both the affluent consumer and the military are treated with solicitude and command an unreasonably large share of increments to social output. "Benign neglect" of the underclass, and social polarization, are the natural counterparts of this system of priorities.

In the U.S. the really depressed underclass is relatively small, but so is the group receiving the benefits from the system of creeping tax preferences. As Philip Stern points out in his *Rape of the Taxpayer*, only 1 in 100 taxpayers get any substantial income from capital gains, and only 1 in 10 gets *any* such income, yet the Congress persists in taxing capital gains only half as severely as wage and salary income. Stern explains this as a result of the extreme dependence of politicians on campaign funding by the wealthy. At least as important is the domination of the media by the upper 5 percent of income receivers and their refusal to focus on income distribution and tax inequities as first-order issues. This has helped pacify the blue and white collar classes, who have also received enough benefits, hope, and opportunities for "making it," as well as ideological conditioning, to identify with the system and its prime beneficiaries. These middle- and lower-middle-classes have become more restive in the last few years under the pressure of inflation, declining real wages and the political lessons of Watergate. But the options offered to them by their leaders, the media, and the political system, are exceedingly narrow, and the issue of "crime in the streets," a self-fulfilling product of benign neglect, preoccupies many. (Contrary to Michael Novak, this issue is a tool serviceable only to the diversionary efforts of status quo politicians — or worse.)

There are some indications of a regression in relative income shares in recent years. According to Peter Henle of the U.S. Department of Labor, earnings data show "a slow but persistent trend toward greater inequality in a period, 1958–1970, of steadily rising incomes." The slight decline of money income of the top 5 percent and 20 percent of families reversed itself about 1967 and edged upward through 1972, and the share of the lowest fifth peaked in 1968–69. Average weekly spendable real earnings of production workers in the U.S. declined or remained stationary in five of the eight years 1966–73. The *Economic Report of the President* chose not to feature the interesting statistic showing that the decline in numbers below the poverty line ended in 1969, rose in 1970 and 1971 and returned to the 1969 level in 1972. The recent sharp upswing in prices has almost certainly reduced the real incomes of the lower two-fifths of income-receiving units since 1972.

The stable shares of the pre-Nixon years was based on consensus politics plus expansionary full employment policies, rooted mainly in military expenditures. Even before Nixon, tight money under Johnson had pushed interest rates up to new heights, with direct upward income redistribution effects and a depressant (regressive) impact on new middle-income housing — lower-income housing was already negligible. Johnson also introduced the large-scale use of social welfare "quiescence"-inducing programs to the middle- and lower-income-classes, financed out of their own pockets by regressive social security taxes. Nixon continued this scheme while also systematically eliminating direct federal contributions to health, education and welfare ("fat").

With Nixon, business domination of government reached a pinnacle reminiscent of the 1920s, and a deliberate "income counter-revolution" was begun and accelerated in the early second term. This was most clearly reflected in the 1974 budget, billed in Nixon double-speak as returning "power to the people"! Nixon's early reliance on tight money and unemployment to control inflation, if carried out with sufficient vigor, might have weakened labor's bargaining position; and his restructuring of government expenditures and taxes at the expense of the weak and poor was an important and partially successful effort at getting the income distribution back to the 1929 degree of inequality. Nixon never possessed sufficient power, however, to use unemployment and state force to really weaken the unions enough to make a dent in inflation from that direction.

The fiscal regression process was slowed up by the sapping of Nixon's political strength and the accompanying disarray of his allies. It is an unsettled question whether Nixon's problems arose out of Watergate, or whether Watergate proved so tenacious because of Nixon's failures on the domestic economic front. With the post-election dismantling of his jerry-built structure of controls, Nixon ran out of easy opponents and opportunistic policies. The truck drivers were more difficult to cope with than the peace marchers, and like Herbert Hoover before him, Nixon simply exhausted the supply of feasible conservative options. The less aggressive, more open, but equally conservative Mr. Ford has shown no propensity toward bold innovation in the field of economic policy. The result is that we have an inflation more rapid than would probably have prevailed under a McGovern Administration! But inflation redistributes income from the poor and lower middle classes to the more affluent; from weak bargainers and people with fixed money incomes to owners of real property and speculators. The "income counter-revolution" thus continues in a new form, by conservative policy default, which nevertheless amounts to an act of choice.

The distribution of income reflects, first and foremost, the structure of interest and power in a society. When that power is consolidated more firmly in the hands of a wealthy minority, as after the Brazilian coup of 1964, the Dominican Republic invasion of 1965, or the Chilean counter-revolution of 1973, the income distribution moves sharply in the direction of increased inequality. Greater income equity, and the majority interest in general, in most Third World States, call for *real* revolution, with a transfer of power from traditional elites to people committed to the interests of the majority. If it be said that this would mean "totalitarianism" in the Third World, the reply is that totalitarianism in a particularly obnoxious form is prevalent now, and with official U.S. support. The best we can hope for in most countries is a relatively benign leadership with roots in and a real concern for the masses, in contrast with the now widespread Free World system of corrupt, extravagant, brutalizing, "grab and run" elite leadership. A comparison of the provision of health services in China and North Vietnam, where they are organized systematically for prevention and for ready availability to the rural masses, with South Vietnam and Indonesia, where the governments have no interest in such mundane matters, illustrates the point. The most important single contribution the American people could make toward improvement in income distribution and welfare in the Third World is, therefore, negative: seeing that their government in Washington terminates its long support for neo-colonialism.

In the U.S. itself, the income distribution improved slightly from 1929–1945, mainly as a result of the devastating effects of the depression on property values and incomes, plus the higher taxes and full employment of World War II. It failed to improve thereafter, and began a small but perceptible move toward increased inequality after 1968. It is obvious that the substantial growth and huge real income now produced in the U.S. have been used in such a way as to leave both a great many people unhappy and a huge array of unsolved problems. The high and relatively stable degree of inequality in the U.S. reflects the success of dominant, mainly business interest groups, in maintaining political and social power and in defining public and private priorities. Breaking the grip of these interests and values is no easy matter, the growth of recent decades having strengthened many vested interests and narrowed our range of choice. Even a huge misadventure such as Vietnam failed to loosen the grip of the military–industrial complex on our disposition of resources. Even the great profit windfalls of the oil companies and mass public hostility accompanying the shortages has yet to result in a significant reduction in the tax privileges of that industry. And even a George McGovern, with his modest liberal reformism, appears to have been beyond the pale of acceptability at this juncture.

It is not easy to be optimistic about prospects for improvement in our income distribution or system of priorities. Change, if it comes, will likely arise out of a continued series of shocks and a failure of the system to "deliver," not only to the bottom 20 percent but to the lower 80 percent. Only substantial material blows are apparently capable of breaking through the false consciousness of racism, of Meany-*Commentary* liberalism (with its emphasis on Red–New Deal threats), to a unification on the basis of real interests and issues. It is a testimony to the power of status quo forces in America that one should see as the next step in improvement, not the development of a new humanism, but merely a capacity on the part of ordinary people to pursue their own real interests!

9. UNCLE SAM'S WELFARE PROGRAM
— FOR THE RICH

Philip M. Stern

Most Americans would probably be intensely surprised to find, in their morning newspaper, headlines such as this one:

CONGRESS SETS $16-PER-YEAR
  WELFARE RATE FOR POOR FAMILIES,
    $720,000 FOR MULTIMILLIONAIRES

Or this one:

NIXON ASKS $103-BILLION
  BUDGET DEFICIT, DOUBLING
    PREVIOUS RED-INK RECORD

The story behind the first of these headlines (the second will be explained later) might read this way:

From *The New York Times* Magazine (April 16, 1972). © 1972 by The New York Times Company. Reprinted by permission.

WASHINGTON, April 16 — Congress completed action today on a revolutionary welfare program that, reversing traditional payment policies, awards huge welfare payments to the super-rich but grants only pennies per week to the very poor.

Under the program, welfare payments averaging some $720,000 a year will go to the nation's wealthiest families, those with annual incomes of over a million dollars.

For the poorest families, those earning $3,000 a year or less, the welfare allowance will average $16 a year, or roughly 30 cents a week.

The program, enacted by Congress in a series of laws over a period of years, has come to be called the Rich Welfare Program, after its principal sponsor, Senator Homer A. Rich. In a triumphant news conference, Senator Rich told newsmen that the $720,000 annual welfare allowances would give America's most affluent families an added weekly take-home pay of about $14,000. "Or, to put it another way," the senator said, "it will provide these families with about $2,000 more spending money every day."

The total cost of the welfare program, the most expensive in the nation's history, amounts to $77.3 billion a year.

Political analysts foresee acute discontent not only among the poor, but also among middle-income families making $10,000 to $15,000 a year. For them, welfare payments under the Rich plan will amount to just $12.50 a week, markedly less than the weekly $14,000 paid to the very rich.

Reporters asked Senator Rich whether wealthy families would be required to work in order to receive their welfare payments, a common eligibility requirement with many welfare programs. Senator Rich seemed puzzled by the question. "The rich? Work?" he asked. "Why, it hadn't occurred to me." Congressional experts advised newsmen that the program contains no work requirement.

Admittedly, the above "news story" sounds implausible, if not unbelievable. Yet the story is essentially true. The facts and figures in it are real. Such a system is, in fact, part of the law of the land. Only the law isn't called a welfare law. It goes by the name of "The Internal Revenue Code of 1954, as Amended" — the basic income-tax law of the United States.

Who gets how much of the "tax welfare" payments from the major "tax preferences" — the loopholes? Until recently, one could only make, at best, an educated guess. But in January [1972] two tax experts at the Brookings Institution in Washington, D.C., Joseph A. Pechman and Benjamin Okner, made a computer analysis of information from actual tax returns (furnished on computer tape, without taxpayer names, by the IRS). Using this data, plus other information from economic surveys, they came up with answers that might astound, or even anger, put-upon taxpayers.

On a per-family basis, a breakdown of the average tax savings of Americans — our "tax welfare" program — looks like this [Table 1].

Table 1

Yearly Income	Yearly "Tax Welfare"
Over $1,000,000	$720,000
$500–1,000,000	$202,000
$100–500,000	$41,000
$50–100,000	$12,000
$25–50,000	$4,000
$15–20,000	$1,200
$10–15,000	$650
$5–10,000	$340
$3–5,000	$48
Under $3,000	$16

Since a tax law takes money from people, rather than paying money to them, what connection does the tax law have with the topsy-turvy welfare system in the news story? The connection lies in the way Congress has played fast and loose with the 16th Amendment to the Constitution, and with the principle of basing taxes on "ability to pay."

The 16th Amendment, which authorized the first United States income tax, empowered Congress to tax "incomes, *from whatever sources derived.*" (Italics mine.) That expresses the Gertrude Stein-ish notion that a dollar is a dollar is a dollar and that, regardless of its source, the dollar endows its lucky recipient with 100 cents of "ability to pay" for food, shoes for the baby, a fraction of a yacht — or for taxes. Hence, in fairness, all dollars, no matter what their origin, should be taxed uniformly. But Congress has decreed differently. It has decreed that dollars earned in an oil or real-estate venture, in a stock-market bonanza, or in interest on a state or local bond, while undeniably effective in buying food, shoes, or yachts, are somehow reduced in potency when it comes to paying taxes — for Congress has exempted such dollars, in whole or in part, from taxation.

The American tax system, which stipulates that rates rise as a person's affluence grows, also holds that a billionaire like oilman Jean Paul Getty — with a reported income of $300,000 *a day* — is better "able to pay" taxes than an impoverished Kentucky coal miner. In fact, under the tax rates supposedly applicable to all citizens, Mr. Getty's $100-million annual income endows him with an "ability to pay" about $70 million to the Internal Revenue Service (on the premise that he should be able to make do on the remaining $30 million each year). But since Mr. Getty's dollars come largely from oil ventures, they are not, by congressional fiat, taxed like other dollars. In consequence, according to what President Kennedy told two United States senators, Mr. Getty's income tax in the early sixties came nowhere near $70 million. It amounted to no more than a few thousand dollars — just about the amount a middle-income engineer or professor would pay.

Now compare the notion of excusing Jean Paul Getty from paying $70 million in taxes — taxes that an equally wealthy non-oil man would legally have to pay — with the notion that Mr. Getty is receiving a $70 million federal welfare check. In both cases the consequences are that:

Mr. Getty is $70 million richer.

The United States Treasury is $70 million poorer than if the full tax had been paid.

The rest of the taxpayers are obliged to pay an added $70 million to make up the difference.

Thus the net effect of a "tax forgiveness" is identical to that of a direct federal handout.

The Brookings study concludes that of the $77.3 billion in tax "handouts," just $92 million goes to the six million poorest families in the nation, while 24 times that amount — $2.2 *billion* — goes to just 3,000 families (those with incomes of more than a million dollars a year). Coincidentally, that $2.2 billion is just the amount Congress voted last year for food stamps for 14.7 million hungry Americans. Moreover, five times that amount in the form of "tax welfare" went to families earning more than $100,000 a year.

The disparity between the "tax welfare" for the wealthy and that granted the poor is even more breathtaking in the case of the "tax preferences" involving so-called "capital gains" — the profits on sales of stocks and bonds, land, buildings, and other kinds of property. When a person cashes in such profits during his lifetime, he pays no more than half the usual tax. Even more striking, all the gains in the value of property a person holds until death are not taxed at all. Some $10 billion entirely escapes taxation in that manner every year.

Since to have capital gains you have to own property (i.e., have the surplus cash to buy same), it's not surprising that only one taxpayer in twelve is able to report any gains, and that three-quarters of such gains are enjoyed by the wealthiest 9 percent of America's taxpayers. Thus, all but the super-rich have a right to be envious, if not startled, by the Brookings figures on the "tax welfare" payments — the average per family tax savings — granted capital-gains recipients [Table 2].

These federal handouts to the wealthy reach the astounding total of nearly $14 billion a year. But even that sum is dwarfed by the tax benefactions that Uncle Sam bestows on all but our poorest citizens the instant they are pronounced man and wife, a happy moment that carries with it the privilege of filing a joint return. The Brookings study reveals,

Table 2

Yearly Income	Yearly "Tax Welfare" from Capital Gains
Over $1,000,000	$641,000
$500–1,000,000	$165,000
$100–500,000	$23,000
$20–25,000	$120
$5–10,000	$8
$3–5,000	$1

startlingly, that the annual total of this giveaway to married couples comes to $21.5 billion.

Some, noting that the Environmental Protection Agency will only be permitted to spend one-fourteenth that amount next year, have difficulty discerning how this $21.5-billion matrimonial "tax dole" benefits the national welfare. If it is supposed to be an incentive to marriage, it is a strange one indeed, since it shows a total indifference to the marital status of the poor, who derive no financial benefit from this tax giveaway whatever. Instead, it offers increasingly generous benefits the higher a couple's income goes, in brackets where it matters little whether two can indeed live as cheaply as one. Two-thirds of this marital "tax welfare" goes to taxpayers making more than $20,000 a year, and less than 3 percent goes to the hardest-pressed married couples — those making less than $10,000 a year. These are the average per-family matrimonial tax savings [Table 3].

Dramatically top-heavy tax largess flows to the super-rich via the fiction, in the tax law, that the $5 billion of interest on state and local bonds is totally nonexistent. Not only is such interest income untaxed; it doesn't

Table 3

Yearly Income	Yearly "Tax Welfare" to Married Couples
Under $3,000	$0
$3–5,000	72 cents
$5–10,000	$24
$25–50,000	$1,479
$100–500,000	$8,212
Over $1,000,000	$11,062

even have to be reported on tax returns. Ownership of such bonds is, understandably, reserved to financial institutions and wealthy individuals, in part because only they have the spare cash to buy such bonds, and in part because these bonds bear comparatively low interest rates that are attractive only to persons in high tax brackets.

As a result, the per-family tax benefactions from this loophole are almost insultingly low for the unmoneyed: an average of only 80 cents a year for families earning $5,000 to $10,000, and just $24 a year even for those in the $25,000–50,000 bracket. But the financial blessing is handsome indeed for the wealthy — $36,000 a year for families with incomes of over $1 million — and it is even more spectacular for the big banks. In 1970 this tax feature saved the Bank of America an estimated $58 million.

All these profligate handouts to the unneedy would be far more publicly apparent if the billions lost to the Treasury through the loopholes came to be regarded in the same jealous, penny-pinching way as the direct outlays that the President requests and Congress votes every year. If that had been the case this past January, newspapers might well have carried a news story such as the following:

WASHINGTON, April 16 — President Nixon today sent Congress the most startling budget in history, calling for a federal deficit of no less than $103 billion, more than twice as high as any previous deficit in American history.

This colossal deficit resulted from Mr. Nixon's inclusion in his annual budget, for the first time, of not only direct outlays from the Treasury but also what the President calls "tax expenditures." These are sums the Treasury does not collect because of various exceptions and preferences embedded in the nation's tax laws. For the current year, such sums amounted to more than $77 billion, Mr. Nixon said.

"It is time the American people faced up to the truth," Mr. Nixon said in his budget message. "Every dollar in taxes that some individual or industry is excused from paying is just as much of a drain on the Treasury, and contributes just as much to federal deficits, as a dollar appropriated by the Congress and spent directly from the Treasury.

"For example," Mr. Nixon said, "nearly $10 billion in 'tax expenditures' is granted every year to stimulate home ownership. This sum ought to be part of the budget of the Department of Housing and Urban Development if we are to get an honest picture of how much we, as a nation, are really spending on America's housing problems."

Of course there was no such fiscal candor in Mr. Nixon's January budget message; nor had there been in those of his predecessors in both parties. But the housing example is a good one, for almost assuredly, few, if any, of the housing specialists in HUD — and few of our elected representatives — are aware that a tax-subsidy program Congress has enacted for homeowners operates in the following manner.

Three families — the Lowlies (who make $7,000 a year), the Comfortables (with a $50,000 income) and the Opulents (they make $400,000 a year) — ask

HUD for help in paying the 7 percent mortgage interest on homes that each family wants to buy. HUD's response is different in each case:

To the Opulents, HUD replies: "HUD will be delighted to pay 5 percent mortgage interest for you, so that when you buy your mansion, you only need pay 2 percent mortgage interest."

To the Comfortables: "HUD will pay half the interest charges, so you can borrow toward your house at 3.5 percent."

To the Lowlies: "We're terribly sorry, but the most we can do is pay 1 percent interest for you, so if you want to borrow to buy that house, you'll have to pay 6 percent."

That seemingly inhumane result, which flows from the tax deductibility of mortgage-interest payments, is inherent in the nature of any tax deduction in a tax system such as ours where tax rates get higher as income rises. It works this way: say Mr. Opulent has a taxable income of $400,100. This puts him in the top tax bracket of 70 percent and it means that he has to pay a tax of $70 on the top $100 of his income. Mr. Lowly, on the other hand, has a taxable income of $7,100, placing him in the 19 percent tax bracket; this imposes a tax of $19 on the top $100 of his more modest income.

Now suppose that each spends $100 on mortgage interest which, being tax-deductible, reduces the taxable income of each by $100. That step lowers Mr. Opulent's tax by $70; that is, $70 that would have gone to Uncle Sam, were it not for the tax deduction, has been diverted to Mr. Opulent's bank account. Uncle Sam has, in effect, footed the bill for $70 of Mr. Opulent's mortgage interest. But in the case of Mr. Lowly, the $100 deduction only lowers his tax by $19. Only $19 is diverted from Uncle Sam to Mr. Lowly's bank account.

Not only does Mr. Opulent get a bigger bang for each tax-deductible buck than Mr. Lowly does, but also Mr. Opulent far outstrips his counterpart in the *number* of bucks he spends yearly for tax-deductible purposes. Mr. Opulent's average annual deductions for mortgage interest, for example, are about 4½ times as large as Mr. Lowly's. According to the Brookings study, the benefits from the various "tax preferences" enjoyed by homeowners (over home renters) come to just 66 cents a year for the least pecunious taxpayers. But the benefits amount to 10,000 times as much — over $6,000 a year — for the nation's wealthiest and best-housed families.

The price tag attached to this inverted subsidy program is enormous: $9.6 billion a year. This is more than twice HUD's total budget and more than fifty times HUD's direct outlays for housing assistance. Clearly, if the $9.6 billion were part of HUD's budget, HUD officials would be embarrassed if they tried to justify a program that gave 66 cents of aid to the neediest citizen and $6,000 to the wealthiest. But since the inequity is embedded in the tax laws, involving no visible outlays, HUD, the President, and the Congress are all spared the embarrassment of annually accounting for this expensive and irrational subsidy. Instead, the $9.6-billion drain on the Treasury will continue just as long as Congress fails to change the law, and congressional *inaction* is demonstrably easier to come by than affirmative congressional action.

The same is true of the tax favors enjoyed by oil companies and investors, which entail an annual "expenditure" of a billion and a half dollars (supposedly to encourage development of our oil resources). But that sum appears nowhere in the Interior Department's natural-resources budget. Perhaps if it did, Secretary of the Interior Rogers C. B. Morton would be spurred to cut back or end this huge "outlay," especially since a recent government-commissioned study showed that the returns on the $1.5 billion were a meager $150 million in additional oil exploration. Any direct subsidy program with a 90 percent waste factor would hardly warm congressional hearts when it came up for annual approval; but oil's multi-billion-dollar tax subsidy is spared that discomfiture.

Translating tax loopholes into "tax expenditures" (i.e., treating the revenues that leak out through the loopholes as if they were direct outlays) can make even the most unexceptionable feature of the tax laws seem questionable. Tax expert Stanley Surrey has explained the effect of that most worthy of all tax features, the deduction for contributions to charity:

Suppose that one Horace Pauper writes the government as follows: "I am too poor to pay an income tax, but the Salvation Army helped me in a time of need and I am contributing $5 to it. Will the government also make a contribution?" The response: "Dear Mr. Pauper: We appreciate your generosity and sacrifice, but in this situation we cannot make the contribution you request."

Suppose that at the same time, Herman Greenbacks, nouveau millionaire, writes to say that of his $500,000 income, he has decided to send $3,000 to the Society for the Preservation of Hog-Calling in Arkansas. He wants to know if the government will help. Reply: "We will be delighted to be of assistance and are at once sending a government check for $7,000 to the Hog-Calling Society."

Here again, this strange situation results from the fact that when a taxpayer in the 70 percent bracket such as Mr. Greenbacks gives $10,000 to charity, it reduces his tax by $7,000 — i.e., it diverts $7,000 from the United States Treasury to the charity. But for Horace Pauper, who has no taxable income to be affected by his generous deduction, there is no tax saving and the government's role is zero.

As if the Greenbacks–Pauper contrast weren't irrational enough, the charitable-deduction feature of the tax law could even give rise to a third situation. Let us say that Roger Croesus, heir to the huge Croesus fortune, writes the government to say that he is selling $2 million in stocks inherited from his grandfather, since he wants to raise cash to pay his taxes and also to buy a yacht. Croesus adds that he feels the Antique Car Society of America is a worthy institution, and that while he has decided not to contribute to the society himself, he is writing to inquire if the government has any interest in doing so. In this case, the government writes as follows:

"Dear Mr. Croesus: We will be delighted to send a $2-million contribution to the Antique Car Society and we will be glad to say that the contribution is in your name. Moreover, in appreciation of your thoughtfulness in suggesting this fine idea to us — and confident that your new yacht will need outfitting — we are sending you a check for $100,000, tax-free, of course."

That unbelievable feat could be accomplished if Mr. Croesus, a taxpayer in the 70 percent bracket, were to give to the cause of antique cars $2 million of stock that was virtually valueless when he inherited it. His tax saving (i.e., the Treasury's contribution) includes $1,400,000 of income tax from the deduction, plus the avoidance of $700,000 in capital-gains tax, for a total of $2,100,000 — or, $100,000 more than his $2-million gift. The result: even after the Treasury has, in effect, paid for his entire contribution, he still enjoys a $100,000 cash profit.

But such quirks in the tax law are overshadowed by the even more gaping tax loopholes we've already discussed, as revealed in the Brookings Institution study. During the coming months, the Brookings findings will take on immense importance if, as expected, the Nixon Administration proposes major revenue-raising through a so-called "value-added tax," or VAT. The VAT is a tax on the "value added" to any product, at each stage of its manufacture or distribution, as that product makes its way to the consumer through various middlemen. Since the VAT is, in essence, a hidden national sales tax, it tends to place a relatively heavy share of the burden on lower- and middle-income taxpayers — a far heavier share than would be the case if the same amount of revenue were raised by closing existing loopholes in the tax law. The Brookings study documents that fact in dramatic fashion.

For example, the $13-to-$16 billion in additional revenue the administration is reportedly considering raising from a VAT coincides almost exactly with the $13.7 billion the Brookings study estimates would be raised by ending the favored taxation on capital gains. Tax reformers can offer a battery of arguments for ending this tax preference, which wholly bypasses eleven out of twelve taxpayers. First, it violates the Basic American Virtues, not to mention elementary standards of fairness, by rewarding the "work" done by *money* vastly more than the work done by men. Why should an already-wealthy multimillionaire pay less tax on, say, a million-dollar stockmarket profit — for which he did not an iota of work — than does an industrious professional person who earns a fraction of that amount by personal ingenuity, talent, and plain sweat?

Second, capital gains represent by far the most gaping escape hatch for the very rich, allowing them to pay, on the average, only half what the federal tax rates indicate they should. Third, ending the capital-gains preference would at one stroke narrow, or close, a variety of tax escape-routes available to only a few selected taxpayers guided by ingenious tax lawyers. Examples of such escape routes are corporate executives' stock options, and tax shelters for high-salaried doctors and other professional men who invest in — but usually never see — cattle farms, or kiwi-nut groves, and the like.

Finally, the dire predictions about the drying up of capital that invariably greet any proposal to alter the taxation of capital gains are, at the least, greatly exaggerated. This is evidenced by the economy's apparently tremorless adjustment to a 10 percent increase in the capital-gains tax enacted in 1969, as well as by the fact that 95 percent of corporations' capital needs are met through plowed-back profits and borrowings, and only 5 percent from stock issues.

The search for alternatives to the VAT is also likely to increase pressure to end or modify the tax exemption of state and local bonds (it's part of Edmund Muskie's otherwise moderate tax-reform program, for example). While zealously cherished by hard-pressed governors and mayors as an inexpensive means of public borrowing (the tax-freee status allows these bonds to carry below-average interest rates), the tax exemption is a grossly inefficient means of subsidizing state and local borrowing costs. Students of the subject calculate that about half this annual $1.2-billion "tax expenditure" is, in effect, wasted, and that both tax justice and governmental economy would be served by replacing the tax exemption with a direct-subsidy program.

The inefficiency of the bond-interest exemption is typical of such "tax expenditures," which, ironically, are spared the traditional scrutiny for "efficiency" that pinch-penny congressmen usually require of direct-spending programs. For example, in 1971, in enacting multibillion-dollar tax "incentives" for corporate exports and plant investment, Congress wastefully granted the incentives to exports and to plant outlays that most corporations would have made anyway — rather than confining the benefits to *increases* in those activities. Thus, those tax subventions are windfalls to corporatons that merely export or invest as usual. Similarly, the oil-depletion allowance, supposedly designed to reward risk-taking, not only goes to the venturesome oil driller but also is freely dispensed to the fortunate landowner — who permits a successful well to be drilled on his property, but who risks absolutely nothing in doing so.

Tax favors granted to the lowly as well as to the mighty often produce both inequity and inefficiency. Take, for example, the additional $750 personal exemption that Congress has voted the aged and the blind. For nonagenarian Charles Stewart Mott, who is said to be worth more than $300 million, that exemption allows him a saving of $525 a year. But for a retiree in St. Petersburg who qualifies for the lowest tax bracket, it saves only $105. And the exemption gives no relief whatsoever to, say, an ancient and impoverished sharecropper whose meager income would not be taxable anyway.

That same perversity applies to the regular exemption available to each taxpayer and his dependents. While its supposed purpose is to spare poor families from being taxed on what they need to meet "some minimum essential living costs," the exemption nonetheless confers some $4 billion in tax handouts to families making over $15,000 a year. Some congressional reformers have proposed replacing the exemption with a flat $150 cut in *taxes* for each dependent. This would be applicable equally to the St. Petersburg bench-sitter and to the nonagenarian multi-millionaire. That step alone — which would increase the taxes of those who earn $10,000 or more, while reducing the taxes of those who are less affluent — would increase federal revenues by nearly $2 billion a year.

Other long-standing "loopholes for the many" are rarely examined with a critical eye, even though they represent immense "tax expenditures" justified by little rhyme or reason. For example, about $10 billion in interest accruing on life-insurance policies is exempt from taxation; this annual "tax expenditure" amounts to $2.7 billion. Nonbusiness personal itemized deductions (for major-medical expenses, charitable contributions, taxes, interest, and the like) excuse another $10 billion from taxation, and the price tag for this is over $4 billion annually. Another rarely discussed but major untaxed item is the return on a homeowner's investment in his own house; this takes the form of rent the homeowner is spared paying to a landlord, rent which the homeowner, in effect, pays to himself. The total of this untaxed "income" amounts to an estimated $15.5 billion annually; failure to tax it represents an unconscious decision on the part of Congress to "spend" more than $4 billion annually on aid to homeowners — with, as usual, far more comfort to mansion-dwellers than to Levittowners.

The basic question raised by the Brookings study is whether the unreviewed annual "tax welfare" of over $77 billion makes sense in a time of budgetary deficits averaging $30 billion a year, and in a time when we are plagued with "social deficits" (in housing, health, and the like) of vastly greater proportions. The Brookings experts propose an essentially preference-free, or "no-loophole," tax system. That would open up some choices that the present sievelike system forbids: it would make it possible to raise added revenues that could be applied to the nation's social needs. Or it could make possible a massive tax-rate reduction; Drs. Pechman and Okner say that in a no-loophole system, the present levels of federal revenues could be collected with tax rates ranging from 7 to 44 percent, instead of the present 14 to 70 percent. Or there could be a combination of both revenue-raising and rate reduction. But whatever the choice, a preference-free system would put an end to irrational multibillion-dollar "tax expenditures" that continue to be perpetuated as long as Congress fails to act. It would also put an end to a tax system that is highly manipulable by the well-to-do (such as the 112 people with incomes over $200,000 who contrived to pay no tax whatever in 1970, despite the supposed congressional effort in 1969 to stop such taxlessness) but that leaves largely helpless the vast majority of taxpayers whose taxes are withheld from their paychecks and whisked away before they even see the money.

What are the prospects for significant tax reform? On a strictly nose-count basis, the cause should be a popular one, especially when it comes to ending such preferences as capital gains (from which just one taxpayer in twelve benefits), or the multibillion-dollar tax favors to large corporations. But past loophole-closing efforts have provoked concentrated lobbying pressure on Congress while generating little public enthusiasm. So, as the Brookings study shows, the tax system is clearly not based on a popular nose count.

Some reformers, however, believe that the tactic President Nixon seems ready to pursue in support of his value-added tax — holding out the bait of using the VAT proceeds to relieve hard-pressed property-taxpayers — may at long last create the vocal "constituency" that could prod Congress into genuine reforms. Offering the proceeds of loophole-closing to reduce property taxes could, in effect, steal Mr. Nixon's bait. Indeed, the prospect of the value-added tax has prodded some legislators who were not heretofore enlisted under the reform banner to search for popular alternatives to the VAT.

Reportedly, under pressure from apparent Democratic successes with the tax-reform issue in the early presidential primaries, Mr. Nixon is considering sweeping reforms instead of the value-added tax. But if he does propose a VAT, it could set off the most basic debate about the tax system in many years and, ironically — despite Treasury Secretary Connally's openly expressed indifference to tax reform ("It leaves me cold") — he and the Nixon Administration might inadvertently give the reform cause the biggest boost it has had in many years.

10. KEEPING THE POOR POOR

Paul Jacobs

Let me begin with a true story about how, for some poor people, pine-apple juice tasted not sweet, but salty. At regular intervals, pineapple juice canneries must clean out the pipes that carry the juice from the crushing to the canning rooms. To do this, a salt solution is forced through the pipes and then flushed out before the new canning process starts again. A few years ago, one large cannery went through this clean-ing operation and began running juice again before it was discovered that the pipes had not been totally purged of the salt solution. But, by that time, thousands of gallons of pineapple juice, all of it slightly salty, had already been processed and canned.

The cans, unlabeled, were sold at a very low price to a food distributor who specializes in handling offbrand and reject merchandise for sale in poor neighborhoods and communities. The distributor put a label on the cans and retailed them for about half the usual price for that size, mak-ing a very good profit for himself. Across the label was printed "NO SWEETENER ADDED," certainly an accurate statement of the juice's con-dition.

In both a real and symbolic sense, this otherwise trivial incident in-volving the sale of salty pineapple juice is characteristic of the relation-ships of the poor to society. The merchandise would have had little or no monetary value outside the poverty market. It seemed cheap to those who purchased it, although in reality, considering its actual value, it was very expensive. No complaints about the saltiness of the juice were re-corded, and its sale was justified by the distributor on the basis that even though the merchandise was imperfect, it was at least available to the poor who might not otherwise have been able to buy any.

Precisely the same set of characteristics are true for most of the life of the poor. As David Caplovitz has clearly demonstrated in his study, *The Poor Pay More*, not only do the poor pay more proportionately for what they get, but what they get for more money is often of inferior quality. Thus, the poverty market can be an extremely profitable one for those who specialize in selling to it, although the rewards are tempered by high risks.

The overall dimensions of the poverty market are reasonably well es-tablished. It includes approximately 35,000,000 people divided into seven million families and four million unrelated individuals. Their total in-

From *New Politics*, vol. 5, pp. 3–16, 19–20, 25–27. Reprinted by permission.

come is estimated at $28,000,000,000. (Oscar Gass in *Commentary*.) But the poor dispose of this income in their own distinctive ways.

To begin with, those who constitute the poverty class spend different proportions of their income for food, shelter, clothing, and medical care than are spent by the remaining four-fifths of the population. Nearly 29 percent of the average poor person's income goes into food expenditures, while those who income exceeds $4,000 a year spend less than 24 percent of it for food. The cost of shelter for the poor is more than 29 percent of their incomes, in contrast to the 17 percent expended by those in the higher income brackets. Ironically, too, although the poor spend a higher proportion of their income for housing, what they get in exchange is always worse than similarly priced — or even lower-priced — middle-income housing.

The differences between the expenditures of the poor and other income groups on clothing and medical care are even sharper: the poor spend one-half as much of their income on clothing as do their economic betters, but a higher proportion on medical care, which, in accordance with the iron law of poverty, is almost always bad. And because the poor have far less money to spend, they are at the same time in much greater debt relative to their income than the middle and upper income brackets. (Interestingly enough, the only items on which both the poor and the rich spend the same proportion of their respective incomes are gifts and contributions.)

The food the poor eat is different from that purchased by the other segments of the population, even taking into account regional preferences; they seek recreation in different ways; they buy in different kinds of stores, although the prices they pay may be just as high or higher, and they buy some items, such as cockroach powder, rarely used by the rest of the consumers. Their overriding economic concerns are short-term rather than long-range ones, for they must worry about whether or not they will have enough money tomorrow rather than after retirement.

Yet these statistical differences do not adequately reflect the fact that poverty creates not only a different life style but a different emotional set as well. Anxiety and uncertainty, derived from their economic situation, dominate the orientation of the poor to the world.

Because of their anxiety and uncertainty certain social types unknown to us become prominent in the lives of the poor. The "mouse man" or the "six-for-fiver," for example, are familiar characters in many poor neighborhoods, just as the "mouse house" (loan company) is an important part of the appliance- and automobile-buying pattern of the poor. And although the "policy" industry is estimated to take in a quarter of a billion dollars annually in New York City alone, the "collectors" who can be found on every Harlem street corner will rarely be seen on the quiet

streets of Riverdale. "Collectors" and "mouse men" live on the economic
anxiety of the poor, without whom they could not thrive.

How large this anxiety factor looms in the lives of the poor is illus-
trated in almost all the problems they face. As we all know too well from
our daily lives, the automobile is one of the most ubiquitous features of
American material culture, and the quiet humming of its engine a great
source of pride to its owner. But the battered, old cars of the poor are
noisy, and the sound of a loud engine rattle, an increasingly noisy rod, or
a grinding bearing strikes panic in the hearts of the poor. If their car
breaks down on the highway, or if it will not start in the morning, they
cannot call the auto club. What may be merely a nuisance to others is a
major disaster to them; they are caught in a trap from which they cannot escape without paying a great price. Generally, they cannot afford to
have their cars fixed, but without a car many of them cannot go to work
or look for employment, the two primary functions for which they need
a car. And so, after they have found a relative or friend who will tow
their disabled car back to their homes, they are forced to try fixing it
themselves. (Public libraries get much less use in poor neighborhoods
than in other areas, but what little use is made of them includes the
frequent borrowing of do-it-yourself repair manuals.)

However, unlike the Model T or Model A Ford, the modern car is not
likely to be fixed by anyone except a skilled mechanic. Indeed, if I have
no other criterion by which to judge the character of a strange neighborhood, the number of junked cars on the streets or in yards serves as an
accurate measure; the more abandoned cars, the poorer the area. After a
while, the rusty and broken-down monuments of junk become so much a
part of the landscape of poverty that no one even notices their presence.

When the poor must somehow face up to purchasing another car, the
magnitude of the problem is likely to be overwhelming. Since approximately 60 percent of all the cars purchased in the United States are
bought on time, automobile financing is a big business. And, as might be
expected, the poor buy far more used than new cars: in 1962, only 9
percent of the new cars purchased on installment payments were bought
by people whose income was below $3,000, but 40 percent of all the
used cars were sold in the poverty market, 75 percent of them at less than
$500. (University of Michigan Survey Research Center, Survey of Cus-
tomer Finances.)

The cheapest way to buy a car — by means of a personal bank loan —
is rarely open to the poor. In order to secure such a loan, at a simple
interest rate, the prospective borrower must put up some collateral, such
as stocks, a savings account, or property — assets rarely held by the poor
as a matter of definition.

The next cheapest method is to get a bank loan on the car. For this, the bank usually requires a down payment of one-third to one-fourth in cash; then it will finance the car, holding a chattel mortgage on it until all the payments have been completed. The interest rates for such loans vary from 4 to 6 percent, depending on whether the bank also purchases paper from dealers, in which case the dealers must be protected. (The dealer will normally try to get 6 percent interest from buyers, although he will bargain about these rates and settle for 5.5 percent or even 5 percent. Then he will sell the sales contract to the banks for 4 percent, keeping the balance in his own reserve funds.)

Recently, I purchased a new car, and the contrast between the way in which that transaction was carried on and what happens when a poor person does the same thing, was most revealing. After I picked out the car I wanted, I called a bank for some information about their low-cost loans. But instead of getting merely information, I got the loan, by telephone, in the space of about five to seven minutes. The bank official asked me where I lived, and after I gave him the address, which is in a "good" section of the city, he asked me if I owned my house. When I replied in the affirmative, he then inquired where I held charge accounts. After I named the stores, which were obviously all "good" ones by his standards, he asked the purchase price of the car and how much I was going to pay in cash. When I told him I would be paying between a quarter and a third down, he informed me I could have the loan without even having to come to the bank. And not once did he ask me what my income was, for my economic position — indeed my entire life pattern — was evident from my residential location and my choice of stores and my tone of voice.

The pattern of life for the poor is equally clear to him; and so poor people are rarely able to get car loans directly from banks, even if they apply in person. Banks don't like to make small loans, for the administrative costs are too high; and they are reluctant to make loans to people whose income is uncertain or whose credit rating is less than exemplary. To the poor, a bank is the place where the teller scowls as he cashes a welfare check and charges 25¢ for the service.

In Los Angeles recently, 8,067 interviews were conducted among all income groups to obtain data concerning the use of banks. Almost 18 percent of the families questioned refused to reveal their income, but 9.1 percent of those who did said they earned less than $250 a month; of this group 47 percent had checking accounts and 51 percent had savings accounts — somewhat higher percentages than the national average for this income level. (The bank that made the survey believes the reason for this was that the sample included a large proportion of retired people whose cash income may be below $250, but whose real income is higher.) Seventy-three percent of those in the $250–$650-a-month group and 91 percent in the $650–$1,000-a-month group had checking accounts.

Quite apart from the wide gap in the use of checking accounts between the poor and other groups, the data also revealed that the bank is not a place in which the poor conduct much business. For instance, 24 percent of all the families in the sample had obtained a loan within the two years prior to the survey, but only 8 percent of the poor had received such loans.

Whatever business the poor do have in banks is likely to involve savings accounts: branch banks located in poor neighborhoods usually have many more savings accounts than checking accounts. Indeed, the poor use their savings accounts as others use their checking accounts; their frequent withdrawals and deposits distinguish branch banks in poor neighborhoods from those located elsewhere.

But for many of the poor, a bank is far too intimidating a place even when they can afford to patronize it. I suspect, too, that the notion that some impersonal agency is keeping a permanent record of one's residence and of how much money one has, keeps away those who are worried about being found by the skip tracers who work for collection or welfare agencies.

The practice of paying bills by check as a matter of routine scarcely exists for the poor. Instead, more than half pay cash or use money orders, purchased either at the post office or, equally likely, from the liquor stores or gas stations which sell the commercial variety.

The commercial money-order business has developed in response to the peculiar need of the poverty market, where marginality is so dominant a theme. Unlike the money orders obtainable in the post office or the banks, commercial ones vary in price, depending on whether the location in which they are sold produces a high or low volume. But even if they are more expensive than bank or postal money orders, they are more convenient for the poor since they can be purchased in handy locations at night or on weekends. Moreover, they do not involve the permanent records associated with a checking account.

The commercial money-order business is a fairly simple one. The company maintains an account in a regular bank and the money order it sells is treated like a check; that is, the bank assumes no responsibility for the transaction beyond what is normal for bank and depositor. This fact is not usually clear to the poor; for the bank's name appears on the money order, which enhances the legitimacy of the transaction. Most of the companies operating in this field are legitimate, but occasionally one does go out of business, leaving the holder of the money order without recourse.

Commercial money-order companies are not regulated by state or federal agencies, and thus can charge whatever price they believe the market will bear. As a result, the rates vary; a company in a "good" location, one with a high volume of sales, can charge higher rates than one in an area where people rely upon post-office money orders or checking accounts. And since these commercial money orders are used almost exclusively to pay bills, they provide another illustration of the dictum that the poor, who can least afford it, pay more, even if only to pay their bills.

That basic principle operates throughout the lives of the poor, no matter what other differences may exist among them. Thus, unless they belong to credit unions, they must finance any substantial purchases through dealers or through finance companies whose rates vary enormously, depending upon what they find the traffic will bear.

Finance-company rates *are* incredible. There is no point in going into a detailed analysis of their operations, for these have been explored and documented by the Congress. (No action has been taken, incidentally, to reduce the exorbitant rates of interest exacted from the poor.) Instead, let me use but one example of the possible range. If a middle-class person borrows $2,500 from a bank on a 36-month personal loan, it will cost him $238.16; financing the purchase of a car at the usual rate of 6 percent will cost him $449.84 for the same period of time. At a loan company, a "mouse house," the normal charge is $674.84. Thus, for the privilege of borrowing the same sum of money, a man with savings or other assets pays $346.68 less than the one without resources.

Not only do the poor pay more for credit, they also run greater risk of losing their purchases. Dealers will normally extend credit to any prospective purchaser so long as he has no record of repossession, even though he may already be in debt to a number of finance companies, as are so many of the poor. So long as the buyer can make a down payment, either with his own money or by getting a loan from a "mouse house," the dealer will sell the commodity. However, if the buyer gets laid off or has an emergency drain on income and falls 30 days behind in payments without attempting to contact whoever is holding the contract, an inexorable process starts. The contract holder hires a "recovery outfit," a company which has the legal authority, under the terms of the contract, to simply repossess the car or television set in any way it can. Normally, in the case of a car, this is done either at the debtor's place of work or at home, late at night, while he is asleep. Appliances or furniture are simply removed from the home.

Once the property is back in the possession of the mortgage holder, the debtor is offered the opportunity to get it back by making up the payments. If he cannot pay, he is sent a "5-day letter" which by law gives him five days to either pay up or refinance, at additional interest charges, of course.

If the debtor does neither, the property reverts to the mortgage holder, who then resells it. After the repossessed item has been sold, the mortgage holder will attempt to recover from the customer the difference between the unpaid balance and the price the property brought at resale.

The recovery attempt is made by a collection agency which gets half of whatever is recovered. The agency goes to court, routinely, to obtain orders to attach the wages of debtors. Just as routinely, the court issues these orders merely on the presentation of the contract and the record of payments, but without notification to the buyer or his representative. The court order is then presented to the debtor's employer, who must go to the administrative expense of withholding the amount specified from the employee's wages and paying it over to the agency. Very often, the employer simply fires the employee rather than be bothered.

The same process operates regardless of the purchaser's income. Obviously, the chances are much greater that the poor, who are generally not well-educated, and whose income is low and irregular, will get caught up in the endless series of credit traps. From the dealer or finance company's viewpoint, the justification for their very high interest rates lies in the risk that the purchaser will be unable to make his payments and will skip town.

Normally, if a credit manager has losses of more than 1 percent a year, he is in danger of losing his own job, for he is apparently using bad judgment about who represents a good credit risk. Yet in some parts of the poverty market, a credit manager who loses less than 10 percent or 12 percent of his customers is considered equally lacking in judgment; he, obviously, is setting too rigorous standards and is thus keeping away potential customers.

The 10 percent or 12 percent loss rate is taken into account when the retail price is established on an item to be sold within the poverty market. In the jewelry industry, for example, a normal markup is 100 percent, but for jewelry sold to the poor, this markup often goes to 300 percent and even higher. Thus, as a rule, a ring, for which a jewelry store pays a $50 wholesale price, is sold for $100 on a cash or short-term credit basis. That same ring will retail for $300 in the poverty market, where the credit jeweler will attempt to get as large a down payment as possible in order to protect himself against the possibility of default on future weekly payments. If the customer can be persuaded to make a $60 down payment, the retailer will have covered the price of the ring and made a modest profit. From then on everything he receives helps swell his profit rate.

The fact that the retailer wants a large number of customers who will enter into such credit arrangements requires that his credit standards be considerably lower than those established by the merchant who caters to middle- and upper-income families. The credit manager in the poverty market demands of his customer only a fixed place of residence and a fixed income, no matter how small, either from a job or from some government agency. In fact, what the retailer is selling is credit itself, and his efforts are bent on trying to keep the customer always in debt to him. He attempts, wherever possible, to draw the customer into the store to make the weekly payments so that he can continue to sell additional merchandise, often by displaying tempting "bargain" items close to the payment counter. In these transactions the price is quoted as a dollar a week rather than some fixed total sum, and the new purchases are urged on the customer on the basis that it will only mean continuing to pay the dollar a week. Every effort is expended to keep the customer on the books continuously in a state of delicate equilibrium in which the desire for goods will outweigh the anxiety associated with the perpetual need to keep up payments.

My own experience living among the poor has been a vivid demonstration of the axiom that the poor pay more, proportionately, in exchange for less. The food stores in poor neighborhoods are more monopolistic than stores in other areas. For one thing, the poor are simply less mobile than middle-class people; shopping around for bargains by bus is much more difficult than shopping by car. The poor are less likely to leave their own neighborhoods and less likely to make a large-scale expenditure on food at any one time. The amount of money they spend on food is the only nonfixed item in their budgets. Thus, they must buy it daily, and never in the larger amounts on which they save money; for what they spend on food may be the carfare they will need tomorrow to get their sick kids to the hospital. It is this need to keep the food budget in a fluid state that accounts, in part, for the low rate of participation in the food-stamp programs: families on welfare, or with uncertain income, cannot spend a sizable sum of money at one time, especially at the beginning of the month when rent, utilities, and other fixed-cost items must be paid.

The kinds of food they buy also reveal the great differences between their life styles and those of the other groups. The poor buy markedly less meat, poultry, eggs, dairy products, fruits, and vegetables than do those in higher income brackets. The only items which they buy in significantly greater amounts are grain products. Dried beans, bread, spaghetti, macaroni, and other starches are what the poor use to fill their stomachs, while their children drink far more soda pop that milk.

Those who specialize in selling in the poverty market can count on certain other characteristic patterns of behavior among their customers. Middle-income people tend to read advertising about sales and to take advantage of them; not so the poor. Nor do they readily buy secondhand merchandise: the Goodwill stores are patronized more by bohemians and the middle class than by the poor. They do not save trading tramps as avidly as middle-class families, and they do not participate in "give-away" programs. They combine an inability to discern real value with a psychic need to buy something new and a financial incapacity to buy more than they require for their immediate purpose. Welfare recipients are often at the mercy of retailers who demand that a fixed amount of goods be purchased before they will cash a relief check. Even worse, they may insist, as a condition of cashing welfare checks, that their customers buy slow-moving items for which the hapless consumer may have little or no use. When that happens, the poor have no choice, for usually they require the cash as quickly as they can get it because some other pressing need is at their throats.

Vulnerability to exploitation of their pervasive anxiety is only one of many special characteristics of the economic situation of the poor. Their economic milieu is also marked by the fact that different kinds of goods and services are available to them than to those in other circumstances. This is, in part, a reflection of their distinctive value system, but to some extent their values are shaped, in turn, by their consumer choices. For instance, reading a morning newspaper (while drinking their nonsalty pineapple juice) is a commonplace, routine act for most Americans, but it is not a characteristic pattern of the poor. Instead, they watch television, and listen to the radio, and these media, almost exclusively, mold their view of the world.

. . . Bad economic circumstances force the poor into seeking abnormal solutions to those economic problems which create far more anxiety for them than the same problems do for the rest of society. Indeed, pitifully few responses are available to what is the basic fact of economic life amongst the poor: that more money must go out each month to pay a myriad of bills from rent and utilities, to furniture payments, to automobile installments, than comes in from wages, salaries, or welfare payments. And since income is capricious while the monthly bills must constantly be met, anxiety is always present; by law, the consequences of nonpayment are inevitable: eviction, the gas shut off, the car or furniture repossessed. Thus, for example, a working mother, without a husband, may have to leave her job because of the unreliability of baby sitters. Once this happens, she and her children are caught in a whirlpool which will suck them all down into despair.

Many people — most, perhaps — who are not poor also go into debt for consumer items such as cars, furniture or appliances, medical care, clothing, jewelry, and so on. But if the low-wage earner is out of work for an extended period, or if his wife loses her job, the very delicate balance between wages and debts is upset and the family gets into real trouble.

When he falls behind in installment payments, a characteristic response of the low-income person is to go to a finance company to "consolidate" his debts and to undertake a series of single monthly payments, presumably according to his ability to pay. As we know, the interest rates are outrageous, but most people in these straits seem to have few alternatives indeed.

For those whose debts continue to escalate despite consolidation, or for those who cannot even get credit from the finance companies, only slender choices remain. One is to give their children away, a practice common among urban Negroes who have simply adapted a Southern rural custom — and out of the same economic motives. If a mother cannot support her children, she will "give" them to a relative, usually the child's grandparents, to raise. Usually, she is expected to provide some money for the child's upkeep, but frequently, of course, she cannot. . . .

More unique to the poor is a sense of gratitude for what others assume to be their natural due. For example, they view installment buying as a privilege to which they are not really entitled — because they do not feel worthy of receiving the fruits of the society. As a result, they are much less likely to grow indignant over the exploitive rates of interest and carrying charges they pay for the right to use merchandise which is not paid for in full. As a consequence of this attitude, the poor are much better customers than the rich from the retailer's point of view: they are not so quick to complain about the quality of the merchandise; they are much more easily intimidated; and they shop far less carefully. The notion of depending upon an organization such as Consumers Union to help protect their interests is completely meaningless to the poor; it assumes a degree of self-consciousness about themselves as consumers which they do not have as yet.

How can the poor become more self-conscious, self-interested consumers? It does little good to educate them about what foods make up a proper nutritional balance when their food budget fails to match the requirements, or when it remains the only item which gives them any financial flexibility. Indeed, the whole notion of a budget implies some ability to plan ahead, to project actions on the basis of a stable income which is enough to meet the reasonable demands put upon it. But the income of the poor is either capricious or inadequate — or both — and only the demands made upon it are stable, fixed by forces and institutions over which they have little or no measure of control.

Thus, I am somewhat pessimistic about the value of educational programs directed toward helping the poor become better consumers. What good will it do to convince the Indians or the Pima reservation in Arizona that their children should drink less pop and eat more meat when very few of the mud "sandwich" houses on the reservation have either electricity or water? Milk and meat spoil in the hot Arizona summer unless they are refrigerated; soda pop and beans do not. What the Pima Indians need is either to cease being poor or to become much more aware of their rights despite their poverty. Such an awareness can come, I believe, only as part of a *general* rise in their living standards, or of a *general* awakening to their rights through some form of political action. . . .

All of us are born into a state of anxiety, and many, or even most, of us must cope, throughout our lives, with deep-rooted feelings of personal inadequacy. For the poor, these feelings are continuously reinforced by

the economic circumstances in which they live and by their relationships
with the rest of society. In an egalitarian society where everyone is living
in poverty, being poor generates neither much anxiety nor strong feelings
of inadequacy. But in a society such as ours, which measures achievement primarily by financial and material standards, to be poor is to be
scorned by others, and even worse, by one's own self. It is for this reason
that in America the taste and smell of poverty are so sour.

11. THE WORKING-CLASS MAJORITY

Andrew Levison

For approximately a quarter of a century, three ideas have dominated
the thinking of liberal intellectuals about the American working class.
One is that blue-collar workers are now outnumbered by white-collar
workers. Another is that rising income levels have eliminated rigid distinctions between blue collar and white, diminishing the importance of
the old working-class political issues. The third is that, smug and well
paid, workers and their unions are now among the most conservative
forces in the nation's political life. Each of these ideas is a myth. First,
blue collars still outnumber white. The "white-collar majority" is the
product of tortured definitions and sometimes deceptive manipulations
of statistics. Second, while the living standards of all Americans have
improved, most blue-collar workers are much closer to poverty than to
affluence. Finally, blue-collar workers are no more conservative than the
middle class on most issues and are more liberal on some, and there is
evidence that they will support liberal political candidates whose programs deal with workers' real problems and grievances.

The persistence of these myths is not an academic issue but one of
practical politics. By clinging to them, liberals have demonstrated a talent
verging on genius for isolating themselves, antagonizing workers, and
defeating genuinely liberal political candidates and programs. The indifference and condescension generated by the myths have created
stumbling blocks for almost every liberal movement of the past decade
— the peace movement and the ecology movement in particular — and
they played a role in twice electing Richard M. Nixon to the Presidency.

From *The Working-Class Majority* (Coward, McCann & Geoghegan). Reprinted by
permission; © 1974 Andrew Levison. Originally in *The New Yorker*.

The myth that America now has a white-collar majority has been taught as fact in college classrooms for years, with the support of most liberal, and even radical, social theorists. For instance, in "The New Industrial State," John Kenneth Galbraith wrote:

By 1965 there were nearly eight million more white than blue collar workers, 44.5 as compared with 36.7 million. During these years the number of professional and technical workers, the category most characteristic of the technostructure, approximately doubled.

Herbert Marcuse endorsed this common misconception in "One-Dimensional Man":

The assimilating trend shows forth in the occupational stratification. In the key industrial establishments the "blue collar" work force declines in relation to the "white collar" element; the number of non-production workers increases.

And in the pop best-seller "Future Shock" Alvin Toffler presents a particularly lyrical version of this idea:

In about 1956 the United States became the first major power in which more than 50 percent of the non-farm labor force ceased to wear the blue collar of factory or manual labor. . . . Within the same lifetime a society for the first time in human history not only threw off the yoke of agriculture, but managed within a few brief decades to throw off the yoke of manual labor as well.

The statistics quoted by such writers are based upon very specific and technical uses of the terms "blue collar" and "white collar" and not on the definitions that these terms still have in ordinary conversation, in which they are synonyms for brawn and brain, for manual labor vs. professional and managerial work. The source of these technical usages is the Census Bureau, which has established the following job categories:

White Collar: Professional, technical, and kindred; managerial and administrative; clerical and sales.
Blue Collar: Craftsmen and foremen; operatives [men who operate machinery], and (non-farm) laborers.
Other: Service, farm laborers.

This sorting looks fine on the surface. If the categories are not crystal clear, they seem adequate. But while for twenty-five years these categories appeared reasonable as a basis for proclaiming the decline of manual labor, it would have become apparent to anyone who went beyond them, to the specific jobs involved, that the white-collar majority was very much like a desert mirage: the more carefully one looked at it, the farther away it was.

Notice that the blue-collar category is limited to only a fraction of all the Americans who are still employed in essentially rote manual labor. "Service" workers are excluded, even though many of them are janitors,

waiters, porters, ushers, elevator operators, doormen, and shoeshine boys
— people who hold some of the lowest-paying and most menial occupations in America. When a given percentage of "blue-collar" workers is
cited, the tendency is to automatically place everyone else, including
these workers, in the middle class. Most of the rest of the people in the
service category are also manual workers: guards, watchmen, cooks,
household help, hospital and other attendants, barbers, policemen, and
firemen. In addition, clerical and sales work, assigned to the white-collar
category, has many working-class jobs concealed within it. The postman
is a clerical worker. So are baggagemen, messenger boys, bill collectors,
newsboys, peddlers, office-machine operators, bus and train dispatchers,
and telegraph operators — all contained in the white-collar category and
hence called middle class. And in 1970 two-thirds of the clerical and sales
workers were women — telephone operators, cashiers, salesgirls, typists,
and others in low-paying, low-status jobs. Some sociologists have tried to
salvage the "middle-class majority" by suggesting that these women
clerical and sales workers are a "new" social group, a lower-middle-class
"salariat" (rather than a proletariat). This is an appealing solution, since
one would hesitate to call them working class. Many writers have been
seduced by this concept, since it seems to apply to a large number of
"career girls" who seem more middle class than working class. The
image of women clerical and sales workers that these writers have is the
New York single girl, perhaps a Vassar graduate, who is working as a
secretary but dreams of "getting into publishing." She lives with two
other young women in an expensive East Side apartment, reads *Ms.*,
takes courses at the New School, smokes pot on occasion, and goes skiing
on weekends. Such an image, however, is misleading. Most women
clerical and sales workers are married, and about half are married to
working-class men. Suddenly the career-girl secretary is joined by a somewhat less romantic figure — the welder's wife who works part time as a
check-out clerk in the A. & P. Instead of *Ms.*, imagine *Reader's Digest;*
instead of the ski slopes it's Wednesday-night bowling; and it's not pot
but one of her husband's beers. To a sociologist who met her on the
street, she would be one of "them," not one of "us."

The best way to clarify this confusion is to look at the occupational
structure for men. Approximately sixty-eight per cent of women aged
eighteen or older are married, and most married women live in the class
and culture of their husbands. Thus, the list of occupations for men alone
gives a much more exact indication of the relative sizes of the working
class and the middle class in America. The following chart [Table 1],
based on Census Bureau figures, shows the proportions quite clearly:

Since there are many working-class jobs hidden in the clerical and
sales grouping, the true working-class figure is probably between sixty
and sixty-two per cent. Thus, three-fifths of America is working class.

Table 1   Major Occupation Groups
For Males in 1969

Middle Class

Professional and Technical	14.6%
Managerial and Proprietor	14.6
Clerical	7.4
Sales	5.8
	42.4%

Working Class

Craftsmen and Foremen	21.4
Operatives	21.4
Laborers	7.6
Service	7.1
	57.5%

The euphoric concept of a middle-class majority, the end of manual labor, and a new age in human history is based on the inclusion in the middle class of steelworkers' wives who go to work as cashiers and sales-girls.

Such figures do leave open the possibility that blue-collar work may be rapidly disappearing and that in a few years we may have a middle-class majority after all. But if we look at the actual number of people in different occupations, one fact is immediately apparent: the number of working-class Americans has not decreased at all; in fact, the census shows that in the two decades since 1950 it has increased by roughly four million. The declining trend the analysts notice is relative; as the population has grown, the working class has increased, but the minority of Americans who are middle class has increased at a faster rate. Between 1950 and 1969, the number of male blue-collar employees increased from twenty-two million to twenty-six million, while the number of white-collar men increased from thirteen million to nineteen million. The white-collar increase is significant, but let us put it in perspective. The relative percentage of blue-collar workers goes down, from 62.4 per cent to 57.5 — a five-per-cent drop in twenty years (not counting the mis-classified clerical and sales workers). First, that still leaves us with twenty-six million working-class American men and nineteen million middle-class American men — a raw social and political fact that cannot be denied. Second, for the middle class just to maintain the same proportion in relation to the working class, an increase of 2.4 million people was required. So only about 3.6 million *more* middle-class employees, beyond that 2.4 million, represent something new in the occupational structure since 1950. Again, the raw number is striking. The whole post-war "revolution" described by so many commentators comes down to less than four million men in a male labor force of about forty-five mil-lion. At this rate, there will be a working-class majority until the next century. At least another generation of Americans will be predominantly working class. Six Presidents and thousands of congressmen will be elected by a working class majority.

If manual workers lived exactly like white-collar workers, however, the fact that they work in factories instead of offices would probably not be of great political significance. And this is what many commentators have told us — that blue-collar workers are now "middle class" or "middle Americans," not affluent but far from poor. For example, Herman P. Miller, in his article "A Profile of the Blue Collar American," in "Blue-Collar Workers: A Symposium on Middle America," published in 1971, wrote, "By 1969 the median annual income of white families headed by blue-collar workers was $10,700." But Miller was talking only about craftsmen, foremen, and operatives — no one else. He excluded service workers, laborers, and people unemployed at the time of the survey — not to mention the somewhat more defensible exclusion of blacks as a special case.

We come up with a very different picture of the American working class if we do not exclude any category of manual worker; if we deal not with averages or medians but with the whole range of working-class-income distribution; and if we examine this distribution in the light of the Bureau of Labor Statistics "standard budgets," which the bureau desig-nates "lower," "intermediate," and "upper," but which actually represent the three socioeconomic cultures in the United States — poverty, working class, and middle class. In 1970, the budget for the lowest of these was $6,960 for a family of four; the intermediate budget — the amount neces-sary for what some unions call a "shabby but respectable life" — was $10,664; and the middle-class budget was $15,551. In 1970, government figures indicate, thirty per cent of the nation's working-class families were living in what was really poverty, with incomes of less than $7,000. Another thirty per cent were above the poverty budget but below that "shabby" intermediate level. Thus, sixty per cent of the working class either were poor or were hovering between poverty and the very modest level of the intermediate budget. A United Auto Workers study shows just how "modest" that budget is: The budget assumes, for example, that a family will own "a toaster that will last for thirty-three years, a refriger-ator and a range that will each last for seventeen years, a vacuum cleaner that will last for fourteen years, and a television set that will last for ten years. The budget assumes that a family will buy a two-year-old car and keep it for four years, and will pay for a tune-up once a year, a brake realignment every three years, and a front-end alignment every four years. . . . The budget assumes that the husband will buy one year-round suit every four years . . . and one topcoat every eight and a half years. . . . It assumes that the husband will take his wife to the movies once every three months, and that one of them will go to the movies alone once a year. The average family's two children are each allowed one movie every four weeks. A total of two dollars and fifty-four cents per person per year is allowed for admission to all other events, from football and baseball games to plays or concerts. . . . The budget allows nothing whatever for savings."

This or less is the condition of sixty per cent of all American workers. The affluent workers, who until recently were supposed to be typical, constitute from twelve to fifteen per cent of the working class, white and black. Eighty-five per cent, then, are not "typical." The average working-class family earns ninety-five hundred dollars — much closer to poverty than to affluence — and this is the income of the entire family, working wife and children included. The average figure does not take into account long-term unemployment, illness, or the income of old people on pensions; it has reference to the working poor, not poverty in general. For many years, the economic condition of workers has been shrugged off with easy references to a handful of plumbers and electricians making eight or ten dollars an hour. But throughout that time other workers have been getting between four dollars and four-fifty an hour, and some even less. In fact, more than any other factor, it is working wives who have made possible even the modest standard of living that the average workers enjoy. It is worth keeping this in mind when one imagines a working-class family that has an income of ten thousand dollars a year. The husband may earn only seven or eight thousand, and his wife may earn the rest.

Blue-collar workers must cope not only with low wages but with frequent unemployment, which neither liberal commentators nor the media have really comprehended. Even in the last few years, as the rate has risen sharply, unemployment has rarely been given much attention in articles about the "blue-collar blues" or discussions of the problems of American workers. It has been mentioned, of course, but has been quickly dismissed. After all, even at the worst point in 1971 unemployment affected only about six per cent of the labor force, and it did not take a great deal of mathematical knowledge to recognize that therefore ninety-four per cent were not laid off. In comparison with conditions in the thirties, it certainly did not sound like a major crisis. Liberals did criticize these figures on the ground that they excluded certain groups from the unemployed, like "discouraged" workers who had given up looking for work, and people who wanted to work full time but could find only a few hours' work a week. Conservatives replied that the six per cent included women, students looking for summer jobs, workers who quit their jobs, and other people for whom unemployment did not have the same impact that it had on the male breadwinner who was suddenly laid off by the company. In February of 1972, the rate for married men, they noted, was only 2.8 per cent. Since blacks constituted a disproportionate number of those who were out of work, most writers concluded that for the "typical" worker unemployment was not a real problem.

But the "annual unemployment rate" that everyone watches so closely is a rather confusing measure; it counts only the people who happen to be unemployed on the day of a survey. In a monthly survey, a sampling of people are asked whether they are working, and the results are counted up. This reveals what percentage of people were without work on a certain day, but not all those who were unemployed earlier in the month or would be later. The annual unemployment rate is simply the average of the twelve surveys per year, rather than a total of all those who were unemployed at some point during the year. Such totals are compiled annually by the Census Bureau and these figures are called the "annual work-experience data." Although these data have far more meaning than the rates, they are almost never used to judge the severity of unemployment. If we ask the simple question "How many people were unemployed at some time last year?" the answer is striking. In 1969, which was before unemployment had become a major issue, eighteen per cent of the operatives, or almost one out of every five, were unemployed for some period of time. In 1970, the figure was twenty-three per cent — or almost one out of every four. The proportions of those affected among blue-collar workers ranged from about thirteen per cent for service employees to more than twenty-five per cent for laborers. (By contrast, for white-collar workers the range was from five per cent for managers and administrators to eleven and a half for clerical workers.)

The conclusion is obvious: Unemployment is tremendously widespread in working-class America. Millions of workers are thrown out of work every year, and among the remainder the fear that they will be next is widespread. There is no doubt that the majority of the nation's workers, even though they keep their jobs, cannot feel any real job security. It must be noted that a significant minority of workers suffer unemployment more than once a year, and therefore the number of different workers who are unemployed is somewhat lower than the figures suggest. On the other hand, the figures do not include workers who are kept idle by bad weather and are not paid during that time.

An important part of the picture is how long unemployment lasts. In 1969, about twenty-three per cent of unemployed blue-collar workers were without work for fifteen or more weeks. In 1970, the proportion rose to more than thirty per cent. One group for whom this issue is of crucial importance is construction craftsmen. Again and again, one hears the refrain "Those people are making seven or eight dollars an hour, or even more — that's over fifteen thousand a year." But not even ten per cent of all construction workers actually made fifteen thousand dollars or more in 1970. The fact is that a majority of construction craftsmen did not make even ten thousand; the median income for construction workers, according to the Census Bureau, was $9,494. In part, this can be accounted for by lower wage rates for nonunion craftsmen. But a more important factor is that construction work involves the highest incidence of unemployment of any sector of the American economy. Almost a quarter of the construction workers — 24.4 per cent — were unemployed at the same time in 1969. In 1970, the percentage rose to more than thirty per cent. On a typical day in that year, nearly one out of every ten construction workers was without a job. The duration of the construction workers' unemployment is also noteworthy. In 1970, more than a third of the unemployed were out of work for almost four months. If construction workers had been paid the same wages as factory workers in 1970, their income would have fallen below the poverty budget. And, even as things were, $9,494 was below the "intermediate budget" of that year.

The belief that in recent times workers have not had serious problems in employment and job security has been at the base of a depressing number of liberal fiascos. The environmental movement, for example, has taken the complacent attitude that "there are other jobs around" in facing the issue of shutting down factories that pollute. But there are not just loads of other jobs around. If there were, twenty-three per cent of all operatives would not have been unemployed during 1970. Since periods of unemployment can rob a worker of the money he has been saving for his children's education, or perhaps make him lose his house, it is clear that he has to fight back, even if he wants clean rivers and clean air. All too often, liberal ecology proponents talk loosely about alternative employment and new jobs for blue-collar workers, but when it comes down to real life the attitude is "Shut down the factory now and we'll figure out something for the worker later." Usually, the something turns out to be nothing — an upshot that is not only unjust but shortsighted. Similarly, the attitude of many liberals toward the construction trades' exclusion of blacks is based on the idea that there are enough jobs for all and the hardhats' opposition to integration is pure racism. In all too many cases, racism is indeed present. But so is the spectre of unemployment. Myra Wolfgang, an international vice-president of the Hotel and Restaurant Employees and Bartenders International Union, has said in an interview in *Dissent*, in 1972, "When twenty-two per cent of the members of your unions are unemployed, as is the case with the carpenters in the Detroit area, this isn't the best time to say to them, 'You should share with blacks.' The blacks and whites who are building tradesmen would all be working if the Nixon Administration met the needs of housing in this country."

Before turning to the third myth, we should consider at further length blacks and another group whose situation I have mentioned only in passing — women. The condition of blacks in America is, ironically, easier to deal with than that of white workers. While most liberals are ignorant of the most basic facts about blue-collar workers, they often remember a few statistics about blacks — that there are about twenty-three million blacks in the United States, that the unemployment rate for blacks is usually double that for whites, and so on. However, the undeniable injustice of unemployment and the consequent reliance on welfare have often produced in the minds of whites an image of a black community composed entirely of unemployed ghetto youths, welfare mothers, and narcotics addicts. The liberal vision of the black community as a unique "underclass" or "culture of poverty" highlights some of the most critical problems, such as bad housing and inadequate medical facilities, but it obscures certain key facts. One is that most black people are not welfare recipients or "street dudes" — they are blue-collar workers who work in some of the dirtiest, lowest-paying, and most dangerous jobs in America. This means that in economic terms the problems of black workers, although significantly worse than the problems of whites, are part of the general pattern of social and economic inequality in America. Most black people are poor not because of unemployment or inadequate welfare payments but because of low wages. Although concern with the poverty of unemployed youths and welfare mothers is valid and important, it should not lead us to ignore the poverty of black janitors and dishwashers, maids and laundry workers. The most important source of black poverty is the exploitation of black workers through low-paying jobs. All too often, the focus on a romanticized culture of poverty ends up by producing a picture amazingly similar to the right-wing myth about all blacks living on welfare. In reality, however, most black people are working long hours in hard jobs for wages that do not even provide a poverty-budget standard of living.

One young Southern black I met who joined a job-training program that paid a salary to people while they learned provides an ironic case in point. He described to me how, in addition to providing training in some skill of rather dubious value, the white instructor spent a good deal of time talking about the cultural factors in unemployment and how he truly understood the trainees' desperation and despair about finding work. The irony was that this young black and several of his friends had been employed before they joined the program, and had joined it because it paid more than the jobs they had held. Their previous work, with a temporary-employment agency, gave them a take-home pay of about nine and a half dollars a day — eight dollars and seventy-five cents after bus fare to the agency and back. To be sure of work, they had to get up at four-thirty in the morning and be at the agency by five-fifteen or five-thirty, although their pay did not start until eight or nine. So here were men who had been spending more than twelve hours a day to earn eight dollars and seventy-five cents now in a training program whose central thesis was that psychological, social, and cultural factors were their real problem, not the eight dollars and seventy-five cents.

In 1972, of twenty-three million blacks the census counted in America, about seven and a half million were adult males. Of these, four and three-quarters million were employed, four hundred and forty thousand were officially designated as unemployed, and more than two million were out of the labor force, many in school, the Army, or jail. This underestimated black unemployment, because the government counted anyone who worked even one day during the week in which the survey was made as "employed," because it included the unemployed who wanted work and sought it but gave up looking in the category "outside the labor force," and because blacks are usually undercounted in census studies. The official unemployment figure was equal to about eight and a half per cent of the black labor force, and a complete figure, including the people who worked only a few hours, would probably be about twelve or fifteen per cent. This is confirmed by a study of black and white unemployment in New York City in 1972 which suggests that about thirteen per cent of blacks are unemployed or employed only part time even though they would work full time if they could find full-time jobs. For black youths, the situation is far worse; in some cities the unemployment figure ranges from twenty-five to forty per cent, and in a few it goes even higher.

And, of course, blacks lucky enough to find full-time jobs do not earn wages approaching those of whites. In 1970, black craftsmen and foremen had a median income of $7,353, compared with a white median of $9,349. The comparisons in other categories were: for operatives, $6,273 and $7,857; for service workers, $5,670 and $7,388; and for laborers, $5,410 and $6,796.

The situation of women can be summed up quickly. The great majority of women employees are unskilled or semiskilled workers who hold rote, repetitive jobs, and many of the "professional" jobs held by women are actually comparable in training and skill levels to the skilled workers' jobs held by men. The most important fact about women's jobs, however, is that in every category women receive thousands of dollars less than men receive for doing approximately the same job. The low wages paid women have two important consequences: First, though the wages paid to wives of blue-collar workers often make the difference between poverty and a less than adequate but tolerable life, women who must live on their own earnings are often unable to do so and must go on welfare. Second, the low wages paid to these women provide the margin of profit for many industries, like clothing or electronics, that are hard pressed by cheap foreign imports. As recently as 1970, women factory workers in these industries often got a starting wage of two dollars and fifteen cents or two dollars and a quarter an hour, which would ordinarily be rejected by a man. The same is true of salesgirls, who often receive only ninety or a hundred dollars a week. Thus, the complaints of the women's liberationists are backed up by very real economic discrepancies. . . .

An issue that may have a decisive influence on the future political role of blue-collar workers is job security. This problem, which is already a significant one, is currently being aggravated by automation, by the energy crisis, and by the move of industry to the suburbs, to the South, and to other countries. As for the energy crisis, its long-term effects are as yet impossible to gauge. Certainly the oil shortage and the Arab oil boycott are but short-term aspects of a bigger problem, and the effects even of these could have been reduced by more imaginative planning — such as an earlier emphasis on small-car production. But the inflation in petroleum prices is part of a broader and more alarming pattern. Prices for a vast range of raw materials and commodities, from food-stuffs to bauxite and copper, have risen precipitously under the impact of the recent world boom in the industrialized countries. This change, which may signalize the end of an era of relatively cheap raw materials, has the potential for a long-range threat to American jobs. But any truly wrenching change would be felt far more in the virtually resourceless countries like Japan, rather than in the United States, which remains one of the most self-sufficient. In fact, our competitive position could actually improve.

Automation is often ignored nowadays, because it did not live up to the predictions made in the nineteen-fifties that it would completely end manual labor within a decade or so. A comprehensive study made in 1967 by the University of Michigan Survey Research Center concluded that "for the years 1962 to 1967 very little unemployment can be attributed *directly* to machine change," a conclusion that may be related to the fact that the years in question were characterized by low levels of unemployment and a rapidly growing gross national product. The study noted, however, that "workers who might have been hired in the absence of technological change are not needed," and that "the last to be hired have to wait longer for a job." This is the hidden effect of automation. Many unions negotiated attrition clauses in their contracts, stipulating that only as workers retired or quit could automatic equipment be introduced, and thus it is the unemployed or the young workers just entering the labor market who feel the impact most. The level of unemployment among black youths sixteen to nineteen years of age, for instance, rose to a stunning 30.2 per cent in 1973.

The persistent move of industry to the suburbs is a key factor in the lives of central-city dwellers, whether blacks or working-class whites. In November, 1970, Paul Zimmerer, the executive director of the Mayor's Committee for Economic and Cultural Development in Chicago, testifying before a House committee on industrial location policy, said, "In Chicago's inner city alone, between 1955 and 1963 there was a net loss of some four hundred manufacturing companies and some seventy thousand manufacturing jobs. . . . Because of discriminatory housing practices, suburban zoning regulations, inadequate mass-transit systems . . . most inner-city workers could not continue to work at relocated manufacturing facilities in the suburbs." In New York, Kenneth Patton, former head of the Economic Development Administration, estimated a loss of two hundred thousand manufacturing jobs over the period from 1950 to 1970. In city after city, the pattern is repeated: factories move to suburban industrial parks that can be reached only by car, thus excluding poor and black workers and eroding the tax base of the central city they have left. There are a variety of perfectly sound reasons for this migration. Many factories function most efficiently when they are spread out horizontally, and land is cheaper in the suburbs. Construction costs are lower there, too, and the congestion of central cities creates serious problems in transporting raw materials and finished goods. But there are some less tangible factors involved. Patton has said, "The decision to locate a facility, particularly in an industrial area, often has at its center the question of evasion." Suburban pollution regulations are often lax and suburban taxes comparatively lower. Local communities often provide additional inducements or services. An inevitable result has been to make the centers of many Northern cities into a kind of urban Appalachia — burned-out pockets of permanent unemployment. Even for those workers who can make the move with their factories, the change has meant either long hours of commuting or the necessity of going deeply into debt for a nearby home.

But industrial migration has not stopped with moves to the suburbs. The relocation of Northern industry in the South has been accelerating. Between 1947 and 1965, employment in the South and the West grew by 57.4 per cent, while in the Middle Atlantic and Northeastern regions it grew by only 20.5 per cent. Supplementing textile mills, the chemical and wood-products industries have become major Southern employers, and the percentage of the Southern population engaged in manufacturing is now close to that of the North. Plants are attracted to the South not only by tax breaks but also by lower wages and the relative weakness of unions there.

And these same advantages, available in even greater measure, are behind the latest trend in industrial migration — the growing "export" of American jobs to other countries. In March of 1973, *Fortune* said that eighty-seven thousand American jobs in the fields of television, radio, and electronic components alone had been lost since 1966 because of the transfer of assembly lines overseas, while Paul Jennings, president of the International Union of Electrical Workers, has put the figure at a hundred and twenty-one thousand jobs. The United Shoe Workers, also hit by foreign imports, have lost sixteen thousand five hundred jobs over a ten-year period. And it has been estimated that a hundred thousand jobs have been lost because of imports in the automobile industry, many of them to American-owned plants in other countries. The trouble is less foreign competition in general than the specific role of the American multinational corporations in the world's economy. What makes "foreign" competition and the loss of blue-collar jobs today a different matter from ostensibly similar problems in previous years is that so many of the cars and electronic components coming into America now are produced by American firms that have set up factories overseas, where wages, fringe benefits, and working conditions are often markedly below those that prevail in the United States. In its effect on the unions, this is nothing but another variant of the "runaway shop" — a firm's transfer of a factory from a high-cost labor area to a low-cost one elsewhere in this country. It is impossible to estimate exactly the number of American jobs that have been lost because of the multinationals. In 1968, a Commerce Department study suggested that only fourteen per cent of imported goods came from American-based multinationals, but this figure clearly underestimated the reality, for it did not include the imports from foreign companies with significant, though minority, American interests. In any event, several hundred thousand jobs have certainly been lost because of job exports.

Curiously, these threats to blue-collar jobs are seen by some social scientists as a positive development. These people envision a long-range trend toward a "service economy," or a "post-industrial state," and identify the decline of manufacturing jobs with upward mobility into the middle class. The emerging "post-industrial society," Daniel Bell has written, "is based on services. . . . What counts is not raw muscle power or energy but information. The central person is the professional, for he is equipped . . . to provide the kinds of skills increasingly in demand. The post-industrial society is defined . . . by the services and amenities, health, education, recreation and the arts, which are now deemed desirable and possible for everyone." Nat Goldfinger, the director of research for the A.F.L.–C.I.O., has pointed out the central flaw in such projections: "Service jobs, most of them, are low-wage, menial jobs. It's not all surgeons and research chemists by any means." As we have seen, much of the white-collar growth has been in clerical and sales occupations, which pay so little that only wives seeking to supplement blue-collar family incomes will fill them. Even if a significant number of workers could find their way into the professional and managerial group, the elimination of factory work could eat away the middle level of American society and create a huge class division, with millions of workers facing unemployment, or, at best, a precipitous drop in income.

A goal on which liberals and black and white workers can agree is the creation of genuine full employment. This goal would also have millions of natural allies in the middle class, because it would ameliorate many of the conditions that affect them. Full employment would be an enormous step toward ending polarization of blacks and whites. By separating the question of jobs for able-bodied men from that of assistance for those who cannot work, it would resolve the welfare issue at a stroke. It would put more money into the black community than any other government program ever could, with obvious improvements in housing and medical care, and a lessening of racial tensions. Finally, it would have a profound impact on the issue of crime, which currently wracks the nation's big cities. Criminals are only a tiny fraction of the unemployed, and there are many criminals who would not be reformed by the prospect of a decent job, but full employment would dry up the vast well of criminal recruits, which is in part created by joblessness and the loss of hope for a decent life.

   The issue is at present locked in a maze of verbal and statistical contradictions. Not only does the government's statistical "unemployment rate" seriously distort the real magnitude of the problem but, from a business point of view, "full employment" does not mean full employment. It means some compromise level of joblessness that will insure stability. Once, this was judged to be 2.5 per cent; today, however, some economists argue that having five per cent of the labor force without jobs is the closest that America can come to full employment. Goldfinger has said, "Full employment, as organized labor views it, means job opportunities at *decent wages* for all those who are able to work and seek employment." The most important part of that definition is the insistence on speaking of jobs and good wages together. It brings out the often forgotten key issue in the whole debate — that the point of jobs is to insure a decent life. The fact is that anyone in the United States could be "employed" in a moment if he offered to wash cars for a nickel, for example, or work as a domestic servant for a dollar a day. The problem is not just jobs but employment at wages that a worker can live on. Black central-city joblessness, in particular, brings this fact into focus. In many big-city newspapers one can find pages of want ads offering jobs for car-wash attendants or dishwashers, and yet many unemployed people will refuse to take them. On this basis, much has been made of "cultural factors" and the "lack of the work ethic." Yet only a few miles away, in the employment office of a General Motors plant, there are hundreds of blacks who have been up since four-thirty in the morning waiting their turn for an interview. Any time a high-wage plant opens up, it is flooded with applicants — sometimes four or five for every opening.

The point is obvious. A serious program for full employment cannot be based on national statistics that lump openings for babysitters, newspaper boys, and hamburger-stand waiters together with stable jobs in industry and the like. The first set of jobs are genuine jobs only for special groups like teen-agers. Other jobs — in the retail trades or in laundry work, say — can be economically viable only for single men or women. None of these jobs can support a family. A million jobs like babysitting and clerking in a store could open up in the black ghetto and young blacks would still line up in the employment offices of factories, looking for work that pays better wages.

A variety of proposals exists for creating full employment, no one of them complete in itself. Perhaps the most popular is creating jobs in the public sector in such fields as medical care, conservation, and education. Jerry Wurf, the head of the American Federation of State, County and Municipal Employees, cites a study which "found [that] some 4.3 million nonprofessional jobs in public and nonprofit agencies could be established to perform useful and needed services." He explains, "These are not 'make-work' slots, but real jobs that need doing."

There have, in fact, been many legislative attempts to begin the creation of jobs, some directly related to welfare recipients and some aimed at the unemployed in general, but the results have barely scratched the surface. The federal public-employment program of 1971 resulted in only a hundred and eighty-five thousand new jobs, all of them temporary, and only a third of them filled by the hard-core unemployed. As of April, 1973, the patchwork of state and federally funded "workfare" programs, which required welfare recipients to accept jobs when offered them, had created sixty-nine hundred public-service jobs — about one factory's worth. But a significant expansion of such programs is a real and practical possibility, even given the current economic uncertainties. In hearings before the Senate Manpower Subcommittee in 1972, a group of economic experts ranging from liberal to conservative made basically similar projections of the costs in such an expansion. More than a million public-service jobs, it was estimated, could be created for about ten billion dollars. Even if one grants that such an estimate is far from precise, and that inflation would make any program more costly today, it is still true that a program on this level could be instituted without deficit financing (and the consequent danger of raising the inflation rate) or enormous tax increases for working Americans. Tax reform and the reallocation of tax money already in government hands could provide the funds.

Some estimates have it, for example, that just the repeal of the "accelerated-depreciation" tax break granted to business in 1971 would pay more than a third of the annual cost of this program. And since ten billion dollars amounts to about four per cent of annual federal expenditures, even the most cosmetic reordering of budget priorities toward social needs could supply sufficient funds. It is ironic that a large-scale program of public-service employment is often portrayed as too innovative and radical an idea to win acceptance, while the government is already creating jobs on a vast scale by financing highways, armaments, and vast aerospace programs. The creation of public-service jobs of the kind envisioned is different only in that the jobs would themselves be of greater social value and would be designed for the urban poor, who most desperately need employment at a decent wage. The creation of a million public-service jobs would be a major step toward full employment, but the program need not be limited to a million jobs. Even in the thirties, with a gross national product, corrected for inflation, roughly one-fifth of what it is today, the American government was able to put some four million Americans to work on federally subsidized public jobs, and it is hard to believe that an equal effort is not possible now.

But public-service employment, if it is to be effective, cannot operate in a vacuum. Without needed changes in the private sector, public-service employment might only result in employed workers changing jobs, rather than in the creation of jobs for the hard-core unemployed. One approach would be to offer tax incentives to business while providing government subsidies to low-income wage earners. However, the practical experience with the "Let business do it" approach in the JOBS Program, a business-government cooperative effort in training ghetto youths for more gainful employment, has not been impressive. In 1972, a study conducted by a joint congressional economic committee found that the program "may have pumped out subsidies to employers who would have hired unskilled laborers anyway, without government aid." And, further, it "has proven virtually useless in periods of high unemployment." In 1968, George Meany, testifying before a congressional committee, accurately predicted that this would occur.

One alternative is to recognize that the location of industries is as much a matter for public and government regulation as the smoke that they spew out of their smokestacks. This issue is also basic to any consideration of job export and consequent unemployment, but it must be seen to include all the ways in which communities are devastated by the movement of jobs. Studies of European countries that have had virtually full employment in the postwar period indicate that a major element in their success is the active role that government has played in economic development. One means of achieving this, known as "indicative planning," involves a strong government presence in planning sessions with management and labor, in which estimates are made of where shortfalls of capital or pockets of poverty will develop in the coming years. This is followed by measures to avoid the occurrence of such problems. In addition, selective wage, price, and profit controls are maintained in the most concentrated areas of the economy, providing a lever with which government can keep large corporations socially responsible. Besides such tested approaches, one future possibility is legislation requiring that a certain proportion of new factories be located where unemployment is highest. More speculative possibilities include direct government subsidies supporting new industry.

· It is precisely the extension of democracy to the main social and economic areas of American life — the creation of a society without injustice toward blue-collar workers — that is the real issue. It is the fulfillment of the democratic ideal that goes all the way back to the French and American Revolutions — the ideal of equality and genuine popular rule which has lain dormant throughout our history. To many, it may appear hopelessly romantic to discuss such issues today. But it is equally unrealistic to discount blue-collar workers as a genuine force for progress.

IV RACISM

It has long been accepted that "race relations" constitute an American social problem. But only recently has the idea taken hold that a system of racism exists, with deep roots in American institutions. One legacy of an unreflective postwar optimism about American society was the belief that racial prejudice and discrimination, like many other problematic aspects of life in the United States, were destined to disappear in the not-so-distant future. A number of sources fed this judgment. First, during this period the race problem was usually defined in terms of the denial of "civil rights." Once the legal barriers to equal opportunity for all races were struck down, the institutional support for racism would presumably be removed and the structure of racial subordination would collapse. And the growing volume of civil-rights legislation during the forties and fifties seemed to signify the increasing willingness of the federal government to take positive action toward reversing the effects of several hundred years of discrimination.

The social and psychological theory of the fifties provided another source of optimism. Most of this theory located the race-relations problem in bigoted "attitudes" and its resolution in strategies designed to change those attitudes. The dominant conception was the notion of "prejudice." A number of classic studies of the 1930s had considered the system of *structural* relations between blacks and whites in American communities – among them John Dollard's *Caste and Class in a Southern Town* and St. Clair Drake's and Horace Cayton's *Black Metropolis*.[1] But the general trend in later works was to see racism primarily as a problem in the minds of individual white people, rather than in the basic organization of political and economic institutions in the United States.

Several related ideas accompanied this view. The first was a tendency to see racism as specific to certain geographical

regions and social groups, that is, the South and the less-
educated and lower or lower middle-class white, and, by implication, to assume that other regions and groups were relatively
free of racism. Research on prejudiced attitudes tended
to support this. Second, since regional "backwardness" was
breaking down under the pressure of industrialization and
urbanization, and since education was being rapidly extended
to all social groups, the social supports of prejudice were
crumbling and we could look forward to continuous improvement in race relations.[2] Improvement would come, therefore,
as a result of psychological changes within the existing social
structure. Finally, the consistent implication was that racial
prejudice and discrimination were basically "unAmerican" –
in the double sense of being foreign to American values (the
American Creed, as Gunnar Myrdal[3] characterized it), and a
kind of historical accident in an otherwise beneficent social
structure.

During the sixties, this view began to lose its credibility,
with the growing awareness of the depth of racial oppression
and powerlessness in the North and of the inability of conventional civil-rights legislation to overcome it. This was powerfully demonstrated in the ghetto uprisings in Watts, Newark,
Detroit, and other cities, and confirmed by the rise of a more
militant and radical movement for black liberation.

All of this resulted in a reinterpretation of the meaning of
racism in the United States, a reappraisal of the significance
of racism in American history, and a recognition that racism
is more deeply entrenched in contemporary American institutions in ways that the civil rights movement barely touched.
The following selections explore these themes in various ways.

The first casualty of American racism was the "Indian." In
"Freedom for the American Indian," Alvin Josephy shows how
the history of relations between whites and Native Americans
has been one of consistent efforts to subordinate Indian lands,
resources, and culture to the needs of the economy as interpreted by whites. Josephy shows that the assault on Indian
lands and resources is not just a shameful episode in the distant past – it continues today. Railroads, coal and power companies, resort developers, and others threaten to turn what is
left of the Indians' former lands – the reservations – into
"white men's domains." Josephy believes the best means of
creating independence for Native Americans is to create genuine tribal governments; but whether this is a realistic goal in
the face of the power of dominant economic and political interests is a real question.

The experience of Mexicans in the United States has been similar to that of the Native Americans in that both had well-established societies and cultures here before the coming of Anglo civilization. Both groups saw much of their land taken and their indigenous cultures threatened and attacked as American capitalism expanded westward. Both are now forced into the lowest rungs of the economy and subjected to attempts to assimilate them into the dominant culture, with its foreign language and often incomprehensible values of competition and individual striving. The selections from Stan Steiner's book, *La Raza*, illustrate various aspects of the Mexican-American experience, from the barrio of Los Angeles to the colonias of South Texas.

The experience of blacks has been shaped by similar economic and political forces, but has taken different forms. Harold Baron describes the situation of blacks in the cities since World War II. From a mainly southern agricultural population before the war, blacks have become a key part of the industrial economy of the North and the West. But they have been locked into what Baron calls a "secondary labor market" — the hardest, dirtiest, and poorest paying jobs; and their economic position is reinforced by a web of other racist institutions, such as the housing market and the schools.

The exploitation of these and other groups in the United States has been accompanied by racial ideologies that explain and justify it on the grounds of the inferiority of the oppressed groups and the superiority of white Western culture and institutions. In the final selection, Robert Blauner provides a general analysis of the tendency of white Western culture to deny or discredit the culture and values of Third World groups. Blauner illustrates the devastating impact of this on the cultures and institutions of the oppressed, but also argues that racism has important functions for the culture of the dominant group itself. Particularly in new and relatively fragmented societies, the downgrading of others becomes a way of fortifying and supporting their own precarious culture. And to the extent that racism is necessary to the integration of the dominant culture, eradicating it will be an even more difficult task than is usually supposed.

REFERENCES

1. John Dollard, *Caste and Class in a Southern Town* (Garden City, N.Y.: Doubleday Anchor, 1949); St. Clair Drake and Horace

R. Cayton, *Black Metropolis: A Study of Negro Life in a Northern City,* rev. ed. (New York: Harper Torchbooks, 1962).

2. For an example of this kind of analysis, see Arnold M. Rose, "Race and Minority Relations," in Robert K. Merton and Robert A. Nisbet, eds., *Contemporary Social Problems* (New York: Harcourt, Brace and World, 1961).

3. Gunnar Myrdal, *An American Dilemma* (New York: Harper and Row, 1962).

12. FREEDOM FOR THE AMERICAN INDIAN

Alvin M. Josephy, Jr.

During the last few years there has been an outpouring of information on American Indians. Books and magazine articles; radio and television documentaries, discussions, and commentaries; movies; and newspaper reports and editorials have focused attention with new and more accurate perspectives on Indian cultural backgrounds, Indian-white history, and present-day Indian needs and aspirations.

One result is that non-Indian Americans today are more understanding than they have ever been of the Indian side of what happened in the *past.* The Native Americans who resisted the intruding whites from the time of Jamestown and Plymouth to the last battle on the plains are now seen as patriotic peoples who struggled righteously for their lives, lands, freedom, religious beliefs, and means of livelihood. Although Indian scholars, still to come, will add breadth and depth to the record from their own cultural and tribal insights, the long history of past shame is clear for all who will read or listen.

Despite all that has been written and said, however, what is more important to the contemporary Indian — his own problems, wants, and goals of *today,* not of the past — seems still confusing to most non-Indian Americans, not alone among the nation's opinion makers and the general public, but in the areas of the federal government that deal with Indian affairs. As a result, sound and harmonious relations between In-

From *The Critic.* © 1973 by the Thomas More Associates, 180 North Wabash Avenue, Chicago, Illinois 60601. Reprinted by permission.

dians and non-Indians appear to many people to be as elusive today as they were to the whites and Native Americans of the past.

The fault is often ascribed to two principal gaps in thinking, one historic and the other cultural. On the historical level, the non-Indian has become aware of what happened in the past, but he feels that that is all over and cannot be undone, and that the Indian of 1973 — a full century after Custer — should "shape up" and be like everyone else. The continuation of reservations puzzles him. Are they concentration camps, or what? He is mystified by the special relationship between the federal government and the Indians that seems to perpetuate, at one and the same time, an incompetent, sometimes corrupt bureaucratic rule by Washington over the Indians, and a helpless, but apparently willing, dependence by the Indians on the federal treasury. Why does it go on? Who is at fault?

The Indians, at the same time, view history differently. Once, they knew, they were free people, thoroughly capable of governing themselves, and all of the present-day United States was theirs. The white man subjugated and dispossessed them. The small portions of land that were left to them (land that had never belonged to anyone else) — or that were given to them by the government, because all of their own territory had been stolen from them — were set aside as reservations for their sole possession and use, with guarantees made to them in solemn treaties that the federal government would protect these reservations for as long as the Indians wished. As payment for the land that was taken, the government promised services — education, health facilities, vocational training, roads, and so forth.

There are about 1,000,000 Indians in the United States today (the estimates of their pre-Columbian population in the same area range from 850,000 up to 9,800,000). About half of them live on reservations and half in urban and rural areas. But almost all of them consider themselves the descendants and inheritors of the peoples who made the treaties with the federal government. To them, not only is the history of the past very much alive, but they are the continuers of that history. Small as their numbers may be, they are the Indian past that is still running like an unbroken thread through our body politic and through many present-day concerns. The land of the reservations is all they have left, but it is still theirs and no one else's. Although it is only a token of what they once had, it is sacred to them for what it means as the repository of their tribal culture, history, and traditions; the burial grounds of their fathers; the homes of their families; the last tie they possess with their mother, the Earth, and with all of nature; the firm root of their existence as Indians and tribal peoples; and the basis of whatever prospects they have for a future as Indians. Their history, up to the present day, has been one of struggle to force the government to live up to its treaty promises and protect the reservations against the erosions and exploitation of non-

Indians. Far from being concentration camps, in short, the reservations are beloved and guarded as homelands by the tribes, and the people can come and go from them as they please.

This sense of an unbroken connection with the historic past reflects the first gap of information between Indians and non-Indians. The Indian is very much aware of the details of the treaties and promises made to his ancestors; the white man, in or out of government, is not. The Indian is also aware of the details of federal–Indian relations from the time when the treaties were made. They include broken promises; zigzagging policies of different administrations in Washington; frauds, lies, and injustices by the score; stern rule by tyrannical agents, missionaries, and army officers; punishments; denial of rations; the stamping out of native languages, religion, and culture; the shanghaiing of children for enforced attendance at distant white men's schools; the smashing of tribal institutions, values, and standards, and the substitution of alien forms; the bringing of poverty with no solutions; and, finally, prejudice, persecutions, neglect, aimlessness, and death. The Indians knew this history, year by year, on one reservation after another. The whites know it only vaguely — in stereotypes and fuzzy generalizations, no more graphic than was the list just recited. The Indian therefore knows exactly what he would like to end; the white man would agree that it should be ended, but he is not exactly sure of what — other than poverty — there is to end.

The cultural gap between Indians and non-Indians is even wider than the historical. Since 1924, Indians have been citizens of the United States. They have the vote and in almost all ways except the most important — the possession of freedom (to be discussed later) — they are considered like all other Americans. They need, use, and enjoy the material traits of modern-day civilization. Some of them are thoroughly acculturated, and even assimilated, into the white man's society. Many are truly bicultural, at home on reservations but equally able to get on in white men's cities. But almost all of them are knowingly and feelingly still Indians, possessors of cultural values, standards, and beliefs that they inherited from their peoples and that differ profoundly from those of the non-Indians.

A whole literature exists on Indian life and beliefs. They differed in some ways from tribe to tribe, but there were many samenesses. The Indians' concepts of their relations to their fellowmen, to the supernatural, and to nature and the Earth were basically somewhat similar among tribes in all areas of the Western Hemisphere. To non-Indians, with a background of Judeo-Christian religion and philosophy and Western European socioeconomic and political development, Indian ways were different and, therefore, inferior. Cooperation rather than competition; group orientation rather than personal ambition; stewardship of nature rather than its conquest; brotherhood with all creation rather than dominion over it —

these were just a few among many of the Indians' ways which were brushed aside and ignored by the white conqueror.

But they did not die. The cultural values, too, are part of the Indian thread that still runs through the United States, believed in and observed by peoples of Indian blood and background, whether they live on reservations or in cities. The proof of their ability to endure exists strikingly in the Atlantic coastal states where Indian tribes were smashed into small and powerless fragments, then overrun, absorbed, and forgotten by non-Indians long before the American Revolution. Today their descendants have emerged as cohesive groups — Penobscots, Micmacs, Malecites, Passamaquoddies in Maine; Wampanoags in Massachusetts; Narragansets in Rhode Island; Niantics, Pequots, Mohegans, and others in Connecticut; Patchogues, Shinnecocks, and Montauks, among others, in New York; Chickahominys, Powhatans, and Rappahannocks in Virginia; Croatans (descendants, perhaps, of those who absorbed Raleigh's "Lost Colony" in 1587) in North Carolina; and many others — still Indians, still proud of their tribal heritages, still clinging to their ancestral cultural values — which continue to be markedly different from those of the rest of American society.

If those values have persisted in the East among people who have been overrun and submerged by the white man for more than two centuries, then how strong they must still be among the more recently conquered peoples, like the Sioux, Cheyenne, Navajos, and many dozens of others in the West, who continue to observe such spiritual ceremonies as the Sun Dance, use their own curers and purify themselves with the sweat bath, go on vision quests, and honor their holy men. And how impossible, it seems to imply, it has been — and will be — for the white man to eradicate them and turn the Indian fully into a white man, living in complete accordance with the white man's cultural values.

Almost all Indians (and, in fairness, some white men) have viewed such an effort as immoral and, indeed, incredibly short-sighted and self-defeating. But the drive and power of the dominant culture have shown neither interest in, nor patience with, the Indians' ways. The white man has not cared to understand Indian culture, much less consider that it could co-exist with his own, and he is totally at sea when the Indian clothes his words and actions in terms of his own culture, as he did recently in stating his purposes during the occupations of Alcatraz Island, the Bureau of Indian Affairs Building in Washington, D.C., and the region of Wounded Knee in South Dakota. There was, of course, nothing novel about the white man's reactions to each of these confrontations. He viewed them as lawless outbursts by radical minorities among the Indians and missed the point entirely that though they were desperate attempts (the only methods left to the Indians) to call the nation's attention to their terrible oppression and suffering (something many whites did un-

derstand), they were even more important as efforts to break the bonds
of their yearnings to save themselves as Indians by saving their Indian
cultural traditions and heritage. Not all Indians approved of the militant
and violent tactics and damage at the Bureau of Indian Affairs and at
Wounded Knee. But most Indians knew what it was all about, agreed
with the aims of the occupiers, and prayed for their safety and success.

In a sense, those recent Indian–white confrontations, accompanied by
patronization, brutal insensitivity, and lack of understanding on the part
of too many whites who were involved, illuminated the depth of the
historical and cultural gaps that still separate Indians and non-Indians.
In a way, also, they climaxed the long centuries of a misguided white
policy toward Indians that began in the first English colonies on the
Atlantic. Until 1890, it was one of assimilate or die. Since then, and until
today, it has been assimilate or stagnate in poverty. Both ideas, one a
continuation of the other, have been at the heart of the nation's Indian
policy since the first Administration of George Washington. The most
benign concept of white men toward Indians has been that of saving
them by turning them, as quickly as possible, into white men — Christian-
izing them, settling them down as farmers or mechanics, cutting their
hair, clothing them as whites, educating them without reference to their
own history, culture, language, or background, and getting them to disappear as white men in the white man's world. Programs changed from
one administration to the next, but each was designed to speed up the
assimilation process — and each, in turn, failed. As part of the process,
the Indian was stripped and robbed of whatever might impede assimilation — among them, his freedom of religion, his tribal institutions, his
mythology and artistic inheritance, and his land and resources. In 1934
he regained his religious freedom. But assimilation is still the aim of
national Indian policy. Hobbled by the historic and cultural gaps which
perpetuate his ignorance and confusion about the Indians' real needs and
goal, the non-Indian American continues to view assimilation as the best
— indeed, the only — destiny for the Indians. He gives this as a mandate
to the federal government, which through appropriate committees in
Congress and the Bureau of Indian Affairs (the executive branch's agency
in the Department of the Interior charged with handling relations with
the Indians), persists in trying to carry it out. In the process, Indian lands
and resources, the basis for continued Indian life, are not protected (the
whittling away of Indian assets increasing, of course, Indian poverty),
and Indian self-determination, even though proclaimed as an Administration goal by President Nixon in July, 1970, is frustrated.

Serious as they have been as impediments blocking the non-Indians'
understanding and support of Indian aims, the historic and cultural gaps
obfuscated the actual mainspring of the nation's traditional Indian policy

and the true motive behind the drive to force Indian assimilation. Stated bluntly, it has been — and continues to be — the acquisitive greed for Indian lands and resources. Many non-Indians undoubtedly believe that the era when the Indians were defrauded and cheated of their lands is over. But the facts are the opposite. Indians have never been permitted rest in their fight to save what they have. Today the assault against the reservations is more massive and threatening to them than at any time in the recent past. Dams are flooding the best parts of their lands. Rights-of-way for railroad lines, transmission lines, highways, and other facilities are slicing through the reservations. Leases for huge real estate developments, white men's resorts, coal strip mines, and power, gasification, and petrochemical plants are being approved for the reservations by the Department of the Interior.

All these developments, plumped down on top of the Indians, industrializing their lands, and making less of the reservation available for them, may be viewed as hastening assimilation. But that is putting the cart before the horse. The real effect is that the reservations are being taken away from the Indians and turned into white men's domains. The methods used, moreover, are the same as those of the past. The Navajos, Hopis, Crows, Northern Cheyennes, and many others have all been victimized by fraud, cheating, lies, and deceit in the leasing of their lands and resources during the last few years.

Scores of Indians are articulate today in expressing their people's needs and demands. Individuals, tribes, and regional and national Indian organizations have grown expert in using the white man's own media to try to communicate what they want. In time, they will undoubtedly bridge the historic and cultural gaps, bringing non-Indians to see their destiny as they see it. But achieving that destiny will be impossible until the mainspring of national Indian policy is, so to speak, smashed, and the taking of Indian lands and resources is checked. The only instrument with which this can be accomplished is what all Americans, save Indians, possess: freedom. Without it, as they now are, their lands, lives, decisions, and fate are at the mercy of a government primarily responsive to outside aggrandizers. Without it, their boundaries of existence narrow and their future as Indians shrivels. To the Indians, there is method in the determination of the government, up to now, to talk self-determination and freedom for them, but in practice to deny it.

What is the relation of the government to the Indians that denies them freedom? In 1934, the Indian Reorganization Act imposed on almost every tribe in the country a uniform type of government, modeled after the white man's ways, with constitutionally-elected tribal officers, a tribal council, or legislature, and tribal courts. For most tribes, it was a tragic mistake. The Indians were used to their own traditional forms of government — whether by clan leaders, traditional chiefs, councils of elders, or some other group or individual — and, in large numbers, they resented and boycotted the alien system that was foisted on them. Constitutions were accepted by small voting minorities in many tribes, and to this day the tribal governments are divisive institutions on numerous reservations, ignored by majorities of the people. Worse still, the powers of the Indian governments were limited. Over all important matters, the Bureau of Indian Affairs maintained absolute control, with the right to approve or veto. Much like the native legislatures in British colonial governments, the tribal councils became little more than ceremonial rubber stamps for the real authority that lay with the white man.

As a consequence, the tribal governments became responsive, and responsible, to the Bureau of Indian Affairs, rather than to their own people. The Bureau, in turn, being responsible to Congress for "no trouble on the reservations," ran the tribes in collusion with pliant and venal tribal officers who basked in the prestige and petty rewards of their positions. This situation, in which reservation peoples often refer to their officeholders as "Uncle Tomahawks" and "Apples" (red outside, white inside), has perpetuated dependence, dulled initiative, and made a sham of real self-determination. Though the present administration regards the tribal councils as the organs of Indian freedom, the real boss is still the Bureau of Indian Affairs.

The question of the authority of the Bureau has been muddied by its position as trustee of Indian lands and resources, a function which almost every tribe wishes it to continue to fulfill. How, asks the Bureau, can we give up ultimate authority and still act responsibly as trustee? The answer lies in an analogy. A bank can be a trustee for a white man's money or property, carry out that function with or without consultation with its client, and have no authority over any other part of that person's life. But, beginning with its trust responsibility over tribal property, the federal government, through the Bureau of Indian Affairs, has insidiously extended its governance over every other portion of an Indian's life. To be convinced, one has only to sit for a day in the outer office of a Bureau agency on any reservation and see the stream of Indians coming in, hat in hand, for advice, approval, and permission in a hundred personal and varied matters. Relatively few Indians turn to their own tribal institutions. They go to the government for approval of wills, for advice on travel, and for a weekly or monthly allowance doled out to them arbitrarily from part of the rental receipts from land leased to whites.

With great truth, Warren H. Cohen and Philip J. Mause wrote in the *Harvard Law Review* in June, 1968: "Although normal expectation in American society is that a private individual or group may do anything unless it is specifically prohibited by the government, it might be said that the normal expectation on the reservation is that the Indians may not do anything unless it is specifically permitted by the government."

This is not freedom.

As a result of the confrontations at the Bureau of Indian Affairs Building and at Wounded Knee, federal–Indian relations are today in a state of crisis. The Indians have made known their needs and demands, but Administration officials and Congress — either through lack of understanding, or because of a determination not to lose control of the Indians and their resources, have responded so far with proposals that are superficial and relatively meaningless — little more than a moving around of chairs, so to speak. None of their reactions go to the heart of relations between the Indians and the federal government, and nothing they propose can therefore succeed in satisfying the Indians or the challenges that the Indians have raised.

Yet the time for a revolutionary change in federal–Indian relations is here and now. The Indians have expressed it, and the form of that change can be stated in the following terms:

1. Within every town, city, county, and state, free Americans have local governments of their own choosing, free of interference by the federal government. Their systems of mayors, town managers, city councils, or whatever, are their own business. Federal officials or agents may be in those areas to carry out the delivery of federal programs to local citizen groups, who may be considered the clients or beneficiaries of the programs. But the local affairs of the people are not the concern of the federal personnel. If there is a local political problem, the people have the means through their own systems of government to handle it themselves. Their governments normally are responsive and accountable to the people. In times of local conflict, the federal officials sit in a corner and read a newspaper. The problem is not theirs.

The Indian tribes must attain the same level of freedom. The dominant society must stand back and enable the people of each tribe to create governments of their own choosing with the full freedom to manage and control their own affairs. If such governments are established, they will of necessity be responsive and responsible to their individual peoples and will provide the basis for what is now missing: The enforcement of the government's trusteeship obligations over lands and resources; protection of treaty rights; the design and execution of development programs that the people really want and will make succeed; educational and other institutions that have meaning for their people; contracting with nongovernmental, as well as governmental, agencies for technical assistance, credit, and services; and the effective safeguarding of their people against discrimination, abuse, and injustices.

2. Simultaneously, the Bureau of Indian Affairs must be stripped of its authority over the tribes and become, in fact as well as in theory, a

service organization, limited in its functions to the delivery of expertise, services, and credit to Indian clients at their request. The present status of the Bureau, on reflection, is ludicrous. In effect, it is charged with being an entire supergovernment over the tribes, with departments and individuals supposedly expert in every phase of modern-day community activity and individual life. It must be expert on the reclamation of strip-mined land, on the buying of school books, on marital problems, on water rights law, on the harvesting of timber, on corporate relations, on the hiring of a lawyer, and on tens of thousands of other matters, many of them vital to Indian concerns. All these spheres of expertise are often centered in one all-powerful bureaucrat or in a small group of his assistants, whose judgments are often autocratically imposed on the Indians, whether they are right or wrong, wanted or unwanted. It is an impossibility to be so infallible, not only in so small an agency, but in one in which mediocrity and incompetence have been hallmarks.

When a tribe needs technical assistance for its people, it should have the freedom to seek the best and, by contract underwritten by the federal government, make its own arrangements with the private, as well as the public sector. But the most important principle must be one, again, of freedom: the B.I.A. personnel, as well as all federal officials, must relate to the Indians and their governments on nontrustee affairs in the same manner in which federal agents relate to non-Indian citizens and their local governments. In Indian matters, they should no longer be permitted to take sides, and they should not have the right to interfere. Their sole duties should be to deliver services adequately funded by the federal government as guaranteed by treaties.

In such a state of affairs, with totally free governments of their own choosing, and with the right to manage and control their own lives as they see fit, Indian initiative will inevitably be unfettered. Compared with the past and present record of the white man thinking for the Indian and doing everything for him — a record replete with maladministration, petty tyranny, and failure — the future will seem like an age of miracles. Even if there are mistakes, internal conflicts, and inefficiency, it can be no worse than what has been and what is. Moreover, it will be the Indians' own business; they have the right, like everyone else, to make mistakes and, by making them, learn and gain experience. If they have truly accountable governments, with such safeguards as methods for referendums, the handling of corruption, and the protection of individual and tribal rights, all must ultimately be far superior to what now exists.

3. To carry out the trustee function, a special management-and-legal apparatus should be created within the federal government, separate from the B.I.A. service delivery organization, responsible to the Indians alone, and charged with a commitment to the trust obligation. Its functions must be the management of trustee affairs and the determined

protection of tribal lands, water rights, and mineral and other resources. Its relationship to the Indians should approximate that of a bank and lawyer to their client, and it should have nothing to do with any other phase of the Indians' life.

This relationship between the federal government and the Indians would provide the underpinnings for the settling and solving of all other matters. There are numerous demands of a bewildering variety that must be negotiated between free Indians and the federal government. The Indians participating in "The Trail of Broken Treaties," which occupied the Bureau of Indian Affairs Building in October, 1972, presented the government with a set of twenty demands which should provide guidelines for such negotiations. They include, among other points, a review and rectification of broken treaties, the enforcement of treaty rights; the re-establishment of a treaty-making relationship between the tribes and the government; and the inclusion of off-reservation Indians and members of tribes not now federally recognized as recipients of programs for Indians.

What has been proposed here is not in conflict with any Indian demand. It is addressed to the non-Indian, in and out of government, who is confused about the present status of the Indian and the substance of what he wants. It calls only for Indian freedom — the prerequisite for meaningful negotiations for everything else.

13. LA RAZA: THE MEXICAN-AMERICANS

Stan Steiner

THE MASKS OF THE INVISIBLE MEN

On a fertile riverbank where a tribe of Indians had built a village of mud and reed huts, a strange band of brown, black, yellow, and red men appeared one day in 1781. These travelers decided to settle amid the native Californians. Industriously they built mud and reed huts of their own, and then proclaimed the tribal village to be a city — *El Pueblo de Nuestra*

Señora la Reina de los Ángeles de Porciuncula. In other words, L.A.

The old faded records of the "Patron de Los Angeles" in the Bancroft Library of Berkeley list these "Spanish settlers" who were the founding fathers of the city:

Nine Mexican Indians
Eight Mulattos
Two Blacks
Two Espanoles
One Mestizo

And there was the gentleman widower by the name of Antonio Rodríguez who alone had come without a wife. Rodriguez was Chinese.

Of the twenty-three "Spanish settlers" who founded Los Angeles only two were Spanish. The earlier expeditions into the Southwest by Don Juan de Oñate, Father Kino, Don Juan Bautista de Anza, and Father Garces had found few white faces. When the lost party of Cabeza de Vaca wandered for a decade through the Southwest in the 1530's, one of those bedraggled men found was Estévanico, the black Moor. One of the first Europeans to set foot in the Southwest was thus an African. On the expeditions of the Spaniards, the men and women recruited from the barrios of Mexican Indians and African slaves outnumbered the Spaniards by two and three to one.

The pueblos they built around quiet plazas were more like those of the Indians than the grandiloquent style of baroque Spain. In their leisurely old houses decendants of the Españoles Mejicanos, the Mexican-born "Spanish," lived for hundreds of years. Nowadays all that remains of the memory of the original settlements is the tourist attractions: the "Old Town Plaza" of Albuquerque and Olvera Street in downtown Los Angeles, but the heirs of the founding fathers have long since been deprived of their cultural inheritance and their property.

History has all but obliterated our dark-skinned forefathers, who, after all, do not fit the romantic image of Spanish courtiers who, in the mythology of the textbooks, settled the Southwest.

"Old Spanish families are an invention of the gringos," wrote Arnold R. Rojas, the descendant of a generations-old Los Angeles family, in his *The Vaquero.*

They are a myth which paisanos have come to believe themselves as Sancho did his enchantment of Dulcinea in *Don Quixote.* . . . The *Californiano* — writers on California to the contrary — called himself a *Sonoreno.* [Sonora, the northernmost province of Mexico, once embraced California.] I have heard third- and fourth-generation descendants of members of the De Anza expedition (in 1777) say, "*Nosotros somos Sonorenos. Sonora es nuestra tierra.*" We are Sonorans, Sonora is our motherland.

When the gringos took over the land, the paisano — if he did not migrate to

Mexico, Chile, or Spain — gathered what few cattle were left him and disappeared into the most distant and isolated places he could find in the West, as far away from the marauding bands of gringos as he could get. Where is he now? Ask the lonely canyons and deserts of the far places. They could tell if they could talk."

In coming to the cities the rural villagers were returning to the homes of their forefathers. They rebuilt the barrios, in the style of the twentieth century, but they were strangers in their own cities.

"Who's got the land? Who's got the money? Who's got everything?" asks Eduardo Pérez. "You Europeans who came here have taken our land away by conquest, have taken our jobs away with machines, have taken our women with false promises. We do not give up our women, but you take them. You have taken everything from us but our color. And you probably are working on that."

The newcomers from the East who had driven the Mexicans out thought of the original settlers as "foreigners." They viewed the "Little Mexicos" of the cities with a mixture of fascination and fear, hatred and envy.

In the twenties, there was an uproar over the barrios. The isolationism of the times, as the country recoiled from the traumas of World War I, and the uneasy peace that was haunted by the specter of the Bolshevik Revolution, had culminated in a national hysteria against the "foreigners." Cries of "The World Is at Our Portals" and "Guard Our Gates" were echoed in the Southwest as "Keep Out the Mongrel Mexicans" and "Lock the Back Door." The mounting revolutions of Mexico, from the fall of Porfirio Díaz in 1910 to the triumph of Pancho Villa in 1917, had frightened newcomers to the Southwest and terrified the real-estate developers.

The rhetoric of racism was voiced nationally by the warning of a Justice of the Supreme Court of New York, Norman Dike, who proclaimed, "Diseased, ignorant and belonging to a greatly lower class, the Mexican elements are lowering the standard of our population as far north as Wyoming." The Mexicans, said the Justice, were "the most undesirable of all of the peoples."

Justice Dike's was one of the more somber voices. The chorus of exclusion reached its highest pitch in a book called *The Alien in Our Midst*, published in 1930. William Green, the president of the American Federation of Labor, and John E. Edgerton, president of the National Federation of Manufacturers, called in unison for those "who are American in blood" to "call the roll of the armies of gunmen in our cities . . . worst criminals . . . anarchists, communists, foreign language newspapers and other lists of disturbers containing unpronounceable or exchanged names" (Edgerton); and "to guard our gates" and ensure that "the Country contains at all times a great preponderance of those of British descent" (Green); for, as the president of the Immigration Study

Commission, C. M. Goethe, wrote in that volume, the "Mexican menace to our homogeneity" threatens "our race purity."

On a fact-finding trip into the barrios of East Los Angeles, during 1927, the historical novelist Kenneth Roberts was shocked to find not only "Mexican half-breed Indians," but "negroid blood" in the "chocolate-colored Mexican peons." In *The Alien in Our Midst* (edited by Madison Grant, Chairman of the New York Zoological Society), the disturbed novelist wrote that the Mexican "mixed breeds [are] unfit to enter the United States," for "they are inferior to immigrants from Central and Southeastern Europe, and incompetent to advance, or even sustain the civilization already established in the United States."

Late that winter Roberts accompanied a "Relief Mission" of East Los Angeles "through two Mexican sections"; he wrote, ". . . in no part of Poland or Southeastern Europe has ever been seen a more ignorant and more destitute class of people than the Mexican peons packed into shacks and hovels that have spread out over those former truck garden districts. . . . The signs are in Spanish, the names are Mexican. They are an acute plague sore on the body politic." Roberts then quoted Professor S. J. Holmes of the University of California: " 'The Mexican is prone to various diseases . . . he brings in various maladies. . . . They are a constant menace to our physical welfare.' "

In the 1930's the barrios were of less interest to the civic authorities. The building booms of the Southwest collapsed in the money-tight depressions, and the lands of the "Little Mexicos" were no longer needed. Many emigrants decided to return to Mexico rather than face the humiliation of bread lines, and for several years the tide of immigration turned. Even the "Lock the Back Door" advocates were silenced by the unexpected turn of the poor away from the promised land.

"I remember back thirty years," says one woman, reliving the Depression years in East Los Angeles.

The leaders of the community in those years were what I call hard-core Mexico Mexicans who did sort of well. They had stores, you know. In those days we had a community organization where there would be dancing and vino and "Viva Mejico!" and the 16th of September and Cinco de Mayo, and the men drunken as the dickens and the gringos, they would be watching, and it would embarrass us. So we decided to keep away from those people. You see, at the time we thought a Mexico Mexican was something to be ashamed of.

There was little hope in the barrios in the dim thirties. The poor stayed within the safety of their homes and fought about scarce jobs and Cinco de Mayo dances; few entered into the upheavals of that decade that shook up the cities.

Life was in limbo until the post-World War II building boom exploded in the barrios. That upset the quiet forever. The old cities of the Southwest, from Texas to California, doubled and tripled and quadrupled in size and population in the wake of the affluence that swept through the deserts after World War II. A sleepy, Sonoran desert town like Tucson, Arizona, moved from 45,454 in 1950 to 236,877 in 1965; old Albuquerque, New Mexico, from 35,500 in 1940 to 201,200 in 1960; the metropolitan area of San Antonio, Texas, from 525,852 in 1950 to 787,000 in 1960.

Once more the old barrios stood in the way of progress and suburban developers. "Very rapid urbanization of the Southwest brought the absorption of [the] Mexican American barrios whose history can be traced to their function as former agricultural labor communities," says the report *Residential Segregation in the Urban Southwest* of the UCLA Mexican American Study Project. Some barrios were bulldozed. The oldest barrio of San Antonio in the heart of the city was leveled to rubble, and the 1,200 families that lived there were evicted to make way for the HemisFair of 1968.

The nemesis of the barrios of Los Angeles has, of course, been the freeways, Chavez Ravine, an old barrio that was bulldozed to make way for freeways, parking lots, and the Dodgers' Stadium, still echoes with the bitterness of the cry painted on the walls: "Remember Chavez Ravine!"

"Naturally they built it in our backyards," Grace Olivarez, a former state leader of Arizona, says of Highway 80, which curves through the backyards of the barrios of South Phoenix, Arizona. "Would you expect them to build a highway through the lawns of Scottsdale, or Goldwater's swimming pool?"

Hemmed in from the outside by the heritage of anti-Mexican racism and built up from the inside by the cultural pride of La Raza, the barrios were a paradox of poverty and strength. The barrios have existed for generations as communities with their own ways of life, their own leaders, their own language and culture and histories. Few outside would see, or would recognize, these hidden resources. The disguises of a colonial people are excellent.

"No one looked 'Mexican' to me when I came to East Los Angeles," Father Luce, a popular Episcopalian minister in the barrios, reports. "In the streets everyone looked so Anglo it startled me. I was determined to find out where the 'Mexicans' were hiding."

Even poverty is hidden. "I didn't know what poverty was until I found out that I was poor," says young David Sanchez, the prime minister of the Brown Berets, who grew up in the barrios of East Los Angeles. A university student, Frank David Cervantes, revisiting the barrios of his childhood in San Antonio, has the same startled thought. "I felt mostly shock and shame seeing this wasteland of poverty in which I had grown up. Until that moment I had never realized my family had lived in a 'slum.'" A judicious observer, Paul Bullock of the Institute of Industrial Relations, University of California, writes in *Poverty in the Ghetto*, "No one can deny that poverty is less 'visible' in Los Angeles."

"Society doesn't want to see us," says Eduardo Pérez. "Technology in the United States is so highly perfected that you cannot see anything you don't want to see. A computer is as blind as the technician who runs it."

La Raza is still referred to as "the invisible minority" in official reports. The barrios are largely unknown and misunderstood by outsiders, even those who devote years to studying them; for the heritage of a colonial mentality blinds outsiders to the reality.

It is no mystery to Eliezer Risco. "When you live in a hostile environment you learn to disguise yourself, so that you are not conspicuous. You wear a mask."

THE MAN WHO WORKED FOR THIRTY YEARS WITHOUT PAY

On the old Montoya Ranch in the hills to the north of Albuquerque, the boy came looking for a job. It was in the summer of 1933. He was then thirteen and he was hired as a ranch hand, for 75 cents a day. Abernicio Gonzales remembers the day with wincing, distant eyes. He remembers his mother had borrowed $50 to pay for the wedding of an older brother. He worked off the debt in about three months. Yet he went on working at the ranch for thirty-three years, and he says he was never paid a penny.

In those Depression days he was happy to have any job. He had been convinced, he says, to go on working for 50 cents a day and board. He was a hard worker; the rancher liked him and promised, since he was so young, to put his wages away for him. That way he would have money to live on when he was too old to work. He reluctantly agreed to this. Whenever the boy asked to see his bank account, he was cowed into silence. He was beaten when he tried to leave the remote ranch. The boy grew to be a man, but he was afraid to run away lest he lose the years of promised savings. He was a serf in the middle of the twentieth century in the United States.

One day in 1966 Gonzales fled from the Montoya Ranch. He was forty-six, penniless, a novice in the world, bewildered by his discovery of hatred. He sued for his thirty-three years of back pay, at 50 cents a day, with 6 percent interest, but obviously no court could repay him for his lost youth and stolen manhood.

A boy may be intimidated. But why would the grown man go on as the boy began? Year after year he lived as if he were a slave. He had enslaved himself. The habits and fears of a man who feels he has no rights bind him to servitude as tightly as if he were chained.

"There are hundreds of people kept in slavery on remote ranches throughout the Southwest of the United States," declares *El Malcriado*, the newspaper of the farm workers. "It is well known. . . ."

No man has fewer rights. The campesino earns less in wages and respect than anyone else. If he is a migrant worker "his earnings are the lowest of our Nation's work force," the Senate Subcommittee on Migratory Labor reports in *The Migratory Farm Labor Problem in the United States* (1967). In recent years these migrants averaged little over $1,100 annually from field work. And they were lucky to add $600 from odd jobs, off season. The hired hands who were regularly employed did somewhat better, but not much.

There are more farm workers in the country than steel workers, auto workers, or aircraft workers. In spite of Rube Goldberg farm machines the census counters say there are 1,400,000 farm workers. Of these over 200,000 are migrants. Since the census counters do not reach the remote ranches, the unseen alleys of the barrios, and the elusive "commuters" from across the Rio Grande, there are undoubtedly many more who are uncounted. Farm workers are a hungry army.

In the fields wages are not only "the lowest," but are getting lower. The output per man on the farm zoomed 270 percent from 1947 to 1964, while wages increased only 64 percent, but in the factories, during the same years, output per man went up 160 percent, while wages increased only 107 percent. Unlike farm workers the factory workers have unions. "The gap between agricultural and nonagricultural earnings has continually widened," reports the Senate Subcommittee. Not only that, but "between 1940 and 1964 gross farm income increased from $11.1 to $42.2 billion. Yet the average farm worker today still earns a daily wage under $9. No other segment of our population is so poorly paid yet contributes so much to our Nation's health and welfare."

> So I tell my friends
> Not to sell themselves;
> He who sells himself
> Always will be the loser.

It is a song of the campesinos by the young grape picker, poet, and singer of El Teatro Campesino, Agustín Lira. He sings:

> Look, look, look, look,
> Look, look, how they work;
> If they stop to rest
> They lose their jobs.

The campesino often feels he is trapped by his labor in the fields of a stranger. Says a campesino in Delano, "You just don't get out of the fields. I think it's very heavy. It's something you are stuck with for the rest of your life. You just can't start anywhere else because you don't have the education, you don't have the experience."

"I am nothing," says another campesino. "My children, they will get an education and they will be someone."

"We have nothing but our hands. Empty hands," a woman says.

It is a feeling of nothingness voiced in the lament of *El Malcriado:*

We have seen how they have taken the work of our hands and our bodies and made themselves rich while we are left with empty hands between the earth and the sky. We who are farm workers have been insulted. We have seen ourselves treated like cattle. We have seen our children treated like inferiors in the schools. We have seen in the face of the cop our inequality before the law. We have known what it is like to be less respected, to be unwanted, to live in a world which did not belong to us.

In a small house on the edge of town the campesino lives quietly. He bothers no one. Usually he stays as far away from the downtown streets as he can. He feels uncomfortable there.

A man says, "They want our business. But they do not like us. We do not go where we are not wanted."

He is an urban man, nonetheless. Most campesinos nowadays live in the cities. Even in the supermetropolis of Los Angeles, a state of California study of employment shows that 7 percent of the men in the barrios of East Los Angeles are farm workers. The myth of the "footloose" and "shiftless" migrant externally wandering in an old jalopy, like a poor, dirty gypsy, no longer exists in the urban Southwest — except in old movies.

Still he does not take part in urban life. He is ignored by the city elites, of whatever group. He pays little in taxes, for his income is too low, and so he has no voice. He is unrepresented in the city where he lives.

"You see, the farm worker is an outsider, even though he may be a resident worker," says Cesar Chavez. "He is an outsider economically, and he is an outsider racially. Most farm workers are of ethnic backgrounds other than white.

"And so, with very few exceptions, they have not been part of the communities where they live. Most of them don't know how or why or by whom laws are made. Who governs them. None of these things. They don't really care," Chavez says.

It is his isolation from the sources of power over his own life that has made the campesino abject. The gap between the two sections of town, much less two societies, has seemed unbridgeable. "Our color, or our language, or our job, have kept us apart," says *El Malcriado.* "And the people who are profiting from our separateness are determined to keep it that way."

A campesino looks around and sees that he is treated as though he were nonexistent. The laws that protect other workers do not apply to him. In the fields the health codes are often ignored. In the farm towns the normal sanitation and civic services often do not reach his little house. Even his ordinary needs on the job — like water to drink and the use of toilets — are ignored. Housing regulations are not enforced in his barrios and *colonias.* "The same labor camps which were used thirty years ago, at the time of the La Follette Committee hearings, are still housing our workers," Chavez tells the Senate Subcommittee on Migratory Labor. "Nothing has changed."

Campesinos are not the invisible men of the ghetto. They are vigorous, sensuous, full of life, strenuous sinews, bright as the sun itself, and at times darkly emotional. In the bars they are boisterous, yelling *"Viva!"* to the TV; and in the churches they are reverent, passionately and publicly. They suffer few identity crises. Yet, these same men will say, "I am nothing!"

The nothingness of the campesino is the recognition of what exists, the way life is. It is not simply self-denial, nor is it the humility of the poor. His is a world of nothings. It descends on the labor camps and barrio homes from the world outside with an almost physical force. Like an impenetrable white fog, it is sometimes so dense it hides the identity of a man from himself.

"I will tell you the truth," says a young campesino in Del Rio, Texas. "When I am among you people, I am not the man I am. I am the man you think I am. A fool!"

"Who emasculated us? I say we emasculate our own manhood," says Rodolfo Gonzales. "For what? The crumbs on the table we have been promised — someday. So we stoop to lick up the crumbs on the floor, saying, 'Yes sir! Yes, sir! Thank you, sir!'"

He scowls. "It's mental stoop labor."

It is "a world of fantasy," Cesar Chavez feels, a "mental attitude" that is the remnant of the old *patrón* syndrome that enslaves the campesinos through their own sense of helplessness and servility, as much as by the power of the ranchers. "It has a lot to do with paternalism. Before, when the employer came by, if the worker was dying of thirst, he would say, 'I'm not thirsty, *patrón.*' And whatever ailed him, or hurt him, he never complained. Now they come back, although they would want a union, more money, [they] keep believing these things. It's really a world of fantasy."

Not all of their fears are fantasies. There is the real fear of the invisible man who feels that he, or a relative, may be deported if he becomes too visible.

In retelling her tale of twenty years in the fields — of illnesses, deaths, hungers, and inhuman treatment — Mrs. Guadalupe Olivarez was questioned by the Senate Subcommittee on Migratory Labor:

Senator Robert Kennedy: "Have you reported it to anybody?"
Mrs. Olivarez: "No, sir."
Senator Robert Kennedy: "Why?"
Mrs. Olivarez: "Well, the one thing I will tell you why, we farm workers, we are afraid."
Senator Robert Kennedy: "Why are you afraid?"

Mrs. Olivarez: "Because I have seen it, sir. Well, I wouldn't mention names. We were not contented about what they did to us in the company we were working for, so we rebelled, and this was sort of a strike. And so there was one woman, you know, who spoke for all of us, and so that woman was fired because she was called an agitator. So, you see, sir, that's why we are afraid to speak."

There is the fear of hunger. . . .

In the kitchens the hunger is visible on the bare tables, in the motley dishes of beans and cereals. The odd and battered pots on the rickety kerosene stoves have a nauseous odor that mingles with the delicious aroma of hot chili cooking. And there is the rancid smell of powdered eggs and surplus food rations. These are the aromas of hunger.

The eyes of the children grow cold in the winter, although the kerosene stoves in the campesinos' homes exude an odorous heat. The work in the fields is seasonal, and during the winter there is not much to do. Men sit and wait. In the farm towns there is little to do but sit and wait — jobs are few, the jobless are many.

It is nonsense to talk of high wages and low wages in work so seasonal. The campesino has to earn enough in the growing and harvesting seasons, his entire family working, to last all winter. His family starves if they cannot save. The income of the campesinos is disputed. Statistics are hard to get. And those that are given are inadequate and inaccurate and contradictory. It is enough to say that they all seem to show that the annual income of the average campesino is about one-third of the national family income of a factory worker.

And this too makes a man fearful. He gets no wage he dare depend on. When the season comes, he never knows what it will bring. The drought and the rain that worry the farmer are worse for the campesino. His family may starve in the winter. So he works harder, travels faster, goes farther, complains less. Once the crops are harvested, there will be little for him to do but sit and wait for the spring.

Waiting demeans a man. He becomes sullen. He is nothing who does nothing.

"People who are hungry have no spirit, have no strength to fight. People who are hungry don't care who makes decisions for them, so long as their families don't starve," Cesar Chavez says. He says it emphatically, unusually so for him, with knowing harshness. "People who are hungry have to eat first of all."

" 'Eating comes before religion and art,' " he says. "That's an old Mexican proverb."

I ask him, "Even before love?"

"No," Chavez says with a half smile, "but certainly before politics. Bread and eggs on the table are the important thing."

In Starr County, Texas, a mother of six children talks of hunger. Her

name is Mrs. E. F. Gutierrez. She has been the director of a Community
Action Program for farm workers, going from barrio to barrio to soothe
the hungry with her words.

"There is out-and-out starvation," she says. "I have been in a home
where I have seen a small, two-year-old child eating oatmeal from the
original paper container, with her fingers. Dry and raw.

"And I said, 'Why don't you put it in a pot and cook it? It will taste
better.'

"And the mother said, 'I don't have a stove.'

"So I said, 'Why don't you mix it with a little water and sugar to make
it taste better?'

"And she said, 'I don't have a cup. I don't have sugar. I don't have a
spoon.' "

In the vineyards of Delano, a farm worker talks of hunger. His lips are
burnt by the sun. When he talks his words expose the scar tissue.

"When a man is hungry, he either gives up, or he becomes ruthless,"
he says.

"A man will kill for food. He will not kill another man. He will kill
himself. If a man becomes ruthless, he destroys love. Without love there
is no family. There is no life. There is nothing.

"Hunger does not kill a man," he says. "I know. The hungry man kills
himself, his senses, his morals, his manhood. I know."

THE REGION OF THE DAMNED

On the empty streets of Rio Grande City, Texas, a gray dust covers everything, like a patina of death. The faces of the people are as gray as the
walls. In the old cowboy hotels and empty bars, with their antique and
wheezing fans, no one talks to a stranger.

"It's a town of ghosts," a gaunt man says. He is called "The Skeleton"
by some.

"Who haunts it?" he is asked.

"The devil," says the gaunt man. "Or maybe the Texas Rangers."

Gilberto Padilla, a taut and intense farm worker from sunny California,
had come to the region of the damned to lead the *huelga* of the cantaloupe pickers and to organize the Farm Workers Union if he could. No
one in this "feudal town," as Padilla calls it, has ever organized a union,
and the *huelga* will be lost in beatings, jailings, and fear.

"We are afraid," a migrant worker says. His look is part of the death.

In the yard of his union office, the rotting house of a campesino, Padilla
looks at the dusty town, the muddy street where the scraggly chickens
peck futilely at the dry, caked tire tracks. "Cesar Chavez said to me,
'There's some problem in Texas. Go and see what's wrong.' That was in
January, 1967. I have been here ever since." He smiles so slightly that

his lips hardly quiver. "We do have 'some problem.' One problem we have is that the Rio Grande Valley is still in the Middle Ages. South Texas is a place of lords and serfs. Or maybe slaves."

A bony cow munches weeds in the wreckage of a junked car. Barking dogs fight over garbage. In bare feet a little girl in sackcloth plays in the mud of the road. Her lips and feet are covered with sores. It looks like any town in Mexico, without the exuberance and bright colors. Nowhere in the United States are there more dead and decayed towns than those of the farm workers in the beautiful valley of the Rio Grande.

"This is the poorest place in the whole country," says Froben Lozada, a local schoolteacher.

Clusters of shacks in the hidden edges of the fields resemble the back country of Guatemala. These are the *colonias* of the poor. Unseen from the highways, the *colonias* are ignored by the towns and counties; they are less tended than the town dump.

An ordinary *colonia*, like any other, is that of Madero (Timber). It is a cross between a Hooverville of the Depression and an Indian village of a century ago.

In a thicket of bushes and trees are huts built of straw and mud, old boards, and road signs. Some of the huts have outhouses. Some have compost heaps in the bushes. Flies swarm by the thousands. On the abandoned cars, where children sleep, chickens squat. Under the trees are old beds with sagging mattresses. There is no room in the huts. There are no stoves. In the winter the people burn wood in washtubs and carry the ashes and coals into the huts for warmth when the temperature drops below freezing, as it often does.

Half of the "houses" in the Lower Rio Grande Valley — 46 percent — have neither plumbing nor hot water, estimates Professor Claude Arenas, of the Department of City and Regional Planning of the University of Texas. At a conference, "Housing Problems in the Valley," sponsored by several federal, state, and local governmental agencies, in the summer of 1968, he tells the audience that 35,000 new houses are needed. But he is pessimistic. "I suspect the situation will get worse. The only question is the rate at which it will get worse."

Across the Rio Grande in Mexico it is the same. Carlos Nuno, an engineer employed by the Mexican Government in the bordertown of Reynosa, tells the conference that 50 percent of the houses in Mexico have "only one room, 60 percent lack water, and 39 percent have no windows." Nuno might be describing any of the *colonias* of Texas.

In the Lower Rio Grande Valley wages have been so depressed they resemble those of the Depression. The random survey of seventy-two farm workers in twelve barrios and *colonias* revealed that forty-six who labored in the cotton and vegetable fields, on hoeing, earned 45 to 75 cents an hour; twenty-six received 45 to 50 cents. The cantaloupe harvesters did better, earning 50 to 85 cents an hour, while the skilled tractor drivers were paid 60 to 90 cents an hour. One man, a cantaloupe picker, reported he earned $1 per hour. His was the highest wage reported. This was in the summer of 1967 when Padilla came to Rio Grande City.

And in Starr County, of which Rio Grande City is the county seat, 75 percent of the families, in 1960, lived beneath the poverty line of $3,000 a year. One-third of the families earned less than $1,000; one-third subsisted on welfare and surplus food.

"Many of the migrant farm workers in the lower Rio Grande Valley were living under conditions close to peonage or slavery," Father Theodore Hesburgh, the chairman of the United States Commission on Civil Rights, and president of Notre Dame University, was reported to have said (the *New York Times,* December 13, 1968) after an investigation of the plight of the *colonias.* That winter "180 rural slum villages with no roads or utilities" were studied. Father Hesburgh was appalled. He instructed the Commission's staff to determine whether the federal antipeonage laws were being violated.

Colonias are a separate world. The irony and anger of their names describe them: Blue Town, Ojo de Agua (Eye of the Water, or Whirlpool), Rancho Alegre (Happy Ranch), Campo Alto (High Field), Relampago (Lightning Bolt), La Paloma (The Dove), La Tijera (The Scissors), La Feria (The Fair).

There are dozens of the *colonias* in the valley, and there are hundreds in southwest Texas. Unseen and uncounted, the families that live in these *colonias* are not even statistics.

Into the region of the doomed comes the union of farm workers, and the Migrant Ministry of the Texas Council of Churches. The Reverend Edgar A. Krueger, a boyish-faced, soft-spoken evangelist of the United Church of Christ, who has worked for eight years in the fields with the migrants, is sent into the valley. He helps found the Colonias del Valle, a "weedroot organization," of twenty-three of the poorest colonies. He begins a self-help program, to build up the communities. "I really believe in self-determination," the young minister says, "so the people in the *colonia* can speak for themselves."

The *Noticias de las Colonias del Valle* (The News of the Colonies of the Valley), a single mimeographed sheet, is issued by the Reverends Edgar Krueger and Nehemias Garcia, the "migrant ministers." "In some areas 70 to 90 percent of the people are without work and without money," reports *Noticias.* "The vast majority of farm worker families have no welfare payments, nor any other financial support when they are without work. Farm workers are excluded from unemployment insurance."

When Christmas comes, the men of the *colonias* who are blessed by charity distribute boxes of food to the hungry families: ten pounds of beans and two pounds of lard for every four to eight people, a box of salt, a can of tomato sauce per person, and two cans of milk for each child under the age of two years. It is a "real Christmas spirit," says the *Noticias*.

"It's worse here than on the Mississippi Delta," says the teacher, Froben Lozada, who has lived and taught in both regions. "The people here are poorer than the poorest blacks. And they are even more thoroughly forgotten by the country. Who ever heard of the *colonias* in the East? Who cares about these people? No one! No one!" Unless you live in the *colonias* you cannot imagine "what a hell hole it is," Lozada says.

A woman organizer for the National Farm Workers' Union in the Rio Grande Valley says, "It's hot here. The weather drains all your strength. The water is bad and the scorpions drive me buggy. They have quite a few of them here, as well as rattlesnakes and rats. This evening Ishmael came in with his little kid who had been bitten by a rat. Tamar was bit by a scorpion yesterday."

The lemon-and-blue sky illuminates the *colonias* with brilliant light. Old carcasses of cars become iridescent. In contrast to the many colors of the sun, the stately palms, and the lushness of the farms in the valleys, the gray hunger seems even more like death.

Under the palm trees the tourists bask in the sun. Come to vacation amid the "palm-lined citrus groves and fresh vegetables in superabundance as far as the eye can see," says a brochure of the Lower Rio Grande Valley Chamber of Commerce. "This is the Fun Coast of Texas." Civic pride has named it "The Magic Valley." "Ever pick a sweet, juicy, ruby red grapefruit or an orange right off a tree?" asks a tourist come-on.

Froben Lozada says, "It would be more accurate to call it the Tragic Valley."

"The Valley, for all practical purposes, is an underdeveloped country," Professor Claudio Arenas says, ". . . similar in economic problems to African and Asian countries. The best solution for the Valley is to model itself after Puerto Rico, or possibly Israel."

Gilberto Padilla, "the Skeleton," is the appropriate man for this ghostly, forgotten valley. On the Day of the Dead, the union newspaper jokingly printed a *calavera* — "skull song" — dedicated to the lean organizer:

> The skeleton came
> And said, "What a shame
> This poor Gil Padilla
> Is so skinny and tame."
>
> But Padilla arose
> And gave such a fight,
> "The devil," he said,
> "I'll come another night."

On the door of his union office there is a black and red flag. He holds it in his hands. The colors are those of the flag of nonviolence of the *huelga* but without the Aztec eagle; it is just black and red, the colors of anarchy and revolution. Is that what the colors mean?

"Here, I think," Padilla says, looking at the flag carefully, "the red stands for blood and the black stands for death."

14. THE DEMAND FOR BLACK LABOR

Harold M. Baron

The changes that took place in the economic deployment of black labor in World War II were clearly an acceleration of developments that had been under way since World War I. In a process of transition, at a certain point the quantity of change becomes so great that the whole set of relationships assume an entirely-different character. Such a nodal point took place during World War II, and there resulted a transformation in the characteristic relations of institutional racism from agrarian thralldom to a metropolitan ghetto system.

Within a generation, few of the concrete economic or demographic forms of the old base remained. In 1940, over three-fourths of all blacks lived in the South, close to two-thirds lived in rural areas there, and just under half were still engaged in agriculture. By 1969, almost as many blacks lived outside the South as still resided in that region, and only 4% of the black laborers remained in agriculture, as they had left the farms at a much more rapid rate than whites. Today, only about a fifth of the total black population live in the rural areas and small towns of the South.

The United States, during the Twentieth Century, has become a distinctively urban nation — or, more accurately, a metropolitan nation with its population centered in the large cities and their surrounding configurations. The first three decades of this century witnessed the rapid urbanization of whites; the next three decades saw an even more rapid urbanization of blacks. In 1940 the proportion of the country's black population living in urban areas (49%) was the same as that proportion of whites had been in 1910. Within 20 years, almost three fourths of all blacks were urban dwellers, a higher proportion than the corresponding one for whites. More specifically, the black population has been relocated

Reprinted by permission of the author.

into the central cities of the metropolitan areas — in 1940, 34% of all blacks resided in central cities; in 1969, 55%. The larger cities were the points of greatest growth. In 1950 black people constituted one out of every eight persons in the central cities of the metropolitan areas of every size classification, and one out of every twenty in the suburbs. By 1969, black people constituted one out of every four in the central city populations of the large metropolitan areas (1,000,000 plus), and about one out of six in the medium-size metropolitan areas (250,000 to 1,000,000), while in the smaller-size metropolitan areas (below 250,000) and the suburbs the proportions remained constant. Today black communities form major cities in themselves, two with populations over 1,000,000, four between 500,000 and 1,000,000, and eight between 200,000 and 500,000.[1] Newark and Washington DC already have black majorities, and several other major cities will most likely join their ranks in the next 10 years.

The displacement of blacks from Southern agriculture was only partially due to the pull of labor demand in wartime. Technological innovation, being a necessary condition of production, acted as an independent force to drive the tenants out of the cotton fields. The push off the land occurred in two phases. Initially, right after the war, the introduction of tractors and herbicides displaced the cotton hands from full-time to seasonal work at summer weeding and harvest. The now part-time workers moved from the farms to hamlets and small towns. During the 1950s mechanization of the harvest eliminated most of the black peasantry from agricultural employment and forced them to move to the larger cities for economic survival.[2]

Elimination of the Southern black peasantry was decisive in changing the forms of racism throughout the entire region, for it meant the disappearance of the economic foundation on which the elaborate superstructure of legal Jim Crow and segregation had originally been erected. Not only did this exploited agrarian group almost vanish, but the power of the large landholders who expropriated the surplus it had produced diminished in relation to the growing urban and industrial interests. While the civil-rights movement and the heroic efforts associated with it were necessary to break the official legality of segregation, it should be recognized that in a sense this particular form of racism was already obsolete, as its base in an exploitative system of production had drastically changed. The nature of the concessions made both by the ruling class nationally and by the newer power groups of the South can be understood only in terms of this fuller view of history.[3]

For the United States as a whole, the most-important domestic development was the further elaboration and deepening of monopoly state capitalism. As the political economy has matured, technological and management innovation have become capital-saving as well as labor-saving. Capital accumulation declines as a proportion of the gross national product, and a mature capitalist economy enters into a post-accumulation phase of development. Under these conditions the disposal of the economic surplus becomes almost as great a problem as the accumulation of it. Corporations promote consumerism through increased sales, effort, planned obsolescence, and advertising. The State meets the problem by increasing its own expenditures, especially in non-consumable military items, by providing monetary support to consumption through subsidies to the well-off, and by spending a certain amount on welfare for the working class and the poor. Markedly-lower incomes would add to the surplus disposal problems and would create economic stagnation as well as risking the most-disruptive forms of class struggle.

Working-class incomes have two basic minimum levels, or floors. One is that which can be considered the level of the good trade-union contract which has to be met even by non-union firms that bid in this section of the labor market. State intervention is usually indirect in the setting of these incomes, but has grown noticeably in the last few years. The other income floor is set by direct government action via minimum-wage and welfare legislation. In the Northern industrial states where trade unions are stronger, both these income floors tend to be higher than in rural and Southern states.

Although in the mature capitalist society both economic and political imperatives exist for a certain limiting of the exploitation of the working class as a whole, each corporation still has to operate on the basis of maximizing its profits. The fostering of a section of the working class that will have to work at the jobs that are paid at rates between those of the two income floors works to meet the needs of profit maximization. Other jobs that fall into this category are those that might pay at the collective bargaining contract level but are subject to considerable seasonal and cyclical unemployment, and those from which a high rate of production is squeezed under hard or hazardous conditions. In all the developed Western capitalist states, there exists a group of workers to fill the jobs that the more politically established sectors of the working class shun. These marginal workers generally are set apart in some way so that they lack the social or the political means of defending their interests. In Western Europe usually they are non-citizens coming from either Southern Europe or Northern Africa. In England they are colored peoples coming from various parts of the Empire.[4] In the urban centers of the United States race serves to mark black and brown workers for filling in the undesirable slots.

Further, in the distribution of government transfer payments each class and status group strives to maximize its receipts. Therefore the powerless tend to receive a smaller proportion of these funds, and those that are delivered to them come in a manner which stigmatizes and bolsters political controls.

Specifically, in the metropolitan centers in America, there is a racial dual labor-market structure.[5] Side by side with the primary metropolitan job market in which firms recruit white workers and white workers seek employment, there exists a smaller secondary market in which firms recruit black workers and black workers seek jobs. In the largest metropolitan areas this secondary black market ranges from one-tenth to one-quarter of the size of the white market. For both the white and black sectors there are distinct demand and supply forces determining earnings and occupational distribution, as well as separate institutions and procedures for recruitment, hiring, training, and promotion of workers.

The distinctiveness of these two labor forces is manifested by many dimensions — by industry, by firm, by departments within firms, by occupation, and by geographical area. Within all industries, including government service, there are occupational ceilings for blacks. In a labor market like that of the Chicago metropolitan area, there are a number of small and medium-size firms in which the majority of the workers are black. However about two-thirds of the small firms and one-fifth of the medium ones hire no blacks at all. In larger firms a dual structure in the internal labor market marks off the position of the black worker along the same lines that exist in the metropolitan labor market.

A review of black employment in Chicago in 1966 finds that blacks tend to work in industries with lower wages, higher turnover, and higher unemployment. Further, they are also over-represented in the industries which exhibit sluggish growth and obviously less chance for advancement. Black men provide a third of the blue-collar workers in such industries as textiles, retail stores, primary metals, and local transportation, while in utilities, advertising, and communication they constitute less than 6%. Black women are even more concentrated in furnishing over half the blue-collar women workers in five industries — personal services, education, retail stores, hotels, and railroads.

In terms of internal labor market segregation, one of the Chicago firms best known as a fair-practice employer has a major installation located in the black community in which blacks constitute 20% of the blue-collar workers and less than 5% of the craftsmen and white-collar workers. A General Motors plant with 7500 workers is reported to have 40% black semi-skilled operatives, but only between 1% and 2% black craftsmen. A foundry firm will have one black clerk out of nearly 100 white-collar workers, while 80% of its blue-collar operators will be black.

The most-detailed information we have on racial dualism for an internal labor market is for the Lackawanna plant of Bethlehem Steel Company near Buffalo.[6] The Lackawanna plant is a major employer of black workers in the Buffalo labor market. In 1968 it employed 2600 out of a total black labor force of about 30,000 for the area. Within the plant blacks constituted about 14% of the work force, which runs in the neighborhood of 19,000. The majority of black employees were assigned to only five of the plant's departments, while only 15% of the whites were in the same units. Within the individual units, blacks were given either the hardest or the lowest-paying jobs. In the plant's Coke Oven Department blacks held 252 out of 343 of the labor jobs, while whites held 118 out of 119 craft jobs. Blacks predominated in the battery and coal-handling units, where the top job paid $3.12 an hour. Whites made up the bulk of the work force in the better-paying by-products and heating units, which had hourly pay rates ranging up to $3.42 and $3.65.

Basic Steel is a high-labor-turnover industry. From April 1, 1966 to December 31, 1967 the Lackawanna plant hired about 7,000 workers. Black job-seekers obviously identified the firm as being active in this labor market. Although 30% to 50% of the job applicants were black, the initial screening ended up with only 20% blacks among those newly hired. Prospects were screened by a general-aptitude test, the passing score for which was not validated by any measure of performance. As the labor market tightened, the passing score lowered. About an eighth of those hired were hired without taking the test, and 96% of this category were whites. The Supervisor of Employment also gave clear preference to residents of Angola, a nearly all-white suburb. Once on the payroll, a majority of the newly-hired blacks were assigned to one of the five departments in which most of the black workers already were placed. Only 20% of newly-hired whites were assigned to these departments, all of which were among the hotter and dirtier locations in the plant.

The dual labor market operates to create an urban-based industrial labor reserve that provides a ready supply of workers in a period of labor shortage and can be politically isolated in times of relatively high unemployment. In a tight labor market the undesirable jobs that whites leave are filled out of this labor reserve so that in time more job categories are added to the black sector of the labor market. If the various forms of disguised unemployment and sub-employment are all taken into account, black unemployment rates can run as high as three or four times those of whites in specific labor markets in recession periods. The welfare and police costs of maintaining this labor reserve are high, but they are borne by the State as a whole and therefore do not enter into the profit calculations of individual firms.

This special exploitation of the black labor force also leads to direct economic gains for the various employers. Methodologically it is very difficult to measure exactly the extra surplus extracted due to wage discrimination, although in Chicago it has been estimated that unskilled black workers earn about 17% less on similar jobs than unskilled white workers of comparable quality.[7] While in a historical sense the entire differential of wage income between blacks and whites can be attributed to discrimination, the employer realizes only that which takes place in the present in terms of either lesser wage payments or greater work output. Estimates of this realized special exploitation range on the order of 10% to 20% of the total black wage and salary income.[8]

The subordinate status of the black labor market does not exist in isolation, but rather is a major part of a whole complex of institutional controls that constitute the web of urban racism.[9] This distinctive modern form of racism conforms to the 300-year-old traditions of the culture of control for the oppression of black people, but now most of the controls are located within the major metropolitan institutional networks — such as the labor market, the housing market, the political system. As the black population grew in the urban centers a distinctive new formation developed in each of these institutional areas. A black ghetto and housing market, a black labor market, a black school system, a black political system, and a black welfare system came into being — not as parts of a self-determining community, but as institutions to be controlled, manipulated, and exploited. When the black population did not serve the needs of dominant institutions by providing a wartime labor reserve, they were isolated so that they could be regulated and incapacitated.

This model of urban racism has had three major components with regard to institutional structures: (1) Within the major institutional networks that operate in the city there have developed definable black sub-sectors which operated on a subordinated basis, subject to the advantage, control, and priorities of the dominant system. (2) A pattern of mutual reinforcement takes place between the barriers that define the various black sub-sectors. (3) The controls over the lives of black men are so pervasive that they form a system analogous to colonial forms of rule.

The history of the demand for black labor in the post-war period showed the continued importance of wartime labor scarcities. The new job categories gained during World War II essentially were transferred into the black sectors of the labor market. Some war industries, like shipbuilding, of course, dropped off considerably. In reconversion and the brief 1948–1949 recession blacks lost out disproportionately on the better jobs. However the Korean War again created an intense labor shortage, making black workers once more in demand, at least until the fighting stopped. The period of slow economic growth in 1955 to the early 1960s saw a deterioration in the relative position of blacks as they experienced very-high rates of unemployment and their incomes grew at a slower rate than those of whites. The civil-rights protests had generated little in the way of new demand. Only the coincidence of the rebellions of Watts, Newark, and Detroit with the escalation of the Vietnam War brought about a sharp growth in demand for black labor.

All the available evidence indicates that there has been no structural change of any significance in the deployment of black workers, most especially in private industry. Certain absolute standards of exclusion in professional, management, and sales occupations have now been removed, but the total growth in these areas has been slight except where a black clientele is serviced, as in the education and health fields. The one significant new demand in the North has been that for women clerical workers. This arises from a shortage of this particular kind of labor in the central business districts, which, being surrounded by the black community, are increasingly geographically removed from white supplies of these workers. About 90% of Chicago's black female white-collar workers work either in their own communities or in the central business districts, and are not employed in the rapidly growing outlying offices. In the South the whole pattern of racial regulation in the major cities is shifting over to a Northern model, so that the basic situation of black workers in Atlanta or Memphis is approaching that of the North about a decade ago.

Until the uprisings in the mid-60s, management of racial affairs was carried out either by the unvarnished maintenance of the status quo (except when black workers were needed) or by an elaborate ritual of fair practices and equal employment opportunity. The latter strategy operated as a sort of sophisticated social Darwinism to make the rules of competition for the survival of the fittest more equitable. Actually it blurred institutional realities, channeling energies and perceptions into individualized findings of fact. The black protest movement finally forced a switch to a policy of affirmative action that is supported by legal encouragement. In either case no basic structures have actually been transformed. As a review of studies on the current racial status in several industries finds: "Over the long haul, however, it is apparent that the laws of supply and demand have exercised a greater influence on the quantitative employment patterns of blacks than have the laws of the land."[10]

REFERENCES

1. These estimates are as of 1969. Data from the 1970 census were not available at the time of writing.

2. Richard H. Day: "The Economics of Technological Change and the Demise of the Sharecropper," *American Economic Review* (June 1967), Pages 427–449; Seymour Melman: "An Industrial Revolution in the Cotton South," *Economic History Review*, Second Series (1949), Pages 59–72.

3. Analysis of the relation of economic and class shifts in the South to the civil-rights movement and the nature of its limited victories from 1954 to 1965 has been seriously neglected. Anyone undertaking such a study should keep in mind V. I. Lenin's fundamental law of revolution: "It is not enough for revolution that the exploited and oppressed masses should understand the impossibility of living in the old way and demand changes, it is essential for revolution that the exploiters should not be able to live and rule in the same way." (Left Wing Communism)

4. David J. Smyth and Peter D. Lowe: "The Vestibule to the Occupational Ladder and Unemployment: Some Econometric Evidence on United Kingdom Structural Unemployment," *Industrial and Labor Relations Review* (July 1970), Pages 561–565.

5. This and following paragraphs on the dual labor market are basically a summary of Harold M. Baron and Bennett Hymer: "The Negro Worker in the Chicago Labor Market," in Julius Jacobson (editor): *The Negro and the American Labor Movement* (New York, 1968), Pages 232–285.

6. The following facts come from the *United States of America Versus Bethlehem Steel Company and Associates*, US District Court, Western District of New York, Civ–1967–436, Stipulation of Facts, July 1, 1968 and Second Stipulation of Facts, September 20, 1968.

7. D. Taylor: "Discrimination and Occupational Wage Differences in the Market for Unskilled Labor," *Industrial and Labor Relations Review* (April 1968), Pages 375–390.

8. For a recent estimate see Lester Thurow: *The Economy of Poverty and Discrimination* (Washington, 1969). He finds the gains due to wage discrimination were $4,600,000,000 in 1960. Advantages to white workers due to higher employment rates were $6,500,000,000.

9. For an extended treatment of the institutionalization of racism in the metropolis see Harold Baron: "The Web of Urban Racism," in Louis Knowles and Kenneth Prewitt (editors): *Institutional Racism in America* (New York, 1969), Pages 134–176.

10. Vernon M. Briggs Junior: "The Negro in American Industry: A Review of Seven Studies," *Journal of Human Resources* (Summer 1970), Pages 371–381.

15. RACISM AND CULTURE

Robert Blauner

RACISM AS THE NEGATION OF CULTURE

Racism can be defined as a propensity to categorize people who are culturally different in terms of noncultural traits, for example, skin color, hair, structure of face and eye. Obviously the human failing of imputing social significance to these differences — a failing Western Europeans have had to an extreme — underlies the fatefulness of race in recent history. By its very logic racial thinking emphasizes the variations between groups rather than the things they have in common. Further, it tends either to ignore the existence of culture or social heritage or, more often, to minimize its importance in accounting for real differences. Since virtually every nation, tribe, or ethnic group defines its uniqueness in terms of culture — its history, religion, ritual, art, philosophy or world view — rather than in terms of "blood," racism as a view of reality violates the autonomy and self-determination of peoples. It rejects their own definition of themselves and substitutes one based on the framework of the oppressor.

One tradition of British colonials was to call all indigenous people of color "niggers" despite the incredible diversity in history and culture among the Africans, Indians, Burmese, and Chinese who received this appellation. In England today West Indians, Africans, Pakistani, and East Indians are lumped together as "blacks." In a similar manner American GI's in "police actions" in Asia have used the term "gook" to refer, successively, to Koreans, Chinese, and Vietnamese. These racial definitions have permitted whites to order a universe of unfamiliar peoples without confronting their diversity and individuality, which are products of rich and distinct cultural traditions. Such a propensity to excessive categorization is fundamental to racism; another example is the tendency to view members of the same minority in global generalized terms when the group may be quite differentiated in a variety of ways.

More important than such mental mechanisms have been the actions of white Europeans as they colonized the world, and the objective consequences of their acts. Especially in the early period, the colonial powers set out to weaken the cultures of the colonized. Missionaries, often the advance guard of Western expansion, were fortified by an almost fanatical belief in the virtues of European religion, morality, and customs. Such an ingrained sense of moral rectitude was responsible for the inability of many Europeans to comprehend other ways of life and led to barbaric attacks on pagan artifacts and social institutions. In Goa and a number of other Asian cities, for example, Western missionaries destroyed Hindu temples, shrines, and priceless works of art. In Central Africa they attempted to outlaw the *lobala,* an exchange of cattle in the betrothal ceremony, on the grounds that it was a bride-purchase, a mercenary custom that profaned the marriage sacrament. The *lobala* was the institution around which the entire social organization of these cattle-raising tribes revolved; its elimination would have meant a total breakdown in social order. Every competent survey of Western colonialism reveals countless similar examples.

The depreciation of the cultural integrity of non-Western people appears to be a result of specific values and emphases within the Western ethos, not just a matter of ignorance, arrogance, and ill will. The leading concepts of Western culture, intensified in Protestantism, include control and dominance, property and appropriation, competition and individualism. These values have worked well in support of racial oppression and cultural domination: equalitarian and democratic themes have been weak countertrends at best. Particularly important has been the conflict between the Western technological orientation or engineering mentality and the more organic, harmonious notions of the relation between man and nature that were held by the societies dominated by colonialism. The aggressive implementation of such an exploitative attitude toward the external world often disrupted non-Western ways of life and contributed to the white man's depreciation of people of color.

For the European mentality:

the apparent inability of the African to dominate his environment provided perhaps the basic proof of his backwardness. . . . Nothing, as Lord Bryce remarked, was more surprising to the European than the fact that savages left "few marks of their presence" on their physical environment. . . . The savage, he argued, had "no more right to claim that the land was made for him than have the wild beasts of the forest who roar after their prey and seek their meat from God." Bryce's view was standard.

Similar arguments belittling the native Americans' claim to their continent were popular in the United States. Englishmen evaluated other cultures primarily in terms of their mastery of nature — but the mastery had to be achieved in the British manner. African footpaths were winding and therefore objects of ridicule: "The straight line, a man-made construct, was indicative of order and environmental control."

THE TENSION BETWEEN RACE AND ETHNICITY

Systems of racial oppression tend to undermine ethnic groups and ethnicity as a principle of social organization. One of the most profound consequences of colonialism was its creation of races and racism through weakening the relevance of other human distinctions. The extreme case was slavery in the New World.

It is an error to assume that slave traders and plantation owners always saw their captives as an undifferentiated mass of black Africans. In North America, as well as in the Caribbean and Brazil, a crude working knowledge of African tribal diversity and social character existed. Thus some West African peoples were viewed as good workers, whereas others were considered less desirable because it was believed that they were more likely to rebel, escape, fall ill, or even commit suicide in the state of bondage. Yet the logic of slavery had to weaken, if it did not necessarily eliminate, the long-run significance of ethnic ties. Cultural groups were broken up, in part because it was the more convenient administrative arrangement, in part because traders and planters were aware that tribal fragmentation would reduce the ability of slaves to communicate and resist. With time it became "natural" to treat the bondsmen as a more or less homogeneous mass of Africans. This took place earlier and more thoroughly in the United States because favorable economic conditions made it possible to reproduce the slave population through natural increase, which ended the need for new imports from Africa. In Brazil and the Caribbean, slaves were more typically worked to death; continuous replenishment through the slave trade maintained the relevance of African ethnicity much longer.

The slave system created the "New World Negro" out of a mélange of distinct cultural groups. In a similar fashion, racial practices common to the European powers in Africa — despite their different colonial policies — created the identities of Negro and African and a corresponding sense of Blackness and African-ness among the disparate populations south of the Sahara. Sithole quotes a saying of the Ndau-speaking people of Rhodesia: " '*Muyungu ndiye ndiye*' — 'the white man is the same the world over.' By this they mean to say that the white man the world over likes to rule and humiliate the black man." It is important to stress that race awareness and racial thinking of this type were almost nonexistent in Africa before white rule. A critical consequence of Western colonialism has been to bring racial divisions and racial thinking to parts of the world and to social groups where they previously held little sway. This cannot be dismissed as false consciousness, a purely mental trip, for to the extent that the West introduced systems of labor and social organization in which color rather than kinship or ethnic group determined social position, race became a socioeconomic reality at the expense of cultural definitions.

It was not possible to override ethnic and cultural differences in the classical situation of overseas colonialism. Ethnic groups were rooted in the land and the natural clusterings of people. Western cultural domination had relatively little direct effect on the traditional ways of life of the Asian and African masses. It was the "assimilated" elites, taught in missionary schools or other centers of Western education, for whom ethnic loyalties became less than central. Furthermore, the Western powers often fostered ethnic divisions and exacerbated cultural conflict by importing nonindigenous peoples to serve certain functions. The British policy of indirect rule was based on maintaining the traditional authority of tribal chieftains as long as they remained subservient to colonial power. The French used militia and policemen from one colony, for example Senegal, to put down disturbances in other territories. The English brought East Indians to their colonies in the West Indies, Africa, and Asia to work as laborers and to fulfill administrative and business roles; people from the Middle East often became small traders in African and Asian colonies.

In addition to races, racism, cultural pluralism, and ethnic conflict, nations and nationalism were further unanticipated consequences of Western colonial rule. Movements of reaction against the colonial cultural attack were especially significant for emerging national consciousness. The first and most characteristic cultural resistance was the maintaining of values and ways of life in the face of Westernization. Where disruption of culture did take place, new religious movements and cults often emerged, based on some combination of old and new, but carrying within them an overt or covert attack on white domination and values. Such religious developments were followed by politically oriented and often race-conscious movements such as *négritude*, which sought to restore the validity and dignity of the cultural heritages impugned by Western racism and to challenge its cultural domination. These forms of cultural resistance contributed to the developing abilities of colonized people to organize for national independence.

Race replaced ethnicity most completely in slave and postslavery societies, above all in the United States. Many of the ambiguities of American race relations stem from the fact that two principles of social division, race and ethnicity, were compressed into one. With their own internal ethnic differences eliminated, people of African descent became a race in objective terms, especially so in the view of the white majority. Afro-Americans became an ethnic group also, one of the many cultural segments of the nation. The ethnicity of Afro-America, however, is either overlooked, denied, or distorted by white Americans, in part because of the historic decision to focus on the racial definition, in part because of the racist tendency to gainsay culture to people of color beyond what they may have assimilated directly from the European tradition. This merging of ethnicity with race, in the eyes of people of color as well as of whites, made it inevitable that racial consciousness among blacks would play a central part in their historic project of culture building, and that their institutions, politics, and social character would be misinterpreted in a restricted racial paradigm.

For those Africans who escaped the slave trade and remained at home, ethnic realities have persisted. Because the colonialists drew their boundaries in disregard for cultural facts, ethnic groups are major social forces in the internal differentiation of African nations today. A paradox of the colonial encounter with culture lies in the fact that the stronger ethnicity in the classical situation has resulted in a weakening of the national unity of many new independent states — though cultural continuity has undoubtedly strengthened social institutions and personal identities — whereas in the United States the more complete development of the racial basis of collective identity among Afro-Americans, which weakened group and individual integrity, ironically created the conditions for a more unified regrouping and a new sense of peoplehood unimpaired by ethnic division.

Up to now I have focused on racism's impact on the cultures of the oppressed. How racism relates to the oppressor's culture is another crucial, though relatively unexplored, issue. It is plausible to assume that the finding of modern psychology that people who are least secure and integrated in personality structure have the greatest need for racist and other distorted belief systems might apply also to nations and their cultures. The special intensity of racial feeling among settler populations and in the cultures of new societies that develop by fragmentation from older national traditions seems to confirm this insight. The new society is characterized by a weakness in cultural identity, a lack of great tradition, an absence of a sense of distinctiveness. Winthrop Jordan has suggested that racist thought contributed to the resolution of such cultural problems among the white American settlers who used African people as "contrast conceptions" to help define themselves. The fear of chaos, even of reversion to barbarism, that comes from the weakness of civil constraints in frontier situations is dealt with by projecting all the undesirable (but dangerously appealing) possibilities associated with savagery and uncivilized animal existence on a scapegoat race. The colonial society of overseas Europeans was even less integrated culturally than the new society in America; in such a context racism and obsessive denigration of the native population became the single most important unifying thread in the lives of the white group. Racial oppressors, in the process of attacking the cultural realities of the oppressed, are engaged in fortifying their own precarious cultures; this tradeoff is another example of the exploitative thrust of white Europe in its historical encounter with peoples of color. Those who believe that racial oppression is on its way out, or can be readily eliminated in American life through reforms that guarantee greater equality in living standards and political participation, fail to reckon with the "integrating" role that racism performs for the society and the depths to which it has penetrated the national culture.

SEXISM   V

Future historians may interpret the 1960s not so much as a decade of protest but as a decade affirming the politics of identity and experience. In the Old Left, analysis preceded experience; in the New Left, experience preceded analysis. Experience provided a sense of self, a sense of group identity, and a definition of the enemy. White civil-rights workers shared the southern black experience and reacted with the outrage characteristic of well-to-do whites. Blacks, less impressed with America's stated ideals, were less outraged than fed up with white-imposed norms, myths, and values and pressed forward with the affirmation of black culture and identity.

For a decade that underwent civil-rights struggles, black militancy, antiwar protests, and campus disturbances, it seemed unlikely that yet another social movement could take hold and grow; but the consciousness of feminine oppression could and did, with enormous impact over remarkably few years. The swift ascent of the women's liberation movement is a tribute to the power of the politics of experience.

Black militancy, the student movement, the antiwar movement, youth militancy, and radicalism all affirmed freedom, equality, and liberation, but none of these was thought to be particularly necessary or applicable to women, especially by radical men. Ironically, it was political experience with radical men that led to the consciousness of radical women as distinctly oppressed, and therefore as a group with distinctive interests. Ellen Willis described the initial break-away confrontation between New Left white men and women during the anti-inaugural demonstration against President Nixon in 1969:

Mobe's ad in the *Guardian* calls for an end to the war and freedom for black and Spanish people: no mention of Women's Liberation.

195

Women in another group want to ask men to destroy their voter cards. Apparently they have interpreted the action as a simple protest against electoral politics, rather than a specifically feminist rejection of appeasement-by-ballot.

I get the funny feeling that we're being absorbed. Will we get the chance to deliver our message, or are we just there to show our support for the important (i.e., male-oriented) branches of the Left? Our group decides to confront this issue with a speech attacking male chauvinism in the movement.

Dave Dellinger introduces the rally with a stirring denunciation of the war and racism.

"What about women, you schmuck," I shout.

"And, uh, a special message from Women's Liberation," he adds. Our moment comes. M., from the Washington group, stands up to speak. This isn't the protest against movement men, which is second on the agenda, just fairly innocuous radical rhetoric—except that it's a good-looking woman talking about women. The men go crazy. "Take it off!" "Take her off the stage and fuck her!" They yell and boo and guffaw at unwitting double-entendres like "We must take to the streets." When S. (Shulamith Firestone), who is representing the New York group, comes to the mike and announces that women will no longer participate in so-called revolution that does not include the abolition of male privilege, it sounds like a spontaneous outburst of rage (rather than like a deliberate statement of the politics of Women's Liberation). By the time we get to the voter-card business, I am shaking. If radical men can be so easily provoked into acting like rednecks (a Women's Liberation group at the University of North Carolina was urinated on by male hecklers at a demonstration), what can we expect from others? What have we gotten ourselves into? Meanwhile Dellinger has been pleading with us to get off the stage "for your own good." Why isn't he telling them to shut up?[1]

If consciousness raising was a first and essential prelude to the growth of the women's movement, analysis of the structural and institutional sources of women's oppression was equally necessary. The selections in this chapter are essentially analytical. Thus, Juliet Mitchell's work is an attempt to unite feminism with socialism. As she says, "Feminism.. . . is the terrain on which a social analysis works."[2] Mitchell's socialist analysis argues that women as an oppressed group possess a distinctively complex reality, which can be encompassed only by an understanding of the four basic social structures impinging on their lives: production, reproduction, sexuality, and socialization. These, she argues, must all be transformed for the liberation of women to be achieved.

One of these areas, production, is discussed by Francine D.

Blau. Her selection documents both the historical and contemporary significance of women in the labor force. Women, in this analysis, constitute a "reserve army of the unemployed" whose talents are both exploited and systematically underused.

Why women's talents are underutilized involves a social conception of the proper role of women into which women as well as men are socialized. As Jo Freeman points out, girls speak, read, and count earlier than boys and generally excel until they become aware of what their adult status is supposed to be. When status is gained through marriage, rather than through personal achievement, women are not motivated toward occupational success. The improvement in the position of women can be achieved only by an understanding of the constrictions of traditional roles and their conscious rejection. That is why consciousness raising has been so emphasized and so influential in the women's liberation movement.

Arlie Russell Hochschild does not dispute that women are discriminated against or trained early to avoid success and authority. Nevertheless she proposes an alternative explanation for women being underrepresented in top career jobs, for example, at major universities. Her explanation stresses the positive value of a traditional housewife and mother who relieves her husband of household chores and child-care. She thus interprets the family as a service agency for such institutional employers as the university, an agency unavailable to career women who must function within the organization and value system of the traditional male career scheme.

Suzannah Lessard's selection describes the impact of traditional sex roles in another area — the social response to homosexuality. Gay people are discriminated against in employment, in the armed forces, and in the criminal law; many psychiatrists (and others) still view homosexuality as a "sickness" to be "cured"; and degrading stereotypes about homosexual behavior permeate American culture. But as Lessard points out, these practices are no longer going unchallenged; the emerging movement for gay liberation, along with the women's movement, is increasingly challenging traditional conceptions of masculinity and femininity.

REFERENCES

1. Quoted by Juliet Mitchell, *Woman's Estate* (New York: Pantheon, 1971).

2. *Ibid.*, p. 96.

16. WOMAN'S ESTATE

Juliet Mitchell

Radical feminism attempts to solve the problem of analyzing the oppression of women by making it *the* problem. The largest, first, and foremost. While such a theory remains descriptive of the experience, it *does* nevertheless stress the magnitude of the problem. What we need is a theory that is at once large enough and yet is capable of being specific. We have to see *why* women have always been oppressed, and *how* they are oppressed now, and how differently elsewhere. As radical feminists demand, we must dedicate ourselves to a theory of the oppression of all women and yet, at the same time, not lose sight of the historical specificity in the general statement. We should ask the feminist questions, but try to come up with some Marxist answers.

The situation of women is different from that of any other oppressed social group: they are half of the human species. In some ways they are exploited and oppressed like, and along with, other exploited classes or oppressed groups — the working class, blacks, etc. Until there is a revolution in production, the labor situation will prescribe women's situation within the world of men. But women are offered a universe of their own: the family. Women are exploited at work, and relegated to the home: the two positions compound their oppression. Their subservience in production is obscured by their assumed dominance in their own world — the family. What is the family? And what are the actual functions that a woman fulfills within it? Like woman herself, the family appears as a natural object, but is actually a cultural creation. There is nothing inevitable about the form or role of the family, any more than there is about the character or role of women. It is the function of ideology to present these given social types as aspects of Nature itself. Both can be exalted, paradoxically, as ideals. The "true" woman and the "true" family are images of peace and plenty: in actuality they may both be sites of violence and despair. The apparently natural condition can be made to appear more attractive than the arduous advance of human beings towards culture. But what Marx wrote about the bourgeois myths of the Golden Ancient World describes precisely women's realm.

. . . in one way the child-like world of the ancients appears to be superior; and this is so, insofar as we seek for closed shape, form and established limitation. The ancients provide a narrow satisfaction, whereas the modern world leaves us unsatisfied, or, where it appears to be satisfied with itself, is *vulgar* and *mean*.[1]

The ideology of "woman" presents her as an undifferentiated whole — "a woman," alike the world over, eternally the same. Likewise the "concept" of the family is of a unit that endures across time and space, there have always been families. . . . Within its supposed permanent structure, eternal woman finds her place. So the notion goes. . . . Any analysis of woman, and of the family, must uncoil this ideological concept of their permanence and of their unification into a monolithic whole, mother and child, a woman's place . . . her natural destiny. Theoretical analysis and revolutionary action must destructure and destroy the inevitability of this combination.

Past socialist theory has failed to differentiate woman's condition into its separate structures, which together form a complex — not a simple — unity. To do this will mean rejecting the idea that woman's condition can be deduced derivatively from the economy (Engels), or equated symbolically with society (early Marx). Rather, it must be seen as a *specific* structure, which is a unity of different elements. The variations of woman's condition throughout history will be the result of different combinations of these elements — we will thus have not a linear narrative of economic development (De Beauvoir), for the elements will be combined in different ways at different times. In a complex totality each independent sector has its own autonomous reality though each is ultimately, but only ultimately, determined by the economic factor. This complex totality means that no contradiction in society is ever simple. As each sector can move at a different pace, the synthesis of the different time scales in the total structure means that sometimes contradictions cancel each other out, and sometimes they reinforce one another. Because the unity of woman's condition at any time is in this way the product of several structures, moving at different paces, it is always "overdetermined."[2]

The key structures of woman's situation can be listed as follows: production, reproduction, sexuality, and the socialization of children. The concrete combination of these produce the "complex unity" of her position; but each separate structure may have reached a different "moment" at any given historical time. Each then must be examined separately in order to see what the present unity is, and how it might be changed. The notes that follow do not pretend to give a historical account of each sector. They are only concerned with some general reflections on the different roles of women and some of their interconnections.

PRODUCTION

The biological differentiation of the sexes into male and female and the division of labor that is based on this have *seemed*, throughout history, an interlocked necessity. Anatomically smaller and weaker, woman's physiology and her psychobiological metabolism appear to render her a less useful member of a work force. It is always stressed how, particularly in the early stages of social development, man's physical superiority gave him the means of conquest over nature which was denied to women. Once woman was accorded the menial tasks involved in maintenance while man undertook conquest and creation, she became an aspect of the things preserved: private property and children. Marx, Engels, Bebel, De Beauvoir — the major socialist writers on the subject — link the confirmation and continuation of woman's oppression after the establishment of her physical inferiority for hard manual work with the advent of private property. But woman's physical weakness has never prevented her from performing work as such (quite apart from bringing up children) — only specific types of work, in specific societies. In primitive, ancient, oriental, medieval, and capitalist societies, the *volume* of work performed by women has always been considerable (it has usually been much more than this). It is only its form that is in question. Domestic labor, even today, is enormous if quantified in terms of productive labor.[3] It has been calculated in Sweden that 2,340 million hours a year are spent by women in housework, compared with 1,290 million hours in industry. The Chase Manhattan Bank estimated a woman's overall working week averaged 99.6 hours. In any case women's physique alone has never permanently or even predominantly relegated them to menial domestic chores. In many peasant societies, women have worked in the fields as much as, or more than, men.

Physical Weakness and Coercion

The assumption behind most socialist analyses is that the crucial factor starting the whole development of feminine subordination was women's lesser capacity for demanding physical work. But in fact, this is a major oversimplification. Even in these terms, historically it has been woman's lesser capacity for violence as well as for work that has determined her subordination. In most societies woman has not only been less able than man to perform arduous kinds of work, she has also been less able to fight. Man not only has the strength to assert himself against nature, but also against his fellows. *Social coercion* has interplayed with the straightforward division of labor, based on biological capacity, to a much greater extent than is generally admitted. Women have been *forced* to do "women's work." Of course, this force may not be actualized as direct aggression. In primitive societies women's lesser physical suitability for the hunt is assumed to be evident. In agricultural societies where women's inferiority is socially instituted, they are given the arduous task of tilling and cultivation. For this coercion is necessary. In developed civilizations, and more complex societies, woman's physical deficiencies again become relevant. Women are thought to be of no use either for war or in the construction of cities. But with early industrialization, coercion once more becomes important. As Marx wrote: "Insofar as machinery dispenses with muscular power, it becomes a means of employing laborers of slight muscular strength, and those whose bodily development is incomplete, but whose limbs are all the more supple. The labor of women and children was, therefore, the first thing sought for by capitalists who used machinery."[4]

René Dumont points out that in many zones of tropical Africa today men are often idle, while women are forced to work all day. "The African woman experiences a threefold servitude: through forced marriage; through her dowry and polygamy, which increases the leisure time of men and simultaneously their social prestige; and finally through the very unequal division of labor."[5] This exploitation has no "natural" source whatever. Women may perform their "heavy" duties in contemporary African peasant societies, not for fear of physical reprisal by their men, but because these duties are "customary" and built into the role structures of the society. A further point is that coercion implies a different relationship from coercer to coerced than does exploitation. It is political rather than economic. In describing coercion Marx said that the master treated the slave or serf as the "inorganic and natural condition of its own reproduction." That is to say, labor itself becomes like other natural things — cattle or soil:

The original conditions of production appear as natural prerequisites, *natural conditions of the existence of the producer,* just as his living body, however reproduced and developed by him, is not originally established by himself, but appears as his *prerequisite.*[6]

This is preeminently woman's condition. For far from woman's *physical* weakness removing her from productive work, her *social* weakness has in these cases evidently made her the major slave of it.

This truth, elementary though it may seem, has nevertheless been constantly ignored by socialist writers on the subject, with the result that there is an unfounded optimism in their predictions of the future. For, if it is just the biological incapacity for the hardest physical work which has determined the subordination of women, then the prospect of an advanced machine technology, abolishing the need for strenuous physical exertion, would seem to promise, therefore, the liberation of women. For a moment industrialization itself thus seems to herald women's liberation. Engels, for instance, wrote:

The first premise for the emancipation of women is the reintroduction of the entire female sex into public industry. . . . And this has become possible only as a result of modern large-scale industry, which not only permits of the participation of women in production in large numbers, but actually calls for it and, moreover, strives to convert private domestic work also into a public industry.[7]

What Marx said of early industrialism is no less, but also *no more,* true of an automated society:

. . . it is obvious that the fact of the collective working group being composed of individuals of both sexes and all ages, must necessarily, *under suitable conditions,* become a source of human development; although in its spontaneously developed, brutal, capitalist form, where the laborer exists for the process of production, and not the process of production for the laborer, that fact is a pestiferous source of corruption and slavery.[8]

Industrial labor and automated technology both promise the preconditions for women's liberation alongside man's — but no more than the preconditions. It is only too obvious that the advent of industrialization has not so far freed women in this sense, either in the West or in the East. De Beauvoir hoped that automation would make a decisive, qualitative difference by abolishing altogether the physical differential between the sexes. But any reliance on this in itself accords an independent role to technique which history does not justify. Under capitalism, automation could possibly lead to an ever-growing structural unemployment which would expel women (along with immigrants) — the latest and least integrated recruits to the labor force and ideologically the most expendable for a bourgeois society — from production after only a brief interlude in it. Technology is mediated by the total structure, and it is this which will determine woman's future in work relations. It is the relationship between the social forces and technology that Firestone's "ecological" revolution ultimately ignores.

Physical deficiency is not now, any more than in the past, a sufficient explanation of woman's relegation to inferior status. Coercion has been ameliorated to an ideology shared by both sexes. Commenting on the results of her questionnaire of working women, Viola Klein notes: "There is no trace of feminine egalitarianism — militant or otherwise — in any of the women's answers to the questionnaire; nor is it even implicitly assumed that women have a 'Right to Work.' "[9] Denied, or refusing, a role in *production,* woman does not even create the preconditions of her liberation. But even her presence in the work force does not erode her oppression in the family.

THE REPRODUCTION OF CHILDREN

Women's absence from the critical sector of production historically, of course, has been caused not just by their assumed physical weakness in a context of coercion — but also by their role in reproduction. Maternity necessitates withdrawals from work, but this is not a decisive phenomenon. It is rather women's role in reproduction which has become, in capitalist society at least, the spiritual "complement" of men's role in production. Bearing children, bringing them up, and maintaining the home — these form the core of woman's natural vocation, in this ideology. This belief has attained great force because of the seeming universality of the family as a human institution. There is little doubt that Marxist analyses have underplayed the fundamental problems posed here. The complete failure to give any operative content to the slogan of "abolition" of the family is striking evidence of this (as well as of the vacuity of the notion).

The biological function of maternity is a universal, atemporal fact, and as such has seemed to escape the categories of Marxist historical analysis. However, from it is made to follow the so-called stability and omnipresence of the family, if in very different forms.[10] Once this is accepted, women's social subordination — however emphasized as an honorable, but different role (cf. the equal-but-"separate" ideologies of Southern racists) — can be seen to follow inevitably as an *insurmountable* biohistorical fact. The causal chain then goes: maternity, family, absence from production and public life, sexual inequality.

The lynch-pin in this line of argument is the idea of the family. The notion that "family" and "society" are virtually coextensive or that an advanced society not founded on the nuclear family is now inconceivable, despite revolutionary posturings to the contrary, is still widespread. It can only be seriously discussed by asking just what the family is — or rather what women's role in the family is. Once this is done, the problem appears in quite a new light. For it is obvious that woman's role in the family — primitive, feudal, or bourgeois — partakes of three quite different structures: reproduction, sexuality, and the socialization of children. These are historically, not intrinsically, related to each other in the present modern family. We can easily see that they needn't be. For instance, biological parentage is not necessarily identical with social parentage (adoption). Thus it is essential to discuss not the family as an unanalyzed entity, but the separate *structures* which today compose it but which tomorrow may be decomposed into a new pattern.

As I have said, reproduction is seen as an apparently constant atemporal phenomenon — part of biology rather than history. In fact this is an illusion. What is true is that the "mode of reproduction" does not vary with the "mode of production"; it can remain effectively the same through a number of different modes of production. For it has been defined till now by its uncontrollable, natural character and to this extent has been an unmodified biological fact. As long as reproduction remained a natural phenomenon, of course, women were effectively doomed to social exploitation. In any sense, they were not "masters" of a large part of their lives. They had no choice as to whether or how often they gave birth to children (apart from precarious methods of contraception or repeated dangerous abortions); their existence was essentially subject to biological processes outside their control.

Contraception

Contraception, which was finally invented as a rational technique only in the nineteenth century, was thus an innovation of world-historic importance. It is only just now beginning to show what immense consequences it could have, in the form of the Pill. For what it means is that at last the mode of reproduction potentially could be transformed. Once child-bearing becomes totally voluntary (how much so is it in the West, even today?) its significance is fundamentally different. It need no longer be the sole or ultimate vocation of woman; it becomes one option among others.

History is the development of man's transformation of nature, and thereby of himself — of human nature — in different modes of production. Today there are the technical possibilities for the transformation and "humanization" of the most natural part of human culture. This is what a change in the mode of reproduction could mean.

We are far from this state of affairs yet. In Italy the sale of contraceptives remains illegal. In many countries it is difficult to get reliable means. The oral contraceptive is still the privilege of a moneyed minority in a few Western countries. Even here the progress has been realized in a typically conservative and exploitative form. It is made only for women, who are thus "guinea pigs" in a venture which involves both sexes.

The fact of overwhelming importance is that easily available contraception threatens to dissociate sexual from reproductive experience — which all contemporary ideology tries to make inseparable, as the *raison d'être* of the family.

Reproduction and Production

At present, reproduction in our society is often a kind of sad mimicry of production. Work in a capitalist society is an alienation of labor in the making of a social product which is confiscated by capital. But it can still sometimes be a real act of creation, purposive and responsible, even in the conditions of the worst exploitation. Maternity is often a caricature of this. The biological product — the child — is treated as if it were a solid product. Parenthood becomes a kind of substitute for work, an activity in which the child is seen as an object created by the mother, in the same way as a commodity is created by a worker. Naturally, the child does not literally escape, but the mother's alienation can be much worse than that of the worker whose product is appropriated by the boss. The child, as an autonomous person, inevitably threatens the activity which claims to create it continually merely as a *possession* of the parent. Possessions are felt as extensions of the self. The child as a possession is supremely this. Anything the child does is therefore a threat to the mother herself, who has renounced her autonomy through this misconception of her reproductive role. There are few more precarious ventures on which to base a life.

Furthermore, even if the woman has emotional control over her child, legally and economically both she and it are subject to the father. The social cult of maternity is matched by the real socioeconomic powerlessness of the mother. The psychological and practical benefits men receive from this are obvious. The converse of woman's quest for creation in the child is man's retreat from his work into the family: "When we come home, we lay aside our mask and drop our tools, and are no longer lawyers, sailors, soldiers, statesmen, clergymen, but only men. We fall again into our most human relations, which, after all, are the whole of what belongs to us as we are ourselves."[11]

Unlike her nonproductive status, her capacity for maternity *is* a definition of woman. But it is only a physiological definition. Yet so long as it is allowed to remain a substitute for action and creativity, and the home an area of relaxation for men, woman will remain confined to the species, to her universal and natural condition.

SEXUALITY

Sexuality has traditionally been the most tabooed dimension of women's situation. The meaning of sexual freedom and its connection with women's freedom is a subject which few socialist writers have cared to broach. "Socialist morality" in the Soviet Union for a long time debarred serious discussion of the subject within the world communist movement. Marx himself — in this respect somewhat less liberal than Engels — early in his life expressed traditional views on the matter:

. . . the sanctification of the sexual instinct through exclusivity, the checking of instinct by laws, the moral beauty which makes nature's commandment ideal in the form of an emotional bond—(this is) the spiritual essence of marriage.[12]

Yet it is obvious that throughout history women have been appropriated as sexual objects, as much as progenitors or producers. Indeed, the sexual relationship can be assimilated to the statute of possession much more easily and completely than the productive or reproductive relationship. Contemporary sexual vocabulary bears eloquent witness to this — it

is a comprehensive lexicon of reification — "bird, fruit, chick. . . ." Later
Marx was well aware of this: "*Marriage* . . . is incontestably a form of
exclusive private property."[13] But neither he nor his successors ever tried
seriously to envisage the implications of this for socialism, or even for a
structural analysis of women's conditions. Communism, Marx stressed in
the same passage, would not mean mere "communalization" of women
as common property. Beyond this, he never ventured.

Some historical considerations are in order here. For if socialists have
said nothing, the gap has been filled by liberal ideologues. Fairly recently, in his book, *Eros Denied,* Wayland Young argues that Western
civilization has been uniquely repressive sexually, and, in a plea for
greater sexual freedom today, compares it as some length with oriental
and ancient societies. It is striking, however, that his book makes no
reference whatever to women's status in these different societies, or to
the different forms of marriage-contract prevalent in them. This makes
the whole argument a purely formal exercise — an obverse of socialist
discussions of women's position which ignore the problem of sexual
freedom and its meanings. For while it is true that certain oriental or
ancient (and indeed primitive) cultures were much less puritanical than
Western societies, it is absurd to regard this as a kind of "transposable
value" which can be abstracted from its social structure. In effect, in
many of these societies sexual openness was accompanied by a form of
polygamous exploitation which made it, in practice, an expression simply
of masculine domination. Since art was the province of man, too, this
freedom finds a natural and often powerful expression in art — which is
often quoted as if it were evidence of the total quality of human relationships in the society. Nothing could be more misleading. What is necessary, rather than this naïve, hortatory core of historical example, is some
account of the covariation between the degrees of sexual liberty and
openness, and the position and dignity of women in different societies.

Sexuality and the Position of Women:
Some Historical Examples

Some points are immediately obvious. The actual history is much more
dialectical than any liberal account presents it. Unlimited juridical
polygamy — whatever the sexualization of the culture which accompanies
it — is clearly a total derogation of woman's autonomy, and constitutes an
extreme form of oppression. Ancient China is a perfect illustration of
this: a sensual culture and a society in which the father as head of the
household wielded an extraordinary despotism. The Chinese pater-
familias was "a liturgical (semi-official) policeman of his kin group."[14]
In the West, however, the advent of monogamy was in no sense an

absolute improvement. It clearly did not create a one-to-one equality —
far from it. Engels commented accurately:

> Monogamy does not by any means make its appearance in history as the
> reconciliation of man and woman, still less as the highest form of such a recon-
> ciliation. On the contrary, it appears as the subjugation of one sex by the other,
> as the proclamation of a conflict between the sexes entirely unknown hitherto
> in prehistoric times.[15]

But in the Christian era, monogamy took on a very specific form in the
West. It was allied with an unprecedented regime of general sexual repression. In its Pauline version, this had a markedly antifeminine bias,
inherited from Judaism. With time this became diluted — feudal society,
despite its subsequent reputation for asceticism, practiced formal monogamy with considerable actual acceptance of polygamous behavior, at
least within the ruling class. But here again the extent of sexual freedom
was only an index of masculine domination. In England, the truly major
change occurred in the sixteenth century with the rise of militant puritanism and the increase of market relations in the economy. Lawrence
Stone observes:

> In practice, if not in theory, the early sixteenth-century nobility was a
> polygamous society, and some contrived to live with a succession of women
> despite the official prohibition on divorce. . . . But impressed by Calvinist
> criticisms of the double standard, in the late sixteenth century public opinion
> began to object to the open maintenance of a mistress.[16]

Capitalism and the attendant demands of the newly emergent bourgeoisie
accorded woman a new status as wife and mother. Her legal rights improved; there was vigorous controversy over her social position: wife-
beating was condemned. "In a woman the bourgeois man is looking for a
counterpart, not an equal."[17] At the social periphery woman did occasionally achieve an equality which was more than her feminine function
in a market society. In the extreme nonconformist sects women often
had completely equal rights: the Quaker leader Fox argued that the Re-
demption restored Prelapsarian equality and Quaker women thereby
gained a real autonomy. But once most of the sects were institutionalized,
the need for family discipline was reemphasized and woman's obedience
with it. As one historian, Keith Thomas, says, the Puritans "had done
something to raise women's status, but not really very much."[18] The
patriarchal system was retained and maintained by the new economic
mode of production — capitalism. The transition to complete effective
monogamy accompanied the transition to modern bourgeois society as
we know it today. Like the capitalist market system itself, it represented
a historic advance, at great historic cost. The formal, juridical equality
of capitalist society and capitalist rationality now applied as much to
the marital as to the labor contract. In both cases, nominal parity masks

real exploitation and inequality. But in both cases the formal equality is itself a certain progress, which can help to make possible a further advance.

Sexuality and the Position of Women: Today

The situation today is defined by a new contradiction. Once formal conjugal equality (monogamy) is established, sexual freedom as such — which under polygamous conditions was usually a form of exploitation — becomes, conversely, a possible force for liberation. It then means, simply, the freedom of both sexes to transcend the limits of present sexual institutions.

Historically, then, there has been a dialectical movement in which sexual expression was "sacrificed" in an epoch of more-or-less puritan repression, which nevertheless produced a greater parity of sexual roles and in turn creates the precondition for a genuine sexual liberation, in the dual sense of equality *and* freedom — whose unity defines socialism.

Love and Marriage

This movement can be verified within the history of the "sentiments." The cult of *love* only emerges in the twelfth century in opposition to legal marital forms and with a heightened valorization of women (courtly love). It thereafter gradually became diffused, and assimilated to marriage as such, producing that absurdity — a *free* choice for *life*. What is striking here is that monogamy, as an institution in the West, anticipated the idea of love by many centuries. The two have subsequently been officially harmonized, but the tension between them has never been abolished. There is a formal contradiction between the voluntary contractual character of "marriage" and the spontaneous uncontrollable character of "love" — the passion that is celebrated precisely for its involuntary force. The notion that it occurs only once in every life, and can therefore be integrated into a voluntary contract, becomes decreasingly plausible in the light of everyday experience — once sexual repression as a psycho-ideological system becomes at all relaxed.

Obviously, the main breach in the traditional value pattern has, so far, been the increase in premarital sexual experience. This is now virtually legitimized in contemporary society. But its implications are explosive for the ideological conception of marriage that dominates this society: that it is an exclusive and permanent bond. An American anthology, *The Family and the Sexual Revolution*, reveals this very clearly:

> As far as extramarital relations are concerned, the antisexualists are still fighting a strong, if losing, battle. The very heart of the Judaeo-Christian sex ethic is that men and women shall remain virginal until marriage and that they shall be completely faithful after marriage. In regard to premarital chastity, this ethic seems clearly on the way out, and in many segments of the populace is more and more becoming a dead letter.[19]

The current wave of sexual liberalization, in the present context, *could* become conducive to the greater general freedom of women. Equally, it could presage new forms of oppression. The puritan-bourgeois creation of "counterpart" (not equal) has produced the *precondition* for emancipation. But it gave statutary legal equality to the sexes at the cost of greatly intensified repression. Subsequently — like private property itself — it has become a brake on the further development of a free sexuality. Capitalist market relations have historically been a precondition of socialism; bourgeois marital relations (contrary to the denunciation of the *Communist Manifesto*) may equally be a precondition of women's liberation.

SOCIALIZATION OF CHILDREN

Woman's biological "destiny" as mother becomes a cultural vocation in her role as socializer of children. In bringing up children, woman achieves her main social definition. Her suitability for socialization springs from her physiological condition: her ability to produce milk and occasional relative inability to undertake strenuous work loads. It should be said at the outset the suitability is not inevitability. Several anthropologists make this clear. Lévi-Strauss writes:

In every human group, women give birth to children and take care of them, and men rather have as their specialty hunting and warlike activities. Even there, though, we have ambiguous cases: of course, men never give birth to babies, but in many societies . . . they are made to act as if they did.[20]

Evans-Pritchard's description of the Nuer tribe depicts just such a situation. Margaret Mead comments on the element of wish fulfillment in the assumption of a *natural* correlation of feminity and nurturance:

We have assumed that because it is convenient for a mother to wish to care for her child, this is a trait with which women have been more generously endowed by a careful teleological process of evolution. We have assumed that because men have hunted, an activity requiring enterprise, bravery and initiative, they have been endowed with these useful attitudes as part of their sex temperament.[21]

However, the cultural allocation of roles in bringing up children — and the limits of its variability — is not the essential problem for consideration. What is much more important is to analyze the nature of the socialization process itself and its requirements.

The sociologist Talcott Parsons, in his detailed analysis claims that it is essential for the child to have two "parents," one who plays an "expressive" role, and one who plays an "instrumental" role.[22] The nuclear family revolves around the two axes of generational hierarchy (parents and children), and of the two parental roles (mother-expressive and father-instrumental). The role division derives from the mother's ability and the father's inability to breast-feed. In all groups, Parsons and his colleagues assert, even in those primitive tribes where the father appears to nurture the child (such as those discussed by Evans-Pritchard and Mead), the male plays the instrumental role *in relation* to the wife–mother. At one stage the mother plays an instrumental and expressive role *vis-à-vis* her infant: this is in the very first years when she is the source of approval and disapproval as well as of love and care. However, after this, the father, or male substitute (in matrilineal societies the mother's brother) takes over. In a modern industrial society two types of role are clearly important: the adult role in the family of procreation, and the adult occupational role in outside work. The function of the family as such reflects the function of the women within it; it is primarily expressive. The person playing the integrated-adaptive-expressive role cannot be off all the time on instrumental-occupational errands — hence there is a built-in inhibition of the woman's work outside the home. Parsons' analysis makes clear the exact role of the maternal socializer in contemporary American society.[23] It fails to go on to state that other aspects and modes of socialization are conceivable. What is valuable in Parsons' work is simply his insistence on the central importance of socialization as a process which is constitutive of any society (no Marxist has provided a comparable analysis). His general conclusion is that:

> It seems to be without serious qualification the opinion of competent personality psychologists that, though personalities differ greatly in their degrees of rigidity, certain broad fundamental patterns of "character" are laid down in childhood (so far as they are not genetically inherited) and are not radically changed by adult experience. The exact degree to which this is the case or the exact age levels at which plasticity becomes greatly diminished, are not at issue here. The important thing is the fact of childhood character formation and its relative stability after that.[24]

Infancy

This seems indisputable: one of the great revolutions of modern psychology has been the discovery of the decisive specific weight of infancy in the course of an individual life — a psychic time disproportionately greater than the chronological time. Freud began the revolution with his work on infantile sexuality; Melanie Klein radicalized it with her work on the first year of the infant's life. The result is that today we know far more than ever before how delicate and precarious a process the passage from birth to childhood is for everyone. It would seem that the fate of the adult personality can be largely decided in the initial months of life. The preconditions for the later stability and integration demand an extraordinary degree of care and intelligence on the part of the adult who is socializing the child, as well as a persistence through time of the same person.

These undoubted advances in the scientific understanding of childhood have been widely used as an argument to reassert women's quintessential maternal function, at a time when the traditional family has seemed increasingly eroded. The psychologist, Bowlby, studying evacuee children in World War II, declared: "Essential for mental health is that the infant and young child should experience a warm, intimate, and continuous relationship with his mother,"[25] setting a trend which has become cumulative since. The emphasis of familial ideology has shifted from a cult of the biological ordeal of maternity (the pain which makes the child precious, etc.) to a celebration of mother care as a social act. This can reach ludicrous extremes:

> For the mother, breast-feeding becomes a complement to the act of creation. It gives her a heightened sense of fulfillment and allows her to participate in a relationship as close to perfection as any that a woman can hope to achieve. . . . The simple fact of giving birth, however, does not of itself fulfill this need and longing. . . . Motherliness is a way of life. It enables a woman to express her total self with the tender feelings, the protective attitudes, the encompassing love of the motherly woman.[26]

The tautologies, the mystifications, the sheer absurdities point to the gap between reality and ideology.

Family Patterns

This ideology corresponds in dislocated form to a real change in the pattern of the family. As the family has become smaller, each child has become more important; the actual *act* of reproduction occupies less and less time, and the socializing and nurturance process increase commensurately in significance. Contemporary society is obsessed by the physical, moral and sexual problems of childhood and adolescence. Ultimate responsibility for these is placed on the mother. Thus the mother's reproductive role has retreated as her socializing role has increased. In the 1890's in England a mother spent fifteen years in a state of pregnancy and lactation: in the 1960's she spent an average of four years. Compulsory schooling from the age of five, of course, reduces the maternal function very greatly after the initial vulnerable years.

The present situation is then one in which the qualitative importance of socialization during the early years of the child's life has acquired a much greater significance than in the past — while the quantitative amount of a mother's life spent either in gestation or child-rearing has greatly diminished. It follows that socialization cannot simply be elevated to the woman's new maternal vocation. Used as a mystique, it becomes an instrument of oppression. Moreover, there is no inherent reason why the biological and social mother should coincide. The process of socialization is, in itself, invariable — but the person of the socializer can vary. Observers of collective methods of child-rearing in the kibbutzim in Israel note that the child who is reared by a trained nurse (though normally maternally breast-fed) does not suffer the backwash of typical parental anxieties and thus may positively gain by the system. This possibility should not be fetishized in its turn. (Jean Baby, speaking of the post-four-year-old child, goes so far as to say that "complete separation appears indispensable to guarantee the liberty of the child as well as the mother."[27]) But what it does reveal is the viability of plural forms of socialization — neither necessarily tied to the nuclear family, nor to the biological parent, or rather to *one* of the biological parents — the mother.

CONCLUSION

The lesson of these reflections is that the liberation of women can only be achieved if *all four* structures in which they are integrated are transformed — production, reproduction, sexuality, and socialization. A modification of any of them can be offset by a reinforcement of another (as increased socialization has made up for decreased reproduction). This means that a mere permutation of the form of exploitation is achieved. The history of the last sixty years provides ample evidence of this. In the early twentieth century, militant feminism in England and the USA surpassed the labor movement in its violence. The vote — a political right — was eventually won. Nonetheless, though a simple completion of the formal legal equality of bourgeois society, it left the socioeconomic situation of women virtually unchanged. The wider legacy of the suffrage was practically nil: the suffragettes, by and large, proved unable to move beyond their own initial demands, and many of their leading figures later became extreme reactionaries. The Russian Revolution produced a quite different experience. In the Soviet Union in the 1920's, advanced social legislation aimed at liberating women above all in the field of sexuality; divorce was made free and automatic for either partner, thus effectively liquidating marriage; illegitimacy was abolished, abortion was free, etc. The social and demographic effects of these laws in a backward, semiliterate society bent on rapid industrialization (needing, therefore, a high birthrate) were — predictably — catastrophic.[28] Stalinism soon produced a restoration of traditional iron norms. Inheritance was reinstated, divorce made inaccessible, abortion illegal, etc.

The State cannot exist without the family. Marriage is a positive value for the Socialist Soviet State only if the partners see in it a lifelong union. So-called free love is a bourgeois invention and has nothing in common with the principles of conduct of a Soviet citizen. Moreover, marriage receives its full value for the State only if there is progeny, and the consorts experience the highest happiness of parenthood. (From the official journal of the Commissariat of Justice of 1939.)[29]

Women still retained the right and obligation to work, but because these gains had not been integrated into the earlier attempts to free sexuality and abolish the family no general liberation has occurred.

In China today there is still another experience. At this stage of the revolution all the emphasis is being placed on liberating women in *production*. This has produced an impressive social promotion of women. But it seems to have been accompanied by a tremendous repression of sexuality and a rigorous puritanism (rampant in civic life). This corresponds not only to the need to mobilize women massively in economic life, but to a deep cultural reaction against the brutality, corruption, and prostitution prevalent in Imperial and Kuo Min Tang China (a phenomenon unlike anything in Czarist Russia). Because the exploitation of women was so great in the *ancien régime* women's participation at village level in the Chinese Revolution was uniquely high. As for reproduction, the Russian cult of maternity in the 1930's and 1940's has not been repeated for demographic reasons: indeed, China may be one of the first countries in the world to provide free State-authorized contraception on a universal scale to the population. Again, however, given the low level of industrialization and fear produced by imperialist encirclement, no all-round advance could be expected.

Probably it is only in the highly developed societies of the West that an authentic liberation of women can be envisaged today. But for this to occur, there must be a transformation of *all* the structures into which they are integrated, and all the contradictions must coalesce, to explode — *a unité de rupture*. A revolutionary movement must base its analysis on the uneven development of each structure, and attack the weakest link in the combination. This may then become the point of departure for a general transformation. What is the situation of the different structures today? What is the concrete situation of the women in each of the positions in which they are inserted?

REFERENCES

1. Karl Marx, *Precapitalist Economic Formations*, ed. Hobsbawm (Lawrence, and Wishart, 1964), p. 85.

2. See Luis Althusser, "Contradiction and Overdetermination," in *For Marx* (London: Allen Lane, 1970). To describe the movement of this complexity, as I have mentioned above, Althusser uses the Freudian term "overdetermination."

The phrase "*unité de rupture*" (mentioned below) refers to the moment when the contradictions so reinforce one another as to coalesce into the conditions for a revolutionary change.

3. Apologists who make out that housework, though time-consuming, is light and relatively enjoyable, are refusing to acknowledge the dull and degrading routine it entails. Lenin commented crisply: "You all know that even when women have full rights, they still remain factually downtrodden because all housework is left to them. In most cases housework is the most unproductive, the most barbarous and the most arduous work a woman can do. It is exceptionally petty and does not include anything that would in any way promote the development of the woman." (*Collected Works*, Vol. XXX, p. 43.)

4. Karl Marx, *Capital*, I, p. 394.

5. René Dumont, *L'Afrique Noire est Mal Partie*, 1962, p. 210.

6. Karl Marx, *Precapitalist Economic Formations*, op. cit., p. 87.

7. Friedrich Engels, *op. cit.*, II, pp. 233, 311.

8. Karl Marx, *Capital*, I, p. 394.

9. Viola Klein, "Working Wives," *Institute of Personnel Management Occasional Papers*, No. 15, 1960, p. 13.

10. Philippe Ariès in *Centuries of Childhood*, 1962, shows that though the family may in some form always have existed it was often submerged under more forceful structures. In fact according to Ariès it has only acquired its present significance with the advent of industrialization.

11. J. A. Froude, *Nemesis of Faith*, 1849, p. 103.

12. Karl Marx, "Chapitre de Mariage," *Oeuvres Complètes*, ed. Molitor, *Oeuvres Philosophiques*, I, p. 25.

13. Karl Marx, *Private Property and Communism*, op. cit., p. 153.

14. Karl Wittfogel, *Oriental Despotism*, 1957, p. 116.

15. Friedrich Engels, *op. cit.*, II, p. 224.

16. Lawrence Stone, *The Crisis of the Aristocracy*, 1965, pp. 663–664.

17. Simone de Beauvior, *La Marche Longue*, 1957, trans. *The Long March*, 1958, p. 141.

18. Keith Thomas, "Women and the Civil War Sects," *Past and Present*, No. 13, 1958, p. 43.

19. Albert Ellis, "The Folklore of Sex," in *The Family and the Sexual Revolution*, ed. E. M. Schur, 1966, p. 35.

20. Claude Lévi-Strauss, "The Family," in *Man, Culture and Society*, ed. H. L. Shapiro, 1956, p. 274.

21. Margaret Mead, "Sex and Temperament," in *The Family and The Sexual Revolution*, op. cit., pp. 207–208.

22. Talcott Parsons and Robert F. Bales, *Family, Socialization and Interaction Process*, 1956, p. 47. "The area of instrumental function concerns relations of the system to its situation outside the system . . . and 'instrumentally' establishing the desired relations to *external* goal-objects. The expressive area concerns the 'internal' affairs of the system, the maintenance of integrative relations between the members, and regulation of the patterns and tension levels of its component units."

23. One of Parsons' main theoretical innovations is his contention that what the child strives to internalize will vary with the content of the reciprocal role

relationships in which he is a participant. R. D. Laing, in *Family and Individual Structure,* 1966, contends that a child may internalize an entire system — i.e., "the family."

24. Talcott Parsons, *The Social System,* 1952, p. 227. There is no doubt that the Women's Liberation Movement, with its practical and theoretical stress on the importance of child care, has accorded the subject the seriousness it needs. See, for instance, "Women's Liberation: Notes on Child Care" produced by the Women's Center, 36 West 22nd St., New York.

25. John Bowlby, cit. Bruno Bettelheim: "Does Communal Education Work? The Case of the Kibbutz," in *The Family and the Sexual Revolution, op. cit.,* p. 295. These evacuee war children were probably suffering from more than mother-loss, e.g., bombings and air raids.

26. Betty Ann Countrywoman, *Redbook,* June, 1960, cit. Betty Friedan, *The Feminine Mystique* (Penguin, 1965), p. 51.

27. Jean Baby, *Un Monde Meilleur* (Maspero, 1964), p. 99.

28. For a fuller account of this see Chapter IVA of Kate Millett's *Sexual Politics.*

29. *Sotsialisticheskaya Zakonnost,* 1939, No. 2, cit. N. Timasheff: "The Attempt to Abolish the Family in Russia," in *The Family,* ed. N. W. Bell and E. F. Vogel, 1960, p. 59.

17. WOMEN IN THE LABOR FORCE: AN OVERVIEW

Francine D. Blau

Women have traditionally engaged in three types of economically productive work. First, they have produced goods and services for their family's own consumption; second, they have engaged in household production for sale or exchange on the market; third, they have worked for pay outside the home. The process of industrialization has brought about a reallocation in the relative importance of these three types of economic activities, greatly increasing the absolute and relative number of women who seek and obtain paid employment. In this paper we shall briefly trace this evolution in the working woman's role and summarize the trends in women's involvement in work outside the home. We shall then examine the status of women in the labor market in terms of their em-

From *Women: A Feminist Perspective,* edited by Jo Freeman. Reprinted by permission of the author.

ployment and earnings. Finally, we shall attempt to draw some conclusions regarding the changes that must be made in employment patterns if women are to gain equality in the labor market.

HISTORICAL PERSPECTIVES

In the preindustrial economy of the American Colonial period, work was frequently allocated on the basis of sex, but there could be little question that the work of women was as essential to the survival of the community as that of men. Unlike England and the Continental countries, where women were routinely employed as reapers, mowers, and haymakers, the Colonies left their agricultural work mostly to the men, at least among the nonslave population.[1] This departure from the customs of the mother country may have been due to the economic importance of the household industries carried on primarily by women and children, who produced most of the manufactured goods for the Colonies. In addition to cleaning, cooking, and caring for their children, Colonial women considered spinning, weaving, and making lace, soap, shoes, and candles part of their ordinary housekeeping duties, for the Colonial economy at first provided no other source for these goods and services.[2]

Moreover, the pressures of a struggling frontier society, faced with a continual labor shortage and imbued with a puritanical abhorrence of idleness, opened up a wide range of business activities to women. They could be found working as tavern keepers, store managers, traders, speculators, printers and publishers, as well as in the more traditional women's occupations of domestic servant, seamstress, and tailor.[3] But many of the Colonial businesswomen were widows, frequently with small children to provide for, who carried on their husband's enterprise after his death.[4] In some cases opportunities for women to remain single and self-supporting were curtailed, perhaps because of women's economic value in the home. For example, in early New England female family heads were given their proportion of planting land, and in Salem even unmarried women at first also received a small allotment. "The custom of granting 'maid's lotts,' however, was soon discontinued in order to avoid 'all presedents and evil events of graunting lotts unto single maidens not disposed of.' "[5]

Although conditions peculiar to the Colonies may have contributed to the relatively high status of American women, the more general point has been made that before the Industrial Revolution separated the home from the place of work, women were able to take a more active role in the economic life of the community.[6] The broad thrust of industrialization may indeed have diminished the participation of women in certain kinds of economically productive work. Particularly in America, how-

ever, women played a crucial role in the development of the first important manufacturing industry, the textile industry.

During the seventeenth century, when spinning and weaving were
household industries done primarily by women and children, each household provided its own raw materials and produced chiefly to meet its
own needs. But it was not uncommon for women to market part of their
output, selling it directly to their own customers or to shopkeepers for
credit against their account.[7] With the expansion of the industry in the
latter half of the eighteenth century, it became more common for women
to be employed by merchants to spin yarn in their own home. Under
this commission system the merchants would sell the yarn or put it out
again to be woven into cloth. The first factories in America embodied
no new technology. They were "merely rooms where several looms were
gathered and where a place of business could be maintained." Women
delivered yarn they had spun at home to these establishments and were
paid for it there.[8]

The first textile factory to incorporate power machinery was established
in Pawtucket, Rhode Island, in 1789 by Samuel Slater, a British immigrant. Slater's factory used a water-powered spinning frame. By 1800
fifteen mills had been established in New England for the carding and
spinning of yarn. When the power loom was introduced in 1814, the
whole process of cloth manufacture could be carried on in the new factories.[9] But if cloth was no longer made solely in the home, it was still
made primarily by women and children, who constituted the bulk of the
new industrial work force.

The earliest factories did not open any new occupations to women. So long as
they were only "spinning mills" there was merely a transferring of women's
work from the home to the factory, and by the time that the establishment of
the power loom had made weaving also a profitable factory operation, women
had become so largely employed as weavers that they were only following this
occupation, too, as it left the home. It may, in brief, be said that the result of
the introduction of the factory system in the textile industries was that the work
which women had been doing in the home could be done more efficiently
outside of the home, but women were carrying on the same processes in the
making of yarn or cloth.[10]

Perhaps even more interesting than the pioneering role of women in the
industry is the reaction of illustrious contemporaries to the employment
of women outside the home. Alexander Hamilton, for example, claimed
that one of the great advantages of the establishment of manufacturing
was "the employment of persons who would otherwise be idle (and in
many cases a burthen on the community). . . . It is worthy of particular
remark, that, in general, women and children are rendered more useful,
and the latter more early useful, by the manufacturing establishments,
than they would otherwise be."[11] The notion that a farmer's masculinity

might be threatened by the entry of his wife and children into paid employment apparently did not trouble American men of the time. Hamilton noted, on the contrary, that men would benefit from having a new source of income in the family.[12] Others claimed that the new factories not only opened up a new source of income but also built character in their employees:

The rise of manufactures was said to have "elevated the females belonging to the families of the cultivators of the soil from a state of penury and idleness to competence and industry". . . . In the same spirit of unreasoning exaggeration the women in villages remote from manufacturing centers were described as "doomed to idleness and its inseparable attendants, vice and guilt."[13]

Since the economy of the United States during this period, was predominantly agricultural, with an extremely favorable land-to-labor ratio, women and children were virtually the only readily available source of labor for the infant manufacturing industry. This would seem to be an important factor in the approval with which the entry of women into the wage-labor force was greeted. The existence of a factor of production, women, which was more productive in the new industrial pursuits than in the home, was cited as an argument for the passage of protective tariffs to encourage the development of the textile industry in a country that appeared to have a clear comparative advantage in agriculture.[14]

Of course, present day attitudes toward women working outside the home are not nearly so encouraging. While a careful investigation of the causes for the change remains to be undertaken, it seems reasonable to suggest that the gradual diminution of the supply of unsettled land coupled with the waves of immigrants that provided a more abundant source of labor shifted public concern to the problem of providing sufficient employment for men. In any case, by the turn of the century sentiment against the "intrusion" of women into the industrial work force was strong enough to compel Edith Abbott to answer this charge specifically in her classic study, *Women in Industry*. Her words add a valuable perspective to contemporary discussions of the issue as well:

Women have been from the beginning of our history an important factor in American industry. In the early days of the factory system they were an indispensable factor. Any theory, therefore, that women are a new element in our industrial life, or that they are doing "men's work," or that they have "driven out the men," is a theory unsupported by the facts.[15]

A careful investigation of the facts also leads us to further qualify the statement that the separation of the home from the place of work during the Industrial Revolution tended to reduce the participation of American women, particularly married women, in many kinds of economically productive work. For one thing, though it is estimated that in 1890 only 5 percent of married women had jobs outside the home,[16] this pattern did not prevail among all groups in the female population. For another, various types of work done in the home continued to be important in the economy throughout the nineteenth century.

The two major groups of married women for whom work outside the home was fairly common were black women, the majority of whom still lived in the South, and immigrant women in the textile-manufacturing towns of New England. In 1890 one quarter of black wives and two-thirds of the large number of black widows were gainfully employed. Most of these women worked either as field hands or as domestic servants, the same kinds of jobs black women had always done under slavery.[17] Undoubtedly the tendency of black wives to engage in market activity can be explained in large part by the low incomes of black men.

The women who worked in the New England textile mills were carrying on the long tradition of the participation of women in this industry. In two Massachusetts towns, Fall River and Lowell, for example, nearly one-fifth of all married women worked outside the home in 1890. Most were first- or second-generation immigrants of French-Canadian or Irish ancestry. The low wages of men working in the textile mills frequently made it necessary for other family members, including children, to work in the mills too. Thus it was often for family reasons as well as financial reasons that married women went to work: "Since many of the older children worked in the mills, their mothers were not needed at home to care for them. Indeed, a mother whose children worked could look after them better if she went to work in the same mill."[18]

In addition to women from these two groups, married women from many sectors of the population were forced to seek market work when they suffered certain kinds of misfortunes against which there was little social protection in the nineteenth and early twentieth centuries. Some indication of the kinds of problems these women faced can be gained from the results of a study conducted by the United States Bureau of Labor Statistics in 1908:

Among one group of 140 wives and widows who were employed in the glass industry, 94 were widows, or had been deserted, or were married to men who were permanently disabled. Thirteen were married to drunkards or loafers who would not work. The husbands of ten were temporarily unable to work because of sickness or injury. Seventeen were married to unskilled laborers who received minimum wages for uncertain employment. Only six were married to regularly employed workers above the grade of unskilled labor.[19]

The types of employment and working conditions of urban women who earned money for work done in the home varied widely. Some women took in boarders or did laundry or sewing. Others, in New York, Chicago, and other major cities, eked out a meager existence doing home work in the garment industry, while Bohemian and German women in New

York's upper East Side tenements provided a cheap source of labor for the cigar industry.[20]

Another element of home work, the production of goods and services for the family's own use, remained extremely important throughout the nineteenth century, even in urban areas. Women frequently kept livestock and poultry and raised fruits and vegetables in small home gardens. Even foodstuffs bought at the market were usually in their natural, unprocessed form. Preserving, pickling, canning, and jelly making, as well as baking the family bread, were normal household duties. Much of the family's clothing, curtains, and linens were sewn or knitted in the home. And, of course, the housekeeping tasks of cleaning, washing, and cooking were all undertaken without the benefit of modern appliances.[21]

THE FEMALE LABOR FORCE SINCE 1890

If the process of industrialization has meant that many of the goods and services women have traditionally produced in the home have increasingly been provided by the market economy, it has also brought about the incorporation of ever-increasing numbers of women into the paid labor force. Since fairly reliable data on the female labor force did not become available until 1890, we shall confine our discussion of the trends in female labor force participation to the period 1890–1970. The figures in Table 1 indicate a relatively slow rate of increase in the proportion of women of working age that were in the labor force in the early decades of this period.[22] Between 1940 and 1970, however, more dramatic changes in women's labor force status occurred. In 1940 less than 29 percent of the female population 16 years of age and over was in the labor force. By 1970 the figure had risen to 43 percent, and nearly half of all women between the ages of 16 and 64 were working or seeking work. Women workers increased from one quarter to nearly two-fifths of the civilian labor force.

When we take into account the World War II experience, however, these changes look less impressive. Between 1940 and 1945 the female labor force expanded by 5.5 million, and 38 percent of all women 16 years of age and over were working. As the 1947 figures indicate, considerable ground was lost in the immediate postwar period. In fact, it was not until 1953 that the absolute number of women workers surpassed its wartime peak. Participation rates did not regain their 1945 levels until 1961.[23]

The long-term growth in the female labor force that has occurred since 1940 was accomplished primarily by the entry of new groups of women into the labor market. Before 1940 the typical female worker was young and single. The peak age-specific participation rate occurred among

Table 1   Women in the Civilian Labor Force, Selected Years,
           1890–1970

Year	No. (in thousands)	As percentage of all workers	As percentage of female population
1890	3,704	17.0	18.2
1900	4,999	18.1	20.0
1920	8,229	20.4	22.7
1930	10,396	21.9	23.6
1940	13,783	25.4	28.6
1945	19,290	36.1	38.1
1947	16,664	27.9	30.8
1950	18,389	29.6	33.9
1955	20,548	31.6	35.7
1960	23,240	33.4	37.7
1965	26,200	35.2	39.2
1970	31,520	38.1	43.3

Sources: U.S. Dept. of Labor, Women's Bureau, 1969 Handbook on Women Workers, p. 10; U. S. Dept. of Labor, Manpower Administration, Manpower Report of the President, April 1971, pp. 203, 205.

Note: Pre-1940 figures include women 14 years of age and over; figures for 1940 and after include women 16 years of age and over.

women 20 to 24 years of age. . . . In the next twenty years older married women entered or re-entered the labor force in increasing numbers, while the labor force participation rates of women between 20 and 34 years of age remained relatively constant. Since 1960 there has been a sizable increase in the participation rates of all women under 65. The fastest increase, however, has occurred among young married women, many with preschool-age children.

The result of the sequential entry into the labor force of black and immigrant women, young single women from all ethnic groups, and older married women, and most recently the increased labor force participation of the younger group of married women, is that the female labor force has come to resemble much more closely the total female population. That is, women who engage in market work have been drawing closer to the total female population in terms of their racial composition, age, educational attainment, marital and family status and other characteristics.[24] Thus it is rapidly becoming more difficult to consider working women as in some sense an unrepresentative or atypical group.

Valerie Oppenheimer has identified the growth in the sex-specific demand for women workers as an important factor in the increase in the female labor force and in its changing composition. As we shall see in greater detail in the next section, the employment of women is restricted chiefly to a limited number of industries and occupational categories. The growing importance of service industries and white-collar work has provided greatly expanded employment opportunities for women, within the framework of the sexually segregated labor market. Moreover, the increase in these jobs, coupled with the appearance of new female occupations between 1940 and 1960, created a demand that greatly exceeded the supply of young single women workers, once the backbone of the female labor force. Thus, as Oppenheimer concludes,

The combination of the rising demand for female labor and the declining supply of the typical worker opened up job opportunities for married women and older women that had not previously existed. . . . The great influx of older married women into the labor force, was, in good part a *response* to increased job opportunities—not the creator of such opportunities.[25]

Oppenheimer also points out that under the pressures of labor shortages, employers were forced to abandon their prejudices against employing older married women.[26] Further research may show that a similar process has operated to the benefit of young married women in the period since 1960. There is some evidence that employers have been reluctant to hire married women with young children, either because they feared such women would have high rates of absenteeism or because they made a moralistic judgment that mothers of preschool-age children should remain at home.[27] Some employers may have been forced to discard these concerns in order to meet their demand for female labor, thus making possible the rapid increase in the labor force participation of women in this group that has occurred in recent years.

If, as Oppenheimer contends, the growing demand for women workers was a crucial factor in the expansion of the female labor force, the question arises whether large numbers of women are outside the labor force simply because sufficient opportunities for work have not been present. The extreme responsiveness of women to the demands created by the emergency conditions of World War II and the evidence that the female labor force tends to grow more quickly during upswings in the business cycle than during recessions would support this view.[28] If we further take into account the extremely limited availability of child care centers and the narrow range of jobs open to women, it becomes difficult to regard the decision whether or not to seek paid employment solely as a matter of free choice or personal preference for many women.

Occupational Distribution

Table 2 shows the distribution of female and male workers by occupation in 1971.

Table 2 Occupational Distribution of the Labor Force, by Sex, 1971

Occupation Group	Distribution (%)	
	Males	Females
Total employed	100.0	100.0
White-collar workers	40.9	60.6
Professional and technical	13.7	14.5
Managers, officials and proprietors	14.6	5.0
Clerical workers	6.7	33.9
Sales workers	5.9	7.2
Blue-collar workers	45.9	15.4
Craftsmen and foremen	19.9	1.3
Operatives	18.3	13.3
Nonfarm laborers	7.7	0.8
Service workers	8.2	22.3
Private household workers	0.1	4.9
Other service workers	8.1	17.4
Farmworkers	5.1	1.7
Farmers and farm managers	3.2	0.3
Farm laborers and foremen	1.9	1.4

Source: U.S. Dept. of Labor, Manpower Administration, *Manpower Report of the President,* March 1972, p. 173.

The patterns of employment displayed by the two groups diverged widely: almost 70 percent of male white-collar workers, or 28 percent of all working men, were in the professional and technical or managerial category, whereas only about 32 percent of female white-collar workers, or 20 percent of all working women, were in one of these categories. Furthermore, while a slightly greater proportion of women than men were employed as professional or technical workers, the majority of the women in this category were concentrated in the two traditionally female professions of elementary or secondary school teacher and nurse.[29] Nearly 56 percent of female white-collar workers, or over one-third of all employed women, were working in clerical jobs.

Men also had a larger share of the higher-paying, higher-status blue-collar jobs. Only 8 percent of female blue-collar workers, or 1.3 percent of all working women, were employed as craftsmen or foremen. By contrast, over 40 percent of male blue-collar workers, or 20 percent of all working men, were employed as craftsmen or foremen. The percentage of women workers in the generally low-paying service-worker category was much greater than the percentage of men. In 1971 some 22 percent of all working women held service jobs, as compared to 8 percent of working men.

The occupational distribution of nonwhite women was even more skewed toward the bottom of the occupational ladder. Fifty percent held service jobs in 1968, and fully half of this group were private household workers, the lowest-paying occupation. Only 30 percent of nonwhite women were white-collar workers, as compared to 60 percent of the total female labor force.[30]

A more specific examination of the occupational distribution of female employees highlights two aspects of the position of women in the labor market. First, women workers are heavily concentrated in an extremely small number of occupations. Half of all working women were employed in just 21 of the 250 detailed occupations listed by the Bureau of the Census in 1969. Just five occupations — secretary–stenographer, household worker, bookkeeper, elementary school teacher, and waitress — accounted for one quarter of all employed women. Men workers were much more widely distributed throughout the occupational structure, with half of them employed in 65 occupations.[31] Second, most women work in predominantly female jobs. A list of the occupations in which 70 percent or more of the workers were women was compiled by Oppenheimer from 1900 and 1960 census figures. She found that in both years well over half of all working women were in these "women's jobs."[32] The only major change over the period was an increase in the number of occupations on the list.

A study by Edward Gross further supports the conclusion that occupational segregation is as severe now as it was in 1900. Gross constructed an "index of segregation" for each census year between 1900 and 1960. The index for any given year can be construed as the percentage of women (or men) who would have to change jobs in order for the occupational distribution of women workers to match that of men. Despite two world wars and a major depression, the index shows a remarkable stability over the years, ranging from a low point of 65.6 percent for 1950 to a high point of 69.0 percent for 1910 and 1940 — a difference of less than 4 percent. The absolute magnitude of the indices is also striking, for it indicates that about two-thirds of the female labor force would have had to change jobs in any given census year for the occupational distribution of women to correspond to that of men. According to this measure, indeed, the segregation of occupations by sex has been even more severe than segregation by race. In 1960 the index of racial segregation was 46.8 percent, as compared to 68.4 percent for sexual segregation. Gross concludes:

Those concerned with sexual segregation as a social problem can take small comfort from these figures. They suggest that the movement of women into the labor market has not meant the disappearance of sexual typing in occupation.

Rather, the great expansion in female employment has been accomplished through the expansion of occupations that were already heavily female, through the emergence of wholly new occupations (such as that of key punch operator) which were defined as female from the start, and through females taking over previously male occupations. This last may be compared to the process of racial invasion in American cities. From the group's point of view, such invasion provides new opportunities but still in a segregated context.[33]

Earnings

In 1971 the annual median earnings of working women were $2,986, only 40 percent of the annual median earnings of working men. Part of this difference is due to the greater prevalence of part-time work among women. Even women who worked full-time, year-round, however, had a median income of only $5,593, or 60 percent of that of working men.[34] Nonwhite women were even more disadvantaged. The median income of those who were full-time, year-round workers was only $3,677 in 1968, or 46 percent of the median income of white men.[35] Furthermore, the gap between the earnings of women and men increased between 1956 and 1969, and has narrowed only slightly since.[36]

A further measure of the problem can be gained by comparing the earnings distribution of female and male workers. In 1970, 45 percent of the women working full-time, year-round, earned less than $5,000, and 12 percent earned less than $3,000. Only 14 percent of the men earned less than $5,000, and only 5 percent earned less than $3,000. At the upper end of the income scale, 1 percent of the women working full-time, year-round, earned over $15,000, as compared to 14 percent of the men.[37] These earnings differentials persist even when we control for major occupation group. In 1971 full-time women sales workers earned only 42 percent as much, based on median income, as men sales workers; women in a managerial capacity earned 53 percent as much as men; women craftsmen and foremen, 56 percent; women service workers (except private household workers), 58 percent; women operatives, 60 percent; women clerical workers, 62 percent; and women professional or technical workers, 66 percent.[38]

Since earnings are directly tied to both work experience and job tenure, the intermittent labor force participation of women workers and their shorter average length of time on a particular job would lead us to expect some differences in median earnings between women and men workers.[39] The observed earnings differentials, however, exceed what could be expected to result from these factors. These extremely high differentials can best be understood in terms of the sexual segregation of the labor market discussed in the preceding section. Women are heavily concentrated in predominantly female occupational categories. Even when women and men are in the same occupation, they are likely to be employed in different industries or establishments.[40] At the risk of some oversimplification, the effect of the resulting "dual labor market" on women's earnings can be explained in terms of supply and demand.

The demand for women workers is mainly restricted to a small number of sexually segregated occupations. At the same time, the supply of women available for work is highly responsive to small changes in the wages offered as well as to employment opportunities in general. Moreover, employers can attract more women into a job simply by increasing the flexibility of work schedules. In all likelihood, the same situation exists even in the traditional women's jobs that require a high level of general education. The reserve pool of qualified women outside the labor market who would be willing to enter it if the price or the job were right certainly exerts a downward pressure on earnings.

In the framework of Marxist analysis, the women outside of the labor force may be viewed as a kind of "reserve army of the unemployed" that is guaranteed its subsistence through the institutions of marriage and the family. Since the labor market is sexually segregated, however, this reserve acts most directly to hold down the earnings of women workers and only indirectly affects the more protected group of men workers. Thus it is not surprising that the rapid expansion of the female work force in recent years has corresponded to an increasing gap between the earnings of women and men. Of course, this does not suggest that women and men never work together on the same job in the same establishment, or that even in that case wage differentials do not exist. Rather it suggests that the practice of unequal pay for equal work is made possible by the limited job opportunities open to women, who have little choice but to accept the disparity. Moreover, nominal differences in job definitions sometimes provide a further excuse for unequal pay even in the case of comparable work.

There are some who argue that women do not need to earn as much as men, and hence that the low earning power of working women is not a significant social problem. Single women who work are only biding their time before marriage, so the argument goes, and married women are only supplementing their husbands' already ample incomes. The assumptions underlying this view — that single women do not need to make a living wage or to be able to save for the future, and that all husbands earn enough to provide adequately for their wives and children — are left unexamined.

We shall cite evidence showing that work is a financial necessity for significant numbers of women, but two additional points should be made at the outset. First, in a society in which value often means monetary value, it is extremely unlikely that women can attain "equality," however that may be defined, without equal earning opportunities. Second, a significant change in women's social status would seem to require the real possibility of economic independence for women, and not simply limited earning opportunities at low income levels.

Returning to the initial point, some indication of the financial importance of paid employment for women can be gained from data on the female labor force. Of the women in the labor force in March 1971, 23 percent were single and an additional 19 percent were widowed, divorced, or separated from their husbands. Of the married women, who constituted the remaining 58 percent, 23 percent had husbands whose incomes were below $5,000. Undoubtedly most of these women, and many whose husbands earned more than $5,000, were also working for compelling economic reasons.[41]

The plight of female-headed families is particularly serious. Although these families constituted only about 11 percent of all American families in 1969, they accounted for 47 percent of all poor families with children in that year. Nearly one-third of all black families were headed by women in March 1970, and 60 percent of these had incomes below the poverty line.[42] Thus any discussion of the issue of poverty that does not concern itself with the disadvantaged position of women in the labor market can hardly be regarded as a serious attempt to deal with the problem.

CONCLUSION

The data presented so far amply demonstrate that women are not at the present time equal participants in the labor market. The question that remains, of course, is what policies are necessary to enable women to attain economic equality? A wide variety of changes in prevailing occupational structures and institutional arrangements must be made if this goal is to be achieved. Clearly, however, the elimination of occupational segregation is one of the most important steps. As we have seen, occupational segregation restricts the employment opportunities open to women; it results in lower earnings for women, owing to the oversupply of labor available for "women's jobs"; and it permits the low status accorded women by society at large to be carried over to predominantly female occupations, which are generally regarded as less prestigious or important than other occupations.

Of course, the finding that occupational segregation is an obstacle to the attainment of economic equality for women is hardly surprising, since there is no reason to assume that the doctrine of "separate but equal" should be any more valid for women than it has proved to be for other groups in our society. Yet, to define the problem in these terms is extremely useful because it points to policies that would affect all working women, not just those at the upper levels. It means, for example, that we must have more women sales workers in wholesale trade, more women electricians, more women chefs, as well as more women doctors, lawyers, and business executives. It also means that more men must move into predominantly female jobs.

Since women presently constitute nearly two-fifths of the civilian labor force and since they are so heavily concentrated in predominantly female jobs, complete integration is a task of enormous proportions. Once a substantial movement of women into the male sector of the labor market took place, however, we could expect the incomes of women in predominantly female occupations to increase, since the supply of labor for these jobs would no longer be so abundant. This in turn should attract men into presently female occupations. Thus the long-range benefits of a sizable movement toward increased integration could be very great.

REFERENCES

1. Edith Abbott, *Women in Industry* (New York: Appleton, 1910), pp. 11–12.

2. Eleanor Flexner, *Century of Struggle: The Women's Rights Movement in the United States* (New York: Atheneum, 1968), p. 9.

3. Abbott, pp. 13–18. "It should be noted that the domestic servant in the seventeenth and eighteenth centuries was employed for a considerable part of her time in processes of manufacture and that, without going far wrong, one might classify this as an industrial occupation." *Ibid.*, p. 16.

4. Flexner, p. 9.

5. Abbott, pp. 11–12.

6. Viola Klein and Alva Myrdal, *Women's Two Roles* (London: Routledge & Kegan Paul, 1956), p. 1.

7. Abbott, pp. 18–19.

8. *Ibid.*, p. 19, and for quote, p. 37.

9. Elizabeth Faulkner Baker, *Technology and Women's Work* (New York: Columbia Univ. Press, 1964), p. 5.

10. Abbott, p. 14.

11. Alexander Hamilton, *Report on Manufactures*, vol. 1, cited in Baker, p. 6.

12. Hamilton, *Report on Manufactures*, cited in Abbott, p. 50.

13. Abbott, p. 57.

14. "To the 'Friends of Industry,' as the early protectionists loved to call themselves, it was . . . a useful argument to be able to say that of all the employees in our manufacturing establishments not one fourth were able-bodied men fit for farming." Edith Abbott, *Women in Industry* (New York: Appleton, 1910), p. 51. The same author noted (p. 52, n. 1) that "manufactures are lauded because of their 'subserviency to the public defense; their employment of women and children, machinery, cattle, fire, fuel, steam, water, and even wind — instead of our ploughmen and male laborers.'"

15. Abbott, p. 317.

16. Robert W. Smuts, *Women and Work in America* (New York: Columbia Univ. Press, 1959), p. 23.

17. *Ibid.*, pp. 10, 56.

18. *Ibid.*, p. 57.

19. *Ibid.*, p. 51.

20. *Ibid.*, pp. 14–17.

21. *Ibid.*, pp. 11–13.

22. There is some question whether there was any increase at all in female labor force participation during the 1890–1930 period. The 1910 census, in which enumerators were given special instructions *not* to overlook women workers, especially unpaid family workers, yielded a participation rate of 25 percent. Robert W. Smuts has argued that women workers were undercounted in the 1900, the 1920, and perhaps the 1930 census as well, but that over the period, gradual improvements in technique, broader definitions of labor force status, and a redistribution of the female work force from unpaid farm work to paid employment resulted in an apparent rather than a true increase in the female participation rate. Smuts, "The Female Labor Force," *Journal of the American Statistical Association*, March 1960, pp. 71–79. For a discussion of this issue see Valerie Kincade Oppenheimer, *The Female Labor Force in the United States* (Berkeley: Univ. of Calif., Institute of International Studies, 1970), pp. 3–5.

23. U.S. Dept. of Labor, Manpower Administration, *Manpower Report of the President*, March 1970, p. 217.

24. Janice Neipert Hedges, "Women and Manpower Demands in the 1970's," *Monthly Labor Review*, June 1970, p. 21.

25. Oppenheimer, *Female Labor Force*, p. 187.

26. *Ibid.*, p. 188.

27. See for example, Georgina M. Smith, *Help Wanted — Female: A Study of Demand and Supply in a Local Job Market for Women* (Rutgers, N.J.: Rutgers Univ., Institute of Management and Labor Relations, 1964), pp. 18–19.

28. See Gertrude Bancroft McNally, "Patterns of Female Labor Force Activity," *Industrial Relations*, May 1968, pp. 204–18.

29. Hedges, pp. 22–23.

30. U.S. Dept. of Labor, Women's Bureau, *1969 Handbook on Women Workers*, Bulletin 294 (Washington, D.C.: GPO, 1969), pp. 105–6.

31. Hedges, p. 19.

32. Valerie Kincade Oppenheimer, "The Sex-Labeling of Jobs," *Industrial Relations*, May 1968, Table 6, p. 220.

33. Edward Gross, "Plus Ca Change . . . ? The Sexual Structure of Occupations Over Time," *Social Problems*, Fall 1968, p. 202.

34. *Economic Report of the President*, Jan. 1973, p. 103.

35. U.S. Dept. of Commerce, Bureau of the Census, *Current Population Reports*, p. 60.

36. *Economic Report of the President*, Jan. 1973, p. 103.

37. *Current Population Reports*, P-60, No. 80.

38. *Economic Report of the President*, Jan. 1973, table 28, p. 104.

39. In addition, full-time hours for women tend to be less than those of men

on the average. For the effect of adjustment for this factor on the earnings differential, see *ibid.*

40. See, for example, Donald McNulty, "Differences in Pay Between Men and Women Workers," *Monthly Labor Review,* Dec. 1967.

41. Elizabeth Waldman and Kathryn R. Gover, "Marital and Family Characteristics of the Labor Force," *Monthly Labor Review,* April 1972, p. 5; Janice Neipert Hedges and Jeanne K. Barnett, "Working Women and the Division of Household Tasks," *ibid.,* p. 10.

42. Robert L. Stein, "The Economic Status of Families Headed by Women," *Monthly Labor Review,* Dec. 1970, pp. 4–5.

18. THE BUILDING OF THE GILDED CAGE

Jo Freeman

Hidden somewhere in the byways of social science is an occasionally discussed, seldom studied, frequently employed, and rarely questioned field generally referred to as social control. We have so thoroughly absorbed our national ideology about living in a "free society" that whatever else we may question, as radicals or academics, we are reluctant to admit that all societies, ours included, do an awful lot of controlling *everyone's* lives. We are even more reluctant to face the often subtle ways that our own attitude and our own lives are being controlled by that same society.

This is why it has been so difficult for materially well-off, educated whites — women as well as men — to accept the idea that women are oppressed. "Women can have a career (or do something else) if they really want to" is the oft-heard refrain. "Women are where they are because they like it" is another. There are many more. "Women are their own worst enemies." "Women prefer to be wives and mothers rather than compete in the hard, aggressive male world." "Women enjoy being feminine. They like to be treated like ladies." These are just variations on the same "freedom of choice" argument which maintains that women are free (don't forget, we are living in a *free* society) to do what they want and never question why they think they want what they say they want.

But what people think they want is precisely what society must control if it is to maintain the *status quo*. As the Bems put it, "We overlook the fact that the society that has spent twenty years carefully marking the woman's ballot for her has nothing to lose in that twenty-first year by pretending to let her cast it for the alternative of her choice. Society has controlled not her alternatives but her motivation to choose any but one of those alternatives."[1]

There are many mechanisms of social control and some are more subtle than others. The socialization process, the climate of opinion in which people live, the group ideology (political or religious), the kind of social structures available, the legal system, and the police are just some of the means society has at its disposal to channel people into the roles it finds necessary for its maintenance. They are all worthy of study, but here we are only going to look at two of them — one overt and one covert — to see what they can tell us about women.

The easiest place to start when trying to determine the position of any group of people is with the legal system. This may strike us as a little strange since our national ideology also says that "all men are equal under the law" until we remember that the ideology is absolutely correct in its restriction of this promise to "men." Now there are three groups who have never been accorded the status and the rights of manhood — blacks, children (minors), and women. Children at least are considered to be in their inferior, dependent status only temporarily because some of them (white males) eventually graduate to become men. Blacks (the 47 percent who are male) have "been denied their manhood" since they were kidnapped from Africa and are currently demanding it back. But women (51 percent of the population, black and white) — how can a woman have manhood?

This paradox illustrates the problem very well: because there is a long-standing legal tradition, reaching back to early Roman law, which says that women are perpetual children and the only adults are men. This tradition, known as the "Perpetual Tutelage of Women"[2] has had its ups and downs, been more or less enforced, but the definition of women as minors who never grow up, who therefore must always be under the guidance of a male (father, brother, husband, or son), has been carried down in modified form to the present day and vestiges of it can still be seen in our legal system.

Even Roman law was an improvement over Greek society. In that cradle of democracy only men could be citizens in the polis. In fact most women were slaves, and most slaves were women.[3] In ancient Rome both the status of women and slaves improved slightly as they were incorporated into the family under the rule of *Patria potestas* or Power of the Father. This term designated not so much a familial relationship as a property relationship. All land was owned by families, not individuals, and was under the control of the oldest male. Women and slaves could not assume proprietorship and in fact frequently were considered to be forms of property. The woman in particular had to turn any income she might receive over to the head of the household and had no rights to her own children, to divorce, or to any life outside the family. The relationship of woman to man was designated by the concept of *manus* (hand) under which the woman stood. Women had no rights under law — not even legal recognition. In any civil or criminal case she had to be represented by the *Pater* who accepted legal judgment on himself and in turn judged her according to his whims. Unlike slaves, women could not be *emancipated* (removed from under the hand). She could only go from under one hand to another. This was the nature of the marital relationship. (From which comes our modern practice "to ask a woman's father for her *hand* in marriage.) At marriage a woman was "born again" into the household of the bridegroom's family and became the "daughter of her husband."[4]

Although later practice of Roman law was much less severe than the ancient rules, some of the most stringent aspects were incorporated into canon law and from there passed to the English common law. Interpretation and spread of the Roman law varied throughout Europe, but it was through the English common law that it was brought to this country and made part of our own legal tradition.

Even here history played tricks on women. Throughout the sixteenth and seventeenth centuries tremendous liberalizations were taking place in the common-law attitude toward women. This was particularly true in the American colonies where rapidly accelerating commercial expansion often made it profitable to ignore the old social rules. In particular, the development of property other than land facilitated this process, as women had always been held to have some right in *movable* property while only male heirs could inherit the family lands.[5]

But when Blackstone wrote his soon-to-be-famous *Commentaries on the Laws of England,* he chose to ignore these new trends in favor of codifying the old common-law rules. Published in 1765, his work was used in Britain as a textbook. But in the Colonies and new Republic it became a legal Bible. Concise and readable, it was frequently the only book to be found in most law libraries in the United States up until the middle of the nineteenth century, and incipient lawyers rarely delved past its pages when seeking the roots of legal tradition.[6] Thus when Edward Mansfield wrote the first major analysis of *The Legal Rights, Liabilities and Duties of Women* in 1845, he still found it necessary to pay homage to the Blackstone doctrine that "the husband and wife are as one and that one is the husband." As he saw it three years before the Seneca Falls Convention would write the *Woman's Declaration of Independence,* it appears that the husband's control over the person of his wife is so complete that he may claim her society altogether; that he may reclaim her if she goes away or is detained by others; that he may use constraint upon her liberty to prevent her going away, or to prevent improper conduct; that he may maintain suits for injuries to her person; that she cannot sue alone; and that she cannot execute a deed or valid conveyance without the concurrence of her husband. In most respects she loses the power of personal independence, and altogether that of separate action in legal matters.[7]

The husband also had almost total control over all the wife's real and personal property or income.

Legal traditions die hard even when they are mythical ones. So the bulk of the activities of feminists in the nineteenth century were spent chipping away at the legal nonexistence that Blackstone had defined for married women. Despite the passage of Married Women's Property Acts and much other legislative relief during the nineteenth century, the core idea of the common law that husbands and wives have reciprocal — not equal — rights and duties remains. The husband must support the wife and children, and she in return must render services to the husband. Thus the woman is legally required to do the domestic chores, to provide marital companionship and sexual consortium. Her first obligation is to him. If he moves out of town, she cannot get unemployment compensation if she quits her job to follow him, but he can divorce her on grounds of desertion if she doesn't. Likewise, unless there has been a legal separation, she cannot deny him access to their house even if she has good reason to believe that his entry on a particular occasion would result in physical abuse to her and her children. He must maintain her, but the amount of support beyond subsistence is at his discretion. She has no claim for direct compensation for any of the services rendered.[8]

Crozier commented on this distribution of obligations:

Clearly, that economic relationship between A and B whereby A has an original ownership of B's labor, with the consequent necessity of providing B's maintenance, is the economic relationship between an owner and his property rather than that between two free persons. It was the economic relationship between a person and his domesticated animal. In the English common law the wife was, in economic relationship to the husband, his property. The financial plan of marriage law was founded upon the economic relationship of owner and property.[9]

This basic relationship still remains in force today. The "domesticated animal" has acquired a longer leash, but the legal chains have yet to be broken. Common-law practices, assumptions, and attitudes still dominate the law. The property, real and personal, brought by the woman to the marriage now remains her separate estate, but such is not always the case for that acquired during the marriage.

There are two types of property systems in the United States — common law and community. In the nine community-property states (Arizona, California, Hawaii, Idaho, Louisiana, Nevada, New Mexico, Texas, and Washington) all property or income acquired by either husband or wife is community property and is equally divided upon divorce. However "the general rule is that the husband is the head of the 'community' and the duty is his to manage the property for the benefit of his wife and family. Usually, as long as the husband is capable of managing the community, the wife has no power of control over it and, acting alone, cannot contract debts chargeable against it."[10] In two of the states (Texas and Nevada) the husband can even dispose of the property without his wife's consent. Included in the property is the income of a working wife which, under the law, is managed by the husband with the wife having no legal right to a say in how it shall be spent.

In common-law states each spouse has a right to manage his own income and property. However, unlike community-property states, this principle does not recognize the contribution made by a wife who works only in the home. Although the wife generally contributes domestic labor to the maintenance of the home far in excess of that of her husband she has no right to an allowance, wages, or an income of any sort. Nor can she claim joint ownership upon divorce.[11]

Marriage incurs a few other disabilities as well. A married woman cannot contract on the same basis as her husband or a single woman in most states. In only five states does she have the same right to her own domicile. In many states a married woman can now live separately from her husband but his domicile is still her address for purposes of taxation, voting, jury service, etc.[12]

Along with the domicile regulations, those concerning names are most symbolic of the theory of the husband's and wife's legal unity. Legally, every married woman's surname is that of her husband and no court will uphold her right to go by a different name. Pragmatically, she can use another name only so long as her husband does not object. If he were legally to change his name, hers would automatically change too, though such would not necessarily be the case for the children. "In a very real sense, the loss of a woman's surname represents the destruction of an important part of her personality and its submersion in that of her husband."[13]

When we move out of the common law and into the statutory law we find an area in which, until recently, the dual legal status of women has increased in the last seventy years. This assault was particularly intense around the turn of the century, but has solidified considerably since then. Some of the earliest sex-discriminatory legislation was against prostitutes; but this didn't so much prohibit the practice of their profession as regulate their hours and place of work. The big crackdown against prostitutes didn't come until World War I when there was fear that the soldiers would contract venereal disease.[14]

There was also a rise in the abortion laws. Originally abortion was illegal only when performed without the husband's consent and the only crime was a "wrong to the husband in depriving him of children."[15] Prior to passage of the nineteenth-century laws which made it a criminal offense it was largely regarded as a Church offense punishable by religious penalties.[16]

The most frequent new laws were sex-specific labor legislation. Under common law and in the early years of this country there was very little restrictive legislation on the employment of women. It was not needed. Custom and prejudice alone sufficed to keep the occupations in which women might be gainfully employed limited to domestic servant, factory worker, governess, and prostitute. As women acquired education and professional skills in the wake of the Industrial Revolution, they increasingly sought employment in fields which put them in competition with men. In some instances men gave way totally and the field became dominated by women, losing prestige, opportunities for advancement, and pay in the process. The occupation of secretary is the most notable. In most cases men fought back and were quick to make use of economic, ideological, and legal weapons to reduce or eliminate their competition. "They excluded women from trade unions, made contracts with employers to prevent their hiring women, passed laws restricting the employment of married women, caricatured working women, and carried on ceaseless propaganda to return women to the home or keep them there."[17]

The restrictive labor laws were the main weapon. Among the earliest were those prohibiting women from practicing certain professions, such as law and medicine. But most were directed toward regulating work conditions in factories. Initially such laws were aimed at protecting both men and women workers from the sweatshop conditions that prevailed during the nineteenth century. The extent to which women, and children, were protected more than men varied from state to state, but in 1905 the heated struggle to get the state to assume responsibility for the welfare of workers received a major setback. The Supreme Court invalidated a New York law that no male or female worker could be required or permitted to work in bakeries more than sixty hours a week and in so doing made all such protective laws unconstitutional.[18]

Three years later the Court upheld an almost identical Oregon statute that applied to females only, on the grounds that their physical inferiority and their function as "mothers to the race" justified special class legislation.[19] With this decision as a precedent, the drive for protective legislation became distorted into a push for laws that applied to women only. It made some strange allies, who had totally opposing reasons for supporting such laws. On the one hand social reformers and many feminists were in favor of them on the principle that half a loaf was better than none and the hope that at some time in the future the laws would apply to men as well.[20] Many male union leaders were also in favor of them, but not because they would protect women. As President Strasser of the International Cigarmakers Union expressed it, "We cannot drive the females out of the trade but we can restrict this daily quota of labor through factory laws."[21]

Strasser soon proved to be right, as the primary use of "protective" laws has been to protect the jobs of men by denying overtime pay, promotions, and employment opportunities to women. The Supreme Court has long since rejected its ruling that prevented protective legislation from applying to men yet there has been no move by male workers to have the laws extended to them. Most of the real benefits made available by such laws have been obtained through federal law or collective bargaining, while the state restrictive laws have been quoted by unions and employers alike to keep women in an inferior competitive position. The dislike of these laws left by the women they affect can be seen in the numerous cases challenging their legitimacy that have been filed since Title VII of the Civil Rights Act was passed (prohibiting sex discrimination in employment).

These laws do more than restrict the hours which women may work. An examination of the state labor laws reveals a complex, confusing, inconsistent chaos. Thirteen states have minimum-wage laws which apply only to women and minors, and two which apply only to women. Adult women are prohibited from working in specified occupations or under certain working conditions considered hazardous in twenty-six states; in ten of these women cannot work in bars.[22]

Laws restricting the number of hours a woman may work — generally to eight per day and forty-eight per week — are found in forty-one states and the District of Columbia. Twenty states prohibit night work and limitations are made in twelve on the amount of weight that can be lifted by a woman. These maximums range from fifteen to thirty-five pounds (the weight of a small child).[23]

The "weight and hours" laws have proved to be the most onerous and are the ones usually challenged in the courts. In *Mengelkoch et al. v. the Industrial Welfare Commission of California and North American Aviation, Inc.*, the defending corporation had admitted that the women were denied overtime and promotions to positions requiring overtime, justifying their actions by the California maximum-hours law. In *Roig v. Southern Bell Telephone and Telegraph Co.*, the plaintiffs are protesting that their current job is exempt from the Louisiana maximum hours but that the higher-paying job to which they were denied promotion is not. One major case which challenged the Georgia weightlifting law is *Weeks v. Southern Bell Telephone and Telegraph.* It received a favorable ruling from the Fifth Circuit Court but the plaintiff has yet to be given the promotion for which she sued.

But perhaps most illustrative of all is an Indiana case,[24] in which the company tried to establish maximum weightlifting restrictions even though its plant and the plaintiffs were located in a state which did not have such laws. By company policy, women were restricted to jobs whose highest pay rate was identical with the lowest pay rate for men. Many of the women, including the defendants, were laid off while men with less seniority were kept on, on the grounds that the women could not lift over thirty-five pounds. This policy resulted in such anomalies as women having to lift seventeen and one-half tons of products a day in separate ten-pound loads while the male supervisors sat at the head of the assembly line handling the controls and lifting one forty-pound box of caps each hour. "In a number of other instances, women were doing hard manual labor until the operations were automated; then they were relieved of their duties, and men were employed to perform the easier and more pleasant jobs."[25] In its defense, the company claimed it reached this policy in accordance with the union's wishes but the Seventh Circuit Court unanimously ruled against it anyway. This is only one of many instances in which corporations and male-run unions have taken advantage of "protective" legislation in order to protect themselves from giving women equal job opportunities and equal pay.

With the passage of Title VII the restrictive labor legislation is slowly being dissolved by the courts. But these laws are just vestiges of what has been an entirely separate legal system applicable particularly to women. At their base lies the fact that the position of women under the Constitution is not the same as that of men. The Supreme Court has ruled several times that the Fourteenth Amendment prohibits any arbitrary class legislation, except that based on sex. The last case was decided in 1961, but the most important was in 1874. In *Minor v. Happerset* (88 U.S. 21 Wall. 162 1873), the Court first defined the concept of "second-class citizenship" by saying that some citizens could be denied rights which others had. The "equal protection" clause of the Fourteenth Amendment did not give women equal rights with men.

Other groups in society have also had special bodies of law created for them as a means of social control. Thus an examination of the statutes can clearly delineate those groups which society feels it necessary to control.

The statutes do not necessarily indicate *all* of the groups which a particular society excludes from full participation, but they do show those which it most adamantly excludes. In virtually every society that has existed, the caste cleavages, as distinct from the class lines, have been imbedded in the law. Differentiating between class and caste is often difficult as the two differ in degree that only at the extremes is seen as a difference in kind. It is made more difficult by our refusal to acknowledge that castes exist in our society. Here too we have allowed our thinking to be subverted by our national ideology. Our belief in the potentiality, if not the current existence, of high social mobility determined only by the individual's talents, leads us to believe that mobility is hampered by one's socioeconomic origins but not that it is made impossible if one comes from the wrong caste. Only recently have we reluctantly begun to face the reality of the "color line" as a caste boundary. Our consciousness of the caste nature of the other boundaries, particularly that of sex, is not yet this high.

The law not only shows the caste boundaries, it also gives a fairly good history of the changes in boundaries. If the rigidity of caste lines fades into more permeable class lines, the legislation usually changes with it. The Middle Ages saw separate application of the law to the separate estates. In the early years of this country certain rights were reserved to those possessing a minimum amount of property. Today, nobility of birth or amount of income may affect the treatment one receives from the courts, but it is not expressed in the law itself. For the past 150 years, the major caste divisions have been along the lines of age, sex, and ethnic origin; these have been the categories for which special legislation has existed.

The law further indicates when restricted castes are seen to be most threatening and the ways in which they are felt to be threatening. If members of a group will restrict their own activities, or these activities are inconsequential, law is unnecessary. No law need be made to keep people out of places they never considered going. It is when certain prerogatives are threatened by an out-group that it must be made illegal to violate them. Thus Jim Crow laws were not necessary during slavery and restrictive labor legislation was not extensively sought for until women entered the job market in rapidly accelerating numbers at the end of the nineteenth century.

Frequently, members of the lower castes are lumped together and the same body of special law applied to all. Most of the labor legislation discussed earlier applies to "women and minors." The state of New York once worded its franchise law to include everyone but "women, minors, convicts, and idiots." When a legal status had to be found for Negro slaves in the seventeenth century, the "nearest and most natural analogy was the status of women."[26] But the clearest analogy of all was stated by the Southern slave-owning class when trying to defend the system prior to the Civil War. One of the most widely read rationalizations was that of George Fitzhugh who wrote in his 1854 *Sociology for the South* that "The kind of slavery is adapted to the men enslaved. Wives and apprentices are slaves, not in theory only, but often in fact. Children are slaves to their parents, guardians, and teachers. Imprisoned culprits are slaves. Lunatics and idiots are slaves also."[27]

The progress of "outcastes," particularly those of the wrong race and sex, also has been parallel. The language of the Nineteenth Amendment was borrowed directly from that of the Fifteenth. The "sex" provision of Title VII (only the second piece of corrective legislation pertaining to women that has been passed)[28] was stuck into the Civil Rights Act of 1964 as a joke by octogenarian representative Howard W. Smith of Virginia.[29]

Many of the same people were involved in both movements as well. Sojourner Truth and Douglass were staunch feminists. Douglass urged the first Convention at Seneca Falls in 1848 to demand the franchise when many of the women were reluctant to do so. Similarly, the early feminists were ardent abolitionists. The consciousness of two of the most active is dated from the World Anti-Slavery Convention in London in 1840 when Lucretia Mott and Elizabeth Cady Stanton were compelled to sit in the galleries rather than participate in the convention.[30] Many of today's new feminists also come out of an active background in the civil-rights and other social movements.[31] Almost without exception, when one of the lower castes in our society begins to revolt, the others quickly perceive the similarities to their own condition and start the battle on their own grounds.

Thus it is not surprising that these groups quickly find that they have more in common than having a similar legal situation. All of them, when comparing themselves to the culture of the middle-aged white male,[32] find that they are distinctly in the minority position. This minority position involves a good deal more than laws and a good deal more than economic and social discrimination. Discrimination *per se* is only one aspect of oppression and not always the most significant one. There are many other social and psychological aspects. Likewise, being subject to separate laws and poorer access to the socioeconomic system are only some of the characteristics of being in a minority group. This point has been well explored by Hacker and the chart she developed to sum up the similarities between women and blacks is reproduced [here].[33]

The Negro analogy has been challenged many times on the grounds that women do not suffer from the same overt segregation as blacks. This point is well noted. But it is important to realize that blatant discrimination is just one mechanism of social control. There are many more subtle ones employed long before such coercion becomes necessary. It is only when these other methods fail to keep a minority group in its place that harsher means must be found. Given that a particular society needs the subservience of several different groups of people it will use its techniques to a different degree with each of them depending on what is available and what they are most susceptible to. It is a measure of the

Table 1   Castelike Status of Women and Negroes

Negroes	Women
1. High Social Visibility	
Skin color, other "racial" characteristics	Secondary sex characteristics
(Sometimes) distinctive dress — bandanna, flashy clothes	Distinctive dress, skirts, etc.
2. Ascribed Attributes	
Inferior intelligence, smaller brain, less convoluted, scarcity of geniuses	Inferior intelligence, smaller brain, less convoluted, scarcity of geniuses
More free in instinctual gratifications; more emotional, "primitive," and childlike; imagined sexual prowess envied	Irresponsible, inconsistent, emotionally unstable; lack strong superego; women as "temptresses"
Common stereotype "inferior"	"Weaker"
3. Rationalizations of Status	
Thought all right in his place	Woman's place is in the home
Myth of contented Negro	Myth of contented woman — "feminine" woman is happy in subordinate role
4. Accommodation Attitudes	
Supplicatory whining intonation of voice	Rising inflection, smiles, laughs, downward glances
Deferential manner	Flattering manner
Concealment of real feelings	"Feminine wiles"
Outwit "white folks"	Outwit "menfolk"
Careful study of points at which dominant group is susceptible to influence	Careful study of points at which dominant group is susceptible to influence
Fake appeals for directives; show of ignorance	Appearance of helplessness
5. Discriminations	
Limitations on education — should fit "place" in society	Limitations on education — should fit "place" in society
Confined to traditional jobs — barred from supervisory positions; their competition feared; no family precedents for new aspirations	Confined to traditional jobs — barred from supervisory positions; their competition feared; no family precedents for new aspirations
Deprived of political importance	Deprived of political importance
Social and professional segregation	Social and professional segregation
More vulnerable to criticism	More vulnerable to criticism, e.g., conduct in bars
6. Similar Problems	

Roles not clearly defined, but in flux as result of social change; conflict between achieved status and ascribed status blacks' resistance to the definition which white society has tried to impose on them that such violent extremes have had to be used to keep the caste lines intact.

Women, however, have not needed such stringent social chains. Their bodies can be left free because their minds are chained long before they became functioning adults. Most women have so thoroughly internalized the social definitions that their only significant role is to serve men as wives and raise the next generation of men and their servants that no laws are necessary to enforce this.

The result is that women, even more than other minority groups, have their identities derived first as members of a group and only second, if at all, as unique persons.

Consider the following—when a boy is born, it is difficult to predict what he will be doing twenty-five years later. We cannot say whether he will be an artist or a doctor or a college professor because he will be permitted to develop and fulfill his own identity. But if the newborn child is a girl, we can predict with almost complete certainty how she will be spending her time twenty-five years later. Her individuality does not have to be considered; it is irrelevant.[34]

Yet until very recently, most women have refused to recognize their own oppression. They have openly accepted the social definition of who and what they are. They have refused to be conscious of the fact that they are seen and treated, before anything else, as women. Many still do. This very refusal is significant because no group is so oppressed as one which will not recognize its own oppression. Women's denial that they must deal with their oppression is a reflection of just how far they still have to go.

There are many reasons why covert mechanisms of social control have been so much more successful with women than with most other minority groups. More than most they have been denied any history. Their tradition of subjection is long and even this history is purged from the books so women cannot compare the similarities of their current condition with that of the past. In a not-so-subtle way both men and women are told that only men make history and women are not important enough to study.

Further, the agents of social control are much nearer to hand than those of any other group. No other minority lives in the same household with its master, separated totally from its peers and urged to compete with them for the privilege of serving the majority group. No other minority so thoroughly accepts the standards of the dominant group as its own and interprets any deviance from those values as a sign of degeneracy. No other minority so readily argues for the maintenance of its own position as one that is merely "different" without questioning whether one must be the "same" to be equal.

Women reach this condition, this acceptance of their secondary role as right and just, through the most insidious mechanism of social control yet devised — the socialization process. That is the mechanism that we want to analyze now.

To understand how most women are socialized we must first understand how they see themselves and are seen by others. Several studies have been done on this. Quoting one of them, McClelland stated that "the female image is characterized as small, weak, soft, and light. In the United States it is also dull, peaceful, relaxed, cold, rounded, passive, and slow."[35] A more thorough study which asked men and women to choose out of a long list of adjectives those which most clearly applied to themselves showed that women strongly felt themselves to be such things as uncertain, anxious, nervous, hasty, careless, fearful, dull, childish, helpless, sorry, timid, clumsy, stupid, silly, and domestic. On a more positive side women felt they were: understanding, tender, sympathetic, pure, generous, affectionate, loving, moral, kind, grateful, and patient.[36]

This is not a very favorable self-image but it does correspond fairly well with the social myths about what women are like. The image has some nice qualities, but they are not the ones normally required for that kind of achievement to which society gives its highest social rewards. Now one can justifiably question both the idea of achievement and the qualities necessary for it, but this is not the place to do so. Rather, because the current standards are the ones which women have been told they do not meet, the purpose here will be to look at the socialization process as a mechanism to keep them from doing so. We will also need to analyze some of the social expectations about women and about what they define as a successful *woman* (not a successful person) because they are inextricably bound up with the socialization process. All people are socialized to meet the social expectations held for them and it is only when this process fails to do so (as is currently happening on several fronts) that it is at all questioned.

First, let us further examine the effects on women of minority-group status. Here, another interesting parallel emerges, but it is one fraught with more heresy than any previously observed. When we look at the *results* of female socialization we find a strong similarity between what our society labels, even extols, as the typical "feminine" character structure and that of oppressed peoples in this country and elsewhere.

In his classic study *The Nature of Prejudice,* Allport devotes a chapter to "Traits due to Victimization." Included are such personality characteristics as sensitivity, submission, fantasies of power, desire for protection, indirectness, ingratiation, petty revenge and sabotage, sympathy, extremes of both self and group hatred and self and group glorification, display of flashy status symbols, compassion for the underprivileged, identification with the dominant groups' norms, and passivity.[37] Allport was primarily concerned with Jews and Negroes, but compare his characterization with the very thorough review of the literature on sex differences among young children made by Terman and Tyler. For girls, they listed such traits as: sensitivity, conformity to social pressures, response to environment, ease of social control, ingratiation, sympathy, low levels of aspiration, compassion for the underprivileged, and anxiety. They found that girls compared to boys were more nervous, unstable, neurotic, socially dependent, submissive, had less self-confidence, lower opinions of themselves and of girls in general, and were more timid, emotional, ministrative, fearful, and passive.[38] These are also the kinds of traits found in the Indians when under British rule,[39] in the Algerians under the French,[40] and elsewhere.

Two of the most essential aspects of this "minority-group character structure" are the extent to which one's perceptions are distorted and one's group is denigrated. These two things in and of themselves are very effective means of social control. If one can be led to believe in one's own inferiority then one is much less likely to resist the status that goes with that inferiority.

When we look at women's opinions of women we find the notion that they are inferior prevalent just about everywhere. Young girls get off to a very good start. They begin speaking, reading, and counting sooner. They articulate more clearly and put words into sentences earlier. They have fewer reading and stuttering problems. Girls are even better in math in the early school years. They also make a lot better grades than boys do until late high school. But when they are asked to compare their achievements with those of boys, they rate boys higher in virtually every respect. Despite factual evidence to the contrary, girls' opinion of girls grows progressively worse with age while their opinion of boys and boys' abilities grows better. Boys, likewise, have an increasingly better opinion of themselves and worse opinion of girls as they grow older.[41]

These distortions become so gross that, according to Goldberg, by the time girls reach college they have become prejudiced against women. He gave college girls sets of booklets containing six identical professional articles in traditional male, female, and neutral fields. The articles were identical, but the names of the authors were not. For example, an article in one set would bear the name "John T. McKay" and in another set the same article would be authored by "Joan T. McKay." Questions at the end of each article asked the students to rate the articles on value, persuasiveness, and profundity and the authors for writing style and competence. The male authors fared better in every field, even in such "feminine" areas as art history and dietetics. Goldberg concluded that "Women are prejudiced against female professionals and, regardless of the actual accomplishments of these professionals, will firmly refuse to recognize them as the equals of their male colleagues."[42]

But these unconscious assumptions about women can be very subtle and cannot help but support the myth that women do not produce high-quality professional work. If the Goldberg findings hold in other situations, and the likelihood is great that they do, it explains why women's work must be of a much higher quality than that of men to be acknowledged as merely equal. People in our society simply refuse to believe that a woman can cross the caste lines and be competent in a "man's world."

However, most women rarely get to the point of writing professional articles or doing other things which put them in competition with men. They seem to lack what psychologists call the "achievement motive."[43] When we look at the little research that has been done we can see why this is the case. Horner's recent study of undergraduates at the University of Michigan showed that 65 percent of the women but only 10 percent of the men associated academic success with having negative consequences. Further research showed that these college women had what Horner termed a "motive to avoid success" because they perceived it as leading to social rejection and role conflict with their concept of "femininity."[44] Lipinski has also shown that women students associate success in the usual sense as something which is achieved by men, but not by women.[45] Pierce suggested that girls did in fact have achievement motivation but that they had different criteria for achievement than did boys. He went on to show that high achievement motivation in high-school women correlates much more strongly with early marriage than it does with success in school.[46]

Some immediate precedents for the idea that women should not achieve too much academically can be seen in high school for it is here that the performance of girls begins to drop drastically. It is also at this time that peer-group pressures on sex-role behavior increase and conceptions of what is "properly feminine" or "masculine" become more narrow.[47] One need only recall Asch's experiments to see how peer-group pressures, coupled with our rigid ideas about "femininity" and "masculinity," could lead to the results found by Horner, Lipinski, and Pierce. Asch found that some 33 percent of his subjects would go contrary to the evidence of their own senses about something as tangible as the comparative length of two lines when their judgments were at variance with those made by the other group members.[48] All but a handful of the other 67 percent experienced tremendous trauma in trying to stick to their correct perceptions.

These experiments are suggestive of how powerful a group can be in imposing its own definition of a situation and suppressing the resistance of individual deviants. When we move to something as intangible as sex-role behavior and to social sanctions far greater than simply the displeasure of a group of unknown experimental stooges, we can get an idea of how stifling social expectations can be. It is not surprising, in light of our cultural norm that a girl should not appear too smart or surpass boys in anything, that those pressures to conform, so prevalent in adolescence, prompt girls to believe that the development of their minds will have only negative results.

But this process begins long before puberty. It begins with the kind of toys young children are given to play with, with the roles they see their parents in, with the stories in their early reading books, and the kind of ambitions they express or actions they engage in that receive rewards from their parents and other adults. Some of the early differentiation along these lines is obvious to us from looking at young children and reminiscing about our own lives. But some of it is not so obvious, even when we engage in it ourselves. It consists of little actions which parents and teachers do every day that are not even noticed but can profoundly affect the style and quality of a child's developing mind.

Adequate research has not yet been done which irrefutably links up child-rearing practices with the eventual adult mind, but there is evidence to support some hypotheses. Let us take a look at one area where strong sex differences show up relatively early — mathematical reasoning ability. No one has been able to define exactly what this ability is, but it has been linked up with number ability and special perception or the ability to visualize objects out of their context. As on other tests, girls score higher on number ability until late high school, but such is not the case with analytic and special perception tests. These tests indicate that boys perceive more analytically while girls are more contextual — although the ability to "break set" or be "field independent" also does not seem to appear until after the fourth or fifth year.[49]

According to Maccoby, this contextual mode of perception common to women is a distinct disadvantage for scientific production. "Girls on the average develop a somewhat different way of handling incoming information — their thinking is less analytic, more global, and more perseverative — and this kind of thinking may serve very well for many kinds of functioning but it is not the kind of thinking most conducive to high-level intellectual productivity, especially in science."[50]

Several social-psychologists have postulated that the key developmental characteristic of analytic thinking is what is called early "independence and mastery training," or "whether and how soon a child is encouraged to assume initiative, to take responsibility for himself, and to solve problems by himself, rather than rely on others for the direction of his activities."[51] In other words, analytically inclined children are those who have not been subject to what Bronfenbrenner calls "oversocialization,"[52] and there is a good deal of indirect evidence that such is the case. Levy has observed that "overprotected" boys tend to develop intellectually like girls.[53] Bing found that those girls who were good at special tasks were those whose mothers left them alone to solve the problems by themselves while the mothers of verbally inclined daughters insisted on helping them.[54] Witkin similarly found that mothers of analytic children had encouraged their initiative while mothers of non-analytic children had encouraged dependence and discouraged self-assertion.[55] One writer commented on these studies that

This is to be expected, for the independent child is less likely to accept superficial appearances of objects without exploring them for himself, while the dependent child will be afraid to reach out on his own and will accept appearances without question. In other words, the independent child is likely to be more *active*, not only psychologically but physically, and the physically active child will naturally have more kinesthetic experience with spatial relationships in his environment.[56]

When we turn to specific child-rearing practices we find that the pattern repeats itself according to the sex of the child. Although comparative studies of parental treatment of boys and girls are not extensive, those that have been made indicate that the traditional practices applied to girls are very different from those applied to boys. Girls receive more affection, more protectiveness, more control and more restrictions. Boys are subjected to more achievement demands and higher expectations.[57] In short, while girls are not always encouraged to be dependent *per se,* they are usually not encouraged to be *independent* and physically active.

Such findings indicate that the differential treatment of the two sexes reflects in part a difference in goals. With sons, socialization seems to focus primarily on directing and constraining the boys' impact on the environment. With daughters, the aim is rather to protect the girl from the impact of environment. The boy is being prepared to mold his world, the girl to be molded by it."[58]

This relationship holds true cross-culturally even more than it does in our own society. In studying child socialization in 110 nonliterate cultures, Barry, Bacon, and Child found that "Pressure toward nurturance, obedience, and responsibility is most often stronger for girls, whereas pressure toward achievement and self-reliance is most often stronger for boys."[59] They also found that strong differences in socialization practices were consistent with highly differentiated adult sex roles.

These cross-cultural studies show that dependency training for women is widespread and has results beyond simply curtailing analytic ability. In all these cultures women were in a relatively inferior status position compared to males. In fact, there was a correlation with the degree of rigidity of sex-role socialization, and the subservience of women to men.

In our society also, analytic abilities are not the only ones valued. Being person-oriented and contextual in perception are very valuable attributes for many fields where, nevertheless, very few women are found. Such characteristics are valuable in the arts and the social sciences where women are found more than in the natural sciences — yet even here their achievement is still not deemed equivalent to that of men. One explanation of this, of course, is the repressive effect of role conflict and peer-group pressures discussed earlier. But when one looks further it appears that there is an earlier cause here as well.

As several studies have shown, the very same early independence and mastery training which has such a beneficial effect on analytic thinking also determines the extent of one's achievement orientation[60] — that drive which pushes one to excel beyond the need of survival. And it is precisely this kind of training that women fail to receive. They are encouraged to be dependent and passive — to be "feminine." In that process the shape of their mind is altered and their ambitions are dulled or channeled into the only socially rewarded achievement for a woman — marriage.

Now we have come almost full circle and can begin to see the vicious nature of the trap in which our society places women. When we become conscious of the many subtle mechanisms of social control — peer-group pressures, cultural norms, parental training, teachers, role expectations, and negative self-concept — it is not hard to see why girls who are better at most everything in childhood do not excel at much of anything as adults.

Only one link remains and that requires taking a brief look at those few women who do manage to slip through a chance loophole. Maccoby provided the best commentary on this when she noted that the girl who does not succumb to overprotection and develop the appropriate personality and behavior for her sex has a major price to pay: the anxiety that comes from crossing the caste lines. She feels that "it is this anxiety which helps to account for the lack of productivity among those women who do make intellectual careers — because (anxiety) is especially damaging to creative thinking." The combination of all these factors together tell "something of a horror story." It would appear that even when a woman is suitably endowed intellectually and develops the right temperament and habits of thought to make use of her endowment, she must be fleet of foot indeed to scale the hurdles society has erected for her and to remain a whole and happy person while continuing to follow her intellectual bent.[61]

The plot behind this horror story should by now be clearly evident. There is more to oppression than discrimination and more to the condition of women than whether or not they want to be free of the home. All societies have many ways to keep people in their places, and we have only discussed a few of the ones used to keep women in theirs. Women have been striving to break free of these bonds for many hundreds of years and once again are gathering their strength for another try. It will take more than a few changes in the legal system to significantly change the condition of women, although those changes will be reflective of more profound changes taking place in society. Unlike blacks, the women's liberation movement does not have the thicket of Jim Crow laws to cut through. This is a mixed blessing. On the one hand, the women's liberation movement lacks the simple handholds of oppression which the early civil-rights movement had; but at the same time it does not have to waste time wading through legal segregation before realizing that the real nature of oppression lies much deeper. It is the more basic means of social control that will have to be attacked as women and men look into their lives and dissect the many factors that made them what they are. The dam of social control now has many cracks in it. It has held women back for years but it is about to break under the strain.

REFERENCES

1. Sandra and Daryl Bem, "We're All Non-Conscious Sexists," *Psychology Today* (November 1970), p. 26.

2. Sir Henry Sumner Maine, *Ancient Law* (London: Murray, 1905), p. 135.

3. Alvin W. Gouldner, *Enter Plato* (New York: Basic Books, 1965), p. 10.

4. Numa Denis Fustel de Coulanges, *The Ancient City* (Garden City, N.Y.: Doubleday, 1873), pp. 42–94.

5. Richard B. Morris, *Studies in the History of American Law* (Philadelphia: Mitchell, 1959), pp. 126–128.

6. Mary Beard, *Woman as Force in History* (New York: Macmillan, 1946), pp. 108–109.

7. Edward Mansfield, *The Legal Rights, Liabilities and Duties of Women* (Salem, Mass.: Jewett, 1845), p. 273.

8. Sophonisba Breckinridge, *The Family and the State* (Chicago: University of Chicago Press, 1934), pp. 109–110.

9. Blanche Crozier, "Marital Support," 15 *Boston University Law Review* 28 (1935).

10. Philip Francis, *The Legal Status of Women* (New York: Oceana, 1963), p. 23.

11. Citizens Advisory Council on the Status of Women, *Report of the Task Force on Family Law and Policy*, 1968, p. 2.

12. *Ibid.*, p. 39.

13. Leo Kanowitz, *Women and the Law: The Unfinished Revolution* (Albuquerque: University of New Mexico Press, 1969), p. 41.

14. George Gould and Ray F. Dickenson, The American Social Hygiene Association, *Digest of State and Federal Laws Dealing with Prostitution and Other Sex Offenses*, 1942.

15. Bernard M. Dickens, *Abortion and the Law* (Bristol: MacGibbon & Kee, 1966), p. 15.

16. Alan F. Guttmacher, "Abortion — Yesterday, Today and Tomorrow," in

A. F. Guttmacher, ed., *The Case for Legalized Abortion Now* (Berkeley: Diablo Press, 1967), p. 4.

17. Helen Mayer Hacker, "Women as a Minority Group, *Social Forces,* 31 (October 1951), p. 67.

18. *Lockner v. New York,* 198 U.S. 45 (1905).

19. *Mueller v. Oregon,* 208 U.C. 412 (1908).

20. British feminists always opposed such laws for their country on the grounds that any sex-specific laws were fraught with more evil than good.

21. Alice Henry, *The Trade Union Woman* (New York: Appleton, 1915), p. 24.

22. U.S. Department of Labor, *Summary of State Labor for Women* (February 1967), *passim.*

23. *Ibid.*

24. *Sellers, Moore and Case v. Colgate Palmolive Co. and the International Chemical Workers Union, Local No. 15,* 272 Supp. 332; Minn. L. Rev. 52: 1091.

25. *Brief for the Plaintiffs/Appellants in the Seventh Circuit Court of Appeals,* No. 16, 632, p. 5.

26. Gunnar Myrdal, *An American Dilemma* (New York: Harper, 1944), p. 1073.

27. George Fitzhugh, *Sociology for the South* (Richmond, Va.: Morris, 1854), p. 86.

28. The first was the Equal Pay Act of 1963 which took 94 years to get through Congress.

29. Caroline Bird, *Born Female: The High Cost of Keeping Women Down* (New York: McKay, 1968), Chapter I.

30. Eleanor Flexner, *Century of Struggle* (New York: Atheneum, 1959), p. 71. They were joined by one white and one black man, William Lloyd Garrison and John Cronan.

31. Jo Freeman, "The New Feminists," *The Nation* (Feb. 24, 1969), p. 242.

32. Myrdal, *op. cit.,* p. 1073.

33. Hacker, *op. cit.,* pp. 10–19.

34. Bem and Bem, *op. cit.,* p. 7.

35. David McClelland, "Wanted: A New Self-Image for Women," *The Women in America,* ed. by Robert J. Lifton (Boston: Beacon Press, 1965), p. 173.

36. Edward M. Bennett and Larry R. Cohen, "Men and Women: Personality Patterns and Contrasts," *Genetic Psychology Monographs,* Vol. 59, 1959, pp. 101–155.

37. Gordon W. Allport, *The Nature of Prejudice* (Reading, Mass.: Addison-Wesley, 1954), pp. 142–161.

38. Lewis M. Terman and Leona E. Tyler, "Psychological Sex Differences," *Manual of Child Psychology,* ed. by Leonard Carmichael (New York: Wiley, 1954), pp. 1080–1100.

39. Lewis Fisher, *Gandhi* (New York: New American Library, 1954).

40. Franz Fanon, *The Wretched of the Earth* (New York: Grove Press, 1963).

41. S. Smith, "Age and Sex Differences in Children's Opinion Concerning Sex Differences," *Journal of Genetic Psychology*, 54 (1939), pp. 17–25.

42. Philip Goldberg, "Are Women Prejudiced Against Women?" *Transaction*, (April 1969).

43. McClelland, *op. cit., passim.*

44. Matina S. Horner, "Woman's Will to Fail," *Psychology Today*, 3:6 (November 1969), p. 36. See also: Matina S. Horner, *Sex Differences in Achievement Motivation and Performance in Competitive and Non-Competitive Situations*, unpublished doctoral dissertation, University of Michigan, 1968.

45. Beatrice Lipinski, *Sex-Role Conflict and Achievement Motivation in College Women*, unpublished Ph.D. dissertation, University of Cincinnati, 1965.

46. James V. Pierce, "Sex Differences in Achievement Motivation of Able High School Students," Cooperative Research Project No. 1097, University of Chicago, December 1961.

47. Lionel J. Neiman, "The Influence of Peer Groups upon Attitudes Toward the Feminine Role," *Social Problems*, 2 (1954), pp. 104–111.

48. S. E. Asch, "Studies of Independence and Conformity: A Minority of One Against a Unanimous Majority," *Psychological Monographs*, 70 (1956), No. 9.

49. Eleanor E. Maccoby, "Sex Differences in Intellectual Functioning," *The Development of Sex Differences*, ed. by E. Maccoby (Stanford University Press, 1966), p. 26ff. The three most common tests are the Rod and Frame Test which requires the adjustment of a rod to a vertical position regardless of the tilt of a frame around it; the Embedded Figures Test which determines the ability to perceive a figure embedded in a more complex field; and an analytic test in which one groups a set of objects according to a common element.

50. Eleanor E. Maccoby, "Woman's Intellect," in *The Potential of Women*, ed. by Farber and Wilson (New York: McGraw-Hill, 1963), p. 30.

51. Maccoby, *ibid.*, p. 31. See also: Julia A. Sherman, "Problems of Sex Differences in Space Perception and Aspects of Intellectual Functioning," *Psychological Review*, 74:4 (July 1967), pp. 290–299; and Philip E. Vernon, "Ability Factors and Environmental Influences," *American Psychologist*, 20:9 (September 1965), pp. 723–733.

52. Urie Bronfenbrenner, "Some Familial Antecedents of Responsibility and Leadership in Adolescents," in *Leadership and Interpersonal Behavior*, ed. by Luigi Petrullo and Bernard M. Bass (New York: Holt, Rinehart and Winston, 1961), p. 260.

53. D. M. Levy, *Maternal Overprotection* (New York: Columbia University Press, 1943).

54. Maccoby, "Woman's Intellect," *op. cit.*, p. 31.

55. H. A. Witkin, R. B. Dyk, H. E. Patterson, D. R. Goodenough, and S. A. Karp, *Psychological Differentiation* (New York: Wiley, 1962).

56. James Clapp, "Sex Differences in Mathematical Reasoning Ability," unpublished paper, 1968.

57. R. R. Sears, E. Maccoby, and H. Levin, *Patterns of Child Rearing* (Evanston, Ill.: Row and Peterson, 1957).

58. Bronfenbrenner, *op. cit.*, p. 260.

59. Herbert Barry, M. K. Bacon, and Irving L. Child, "A Cross-Cultural

Survey of Some Sex Differences in Socialization," *Journal of Abnormal and Social Psychology*, 55 (November 1957), p. 328.

60. Marian R. Winterbottom, "The Relation of Need for Achievement to Learning Experiences in Independence and Mastery," *Basic Studies in Social Psychology*, ed. by Harold Proshansky and Bernard Seidenberg (New York: Holt, Rinehart and Winston, 1965), pp. 294–307.

61. Maccoby, *op. cit.*, p. 37.

19. INSIDE THE CLOCKWORK OF MALE CAREERS

Arlie Russell Hochschild

I would like to start by asking a simple and familiar question: Why, at a public university like the University of California at Berkeley in 1972, do women compose 41 percent of the entering freshmen, 37 percent of the graduating seniors, 31 percent of the applicants for admission to graduate school, 28 percent of the graduate admissions, 24 percent of the doctoral students, 21 percent of advanced doctoral students, 12 percent of Ph.D.'s, 38 percent of instructors, 9 percent of assistant professors, 6 percent of associate professors, and 3 percent of full professors (Erwin–Tripp, 1973)? This classic pattern is typical for women at all major universities, and the situation in nearly all of them is, as in Berkeley, worse than it was in 1930 (Graham, 1971).[1]

I have heard three standard explanations for this classic pattern, but I doubt that either gets to the bottom of the matter. One explanation is that the university discriminates against women. If only tomorrow it could halt discrimination and become an impartial meritocracy, there would be many more academic women. There is no question that discrimination goes on, but I think the issue runs deeper — the system eliminates women not so much through malevolent disobedience to good rules as through making up rules to suit half the population in the first place.

The second explanation is that women are trained early to avoid success and authority, and cool themselves out by a sort of "autodiscrimination." It is admittedly hard to distinguish between women who remove themselves from the university and women who are removed or who are

From *Women & the Power to Change*, edited by Florence Howe. Copyright © 1975 by the Carnegie Commission on Higher Education. Used with permission of McGraw-Hill Book Company.

moved to remove themselves. For there are innumerable aspects of graduate school that are quite discriminatory, but simply in a general way *discouraging* — the invisibility of women among the teachers and writers of the books one reads, the faces framed on the walls of the faculty club, the paucity of women at the informal gathering over beer after the seminar. There is also the continual, semiconscious work of sensing and avoiding professors who are known to dislike or discredit women or particular types of women. But this too is a symptom of the deeper problem.

The third explanation is that women in universities lack good role models. What we have now is a scattering of women who have found private solutions to a public problem. They provide models of personal struggle and overwork (e.g., the amazon model of the woman who "does everything"), but any useful model is a model of a normal woman in a reasonable *situation;* its models of situations we need, and those we will lack until the system itself changes.

These three explanations for why there are so few women are not in themselves wrong. They are simply partial. Underlying the problems each of these explanations points to is a more profound problem: namely, that the classic profile of the academic career is cut to the image of the traditional man with his traditional wife. To ask why more women are not full professors, or "full" anything else in the upper reaches of the economy, we have to ask first what it means to be a male full professor — socially, morally, and humanly — and what kind of system makes them into what they become.

The academic career is founded on some peculiar assumptions about the relation between doing work and competing with others, competing with others and getting credit for work, getting credit and building a reputation, building a reputation and doing it while you're young, doing it while you're young and hoarding scarce time, hoarding scarce time and minimizing family life, minimizing family life and leaving it to your wife — the chain of experiences that seems to anchor the traditional academic career. Even if the meritocracy worked perfectly, even if women did not cool themselves out, I suspect there would remain in a system that defines careers this way only a handful of women at the top.

There are two important assumptions behind the male career. One is the assumed relation between work and what competition turns work into — the quest for reputation. The second is the assumed relation between reputation and time. In universities today, the stress is less on work than on "getting credit for" work. It is less on solving an intellectual problem than on being "the first" recognized as solving the problem. To borrow from movement language, one can manage to get a reputation in the "star system," and knowing you have to want to become one, or becoming even a minor star is what women learn in man-made careers.

A reputation is measured against time — that is, against the year one is born. Age discrimination is not some separate extra unfairness thoughtlessly tacked on to universities; it follows from the bottommost assumptions about university careers. If jobs are scarce and promising reputations important, who wants a 50 year old mother of three with a dissertation almost completed? Time becomes a scarce resource that one hoards greedily, and time becomes the thing one talks about when one is wasting it. If "doing one's work" is a labor of love, love itself comes to have an economic and honorific base. One's attitude toward it becomes an indelible part of the career — *self*. Male styled careers introduce women to a new form of time consciousness; it is not age measured against beauty as in our "first" training, but age measured against the finely measured credits that construct a reputation. If work, conceptualized as a career, becomes a measured line, the line often appears to be a rising one. Very often the rising career line is also, despite a residual cynicism about power, associated with a pleasant belief in the progress of the world. Even those who have refused to fit this profile know very well that they are measured against it by others who rise to the top, and, from this top-of-the-career world view, set the prevailing standards.

The new importance of time to work is related to the unimportance — for men — of families. Families subtract time from work. And at present men and women have different ties to the family. I think this is not accidental, for the university (a comparatively flexible institution at that) seeks to immunize itself against the vicissitudes of human existence that are out of its control. Some of these vicissitudes are expressed and absorbed in the family: birth at one end of the life cycle and death at the other. Lower ages at retirement handle the "problem" of death, and the exclusion of women the "problem" of birth. (If it could, the university would also guard against other human traumas, sickness, insanity, post-divorce depression, now removed from it by sabbaticals and leaves of absence.) The family is in some sense a preindustrial institution and lives in a private, more flexible time, remote from the immortal industrial clock. The family absorbs vicissitudes that the workplace discards.

It is the university's welfare agency, and women are its social workers. That is to say, the family serves a function for the university, and at present women have more to do with the family than men. As a result, Machiavelli's advice suits them less well. Women Ph.D.'s in the United States spend about 28 hours per week on household tasks (Graham, 1971). Also, the twenties and sometimes the thirties are normally a time to bear and raise children. But it is at precisely this stage that one begins to hear talk about "serious contribution to the field" and "reputation," which are always more or less promising than those of another of one's age. The result is apparent from a glance at a few crucial details cemented to her curriculum vita: How long did she take for the degree?

Full-time, continuous work? Previous jobs, the best she could get? But the result shows too in how she sees herself in a career. For most academic women have been socialized at least twice, once to be women (as housewives and mothers) and once again to be like men (in traditional careers). The second socialization raises the issue of *assimilation* to the male culture associated with academic life; the first socialization raises the issue of what women abandon in the process. The question we must unbury lies between the first socialization and the second: How much do women want careers to change them and how much do women want to change careers?

THE CAREER CULTURE AND THE FAMILY

The links between competition, career, reputation, and time consciousness extend to life that is at once outside the university but inside the career culture: that is, to the family and to the faculty wife. The university has no *formal* administrative policy toward the families of its members. I have never heard of the university equivalent to the "farming out system" in early industry, or of families being brought into the university the way they were taken into nineteenth-century factories. Certainly we do not hear of a family winning a Ford Foundation grant, aunts and uncles doing the interviewing, husband and wife the analysis and writing, leaving footnotes to the children. While books have been typed, if not partly written, by wives, the family in the university has never been the productive *unit* of it.

Nonetheless, I think we have what amounts to a tacit policy toward the family. Let us consider the following: *if all else were equal,* who would be most likely to survive under the career system — a man married to a full-time housewife and mother; or a man whose wife has a nine-to-five job and the children in day care; or a man who works part-time, as does his wife, while their children are small? I think the general principle that determines the answer is this: *To the extent that his family (1) does not positively help him in his work or (2) makes demands on his time and psychic energy that compete with those devoted to his job, they lower his chances for survival. This is true insofar as he is competing with other men whose wives either aid them or do not interfere with their work.* Other things being equal, the university rewards the married family-free man.

But intellectual productivity is sometimes discussed as if it were a gift from heaven to the chosen few, which had nothing to do with families or social environment at all. If we inspect the social context of male productivity, we often find nameless women and a few younger men feeding the "productive one" references, computer outputs, library books, and cooked dinners. Women, single or married, are in competition not simply with men, but with the *heads of small branch industries.*

A few book prefaces tell the familiar story. A book on racial oppression written in 1972:

Finally, I would like to thank my wife ———, who suffered the inconveniences that protracted writing brought about with as much graciousness as could be expected, and who instructed our children, ——— and ———, to respect the privacy of their father's work.

An earlier book, 1963: In many ways my wife Suzanne should be coauthor. She shared the problems of planning and carrying out the field work, and the life of a wife-mother-interviewer in another culture was more demanding than either of us might have imagined. Although she did not take part in the actual writing, she has been a patient sounding board, and her concern with individual cases provided a needed balance to my irrepressible desire to paint the broad picture.

Still one more, 1962: ———, to whom I was then married, helped in the field work, and a number of the observations in the book are hers.

These are excellent books, and they have taught me a great deal, but then so have the prefaces to them.

If this puts liberated men at a competitive disadvantage, needless to say it does the same to liberated women. It is a familiar joke in women's circles to say, "What I really need is a wife." Young women in graduate school today are, according to the 1969 Carnegie survey, much more likely (63 percent) to have husbands in academe than are men to have academic wives (14 percent). Typed page for typed page, proofread line for proofread line, soothing hour for soothing hour, I suspect that, all else being equal, a traditional male, minus a modern woman, is more likely than anyone else to end up a branch manager.

This total situation is often perceived as a "woman's problem," her role conflict, as if that conflict were detachable from the career system itself. It is her problem to choose between a few prepackaged options: being a housewife, or professor, or trying to piece together a collage of wife, mother, and *traditional* career. The option we do not hear about, one that would make it a man's problem or a university problem as well, is parenthood with a radically new sort of career. Affirmative action plans aren't talking about this.

Given the academic career as it is now, women can only improvise one or another practical solution for fitting their families to their careers. Many professional women of my generation either waited to have children until two years into their first "real" job or had them before beginning graduate school. One had her children in-between and resolved the dual pressures by using her children as data for her books. Those who waited until they were in their late twenties or early thirties often did so precisely to avoid premature discrimination, only to discover that the real pressure point lay not behind but slightly ahead. Nearly half the women who remain in academic life solve the problem by not marrying or not rearing children at all. In a 1962 study of 21,650 men and 2,234 women scientists and engineers, women were six times more likely than men never to marry. Those women who married were less likely than their male colleagues to raise a family: 36 percent of women and 11 percent of men had no children. Those women who did have children had fewer: the families of women scientists and engineers were, compared with those of their male counterparts, one child smaller (David, 1973). Among graduate students, the proportion who consider dropping out increases for women with each new child born, but remains the same for men.[2] Another study of women who received their doctorates between 1958 and 1963 in a number of fields found that only 50 percent of the women had married by 1967. Among the men, 95 percent were married (Simon et al., 1967).

Half of the women and nearly all of the men married; it's a painful little statistic, and I say that without being derogatory to single women. It is one thing for a woman to freely *decide* against marriage or children as issues on their own merits. But it is quite another matter to be forced into the choice because the career system is shaped for and by the man with a family who is family-free.[3]

SITUATION AND CONSCIOUSNESS

It is for a minority of academic women with children that the contradictions exist in their full glory. My own solution may be uncommon, but not the general contours of my dilemma. When I first decided to have a child at the age of 31, my thoughts turned to the practical arrangements whereby I could continue to teach, something that means a great deal to me. Several arrangements were possible, but my experiment was a preindustrial one — to introduce the family back into the university, to take the baby with me for office hours on the fourth floor of Barrows Hall. From two to eight months, he was, for the most part, the perfect guest. I made him a little cardboard box with blankets where he napped (which he did most of the time), and I brought along an infant seat from which he kept an eye on key chains, colored notebooks, earrings, and glasses. Sometimes waiting students took him out into the hall and passed him around. He became a conversation piece with shy students, and some returned to see him rather than me. I put up a fictitious name on the appointment list every four hours and fed him alone or while on the telephone.

The baby's presence proved to be a Rorschach test, for people reacted very differently. Older men, undergraduate women, and a few younger men seemed to like him and the idea of his being there. In the next office there was a distinguished professor of 74; it was our joke that he would stop by when he heard the baby crying and say, shaking his head, "Beating the baby again, eh?" Publishers and book salesmen in trim suits and exquisite sideburns were generally shocked. Graduate student women would often inquire about him tentatively, and a few feminists were put off, perhaps because babies are out of fashion these days, perhaps because his presence seemed "unprofessional."

One incident brought into focus my identity and the university's bizarre power to maintain relationships in the face of change. It happened about a year ago. A male graduate student had come early for his appointment. The baby had slept longer than usual and got hungry later than I had scheduled by Barrows Hall time. I invited the student in. Since we had never met before, he introduced himself with extreme deference. He seemed acquainted with my work and tastes in the field, and as I am often tempted to do, I responded to that deference by behaving more formally than I otherwise might. He began tentatively to elaborate his interests in sociology and to broach the subject of asking me to serve on his orals committee. He had the onerous task of explaining to me that he was a clever student, a trustworthy and obedient student, but that academic fields were not organized as he wanted to study them; and of asking me, without knowing what I thought, whether he could study Marx under the rubric of the sociology of work.

In the course of this lengthy explanation, the baby began to cry. I gave him a pacifier and continued to listen all the more intently. The student went on. The baby spat out the pacifier and began to wail. Finally, trying to be casual, I began to feed him. He wailed now the strongest, most rebellious wail I had ever heard from this small armful of person.

The student uncrossed one leg and crossed the other and held a polite smile, coughing a bit as he waited for this little crisis to pass. I excused myself, and got up to walk back and forth with the baby to calm him down. "I've never done this before. It's just an experiment," I remember saying.

"I have two children of my own," he replied. "Only they're not in Berkeley. We're divorced and I miss them a lot." We exchanged a human glance of mutual support, talked of our families more, and soon the baby calmed down.

A month later when John had signed up for a second appointment, he entered the office, sat down formally. "As we were discussing last time, Professor Hochschild. . . ." Nothing further was said about the prior occasion, but more astonishing to me, nothing had changed. I was still Professor Hochschild and he was still John. Something about power lived on regardless.

In retrospect, I felt a little like one of the characters in *Dr. Dolittle and the Pirates,* the pushme-pullyu, a horse with two heads that see and say different things. The pushme head was relieved that motherhood had not reduced me as a professional. But the pullyu wondered what the pervasive power differences were doing there in the first place. And why weren't children in offices occasionally part of the "normal" scene?

At the same time I also felt envious of the smooth choicelessness of my male colleagues who did not bring their children to Barrows Hall. I sometimes feel this keenly when I meet a male colleague jogging on the track (it's a popular academic sport because it takes little time) and then meet his wife taking their child to the YMCA kinder-gym program. I feel it too when I see wives drive up to the building in the evening, in the station wagon, elbow on the window, two children in the back, waiting for a man briskly walking down the steps, briefcase in hand. It seems a particularly pleasant moment in the day for them. It reminds me of those Friday evenings, always a great treat, when my older brother and I would pack into the back of our old Hudson, and my mother with a picnic basket would drive up from the suburbs to Washington, D.C., at five o'clock to meet my father, walking briskly down the steps of the State Department, briefcase in hand. We picnicked at the Cherry Basin surrounding the Jefferson Memorial, my parents sharing their day, and in that end-of-the-week mood, we came home.

Whenever I see similar scenes, something inside rips in half, for I am neither and both the brisk-stepping carrier of a briefcase and the mother with a packed picnic lunch. The university is designed for such men, and their homes for such women. It looks easier for them and part of me envies them for it. Beneath the envy lies a sense of my competitive disadvantage vis-à-vis the men to whom I am compared and to whom I compare myself. Also beneath it, I am aware of the bizarreness of my experiment with the infant box, and paradoxically aware too that I am envious of a life I would not really like to live.

The invisible half of this scene is, of course, the woman in the station wagon. She has "solved" the problem in one of the other possible ways. But if both her way and my way of solving this "problem" seem to lead to strains, it may be that the problem is not only ours. It may be the inevitable result of a public system arranged not for women with families but for family-free men.

THE WHOLE OF THE PROBLEM:
THE PARTS OF THE SOLUTION

The problem for American women today is not so much going to work, since over 40 percent of women of working age are in the labor force already and nine out of ten women work some time in their lives. The problem is now one of moving *up*, and that means moving into careers. More fundamentally, the problem for women in academic or other sorts of careers is to alter the link between family and career, and more generally, between private and public life. Several alternatives seem both possible and just. First, women might adopt a relation to home and family indistinguishable from that of their male competitors. Women could marry househusbands if they can find them, or hire a substitute wife-mother in their absence. Academic women could thereby establish a two-roled life for another person (a husband), or divide such roles between husband and housekeeper. If the housekeeper were well paid and unionized, perhaps we could still talk about justice; otherwise I think not. But neither a housekeeper nor a child-care center would solve the problem completely, since tending the sick, caring for the old, writing Christmas cards, and just being there for people in their bad moments — what wives do — still need doing. In my view, even when we have eliminated the needless elaboration of a wife's role, a humanly satisfying life requires that someone do these things.

Second, academic men who want careers might give up marriage or children, just as many academic women have. If the first alternative makes women more like men, this one makes men more like academic women, in extending to them the familiar two-box choice of family or career. This would be more just, but I doubt it would be popular among men.

One can understand women who opt for the first alternative, given the absence of other choices. Insofar as it involves a reverse family imperialism, however, I do not see why it is any better than the original male one. Because I value at least the option of family life, I cannot endorse the second solution either. Since neither appeals to me as a long-range solution, I am led to a third alternative: the possibility of an egalitarian marriage with a radically different career to go with it. This means creating a different system in which to work at this different career, a system that would make egalitarian marriage *normal*.

The university makes virtually no adjustments to the family, but the traditional family makes quite a few to the university. And it is not so much the brisk-stepping man with the briefcase as it is his wife with the picnic basket who makes the adjustments for "the family's sake" (somehow amorphously connected to his career.) I think the reason for this is that it is easier to change families than universities. But the contradictions of changing families without changing careers leads to either migraine headaches or hearty, rebellious thoughts.

Any vision of changing something as apparently implacable as the career system may seem at first ludicrous or utopian. But as Karl Mannheim (1936) once pointed out, all movements for social change need a utopia, built of parts borrowed from different or theoretical societies.

This need not be a utopia for dreaming that remains separate from waking life, but a utopia that, like reading a good book, shows us where and how far we have to go, a vision that makes sense of frustration by analyzing its source. In the 1970s, when utopias already seem quaint, when public visions seem a large shadow over many small private aims, when jobs are scarce and competition magnified, now in the 1970s more than ever we need a guiding vision.

For a start, all departments of 20 full-time men could expand to departments of 40 part-time men and women. This would offer a solution to our present dilemma of trying to meet the goals of affirmative action within a "steady state" (or declining) economy. It would mean more jobs for women and men. It would democratize and thus eliminate competitive disadvantages and offer an opportunity to some of those women in the station wagon. In many fields, research would leap ahead if two people rather than one worked on problems. Teaching would certainly not be hurt by the arrangement and might benefit from the additional energies.

While administrative arrangements would be manageable, I can imagine queries about efficiency. Is it economical to train 40 Ph.D's to work part-time when 20 could do the same amount of work? And what of those who simply do not want part-time work? One can point to the new glut of Ph.D.'s and argue that if those currently teaching in universities were to divide and share their jobs, many more might gain the chance to work. The effect would not eliminate but reduce competition for university jobs.

Part-time work is very often more like three-fourths-time work, for one teaches students rather than classes. If a graduate student moves to Ecuador and sends me his paper, I read it. If a former student comes around to the house, I talk to her. If there is a meeting, I don't leave halfway through the hour. Part-time often turns out to be a release in quantity to improve quality.

But that raises the financial issue. The sorry fact is that, for financial reasons, most men and some women do not want half-time work. A male professor may work long hours when his children are young and there are doctor bills, and again when they are in college and there are tuition bills. But two part-time workers earn two part-time salaries, and there are social disadvantages to the one overworked–one underworked family pattern.

Hearsay has it that a group of MIT male assistant professors, who had worked late evenings because they were in competition with each other for advancement while their wives took care of the children, made a pact to cut down their hours and spend more time with their young children. Maybe many private pacts could lead to a larger public one, but only when those who set the standards are part of it.

While one may debate the virtues or defects of competition, it is an aspect of university life that we need not take for granted, that can be, and I think should be, modified. Some elements of my own utopia are borrowed from the Cuban experiment, since it bears on the issue of competition. The Cuban revolution made its share of mistakes, and not all of its successes are applicable to a rich industrial country. But the basic lesson to be learned from Cuba is that competition can be modified not only by splitting jobs (which it did not try to do), but by creating jobs to fit social needs. This may seem a bit far afield in an essay on universities, but my analysis brings me to it. For in my view, we cannot change the role of women in universities without changing the career system based on competition, and we can't change that competitive structure without also altering the economy, the larger fit of supply and demand of workers. We need thus to explore the experiments in altering that.

I visited the University of Havana in the summer of 1967 and joined some students and faculty who were working together doing "productive labor" (they don't think this phrase is redundant), planting coffee plants in the belt surrounding Havana. As we moved along the rows, people talked about the university before the revolution. It sounded in some ways like a more intense version of Berkeley in both the 1960s and 1970s.

The competition was so fierce for the few professional jobs in the cities that rich students bought grades. (That is only one step removed from the profitable cynicism of the term paper industries, like "Quality Bullshit" in Berkeley, where a student can buy a custom-written paper from some unemployed graduate students.)

At the same time, Cuban students hung around the university cafes dropping out and back in again, wondering who they were. Before 1958 there were some 3,000 students at the University of Havana trying to enter the diplomatic service, while there was only a handful of electrical engineers in the whole country. The revolution put the university in touch with economic realities, and it changed those economic realities by inventing jobs where there was a social need for them. Since the revolution, the task has not been to restrict admission, but to supply the tremendous need for doctors, dentists, teachers, and architects as clients of the poor, paid by the government. The revolution simply recognized and legitimated a need that had always been there.

Corresponding to the supply of graduates American universities turn out each year, there is, I believe, a "social need." There is, for example, a great need for teachers in crowded classrooms, and yet we speak of the teacher "surplus." Despite the AMA, and the fierce competition to enter medical school, we need doctors, especially in ghettos and in prisons. We need quality day care, community organizers, traveling artists. Yet there are, we say, "too many people" and "not enough jobs." If social need coincided with social demand for skills, if market value were coextensive with use value, we could at least in some fields eliminate *needless* competition generated outside the university, which affects what goes on inside as well. I personally do not think "education for leisure" is the answer, for it ignores all the social ills that persist even in a rich industrial country, not to mention those outside it. If we redefine what a social need is, and design jobs to meet social needs, we also reduce the exaggerated competition we see in universities, a competition that inevitably moves women out. If the division of jobs alleviates competition among academics, the creation of jobs can alleviate competition among would-be workers, including, of course, professors.[4]

There is another lesson to be learned from Cuba, too. Insofar as American career women become like career men, they become oriented toward success and competition. Just as manhood has traditionally been measured by success, so now academic womanhood is defined that way. But manhood, for the middle-class American academic man, is based *more* on "doing well" than on "doing good." Manhood in professional circles is linked to an orientation toward "success," which is kept scarce and made to seem valuable. Men are socialized to competition because they are socialized to scarcity. It is as if sexual identity, at least in the middle class, were not freely given by nature, but conserved only for those who earn it. Manhood at birth seems to be taken from men, only for them to re-win it. The bookish boy is defined as girlish and then, with a turnabout, earns his manhood as a creative scholar in the university. To fail to "do well" at this is to be robbed in degrees of manhood.

I think there is a human propensity to achieve competence, what Thorstein Veblen (1914) called simply an "instinct for workmanship," but it comes to have a secondary meaning for *manhood*. The competition that takes the form of secrecy attached to new ideas before they are in final draft for the publisher, the vita talk, the 60-hour work weeks, the station wagon wife, all are related to this secondary meaning of work, this second layer of value associated with success and manhood. It is this second meaning that women feel they must analogously adopt and compete with.

Yet the reputation so won is often totally detached from social usefulness or moral purpose. For such men, *morality* has become a *luxury*. Women who learn to aspire to this deficiency lose what was valuable from our first training – a training not only to be invisible, but, in a larger sense, to "do good" rather than simply to "do well." Insofar as women, like other marginal groups, *overconform* in the attempt to gain acceptance, we find ourselves even more oriented toward success, and less toward morality, than some men.

The Cuban revolution seems to me to have solved at least this dilemma, simply by trying structurally to equate "doing well" with "doing good," achievement with moral purpose. The assimilation of Cuban women entering a male-dominated economy does not seem to mean the eclipse of morality. Cuban women have not escaped the doll's house to enter a career of "bourgeois individualism"; they have, despite other problems, escaped that as well.

Conclusion

To talk as I have about the evils of the system as they affect a handful of academic women is a little like talking about the problems of the suburb while there are people trying to escape the ghetto. But there are problems both with trying to find a meaningful career and with having one on the system's terms. The two problems are more than distantly related. Both finding an academic job and remaining humane once you have had one for a while are problems that lead ultimately to the assumptions about families that lie behind careers. At present, women are either slowly eliminated from academic life or else forced imperceptibly to acquire the moral and psychic disabilities from which male academics have had to suffer.

If we are to bring more women into the university at every level, we shall have to do something more extreme than most affirmative action plans have imagined: change the present entente between the university and its service agency, the family. If we change this, we also introduce into academe some of the values formerly the separate specialty of women. We leave the ethos of "making it" with another ethos of care-taking and cooperation, leaven the *gesellschaft* with the values of *gemein-schaft*. It is, after all, not simply women but some feminine values that have been discriminated against. It is not simply that we lack role models who happen to be women, but that we lack exemplars of this alternative ethos.

What I am trying to say is that social justice, giving women a fair break, is a goal that speaks for itself, and a goal that calls for men doing their fair share in private life and for women getting their fair chance in public life. But there are two ways of creating this social justice. One involves fitting into the meritocracy as it is; the other aims to change it. Insofar as we merely extend "bourgeois individualism" to women, ask for "a room of one's own," a reputation, sparring with the others, we fit in nicely with the normal distortion of the importance of success versus moral purpose, the experience of time, or quality of talk that men experience.

The very first step is to reconsider what parts in the cultural recipe of our first socialization to nurturance and caring are worth salvaging in ourselves, and the second step is to consider how to extend and institutionalize them in our place of work. The second way of creating social justice less often speaks up for itself: it is to democratize and reward that cooperative, caretaking, morally concerned, not-always-lived-up-to womanly virtue of the past. We need *that* in careers, that among our full professors of either sex. My utopian university is not a Tolstoyan peasant family, but it is also not vita talking to vita. It requires a move in the balance between competition and cooperation, doing well and doing good, taking time to teach a child to swim and taking time to vote in a department meeting. When we have made that change, surely it will show in book prefaces and office talk.

REFERENCES

1. See Alice S. Rossi and Ann Calderwood (eds.), *Academic Women on the Move* (1973); Susan Mitchell, *Women and the Doctorate* (1968); and a publication based on the recent massive survey sponsored by the Carnegie Commission: Saul Feldman, *Escape from the Doll's House: Women in Graduate and Professional School Education* (1974). See also Carnegie Commission on Higher Education, *Opportunities for Women in Higher Education* (1973).

2. According to Carnegie data, 57 percent of men with no children, 58 percent with one, 58 percent with two, and 59 percent with three considered quitting for good in the last year. For women, it was 42 percent with no children, 48 percent for one, 42 percent for two, and 57 percent for three. Three seems to be a crucial number. Among graduate students nationally between 1958 and 1963, 44 percent of men and 55 percent of women actually did drop out, but 49 percent of men with children and 74 percent of women with children did so (Sells, forthcoming doctoral dissertation).

Simon et al. (1967) found that married women without children were slightly less likely to have published a book than were married women with children. Age was not considered, and of course it might account for this otherwise unexpected finding. Forty percent of unmarried, 47 percent of married, and 37 percent of married mothers were assistant professors; 28 percent, 16 percent, 15 percent were associates; and 18 percent, 8 percent, and 8 percent were full professors (Simon et al., 1967). Fifty-eight percent of unmarried women, 33 percent of married, and 28 percent of married women with children (among those earning their degrees in 1958–59) had tenure. Another study comparing men and women showed that 20 years after getting their degrees, 90 percent of the men, 53 percent of the single women, and 41 percent of the married women had reached a full professorship (Rossi, 1970).

3. A woman's college that has administered questionnaires each year since 1964 to entering freshmen found that 65 percent of the class of 1964 wanted to be a housewife with one or more children. In the following years, the percentage dropped steadily: 65, 61, 60, 53, 52, 46, and 31. The proportion who wanted career and marriage with children doubled, from 20 to 40 percent. The difference between Stanford women surveyed in 1965 and in 1972 is even more dramatic: in all, only 18 percent mentioned the role of wife and mother as

part of their plans for the next five years (see Carnegie Commission, 1973).

4. How a nation or university "legislates" that supply meets demand for jobs without becoming authoritarian raises not simply an administrative but a serious political issue to which I have no easy answer. Here I only mean to show that dividing up old jobs and creating new ones is a possible way of alleviating competition that underlies the career system.

BIBLIOGRAPHY

Astin, Helen: *The Woman Doctorate in America,* Russell Sage Foundation, New York, 1969.

Bernard, Jessie: *Academic Women,* World Publishing Company, New York, 1966.

Carnegie Commission on Higher Education: *Opportunities for Women in Higher Education,* McGraw-Hill Book Company, New York, 1973.

David, Deborah: "Marriage and Fertility Patterns of Scientists and Engineers: A Comparison of Males and Females," paper delivered at the American Sociological Association Convention, New York, September 1973.

Ervin-Tripp, Susan M.: "Report of the Committee on the Status of Women," University of California, Berkeley, May 21, 1973.

Feldman, Saul: *Escape from the Doll's House: Women in Graduate and Professional School Education,* McGraw-Hill Book Company, New York, 1974.

Graham, Patricia A.: "Women in Academe," in Athena Theodore (ed.), *The Professional Woman,* Schenkman Publishing Co., Inc., Cambridge, Mass., 1971, pp. 720–740.

Kerr, Clark: *The Uses of the University,* Harvard University Press, Cambridge, Mass., 1963.

Kriegel, Leonard: *Working Through,* Saturday Review Press, New York, 1972.

Lee, Dorothy: *Freedom and Culture,* Prentice-Hall, Englewood Cliffs, N.J., 1965.

Lehman, H.: *Age and Achievement,* Princeton University Press, Princeton, N.J., 1953.

Lehman, H.: "More About Age and Achievement," *The Gerontologist,* vol. 2, no. 3, 1962.

Lehman, H.: "The Production of Masterworks Prior to Age Thirty," *The Gerontologist,* vol. 5, no. 1, pp. 24–29, 1965.

Lofting, Hugh: *Dr. Dolittle and the Pirates,* Beginner Books, a division of Random House, Inc., New York, 1968.

Mannheim, Karl: *Ideology and Utopia, an Introduction to the Sociology of Knowledge,* L. Wirth and E. Shils (trans.), Harcourt, Brace, London, 1936.

Mitchell, Susan: *Women and the Doctorate,* U.S. Department of Health, Education and Welfare, Office of Education, Bureau of Research, Washington, D.C., 1968.

Papanek, Hanna: "Men, Women, and Work: Reflections on the Two-Person Career," in Joan Huber (ed.), *Changing Women in a Changing Society,* The University of Chicago Press, Chicago, 1973.

Rossi, Alice S.: "Status of Women in Graduate Departments of Sociology," *The American Sociologist,* vol. 5, pp. 1–12, February 1970.

Rossi, Alice S., and Ann Calderwood (eds.): *Academic Women on the Move,* Russell Sage Foundation, New York, 1973.

Sells, Lucy: Forthcoming doctoral dissertation, University of California, Berkeley.

Simon, Rita J., Shirley M. Clark, and Kathleen Galway: "The Woman Ph.D.: A Recent Profile," *Social Problems,* vol. 15, pp. 221–236, 1967.

Veblen, Thorstein: *The Instinct of Workmanship and the State of the Industrial Arts,* Viking Press, New York, 1914.

20. GAY IS GOOD FOR US ALL

Suzannah Lessard

"Oh no, not the fairies too!" said a woman watching the Gay Liberation Movement march up Sixth Avenue last June, with a quizzical, good-humored expression on her face, as though they were so many puppies. "I'm from Ohio. I think it's funny," said a tourist. "I'd like to kick the shit out of them," said a clean, tense young man turning on his heel. No one quite knew how to react. Few grasped the implications or viewed it as more than either a circus or an abomination. But the marchers were confident. They had taken the trick out of the trick mirror; the invisible homosexual was now massively visible. With what seemed hardly more than a flick of the wrist they had upturned a whole new complex of bigotry and exclusion into broad sunlight, and the astonished prejudices could do little more than blink.

And once again, with the emergence of the Gay Movement, the old image of society as a vertical structure with one group holding another in subjugation was transformed into something more like a many-leveled house of cards, suits straining against each other, Queens standing on Knaves, one-eyed Jacks trumping Queens, the ceiling of one set forming the floor of another, with only one simple element in the complex of relationships — the position in the throne room of the white, male, hetero-sexual King.

The movement was born one night in August, 1969, when the New

York police raided the Stonewall Inn, a gay bar on Christopher Street. It was by no means the first time — few of the many gay bars in the Village vicinity were immune to the arbitrary raids which usually ended in several arrests and many more bruises and broken heads. But this time, to the amazement of the Sixth Precinct, the homosexuals refused to take their punishment passively. The sissies fought back. Word of the brawl traveled, the gay community turned out in force, and the battle spread from the bar into what came to be known as the Christopher Street Riot, a free-for-all in which cars were overturned, fires lit, and police sent to the hospital. After that the image of the homosexual in the eyes of the world, and, more important, in his own eyes as well, was irrevocably altered.

Prior to Christopher Street, the two major homosexual organizations, the Mattachine Society and the Daughters of Bilitis, were small and necessarily timid. Though Mattachine did make statements to the effect that homosexuality was neither pathological nor depraved, its objectives were in fact limited to helping the homosexual adjust within the society, providing social activities and legal and medical help, and backing conservative campaigns to change the more flagrant anti-homosexual laws. They were limited because their members were limited: homosexuals tended to be isolated and inhibited, having taken the one course they could really afford, which was to pass for heterosexual in order to pursue careers and life within the society, both of which would likely be destroyed were their homosexuality exposed. So their endeavor was not to battle the dragon but to sneak around it, to "get by" with a minimum of pain.

Furthermore, most people view the homosexual as a criminal and a pervert, an attitude deeply embedded in the culture; and it would take rare assurance for a homosexual not to let this attitude pervade his own image of himself and further deter his drive to challenge it.

OUT OF THE CLOSET INTO THE STREET

Out of Christopher Street the Gay Liberation Front was formed. In New York and subsequently in every major city in the country, the Front recruited, held workshops, and started newspapers. Many of the members were also part of the New Left, and, like the women, they started by confronting prejudice among their peers, educating them to the oppressiveness of their attitudes and the problems of the homosexual. After 10 months they had grown big enough and become inwardly confident enough to organize a mass march up Sixth Avenue in New York. It was touch and go down to the wire, however. No one knew until the last minute whether more than a handful would actually show up, and few thought the march would reach its destination in Central Park without a violent confrontation with bystanders or the police.

But thousands and thousands turned out for the first big holiday from the closet. The festive mood was intoxicating. People in their Sunday best, their hippie best, lots of workshirt and jeans types, a few fantastic costumes — they looked more like a peace march to whom the President had just capitulated than *homosexuals*. They just didn't *look* queer, and that fact registered everything from horror to discomfort to plain surprise on the faces of people on the sidelines. As one marcher put it, "So much has been accomplished in terms of who we are. We are people." And not only were they people, but they were evidently quite happy. The happy homosexual was supposed to be an impossibility. These together struck a solid blow at the assumption that homosexuality is in itself distorting, sad, and sick. Rather, it becomes clear that the conditions under which society forces it to exist are the causes of all those traits — deviousness, self-deprecation, unstable relationships — that we have been accustomed to linking inextricably with the way of life.

This seemed to have been a discovery for the marchers as well. After lives of secrecy and guilt, coming out into the open with the assertion "Gay is Good" gave them a healthy sense of self many hadn't known for years. "Coming out has been a delight," a woman recently told me. "It's difficult to imagine what it was like before. We are conditioned not to remember pain."

The briefest glance uncovers the depth of prejudice which the movement hopes to vanquish. The psychoanalytic tradition describes homosexuality entirely in terms of sickness, arrested development, unhealthy parental relationships, etc. Upon learning that a friend is homosexual, most of us, however sympathetic, have a tendency to conjure up an image of his mother. We assume that something has gone wrong, that the person has become homosexual for negative reasons, because he was unable to deal with some problem, and hence his choice represents a failure of sorts. The masculinity cult in America colors all our attitudes. Qualities like courage, effectiveness, and leadership are considered superior and are associated with virility, and conversely, the "feminine virtues" of tenderness, docility, and patience are considered of less importance. Men are expected to embody virility, and women maternity. Deviates from these roles are thought to be "half a man" or "half a woman" — and inferior in areas which have nothing whatever to do with sexuality. To most straight people, it is simply self-evident that a heterosexual is "better" than a homosexual. The notion that it's not a misfortune to have a child become a homosexual is as strange as the suggestion of one member of the movement that when a child discovers he is homosexual, the parents, not the child, should go to a psychiatrist to try to overcome their hang-ups about homosexuality.

The legal tradition is even harsher. In all states but one (Illinois), sodomy is a crime with sentences running as high as 10 years' minimum and referred to in such phrases as "infamous crime against nature." Under this legal umbrella, discriminatory hiring practices exist unchallenged. For instance, the Civil Service Commission handbook on personnel states flatly that a homosexual is not suitable for service because his condition would automatically impair his efficiency as well as "inhibiting" those who were forced to work with him. This policy was recently overturned in a District of Columbia Court of Appeals, but the decision applies only to hiring within the D.C. Circuit. Further, because many homosexuals are reluctant to expose themselves to publicity, Civil Service has been able to pursue its old policy within the District with few challenges.

The armed forces also have policies to the effect that homosexuality is an incapacitating condition which undermines discipline and makes the individual incapable of leading a constructive life. These policies have led to the dishonorable discharge of many men as well as Wacs and Waves. The women's services are one of the few areas where intense job discrimination against lesbians exists. In most cases lesbians, who can in any event hide their homosexuality more easily than men, are discriminated against primarily as women.

Beyond these formalities, antihomosexuality permeates the popular culture. "Faggot" is a universal term of derision. Wherever homosexuals are portrayed in movies they are ridiculous or desperate or disgusting. The old man in "Midnight Cowboy" was revolting, and Joe Buck responded "naturally" when he hit him. The host in "Boys in the Band" was pathetic. Both lesbians in "Five Easy Pieces" looked ugly in a movie full of pretty people. These versions of the homosexual generally go unquestioned. They fulfill our preconceived notions and affirm heterosexual superiority.

It seems clear that this overall attitude is irrational, that there is no necessary connection between worthiness and sexuality, and that whether or not one considers homosexuality a sickness these policies and attitudes are a barbarous response. It would seem that attitudes towards homosexuality are far more unacceptable, far more degrading to those who hold them — as well as those who endure them — than homosexuality itself could ever be.

SISTERS

Bonds between Gay Lib and Women's Lib grew early. It was a natural affiliation; they both were rebelling against roles predetermined by sex and felt oppressed by the chauvinistic heterosexual male. Both worked to develop a sense of self-worth against the long-accepted condition of second-class citizenship. The women were also struggling with the influence of the psychoanalytic tradition which, as Kate Millett put it in speaking of Freud, "assumed that to be born female was to be born castrated" and therefore innately inferior to the potent male. It was not a smooth affiliation, however. Straight women found they had to struggle with sex chauvinism in dealing with the gay men and were, in turn, guilty of resisting the lesbian within their own ranks for fear the movement, which was already being ridiculed as "a bunch of dykes," would be discredited. However, despite the resistance they encountered in Women's Lib groups, the larger percentage of activist lesbians has chosen Women's Liberation as their primary point of identification and Gay Liberation second, thus bringing the gay struggle into the heart of the women's movement.

On the whole, society seems to be less outraged by lesbians than by male homosexuals. After all, within the context of sex roles, the male is rejecting kingship, thus blaspheming what society holds most holy — whereas the lesbian is rejecting servitude, a futile act for one born with the indelible marks of a servant. Secondly, it has long been the prejudice of Western tradition that women endure rather than enjoy sex (Freud insisted that their only pleasure came from a masochistic enjoyment of pain) and hence sex between women is nonsensical. Thirdly, because a woman's homosexuality is far less manifest, to the extent that she can apparently function perfectly within a marriage, lesbians seem to be a rarity rather than a social "problem." If anything, men find lesbians titillating, à la James Bond, Pussy Galore — a challenge, something to be conquered, coerced into the proper reverence for their irresistible powers. On the other side of the coin, lesbians are the gravest threat to the sex role power structure, for they are at the bottom of the pack, the ace if you will, and independent of men — so that in rebelling they have nothing to lose. This is what has brought them into a unique position within the women's movement. As a Radicalesbian statement put it, "Lesbian is the word that holds women in line."

The resistance to homosexuals within the Women's Lib movement has not been overcome in all factions. The more establishment oriented, such as the National Organization for Women, have adamantly insisted on their heterosexual purity (though even NOW is expected to come out with a statement on lesbians in the next month reversing its policy). But in the more radical groups, lesbians have evolved a very special role for themselves. As one woman said, "As lesbians we are truly independent of men, and it's very important for straight women to see that that's possible. We just aren't dependent on that candy bar" — the candy bar being the hope for some form of masculine approval. Some women have even gone so far as to become "political lesbians" — that is, to become lesbians on purpose so as to utterly sever their dependence on men, presumably in order to eventually reenter relationships with men from a position of equal inner strength. That is certainly an extreme; a more moderate measure is for a woman to reply to the question of whether she is or is not a lesbian in the affirmative regardless of fact, thus reducing the word to meaninglessness and eliminating the fear of being called a "dyke" for stepping out of the homebody, "real woman" role which society has cut out for her.

So, though the relationship has been trouble-fraught (in some places they're not speaking to each other), Gay Lib and Women's Lib have played crucial roles in each other's development. Together they expose the underbelly of society in a more extensive, penetrating way than either could alone, uncovering the depth and extent to which predetermined masculine/feminine roles have governed social dynamics, not only allowing but often forcing one group of people to exploit another.

Ho-Ho-Homosexual

A sector of Gay Lib has extended its horizons beyond Women's Lib. A strong element in the Gay Liberation Front of New York brought radical politics explicitly into the Gay platform, ultimately causing a split within the New York group. A break-off group, the Gay Activists Alliance (GAA) was then formed. The GAA limits its activities to gay liberation per se and works, though militantly, within the system, while the GLF men consider themselves revolutionaries first. Though groups in other cities haven't split, the same elements exist in all, the more militant factions resolving their position within the whole by forming radical caucuses. GLF women in general identify primarily with the Women's Lib movement; the more revolutionary lesbians having formed their own group, Radicalesbians, which like the GLF/New York men identifies primarily with political revolution. These groups are by no means mutually exclusive.

The revolution-oriented gay men and women explain their fusion of the two causes thus (their arguments being greatly reduced here): the basic unit of the sex role structure is the family in which the woman performs menial chores for the man, who is thus freed to pursue more lofty ambitions. The family is also the basic consumer unit of the capitalist system, which stresses the connection between worthiness (you can read power here) and the acquisition of objects. This is directly related to the sex role nature of the family, in that among the objects a man accumulates is his wife (this is a version of the thesis that men treat women primarily as sex objects), hopefully beautiful, efficient, and at the service of his pleasure. This relationship between the acquisition of goods and power over women is emphasized unequivocally in advertising, the lubricant of capitalism in its function of engendering greed. Capitalism, then, is based on the assumption that people are greedy for goods — and the power that goods bring. It assumes that these basic facts cannot be changed, that social planning can only be corrective within the system, not redirective. The result of this power-acquisitive urge has been racism, imperialism, and sexism. Revolution says these "facts of nature" can be changed, but to do so you have to raze the system which nourishes them. In other words, to achieve true gay liberation you have to do away with capitalism which, in its present form, is deeply intertwined with sexism — just as in order to achieve black liberation you must dissolve the system, because in the same power-oriented manner it induces people of one race to beat up on another. And this is why the causes of the nigger, the dyke, the bitch, and the faggot are one and the same and why these Causes Incorporated must be geared to the overthrow of capitalism.

It is easy to punch holes in this argument, to call it simplistic, metaphorical, in parts fanciful, but that would be, I think, a dodge to avoid recognizing a certain genius at work in it. The genius is in great need of refinement, granted, but it is there. My reaction to the argument at this point is that somehow it doesn't manage to produce its own kernel. And while I'm no great defender of capitalism it seems clear that sexism, racism, and imperialism have occurred under every system, Marxism included, and that by doing away with capitalism you will by no means insure yourself against these evils. The revolutionary gays will agree with me there, but counter that while oppression can certainly exist without capitalism, the particular form of capitalism which has actually evolved is so deeply rooted in oppression that it would be impossible to purge the system without in effect destroying it.

The merging of Gay Lib and Women's Lib directly with revolution raises another issue: how do you describe these groups — are they a class, a caste, or what? This is more than a semantic issue, because the confusion in definition represents, I think, a real confusion within these groups in terms of who they are. The terms class and caste are really relevant only in a metaphorical sense; the social structure one combats as a gay person or a woman is far more kaleidoscopic, more mercurial than what one combats as an economically oppressed person. "People use the economic thing to negate the gay movement," said a black member of GLF. "They don't stop to consider how many gay people belong to economically oppressed groups." NOW is currently waging a battle with the FCC over the equal priority of sex and race discrimination in hiring practices: "Without equal enforcement against sex discrimination, employers are encouraged to discriminate on every other one of the prohibited bases — race, color, creed, and national origin — as long as they do so against women." But because women and homosexuals have numbers among the oppressed class does not make them as a group an oppressed class, though the dynamics of discrimination described above are very real and suggest the nature of the bond, of the common denominator which they share. Women and homosexuals, respectively, belong to groups, or kinds, with certain common traits which society has arbitrarily invested with symbolic meaning — i.e., that your value as a lawyer, doctor, thinker, is discernible through those traits — female, homosexual — which actually tell nothing whatever about your value in those capacities.

But whatever the exact role and definition of any group within the structure, all discriminations, as suggested by the NOW statement, aid and nourish each other — witness the KKK slogan "Don't be half a man, join the Klan" — and, conversely, there is a kinship between all oppressed groups. When one group relates its condition to another, however metaphorically, there is a sudden subjective realization of kinship which transcends all antagonisms.

INSTITUTIONS IN CRISIS

THE ENVIRONMENT   VI

One of the most important social developments of the last decade has been the emergence of a diverse and widespread ecology movement, as great numbers of American people woke up to the fact that their rivers, lakes, oceans, and air were rapidly deteriorating under the impact of economic "progress." Today, the deepening tragedy of environmental destruction, and the crying need to do something about it, are widely felt in American society. But there is little agreement on the causes of the environmental crisis or on the best means for its solution.

Two main approaches have emerged during the past few years: The first, widespread in the early ecology movement and still widely held by many writers on environmental issues, holds that environmental problems are the inevitable result of a high level of industrialization, expanding population, and our supposed craving for more and more consumer goods. From this perspective, the basic problem is *people* — too many of them, consuming too much and making extravagant demands on the earth's limited resources. And the remedy (if there is one) is seen in terms of self-renunciation; we must learn to do with less — less population, less energy consumption, fewer material goods, reduced aspirations. Many people who share this perspective, in fact, see *no* likely solutions to the environmental crisis, and urge us to withdraw into our own private worlds and enjoy ourselves while we can, in the limited time before the general catastrophe.

The second approach focuses more on the specific social, political, and economic forces that shape the crisis of the environment. While granting that such things as the sheer number of people and the growth of industry generally lead

to deep and complex ecological problems in any political and
economic system, this perspective suggests that the depth and
extent of the environmental crisis in the United States, as well
as the resistance to developing effective means of dealing with
it, are reflections of the drive for private profit at the heart of
the American economy. The quest for profit is not responsible
for all of our environmental problems, but it does aggravate
those that already exist and creates new ones all its own.

How does the drive for profit result in destruction of the
environment? The selections in this chapter illustrate several
ways in which this happens. In the selection from his book
The Closing Circle, Barry Commoner develops a general argument explaining the relation between pollution and profit in
the capitalist economy. According to Commoner, the key
problem is the profitability of introducing new technologies —
technologies that may have a devastating impact on the natural
environment and even on the functioning of the industry itself,
but that provide a very high rate of profit for the corporations,
at least over the short run. In Commoner's view, the dramatic
destruction of the environment in the years since World War
II was primarily the result of the explosion of these new technologies, which enriched the large corporations while im-
poverishing everyone else.

This key point — that what is bad for the environment may
be "good business" from the point of view of the giant corporations — is detailed in the next two selections. In Supership,
Noel Mostert provides a direct illustration of the process described by Commoner. The oil companies' search for ever
higher profits has led them to develop ever larger and more
complex supertankers to meet increased demands for energy.
As these ships get bigger and bigger, they are more carelessly
and shoddily constructed, more poorly staffed, and their operating principles less well understood. The result, as Mostert
graphically shows, has been an almost incredible record of
repeated wrecks, explosions, and oil spills, which have taken
a tremendous toll in lives and environmental destruction, and
which promise to become worse in the future.

Finally, in his study of the history of American ground
transport, Bradford Snell provides a shocking story of corporate complicity in the destruction of the environment on a
massive scale. It's well known that the dominance of the
automobile has been the source of much of our air pollution
problem — as well as the more general distortion of the urban
and rural landscape produced by freeways, parking lots, and

the other artifacts of automotive civilization. But Snell shows that the rise of the private automobile and the decline of other, more efficient, and less polluting means of transportation was in large part the result of a conscious policy by the auto and oil corporations — especially General Motors — to destroy systematically other forms of ground transportation in order to create dependency on the automobile. His study speaks volumes about the relation between corporate profit and the deepening destruction of the natural and social environment in the twentieth century.

21. THE ECONOMIC MEANING OF ECOLOGY

Barry Commoner

What is the connection between pollution and profit in a private enterprise economic system such as the United States? Let us recall that in the United States intense environmental pollution is closely associated with the technological transformation of the productive system since World War II. Much of our pollution problem can be traced to a series of large scale technological displacements in industry and agriculture since 1946. A number of the new, rapidly growing productive activities are much more prone to pollute than the older ones they have displaced.

Thus, since World War II, in the United States, private business has chosen to invest its capital preferentially in a series of new productive enterprises that are closely related to the intensification of environmental pollution. What has motivated this pattern of investment? According to Heilbroner:

Whether the investment is for the replacement of old capital or for the installation of new capital, the ruling consideration is virtually never the personal use or satisfaction that the investment yields to the owners of the firm. Instead, the touchstone of investment decisions, is *profit*.

The introduction of new technology has clearly played an important role in the profitability of postwar business enterprise. The economic factor that links profit to technology is *productivity*, which is usually defined as the output of product per unit input of labor. Productivity has grown rapidly since World War II and, according to Heilbroner, this is largely due to the introduction of new technologies in that period of time. The following relationship seems to be at work: new investment in the postwar economy, as expected, has moved in directions that appeared to promise, and in fact yielded, increased profit; these investments have been heavily based on the introduction of new technology, which is a major factor in the notable increase in productivity, the major source of profit.

If these relationships have been operative in the technological displacements that, as we have seen, have played such an important role in generating the environmental crisis in the United States, then we would expect to find, in the appropriate statistics, that production based on the new technology has been more profitable than production based on the old technology it has replaced. That is, the new, more polluting technologies should yield higher profits than the older, less polluting technologies they have displaced.

The available data seem to bear out this expectation. A good example is the pervasive displacement of soap by synthetic detergents. As it happens, United States government statistics report economic data on the combined soap and detergent industry. In 1947, when the industry produced essentially no detergents, the profit was 30 per cent of sales. In 1967, when the industry produced about one-third per cent soap and two-thirds per cent detergents, the profit from sales was 42 per cent. From the data for intervening years it can be computed that the profit on pure detergent sales is about 52 per cent, considerably higher than that of pure soap sales. Significantly, the industry has experienced a considerable increase in productivity, labor input relative to output in sales having declined by about 25 per cent. Clearly, if profitability is a powerful motivation, the rapid displacement of soap by detergents — and the resultant environmental pollution — has a rational explanation. This helps to explain why, despite its continued usefulness for most cleaning purposes, soap has been driven off the market by detergents. It has benefitted the investor, if not society.

The synthetic chemical industry is another example that illustrates some of the reasons for the profitability of such technological innovations. This is readily documented from an informative volume on the economics of the chemical industry published by the Manufacturing Chemists' Association. The chemical industry, particularly the manufacturers of synthetic organic chemicals, during the 1946–66 period recorded an unusually high rate of profit. During that period, while the average return on net worth for all manufacturing industries was 13.1 per cent, the chemical industry averaged 14.7 per cent. The MCA volume offers an explanation for this exceptionally high rate of profit. This is largely based on the introduction of newly developed materials, especially synthetic ones. For about from four to five years after a new, innovative chemical product reaches the market, profits are well above the average (innovative firms enjoy about twice the rate of profit of noninnovative firms). This is due to the effective monopoly enjoyed by the firm that developed the material, that permits the establishment of a high sales price. After four to five years, smaller competitors are able to develop their own methods of manufacture; as they enter the market, the supply increases, competition intensifies, the price drops, and profits decline. At this point the large innovative firm, through its extensive research and development effort, is ready to introduce a new synthetic substance and can recover a high rate of profit. And so on. As the MCA volume points out: "The maintenance of above average profit margins requires the continuous discovery of new products and specialties on which high profit margins may be earned while the former products in that category evolve into commodity chemicals with lower margins." It is therefore no accident that the synthetic organic chemical industry has one of the highest rates of investment in research and development (in 1967, 3.7 per cent of sales, as compared with an average of 2.1 per cent for all manufacturing industries).

Thus, the extraordinarily high rate of profit of this industry appears to be a direct result of the development and production at rapid intervals of new, usually unnatural, synthetic materials — which, entering the environment, for reasons already given, often pollute it. This situation is an ecologist's nightmare, for in the four to five year period in which a new synthetic substance, such as a detergent or pesticide, is massively moved into the market — and into the environment — there is literally not enough time to work out its ecological effects. Inevitably, by the time the effects are known, the damage is done and the inertia of the heavy investment in a new productive technology makes a retreat extraordinarily difficult. The very system of enhancing profit in this industry is precisely the cause of its intense, detrimental impact on the environment.

It is significant that since 1966, the profit position of the chemical industry has declined sharply. Industry spokesmen have themselves described environmental concern as an important reason for this decline. For example, at recent congressional hearings, an industry official pointed out that a number of chemical companies had found pesticide manufacturing decreasingly profitable because of the need to meet new environmental demands. Because of these demands, costs of developing new pesticides and of testing their environmental effects have risen sharply. At the same time, cancellation or suspension of official pesticide registrations increased from 25 in 1967 to 123 in 1970. As a result, a number of companies have abandoned production of pesticides, although over-all production continues to increase. One company reported that it had dropped pesticide production "because investments in other areas promised better business."

Another explicit example of the impact of environmental concern on the profitability of new chemicals is NTA, a supposedly nonpolluting substitute for phosphate in detergents. Under the pressure of intense public concern over water pollution due to detergent phosphates, the industry developed NTA as a replacement. Two large firms then proceeded to construct plans for the manufacture of NTA — at a cost of about $100 million each. When the plants were partially built, the United States Public Health Service advised against the use of NTA, because of evidence that birth defects occur in laboratory animals exposed to NTA. The new plants had to be abandoned, at considerable cost to these firms. As a result of such hazards, research and development expenditures in the chemical industry have recently declined — a process which is likely to reduce the industry's profit position even more.

Nitrogen fertilizer provides another informative example of the link between pollution and profits. In a typical United States Corn Belt farm, a yield that is more than from 25 to 30 bushels per acre below present averages may mean no profit for the farmer, . . . [P]resent corn yields depend on a high rate of nitrogen application. Under these conditions, the uptake of nitrogen by the crop is approaching saturation, so that an appreciable fraction of the fertilizer drains from the land and pollutes surface waters. In other words, under present conditions, it appears that the farmer *must* use sufficient fertilizer to pollute the water if he is to make a profit. Perhaps the simplest way to exemplify this tragic connection between economic survival and environmental pollution is in the words of one thoughtful farmer in recent testimony before the Illinois State Pollution Control Board:

> Money spent on fertilizer year in and year out is the best investment a farmer can make. It is one of our production tools that hasn't nearly priced itself out of all realm of possibility as is the case with machinery and other farm inputs. Fertilizer expense in my case exceeds $20 per acre, but I feel I get back one to three dollars for every dollar spent on fertilizer. . . . I doubt that I could operate if I lost the use of fertilizers and chemicals as I know them today. I hope adequate substitutes are developed and researched if the government decides our production tools are a danger to society.

National statistics support this farmer's view of the economic importance of fertilizers or pesticides. These statistics show that whereas such chemicals yield three or four dollars per dollar spent, other inputs — labor and machinery, for example — yield much lower returns.

This is evidence that a high rate of profit is associated with practices that are particularly stressful toward the environment and that when these practices are restricted, profits decline.

Another important example is provided by the auto industry where the displacement of small, low-powered cars by large, high-powered ones is a major cause of environmental pollution. Although specific data on the relationship between profitability and crucial engineering factors such as horsepower do not appear to be available, some more general evidence is at hand. According to a recent article in *Fortune* magazine:

As the size and selling price of a car are reduced, then, the profit margin tends to drop even faster. A standard United States sedan with a basic price of $3,000, for example, yields something like $250 to $300 in profit to its manufacturer. But when the price falls by a third, to $2,000, the factory profit drops by about half. Below $2,000, the decline grows even more precipitous.

Clearly, the introduction of a car of reduced environmental impact, which would necessarily have a relatively low-powered, low-compression engine and a low over-all weight, would sell at a relatively low price. It would therefore yield a smaller profit relative to sales price than the standard heavy, high-powered, high-polluting vehicle. This may explain the recent remark by Henry Ford II, that "minicars make miniprofits."

. . . [P]rominent among the large-scale technological displacements that have increased environmental impacts are certain construction materials: steel, aluminum, lumber, cement, and plastics. In construction and other uses, steel and lumber have been increasingly displaced by aluminum, cement (in the form of concrete), and plastics. In 1969 the profits (in terms of profit as per cent of total sales) from steel production (by blast furnaces) and lumber production were 12.5 per cent and 15.4 per cent respectively. In contrast, the products that have displaced steel and lumber yielded significantly higher profits: aluminum, 25.7 per cent; cement, 37.4 per cent; plastics and resins, 21.4 per cent. Again, displacement of technologies with relatively weak environmental impacts by technologies with more intensive impacts is accompanied by a significant increase in profitability.

A similar situation is evident in the displacement of railroad freight haulage (relatively weak environmental impact) and truck freight haulage (intense environmental impact). In this case, economic data are somewhat equivocal because of the relatively large capital investment in railroads as compared to trucks (the trucks' right-of-way being provided by government-supported roads). Nevertheless, truck freight appears to yield significantly more profit than railroad freight; the ratio of net income to shareholders' and proprietors' equity in the case of railroads is 2.61 per cent, and for trucks, 8.84 per cent (in 1969).

In connection with the foregoing examples, in which profitability appears to increase when a new, more environmentally intense technology displaces an older one, it should be noted that not all new technologies share this characteristic. For example, the displacement of coal-burning locomotives by diesel engines *improved* the environmental impact of rail-roads between 1946 and 1950, for diesel engines burn considerably less fuel per ton-mile of freight than do coal-burning engines. Unfortunately, this improvement has been vitiated by the subsequent displacement of railroad freight haulage by truck freight, and at the same time made no lasting improvement in the railroads' economic position. It is also evident that certain new technologies, which are wholly novel, rather than dis-placing older ones — for example, television sets and other consumer elec-tronics — may well be highly profitable without incurring an unusually intense environmental impact. The point of the foregoing observations is not that they establish the rule that increased profitability inevitably means increased pollution, but only that many of the heavily polluting new technologies have brought with them a higher rate of profit than the less polluting technologies they have displaced.

Nor is this to say that the relationship is intentional on the part of the entrepreneur. Indeed, there is considerable evidence, some of which has been cited earlier, that the producers are typically unaware of the poten-tial environmental effects of their operation until the effects become manifest, after the limits of biological accommodation have been ex-ceeded, in ecological collapse or human illness. Nevertheless, despite these limitations, these examples of the relationship between pollution and profit-taking in a private enterprise economic system need to be taken seriously, I believe, because they relate to important segments of the economic system of the world's largest capitalist power.

In response to such evidence, some will argue that such a connection between pollution and profit-taking is irrational because pollution de-grades the quality of the environment on which the future success of even the most voracious capitalist enterprise depends. In general, this argument has a considerable force, for it is certainly true that industrial pollution tends to destroy the very "biological capital" that the ecosys-tem provides and on which production depends. A good example is the potential effect of mercury pollution from chloralkali plants on the suc-cessful operation of these plants. Every ton of chlorine produced by such a plant requires about 15,000 gallons of water, which must meet rigorous standards of purity. This water is obtained from nearby rivers or lakes, in which purity is achieved by ecological cycles, driven by the metabolic activities of a number of microorganisms. Since mercury compounds are highly toxic to most living organisms, the release of mercury by chlor-alkali plants must be regarded as a serious threat to the sources of pure water on which these plants depend. Nevertheless, it is a fact that in this and other instances, the industrial operation — until constrained by out-side forces — has proceeded on the seemingly irrational, self-destructive course of polluting the environment on which it depends.

A statistician, Daniel Fife, has recently made an interesting observation that helps to explain this paradoxical relationship between the profitability of a business and its tendency to destroy its own environmental base. His example is the whaling industry, which has been driving itself out of business by killing whales so fast as to ensure that they will soon become extinct. Fife refers to this kind of business operation as "irresponsible," in contrast with a "responsible" operation, which would only kill whales as fast as they can reproduce. He points out that even though the irresponsible business will eventually wipe itself out, it *may be profitable to do so* — at least for the entrepreneur, if not for society — if the extra profit derived from the irresponsible operation is high enough to yield a return on investment elsewhere that outweighs the ultimate effect of killing off the whaling business. To paraphrase Fife, the "irresponsible" entrepreneur finds it profitable to kill the goose that lays the golden eggs, so long as the goose lives long enough to provide him with sufficient eggs to pay for the purchase of a new goose. Ecological irresponsibility can pay — for the entrepreneur, but not for society as a whole.

The crucial link between pollution and profits appears to be modern technology, which is both the main source of recent increases in productivity — and therefore of profits — and of recent assaults on the environment. Driven by an inherent tendency to maximize profits, modern private enterprise has seized upon those massive technological innovations that promise to gratify this need, usually unaware that these same innovations are often also instruments of environmental destruction. Nor is this surprising, for . . . technologies tend to be designed at present as single-purpose instruments. Apparently, this purpose is unfortunately, too often dominated by the desire to enhance productivity — and therefore profit.

Obviously, we need to know a great deal more about the connection between pollution and profits in private enterprise economies. Meanwhile, it would be prudent to give some thought to the meaning of the functional connection between pollution and profits, which is at least suggested by the present information.

The general proposition that emerges from these considerations is that environmental pollution is connected to the economics of the private enterprise system in two ways. First, pollution tends to become intensified by the displacement of older productive techniques by new, ecologically faulty, but more profitable technologies. Thus, in these cases, pollution is an unintended concomitant of the natural drive of the economic system to introduce new technologies that increase productivity. Second, the cost[s] of environmental degradation are chiefly borne not by the producer, but by society as a whole, in the form of "externalities." A business enterprise that pollutes the environment is therefore being subsidized by society; to this extent, the enterprise, though free, is not wholly private.

22. SUPERSHIP

Noel Mostert

In May 1970, the 50,380-ton Norwegian tanker *Polycommander,* carrying a full cargo of crude oil, ran aground and burst into flames at Muxieirio Point, on the Spanish Atlantic coast near Vigo. The oil spillage amounted to about sixteen thousand tons, or one-third her cargo; it caught alight on the sea, and the flames created by this burning oil were so fierce that they caused a "fire storm": a heat disturbance of such intensity that it raised hurricane force winds in the immediate vicinity of the stricken ship. The winds whirled aloft a huge amount of oil, spraying it into a fine mist, and bore it up to high altitudes. The mist condensed into drops and some days later a black rain began to fall upon the coast — upon its farmlands and upon the villages of Panjón and Bayona. Damage to homes, gardens, and crops was extensive and cattle died of eating oil-covered grass; it all would have been much worse had it not been for the fact that most of the black rain fell on uninhabited bush and hill country.

As tanker and pollution accidents go, the Vigo incident was comparatively minor, though not of course to the inhabitants of Panjón and Bayona. The *Polycommander* itself was a small ship compared to the general run of tankers these days, and not to be classed in the super-tanker category. The startling and horrible results of the fire, however, made the accident unique. The damage caused, conservatively calculated to be in the region of $480,000, was scarcely comparable to the devastation caused by the *Torrey Canyon* and other similar accidents, but it certainly added a new dimension to the general concern, not to say apprehension, about tanker disasters, all of which must henceforth be projected to include the consequences of the same sort of thing happening to the biggest of ships. Who can visualize the consequences of a *Polycommander*-type fire storm rising from a broken million tonner upon the green pastures and forests of Maine, Nova Scotia, and New-foundland? It would of course require some extraordinary circumstance to break the entire frame of such a vessel, but it is not unreasonable to suppose that at least two of its giant tank-sections could be torn open and set ablaze in a collision. God knows, the fire ball created by just one of them is more than the mind can grasp.

The means that tankers have of causing havoc upon the sea are many and varied, ranging from spectacular mishaps such as the *Torrey Canyon's* to the insidiously accumulative effect of constant leaks, spills, and irresponsible dumping of tank slops at sea. Every tanker, however well managed, drops some of its oil into the sea in some form or another; badly managed ships are ceaseless polluters and, like garden snails, can often be followed by the long iridescent trail of their waste.

The subject of pollution of the oceans has become a vast and complex one since it involves such an enormous variety of effluents going into the sea from rivers, coastal towns, and cities, indiscriminate dumping of noxious commodities, and leaks from offshore oil rigs. Examples are legion. West Germany and other Rhine countries send half a million tons of waste chemicals down the Rhine every year for dumping in the North Sea. In 1969 some twelve thousand seabirds as well as thousands of fish and seals died mysteriously in the Irish Sea. A plankton and fish survey conducted from the Antarctic to the Arctic in 1970 by the Wood's Hole Oceanographic Institute, Massachusetts, revealed that plankton throughout the entire Atlantic ocean already contain unsuspectedly high levels of an industrial pollutant related to the pesticide DDT.

Oil, however, remains the single biggest pollutant and tankers the single biggest dispenser of it.

Nobody knows how much oil is going into the sea every year. Official estimates tend to be conservative against those of marine conservationists, but they are disturbing enough. An estimate of the amount of petroleum products going into the oceans was presented to the Ocean Affairs Board of the National Academy of Sciences in Washington in May 1973. This analysis, based on available official estimates, indicated that about 1,370,000 tons of oil are discharged into the sea every year during routine operations of tankers and other ships; in addition, accidents dumped another 350,000 tons. On the conservationist side, there have been many warnings during the last few years about the depletion and ruin of the oceans, but one of the most forceful was that of Professor Jacques Piccard, the Swiss oceanographer, on the eve of the United Nations conference on the human environment, held at Stockholm in 1972, when, speaking on behalf of the Secretariat, he said that many experts now believe that life in the seas could be extinguished within the next twenty-five to thirty years unless man stops polluting them. His own estimate was that something between 5 and 10 millions tons of petroleum products were going into the oceans every year, with tanker dumping being responsible for at least 1 million tons of this. If, in the absence of definite figures, we accept the true amount of dumping as something between Piccard's estimate and the American one, the position is serious indeed, because most of the oil is being dumped in estuaries, offshore waters, and other areas where the true fertility of the sea is concentrated.

Plankton is surface matter. It is the basic life of the sea and consists of phytoplankton, the "grass" of the sea, that generates through photosynthesis at least one third of the world's oxygen, and zooplankton, the

minute organisms that form the lower animal life of the sea; the phytoplankton convert the water's nutrients into the sugars, starches, and
proteins upon which all sea creatures ultimately depend through their
intertwined cycles. Zooplankton feed upon the phytoplankton, and those
that feed upon the zooplankton in turn feed others. Seabirds fall from the
sky and feed selectively upon this thriving cycle. As Professor Piccard
himself pointed out, all that needs to be done to disrupt the marine cycle
fatally is to destroy the phytoplankton, which oil skim so easily does.

To what degree and how often do we have to bruise this delicate living
surface of the oceans with oil and other pollutants before the whole
system collapses or is destructively and irreversibly diminished?

There are many areas of the oceans where the surface life of the water
now seldom has a chance to remain free of pollution for more than a few
weeks, or even days. Considering how far the Atlantic plankton already
appear to be polluted, the general diminution of life over big stretches
of the open and apparently unscathed seas might be far more advanced
than we could suspect. If it is, then it would represent, surely, man's
single most calamitous act.

That the very seas should be considered a wasting asset must surely be
the essential nightmare of the whole business of the despoliation of this
planet which daily is perpetrated before our eyes, about our ears, and
inside our nostrils. It is simply that the salt seas are for almost all of us
the perpetual assurance of an accessible freshness and cleanness; and, I
suppose, there is in this as well the remnant of an atavistic instinct defensive of our remote origin, a much-needed conviction of their inviolabil-
ity, that whatsoever other havoc we wreak, however deeply we pile the
ashes, the seas still will rise and fall and safely breathe in their depths.
But their wastage is happening so fast in the Mediterranean around
where I live that it has become almost a visible phenomenon; certainly
the condition of this sea deteriorates perceptibly season after season. The
Baltic is worse, already scientifically dead over much of its bottom, useless as a fish source where once it was the home of the herring and the
source of the Hanseatic fortunes; and, although it means less to me personally as a sea, as I have crossed it only once and then through fog and
ice, its condition strikes me as a terrible augury for the whole body of our
waters.

There are whole stretches of the Mediterranean where I no longer will
enter the water. A lot of the reason for this is local sewage and industrial-
waste arrangements. Seventy-five percent of Italian sea waters are more
or less seriously polluted. Spain's Costa del Sol, where I have happily
bathed during the past decade, no longer tempts. One often feels that
hepatitis is an endemic there in summer as the common cold in Britain
during the winter. But it is the oil that really creates feelings of violence.
Local self-interest and the value of the tourist industry might clean up
the sewage, but one can't see it doing much as regards the oil. One of the

finest beaches in southern Spain used to be the strip of clean white sand between Gibraltar and Algeciras, the rim of the Bay of Algeciras. Five years ago a large refinery was built and it is managed, it would appear, with scant respect for the local environment. The Straits of Gibraltar, which half a decade ago were virtually as unspoiled as in the days of Homer, are now constantly and densely polluted and its fast currents carry this mess either deep into the Mediterranean or out into the Atlantic. The Moroccan fishermen have seen their catches dwindle and I myself have watched the gull population in the area diminish year by year to vanishing point. And it becomes an angry pain when I come down to the Moroccan coastline more or less opposite the seat of this havoc, that is to say between Cape Malabata and Ceuta, where some of the best beaches in the world are to be found, only to find the sands and rocks blackened by oil or to see a miles-long slick moving along the offshore currents, like an endless loathsome serpent seeking a likely place to come ashore and leave its offal. There are times when the water seems to be of that full blackness which promises to be our ultimate reward: a viscous shroud spread along every shore and reaching to all horizons. If this seems farfetched one only need return to the million-tonner idea and ask oneself what the actuality would be if one of those behemoths-to-be lay wrecked and breaking upon any of our shores. One ship could spill in one place what Professor Piccard now estimates the world's tankers and other vessels do over the period of a year.

The position is disastrous enough simply as a result of the casual spillage that now goes into the sea everywhere. There is not an ocean in the world that at this moment of my writing, or your reading, does not bear countless slicks distributed across its entire surface ranging in size from a few yards to many miles. In his log aboard his raft *Ra*, the Norwegian explorer Thor Heyerdahl reported that drifting black lumps of oil were "seemingly never ending" across the Atlantic. In 1970 the British yachtsman Sir Francis Chichester, after a Mediterranean voyage, wrote this letter to *The Times:*

I have just returned from a 4,600-mile try-out sail in my *Gipsy Moth* V to the Mediterranean and back. Time after time we sailed through patches or slicks of oil film on the surface. Seas coming aboard the yacht left clots of black oil on the deck and stained the sails. I noticed signs or effects of oil at intervals all the way from the Solent to Gibraltar and in the Mediterranean itself between Gibraltar and Majorca. I mention this because I think it is probably more noticeable from a small low yacht than from a steamer. Does it mean that in time, if it continues to increase, the oil effect will kill life in the sea?

In a report on sea pollution in *Science* in 1970, three marine scientists, M. H. Horn, J. M. Teal, and R. H. Backus, said:

Taken all together our observations indicate that lumps of petroleum exist in surprisingly large amounts on the sea surface. These lumps form a chronic type of oil pollution which may significantly affect the marine ecosystem. It is evident that a concerted research by interested oceanographers from around the world will be required to assess quantitatively the distribution of oil on and in the ocean, to understand the physical, chemical, biological and microbiological processes involved in its dispersion and eventual disposition, and to estimate the effects upon the marine ecosystem. . . .

We are still very far from even beginning to understand the effects of oil, but at least our assessment of the *quantity* of it is improving. A recent American survey has found that at least 80,000 tons of *indestructible* tarry residues are to be found floating upon approximately ten percent of the total oceanic surface of the earth, including the Arctic and the Antarctic, a permanent legacy of the millions of tons of oil that have gone into the sea in recent years and disintegrated or been absorbed. The concentrations vary. They are estimated at twenty kilograms per square kilometer in the Mediterranean and one kilogram per square kilometer in the North Atlantic.

International concern about pollution at sea already is fifty years old. The contamination of the seas by oil during World War One disturbed Congress so much that it proposed an international conference, which was held in 1926. The *Torrey Canyon* may have initiated the first intensive study and concern about the effects of oil pollution but it also brought its own confusion to the matter because the detergents used for cleaning up the seas and coasts on the British side of the Channel caused as much damage as the oil itself, sometimes more. There is not enough data by which to assess the effects of pollution accurately because we haven't yet begun to explore the full range of its interactions in the sea. We do know that all crude oils are poisonous to all marine organisms, but we need to know at least to some extent the degree to which they are poisonous to the different flora and fauna and, above all, their long-term consequences.

Crude oil is one of the most complicated natural chemical mixtures on earth, its components vary from locality to locality. It has so many chemical and physical properties, so many agents of solubility, volatility, and toxicity, that its interactions with the sea's own abundant range of salinity, temperature, and other changes pose seemingly limitless possibilities. What we do know is bad enough. Oil poisons, smothers, burns, coats, taints; among many consequences, it can start carcinogenic processes in sea animals, affect reproduction, and cause genetic change; it affects respiratory organs and clogs the filtering mechanisms of fish; it affects, as we have seen at the Cape, the balance and independence of a bird such as the penguin; it causes imbalance in the cycles of plant life, when it doesn't kill it altogether; its degrading process consumes large quantities of dissolved oxygen, which is vital to the life in the sea.

The uncertainties that exist about oil pollution were indicated after two big American spills in 1969, the one at Santa Barbara and the other at Falmouth, Massachusetts, when there appeared to be strong scientific disagreement about the effects on marine life. Dr. Dale Straughan of the University of Southern California's Allan Hancock Foundation said in her report on the biological effects of the Santa Barbara spill that tests had failed to reveal any effects of oil pollution on the Santa Barbara channel's zooplankton and phytoplankton and that, similarly, sea plants and the production of fish and larvae were not lastingly affected. The principal reason for the low animal mortality rate, Dr. Straughan said, was that toxins are the lightest components of oil and can rapidly evaporate. This conclusion was, however, apparently contradicted by Dr. Max Blumer of the Wood's Hole Oceanographic Institute in Massachusetts after he had studied the results of the spill off West Falmouth, where he found that the toxic elements of the oil were actually the most persistent.

These contradictions were not quite as confusing as they seem. Experience of oil spills shows that they vary enormously, and capriciously, in their effects. "Each spill will have its own characteristics, its own family of problems," the Canadian report on the stranding of the tanker *Arrow* off Nova Scotia in 1970 declared.

In the first place, the oil that is being spilled on the sea is of many kinds; even crude oil is of many different types. Of them all, the crude oil that was spilled off Santa Barbara is, in the short term at least, less obviously devastating than refined oils, which were spilled at Falmouth. This latter spill involved between 160,000 and 170,000 gallons. Three days after the spill oceanographers trawled the area and found that 95 percent of their catch was dead. A year later, life on the seabed was still dying.

The toxins in refined oil and crude seem to be quite different in their effect and action. If, as Dr. Blumer found out at Falmouth, the toxins of refined oil are more persistent at the sea of spillage than crude, it does not necessarily mean that those in crude oil are less dangerous. In fact, the very swiftness of their dissipation may make them even more dangerous under certain circumstances in that they not only evaporate from the surface but also dissolve quickly into seawater itself. Crude oil is most toxic soon after it is spilled, which is the main reason for burning it in a wreck or sinking the vessel with the cargo inside or at least getting the crude out as soon as possible. At this point it contains a large amount of aromatics, including benzene, which is poisonous. The oil's naphthenic acids are highly poisonous as well and have the effect of coagulating a fish's protein. Long after beaches have been scoured and cleaned these toxins may lie in the sediment of the sea bottom and seep out slowly through the action of water movement and currents, thus maintaining a flow of poison over a protracted period. This is a danger that

Santa Barbara may yet have to confront: the area experienced the heaviest rains in forty years at the time of the spill, and silt that washed into the sea stuck to the oil and sank with it to the bottom; the silt thereby became one of the main cleansing agents. But if most of the oil now lies in the sediment at the bottom of the Santa Barbara channel, some of its effects may well be long delayed. In the *Torrey Canyon* affair, the French were congratulated for doing better than the British in disposing of oil before it struck heavily at their coasts. They dropped chalk on the oil, which had the same effect as the Santa Barbara silt and carried the oil to the bottom of the sea. It has been reported that the oil occasionally returns to the surface, but this is hard to verify because of the persistent pollution in the English Channel. At any rate the oil is still at the bottom and will only be very gradually dispersed over many years. It was for these reasons that chalk, which is one of the cheapest and easiest ways of disposing of oil on the water, was not used by the Canadians during the *Arrow* cleanup. In their official report on the *Arrow*, the Canadians gave as their reason the fact that they were afraid of damage to sea bottom flora and fauna and the possibility of the oil's coming to the surface later; they concluded: "It is believed that further work is required on the fate of oil treated in this way before serious consideration is given to the use of sinking agents in future spills."

Again in the case of the *Torrey Canyon*, there was some early belief that the effects of oil pollution were not as lethal as first supposed and one of the arguments was that shellfish in areas that had not been treated with detergent fed on the oil and so helped clear large stretches of coast. But in her evidence to the Canadian inquiry on the *Arrow*, Dr. Molly Spooner said that laboratory experiments on fish that had ingested sublethal amounts of oil indicated that the oil might be having carcinogenic effects on them. Elsewhere, experiments with oysters showed that when water-soluble fractions of oil were introduced into their water, the amount of water filtered by the oysters decreased from between 207 and 310 liters a day to between 2.9 and 1.0 liters after eight to thirteen days. It is hard not to wonder therefore to what degree the Cornish shrimp actually benefited from their diet of *Torrey Canyon* crude.

Both the *Torrey Canyon* and the *Arrow* carried crude oil, but even these two experiences can't really be compared because the *Arrow's* cargo was of a type known as Bunker C, which is relatively nontoxic compared to other forms of crude. Bottom life in Chedabucto Bay was not affected by the spill. The lobster season opened on schedule and the catch was normal. The herring catch was above normal. Clamming, however, was closed down. Three months after the accident there was a 25 percent kill of clams because of suffocation caused by plugging of their airholes by oil. The principal victims of the *Arrow* were more than seven thousand seabirds, the majority of them killed on Sable Island, off the

Atlantic coast of Nova Scotia and 125 miles from the wreck. It was the *Arrow's* slick of course that killed them. The Canadian report on the *Arrow* concluded that "despite the relatively large amount of oil released from the wreck, the overall or lasting effect on the wildlife and fishlife of the bay was not significant." What it did not, and could not, account for was the damage done by the *Arrow's* slick on its way to and beyond Sable Island.

There has been an understandable tendency in all oil spills so far to regard the limits of the catastrophe as roughly the area visibly contaminated by oil, as well as its underlying depths. What any given locality suffers when oil comes ashore is very much determined by local tides, currents, winds, temperature, and other weather and climatic phenomena. In the Persian Gulf, much of the toxicity of spilled crude is removed by the swift rate of evaporation in that region's heat, which also helps the disintegration of the oil on the surface. What afflicted areas in more temperate climates usually look for is similar help from local weather conditions to save their beaches and tidal zones from inundation. Sir George Deacon, former director of Britain's National Institute of Oceanography, has said that "instead of the *Torrey Canyon* oil drifting inevitably to our coasts there was at any time only a fifty-fifty chance, depending on the wind." This is probably true for most coastal communities where wind and tide conditions are strong and where, if pollution threatens, the hope invariably is that the oil will change course and head somewhere else, out to sea, and the response always is relief if the slick finally is seen traveling toward the horizon. By and large, I suppose, we all live for today.

One might feel somewhat more sanguine about this if some way had been found for dealing with slicks at sea. None has that one could call truly effective. Practically all ways of dealing with oil spillage concern handling it on beaches, offshore, or on reasonably accessible areas of the sea. Nor are any of these fully effective. When they were working on the *Arrow* the Canadians found that, on the beaches and in the shallows, straw and peat moss served as the best and safest absorbents. On the water the device they found most useful was the so-called slick-licker, a sort of conveyor belt that literally licks up the oil from the surface. The use of these contraptions is limited by weather and circumstances: it would take an awful lot of licking to remove from the sea's surface a slick such as the *Wafra's*, which was thirty-five miles long, several miles wide, and several inches thick. All manner of other devices have been invented or improvised for damming, scooping, or holding spilled oil, but each has its limitations, and none would be of any practical use on a major slick on the open sea, least of all on a troubled sea such as that around the Cape, or off Maine and Nova Scotia in winter.

The best answer of all is to burn a slick, but oil floating on rough or choppy water picks up large quantities of seawater and there is little hope of burning slicks that have been exposed to weather for more than a few hours, which was another conclusion made by those working on the *Arrow*. A possible solution is one now under investigation, namely to provide bacteria that feed on oil and themselves die when they have consumed it all. Until something like it is found no one perhaps should feel too grateful that any threatened pollution by oil slick has vanished seaward under propulsion of wind and tide. If the beaches are saved, what else is doomed?

It is virtually impossible to document the incidence of slicks, but the British Advisory Committee on Oil Pollution of the Sea in 1973 reported that in the previous year the length of the British coastline polluted by oil had increased by a quarter. Twenty-one slicks came ashore in the area near the Straits of Dover in 1971. Sixty miles of coastline in Lancashire and the Irish Sea were hit by thirty-three slicks in 1972. Probably most of this sort of thing comes from the flushing out of ships' tanks as they head for the Persian Gulf or wherever to fetch another cargo after discharging their last. Some wait until they get to the deeper ocean; many don't. In the long run, one might well ask, What difference does it make? After the *Torrey Canyon* disaster there was a sharp increase of reports of ships seen discharging oil in the English Channel off the British and French coasts even though it was an offense punishable by a fine of up to one thousand pounds (since raised to fifty thousand pounds); the British coastal authorities believed that these were all ships taking advantage of the disaster and hoping that *Torrey Canyon* would be blamed for their own sludge. The same happened after the *Arrow* disaster off the Nova Scotia coast. Tankers cleaned out their tanks at night in the vicinity of the wreck to enable them to get rid of their oily swill without detection. With such scruples, what hope have we got? None, it would appear, if we have to depend upon much of the modern maritime conscience.

There is no effective international or even national means of dealing with such a problem. Enough oil clings to the sides of a ship's tanks after they have been emptied to form up to one percent of the cargo which, in the case of a 200,000 tonner, means as much as two thousand tons of oil, though in practice it is usually something between one thousand and two thousand tons. Unscrupulous masters might flush all of this into the sea and, without question, often do, causing destructive slicks.

There is still no blanket international law against dumping oil at sea, but there is one against pumping out off coastlines. IMCO, the Inter-Governmental Maritime Consultative Organization, is of course the instrument for pushing these measures into existence. Even when it finally gets a total prohibition against dumping of all oil at sea, however, the force of such an international law will be an elusive thing. There is no effective means of enforcing it upon the seas. Any vigor it might possess must depend upon the zeal of individual governments, which is a variable quantity, to say the least. As it is, judging from the time it takes to get any legislation on the sea generally approved, one feels that the vigor and survival of the oceans has a low priority with most members of IMCO.

In 1954 IMCO suggested to its members that a ban should be imposed upon dumping sludge or any other form of oil fifty miles off any coast. It took eight years to get this ratified.

By that time, however, the major oil companies, ever prudent of their image and in face of gathering public dismay about the state of the seas, had voluntarily introduced a simple system called "load-on-top" to eliminate most of the oily sludge left in their ships' tanks without emptying it into the sea. In this system the seawater used for washing all the tanks is pumped into special "slop" tanks where the oil eventually rises to the surface. This oil is mixed with the next cargo and the residual water only is put into the sea. Great precaution is taken even with this water, whose oily content varies. In 1970 IMCO put up a fresh proposal, which suggests that no tanker be allowed to dump more than one-fifteenth-thousandth of its total cargo capacity. This would amount to about thirteen tons in a 200,000 tonner, which would cover the oil content of residual water. IMCO's proposal is that this water should never be of a strength greater than one hundred parts oil to one million parts water, and that it should never be dumped at a rate of more than sixty liters per mile. Given the rate of increase in world oil consumption, IMCO feels that even this is too much and wants, by the end of this decade, to have in effect a complete ban on any oil whatsoever going into the sea. Considering that world oil consumption will have almost doubled again by then, it would seem to be a brave but wishful hope, particularly since the performance on current measures has not been impressive: by mid-1974 only twenty of IMCO's members had approved the residual water measure.

Tanker specialists in London, including spokesmen for the British Chamber of Shipping and for Shell, which initiated the load-on-top principle in the mid-sixties, believe that eighty percent of the world's tankers are capable of using the system (that is, that they have the tank space to use for slops) but estimate that probably only about fifty percent actually do so, which means that their oil goes into the sea.

In the end, much depends upon the vigilance of coastal states themselves. All British ships keep oil record books, in which every bit of oil on board, whether fuel or cargo, must be fully accounted for to British inspectors. The U.S. Coast Guard runs air patrols one hundred miles off the coast to watch for offenders, who are easily traced simply by following a slick all the way up to the very wake of the ship. If an offender puts into port it can be penalized under national laws but if it is spotted dumping oil at sea and continues on into international waters the only recourse is to make a complaint to the nation whose flag it flies. The IMCO rules specify that the owner nation must apply penalties. Unfortunately a large proportion of the world's tankers fly one or the other of the so-called flags of convenience, which means that they are registered in small nonseafaring nations such as Liberia, Panama, Costa Rica, Honduras, Lebanon, and Cyprus. Any flag of convenience master choosing to dump oil sludge would not feel unduly perturbed about the punitive consequences at his home port, whose conscience and standards on these matters might be questionable, and which anyway his ship probably never has visited, or ever is likely to.

As the British Field Studies Council report on devastation around refineries indicated, small steady slicks do more damage than one big spill if they are persistent in an area. The steady dumping of sludge, tank washings, and other forms of oil upon the sea might be having the same effects there. There is certainly no reason to suppose that the effects are less. There is indeed some evidence to suggest the contrary. Slicks have become so persistent in British offshore waters because of the tanker traffic that great anxiety has been expressed over the future of British seabirds. A breeding survey financed in 1970 by the Torrey Canyon Appeal of the World Wildlife Fund and the Royal Society for the Protection of Birds found that guillemots, razorbills, and puffins are threatened by extinction around British coasts unless something is done about oil pollution; and most of the damage to the seabird communities was found to have been caused long before oil slicks actually reached the British shores.

The steady pollution of the southern seas off the Cape of Good Hope since tankers stopped using Suez similarly has threatened the extinction of at least one species of penguin, the jackass penguin. Tens of thousands of penguins and seals and seabirds, belonging to species that breed in the mild waters and rich feeding grounds off the South African coasts, have been wiped out by steady oil spillage and by accidents such as that of the *Wafra.*

So far the world has not seen an oil tanker spill bigger than the *Torrey Canyon's,* although there have been many devastating lesser ones. The VLCCs have escaped involvement in a major pollution incident, despite an unhappy record of breakdowns and accidents, at least one of which came very close to creating the precedent that everyone fears and expects at some point. In the fall of 1970 the British VLCC *Esso Cambria,* with 241,000 tons of crude oil in her tanks, ran ashore in the Persian Gulf because of negligent navigation by her chief officer. She fortunately ran onto a shoal instead of rocks; even so, two of her tanks were broken and she spilled 1,500 tons of oil, which she'd loaded the previous day.

In recent years safety at sea has been deteriorating steadily. The rate of ship accidents has been rising to an alarming degree, and tankers are very much part of the problem. In 1971 tonnage totally lost by the world merchant fleet was the highest in civil times since records were first kept in 1891; it amounted to just over one million tons, and was the equivalent of one sixth of the losses in the Atlantic in 1942, the worst year of the war for U-boat activity. Tankers accounted for one third of the tonnage lost: twenty-two in number, totaling 328,337 tons. Casualty figures since have remained close to these levels.

In the two-month period November–December 1972, for example, the 12,440-ton Rumanian tanker *Ploiesti* sank in the Straits of Messina after collision, with the loss of three lives; the 100,000-ton Liberian tanker *World Hero* collided with a Greek warship, which sank with a loss of forty-four lives; the 8,816-ton Singapore tanker *Cosmopolitan* was extensively damaged by fire in its home port; the 12,000-ton Norwegian tanker *Texaco Britannia* was extensively damaged by an explosion at Keelung that killed eleven men and injured forty-two; the 12,000-ton Italian tanker *San Nicola* exploded off Brindisi, killing three men; the 200,000-ton fully laden British tanker *Fina Britannia* was taken in tow in the Indian Ocean after breaking down; the 63,000-ton laden Korean tanker *Sea Star* caught fire, exploded, and sank in the Persian Gulf after colliding with the Brazilian tanker *Horta Barbosa*, with the loss of twelve men; the 1,500-ton Swedish tanker *Nova* sank off Ystad after colliding with a Greek freighter, with one man lost; the laden 26,000-ton Italian tanker *Bello* exploded and burned out in the Mediterranean; and the 85,982-ton Spanish tanker *Alvaro de Bazan* caught fire in the engine room in the Persian Gulf, was left drifting and powerless, and eventually towed to Bombay, which offered the nearest dock. A total of seventy-one men lost their lives in this dreary but by no means unusual record of calamity and destruction.

In the first quarter of 1974, according to the Tanker Advisory Center, New York, there were three hundred twenty-six tanker casualties throughout the world compared with three hundred twenty in the same period of 1973. One ship, a 133,000-ton Italian tanker, was a total loss after an explosion in her tanks. Included in these casualties were eighteen tankers disabled by fires and explosions, twenty-nine which suffered weather damage, twenty-nine which stranded, and fifteen involved in collisions. Twenty-five persons died or were missing and nine were seriously injured in all these incidents.

The main danger to ships throughout the ages of sail was shipwreck, either through stranding or bad weather. Steam allowed ships to choose the most direct routes, which meant that on busy trades they were choosing the same track and were in much closer proximity than sail had brought them. Collision therefore became the main risk at sea, especially off headlands and in narrow waterways where many routes converged.

Since the late fifties the rate of collision has been climbing steadily. The fact that such a high proportion of these, indeed of all accidents, happens to tankers has made the casualty phenomenon at sea an international menace and a matter of critical concern beyond merely maritime circles.

A British survey of tanker accidents published in 1973 showed that during the ten-year period 1959 to 1968 a total of 11,501 ship accidents occurred in northwest European waters; 2,749 of these involved tankers. During that period 13,379 accidents occurred to tankers throughout the world. The total tanker population during that time was 50,559. It is this high rate of accidents to tankers that makes safety at sea an international problem going beyond merely maritime circles. Most of the big oil spills that have occurred since the loss of the *Torrey Canyon* have come from ships that collided with each other or went aground.

In a detailed study of fifty recent ship accidents published at the end of 1972, the British Chamber of Shipping said that most of the collisions involved were attributable to appalling seamanship and could have been avoided if alertness and prudence had been shown, while all the groundings were directly attributable to bad navigation. Shell Oil, in a detailed study of forty serious tanker accidents that involved pollution, found that the common link between all was that "people made silly mistakes."

A very large number of the mistakes seem to be made by ships flying one of the flags of convenience. These countries, together with others such as Greece, Formosa, and the Philippines, have dominated the marine casualty lists for some years; each year for the past five years Liberia has had the biggest total losses of any country.

Twenty years ago world shipping was largely a western European business, with Britain firmly in the lead as the biggest owner and operator of ships; outside Europe, America and Japan were the only major shipping nations. Liberia now has the world's largest merchant marine, followed by Japan and Britain, and her lead is rapidly increasing; flag of convenience fleets have regularly grown at rates more than twice those of world fleets as a whole. Liberia and Panama together now own, on paper, nearly a quarter of world shipping. Tankers dominate these expatriate fleets.

Thirty-five to 40 percent of the Liberian tonnage is American-owned, and an additional 10 percent of it is American-financed, which helps explain where the American merchant fleet, in steady decline since the end of the war, has taken itself. According to law, American-flag ships must be built in the United States and must be three-quarters manned by Americans. American shipbuilding costs used to be double those elsewhere (inflation abroad has helped make them competitive again), and American seamen's wages are still higher than elsewhere. American users of the flags of convenience, and they include Gulf, Esso, Texaco, Getty

Oil, Tidewater, and Union Oil, have argued that they act not for convenience but out of necessity. Their plea has been that without the flags of convenience the American merchant fleet would have substantially vanished by now, because of costs. They have pleaded in fact that theirs is a patriotic stance in that they ensure the survival of a merchant fleet that would be vital in a war. How this squares with the fact of fewer trained American seamen, or how they would ensure the loyalty of their foreign crews and continued possession of their ships in such an emergency has never been explained.

Flag of convenience operators often say that their ships, especially many of those under the Liberian flag, are among the largest, best-equipped, and most modern in the world. This may be true. But ships are only as good as the men who run them, and the record is not impressive. Old ships traditionally have a higher casualty rate than new ones. Liberian losses between 1966 and 1970 not only averaged twice as high as those of the other major maritime nations, but, contrary to the rule, the ships they were losing were on the whole new ones, certainly newer than the ones lost by the other principal merchant marines: the average age of Liberian losses in that four-year period was 8.7 years, while that of the Japanese and Europeans averaged 12 years.

To a disconcerting degree, oil cargoes have been delivered in recent years by improperly trained and uncertificated officers aboard ships navigating with defective equipment. One of the biggest of all tanker accidents involved an American-owned Liberian ship which was in charge of an officer who had no certificate whatsoever.

After the Liberian tanker *Arrow* ran ashore in Chedabucto Bay, a three-man committee of inquiry, which was led by Dr. P. D. McTaggart-Cowan, executive director of the Science Council of Canada, found that the *Arrow*, owned by Aristotle Onassis, had been operating with almost none of its navigation equipment serviceable. The radar had ceased to function an hour before the ship struck; the echo sounder had not been in working condition for two months; and the gyrocompass, which is used to steer by and to keep the ship on course, had a permanent error of three degrees west. The officer on watch at the time of the accident, the ship's third officer, had no license. The commission of inquiry said none of the crew had any navigational skill except the master, "and there are even doubts about his ability." In its final report the commission said: "We are well aware of the fact that no form of transportation can be 100 per cent safe but from the record available to us the standard of operation of the world's tanker fleets, particularly those under flags of convenience, is so appalling and so far from the kind of safety which science, engineering and technology can bring to those who care, that the people of the world should demand immediate action."

If one judges by Liberia's recent record, it often seems to make little

difference aboard a Liberian ship whether it has the newest equipment or
the oldest; too often those in charge of an ultramodern bridge don't
know how to use what's there, or don't know how to repair anything that
breaks down, or, worse, don't even bother to report a fault when they
get to port. Even in the case of well-qualified men commanding ships of
the highest standard, as was the case with the Torrey Canyon, their judgment, responsibility, and seamanship in the long run can be affected and
impaired by terms of service that would not be tolerated on any ship
flying the American flag, or that of any of the other major maritime powers. When he drove the Torrey Canyon aground on the Scilly Isles, the
ship's Italian master, who had behind him an outstanding reputation and
record as a seaman, already had served 366 days on board.

As the British and French governments discovered when they sought
to find someone to hold responsible for the accident, the task of trying to
pin down a flag of convenience ship within any accessible frame of legal
jurisdiction is well-nigh impossible. The Torrey Canyon was owned by
the Barracuda Tanker Corporation, a financial offshoot of the Union Oil
Company of California, which leased the ship and had, in turn, subleased
it to British Petroleum Trading Limited, which was a subsidiary of the
British Petroleum Company. The ship, built in the United States, and
rebuilt in Japan, was registered in Liberia, insured in London, and
crewed by Italians. For an international lawyer any suit involving such
a vessel must, one assumes, be the sort of stuff of which dreams of eternal
litigation are made. The British and French, however, took a simple
course. They pretended they weren't looking and, when one of Torrey
Canyon's sister ships, the Lake Palourde, ambled into the first port where
the law was held to be firm, they pounced and had her arrested until the
insurers, the only accessible body with responsibility, paid up $7,500,000
as a settlement for damage.

Starting with Torrey Canyon, most of the major oil spillage calamities
of the past six years have involved Liberian ships. These have included
the Ocean Eagle, whose wreck fouled the beaches of San Juan, Puerto
Rico, in 1967; the Arrow, which coated sixty miles of Nova Scotia shore-
line in 1970; and the Juliana, which in 1971 gave Japan its worst oil spill
when it broke in two after hitting a breakwater off the port of Niigata. In
October 1970, two fully laden supertankers the 77,648-ton Pacific Glory,
Chinese owned, and the 95,445-ton Allegro, Greek owned, both flying the
Liberian flag, and between them carrying 170,000 tons of crude oil, ran
into each other off the Isle of Wight. The Pacific Glory suffered a violent
explosion and was burned out; fourteen of her crew died. Most of the oil
in their tanks fortunately remained intact. The third officers of both ships
were on watch at the time; the Allegro's third officer, a Greek, had no
certificate whatsoever. Two of her engineers, Greek as well, had no
certificates either. Two of Pacific Glory's engineers also had no certifi-

cates. This was, at the time, the worst maritime collision on record, but it lost this distinction in August 1972, when two Liberian-flag super-tankers, the 95,000-ton American owned *Oswego Guardian*, fully laden, collided with the 100,000-ton Greek-owned *Texanita* northeast of Cape Town in the Indian Ocean. The *Texanita*, which was empty, exploded with such violence that it rocked buildings and woke people forty miles inland from the coast, which itself was twenty-three miles distant from the accident. The *Texanita* broke in two and vanished within four minutes. Thirty-three men died with the *Texanita*, and one aboard the *Oswego Guardian*. Both ships were traveling at high speed through fog so dense that the master of the *Texanita*, who survived, couldn't see the masts of his own ship; although they had observed each other on radar, neither ship reduced speed. *Texanita* made only two attempts to plot the course of the approaching ship, the second when it was only four miles off, and *Oswego Guardian* made no attempt whatsoever to plot the other ship.

The chief officer of a Norwegian freighter, the *Thorswave*, later provided what might be the first electronic eyewitness account of a major maritime disaster. His own ship was in the vicinity and he had watched the accident develop on his radar screen. "I saw these two ships coming closer together," he told the *Cape Argus* in Cape Town. "Then the two dots came into one. Just then we heard this terrific explosion and felt our own ship shake twice. I thought there was something wrong with our own ship because the explosion was so loud. A minute or two after this I saw the two dots coming away from each other. Then one dot suddenly disappeared from the screen."

Immediately after the collision, the master of the *Oswego Guardian* ordered his ship at full speed away from the scene. No attempt was made to pick up survivors, who owed their lives to other vessels in the area including the *Thorswave*. The *Oswego Guardian's* SOS call gave a wrong position, which was not discovered until six hours after the accident; no correction was ever sent out. The *Texanita's* master lost his license for eighteen months; the master of the *Oswego Guardian*, a Chinese, had his revoked.

Half the ship collisions in the world take place in the area bounded by the Elbe and the English Channel. Most of these are head-on and by far the majority of them occur in or near the Straits of Dover where, at any given moment, some forty ships usually are moving. Dodging this situation as well as the many wrecks and sandbanks in the area has become the principal nightmare for all supertanker and VLCC masters; and it is one they constantly confront because Rotterdam is the main tanker terminal for Europe and the most common destination for tankers inbound from the Persian Gulf. Tankers, as one might expect, are the ships most commonly involved in accidents there, especially flag of convenience ones, and usually because of appalling seamanship and standards aboard them.

Between October 1970 and April 1971, for example, ten tankers carrying among them some 300,000 tons of crude oil were involved in serious accidents in the area. Half of them were Liberian and they included the *Pacific Glory* and *Allegro*. On March 3, 1971, the Liberian tanker *Trinity Navigator,* carrying 32,000 tons of oil, ran aground off Berry Head, England, and was refloated after five hours by a British Channel pilot who later said that the ship's radar was out of order and that she had no VHF radio for local communication. The Chinese crew in any event spoke no English, the international language of the sea as much as it is of the air. Coast guards and a pilot boat that signaled to her by lamp advising that she was on a dangerous course got no reply. On April 4, 1971, the Liberian tanker *Panther,* carrying 25,000 tons of oil, grounded on the Goodwin Sands and was freed two weeks later by tugs. Her radar too was reported defective by the pilot who boarded her. A Trinity House master mariner, Captain W. L. D. Bayley, writing in *Safety at Sea,* in its issue of December 1969, said that supertankers with faulty VHF or radar were so numerous that channel pilots had ceased to report them. A further instance of almost total inadequacy was provided when the Greek-owned and Cyprus-registered tanker *Aegis Star* ran aground on the Swedish coast in November 1972. A surveyor who boarded her after she had been refloated found that her gyrocompass, echo sounder, radar, automatic log, speed indicator, and rudder indicator were all out of order, according to a report in the British shipping journal *Fairplay.*

A senior Trinity House Channel pilot, Captain N. R. Knowles, told me recently that, far from improving, things were in fact getting worse, and described an incident involving a Liberian vessel inbound for Dunkirk which had been advised that she would have to stay outside because no berth was available. As pilotage is not compulsory and many ships, flag of convenience ones especially, avoid taking aboard pilots for the English Channel run because of the extra expense, the ship in question had not asked for a pilot when she made the approaches. Fighting a gale off Dunkirk, she searched for anchorage by steaming north, and then back down the Channel to Beachy Head on the English side. Her fifty-seven-year-old master finally sent an urgent appeal for a pilot to show him to safe anchorage on the English coast. He was near exhaustion when the pilot boarded. He was the only officer on board with a mariner's certificate; his first officer had been at sea only three and a half years. Aside from the threat that such an improperly manned ship presented to tanker traffic in the area, Knowles said, she herself was typical of many tankers he'd boarded.

The menace of such vessels and their substandard operation was one of the principal factors behind the introduction of two-lane traffic in sixty-six busy maritime areas throughout the world at the beginning of this decade. Ships now are required to move in these double lanes of one-way traffic when laying course through these areas, which include the English Channel, the Cape of Good Hope, the Malacca Straits, the San Francisco and New York harbors, the Baltic, the Straits of Gibraltar. It was felt that this system would at least help minimize the risks to heavily laden supertankers. Unfortunately the lanes are ignored by many ships (referred to as "cowboys" by those who stick to their proper lane) and the results can be tragic.

On January 11, 1971, a 12,000-ton Peruvian freighter, *Paracas*, entered the English Channel and, instead of using the northbound lane off the French coast as she was supposed to do, took the shorter and more convenient downbound lane along the English coast. She struck the Panamanian tanker *Texaco Caribbean* and the resulting explosion shattered windows five miles away in Folkestone. Nine men went down with the ship.

The British coastal authorities marked the sunken *Texaco Caribbean* with three vertical green lights as a wreck warning. The following day a German freighter, the *Brandenburg*, outbound for North America, hit the wreck and sank with the loss of more than half her thirty-one-man crew. The British added a lightship and five light buoys to the green lights on the site, but on February 28 a Greek freighter, *Niki*, struck the two ships and herself went down, taking her entire crew of twenty-two. A second lightship and nine more buoys were added to the collection of wrecks, but on March 16 an unidentified supertanker ignored a barrage of rockets and flashing lamps from the guard ships, ran through one row of buoys and, to everyone's surprise, got away with it and vanished. Within a two-month period, sixteen ships were reported by British coastal authorities for having ignored the elaborate arrangement of lights and signals and entered the area of the wrecks, which have since been demolished.

It is a situation that can only get much, much worse as world trade and world fleets expand. Today's run-of-the-mill superships, the 200,000 tonners, will be tomorrow's traders of low degree. The write-off life of a VLCC is about ten years. Most of the first wave of 200,000–250,000 tonners already have seen half that. Superships aren't built to last. As they get older they begin to fall apart, to break down, and repairs and maintenance, not to speak of long tows, become too expensive to justify their retention in the service of any well-managed fleet. As the next big wave of investment starts creating the next plateau in tanker size, probably with the 500,000 tonners, the older ships will be handed down in job lots to the next generation of newcomers seeking a fortune in oil ships. So it presumably will continue, with demand and profits waxing and the oceans, alas, waning, unless some extraordinary international effort is made to control standards at sea. There seems a strange sinister touch of alchemy about it all — of black gold turned to golden gold and the lot ending up as purest dross, which will be the quality of the environment, and of life within it, we eventually will be left with.

23. AMERICAN GROUND TRANSPORT

Bradford Snell

The manufacture of ground transportation equipment is one of this Nation's least competitive industrial activities. . . .

Ground transport is dominated by a single, diversified firm to an extent possibly without parallel in the American economy. General Motors, the world's largest producer of cars and trucks, has also achieved monopoly control of buses and locomotives which compete with motor vehicles for passengers and freight. Its dominance of the bus and locomotive industries, moreover, would seem to constitute a classic monopoly. Although GM technically accounts for 75 percent of current city bus production, its only remaining competitor, the Flxible Co., relies on it for diesel propulsion systems, major engine components, technical assistance, and financing. In short, Flxible is more a distributor for GM than a viable competitor; virtually its sole function is the assembly of General Motors' bus parts for sale under the Flxible trade name. Likewise, in the production of intercity buses, its only remaining competitor, Motor Coach Industries, is wholly dependent upon GM for diesel propulsion systems and major mechanical components. In addition, General Motors accounts for 100 percent of all passenger and 80 percent of all freight locomotives manufactured in the United States. Such concentration in a single firm of control over three rival transportation equipment industries all but precludes the existence of competitive conduct and performance.

The distribution of economic power in this sector is remarkably asymmetrical. . . . [E]conomic power is fundamentally a function of concentration and size. In terms of concentration, the ground transport sector is virtually controlled by the Big Three auto companies. General Motors, Ford, and Chrysler account for 97 percent of automobile and 84 percent of truck production; GM alone dominates the bus and rail locomotive industries. Accordingly, the automakers have the power to impose a tax, in the form of a price increase, on purchasers of new cars to underwrite political campaigns against bus and rail systems.

In terms of size, there is an enormous divergence between the competing automotive and nonautomotive industries. Moreover, General Motors' diversification program has left only a small portion of the bus and rail industries in the hands of independent producers. As measured by aggregate sales, employment, and financial resources, therefore, the independent bus and rail firms are no match for the automakers. The Big Three's aggregate sales of motor vehicles and parts amount to about $52 billion each year, or more than 25 times the combined sales of trains, buses, subway and rapid transit cars by the four largest firms other than GM which produce bus and rail vehicles: Pullman and Budd (railway freight and passenger cars, subway and rapid transit cars); Rohr (buses and rapid transit cars); General Electric (commuter railcars and locomotives). The Big Three automakers employ nearly 1½ million workers, or more than three times as many as their four principal rivals: General Motors alone maintains plants in 19 different states. The Big Three also excel in their ability to finance lobbying and related political activities. GM, Ford, and Chrysler annually contribute more than an estimated $14 million to trade associations which lobby for the promotion of automotive transportation. By contrast, their four leading rivals contribute not more than $1 million, or less than one-tenth this amount, to rail transit lobbies. The magnitude of their sales, employment, and financial resources, therefore, affords the automakers overwhelming political influence.

It may be argued, moreover, that due to their conflicting interlocks with the motor vehicle manufacturers, these bus and rail firms would be reluctant to set their economic and political resources against them. Eighty percent of Budd's sales, for example, consist of automotive components purchased by the Big Three; Rohr, which also owns the Flxible Co., is wholly dependent upon GM for major bus components; Pullman derives more income from manufacturing trailers for highway trucks than from selling freight cars to the railroads; and General Electric manufactures a vast range of automotive electrical equipment, including about 80 percent of all automotive lamps. In sum, the independent bus and rail equipment manufacturers are probably unable and possibly unwilling to oppose the Big Three automakers effectively in political struggles over transportation policy.

Lacking a competitive structure, the group of industries responsible for providing us with ground transportation equipment fail to behave competitively. Diversification by General Motors into bus and rail production may have contributed to the displacement of these alternatives by automobiles and trucks. In addition, the asymmetrical distribution of economic and political power may have enabled the automakers to divert Government funds from rail transit to highways.

The Big Three automakers' efforts to restrain nonautomotive forms of passenger and freight transport have been perfectly consistent with profit maximization. One trolley coach or bus can eliminate 35 automobiles; 1 streetcar, subway, or rapid transit vehicle can supplant 50 passenger cars; an interurban railway or railroad train can displace 1,000 cars or a fleet of 150 cargo-laden trucks. Given the Big Three automakers' shared monopoly control of motor vehicle production and GM's diversified control of nonautomotive transport, it was inevitable that cars and trucks would eventually displace every other competing form of ground transportation.

The demise of nonautomative transport is a matter of historical record. By 1973 viable alternatives to cars and trucks had all but ceased to exist. No producers of electric streetcars, trolley coaches, or interurban electric trains remained; only two established railcar builders (Pullman and Rohr) were definitely planning to continue production; a single firm (General Electric) still manufactured a handful of electric locomotives; and General Motors accounted for virtually all of an ever-shrinking number of diesel buses and locomotives.

There were, of course, a number of factors involved in this decline. For example, the popularity of motor vehicles, due in large part to their initial flexibility, most certainly affected public demand for competing methods of travel. On the other hand, the demise of bus and rail forms of transport cannot, as some have suggested, be attributed to the public's desire to travel exclusively by automobile. Rather, much of the growth in autos as well as trucks may have proceeded from the decline of rail and bus systems. In short, as alternatives ceased to be viable, automobiles and trucks became indispensable.

The sections which immediately follow relate in considerable detail how General Motors' diversification into bus and rail production generated conflicts of interest which necessarily contributed to the displacement of alternatives to motor vehicle transportation. A subsequent section will consider how asymmetry in the ground transport sector led to the political restraint of urban rail transit.

Before considering the displacement of bus and rail transportation, however, a distinction between intent and effect should be carefully drawn. This study contends that certain adverse effects flow inevitably from concentrated multi-industry structures regardless of whether these effects were actually intended. Specifically, it argues that structural concentration of auto, truck, bus, and rail production in one firm necessarily resulted in the promotion of motor vehicles and the displacement of competing alternatives. Whether that firm's executives in the 1920's actually intended to construct a society wholly dependent on automobiles and trucks is unlikely and, in any case, irrelevant. That such a society developed in part as the result of General Motors' common control of competing ground transport industries is both relevant and demonstrable.

1. The Substitution of Bus for Rail Passenger Transportation. By the mid-1920's, the automobile market had become saturated. Those who desired to own automobiles had already purchased them; most new car sales had to be to old car owners. Largely as a result, General Motors diversified into alternative modes of transportation. It undertook the production of city and intercity motor buses. It also became involved in the operation of bus and rail passenger services. As a necessary consequence, it was confronted with fundamental conflicts of interest regarding which of these several competing methods of transport it might promote most profitably and effectively. Its natural economic incentives and prior business experience strongly favored the manufacture and sale of cars and trucks rather than bus, and particularly rail, vehicles. In the course of events, it became committed to the displacement of rail transportation by diesel buses and, ultimately, to their displacement by automobiles.

In 1925, General Motors entered bus production by acquiring Yellow Coach, which at that time was the Nation's largest manufacturer of city and intercity buses. One year later, it integrated forward into intercity bus operation by assisting in the formation of the Greyhound Corp., and soon became involved in that company's attempt to convert passenger rail operations to intercity bus service. Beginning in 1932, it undertook the direct operation and conversion of interurban electric railways and local electric streetcar and trolleybus systems to city bus operations. By the mid-1950's, it could lay claim to having played a prominent role in the complete replacement of electric street transportation with diesel buses. Due to their high cost of operation and slow speed on congested streets, however, these buses ultimately contributed to the collapse of several hundred public transit systems and to the diversion of hundreds of thousands of patrons to automobiles. In sum, the effect of General Motors' diversification program was threefold: substitution of buses for passenger trains, streetcars and trolleybuses; monopolization of bus production; and diversion of riders to automobiles.

Immediately after acquiring Yellow Coach, General Motors integrated forward into intercity bus operation. In 1926, interests allied with GM organized and then combined with the Greyhound Corp. for the purpose of replacing rail passenger service with a GM-equipped and Greyhound-operated nationwide system of intercity bus transportation. By mutual arrangement, Greyhound agreed to purchase virtually all of its buses from GM, which agreed in turn to refrain from selling intercity buses to any of Greyhound's bus operating competitors. In 1928, Greyhound announced its intention of converting commuter rail operations to intercity bus service. By 1939, six major railroads had agreed under pressure from Greyhound to replace substantial portions of their commuter rail service with Greyhound bus systems: Pennsylvania RR (Pennsylvania Greyhound Lines), New York Central RR (Central Greyhound Lines), Southern Pacific RR. (Pacific Greyhound Lines), New York, New Haven & Hartford RR. (New England Greyhound Lines), Great Northern RR. (Northland Greyhound Lines), and St. Louis Southwestern Railway (Southwestern Greyhound Lines). By 1950, Greyhound carried roughly half as many intercity passengers as all the Nation's railroads combined.

During this period, General Motors played a prominent role in Greyhound management. In 1929, for example, it was responsible for the formation, direct operation, and financing of Atlantic Greyhound, which later became Greyhound's southeastern affiliate. Three years later, in 1932, when Greyhound was in serious financial trouble, it arranged for a million dollar cash loan. In addition, I. B. Babcock, the president of GM's bus division, served on Greyhound's board of directors until 1938, when he was replaced by his successor at GM, John A. Ritchie. Until 1948, GM was also the largest single shareholder in the Greyhound Corp. In short, through its interlocking interests in and promotion of Greyhound, General Motors acquired a not insignificant amount of influence over the shape of this Nation's intercity passenger transportation. As the largest manufacturer of buses, it inevitably pursued a policy which would divert intercity traffic from rails to the intercity buses which it produced and Greyhound operated. Although this policy was perfectly compatible with GM's legitimate interest in maximizing returns on its stockholders' investments, it was not necessarily in the best interest of the riding public. In effect, the public was substantially deprived of access to an alternative form of intercity travel which, regardless of its merits, was apparently curtailed as a result of corporate rather than public determination.

After its successful experience with intercity buses, General Motors diversified into city bus and rail operations. At first, its procedure consisted of directly acquiring and scrapping local electric transit systems in favor of GM buses. In this fashion, it created a market for its city buses. As GM General Counsel Henry Hogan would observe later, the corporation "decided that the only way this new market for (city) buses could be created was for it to finance the conversion from streetcars to buses in some small cities." On June 29, 1932, the GM-bus executive committee formally resolved that "to develop motorized transportation, our company should initiate a program of this nature and authorize the incorporation of a holding company with a capital of $300,000." Thus was formed United Cities Motor Transit (UCMT) as a subsidiary of GM's bus division. Its sole function was to acquire electric streetcar companies, convert them to GM motorbus operation, and then resell the properties to local concerns which agreed to purchase GM bus replacements. The electric streetcar lines of Kalamazoo and Saginaw, Mich., and Springfield, Ohio, were UCMT's first targets. "In each case," Hogan stated, GM "successfully motorized the city, turned the management over to other interests and liquidated its investment." The program ceased, however, in 1935 when GM was censured by the American Transit Association (ATA) for its self-serving role, as a bus manufacturer, in apparently attempting to motorize Portland's electric streetcar system.

As a result of the ATA censure, GM dissolved UCMT and embarked upon a nationwide plan to accomplish the same result indirectly. In 1936 it combined with the Omnibus Corp. in engineering the tremendous conversion of New York City's electric streetcar system to GM buses. At that time, as a result of stock and management interlocks, GM was able to exert substantial influence over Omnibus. John A. Ritchie, for example, served simultaneously as chairman of GM's bus division and president of Omnibus from 1926 until well after the motorization was completed. The massive conversion within a period of only 18 months of the New York system, then the world's largest streetcar network, has been recognized subsequently as the turning point in the electric railway industry.

Meanwhile, General Motors had organized another holding company to convert the remainder of the Nation's electric transportation systems to GM buses. In 1936, it caused its officers and employees, I. B. Babcock, E. J. Stone, E. P. Crenshaw, and several Greyhound executives to form National City Lines, Inc. (NCL). During the following 14 years General Motors, together with Standard Oil of California, Firestone Tire, and two other suppliers of bus-related products, contributed more than $9 million to this holding company for the purpose of converting electric transit systems in 16 states to GM bus operations. The method of operation was basically the same as that which GM employed successfully in its United Cities Motor Transit program: acquisition, motorization, resale. By having NCL resell the properties after conversion was completed, GM and its allied companies were assured that their capital was continually reinvested in the motorization of additional systems. There was, moreover, little possibility of reconversion. To preclude the return of electric vehicles to the dozens of cities it motorized, GM extracted from the local transit companies contracts which prohibited their purchase of ". . . any new equipment using any fuel or means of propulsion other than gas."

The National City Lines campaign had a devastating impact on the quality of urban transportation and urban living in America. Nowhere was the ruin more apparent than in the Greater Los Angeles metropolitan area. Thirty-five years ago it was a beautiful region of lush palm trees, fragrant orange groves, and clean, ocean-enriched air. It was served then by the world's largest interurban electric railway system. The Pacific Electric system branched out from Los Angeles for a radius of more than 75 miles reaching north to San Fernando, east to San Bernardino, and south to Santa Ana. It's 3,000 quiet, pollution-free, electric trains annually transported 80 million people throughout the sprawling region's 56 separately incorporated cities. Contrary to popular belief, the Pacific Electric, not the automobile, was responsible for the area's geographical development. First constructed in 1911, it established traditions of suburban living long before the automobile had arrived.

In 1938, General Motors and Standard Oil of California organized Pacific City Lines (PCL) as an affiliate of NCL to motorize west coast electric railways. The following year PCL acquired, scrapped, and substituted bus lines for three northern California electric rail systems in Fresno, San Jose, and Stockton. In 1940 GM, Standard Oil, and Firestone "assumed the active management of Pacific (City Lines)" in order to supervise its California operations more directly. That year, PCL began to acquire and scrap portions of the $100 million Pacific Electric system including rail lines from Los Angeles to Glendale, Burbank, Pasadena, and San Bernardino. Subsequently, in December 1944, another NCL affiliate (American City Lines) was financed by GM and Standard Oil to motorize downtown Los Angeles. At the time, the Pacific Electric shared downtown Los Angeles trackage with a local electric streetcar company, the Los Angeles Railway. American City Lines purchased the local system, scrapped its electric transit cars, tore down its power transmission lines, ripped up the tracks, and placed GM diesel buses fueled by Standard Oil on Los Angeles' crowded streets. In sum, GM and its auto-industrial allies severed Los Angeles' regional rail links and then motorized its downtown heart.

Motorization drastically altered the quality of life in southern California. Today, Los Angeles is an ecological wasteland: The palm trees are dying from petrochemical smog; the orange groves have been paved over by 300 miles of freeways; the air is a septic tank into which 4 million cars, half of them built by General Motors, pump 13,000 tons of pollutants daily. With the destruction of the efficient Pacific Electric rail system, Los Angeles may have lost its best hope for rapid rail transit and a smog-free metropolitan area. "The Pacific Electric," wrote UCLA Professor Hilton, "could have comprised the nucleus of a highly efficient rapid transit system, which would have contributed greatly to lessening the tremendous traffic and smog problems that developed from population growth." The substitution of GM diesel buses, which were forced to compete with automobiles for space on congested freeways, apparently benefited GM, Standard Oil, and Firestone, considerably more than the riding public. Hilton added: "the (Pacific Electric) system, with its extensive private right of way, was far superior to a system consisting solely of buses on the crowded streets." As early as 1963, the city already was seeking ways of raising $500 million to rebuild a rail system "to supersede its present inadequate network of bus lines." A decade later, the estimated cost of constructing a 116-mile rail system, less than one-sixth the size of the earlier Pacific Electric, had escalated to more than $6.6 billion.

By 1949, General Motors had been involved in the replacement of more than 100 electric transit systems with GM buses in 45 cities including New York, Philadelphia, Baltimore, St. Louis, Oakland, Salt Lake City, and Los Angeles. In April of that year, a Chicago Federal jury convicted GM of having criminally conspired with Standard Oil of California, Firestone Tire and others to replace electric transportation with gas- or diesel-powered buses and to monopolize the sale of buses and related products to local transportation companies throughout the country. The court imposed a sanction of $5,000 on GM. In addition, the jury convicted H. C. Grossman, who was then treasurer of General Motors. Grossman had played a key role in the motorization campaigns and had served as a director of PCL when that company undertook the dismantlement of the $100 million Pacific Electric system. The court fined Grossman the magnanimous sum of $1.

Despite its criminal conviction, General Motors continued to acquire and dieselize electric transit properties through September of 1955. By then, approximately 88 percent of the nation's electric streetcar network had been eliminated. In 1936, when GM organized National City Lines, 40,000 streetcars were operating in the United States; at the end of 1955, only 5,000 remained. In December of that year, GM bus chief Roger M. Kyes correctly observed: "The motor coach has supplanted the interurban systems and has for all practical purposes eliminated the trolley (streetcar)."

The effect of General Motors' diversification into city transportation systems was substantially to curtail yet another alternative to motor vehicle transportation. Electric street railways and electric trolley buses were eliminated without regard to their relative merit as a mode of transport. Their displacement by oil-powered buses maximized the earnings of GM stockholders; but it deprived the riding public of a competing method of travel. Moreover, there is some evidence that in terms of air pollution and energy consumption these electric systems were superior to diesel buses. In any event, GM and its oil and tire coconspirators used National City Lines as a device to force the sale of their products regardless of the public interest. As Professor Smerk, an authority on urban transportation, has written, "Street railways and trolley bus operations, even if better suited to traffic needs and the public interest, were doomed in favor of the vehicles and material produced by the conspirators."

General Motors' substitution of buses for city streetcar lines may also have contributed in an indirect manner to the abandonment of electric railway freight service. During the 1930's merchants relied extensively on interurban electric railways to deliver local goods and to interchange distant freight shipments with mainline railroads. The Pacific Electric, for example, was once the third largest freight railroad in California; it interchanged freight with the Southern Pacific, the Union Pacific and the Santa Fe. In urban areas, these railways often ran on local streetcar trackage. The conversion of city streetcars to buses, therefore, deprived them of city trackage and hastened their replacement by motor trucks, many of which, incidentally, were produced by GM.

General Motors also stood to profit from its interests in highway freight transport. Until the early 1950's, it maintained sizable stock interests in two of the Nation's largest trucking firms, Associated Transport and Consolidated Freightways, which enjoyed the freight traffic diverted from the electric railways. By 1951, these two companies had established more than 100 freight terminals in 29 states coast-to-coast and, more than likely, had invested in a substantial number of GM diesel-powered trucks.

GM's diversification into bus and rail operations would appear not only to have had the effect of foreclosing transport alternatives regardless of their comparative advantages but also to have contributed at least in part to urban air pollution problems. There were in fact some early warnings that GM's replacement of electric-driven vehicles with diesel-powered buses and trucks was increasing air pollution. On January 26, 1954, for instance, E. P. Crenshaw, GM bus general sales manager, sent the following memorandum to F. J. Limback, another GM executive:

> There has developed in a number of cities "smog" conditions which has resulted in Anti-Air Pollution committees, who immediately take issue with bus and truck operations, and especially Diesel engine exhaust. In many cases, efforts are being made to stop further substitution of Diesel buses for electric-driven vehicles. . . .

Three months later, in April 1954, the American Conference of Governmental Industrial Hygienists adopted a limit of 5 parts per million for human exposure to nitrogen oxides. Diesel buses, according to another report by two GM engineers, emitted "oxides of nitrogen concentrations over 200 times the recommended" exposure limit. Nevertheless, the dieselization program continued. Crenshaw reported to Limback in 1954:

> The elimination of street-cars and trolley-buses and their replacement by our large GM 51-passenger Diesel Hydraulic coaches continues steadily . . . in Denver, Omaha, Kansas City, San Francisco, Los Angeles, New Orleans, Honolulu, Baltimore, Milwaukee, Akron, Youngstown, Columbus, etc.

2. *The Displacement of Bus Transit by Automobiles.* Diversification into bus production and, subsequently, into bus and rail operation inevitably encouraged General Motors to supplant trains, streetcars and trolleybuses with first gasoline and then diesel buses. It also contributed to this firm's monopolization of city and intercity bus production. The effect of GM's mutually exclusive dealing arrangement with Greyhound,

for example, was to foreclose all other bus manufacturers and bus operating concerns from a substantial segment of the intercity market. At least by 1952, both companies had achieved their respective monopolies: GM dominated intercity bus production and Greyhound dominated intercity bus operation. By 1973, GM's only competitor, Motor Coach Industries (established in 1962 by Greyhound as the result of a Government antitrust decree) was wholly dependent on it for major components; and Greyhound's only operating competitor, Trailways, had been forced to purchase its buses from overseas. In the process, a number of innovative bus builders and potential manufacturers, including General Dynamics' predecessor (Consolidated Vultee) and the Douglas Aircraft Co., had been driven from the industry.

Likewise, in the city bus market, GM's exclusive bus replacement contracts with National City Lines, American City Lines, Pacific City Lines, the Omnibus Corporation, Public Transport of New Jersey and practically every other major bus operating company foreclosed competing city bus manufacturers from all but a handful of cities in the country and assured GM monopoly control of this market as well. Since 1925 more than 50 firms have withdrawn from city bus manufacturing including Ford, ACF-Brill, Marmon-Herrington, Mack Trucks, White Motor, International Harvester, Studebaker Twin Coach, Fifth Avenue Coach, Chrysler (Dodge), and Reo Motors. By 1973, only the Flxible Company, which had been established and controlled until 1958 by C. F. Kettering, a GM vice-president, remained as effectively a competitor–assembler of GM city buses. One other firm, AM General (American Motors), had announced its intention to assemble GM-powered city buses for delivery in late 1973. The ability of this firm, or for that matter Flxible and Motor Coach Industries, to survive beyond 1975, however, was seriously doubted by industry observers. That year a Government antitrust decree compelling GM to supply bus assemblers with diesel engines, transmissions and other major components will expire.

Monopolization of bus production and the elimination of electric street transportation has brought an end to price and technological competition in these industries. In this regard, several cities led by New York have filed a lawsuit charging that General Motors sets higher-than-competitive prices for its diesel buses and receives millions of dollars annually in monopoly profits. The suit also alleges that GM may be disregarding technological innovations in propulsion, pollution control and coach design, which would help attract patrons out of their automobiles.

In light of our dwindling petroleum supplies and mounting concerns about air pollution, the decline of technological competition in bus manufacturing is particularly unfortunate. ACF-Brill, Marmon-Herrington, Pullman-Standard, Twin Coach, and St. Louis Car once built electric buses and electric streetcars. Other firms manufactured steam-driven buses. According to a number of studies, these alternative forms of motive power would be preferable in terms of energy consumption, efficiency, pollution, noise, and durability to the diesel engine. Exclusion of these innovative firms, however, and GM's apparent disinterest in steam- or electric-powered vehicles (whose longer life, fewer parts, and easier repair would drastically reduce her placement sales), have precluded the availability of these technological alternatives today. Moreover, domination of domestic bus manufacturing by the world's largest industrial concern tends to deter entry by smaller, innovative firms. Lear Motors, for example, has developed quiet, low-pollution steam turbines buses; Mercedes-Benz, which sells buses in 160 countries, has produced low-pollution electric buses. Neither these nor any other firms, however, have been able to break into the GM-dominated American bus market. Furthermore, GM's conversion of much of this country's streetcar and interurban trackage to bus routes has precluded the survival of domestic streetcar builders and deterred entry by foreign railcar manufacturers. As a result, there remain few transit alternatives to GM diesel buses. None of the early White or Doble steam buses are still in operation. The last electric streetcars were built in 1953; only one electric bus (built in Canada) has been delivered since 1955. In 1973, only five American cities continued to operate electric buses, and eight ran a handful of ancient streetcars.

General Motors' gross revenues are 10 times greater if it sells cars rather than buses. In theory, therefore, GM has every economic incentive to discourage bus ridership. In fact, its bus dieselization program may have generated that effect. Engineering studies strongly suggest that conversion from electric transit to diesel buses results in higher operating costs, loss of patronage, and eventual bankruptcy. They demonstrate, for example, that diesel buses have 28 percent shorter economic lives, 40 percent higher operating costs, and 9 percent lower productivity than electric buses. They also conclude that the diesel's foul smoke, ear-splitting noise, and slow acceleration may discourage ridership. In short, by increasing the costs, reducing the revenues, and contributing to the collapse of hundreds of transit systems, GM's dieselization program may have had the long-term effect of selling GM cars.

Today, automobiles have completely replaced bus transportation in many areas of the country. Since 1952, the year GM achieved monopoly control of bus production, ridership has declined by 3 billion passengers and bus sales have fallen by about 60 percent. During that same period, GM automobile sales have risen from 1.7 million to more than 4.8 million units per year. By 1972, in a move which possibly signified the passing of bus transportation in this country, General Motors had begun converting its bus plants to motor home production.

3. *The Displacement of Railroad Transportation by Automobiles and Trucks.* As described in the preceding section, General Motors' diversifi-

cation into bus transportation contributed to two developments: The displacement of passengers from rail to bus and eventually to automobile travel, and the shift in freight from rail to trucks. GM's integration into locomotive production was arguably an additional factor in the diversion of rail passengers to automobiles and rail freight to trucks. In 1930, it entered the locomotive industry by acquiring Winton Engine and Electro-Motive. At that time, Winton was the largest manufacturer of heavy diesel engines. Electro-Motive, a principal customer of Winton, was the leading firm in the application of diesel engines to railroad motive power. By combining these firms, GM became the Nation's largest manufacturer of train locomotives.

As the world's largest manufacturer of cars and trucks, General Motors was inherently ill suited to promote train transportation. Indeed, it had every economic incentive to repress this method of travel. A single GM-powered passenger train could displace as many as 1,000 GM cars; a GM-powered freight train could supplant a fleet of 150 GM trucks. From the standpoint of economies, moreover, GM's gross revenues were from 25 to 35 times larger if it sold cars and trucks rather than train locomotives.

In fact, General Motors' diversification into railroads probably weakened this industry's ability to compete with motor vehicles. More specifically, GM eliminated technological alternatives in train motive power which were arguably more efficient than the diesel combustion system it promoted. Its production of diesels rather than electric- or steam-driven locomotives, however, was entirely rational in terms of profit maximization. First, dieselization would vastly increase locomotive sales. A diesel locomotive, for example, lasted one-half as long, did one-third the work, and cost three times more than an electric locomotive. Second, as compared with railroad electrification, dieselization was substantially less of a threat to car and truck transportation. Diesel trains were sluggish, noisy, and generally less attractive to passengers than rapid, quiet, pollution-free electric trains. In addition, they were less powerful and therefore not as efficient in hauling freight. As the Nation's largest shipper of freight, GM was able to exert considerable influence over the locomotive purchasing policies of the Nation's railroads. It used this powerful form of leverage to sell its diesel locomotives. Before long, it had dieselized the entire American railroad industry, and simultaneously had obtained a monopoly in the production of locomotives. As a consequence, alternative forms of motive power, such as electricity which might have enabled the railroads to compete more effectively with cars and trucks, were disregarded.

General Motors dieselized the Nation's railroads by using its freight business to coerce them to purchase its diesel locomotives. In 1935, with barely 2.4 percent of industry sales, it embarked upon a dual plan to monopolize locomotive production and to dieselize the American railroad industry. At that time, electric locomotives outnumbered diesel units 7 to 1, and several firms were developing a steam turbine engine to replace the conventional steam locomotive. In November, GM ordered its traffic division to begin routing freight over railroads which agreed reciprocally to scrap their electric and steam equipment for GM diesels. For the next 35 years it used its formidable leverage as the largest commercial shipper to exclude locomotive competitors and to force the railroads to convert to all-diesel operation. By 1970, it had effectively dieselized the entire industry: steam units were virtually extinct; and diesels, 80 percent of which were manufactured by GM, outnumbered electric locomotives 100 to 1.

The dieselization of America's railroads did not require blatant acts of coercion. Rail executives were fully aware of GM's formidable freight leverage. As an interoffice legal memorandum drafted by GM's antitrust attorneys stated, "GM could, in all probability, have successfully capitalized upon the railroad's sensitivity to reciprocity by frequently reminding them of GM's considerable traffic, and could have done so without ever interfering substantially with the economical routing of traffic." Nevertheless, on occasion, GM may have resorted to blatant pressure.

In November 1948, for instance, Roy B. White, President of the Baltimore & Ohio Railroad, was apparently contacted by Alfred P. Sloan, Jr., Chairman of General Motors, regarding GM's offer to locate one of its warehouses on B. & O.'s tracks in return for B. & O.'s agreement to convert to GM diesels. Later that month, White replied by letter to Sloan to the effect: "Here is your Christmas present . . . we will purchase 300 diesel locomotives . . . we now expect to receive a New Year's gift from you . . . locate your warehouse near our tracks." Likewise, in the fall of 1958 a General Motors official informed Gulf, Mobile & Ohio Railroad that certain GM traffic would not be routed over its lines because other railroads had purchased more GM diesel locomotives than Gulf.

Through its shrewd use of freight leverage, GM eliminated all but one of its competitors by 1970. Westinghouse, a pioneer in railway electrification, announced its departure from the history in 1954. Baldwin-Lima-Hamilton, one of the Nation's oldest railroad builders, but its last locomotive in 1956. Fairbanks-Morse, which attempted to enter in 1944, was forced out by 1958. In 1969, American Locomotive, an aggressive manufacturer of gas turbine, electric, steam turbine as well as diesel locomotives, and the leading exporter of rail equipment, was purchased by one of GM's automotive parts suppliers (Studebaker-Worthington) and immediately withdrawn from locomotive production. By 1973, 99 percent of the locomotive fleet was dieselized and GM's only competitor, General Electric, accounted for less than 17 percent of total production.

The immediate effect of dieselization was suppression of an alternative system of train propulsion: namely, electrification. In 1935, when GM initiated its dieselization program, two of the country's major railroads had electrified their systems and several others contemplated similar action. The New York, New Haven & Hartford had constructed the world's first 11,000-volt, 25-cycle alternating current system along 500 miles of New England track. The Pennsylvania had inaugurated electric passenger and freight train operations between New York and Washington. By dieselizing these and other roads, GM may have curbed in its incipiency a trend toward electrification. By 1960, when virtually every other industrialized Nation in the world was electrifying their trains, America was locked-in to GM diesel locomotives.

The long-term effect of dieselization was impairment of the railroads' ability to compete effectively with cars and trucks. By vastly increasing operating, maintenance and depreciation costs, dieselization contributed to the curtailment of maintenance and service, and eventual bankruptcy of many American railroads. This process was arguably apparent in General Motors' conversion of the New Haven system from electric to diesel power. In 1956, GM reportedly used its freight leverage to coerce the railroad into scrapping all of its electric passenger and freight locomotives in favor of GM diesel passenger units. The conversion was followed by loss of a substantial portion of the New Haven's passenger and freight traffic to cars and trucks. Dieselization may have been the responsible factor. The slower GM diesels were less attractive to New Haven passengers accustomed to rapid electric trains. They were also less powerful and, consequently, less suitable for moving freight than the electric locomotives they replaced. Within a short time the company began to experience serious operating deficits. These deficits coupled with the diesel's higher operating and depreciation costs compelled, in turn, cutbacks in maintenance and service, which generated another round of traffic diversion to cars and trucks.

A subsequent investigation by the Interstate Commerce Commission in 1960 confirmed that in fact dieselization had contributed to the New Haven's severe financial crisis and eventual bankruptcy. Observing that "without an intelligent locomotive policy, no efficient railroad operation can possibly be conducted," the ICC hearing officers stressed the significant economic advantages which the New Haven had derived from the durability, efficiency and extraordinary power of electric locomotives. They noted that the life of an electric locomotive was about twice that of a diesel (30 years versus 15 years, respectively) and, being a less complicated, more efficient and less delicate piece of machinery, was substantially cheaper to operate and maintain. In addition, they emphasized that a single electric locomotive could do the work of three diesels and that new electric locomotives cost only one-third as much as the diesel locomotives sold to the New Haven by General Motors. The examiners found, however, that despite the numerous advantages of electric operation as compared with diesel and contrary to the advice of its own independent engineering consultants, the New Haven had relied instead on General Motors' "ridiculous" representations as to the savings to be derived from dieselization.

According to the ICC officials, GM's claims of anticipated savings proved to be "a mirage." The New Haven's replacement of its electric locomotives with GM diesels generated higher operating, maintenance and depreciation expenses and substantial losses in passenger and freight revenues. During 50 years of electrified operation, it had never failed to show an operating profit. In 1955, the year before dieselization, it earned $5.7 million carrying 45 million passengers and 814 thousand carloads of freight. By 1959, 7 years after GM dieselization began, it lost $9.2 million hauling 10 million fewer passengers and 130 thousand fewer carloads of freight. In 1961, it was declared bankrupt; by 1968, when it was acquired by the Penn Central, it had accumulated a capital deficit of nearly $300 million.

In 1961, the ICC upheld the hearing officers' recommended report on the bankrupt New Haven and censured General Motors for contributing to the railroad's financial ruin. Of the several factors it listed as responsible for the New Haven's downfall, it placed special emphasis on the elimination of electric locomotives. Although it refrained from suggesting that GM was guilty of fraudulent misrepresentation, the Commission found the automakers' estimates of savings from conversion to diesels "erroneous," "inflated," and "manifestly absurd." Referring to the "great advances in railway electrification made in Europe and in the Soviet Union," it concluded with a recommendation that the trustees undertake a study of the economic feasibility of complete reelectrification of the New Haven's main line.

The New Haven was probably not the only casualty of GM's dieselization program. All six of the major railroads serving the Northeast corridor are today bankrupt, and those in the rest of the country are earning an average of less than 2 percent on investment. Had these roads electrified, they might have fared better financially and might have been better able to compete effectively with motor vehicles. That technological option, however, was foreclosed to them as a result, in part, of GM's diversification into railroad locomotives.

Since GM began its dieselization campaign in 1935, the railroads have progressively lost traffic first to buses and then to cars and trucks, most of which are manufactured by GM. In 1939 they carried half a million passengers and accounted for 75 percent of all freight revenues; by 1972 they had lost 50 percent of their passengers to cars, and nearly 75 percent of all freight revenue to trucks. Whether this result was actually intended by GM is irrelevant. Nonetheless, it is difficult to believe that a firm fundamentally interested in marketing cars and trucks would develop an efficient high-speed train system that might diminish their sales.

The impact of dieselization on this Nation's railroads has been the subject of expert scrutiny. H. F. Brown, an international authority on railroad motive power, has concluded that dieselization "was the single most important factor responsible for the demise of America's railroads." Significantly, his studies of America's experience with GM diesels helped persuade Parliament to electrify rather than dieselize the British railway system.

4. The Political Restraint of Rail Transit. General Motors' diversification into streetcar, bus and railroad transportation was very likely a significant factor in their eventual displacement by automobiles and trucks. A second structural feature, the asymmetrical distribution of economic power in the ground transport sector, may also have generated the political restraint of a third alternative to automobile transportation: rail rapid transit (subways).

. . . [S]mall deconcentrated industries are less able to influence government policymaking as effectively as their concentrated rivals. This may explain, in part, the political disregard until quite recently of rail transit as an alternative in congested urban areas to automotive transportation. Due to its high concentration and gigantic sales volume, the auto industry has accumulated hundreds of millions of dollars in revenues from higher-than-competitively-priced motor vehicles. It has used some of these revenues to finance political activities which, in the absence of effective countervailing activities by competing ground transport industries, induced government bodies to promote their product (automobiles) over other alternatives, particularly rail rapid transit.

Every industry, of course, has the constitutionally protected right to petition Government bodies and to mobilize public opinion as a means of shaping Government policies to its own private corporate advantage. This study does not take exception with that privilege. It does, however, suggest that the presence of a relatively large and highly concentrated automotive industry in the important multi-industry ground transportation sector may have resulted in the distortion of political processes to the advantage of this industry and to the disadvantage of the riding public. The effect, in short, may have been to deprive the public of the opportunity of choosing among competing transportation alternatives. More specifically, an imbalanced distribution of political power in favor of the automakers may have encouraged the Government to allocate overwhelmingly disproportionate sums of money to highways rather than to rail systems.

Generally, the automakers' political activities have been twofold in nature: establishment of a powerful lobbying organization to promote the public financing of highways, and participation in competing associations which favored the construction of subways.

On June 28, 1932, Alfred P. Sloan, Jr., president of General Motors, organized the National Highway Users Conference to combine representatives of the Nation's auto, oil, and tire industries in a common front against competing transportation interests. Sloan became its permanent chairman and served in that capacity until 1948, when he was succeeded by the new chairman of GM, Albert Bradley, who continued as its chairman through 1956. Its announced objectives were dedication of highway taxes solely to highway purposes, and development of a continuing program of highway construction.

In a statement issued the following January, NHUC formally proclaimed its political commitment to automotive transportation: "Until now those interested in automotive transportation have fought their battles independently. Participating in the National Highway Users Conference are a large majority of the interested groups. The manufacturers of motorcars and accessories have joined with the users of their equipment in the common cause of defense." The "interested groups" included the Motor Vehicle Manufacturers Association (representing automobile and truck companies), the American Petroleum Institute (spokesman for the oil industry), the American Trucking Association (representing the trucking interests), the Rubber Manufacturers Association (comprising the tire companies) and the American Automobile Association (purporting to speak for the Nation's millions of motorists). Although it disclaimed any intention of lobbying on behalf of these highway interests, it proposed to serve as "an agency for the coordination of activities of interested groups" and to cooperate with "such State organizations as are set up along the same lines as the national body." Implicitly, therefore, its function was to influence Congress and the state legislators where it claimed "the membership may be badly informed or where a considerable part of it may yield to the influence of selfish interests."

During the succeeding 40 years, the National Highway Users Conference has compiled an impressive record of accomplishments. Its effect, if not purpose, has been to direct public funds away from rail construction and into highway building. At the state level, its 2,800 lobbying groups have been instrumental in persuading 44 of the Nation's 50 legislatures to adopt and preserve measures which dedicated State and local gasoline tax revenues exclusively to highway construction. By promoting these highway "trust funds," it has discouraged governors and mayors from attempting to build anything other than highways for urban transportation. Subways and rail transit proposals have had to compete with hospitals, schools and other governmental responsibilities for funding. By contrast, highways have been automatically financed from a self-perpetuating fund which was legally unavailable for any other purpose. Largely as a result, highways, not subways, have been built. From 1945 through 1970, states and localities spent more than $156 billion constructing hundreds of thousands of miles of roads. During that same period, only 16 miles of subway were constructed in the entire country.

Likewise, at the Federal level this organization has been very successful in promoting highways over rail transportation. For example, under the early and exceptionally capable leadership of GM's Sloan and Bradley, it became a principal architect of the world's largest roadbuilding effort, the 42,500-mile, $70-billion Interstate Highway System. During the years prior to passage in 1956 of the Interstate Highway Act, NHUC and allied highway groups had worked assiduously building support among Congressmen, Federal administrators, academicians and engineers. They contributed to congressional campaigns, placed their members in important administrative posts, and granted millions of dollars to highway research.

At the time, few opposed the idea of building a system of interstate highways. Only one witness during more than 2 years of congressional hearings even raised the issue of what effect it might have on the Nation's railroads. In retrospect, a national highway program was unquestionably needed. Whether its tremendous scope and budgetary commitment, however, might preclude Federal financing of alternative rail transport systems was a point which should have been debated at that time. The uneven distribution of political resources between automakers and rail manufacturers may explain why this important question received virtually no political attention.

When Congress finally began hearings on the Interstate Highway Act in 1956, the outcome was a foregone conclusion. Only the manner of financing the program was at issue. In the end, the National Highway Users Conference managed to persuade Congress to adopt the same trust fund arrangement which it had successfully promoted earlier to the state legislatures. The impact of the Federal Highway Trust Fund on transportation spending was similar to that which occurred at the state level. While urban rail proposals were forced to compete for funds with dozens of Federal priorities including national defense, health, and social security, thousands of miles of highways were built automatically with gasoline tax revenues unavailable for any other purpose. From 1956 through 1970, the Federal Government spent approximately $70 billion for highways; and only $795 million, or 1 percent, for rail transit.

Today, the National Highway Users Conference, now known as Highway Users Federation for Safety and Mobility (HUFSAM), works effectively with highway-related groups such as the Motor Vehicle Manufacturers Association (MVMA) to promote the automakers' interest in more highways and less rail transit. With combined annual budgets of nearly $16 million, most of which comes from the Big Three auto companies,

HUFSAM and MVMA fight State and Federal attempts to "divert" highway funds for rail transit purposes. In this regard they are aided by a score of allied highway interests which collectively spend an estimated $500 million a year lobbying to preserve highway trust funds. They are also active in financing research groups which invariably conclude that automobiles, trucks, and, if necessary, "bus transit" complete with underground diesel "busways" can satisfy every ground transportation need.

By comparison, the three leading transit lobby groups are financially weak and torn by the conflicting interests of their membership. The American Transit Association, the largest element of the transit lobby, operates on an annual budget of about $700,000 which must be apportioned between the conflicting political needs of its bus and rail transit manufacturing members. The Railway Institute spends an estimated $600,000 a year. The third and smallest element of the transit body, the Institute for Rapid Transit, operates on a meager budget of about $200,000 a year. In short, HUFSAM and MVMA alone outspend the three principal transit organizations by more than 10 to 1. Furthermore, General Motors, whose personnel organized and continue to direct the highway lobby, has secured the power to influence the policies of two of these three transit groups. Due to its position as the Nation's largest producer of bus and rail vehicles, it is a major financial contributor to both the American Transit Association and the Railway Progress Institute. It is also an influential member of the Institute for Rapid Transit.

Absent a powerful and unequivocal rail transit lobby, those interested in balanced transportation are no match for the organized highway interests. Legislators including Senators Kennedy, Muskie, and Weicker, citizen and municipal groups such as the Highway Action Coalition and the League of Cities, Mayors Alioto (San Francisco), White (Boston), Daley (Chicago), and numerous others have failed repeatedly to shift anything other than token amounts of state and Federal gas tax revenues from highways to rail transit. As an apparent consequence, national transportation policy principally reflects the legislative objective of the automakers: Building more highways which sell more cars and trucks.

Publicly, the automakers proclaim their support for mass transit. They cultivate this seemingly paradoxical image for two reasons. First, a pro-transit posture at a time of petroleum shortages and environmental concerns is good for public relations. Second, and perhaps more importantly, they seek to control and direct the development of nonautomotive transport technology in a manner least threatening to their fundamental interest: selling cars. In this regard, Ford is developing "horizontal elevators" and PRT (personal rapid transit) vehicles capable of moving people short distances within strictly downtown areas. Ford's transit vehicles would compete, therefore, not with automobiles but with pedestrians. Likewise, General Motors is engaged in a continuing effort to divert

Government funds from rapid rail transit, which seriously threatens the use of cars in metropolitan areas, to GM buses, which fail consistently to persuade people to abandon their autos. In place of regional electric rail systems, for instance, it promotes diesel-powered "bus trains" of as many as 1,400 units, each spaced 80 feet apart. Instead of urban electric rail, it advocates the use of dual-mode gas/electric vehicles which would be adapted from GM's minimotor homes. In sum, the automakers embrace transit in order to prevent it from competing effectively with their sales of automobiles.

General Motors' diversification into the bus and rail industries and the asymmetrical distribution of power between automakers and rail builders would appear to have contributed at least in part, therefore, to the decline of competing alternatives to motor vehicles. By 1973 five different forms of nonautomotive transportation had either disappeared or been seriously impaired: electric streetcars, trolley coaches, interurban electric railways, buses, and trains. In short, diversification and asymmetry in ground transport manufacturing may have retarded the development of mass transportation and, as a consequence, may have generated a reliance on motor vehicles incompatible with metropolitan needs.

5. *Current Performance of the Ground Transportation Sector.* Due to its anticompetitive structure and behavior, this country's ground transport sector can no longer perform satisfactorily. It has become seriously imbalanced in favor of the unlimited production of motor vehicles. Unlike every other industrialized country in the world, America has come to rely almost exclusively on cars and trucks for the land transportation of its people and goods. Cars are used for 90 percent of city and intercity travel; trucks are the only method of intracity freight delivery and account for 78 percent of all freight revenues. This substitution of more than 100 million petroleum-consuming cars and trucks for competing forms of alternately powered ground transportation is a significant factor in this sector's unacceptable level of inefficient and nonprogressive performance.

Efficiency in terms of market performance may be defined as a comparison of actual prices or costs with those that would obtain in a competitively structured market. Currently, Americans pay $181 billion per year for motor vehicle transportation. In terms of high energy consumption, accident rates, contribution to pollution, and displacement of urban amenities, however, motor vehicle travel is possibly the most inefficient method of transportation devised by modern man.

More specifically, the diversion of traffic from energy-efficient electric rails to fuel-guzzling highway transport has resulted in an enormous consumption of energy. Rails can move passengers and freight for less than one-fifth the amount of energy required by cars and trucks. The displacement of rails by highways, therefore, has seriously depleted our scarce supplies of energy and has increased by several billion dollars a year the amount consumers must pay for ground transportation. It has been estimated, for example, that the diversion of passengers in urban areas from energy-efficient electric rail to gasoline automobiles results in their paying $18 billion a year more in energy costs alone. In addition, economists have found that the inefficient diversion of intercity freight from rail to trucks costs consumers $5 billion per year in higher prices for goods.

The substitution of highways for rails has also reduced efficiency by imposing higher indirect costs on the public in the form of accidents, pollution, and land consumption. Rail travel is 23 times as safe as travel by motor vehicles. The diversion to highways has cost the public an estimated $17 billion each year in economic damages attributable to motor vehicle accidents. This figure, however, cannot reflect the incalculable human costs of motor vehicle accidents: The violent deaths each year by car and truck of 55,000 Americans, more than all who died in the entire 12 years of our involvement in Vietnam, and the serious injuries to an additional 5 million of our citizens.

Likewise, the costs of urban air pollution have been greatly accentuated by the imbalance in favor of cars and trucks. Motor vehicles annually consume 42 billion gallons of petroleum within the densely populated 2 percent of the U.S. geographic area classified as urban. The consumption of this enormous quantity of fuel in urban areas produces in excess of 60 million tons of toxic pollutants, which in turn cost urban residents more than $4 billion in economic damages.

The presence of high concentrations of these motor vehicle pollutants, particularly oxides of nitrogen, in densely populated areas has also generated a crisis in urban public health. In Los Angeles alone, more than 500 persons die each year of ailments attributable to motor vehicle generated smog. The hazards of carbon monoxide and hydrocarbon emissions from automobiles have been widely acknowledged. Less well known are the potentially more serious effects of oxides of nitrogen produced primarily by diesel trucks and buses in high concentrations on congested city streets. When inhaled, these oxides combine with moisture in the lungs to form corrosive nitric acid which permanently damages lung tissues and accelerates death by slowly destroying the body's ability to resist heart and lung diseases. By contrast, if electric rail transportation were substituted in cities for motor vehicles, urban air pollution might be reduced substantially. Although the burning of fuels to generate this increased electrical energy would produce some pollution, it would pose a substantially less serious hazard to public health. Electric powerplants can often be located in areas remote from population centers. Moreover, the increased pollution by generating facilities would be offset by a reduction in pollution due to oil refinery operations. Furthermore, the abatement of air pollution at a relatively small number of stationary powerplants would represent a far easier task than attempting to install and monitor devices on 100 million transient motor vehicles.

The diversion of traffic from rail to highways has imposed a third cost on consumers — the consumption of vast amounts of taxable urban landscapes from 60 to 65 percent of our cities' land area is devoted to highways, parking facilities, and other auto- and truck-related uses. In downtown Los Angeles, the figure approaches 85 percent. This has led to an erosion in the cities' tax base and, concomitantly, to a decline in their ability to finance the delivery of vital municipal services. Electric rail transportation, by comparison, requires less than one-thirteenth as much space as highways to move a comparable amount of passengers or goods, and in many cases can be located underground.

Progressiveness in terms of market performance is generally understood as a comparison of the number and importance of actual innovations with those which optimally could have been developed and introduced. The substitution of highways for rails has resulted in a decrease in mobility and has precluded important innovations in high-speed urban and intercity ground transportation. The decrease in mobility is most acute in urban areas. The average speed of rush hour traffic in cities dependent on motor vehicles, for example, is 12 miles per hour. Studies indicate that city traffic moved more quickly in 1890. Moreover, 20 percent of our urban population (the aged, youth, disabled, and poor) lack access to automobiles and, due to the nonexistence of adequate public transportation, are effectively isolated from employment or educational opportunities and other urban amenities. Substitution of highways for rails has also retarded innovations in high-speed urban and intercity transport. Technologically advanced rail transit systems, which currently operate in the major cities of Europe and Japan, would relieve congestion and contribute to urban mobility. High-speed intercity rail systems, such as Japan's 150-mile-per-hour electric Tokaido Express, would help relieve mounting air traffic congestion and offer a practical alternative to slower and more tedious travel by car or truck. But the political predilections of the automakers have become the guidelines for American transportation policy. In contrast to the advanced rail transport emphasis of Europe and Japan, this country has persisted in the expansion of highway transport. As a result, America has become a second-rate nation in transportation.

There are strong indications, moreover, that due to mounting concerns about air pollution and a worldwide shortage of petroleum, our motor-vehicle-dominated transportation system will perform even worse in the future. The Environmental Protection Agency has warned that by 1977 motor vehicle emissions in major urban areas may compel a cutback in automobile, truck, and diesel bus use of as much as 60 percent. In addition, the Department of the Interior has forecast that the current petroleum crisis might cripple transportation and cause "serious economic and social disruptions." More precisely, an excessive reliance in the past on fuel-guzzling motor vehicles for transport has contributed to a crisis in energy which now threatens to shut down industries, curb air and ground travel, and deprive our homes of heating oil for winter.

Despite these adverse trends, the automakers appear bent on further motorization. Henry Ford II, for instance, has noted that notwithstanding "the energy crisis, the environmental crisis, and the urban crisis" new car sales in the United States "have increased by more than a million during the past 2 model years." General Motors' chief operating executive has predicted that soon each American will own a "family of cars" for every conceivable travel activity including small cars for trips, recreational vehicles for leisure, and motor homes for mobile living. GM is also engaged in the displacement of what little remains of this Nation's rail systems. To that end, it is developing 750-horsepower diesel engines to haul multiple trailers at speeds of 70 miles per hour along the nearly completed Interstate Highway System. These "truck trains" are slated to replace rail freight service. As substitutes for regional subway systems, GM is also advocating 1,400-unit diesel "bus trains," which would operate on exclusive busways outside cities and in bus tunnels under downtown areas. Both diesel truck trains and underground bus trains, however, would seem grossly incompatible with public concerns about petroleum shortages and suffocating air pollution.

The automakers' motorization program, moreover, is worldwide in scope. The superior bus and rail systems which flourish in the rest of the industrialized world interfere with the sale of cars and trucks by the Big Three's foreign subsidiaries. "The automobile industry put America on wheels," said GM Chairman Gerstenberg in September of 1972. "Today," he added, "expanding markets all around the world give us the historic opportunity to put the whole world on wheels."

THE WORKPLACE VII

During the past 200 years, work has held a central position in the ideas of philosophers and social scientists. Of these, the most influential and enduring commentator was Karl Marx. His analysis of the workplace during the industrial revolution was distinguished by its sympathy for the plight of the industrial worker, its analytical power, and its empirical grounding (derived from observations of the industrial workplace by British Commissions of Inquiry).

Marx wrote during the mid-nineteenth century, when manufacturing had evolved from the family cottage to the "factory" — an appropriately speeded-up word invented to describe the new industrial form. In analyzing the human effects of capitalist industry, Marx emphasized the subordination of the worker's own needs to the requirements of production for profit:

What constitutes the alienation of labour? First, that the work is *external* to the worker, that it is not part of his nature; and that, consequently, he does not fulfill himself in his work but denies himself, has a feeling of misery rather than well-being, does not develop freely his mental and physical energies but is physically exhausted and mentally debased. The worker, therefore, feels himself at home only during his leisure time, whereas at work he feels homeless. His work is not voluntary but imposed, *forced labour*. It is not satisfaction of a need, but only a *means* for satisfying other needs. Its alien character is clearly shown by the fact that as soon as there is no physical or other compulsion it is avoided like the plague.[1]

Should work be interesting and significant, or is work simply an unpleasant task that must be done to live and to provide resources for spending on leisure activities away from the workplace? Is it possible to reform work, that is, to make it less dull, less dangerous, less exhausting? The latter has been one goal of labor unions in Western society. With what success? The two selections on factory work suggest some but not enormous improvement over conditions prevailing in the nineteenth century factory. Working hours are shorter, pay is higher, leisure is possible, but factory work remains monotonous, tiring, subservient, and dangerous. As Studs Terkel's interviews show, white-collar work can also be routinized and boring, but at least the white-collar worker relates partly to people, not just to a machine, on the job.

If factory work is dangerous, mining is often brutal, sometimes deadly. The squalor and harshness of nineteenth century mining and the family life of the miner have been documented by a variety of scholars and writers. Rachel Scott's contemporary description of the same workplace seems hardly to suggest improvement. If anything, there is as much — or more — danger in a twentieth century Idaho silver mine as in a nineteenth century Welsh coal mine.

It is scarcely news that traditional industrial workplaces — the factory, the mine — are less than attractive and inspiring. The young miner dreams of being, for instance, a professional football player. Yet, as the selection by Arnold Mandell shows, behind the colorful uniforms, the cheerleaders, the bands, the patriotic displays, is sheer pain accumulated through the years of broken bones, torn muscles, ligaments, cartilege. Such pain can be controlled only by use (and abuse) of pills of various effects; in particular, analgesics to deaden pain, and stimulants to waken dormant areas of the brain to the aggressiveness required to succeed in this competitive enterprise. Football is a sport. Professional football, like the factory, the bank, and the mine, is a business enterprise run for profit.

REFERENCES

1. Quoted in Shlomo Avineri, *The Social and Political Thought of Karl Marx,* Cambridge, Cambridge University Press, 1971, p. 106.

24. AUTO PRODUCTION — LORDSTOWN

Emma Rothschild

The Lordstown Vega factory began operating in June 1970, to rapturous business acclamation. The factory was not new, but renovated, at a cost of some hundreds of millions of dollars. Since 1966, GM had built Chevrolets at Lordstown, in the low-grade farmland between Pittsburgh and Cleveland; and from the earliest days the Lordstown work force was one of the youngest at any GM plant. By 1970, there were four factories in the Lordstown complex: Chevrolet auto assembly, Fisher body assembly, a new stamping plant, designed by a computer, and a new Chevrolet truck plant. The Chevrolet assembly plant had been redesigned, in accordance with what GM called the "entirely new concept of [Vega] assembly" — people who worked at the old Lordstown plant said that secretive GM engineers appeared at the factory in March 1970, "tearing the whole insides out and ripping up the line," even before the last of the Chevrolet Impalas were assembled.

By midsummer 1970, GM was ready to invite visitors to its new, improved Lordstown factories. Early Vega publicity emphasized the manufacture of the new, competitive car, at its new, competitive factory, and most early reactions were suitably awestruck. GM's labor-saving assembly techniques attracted national attention, as the corporation lamented the high level of U.S. wage rates. "Stomping the Beetle?" the *Wall Street Journal* asked from Lordstown, and announced that "GM resorts to aggressive automation to pare construction costs of mini-car . . . [and hopes to] be able to wring about 10 percent out of the normal labor costs of producing an automobile." Company executives suggested that the high quality of Vegas was made possible by Lordstown assembly efficiency: J. Z. DeLorean of Chevrolet described Vega "quality control," and pronounced in September 1970 that "the high level of enthusiasm among employees at the Lordstown plant is producing craftsmanship to challenge any auto maker in the world."

Corporate pride increased throughout the first year of Vega sales. The Lordstown project was, it seemed, of critical importance not only for the Vega but also for GM's entire campaign to increase productivity. The cover of the 1970 GM Annual Report showed a panorama of the Lordstown assembly plant, with two Vegas parked outside: the report also contained photographs of three men working on the Lordstown line, and of a "solid-state computerized tester" for Vegas.[1] As late as January 1972,

Richard Gerstenberg, the chairman of GM, mentioned the Lordstown operation as a major example of his company's efforts to increase worker productivity: "Every attempt was made [there] to design out costs in the assembly process." Earlier, an auto industry share analyst had summarized corporate hopes for Lordstown production, when he returned from a visit to the factory, "excited" about the prospects for reducing labor costs: "The essential point made was that the Vega line is a prototype, a schooling place for everybody in the GM system. . . . It is the wave of the future."

"Paradise Lost"

GM's presentation of Lordstown as the wave of the automotive future continued until February 1972 — when workers at the Vega factories voted by a 97 percent majority to strike over working conditions. The strike vote came after months of struggle: a change in plant management, layoffs, a disciplinary crackdown, an increase in car defects, complaints by workers about the speeding up of monotonous assembly-line tasks, slowdowns, high absenteeism, repeated allegations by GM of worker sabotage. Workers claimed that supervisors authorized shipment of defective cars; the company claimed that workers attacked the paint, body, upholstery, and controls of the Vegas.

During the three-week strike which followed, and the months of subsequent resentment, GM executives restrained their public enthusiasm for Lordstown technology. But the distance between past expectations and present disaster was too great to be ignored, even by the most awestruck of previous visitors; and for the *Wall Street Journal* the "Utopian" Lordstown factories had become nothing less than a "Paradise Lost," "fall[en] from grace." Public reactions to the strike were well described, six months later, by GM's director of labor relations. With heavy sarcasm, and a determination to "put the record straight," this executive declared that "the Lordstown chapter in the story of industrial life in the twentieth century will single out the Lordstown strike of 1972 as marking the explosion of youth and its rebellion against the management and union establishment." Once prototypes of efficiency, the Lordstown factories had now become prototypes of revolt. Commentators, from CBS and the U.S. Senate to *Motor Trend* and *Playboy*, converged on Lordstown; for one national journal the Vega plant was an "industrial Woodstock," where young workers acted out mysterious modern attitudes to work.

Even GM's labor relations executive was to admit after the Lordstown strike that "changes in the social environment are affecting our business in the area of motivation and behavior of employees," that GM employed, for example, more women, more blacks, and better-educated workers than in the past. But Lordstown workers and GM executives agreed that the famous 1972 strike had to do not only with social psychology but also with production issues, with layoffs, changed working conditions, and changed factory discipline. Most of these changes were the direct result of the same improvements and productive reorganizations that constituted GM's Lordstown "advances" in efficiency, and that made the new factory a "Paradise" for the business press. GM's own copious descriptions of Lordstown production may provide some explanation for worker discontent, and some idea of how advanced the Lordstown technology turned out to be.

LORDSTOWN FORDISM

From the days when Vegas were XP-887 experimental cars, and Lordstown workers built Chevrolet Impalas, GM's Lordstown policy was determined by Fordist exigencies: mechanization of jobs, reorganization of factory life, time, and space around unskilled work, and the modern auto imperative of cutting all costs, everywhere. Henry Ford's production had required the transfer of skills, and jobs, from workers to machines, and the "rationalization" of those jobs that could not be mechanized, and work was now so organized to be as precise, as predictable, and as machinelike as possible. In the Fordist "unity" of "men and machines," jobs followed the rhythms of mechanical production — as at Highland Park, so at Lordstown with its robots and computer controls.

The improvements of Lordstown production together forced a continuous reorganization of work — and their joint momentum can show to what extent Lordstown's designers had relied upon Fordist technology. The expensive Lordstown factories contained an unusually high concentration of mechanical innovations: for the present, cost-conscious auto industry, gloomy about future expansion, it often seems desirable to increase productivity in the cheapest possible ways, without new capital equipment; and, at GM, Mr. "Bookkeeper" Gerstenberg's main complaint about Lordstown was apparently that the corporation had "spent a terrific pile" of money on building the new factories. Yet even the most elaborate technology, such as the vaunted Lordstown robot welders, had progressed only modestly since the youth of mass production. The most ambitious of modern U.S. auto investments, Lordstown was still a product of Fordist practice.

Each of the three major "advances" built into the Lordstown factories — advances in mechanization, in factory planning (as helped by GM's computer designers), and in automatic controls and inspections — either was or could have been imagined by Henry Ford, and each increased the intensity and pace of unskilled work. Subsequent attempts to improve on the built-in and mechanical Lordstown innovations were a logical continuation of Fordist endeavor as refined by forty years of corporate cost efficiency. Henry Ford relied on his factory supervisors to discover when men and machines "wore out" or "needed to be replaced": for General Motors, determined managers could discover lost costs and idle moments overlooked by time-study engineers, and diligent foremen could find those inefficiencies that the managers had overlooked.

Mechanization, the first of the three categories of Lordstown innovation, has troubled the U.S. auto corporations for some fifty years. Now, as in the 1920s, automobiles are made out of thousands of metal and other parts, bolted or screwed or pushed or welded together: and now, as then, the assembling of the different parts is assumed to require some manual dexterity, some lowest human knack of visual coordination. Since the time of Henry Ford, the auto companies have tried to simplify their cars in such a way as to increase the number of assembly jobs which can be performed mechanically, while the development of auto marketing has required greater and greater elaboration in cars. But certain assembly jobs continue to demand an unskilled but barely mechanizable adaptability. People are still better than any but the most sophisticated, and *expensive*, automata at tightening bolts . . . or hanging wheels, or fixing steering columns, or, as two young women were doing at Lordstown a few months after the 1972 strike, jumping off and on the assembly line sliding grilles between the headlights of Vegas.

At Lordstown, the major effort at mechanization consisted of introducing the twenty-six "Unimate" robots which perform much of the welding on Vega bodies. (Before taking the public tour of the Vega factory, visitors are told that they will be particularly anxious to look out for the Unimates. During the tour, company guides cannot talk over the noise of the factory floor, and visitors ask one another whether each successive welding gun is in fact one of the famous robots. But when the group finally reaches them, the Unimates are unmistakable, white and contoured on a dreary iron line. They even move like science fiction automata — or, as one small boy who had joined the tour with his father and grandfather put it, "like little animals, nibbling the cars.")

The Lordstown robots in fact operate according to forty-year-old principles: in 1931 Henry Ford described the newly developed "automatic welding machine" which did the same job (of joining steel parts) as a human worker, and "went through the welding cycle automatically to completion." For Ford, the problem with such devices was their lack of adaptability, and GM's Lordstown experiences also illustrate some of the hazards of even the least adventurous assembly mechanization. As it turned out, the local management had almost as much trouble with its new machines as with its human "operators." One subsidiary machine, whose responsibility was to hand things to the Unimates, broke down repeatedly because of the "strain on key parts." Other new devices were even less dexterous. According to the *Wall Street Journal*, for example, the automatic spray guns that painted Vegas and remembered (or so it was hoped) whether the car to be painted was a coupe, a sedan, or a station wagon, developed a tendency to lose control, spraying paint into the air, the car windows, and assorted nearby holes.

Of these more or less efficient machines which replace unskilled labor, few improve factory working conditions, or change the character of the remaining jobs. DeLorean has written that the Lordstown Unimates "eliminate the obligation of the worker carrying a heavy welding gun around" — but also, and probably more candidly, that "one consideration is that we have mechanized many areas that would normally be areas of potential operator failure." Welding is comparatively easy to automate, and, besides, companies could not expect human workers to perform heavy welding one hundred times an hour. The introduction of automatic equipment sometimes actually creates new and more arduous jobs for unskilled workers. According to the head of the firm that manufactures them, Unimate robots are popular because "many 'subhuman' jobs are just not acceptable to workers today." Yet at Lordstown the Unimates themselves have human helpers — charged with the arguably subhuman job of preparing pieces of work, which they pass to the robot welders. As *Fortune* has described it, one of the "ironies" of automation is that machines often "take over the more skilled jobs, such as machining or welding, leaving the menial tasks for humans": "At Lordstown people pick up the sheet-metal panels and clamp them into position in the welding fixtures. At one time GM considered robotizing this job too. But the panels would have to be presented the robot's clutching hands exactly the same way every time, and the machinery to accomplish this was judged prohibitively expensive." (The blind and clutching Unimates have an evident resemblance to the feeding machines in Chaplin's *Modern Times.* "Don't stop for lunch. Be ahead of your competitors.")

The second category of Lordstown innovation, factory planning, is similarly close to Fordist practice. Even more than the Lordstown attempts at mechanization, the planning of Lordstown production shows to what extent the modern auto corporations are dependent on old technology, and how that dependence affects the character of automotive work. The major principle of Lordstown production is the speed-up, as developed in the 1910s. One hundred and two cars pass along the final assembly line each hour; when the Lordstown line made Chevrolet Impalas it turned out sixty cars an hour, a normal rate, although some other factories now make as many as ninety cars each hour. Workers on the Vega line face a new car every thirty-six seconds — eight hundred

Vegas in each eight-hour shift. Every change in factory arrangement supports the assembly speed-up: jobs, and the simplified Vegas, were redesigned to suit a thirty-six-second rhythm of production.

When GM engineers described the Lordstown project, they seemed particularly proud of their organizational achievements. One of their main ambitions in the project was to use "computer technology" to make each employee's job "easier to perform in a more precise way." It is cheaper to increase the precision and speed of production work than to replace workers with speedy (and perhaps clumsy) robots; and precise work, for auto engineers, usually means increased work. As the president of the Lordstown local union described it, to *The New York Times*, "That's the fastest line in the world. A guy has about forty seconds to do his job. The company does some figuring and they say, 'Look, we only added one thing to his job.' On paper it looks like he's got time. But you've got forty seconds to work with. You add one more thing and it can kill you." (Even off the reorganized Vega line, Lordstown jobs are engineered to a fraction of a second. One woman worker in the Lordstown truck plant explained to me the ways in which work is restricted by organizational "precision": "I work with a twelve-pound air gun tightening bolts, but the guns don't always work. Sometimes I have to drop mine on the floor to make it work. Now every job has been time-studied — so having to drop the gun makes me more work.")

The Lordstown assembly line moves up and down, so that workers do not lose time on unnecessary (unproductive) stretching and bending. Chevrolet's first Lordstown coordinator boasted to *Automotive News*, when the factory opened, that "Even the conveyor system at Lordstown is unique. It has four elevations and varies in height from fourteen to seventy-two inches, according to assembly sequence, in order to bring the job closer to the operator at each station." This coordinator used almost the same words as Henry Ford, who in *My Life and Work* described his attempts at "the reduction of the necessity for thought on the part of the worker and the reduction of his movements to a minimum": "In the early part of 1914 we elevated the assembly line. We had adopted a policy of 'man-high' work; we had one line 26¼ inches and another 24½ inches from the floor." Later, in *Today and Tomorrow*, Ford explained that "stooping to the floor to pick up a tool or a part is not productive labor — therefore, all material is delivered waist-high."[2]

The effect of such refinements, in the 1970s as in the 1920s, is to increase the number of times each job can be performed in an hour, to increase the monotony and intensity of the job, and to increase the concentration required. Descriptions of Lordstown are thick with the sort of calculation that Henry Ford most enjoyed, as he worried over idle moments and wasted motions. If each worker took ten fewer steps each day "you will have saved 50 miles of wasted motion and misspent energy" at Highland Park each day. And Ford paid men to work, not walk. By bringing work nearer to workers, and by such advances as re-designing Vega air cleaners with 8 instead of 49 parts, GM hoped to save around $50 in labor costs on each car, or $20 million a year, or somewhere under two seconds per Vega for each Lordstown worker.

One GM executive, Joseph Godfrey, who is head of the GM Assembly Division which now manages the Lordstown Vega factories, has sum-marized this philosophy of modern Fordism. He complains that human productivity is hard to measure. But, he says, "If a man works sixty minutes an hour, that's full productivity. That's how I measure it." By factory organization, productivity can become "fuller" in Godfrey's sense: if each worker at Lordstown works twenty seconds more in each hour, GM will save around $1 million in a year, or 0.05 percent of its annual profit after tax. (Lordstown planning uses Fordist principles to arrange every inch of factory space, as well as every second of factory time. One woman worker at Lordstown described to me the perils of leaving work at the end of the late shift. The company had built an overpass "so we wouldn't get hit on the way to the parking lot," but the factory is sur-rounded by finished cars: "You're like a mouse in a puzzle looking for a way to get through, the Vegas are parked so close together.")

Automatic control and inspection, the third type of Lordstown innova-tion, follows from these calculations of factory rearrangement. Precision and speed of work are built into the Lordstown machinery — and the machinery is further controlled by computer processes. Such controls are an essential part of most modern auto investment, investment which, un-like the Lordstown program, does not involve expanding production, building new factories, and tearing up old equipment. Cut-price effi-ciency demands that employees do more work for their money: robots are expensive, but even the most stagnant auto corporation can afford the salaries of time-study engineers, and computer time for planning and rearranging. At Lordstown these techniques are used, as well as more expansionary innovations.

The Lordstown computer controllers behave like conventional, if in-exorable, human supervisors. The main system is called ALPACA (As-sembly Line Production and Control Activity), and "gives each operator enough [and presumably no more than enough] time to do his job." This endeavor is, again, purely Fordist. Henry Ford's biographers claim that innovations at Ford factories in the 1920s formed the basis (at least, the mechanical and conceptual rather than the electronic basis) of mod-ern automation: Ford's cadres of foremen were certainly the inspiration for ALPACA. "Inspection," Ford wrote, "is the keynote of our produc-tion."

Another Lordstown control program, Product Assurance Control Sys-tem (PACS) is intended, apparently, to help produce high-quality cars. It was described by a "product quality engineer" in the Chevrolet "quality control department" as consisting of "sixteen optical scanning devices strategically located throughout the plant." It is a "closed-loop system," and ensures that "no unresolved production problem is allowed to continue beyond a specified period." Such computer spy systems are fairly common in modern auto "quality control": much of the equipment used in the automation of production replaces inspectors and supervisors rather than unskilled workers. PACS has, however, been conspicuously unsuccessful in avoiding "unresolved production problems," and some Lordstown workers say that they have themselves seen and pointed out assembly-line defects, which are then ignored both by the computer eyes and by the human foremen. The programs in fact seem less adept at maintaining quality than at more traditional efforts — of supervision and cost control.

The sort of automated supervision attempted in the Lordstown ALPACA and PACS programs is a major objective for much of modern industry. ALPACA is only a small step towards the ideal of what one business journal describes as "the programmed responsive plant," in perfect, almost biological homeostasis, where "people would be found doing many of the things they do now, but largely under the direction of machines." In the auto industry, such a vision of automation can become grotesque. At each stage of Lordstown innovation, in mechanization, planning, and control, GM's engineers were dependent on a Fordist use of unskilled labor. Under automation of supervision, auto factory organization becomes a giant unstable hierarchy, with each level controlled by a more and more elaborate technology of reorganization, and with all controls descending to the factory floor, where unskilled workers use a fifty-year-old, nonmechanizable "knack" to assemble the parts of automobiles. As long as the auto corporations are unable to eliminate monotonous production work, they will continue to look for ever more rigorous techniques of Fordist planning, to increase the intensity and precision and predictability of work. And in the thirty-six-second jobs of Lordstown production such rigor cannot easily be found. Not only are unskilled jobs made harder with each cost saving, but the job of reorganization itself becomes harder, as inches and fractions of inches are saved in each movement, minutes and seconds and fractions of seconds in every hour.

GMAD FORDISM

The last stage in GM's Lordstown reorganization was achieved with the GM Assembly Division (GMAD) takeover of plant management. The arrival of GMAD in October 1971 marked a new intensity in the disturbances that culminated in the Lordstown strike of March 1972; in the five intervening months union members registered five thousand grievances against management. GMAD's role, at Lordstown and elsewhere, was to go beyond the technological rationality of mass auto production, to a rationality of management and factory discipline. The division was founded in 1965 to control the assembly of certain GM cars, usually when more than one make was handled at a single plant.[3] It is now responsible for 75 percent of all GM cars in North America, for most assembly lines, and for such "rationalized" operations as coordinating the national flow of auto components. At Lordstown, as at several other plants previously operated by Chevrolet and Fisher Body, GMAD took control of joining together the final auto-assembly and auto-body-manufacturing plants; this consolidation, according to a GM executive, "rendered meaningless a significant amount of duplication of effort that existed under the previous two-management set-up. No longer was there any need for two maintenance, two material, or two inspection departments, for example."

Beyond such acts of managerial reorganization, GMAD is charged, at Lordstown and throughout the corporation, with a more general rearrangement of factory discipline. At Lordstown this rearrangement took the form of layoffs, increased severity by foremen, the assigning of extra tasks and extra penalties for failure to perform these tasks — the sort of changes that have earned the division a national reputation for ruthless aggression. The Vega factory was designed, from the first, around an assembly-line speed of one hundred or more cars an hour, yet the new GMAD plant manager announced that "[while] there are increases in the amount of work some [workers] are doing . . . in these cases it is overdue." The manager implied that his team of production analysts had discovered tricks of cost efficiency that even the Lordstown computers had failed to imagine: "This plant, like any other new facility, was overstaffed at the start." Each of the rearrangements was designed to prevent the "waste" of time, cash, machinery, or nonproductive moments. One of the most praised mechanical innovations at Lordstown was an electrostatically controlled vat, where Vega bodies could be immersed in paint. When GMAD arrived at the factory, the new management complained that paint was being wasted, because it "would lie in crevices as the body left the vat." GMAD's complaint about Lordstown production jobs was, apparently, that expensive seconds were being wasted, in the crevices of the working day.

The GMAD intensification of discipline is a characteristic extreme expression of modern Fordist attempts to increase auto productivity. Just as factory planning is cheaper than mechanizing jobs, and production control is cheaper than mechanical planning, so managerial discipline is cheaper than inspection or time study or other similar corporate techniques. Managers are trained to identify and eliminate waste moments. And beyond such training, the managers learn (for free) a lasting attitude of tough-mindedness, to be shared by executives and plant managers and middle managers and general supervisors and foremen on the line. (Even management toughness is based on Fordist practice. Samuel Marquis, a Ford apostate who once ran Ford's welfare department, wrote that he resigned from the company in 1921 because "the old group of executives, who at times set justice and humanity above profits and production, were gone, [and] there came to the front men whose theory was that men are more profitable to an industry when driven than led. . . . The humane treatment of employees, according to these men, would lead to the weakening of the authority of the 'boss,' and to the breaking down of discipline in the shop.")

Management tough-mindedness is itself a major issue in present automotive discontent. Workers' grievances at Lordstown concerned not only the speeding up and intensification of jobs, but also the disciplinary character of plant management — where workers must ask, and wait, to leave their jobs for one or two minutes; must ask, and wait for permission to get married on a Saturday; must show a doctor's note if they stay home when they get sick; or a note from the funeral director when they go to their father's burial; or a garage bill if they arrive at work late because their car broke down.[4]

This sort of discipline is not expensive for management, but it is part of the "dehumanization" of auto industry work, in which, as a Lordstown worker said to me, there is one, American, law outside the plant, and a GM law inside. A GM law which for visitors to Lordstown begins in the "employees' parking lot," where the first notice seen is in the blue and white colors of GM's corporate insignia, "This parking lot is under surveillance by closed-circuit television." A law which, at the price of a few printed signs, dominates public tours of the plant. Visitors drive through ranks of peripheral parking lots, for Vegas, trucks, executives, workers, to the employee's entrance; inside, there are more signs, and a thickening atmosphere of institutional life: straight ahead, "Don't Give Outsiders Inside Information," and, to the right of the door, a large graph of "demerits" awarded recently in the department of quality control. A Ford worker told Edmund Wilson, in 1931, that "a man checks his brains and his freedom at the door when he goes to work at Ford's." The Lordstown worker I talked to about GM's law said that America must soon move away from the "company law" to a "new law." "It's a wonder," he said, that people have not yet "tried to humanize or Americanize General Motors."

Management and supervisory toughness is built into the Lordstown factory, like the speed and accuracy of the machinery. People in the local union say that foremen are even harsher at Lordstown than in most plants: "They come here from all over GM," and "they want to get to be general foreman, up all the little steps of the ladder." "They've heard about Lordstown, and they want to say 'I make it go, I'm part of that machine.'"[5] Yet the attitude of Lordstown foremen is itself part of the General Motors, GMAD machine. Supervisors rise through the corporate hierarchy, up all the little steps, by maintaining discipline, and by making "their" workers a functioning part of factory production. The Ford worker told Wilson in 1931 that "the bosses are as thick as treacle and they're always on your neck, because the man above is on their neck and Sorenson [the plant manager] is on the neck of the whole lot"; at Lordstown, as at Ford's early factories, the "rationalization" of work and authority is essential to auto production.

GMAD harshness is, in fact, an expected consequence of Fordist technology, and of Henry Ford's own attitude to human work. Automobile mass production was based on an unescapable but highly regimented use of unskilled work: it is to be expected in such an organization of production that managers and foremen should think of assembly-line work as a nearly subhuman activity, to be disciplined, circumscribed, rationalized. The week GMAD took over at Lordstown, *Automotive News* asked Mr. Godfrey, the head of the division, for his views of the "monotony of mass production": "Monotony," Godfrey answered, "is not quite the right word. There is a good deal of misunderstanding about that, but it seems to me that we have our biggest problems when we disturb that 'monotony.' The workers may complain about monotony, *but years spent in the factories leads me to believe that they like to do their jobs automatically. If you interject new things, you spoil the rhythm of the job, and work gets fouled up." (Italics added) These opinions would have been welcomed by Henry Ford, who himself observed that "the vast majority of men want to stay put. They want to be led. They want to have everything done for them and to have no responsibility" — who wrote "some of our tasks are extremely monotonous . . . but then, also many minds are very monotonous." Godfrey has summarized most lucidly the spirit of GMAD, and of modern Fordism: the implicit hope that production work can be reduced to a disciplined part of a great machine, to work for human automata.

"TREAT ME WITH RESPECT AND I WILL GIVE YOU TOP QUALITY WORK WITH LESS EFFORT"

People at Lordstown find the same conditions of work that Ford workers found in the 1920s and 1930s: the same precise restriction of jobs, as they try to make time to drop their faulty air guns; similar disciplinary attitudes, with notes from the funeral director, and permission to leave the line, and foremen on the necks of other foremen; the same "un-American" laws inside the employees' factory entrance. More than most other industries, the auto business sustains an old pattern of production, where unskilled work is both essential and degraded, and where people literally and metaphorically serve machines. For a group of women workers I talked to at Lordstown, it was exactly this situation, with people less important than machines, that summarized the conditions of Lordstown work: where management offices were air-conditioned, while people worked with machines in extremes of heat and cold, where "GM is the richest company in the world and our roof leaks when it rains," and where "the other day an [electrical] transformer blew up just where I work; we thought the plant had been bombed, and we sat there waiting in the dark for an hour and a half while they tried to get in touch with Detroit to close the plant down." Where the factory nurses say, "You didn't do that to yourself in the plant," so we can't treat it, and the doctors are like "veterinarians," and where "we matter less to them than machines or tools." Where, as one of the women described it, "Some of the machines have written on them 'Treat Me with Respect and I will give you Top Quality Work with Less Effort,' and the GM sign. I said we should have that printed on sweatshirts, and wear them to work . . . but we wouldn't be able to keep them on for five minutes, we'd be sent home for disrespect. We should have a whole lot made, and all wear them together. . . . They couldn't send the whole shop home."

REFERENCES

1. GM's report covers provide a revealing chronology of the company's aspirations. 1969, two colored globes, with the legend that GM products are sold in 169 countries of the world: indicating a hope for profit through international expansion. 1970, Lordstown, and hopes for domestic productivity and second-car marketing. 1971, a tan Chevrolet and a turquoise Buick outside the GM "Emissions Research Center": the hope that traditional auto markets would be sustained by a new sort of obsolescence.

2. At Lordstown, as in photographs of early Ford factories, or in Diego Rivera's Detroit murals, people work beneath an overhead conveyor belt, where the odd parts of Vegas dangle like joints of meat.

3. One advantage of the GMAD arrangement is that it makes GM unsuitable for simple antitrust dissolution, since the car divisions, such as Chevrolet and Buick, have few assembly facilities, and GMAD has nothing else. The division developed from the Buick–Oldsmobile assembly operation established in the 1930's, when it was decided that different cars, at different prices and with different accessories, could be assembled out of the same body components on the same production lines — as Alfred Sloan described it, "a reduction of bodies to three basic standards types."

4. The Lordstown policy on garage bills provides a striking indication of how GM watches out for its wider socioeconomic interests even while maintaining plant "authority." An officer in the local union described the procedure to me: "Everyone needs a car to get to work [the plant is completely remote from public transport, or from much housing] — but if your car breaks down you get a reprimand. If a guy is late because he had to get his car fixed, it is incumbent on him to show a receipt for repairs. Now, this might cost twenty-five dollars, and this man perhaps he's a mechanic and he could have fixed it himself for a dollar fifty."

5. "But it's not true," one worker said, "it's the workers that make it go."

25. WOMEN WORKING

Studs Terkel

GRACE CLEMENTS

She is a sparrow of a woman in her mid-forties. She has eighteen grand-children. "I got my family the easy way. I married my family." She has worked in factories for the past twenty-five years: "A punch press operator, oven unloader, sander, did riveting, stapling, light assembly. . . ." She has been with one company for twenty-one years, ARMCO Corporation.

During the last four years, she has worked in the luggage division of one of the corporation's subsidiaries. In the same factory are made snow-mobile parts, windshield defrosters, tilt caps, sewer tiles, and black paper speakers for radios and TV sets.

"We're about twelve women that work in our area, one for each tank. We're about one-third Puerto Rican and Mexican, maybe a quarter black, and the rest of us are white. We have women of all ages, from eighteen to sixty-six, married, single, with families, without families.

"We have to punch in before seven. We're at our tank approximately one to two minutes before seven to take over from the girl who's leaving. The tanks run twenty-four hours a day."

The tank I work at is six-foot deep, eight-foot square. In it is pulp, made of ground wood, ground glass, fiberglass, a mixture of chemicals and

water. It comes up through a copper screen felter as a form, shaped like
the luggage you buy in the store.

In forty seconds you have to take the wet felt out of the felter, put
the banket on — a rubber sheeting — to draw out the excess moisture,
wait two, three seconds, take the blanket off, pick the wet felt up, balance it on your shoulder — there is no way of holding it without it tearing all to pieces, it is wet and will collapse — reach over, get the hose,
spray the inside of this copper screen to keep it from plugging, turn
around, walk to the hot dry die behind you, take the hot piece off with
your opposite hand, set it on the floor — this wet thing is still balanced
on my shoulder — put the wet piece on the dry die, push this button that
lets the dry press down, inspect the piece we just took off, the hot piece,
stack it, and count it — when you get a stack of ten, you push it over and
start another stack of ten — then go back and put our blanket on the wet
piece coming up from the tank . . . and start all over. Forty seconds.
We also have to weigh every third piece in that time. It has to be within
so many grams. We are constantly standing and moving. If you talk
during working, you get a reprimand, because it is easy to make a reject
if you're talking.

A thirty-inch luggage weighs up to fifteen pounds wet. The hot piece
weighs between three to four pounds. The big luggage you'll maybe
process only four hundred. On the small luggage, you'll run maybe 800,
sometimes 850 a day. All day long is the same thing over and over. That's
about ten steps every forty seconds about 800 times a day.

We work eight straight hours, with two ten-minute breaks and one
twenty-minute break for lunch. If you want to use the washroom, you
have to do that in that time. By the time you leave your tank, you go
to the washroom, freshen up a bit, go into the recreation room, it makes
it very difficult to finish a small lunch and be back in the tank in twenty
minutes. So you don't really have too much time for conversation. Many
of our women take a half a sandwich or some of them don't even take
anything. I'm a big eater. I carry a lunch box, fruit, a half a sandwich, a
little cup of cottage cheese or salad. I find it very difficult to complete
my lunch in the length of time.

You cannot at any time leave the tank. The pieces in the die will burn
while you're gone. If you're real, real, real sick and in urgent need, you
do shut it off. You turn on the trouble light and wait for the tool man to
come and take your place. But they'll take you to a nurse and check it
out.

The job I'm doing is easier than the punch presses I used to run. It's
still not as fast as the punch press, where you're putting out anywhere
to five hundred pieces an hour. Whereas here you can have a couple of
seconds to rest in. I mean *seconds*. (Laughs.) You have about two seconds to wait while the blanket is on the felt drawing the moisture out.
You can stand and relax those two seconds — three seconds at most. You

wish you didn't have to work in a factory. When it's all you know what to do, that's what you do.

I guess my scars are pretty well healed by now, because I've been off on medical leave for two, three months. Ordinarily I usually have two, three burn spots. It's real hot, and if it touches you for a second, it'll burn your arm. Most of the girls carry scars all the time.

We've had two or three serious accidents in the last year and a half. One happened about two weeks ago to a woman on the hydraulic lift. The cast-iron extension deteriorated with age and cracked and the die dropped. It broke her whole hand. She lost two fingers and had plastic surgery to cover the burn. The dry die runs anywhere from 385 degrees to 425.

We have wooden platforms where we can walk on. Some of the tanks have no-skid strips to keep you from slipping, 'cause the floor gets wet. The hose we wash the felter with will sometimes have leaks and will spray back on you. Sometimes the tanks will overflow. You can slip and fall. And slipping on oil. The hydraulic presses leak every once in a while. We've had a number of accidents. I currently have a workman's comp suit going. I came up under an electric switch box with my elbow and injured the bone and muscle where it fastens together. I couldn't use it.

I have arthritis in the joints of some of my fingers. Your hands handling hot pieces perspire and you end up with rheumatism or arthritis in your fingers. Naturally in your shoulder, balancing that wet piece. You've got the heat, you've got the moisture because there's steam coming out. You have the possibility of being burnt with steam when the hot die hits that wet felt. You're just engulfed in a cloud of steam every forty seconds.

It's very noisy. If the tool man comes to talk to you, the noise is great enough you have to almost shout to make yourself heard. There's the hissing of the steam, there's the compressed air, a lot of pressure — it's gotta lift that fifteen pounds and break it loose from that copper screen. I've lost a certain percentage of my hearing already. I can't hear the phone in the yard. The family can.

In the summertime, the temperature ranges anywhere from 100 to 150 degrees at our work station. I've taken thermometers and checked it out. You've got three open presses behind you. There's nothing between you and that heat but an asbestos sheet. They've recently put in air conditioning in the recreation room. There's been quite a little discussion between the union and the company on this. They carry the air conditioning too low for the people on the presses. Our temperature will be up to 140, and to go into an air-conditioned recreation room that might be set at 72 — 'cause the office force is happy and content with it — people on the presses almost faint when they go back. We really suffer.

I'm chairman of the grievance committee.[1] We have quite a few grievances. Sometimes we don't have the support we should have from our people. Sometimes the company is obstinate. For the most part, many of our grievances are won.

Where most people get off at three, I get off at two o'clock. I have an hour to investigate grievances, to work on them, to write them up, to just in general check working conditions. I'm also the editor of the union paper. I do all my own work. I cut stencils, I write the articles, copy the pictures. I'm not a very good freehand artist (laughs), so I copy them. I usually do that in the union office before I go home and make supper. It takes about five hours to do a paper. Two nights.

(Laughs.) I daydream while I'm working. Your mind gets so it automatically picks out the flaws. I plan my paper and what I'm going to have for supper and what we're gonna do for the weekend. My husband and I have a sixteen-foot boat. We spend a lot of weekends and evenings on the river. And I try to figure out how I'm gonna feed twenty, twenty-five people for dinner on Saturday. And how to solve a grievance. . . .

They can't keep the men on the tanks. We've never been able to keep a man over a week. They say it's too monotonous. I think women adjust to monotony better than men do. Because their minds are used to doing two things at once, where a man usually can do one thing at a time. A woman is used to listening to a child tell her something while she's doing something else. She might be making a cake while the child is asking her a question. She can answer that child and continue to put that cake together. It's the same way on the tanks. You get to be automatic in what you're doing and your mind is doing something else.

I was one of the organizers here (laughs) when the union came in. I was as anti-union in the beginning as I am union now. Coming from a small farming community in Wisconsin, I didn't know what a union was all about. I didn't understand the labor movement at all. In school you're shown the bad side of it.

Before the union came in, all I did was do my eight hours, collect my paycheck, and go home, did my housework, took care of my daughter, and went back to work. I had no outside interests. You just lived to live. Since I became active in the union, I've become active in politics, in the community, in legislative problems. I've been to Washington on one or two trips. I've been to Springfield. That has given me more of an incentive for life.

I see the others. I'm sad. They just come to work, do their work, go home, take care of their home, and come back to work. Their conversation is strictly about their family and meals. They live each day for itself and that's about it.

"I tried to get my children to finish vocational school. One of the girls works for a vending machine company, serving hot lunches. She makes good. One of the daughters does waitress work. One of the girls has gone

into factory work. One of the boys is in a factory. He would like to work up to maintenance. One girl married and doesn't do any work at all. My husband is a custodian in a factory. He likes his work as a janitor. There's no pushing him.

"This summer I've been quite ill and they've been fussin' about me. *(Laughs.)* Monday and Tuesday my two daughters and I made over sixty quarts of peaches, made six batches of jam. On Wednesday we made five batches of wild grape jelly. We like to try new recipes. I like to see something different on the table every night. I enjoy baking my own bread and coffee cake. I bake everything I carry in our lunch."

My whole attitude on the job has changed since the union came in. Now I would like to be a union counselor or work for the OEO. I work with humans as grievance committee chairman. They come to you angry, they come to you hurt, they come to you puzzled. You have to make life easier for them.

I attended a conference of the Governor's Commission on the Status of Women. Another lady went with me. We were both union officers. Most of the women there were either teachers or nurses or in a professional field. When they found out we were from labor, their attitude was cold. You felt like a little piece of scum. They acted like they were very much better than we were, just because we worked in a factory. I felt that, without us, they'd be in a heck of a shape. (Laughs.) They wouldn't have anything without us. How could we employ teachers if it wasn't for the factory workers to manufacture the books? And briefcases, that's luggage. (Laughs.)

I can understand how the black and the Spanish-speaking people feel. Even as a farmer's daughter, because we were just hard-working poor farmers, you were looked down upon by many people. Then to go into factory work, it's the same thing. You're looked down upon. You can even feel it in a store, if you're in work clothes. The difference between being in work clothes going into a nice department store and going in your dress clothes. It is two entirely different feelings. People won't treat you the same at all.

I hope I don't work many more years. I'm tired. I'd like to stay home and keep house. We're in hopes my husband would get himself a small hamburger place and a place near the lake where I can have a little garden and raise my flowers that I love to raise. . . .

DOLORES DANTE

She has been a waitress in the same restaurant for twenty-three years. Many of its patrons are credit card carriers on an expense account — conventioneers, politicians, labor leaders, agency people. Her hours are from 5:00 p.m. to 2:00 a.m. six days a week. She arrives earlier "to get things ready, the silverware, the butter. When people come in and ask for you, you would like to be in a position to handle them all, because that means more money for you.

"I became a waitress because I needed money fast and you don't get it in an office. My husband and I broke up and he left me with debts and three children. My baby was six months. The fast buck, your tips. The first ten-dollar bill that I got as a tip, a Viking guy gave to me. He was a very robust, terrific atheist. Made very good conversation for us, cause I am too.

"Everyone says all waitresses have broken homes. What they don't realize is when people have broken homes they need to make money fast, and do this work. They don't have broken homes because they're waitresses."

I have to be a waitress. How else can I learn about people? How else does the world come to me? I can't go to everyone. So they have to come to me. Everyone wants to eat, everyone has hunger. And I serve them. If they've had a bad day, I nurse them, cajole them. Maybe with coffee I give them a little philosophy. They have cocktails. I give them political science.

I'll say things that bug me. If they manufacture soap, I say what I think about pollution. If it's automobiles, I say what I think about them. If I pour water I'll say, "Would you like your quota of mercury today?" If I serve cream, I say, "Here is your substitute. I think you're drinking plastic." I just can't keep quiet. I have an opinion on every single subject there is. In the beginning it was theology, and my bosses didn't like it. Now I am a political and my bosses don't like it. I speak *sotto voce*. But if I get heated, then I don't give a damn. I speak like an Italian speaks. I can't be servile. I give service. There is a difference.

I'm called by my first name. I like my name. I hate to be called Miss. Even when I serve a lady, a strange woman, I will not say madam. I hate ma'am. I always say milady. In the American language there is no word to address a woman, to indicate whether she's married or unmarried. So I say milady. And sometimes I playfully say to the man milord.

It would be very tiring if I had to say, "Would you like a cocktail?" and say that over and over. So I come out different for my own enjoyment. I would say, "What's exciting at the bar that I can offer?" I can't say, "Do you want coffee?" Maybe I'll say, "Are you in the mood for coffee?" Or, "The coffee sounds exciting." Just rephrase it enough to make it interesting for me. That would make them take an interest. It becomes theatrical and I feel like Mata Hari and it intoxicates me.

People imagine a waitress couldn't possibly think or have any kind of aspiration other than to serve food. When somebody says to me, "You're great, how come you're *just* a waitress?" *Just* a waitress. I'd say, "Why, don't you think you deserve to be served by me?" It's implying that he's not worthy, not that I'm not worthy. It makes me irate. I don't feel lowly at all. I myself feel sure. I don't want to change the job. I love it.

Tips? I feel like Carmen. It's like a gypsy holding out a tambourine and they throw the coin. (Laughs.) If you like people, you're not thinking of the tips. I never count my money at night. I always wait till morning. If I thought about my tips I'd be uptight. I never look at a tip. You pick it up fast. I would do my bookkeeping in the morning. It would be very dull for me to know I was making so much and no more. I do like challenge. And it isn't demeaning, not for me.

There might be occasions when the customers might intend to make it demeaning — the man about town, the conventioneer. When the time comes to pay the check, he would do little things, "How much should I give you?" He might make an issue about it. I did say to one, "Don't play God with me. Do what you want." Then it really didn't matter whether I got a tip or not. I would spit it out, my resentment — that he dares make me feel I'm operating only for a tip.

He'd ask for his check. Maybe he's going to sign it. He'd take a very long time and he'd make me stand there. "Let's see now, what do you think I ought to give you?" He would not let go of that moment. And you knew it. You know he meant to demean you. He's holding the change in his hand, or if he'd sign, he'd flourish the pen and wait. These are the times I really get angry. I'm not reticent. Something would come out. Then I really didn't care. "Goddamn, keep your money!"

There are conventioneers, who leave their lovely wives or their bad wives. They approach you and say, "Are there any hot spots?" "Where can I find girls?" It is, of course, first directed at you. I don't mean that as a compliment, 'cause all they're looking for is females. They're not looking for companionship or conversation. I am quite adept at understanding this. I think I'm interesting enough that someone may just want to talk to me. But I would philosophize that way. After all, what is left after you talk? The hours have gone by and I could be home resting or reading or studying guitar, which I do on occasion. I would say, "What are you going to offer me? Drinks?" And I'd point to the bar, "I have it all here." He'd look blank and then I'd say, "A man? If I need a man, wouldn't you think I'd have one of my own? Must I wait for you?"

Life doesn't frighten me any more. There are only two things that relegate us — the bathroom and the grave. Either I'm gonna have to go to the bathroom now or I'm gonna die now. I go to the bathroom.

And I don't have a high opinion of bosses. The more popular you are, the more the boss holds it over your head. You're bringing them business, but he knows you're getting good tips and you won't leave. You have to worry not to overplay it, because the boss becomes resentful and he uses this as a club over your head.

If you become too good a waitress, there's jealousy. They don't come in and say, "Where's the boss?" They'll ask for Dolores. It doesn't make a hit. That makes it rough. Sometimes you say, Aw hell, why am I trying so hard? I did get an ulcer. Maybe the things I kept to myself were twisting me.

It's not the customers, never the customers. It's injustice. My dad came from Italy and I think of his broken English — *injoost*. He hated injustice. If you hate injustice for the world, you hate more than anything injustice toward you. Loyalty is never appreciated, particularly if you're the type who doesn't like small talk and are not the type who makes reports on your fellow worker. The boss wants to find out what is going on surreptitiously. In our society today you have informers everywhere. They've informed on cooks, on coworkers. "Oh, someone wasted this." They would say I'm talking to all the customers. "I saw her carry such-and-such out. See if she wrote that on her check." "The salad looked like it was a double salad." I don't give anything away. I just give myself. Informers will manufacture things in order to make their job worthwhile. They're not sure of themselves as workers. There's always someone who wants your station, who would be pretender to the crown. In life there is always someone who wants somebody's job.

I'd get intoxicated with giving service. People would ask for me and I didn't have enough tables. Some of the girls are standing and don't have customers. There is resentment. I feel self-conscious. I feel a sense of guilt. It cramps my style. I would like to say to the customer, "Go to so-and-so." But you can't do that, because you feel a sense of loyalty. So you would rush, get to your customers quickly. Some don't care to drink and still they wait for you. That's a compliment.

There is plenty of tension. If the cook isn't good, you fight to see that the customers get what you know they like. You have to use diplomacy with cooks, who are always dangerous. (Laughs.) They're madmen. (Laughs.) You have to be their friend. They better like you. And your bartender better like you too, because he may do something to the drink. If your bartender doesn't like you, your cook doesn't like you, your boss doesn't like you, the other girls don't like you, you're in trouble.

And there will be customers who are hypochondriacs, who feel they can't eat, and I coax them. Then I hope I can get it just the right way from the cook. I may mix the salad myself, just the way they want it.

Maybe there's a party of ten. Big shots, and they'd say, "Dolores, I have special clients, do your best tonight." You just hope you have the right cook behind the broiler. You really want to pleasure your guests. He's selling something, he wants things right, too. You're giving your all.

How does the steak look? If you cut his steak, you look at it surreptitiously. How's it going?

Carrying dishes is a problem. We do have accidents. I spilled a tray
once with steaks for seven on it. It was a big, gigantic T-bone, all sliced.
But when that tray fell, I went with it, and never made a sound, dish
and all (softly) never made a sound. It took about an hour and a half to
cook that steak. How would I explain this thing? That steak was sal-
vaged. (Laughs.)

Some don't care. When the plate is down you can hear the sound. I try
not to have that sound. I want my hands to be right when I serve. I pick
up a glass, I want it to be just right. I get to be almost Oriental in the
serving. I like it to look nice all the way. To be a waitress, it's an art. I
feel like a ballerina, too. I have to go between those tables, between
those chairs. . . . Maybe that's the reason I always stayed slim. It is a
certain way I can go through a chair no one else can do. I do it with an
air. If I drop a fork, there is a certain way I pick it up. I know they can
see how delicately I do it. I'm on stage.

I tell everyone I'm a waitress and I'm proud. If a nurse gives service, I
say, "You're a professional." Whatever you do, be professional. I always
compliment people.

I like to have my station looking nice. I like to see there's enough ash
trays when they're having their coffee and cigarettes. I don't like ash
trays so loaded that people are not enjoying the moment. It offends me.
I don't do it because I think that's gonna make a better tip. It offends
me as a person.

People say, "No one does good work any more." I don't believe it. You
know who's saying that? The man at the top, who says the people
beneath him are not doing a good job. He's the one who always said,
"You're nothing." The housewife who has all the money, she believed
housework was demeaning, 'cause she hired someone else to do it. If it
weren't so demeaning, why didn't *she* do it? So anyone who did her
housework was a person to be demeaned. The maid who did all the
housework said, "Well hell, if this is the way you feel about it, I won't
do your housework. You tell me I'm no good, I'm nobody. Well, maybe
I'll go out and be somebody." They're only mad because they can't find
someone to do it now. The fault is not in the people who did the — quote
— lowly work.

Just a waitress. At the end of the night I feel drained. I think a lot of
waitresses become alcoholics because of that. In most cases, a waiter or
a waitress doesn't eat. They handle food, they don't have time. You'll
pick at something in the kitchen, maybe a piece of bread. You'll have a
cracker, a little bit of soup. You go back and take a teaspoonful of something. Then maybe sit down afterwards and have a drink, maybe three,
four, five. And bartenders, too, most of them are alcoholics. They'd go

out in a group. There are after-hour places. You've got to go release your tension. So they go out before they go to bed. Some of them stay out all night.

It's tiring, it's nerve-racking. We don't ever sit down. We're on stage and the bosses are watching. If you get the wrong shoes and you get the wrong stitch in that shoe, that does bother you. Your feet hurt, your body aches. If you come out in anger at things that were done to you, it would only make you feel cheapened. Really I've been keeping it to myself. But of late, I'm beginning to spew it out. It's almost as though I sensed my body and soul had had quite enough.

It builds and builds and builds in your guts. Near crying. I can think about it. . . . (She cries softly.) 'Cause you're tired. When the night is done, you're tired. You've had so much, there's so much going. . . . You had to get it done. The dread that something wouldn't be right, because you want to please. You hope everyone is satisfied. The night's done, you've done your act. The curtains close.

The next morning is pleasant again. I take out my budget book, write down how much I made, what my bills are. I'm managing. I won't give up this job as long as I'm able to do it. I feel out of contact if I just sit at home. At work they all consider me a kook. (Laughs.) That's okay. No matter where I'd be, I would make a rough road for me. It's just me, and I can't keep still. It hurts, and what hurts has to come out.

POSTSCRIPT: *"After sixteen years — that was seven years ago — I took a trip to Hawaii and the Caribbean for two weeks. Went with a lover. The kids saw it — they're all married now. (Laughs.) One of my daughters said, "Act your age." I said, "Honey, if I were acting my age, I wouldn't be walking. My bones would ache. You don't want to hear about my arthritis. Aren't you glad I'm happy?"*

NANCY ROGERS

At twenty-eight, she has been a bank teller for six years. She earns five-hundred dollars a month.

What I do is say hello to people when they come up to my window. "Can I help?" And transact their business, which amounts to taking money from them and putting it in their account. Or giving them money out of their account. You make sure it's the right amount, put the deposits on through the machine so it shows on the books, so they know. You don't really do much. It's just a service job.

We have a time clock. It's really terrible. You have a card that you put in the machine and it punches the time that you've arrived. If you get there after eight-forty-five, they yell and they scream a lot and say, "Late!" Which I don't quite understand, because I've never felt you should be tied to something like a clock. It's not that important. If you're there to start doing business with the people when the bank opens, fine.

I go to my vault, open that, take out my cash, set up my cage, get my stamps set out, and ink my stamp pad. From there on until nine o'clock when the bank opens, I sit around and talk to the other girls.

My supervisor yells at me. He's about fifty, in a position that he doesn't really enjoy. He's been there for a long time and hasn't really advanced that much. He's supposed to have authority over a lot of things but he hasn't really kept informed of changes. The girls who work under him don't really have the proper respect that you think a person in his position would get. In some ways, it's nice. It's easier to talk to him. You can ask him a question without getting, "I'm too busy." Yet you ask a question a lot of times and you don't get the answer you need. Like he doesn't listen.

We work right now with the IBM. It's connected with the main computer bank which has all the information about all the savings accounts. To get any information, we just punch the proper buttons. There are two tellers to a cage and the machine is in between our windows. I don't like the way the bank is set up. It separates people. People are already separated enough. There are apartment houses where you don't know anybody else in the building. They object to your going into somebody else's cage, which is understandable. If the person doesn't balance, they'll say, "She was in my cage." Cages? I've wondered about that. It's not quite like being in prison, but I still feel very locked in.

The person who shares my cage, she's young, black, and very nice. I like her very much. I have fun with her. She's originally from the South. She's a very relaxed type of person. I can be open and not worry I might offend her. I keep telling her she's a bigot. (Laughs.) And she keeps saying, "There are only three kinds of people I dislike — the Italians, the Polacks, and the Jews." (Laughs.) I'll walk up to her and put my hands on her shoulder and she'll say, "Get your hands off me, white girl, don't you know you're not supposed to touch?" It's nice and relaxed kind of — we sit around and gossip about our boyfriends, which is fun.

A lot of people who work there I don't know. Never talk to, have no idea who they are. You're never introduced. I don't even know who the president of the bank is. I don't know what he looks like. It's really funny, because you have to go have okays on certain things. Like we're only allowed to cash up to a certain amount without having an officer okay it. They'd say, "Go see Mr. Frank." And I'd say, "Who's that? Which one? Point him out." The girl who's the supervisor for checking kept saying, "You don't know who he is? You don't know who he is? He's the one over there. Remember him? You waited on him." "Yeah, but I didn't know what his name was. Nobody ever told me."

I enjoy talking to people. Once you start getting regular customers, you take your time to talk — which makes the job more enjoyable. It also makes me wonder about people. Some people are out working like every penny counts. Other people, it's a status thing with them. They really like to talk about it. I had a man the other day who was buying stock. "Oh well, I'm buying fifty-thousand dollars worth of AT&T, and I'm also investing in . . ." He wouldn't stop talking. He was trying to impress me: I have money, therefore I'm somebody.

Money doesn't mean that much to me. To me, it's not money, it's just little pieces of paper. It's not money to me unless I'm the one who's taking the money out or cashing the check. That's money because it's mine. Otherwise it doesn't really mean anything. Somebody asked me "Doesn't it bother you, handling all that money all day long?" I said, "It's not money. I'm a magician. I'll show you how it works." So I counted out the paper. I said, "Over there, at this window, it's nothing. Over there, at that window, it's money." If you were gonna think about it every minute: "Oh lookit, here's five-thousand dollars, wow! Where could I go on five-thousand dollars? Off to Bermuda — " You'd get hung-up and so dissatisfied of having to deal with money that's not yours, you couldn't work.

People are always coming in and joking about — "Why don't you and I get together? I'll come and take the money and you ring the alarm after I've left and say, 'Oh, I was frightened, I couldn't do anything.'" I say, "It's not enough." The amount in my cash drawer isn't enough. If you're going to steal, steal at least into the hundreds of thousands. To steal five or ten thousand isn't worth it.

It's joked about all the time. Sometimes it's kidded about if you do have a difference. Maybe I was paying out a hundred dollars and two bills stuck together and I gave him $110 instead. A lot of times people have come back and said, "I think you gave me ten dollars too much." Like they didn't want me to get in trouble. "She won't balance today and here I am sitting with ten dollars she doesn't have." It's really nice to know people are honest. Quite a few are. Anyway, we're bonded, we're insured for that. The bank usually has a slush fund for making up differences one way or the other.

I've never been held up. We have a foot alarm, one that you just trip with your toe. At the other place, we had a button you push, which was immediately under the counter. Some people, you get a funny feeling about. Like I don't think that's his passbook, it's probably stolen. Most of the time you're never right. (Laughs.)

One of the girls who works here was held up. She just gave the man

the money he wanted. (Laughs.) Which is all you can do. She went up to
our head teller to get more money. She said, "Mr. Murphy, I was just
held up." He said, "Oh sure, uh huh, ha, ha, ha." She said, "No really I
was." (Laughs.) He said, "Ooohhh, you really were, weren't you?"
(Laughs.) Like wow! I don't think they ever caught the person. She didn't
give him all that money. She just gave him what she had in one part of
the drawer and didn't bother to open the other drawers, where most of
that cash was stored.

I really don't know what I'd do. I don't think I'd panic too badly. I'd
be very nervous and upset, but I'd probably do exactly what the man
wanted. If possible, trip the alarm, but that's not going to do much good.
I'd give him the money, especially if he had a gun in his hand or even
giving the slight implication. . . . Money's not worth that much. The
bank's insured by the government for things like that, so there's no real
. . . It'd be exciting, I guess.

A lot of younger girls who are coming in now, they get pushed too
fast. If you've never done it before, it takes time just to realize – you
have to stop and think, especially if it's busy. Here I am doing three
different things. I am taking money out of these people's accounts and
putting part of it into checking and he wants part of it back, plus he
wants to cash a check, and he asks for a couple of money orders. You
got all these things that you have to remember about – that have to be
added and subtracted so everything comes out right.

You force yourself into speeding up because you don't want to make
people wait. 'Cause you're there for one reason, you're there to serve
them. Lots of times there's somebody you know back there and you
want to get rid of these people so you can talk to him. (Laughs.)

In a lot of cases, as far as males, you're gonna be asked out. Whether
you accept or not is something else. I met quite a few people in the bank
who I've gone out with. Sometimes relationships work out very nicely
and you become good friends with these people and it may last for years.
My social life is affected by my job, oh sure. A customer coming in and
saying, "I'm giving a party next week, would you like to come?"

Some places kind of frown on it. But most of them have no control.
One fella I met at the bank, he was from an auditing firm, who I went
out with for a short while. He said, "Don't tell anybody. We're not supposed to go with anybody from the bank we work for." That's weird,
for a job to carry over into your private life.

Banks are very much giving into desexualizing the women who work
there, by putting uniforms on them. Trying to make everybody look the
same. In one way it's nice, it saves on clothes. In another way, it's
boring. Putting on the same thing almost every day is – ech!! Some I've
seen aren't too bad, but in some places they're very tailored and in drab
colors. Uptight is the only word I can think of to describe them. The

place I worked before, it was a navy-blue suit and it was — blach!! (Laughs.)

Most bank tellers are women because of the pay scale. It's assumed that women are paid a little bit lower than men. (Laughs.) There are only two men that work in the area, aside from my supervisor. The head teller, who's been there for years and years and years, and a young fella in charge of all the silver. For most men it's a job that doesn't offer that much kind of advancement. You'd have to be the type that would really just enjoy sittin' back and doing the same thing over and over again. A transaction is a transaction is a transaction.

Some days, when you're aggravated about something, you carry it after you leave the job. Certain people are bad days. (Laughs.) The type of person who will walk in and says, "My car's double-parked outside. Would you hurry up, lady? I haven't got time to waste around here." And you go — "What??? — " You want to say, "Hey, why did you double-park your car? So now you're gonna blame me if you get a ticket, 'cause you were dumb enough to leave it there?" But you can't. That's the one hassle. You can't say anything back. The customer's always right.

Certain people who are having a bad day themselves feel they must take it out on you: "What are you doing there?" "Why are you checking that?" "Why did you have to do that?" You calmly try and explain to them, "That's what's required." You can't please 'em. They make sure you're in as nasty a mood as they are. (Laughs.)

We have quite a bit of talk during coffee breaks. There's speculation: "Do you think this is what happened?" There was a girl who was let go this week. Nobody was told as to the why or wherefore. Nobody really still knows. They keep coming through the bank saying, "We don't want rumors started about such-and-such." But they don't explain it. She doesn't exist any more totally. She's no longer here.

The last place I worked for, I was let go. I told the people I worked with, "If anybody asks tell them I got fired and give them my phone number." One of my friends stopped by and asked where I was at. They said, "She's no longer with us." That's all. I vanished.

When it happened, it was such an abrupt thing. I hadn't really expected it. I was supposed to be an example so that these things wouldn't occur any more. One of the factors was a man I wasn't getting along with. He worked out at the desk. He was — how can I put it? — he was a very handsy person. He was that way toward everybody. I didn't like it. He'd always pick out a time when you were balancing or you were trying to figure something out. You didn't want to be interrupted. At other times, you wouldn't mind, you'd laugh it off.

The reason I was given for being fired was that I was absent too much and had been tardy too often. But I think there was really another reason. The girl who was supervisor was leaving and I was next in seniority. I just don't think they were going to let me go further.

With her the job was everything, it was her whole life. She would stay there till seven in the evening if something went wrong, and come in on Saturdays if they asked her to. When I was done — I'm sorry, I was done for the day.

And I was very open about being different. It started when one of the girls had brought in a little sticker-thing for Valentine's Day. I thought they were cute. So I had just taken a couple of hearts out of one and put it on my name sign on the window, 'cause I liked it. There was never anything really said except "How come that's there?" And I said, "'Cause I like it." A lot of customers'd come in and say, "Wow! She had hearts on her window, she must be a nice girl." It gave them an opportunity to have something to say instead of just feeling they didn't know you and didn't quite know what to say. I think the bank didn't care for that too much. They want everybody to be pretty much the same, kind of conservative, fitting into the norm. I think that was the real reason I was let go.

I think a lot of places don't want people to be people. I think they want you to almost be the machines they're working with. They just want to dehumanize you. Just like when you walk in in the morning, you put the switch on and here you are: "I am a robot. This is what I do. Good morning. How are you? May I help you?" I hate having to deal with people like that.

In some way, I feel my job's important. Especially when you work with people who are trying to save money. It's gratifying for them when they give you the stuff and you mark in their book and there it is — wow! I've accomplished this. And you say, "I'm glad to see you again. You're really doing well." Most of these people here work in restaurants downtown and are secretaries. Lower middle class and a lot of blacks come in this bank. They're a lot more friendly than some of your other people, who are so busy trying to impress one another.

They don't even recognize you. It's like I'm almost being treated as a machine. They don't have time to bother. After all, you're just a peon. I had a black man come up to my window and say, "It's really nice to see somebody working in a place like this who's even halfway relevant." And I thought — wow! (Laughs.) I had my hair up like in little ponytails on the side and just had a pull-over sweater and a skirt on and wasn't really dressed up. I was very taken aback by it. It's the first compliment I had in a long time. It's nice to be recognized. Most places, it's your full name on the window. Some places just have Miss or Mrs. So-and-so. I prefer giving my whole name so people can call me Nancy. (Laughs.) They feel a little more comfortable. Certain officers you refer to by their first names. Other people you don't. Some people you would feel kind of weird saying, "Hey, Charlie, would you come over here and do this for me?" Other people you'd feel strange calling them by their proper name. All men who sit at the desk in the office you refer to as Mister. Okay, he's a vice president, he must be called Mr. So-an-so. Whereas you're just a teller. Therefore he can call you by your first name. Smaller banks tend to be more friendly and open.

When I tell people at a party I work for a bank, most of them get interested. They say, "What do you do?" I say, "I'm a teller." They say, "Oh, hmm, okay," and walk away. I remember getting into a discussion with one person about the war. We were disagreeing. He was for it. I wasn't getting angry because I thought he has his right to his point of view. But the man couldn't recognize that I had the right to mine. The thing finally was thrown at me: "What do you mean saying that? After all, who are you? I own my own business, you just work in a crummy bank." It doesn't compute. Like, unless you're capable of making it in the business world, you don't have a right to an opinion. (Laughs.)

My job doesn't have prestige. It's a service job. Whether you're a waitress, salesperson, anything like that — working directly for the public — it's not quite looked on as being prestigious. You are there to serve them. They are not there to serve you. Like a housemaid or a servant.

One of the girls said, "People who go through four years of college should have it recognized that they have achieved something." A man said, "Don't you think someone who becomes an auto mechanic and is good at it should also be recognized? He's a specialist, too, like the man who goes to be a doctor." Yet he's not thought of that way. What difference? It's a shame that people aren't looked at as each job being special unto itself. I can't work on a car, yet I see people who can do it beautifully. Like they have a feel for it. Some people can write books, other people can do marvelous things in other ways. . . .

REFERENCE

1. It is a local of the UAW.

26. "YES, SIR, THIS HAS CERTAINLY BEEN CONSIDERED A SAFE MINE"

Rachel Scott

May 2, 1972, is a chilly clear day in the mountains of northern Idaho. It is 6:00 A.M. and good daylight at the Sunshine silver mine in Big Creek Canyon. Robert McCoy, a timber repairman, turns his pickup truck into the mine parking lot and heads for the dryhouse to change clothes. It will be an hour before the day shift crew starts down, but he likes to get to the mine early. If a man doesn't like to rush, and McCoy doesn't, it can take half an hour to pull on his T-shirt, overalls, wool socks and steel-toed rubber boots, his helmet and belt and light and battery pack, and maybe a denim jacket to wear in the breezy shaft air going down.

After McCoy finishes changing, he walks up to the portal and pours himself a cup of coffee from his lunch bucket — his "emblem of ignorance," he calls it. Gaunt-faced and slender at fifty-six, he's been mining for thirty years, almost fifteen of them at Sunshine. He looks across the canyon to the ridge above the Crescent mine. In the early morning in spring you can see elk there, just below the snow line, some days as many as ten or twelve head. Yesterday he spotted three, today there are none.

By seven o'clock 173 men are assembled at the Jewell shaft, ready to go down. The "cage" or elevator can carry forty-eight men at a time, and it takes twenty minutes to lower the whole crew to the 3700-foot level, where they board a train that carries them back through a mile-long "drift" or tunnel to the No. 10 shaft. Morning starts out easy. The men are relaxed, no one's hurrying. At No. 10 shaft they have time to talk while the skip tender finishes his coffee. Then they board the skip, or cage, for the final descent — 4200 feet, 5000, 5200, 5600, their helmet lights flashing against the blurred rock sides of the shaft as they hurtle through the black, thirty feet per second. There are two hoists in No. 10 shaft, the "chippy hoist" on the 3700-foot level which hauls the men, and the double-drum hoist on 3100, a thousand-horsepower monster machine, newly installed, tricky to operate. It is used to haul muck — ore and rock — though it is also equipped with a twelve-man cage.

Operating the double-drum is Ira Sliger's job, although some days, like today, he has a partner to assist him. Sliger is sixty years old, looks, as he likes to say, "big enough to eat oats and pull a plow," but forty-four years of metal mining have left their mark. One lung is gone, and the other has been weakened by emphysema — "dust on the lungs," he calls it. All morning Sliger and his partner, Bob Scanlan, sit in the control booth in the cavernous underground hoistroom, hauling muck buckets up and down the shaft according to bell signals from the cager, who supervises the muck loading a half-mile below. Until noon it is an ordinary day. At one o'clock more than half of the crew will be dead.

Shortly after twelve Sliger gets a phone call from a shaft crew on the 4400 level. (The crew had smelled smoke in the shaft and signaled for the 3700 chippy hoist. When it didn't come, and no one answered in the hoistroom, they called Sliger to ask what was wrong.) They don't mention the smoke. Sliger figures the signal system must have gone out. It failed once before in the past week, and he isn't surprised that it has apparently happened again. Underground miners keep their sanity by not worrying too much, and Sliger is philosophical. He turns back to his controls, but immediately there is another call, this from his boss, Gene Johnson, on 3700.

"Where's your cager at?" asks Johnson. "Get him up here as soon as you can."

"What's the trouble, Gene?" asks Scanlan, overhearing.

"There's a fire down there."

Those are chilling words in the confined workings of a deep underground mine, where even a small, contained blaze in an oil drum, or from a single piece of machinery, can generate enough carbon monoxide to kill anyone working "inby" or downwind. And most of the mine is inby the 3700-foot level.

Besides being the main travelway from the No. 10 shaft to the Jewell shaft, the 3700 level also houses the underground foremen's office — the "Blue Room" — and the maintenance shops — the pipe, electric, machine, warehouse, and drill shops. About 11:35 A.M., shortly after they finished lunch, two miners stepped out of the electric shop into the drift, smelled smoke, and yelled "Fire!" Thirty feet down the drift in the Blue Room, foremen Harvey Dionne and Gene Johnson grabbed their helmets and battery packs and ran out into the tunnel. What happened on 3700 during the next thirty minutes cannot be told with any certainty. By one account it was Dionne and Johnson who finally made the decision to evacuate. By another account, it was Dionne and foreman Jim Bush. In any event, before any decision was made, the foremen looked for the fire, following the smoke west toward the Jewell shaft 800 feet until they reached the 910 raise, a verticle shaft which rose 300 feet through old, worked-out portions of the mine. There the smoke seemed heaviest, but they couldn't see where it was coming from. Dionne crawled up onto the timber supports, and from there he could see smoke pouring out of the raise. By his account, he and Johnson talked briefly and decided to evacuate the mine, Johnson starting back to No. 10 shaft to give the evacuation orders and Dionne and two other men heading for the Jewell shaft to close the fire door.

When Gene Johnson calls Sliger, cager Byron Schulz is at the 5600 level pulling muck. Sliger signals a long-short and a 3700 station call. It could have been a routine station call, but when Schulz brings the cage up to 3700, the drift is filled with smoke. And it has been for some time. Fifteen minutes earlier the chippy hoistman had to abandon the hoistroom, unable to see his controls for the smoke. With the chippy hoist out and the 3700 level blocked, the situation is critical. On orders from Gene Johnson, Schulz takes a cage full of miners to the 3100 level, where another tunnel leads to the Jewell shaft, and starts back down for more. Schulz and Greg Dionne, a pipe fitter who came up on the cage from 3700, work together bringing the men up. The small twelve-man cage makes the process unbearably slow, as the deadly carbon monoxide gas and smoke spread quickly, down the shaft, through the mine.

Five thousand feet underground, Robert McCoy finished eating dinner and looked at his watch. It was 11:30, time to go back to work. He worked for half an hour, maybe forty-five minutes, repairing timber at the No. 10 shaft station; then he noticed smoke coming down the shaft. It keeps coming, poisoning the air, and a motor crew drives back into the drift, alerting miners along the way. The miners, about twenty of them, gather at the station and someone hands out self-rescuers (compact breathing devices that convert carbon monoxide to carbon dioxide), which are kept in a box near the station. Soon the air is a blue haze. Still the cage hasn't come. The men move back into the drift and tap a compressed-air line, turning it on full blast. It doesn't help much. They've waited thirty minutes now, and the cage is finally there; too late for some of the men, who later collapse in the 3100 hoistroom. They are so weak that Schulz, the slightly built twenty-one-year-old cager, has to push them onto the cage. They squeeze in tightly, but half of the men, including McCoy, are left behind. He still feels all right, he thinks, and when the cage returns he leaves his self-rescuer behind, in case someone coming out of the drift might need it.

On the 3100 he gets off the skip and walks with another miner a few hundred feet down the drift; then, too weak to go on, they sit down on the side of the tunnel, feeling sick, too sick to be frightened. A man train stops and someone lifts them on. McCoy doesn't see or hear anymore. He is unconscious.

Byron Schulz brings the second load up from 5000, and returns to the 3100 hoistroom at 12:44. He stumbles off the cage, and into the hoistroom, which is filled with the bodies of collapsed miners, some still gasping for air, some dead. Only Schulz and another miner, Doug Wiederrick, are still up. "There's nothing we can do here," says Schulz, and they start out of the hoistroom. But the smoke is thick in the drift. Wiederrick turns back and picks up the telephone and asks topside where they can find fresh air. "The Jewell shaft," he is told. "My God! We'll never make it," he cries, and slumps to the floor. Schulz bends over him and pushes a self-rescuer into his mouth, but the miner spits it out, unconscious. Schulz, alone now, struggles out of the hoistroom and begins the long walk to the Jewell shaft. A thousand feet out he meets a rescue crew wearing oxygen packs coming from the surface.

"They're all dead back there, they're all dead back there," Schulz gasps, over and over. He pleads for oxygen and one member of the team, holding his breath, places his own mask over Schulz's face. At the same time, Don Beehner, another crew member, also pulls his mask to help Schulz. He is down instantly, overcome by the deadly carbon monoxide gas. Blood gushes from his mouth and nose. Within seconds he is dead.

In the hoistroom the smoke began to bother Sliger soon after Johnson called. He put on a self-rescuer and gave one to his partner, Bob Scanlan. They closed the doors of the glass cab in which they worked, but still the smoke came in. When Johnson arrived with the cage from 3700, he ordered Sliger to get out. Sliger turned the controls over to Scanlan, and caught the last train out, the same train that had stopped for McCoy. By the time he reached the surface, less than ten minutes later, topside had lost contact with the hoistroom.

Thirty-one men, including Bob Scanlan, Greg Dionne, Gene Johnson, and Doug Wiederrick, died on the hoistroom floor. Eighty men made it out of the mine that day. Byron Schulz was the last. Of the rest trapped below when the hoistman died, only two men survived. On 4800 level Ron Flory and Tom Wilkinson had waited at the shaft station with other miners, but as the smoke kept billowing down the shaft, they ran back into the drift until they found fresh air, brought in by compressed-air lines. They waited there for seven days in the black silent mine until they were found by rescuers. They survived on sandwiches scavenged from their dead buddies' lunch buckets and water from condensation on the air cooler. The rescue teams worked slowly, severely hampered by dense smoke and intense heat as the fire continued to burn. They did not recover the last body until May 13. The final death toll was ninety-one men. It was the worst disaster in the hard-rock mining industry since 1917.

The Sunshine mine is on the eastern slope of a narrow valley cut through the sparsely forested, smelter-scarred Bitterroot Mountains by Big Creek. Owned and operated by the Sunshine Mining Company, the mine is the biggest silver producer in the country (seven million ounces, worth $10.9 million, in 1971), a huge sprawling network of 110 miles of shafts and tunnels. Only a relatively small section of the mine near the No. 10

shaft has been worked in recent years. The mine is like an anthill, with major drifts following the ore deposits east and west from the No. 10 shaft, the drifts horizontally at intervals of 200 feet, one on top of another, and connected vertically by shafts and raises which provide transportation, ventilation, electricity, and compressed air and water. Leading off the main drifts are small dead-end "stopes," the producing areas of the mine. The drifts follow a major fault line which runs east and west through the mountains. Most of the metals mined in the Coeur d'Alene district — silver, lead, zinc, copper, and antimony — are found in rich deposits along this fault. This twenty-by-thirty-mile area in Shoshone County produces half of the silver mined annually in the United States.

The Sunshine miners are either "day's pay" miners, hourly workers who handle support and maintenance jobs — the motormen, hoistmen, cagers, timber repairmen, electricians, pipe fitters; or they are "gyppo" or contract miners, paid according to the number of feet they drive through the rock. Contract mining is hard work and the most dangerous. "I've seen young fellas come in there, twenty-one years old," says a Sunshine miner, "At thirty-five, forty years, they're stoked out, we call it. They get injured more. They have broken arms and broken legs and broken backs." But it pays well. An average gyppo miner can make $50 a day and the better miners can make $80 to $100 a day.

Gyppo miners work a mining cycle which ends with blasting, so that each new shift finds a pile of blasted rock awaiting it in the slopes. At the start of the shift, the miners, working two to a slope, "bar down," or knock down loose rock from the "ground" — the roof and sides of the blasted area. If the ground is still unstable they may brace it with rock bolts or timber. Then they wet down the rock and "muck out," removing the pay dirt with a machine that scoops it to the nearest raise, where it falls into ore cars below to be hauled out. The remainder of the shift is spent drilling deep holes into the "face" of the rock. At the end of the shift the holes are filled with dynamite and blasted.

Practically every man who lives in the Coeur d'Alene valley has mined at one time or another, and many have worked as loggers, too. Traditionally, hard-rock mining has been a "tramp" occupation, the miners moving from mining camp to mining camp, following the high-paying jobs in the rich metal mines of the West. They move too often to have roots, living in tiny shacks, spending their money for pleasures — drinking, gambling, and whoring. The miners in Coeur d'Alene are more stationary now, but they still live in shacks and trailers up and down the valley. The mines — the Lucky Friday, Star, Crescent, Bunker Hill, Galena, and Sunshine — and the towns they support, are scattered along the Coeur d'Alene River and Interstate 90, which follows the riverbed across the northern panhandle of Idaho.

Every year four or five men die in the mines of the "silver valley" from rockfalls, haulage accidents, falls down shafts. Twenty-four men died in the district's mines between 1966 and 1970, five of them in the Sunshine mine. Bureau of Mines statistics are not available for 1971, but two men died that year in a fire at the Star mine, and one died in a rock-fall at the Sunshine mine. But no one expected a tragedy of the size of the 1972 Sunshine disaster. "Everyone in the hard-rock mines thought this could never happen — nothing of this magnitude," says John Parker, manager of the Bunker Hill lead and zinc mine in Kellogg. That is the typical miner's view, too. "The fact is, this fire was totally unexpected," says Ira Sliger. "In my forty-four years of mining I've never seen anything like it. It didn't smell like anything I'd ever smelled, or look like anything I'd ever seen. It was just one terrible fire and a terrible disaster."

"It was an incredible kind of a freak accident," Carl Burke, a company attorney, told reporters in a parking lot press conference at the mine the day after the fire. He said mine officials believed the fire might have started from spontaneous combustion, smoldering in old timber-filled workings near the 3700-foot level of the mine, possibly for days, before suddenly the pressure of expanding gases burst through the airtight bulkheads used to seal off the worked-out drifts. Then poisonous gases flowed swiftly into the mainstream of the ventilation system.

But Sunshine could not be faulted, Burke said. "We have been one of the forerunners [sic] of the mine health and safety act. What happened here yesterday, when the facts are out, will show it to be a very tragic, but a freak accident." Later Burke would admit: "I don't know if I can factually clarify that I would even scratch that line. I don't know if it's a good one." He would explain that before the fire, company officials had prided themselves on their efforts to improve safety conditions in the mine and within the industry, but "in retrospect, it is clear that whatever we had done was not enough — that the mine at that time was not able to respond to that kind of a disaster." And so the facts began to emerge, they suggested not so much a "freak accident" as a flawed and familiar pattern in industry — of choosing, once too often, to favor production needs over safety precautions. "The trouble is, the whole thing is, if they had let me know about this thirty minutes earlier, most of those men would have been alive today," says Ira Sliger. The evacuation order could have been given when the fire was first discovered, sometime close to 11:35 A.M., but mine foremen looked first for the source of the smoke, delaying evacuation until 12:05 P.M. By then 3700 level was impassable and the chippy hoist inoperable.

Hap Fowler, who was working in the warehouse and made it out, assesses the situation in the same way as Sliger. "The reason those guys died," he says, "no foreman wanted to take the responsibility to get those men out of there early enough. It isn't here at the mines — our people. It starts at New York — the big wheels. If they'd pulled those men out, somebody could have got in a lot of trouble — not by Chase [Marvin Chase is a director and vice president of the company and general manager of mining operations]. Chase is a hell of a nice guy. He would have backed them up. But New York, the big shots back in the East. They would have really picked a bitch. All the bosses know that. If they'd pulled those men out that would mean they would probably lost twenty-five or thirty rounds [of blasting]." And that would have cost thousands of dollars.

Fowler knew about "New York" from personal experience, he says. About a year ago he was working for Jim Atha, then safety engineer, and asked him for some self-rescuers — "the good kind." The reason he wanted them, he says, is that "we didn't have enough. I wanted to get some aluminum ones. These old ones rusted out too fast. Two or three levels didn't have any on them." But Atha told him, "I can't get them."

"I said, 'Why not?'

"He said, 'They cost thirty-five dollars apiece.'

"I said, 'Jesus Christ, man, thirty-five dollars ain't much.'

"He said, 'Well, I got this letter — he pulled out this letter. It was from New York, giving him hell for spending so much." Atha says he doesn't recall ever getting any letter from New York.

The big wheels — the directors of the mining company — are part of a group of investors that seized control of the company in a 1965 proxy fight. The group was led by the late Louis Beryl, a New York insurance broker, who a few years before had participated in a take-over of the United States Smelting Refining and Mining Company. Beryl and his group had barely taken their seats on the Sunshine board before they began casting about for more companies to take over. In 1965 alone, the company attempted, unsuccessfully, to merge with Kerr-McGee Corporation, Independent Coal & Coke, and U.S. Industries. In 1968 the company borrowed $20 million and bought Renwell Industries, a failing Pennsylvania-based electronics firm, for $12 million, including the assumption of a $6 million debt. That might not seem like the best investment in the world for a small Western mining company, unless, of course, you were a Renwell director. Two Sunshine directors had been, and Sunshine stockholders charged, in a suit still pending, that Irwin P. Underweiser, chairman of the board and president of Sunshine, and another Sunshine director benefited from the purchase, which involved an exchange of stock. In 1969 the company bid unsuccessfully for the bankrupt Canandaigua Race Track in upstate New York. Meanwhile, several still pending suits filed by stockholders charged the board members with mismanagement, diverting funds for the directors' personal benefit, and increasing their salaries to exorbitant amounts. Stockholders questioned, for example, the wisdom of an investment of "more than $1,230,843" in the stock of Reading Company, of which three Sunshine directors were also board members. Reading stock has since dropped from a high of 9⅞ in 1971 to a high of 3½ in 1972 and has been running deficts of $9 per share. Says one stockholder, "It looks like, for all practical purposes, they're well on their way to bankruptcy."

Directors' meetings, usually held in New York, were "all concerned with how to invest their money," says one company critic with access to inside information. "Most of the directors showed almost no interest in the mine. It seems like a Greek tragedy that this group is associated with this mine."

It was this management, "totally dedicated to growth through internal expansion, mergers and acquisitions," as the company boasts in its 1971 annual report, which was holding its annual stockholders' meeting in Coeur d'Alene on the morning of May 2. It must have been a difficult meeting for Irwin Underweiser. After several years of stockholders' charges that the directors were "ruining the company," Underweiser had to explain why Sunshine showed a $1.2 million loss for 1971, even though the mine itself made a profit. The losses, he explained, were due to a "write-off in securities" and lower silver prices.

But he had a glowing report for the first quarter of 1972: first quarter earnings were a healthy $122,000. "All indications are that we are definitely on the upswing," he said. But then, in the middle of the meeting, came news of the fire. In the first few days after the fire Underweiser looked pale and troubled. On May 8, however, he told an AP reporter that in spite of the lengthy shutdown the fire would certainly cause, "we may even make a profit on the closure." He said insurance would cover costs of a shutdown of up to six months. And since the mine is the largest U.S. silver producer, the closure could cause a shortage in silver, forcing prices up as much as 10 percent.

Fires are all too common in hard-rock mines, in spite of company and industry statements that such things never happen. An underground fire is to be feared, not so much because of the fire itself, but because it consumes oxygen and produces suffocating carbon monoxide gas. In a metal mine such as the Sunshine, the rock itself will not burn, but the millions of feet of timber, brought into the mine every year as support for the walls and roofs of tunnels and shafts, will burn. Until a few years ago, timbers that were no longer needed were thrown into old worked-out drifts, along with anything else the miners didn't want to haul out of the mine. Then the tunnels were sealed and the timbers left to rot. "Once they are bulkheaded off, you assume they're safe," says Marvin Chase, but he adds, "It's a worry always to everyone that someday something will happen."

Company safety engineer Bob Launhardt says the company was as prepared as it could be for a fire. He says he had "studied quite extensively in the areas of fire prevention," and found that "all major fires in hard-rock mines had been either in the intake air shaft or surface buildings. Never before in hard-rock mining had there been a major fire in other than those places." Bureau of Mines records flatly contradict Launhardt. Although shaft fires are more often deadly because the shafts are thickly timbered and flames can spread quickly, fires starting in other areas have caused major disasters. Launhardt says Sunshine had focused its fire plans on prevention of shaft fires, installing concrete doors in the shaft that could be activated by carbon monoxide detectors. "If it had been in the shaft, this fire would not have got back in the mine," he says. With that protection, and "having a second escapeway," he says, "I felt we were one of the best-prepared mines for a fire."

Perhaps so, but clearly not the best prepared for the type of fire that has often hit the Sunshine mine in the past. The Bureau of Mines has recorded at least three major fires at the mine prior to the May 2 disaster, none of them shaft fires. In 1945 a fire, apparently caused by an electrical short circuit, raged for weeks before it was finally extinguished by flooding the mine. In 1967 another fire started when two miners blasted out timbers to remove them from a raise where they were working. They left for lunch after blasting and returned to find the timbers burning. The fire filled the drift with thick smoke and was not subdued for several hours, although the mine was not evacuated.

Another electrical fire in April of 1971 burned along a power cable for eight feet, then spread into nearby timber. William Spear, an Idaho mine inspector, investigated the fire the next day. He discovered that the mine's fire alarm system — a stench gas which is manually released into the ventilation system — had not been used. It was out of order. Spear reported, in the mild manner characteristic of state and federal investigators, that "most of the people that were asked, said the matter was handled very well, but some thought an evacuation of the mine would have been in better judgment." Though he didn't say so, Spear privately thought the company should have ordered an evacuation. So did local United Steelworkers president Lavern Melton, who protested to management. "The company was defensive," says Melton. "They said they told the men to stand by and then went to see how serious the fire was. They said it would be awful silly to take all these men out and lose all that production for nothing."

Bob Launhardt studied theology in college and received his safety instruction from the industry-supported National Safety Council. Miners call him "cooperative" and "conscientious" but say he is "a little bit too much company." Launhardt believes "the basic thing in accident prevention is the ability to motivate people, to motivate management. Eighty-eight percent of all accidents are the result of human oversight and ten percent are the result of physical failure — now it could be oversight on the part of management." An enlightened philosophy, but it's not carried out in practice. Sunshine's prime safety strategy has been to offer prizes to the crew for so many man-hours worked without a lost-time accident. "They're real nice prizes," says one miner — "electric fry pans, nice sleeping bags, electric can openers." Young miners think the prizes are just so much bullshit, but older miners with families like them. The prizes don't discourage accidents, though.

In spite of the prizes, injury and fatality rates at the Sunshine mine have, since 1960, consistently exceeded national averages. Injury rates have been more than twice as high as the national average for metal mines, and rose from 61.74 injuries per million man-hours in 1960 to 126.49 in 1971. The actual number of disabling injuries (or lost-time accidents) rose from 43 a year in 1965 to 133 in 1971. It is hard to know exactly what has caused the rate to go up, but it may help to know that between 1966 and 1971, in the years since contract mining was introduced, the injury rate averaged 100.33 injuries per million man-hours, up from 86.60 for the previous six years. Launhardt blames the mine's poor record on a rapid labor turnover and unstable rock conditions in the Coeur d'Alene district. A more likely reason, say some miners, is that top management just doesn't give a damn about safety. "A safety engineer in the Sunshine mine has got about as much say as a mucker since about 1960," says Hap Fowler. "Since ol' Charley Angle [a former mine superintendent] left in 1960 our safety began to slow up. He really believed in safety and wanted men to eat it, live it, and think it. We were preached safety twenty-four hours a day. You'd get canned quicker for an unsafe mine practice than for missing a round or getting drunk and laying off. The guys talked safety among themselves. And the bosses talked safety. You don't see that anymore. Since he left it's not that way. Get that muck out, or else. Of course a boss likes to get muck. That's how he gets his reputation.

"The safety man today doesn't get any cooperation from the bosses, and he just hates to say anything and go over their heads. Still the safety guy is the fall guy if anything goes wrong. He should have the power to tramp [fire] a foreman or anything else."

At times, it gets to be too much even for the company safety engineer to take. Paul Johnson, who died in the May 2 fire, was safety engineer in 1968, but he quit after one year. His widow says he resigned because "in general he just felt like he wasn't able to go ahead and do the things he'd like to do. He didn't feel like he had the backing."

Launhardt reportedly has felt the same pressures. Lavern Melton says that more than once when he went to the safety man with complaints

Launhardt responded, "Well, you know the problems that anyone in this job has — the limitations that he has." It didn't matter how conscientiously he went about his job. Without management support he was powerless, and as a result, ineffective. The supervisors knew it and the men knew it. And the accident rates showed it. Then came May 2.

After the fire Launhardt admitted to reporters that the company had never held fire drills, or provided safety meetings of any kind for miners. If the men were concerned about the possibility of a fire, they could read the safety manual, which notes briefly: "This mine is equipped with a stench warning system. Inquire of your supervisor as to the course of action you should follow upon a fire alert." Nor were they taught how to use the self-rescuers. Explained Launhardt: "They would have to be retrained every six months or they would forget how to use them."

Astonishing as these revelations were, the big surprise was yet to come. On May 7, the company announced that ninety-three men were missing, not eighty-two, as they had previously told reporters. The original number had been a guess; since the mine kept no surface record of who was underground, the best they could do was count the number of miners' lamps missing from the dryhouse. The only records had been kept by the shift bosses, and most of them were still underground among the missing. The union had protested against this practice a year before, concerned that men might meet with an accident and not be missed, but according to Lavern Melton management replied: "What we've been doing up to now has worked fine."

In the aftermath of the fire, Sunshine Mining Company officials have maintained that the Sunshine mine is no worse than any other mine, and possibly better than most. They are fond of pointing out that Sunshine did not violate any laws in this disaster. The federal Metal and Non-metallic Mine Safety Act of 1966 did not require fire drills, or specific evacuation procedures, or underground oxygen supplies for hoistmen, or even self-rescuers. By providing self-rescuers underground, they point out, Sunshine was far ahead of many other hard-rock miners. All true enough.

But Sunshine neglects to mention its part in shaping the absurdly lenient mine safety laws that continued to allow them to look "good" with the death of ninety-one men. During congressional hearings on the mine safety act in 1965, H. B. Johnson, then manager of the Sunshine mine, and now director of health and safety for the American Mining Congress, wrote to oppose passage of the act as "an unnecessary imposition of federal regulation." "The industry is best prepared to meet the problem in this area through its own efforts," he argued.

The legislation — the first to provide (or at least promise) protection for non-coal miners — was passed and signed into law in 1966 during the Johnson Administration, but it showed the scars of heavy industry opposition, notably from the American Mining Congress. The AMC is a powerful lobbying group, well financed, hard-nosed, and effective. It represents the interests of such industries as Consolidation Coal (subsidiary of Continental Oil), Kennecott Copper, Anaconda, American Smelting and Refining, American Metal Climax, Bethlehem Steel — in short, almost every American mining interest, hard-rock and coal.

The act entrusted enforcement powers to the Interior Department's Bureau of Mines — the next closest thing to allowing the industry to police itself. The Department of the Interior, as "custodian of the Nation's natural resources," attracts special interests like flies to carrion. Its top officers are filled partly from the ranks of the mining industry and partly by political appointees. Dedicated to a philosophy of "cooperation" with industry, its officials believe in enforcing safety regulations as conservatively as possible, if at all. The new safety law fit well into the bureau's philosophy. It lacked monetary penalties, narrowly limiting enforcement provisions to the power to withdraw workers in case of "imminent danger" or for failure to abate a violation. Standards would be developed by an advisory committee appointed by the Secretary of the Interior, then Stewart Udall. The early advisory committees — there were three because Frank Memmot, the Bureau official in charge of the act and a former American Mining Congress member, had a lot of friends — delayed promulgation of standards until 1969. Under the law the standards would not go into effect for yet another year. And most of the regulations were "advisory," rather than "mandatory," and thus lacked even the feeble weight of the law.

The present committee, appointed in 1970 by then Secretary Walter Hickel, is chaired by James Boyd, chairman of the board of the Copper Range Company and an American Mining Congress spokesman. The committee meets about four times a year, but like its predecessor seldom reaches any conclusions. "If [a proposed standard] isn't unanimous, it's tabled for further discussion," explains Dr. Julian Feiss, executive secretary for the committee. Another committee member is Gordon Miner, vice president and director of the Hecla Mining Company. Hecla owns rights to 33 percent of the Sunshine mine's production and is Sunshine's largest shareholder, holding almost 4 percent of the company's widely held stock.

Secretary of the Interior Rogers C. B. Morton led the parade of department officials who flocked to the scene of the disaster. Morton expressed his sympathy to relatives of the trapped miners and commented to reporters that, "Yes, sir, this has certainly been considered a safe mine." Morton, who in 1968 was chief fund raiser for the Republican Party, also conveyed President Nixon's sympathies. (Nixon sent a telegram to the Mayor of Kellogg the same day, promising "the full spectrum of federal assistance," but later refused to declare the area a major disaster zone, which would have allowed the stricken families to receive federal aid.)

Morton's aide, Lewis Helm was quickly dispatched to the mine to handle the Department's press relations. Assigned to the Office of Communications, Helm wields considerable power at Interior as Morton's chief image maker and troubleshooter. In Idaho Helm was largely successful in his mission — to create the most favorable publicity possible for the Bureau of Mines. His efforts inspired such news stories as one headlined NO MINE DANGERS SEEN in the May 4 issue of the Spokane *Daily Chronicle*. The story quoted Helm, reporting, "None of the several inspections in the past two years at the Sunshine Mine has indicated any potential fire hazards, a U.S. Department of the Interior spokesman said here today. . . ." In fact, the company had been cited repeatedly for violating both federal and state fire regulations, as well as explosives, electrical, ground support, and emergency escapeway standards.

Bureau of Mines deputy director Donald Schlick told a Denver *Post* reporter that the company and the Bureau were unprepared for the fire because "there has never been a metal-mine fire before. We've had small fires before in metal mines, but they were very minor and no one was hurt. No one ever expected a fire the size of the one that hit the Sunshine mine because there's nothing to burn in a metal mine." Schlick, a former industrial engineer for Consolidation Coal, ought to know better. Presumably he has access to Bureau statistics. In the past one hundred years since records have been kept, major metal-mine fires have averaged one every four years, and since Schlick entered his chosen field in 1953 there have been sixty-eight reported metal-mine fires.

The man directly responsible for enforcement of the law is Stanley Jarrett, the sixty-nine-year-old assistant director for metal and nonmetal mine safety. Jarrett is considered extremely knowledgeable on mine safety, and assisted in rescue operations at the mine, directing the effort that led to the rescue of Flory and Wilkinson. But an enforcer he's not. Says a Bureau source, "He'd been in the business all his life and he is industry-oriented and doesn't even know it." Before joining the Bureau in 1969, Jarrett was safety engineer for Kennecott Copper. At an Idaho press conference he refused to comment on whether he thought the mine safety act should be strengthened. A few weeks later the Bureau announced stricter enforcement of the act, more inspectors, and tougher standards, but it was an obvious attempt to undermine a congressional move to "clean house" and transfer jurisdiction of hard-rock mines to the Labor Department under the relatively tougher Occupational Health and Safety Act of 1970. Whoever sanctioned the press release didn't seem to be speaking for Jarrett, who told Bureau mine inspectors at a July meeting that if death and injury rates do not improve, "we'll see legislation like you've never seen, and we don't want it."

It is two months since the fire. The Interior Department's public hearing in Kellogg, Idaho, has been adjourned for lunch and Mrs. Casey Pena and Mrs. Howard Harrison, who both lost their husbands in the fire, are eating at Duffy's Cafe. Even now they can think or talk of little else but the fire. The grisly details of the deaths seem to carry a special significance, the facts — real, concrete — to balance against the unknown horror, the immensity, of ninety-one men, husbands and friends, struggling in the black against an inescapable death. The women dwell on these details, recounting them at length. Mrs. Harrison, a soft-featured woman in her early thirties, recalls a conversation with a miner who helped carry the bodies out. "He says, 'You know, Alice, in one way you're lucky you didn't have to see their bodies.' He said it was the most horrifying, terrible thing he ever saw." The men were so unrecognizable, she says, that the crews had to ask the widows for identifying disfigurements. "Howard's got a scar on his neck from an accident in Sunshine" she indicates, with her finger on her own neck, a long gash from her ear to the base of her neck — "and his foot was crushed from a cave-in at Butte. They wanted to amputate it but he wouldn't let them. It was all mangled, you know."

The women are angry that the death benefits are so low. State workmen's compensation provides a $750 burial award and a maximum $26,550 for a widow without dependent children; a maximum $35,400 with three or more children. The ninety-one men left seventy-seven widows and 181 dependent children. Three more have been born since the disaster. There are also social security benefits, a $5,000 company life insurance premium, a company-sponsored $100,000 educational fund, and a $125,000 union fund, which has been divided between widows and miners laid off by the mine shutdown. Mrs. Pena thinks the benefits should be much higher — at least provide whatever amount the worker would have made in his lifetime. She and Mrs. Harrison are two of about fifty widows represented by a group of lawyers who are considering a possible third party suit, probably against manufacturers of the self-rescuers. Sunshine cannot be sued. Idaho law provides that employers may be held liable only for workmen's compensation claims.

Many of the widows were initially reluctant to join in the legal proceedings, Mrs. Pena says, but "now everybody is calling up. They're realizing that they have a complete new life to live. They feel like they should have what's coming to them." There aren't many jobs for women in mining towns. "There's office work, clerking, waitressing, 'tramming' [a mining term for carrying or hauling] beer, and that's just about it," says one man.

The two widows carry with them the coroner's reports, funeral bills, military service records, and an announcement of a memorial service, listing the names of the dead. The coroner's report shows that Howard Harrison, age thirty-four, died of carbon monoxide asphyxiation in twenty to thirty seconds. Mrs. Harrison is skeptical of the findings. "You know what I wonder?" she says. She speaks softly, almost tenderly. "Did he die that way? Did he cry? Was he scared? Did he try to climb the walls, did he try to dig out?"

Has the disaster affected people in the valley? "Do you want to know what it was like before?" asks Mrs. Harrison. "This was the happiest, jolliest town that was ever on the face of the nation." Her eyes sparkle. "Do you know what it's like now? It's like a living graveyard. I don't think all those men were condemned to die underground. There was one man who was supposed to retire the next week after this happened. Floyd Rais."

"No, it was next April," says Mrs. Pena.

"Was it? And William Hanna was his partner. And Louis Goos, he'd been in a car wreck and the next day he went back to work. He said he had a . . . a . . . lucky — something — on his shoulder. We not only lost our husbands, we lost a lot of good friends."

The people in the silver valley are trying to put the disaster behind them now — some even feel resentment that the inquiries and hearings continue. "It just opens up the wounds," one man says. "It was kind of sad for a while," another miner says, "but life goes on, you know." Men will keep on mining and in time it will again be the happiest, jolliest place, but it will never be quite the same. "The only thing that will bother me about going back to work," says Robert McCoy, "is not seeing all the old faces I've known so long. It's like you went to a party and you knew everybody in the room, and then you went into another room and it was filled with strangers. All these men, electricians, mechanics, all of them. I knew them for years."

"It hurts. It hurts," said Mrs. Mike Williams, who works at the union hall. "I don't know if we'll ever get over it."

27. PRO FOOTBALL FUMBLES
THE DRUG SCANDAL

Arnold Mandell

As practice for the next battering season is about to begin, pro football's drug troubles have been wiped off the sports pages. National Football League Commissioner Pete Rozelle took care of that at his annual pre-Super-Bowl press conference in January of 1975. He assured the press that he'd cleaned up the situation by levying tough penalties against the San Diego Chargers.

All the NFL really accomplished was to show that it cared about the drug crisis as much as anybody. It did not solve the problem. By hiring ex-FBI agents to snoop into players' private lives, it forced NFL teams to squelch any medical effort to control drug abuse. It left the actual drug use among the players unchanged, in my opinion, if not worse. What could have been a practical attack on drug abuse, a vocational disease in football as surely as silicosis is in mining, got shoved off the field after a clumsy, ham-handed press conference at the end of the season. The San Diego Chargers ended up as the sacrificial lambs for the sins endemic to the football business.

Rozelle has a big, tough job, and he does what he believes is right. I am sure that he did not intend to force veteran players into the streets to buy speed, or push the Chargers around, or produce any of the other damaging effects of his policy. Many earnest laymen, not to mention hundreds of professionals, have found drug use to be a problem that defies their standard operating procedures.

Charger Cleanup. But why pick on the Chargers? The Charger management had tried to do something concrete and lasting about drug use and abuse. As an M.D., psychiatrist, and research pharmacologist, I worked to develop the program with Coach Harland Svare and owner Eugene Klein. We got results. We helped many players get clean of some drugs, and helped others cut their dosage.

Until now, I have been very reluctant to publish this case study, the only one of its kind, but far too many fine players and their families suffer from illegal chemicals and the myths about them. And, like 60 million other Americans, I am hooked on the game that pushes human psychology to its limits.

Gifted Screw-Ups. The Chargers definitely needed some kind of help when Svare came, in October of 1972 to my office at the University of

California. His team were already losers, he admitted, but the talent was there. In eight days that summer, he had made an all-time record of trades. Many of his new players had come cheap because they were gifted screw-ups. Svare had deliberately taken this high-risk route in the belief that his empathic coaching could mend the misfits and weld them into a championship team. He thought I might help out as the NFL's first psychiatrist-in-residence.

"Ninety percent of this game is in the mind," Svare assured me. "With all the talent in the League, it's the intangibles that create the winning edge. All these bodies can run the 40 in five seconds or so; they all lift weights, so their muscle mass is maximized. The rest is in the mind. And that's your job."

Some job, and I wasn't even a fan. Yet. Although I approached the problem as a psychiatric consultant to the team, the situation more and more invoked my commitment as a physician for individual players. I had not only to work with them on their hang-ups, but to encourage the strong interpersonal relationships, the group identity of a winning team.

Right-Headed Men. It went well, at first. I hung out in the locker room, observed the men in pain and in victory, on the practice field and keyed up for games. Soon I was accepted, no longer a spook. I was able to help several players with personal problems that were carrying over into the game. I got a vivid sense of the world of professional athletes, of what it takes to make it, of what it means to be a gladiator.

Professional football players are not dumb, but they are different. Brain researchers have demonstrated that, for most of us, the dominant hemisphere of the brain is the left, the one in charge of logical, verbal, mathematical thinking. I would call most football players right-brained; they are intuitive and pictorial in their thought processes. They may not be facile with words, although most test out in the top 25 per cent in IQ, but they are accurate with images.

Their words often define complex interpersonal relationships as objects in space, operating over time. Hear them talk: "I can get out but not away." "I go around the thing but can't get myself to enter." "I'm caught inside and have no key." "I'm the kind that goes in but doesn't stay in." This is a perfectly adequate language, but it is alien to word-spouters who don't happen to be poets.

Hooked on Action. Uncomfortable in a left-brained world, football players generally don't find words persuasive. On the other hand, they are activists; they move lessons into life and try them out quickly. So my talking treatments had to be quick and to the point.

I had been used to hours and hours of talk with patients who would come to conclusions, but often succumb later to fearful inertia. The players moved. They would change their care of their children, talk straight with their wives, straighten out differences with teammates and coaches, start a rigorous conditioning program. Sleep and eat better.

There was a negative side, one I learned from Svare when he talked about the early experiences of many athletes. Even as high-school freshmen, they are forever preoccupied with physical activity and tired from workouts. Less-coordinated boys and girls from the nonjock set stereotype them as dummies, usually out of envy or competitiveness. But athletes also are deified, given special favors, then criticized, threatened and made fearful of losing their standing and perquisites. The alumni and the fans control athletes much as heroin dealers control junkies. Get the nervous system dependent on something special, then threaten it with withdrawal.

Such treatment starts early. Athletes learn that they must perform and please others, or they have no place, no worth. Anger and paranoia thrive under such conditions. Many players become hustling, shucking-and-jiving cynics who can take bizarre pride in screwing the system or even get perverse gratification from losing a critical game. Here, Svare and I miscalculated. The respect and positive expectation practiced by Svare, a genuinely warm and sensitive man, failed to earn enough response from men scarred by exploitation. All the warmth in the world cannot substitute for victory, and the Chargers began to lose early on.

A team defines itself to itself in those first games: "We're winners." "We're losers." "We're fumblers." "We're unlucky." "We're tough." To the players, a loss is a personal rebuke from the Lord, telling them they're worthless. We began to fight an accumulating negative self-image.

The ultimate occupational hazard of football is depression and despair. Activist, nonverbal, assertive men like these are prone to depression, and the physical punishment they take makes them totally vulnerable to it. I've never ceased to be aghast at the injuries and the idea of *playing hurt*, which means, understand, not pretending to be hurt, but playing *while* you are hurt.

Pills for Pain. By the second or third game of a season, I found, *everybody* is hurt. I never saw such injuries, even in my intern years in the emergency rooms of innercity hospitals. Huge bruises spread over big slabs of the body. Shoulder injuries can make any movement or contact excruciating. Most people with a cracked rib cannot tie their shoes; these men tape the cracks up tight and keep hitting with throbbing, aching bodies.

Faced with early losses, the pain and the need to win, most players reached for common antidotes adopted by football players years ago. By the fourth regular season game, I had realized that there was no way to discuss or manipulate the psychological aspects of pro football without grappling with the pervasive, systematic use of mood-altering drugs: uppers, grass, booze. From both common knowledge and the public press it was clear that the League knew about it, but, like most official bodies, tried first to deny reality and later to suppress it. Few laymen like to wrestle with the tangled roots of drug use.

An idealistic young coach in the Physical Education Department on my campus surveyed some 200 players on 16 of the NFL teams. I guess he hoped to acquit the sport of the charges, then being flaunted in the papers and several best-selling novels, that drug use is rampant. Instead, in 1971 to 1973, he got enough information to write a graduate thesis on the use of amphetamines in professional football. His figures show that on any given Sunday, it is likely that half the players are using stimulant drugs to play, all in defiance of a League rule, hastily passed in 1973, against drugs. Prior to that, athletes stoked themselves with club-supplied uppers, usually Dexedrine and Benzedrine.

Chemical Courage. The young coach's data tended to jibe with the ideal personality structure that I was developing for each playing position [see *Saturday Review World,* Oct. 5, 1974]. My computer profiles indicated that the best defense-men were rebels, renegades, structure-haters and rule-breakers. Their positions require fast reactions and reckless, hard-nosed aggression, with less need to act precisely and remember assignments. In short, just the ones you'd expect to be popping uppers, and the coach's survey indeed showed far more defensemen using amphetamines.

Why take them? Because this game requires a man to wind himself up to a high pitch of rage and aggression every Sunday afternoon at 1:00, and do it with a pain-wracked body. To labor up past baseline metabolism to the heights of confidence, energy and rage is a long and painful weekly trek. This gets rough for the older players. The ability to mobilize hate burns out in the late 20s or early 30s unless something agitates the centers of rage and aggression in the brain — alcohol withdrawal, or stimulants, or antidepressants.

Stimulants work in two ways to permit playing hard while in pain. They relieve pain directly; their analgesic effect is like the effect of one's own adrenalin. Stimulants also temporarily clear away lethargy and depression. Any pharmacologist knows that depression facilitates the experience of pain. Many patients with chronic back pain are much relieved by antidepressant medication. More than that, the stimulants induce a state of hypomanic excitement — the energetic, dominant, confident psychological state that most of these men have before the game seasons drain out the bounce. With age, the natural adrenalin response and its effectiveness are reduced, and the veterans find it harder to psych themselves up. Many older players use stimulants, and those who feel the need are desperate.

One professional explained the practical facts. "Doc," he rumbled, "I'm not about to go out there one-on-one against a guy who is grunting and drooling and coming at me with big dilated pupils unless I'm in the same condition."

Hyped Up on TV. Amphetamines, when used for mood alteration, are crude. But they work well enough to represent the first surfacing in mainstream America of the crucial issues of the new psychopharmacology. Drug technology and the younger, knowledgeable users are going to change the role of drugs in our society. Mood-changing chemicals will become, as they already are for those who can doctor-shop, a matter of individual choice. The right to supplement the biochemicals in the brain with stuff from the laboratories will not be questioned.

Selective drug use will become a matter of facts, decision and caution rather than morality. Like abortion, birth control, sex education and cohabitation without marriage, such drugs will become socially accepted options. The day may come when you will expect your surgeon to dose his brain and his hands to their best performance as bomber pilots dose themselves to avoid mistakes on long nuclear flights.

But in our present state of knowledge, amphetamines are dangerous to use because they are such primitive drugs, even in pure preparations. It's extremely hard for a player to strike just the right dose, enough to get him alert, energetic and aggressive without pushing himself into the trip of the babbling speed freak.

Some of the Chargers appeared to overdo their dosages and were betrayed by their own hyped-up behavior. The coaches had trouble making contact with some players to get them to change defensive alignments. You'd see them raving to themselves about going to get 'em and getting suckered every time. You can usually see the effects of speed on the sideline, even through the TV camera: a manic player sitting there, talking a blue streak to himself, rolling his eyeballs and rubbing his hands.

David Segal's recent work in our lab indicates that drug-induced arousal, even the smallest amount, restricts the variety of responses that an animal will make in a new situation. Colin Martindale's research on creativity indicates the same kind of loss from over-arousal among human beings. Some quarterbacks have quit amphetamines because they feel that when high they have trouble making last-minute decisions for calling signals or audibles, at the line of scrimmage. On uppers, repetitive acts seem to replace flexible behavior.

Semitough Sex. On the other side of the problem of getting up, there's the problem of getting back down into relaxation and release. That Sunday pitch of rage and tension doesn't let go when the final minute runs off the clock. Win or lose, postgame depression is severe and prolonged. It magnifies and is magnified by the agonies of bruises, pulled muscles, cracked ribs, trick knees, torn foot muscles, internal tissue damage, hip pointers, low back pain, whiplashed necks, the works. It causes impotence, irritability, insomnia, self-torture.

Every player devises his own means of release. Several recent best-sellers have described heroic bouts with booze, grass and broads. I once thought novels like *Semi-Tough* and *Dallas North Forty* were pure fiction, but they capture the mood with reportorial clarity.

The last half of the 1972 season let us know that we had to do something about drugs, but we were still underestimating pro football's problem when we started preseason workouts in 1973. *The N.Y. Times* and *The San Diego Union* were digging into the subject, partly because a player was suing the Chargers for letting him play on drugs in 1969. But nobody reported the psychological forces that explain heavy use in professional ball. For some reason, psychiatrists who know pharmacology have never built a sound research literature on sports.

Training camp at the University of California's Irvine campus was frighteningly smooth and quiet. No rebellions, no fights, no drunks, not even any women in the rooms. Lights went out at 10 without any arguments. Just stereo jazz going quietly. But now and then the assistant coaches reported a funny smell like burning rope. In retrospect, what we thought was the relaxed, cooperative locker room of a winning team was the beginning of a pot-smoothed disengagement, a silent rebellion, a dodge from the demands of the game and the coaches.

There was unquestionably a lot of grass among the younger players, an extension of the cultural and generational gap that showed up everywhere in the late '60s and early '70s. After the first few games of the season, it became clear that the off-duty downers (and there were sleeping pills and tranquilizers in addition to the pot) were messing up play on the field. We had mistiming, feeble hitting, and a surplus of fumbles.

Svare was worried. I remember him watching game films: "Hell, we get a game plan and some secret pothead will fumble the ball. Or reach up for a pass after it's gone over him. I see those things all the time now. Before, they were a rarity. But what do you do? Was it a mistake or a drug effect? I call the guy aside to talk to him, and get a puzzled, hurt look, even resentment. And the lawyers say that I better have proof before I fine or charge anybody, or the Players Association will be on me."

So we decided to start a drug-education program. My years of experience working with teenagers had shown that moral judgments and threats from legal authorities don't work. Besides, our whole approach was to treat the players with trust and respect rather than the mindless militarism that a good many other coaches take pride in.

Soft Grass, Hard Speed. We had to try education and persuasion. I talked to the team about how marijuana destroys timing and coordination, and dissolves aggression and drive. I also told them how the marijuana metabolites remain stored in their nerve endings as long as a week and may be released by stress at game time. I cajoled them and invoked their hopes for their own futures.

The persuasion worked. The next week there were three fights during practice. Someone swore at the offensive coach, and there were arguments every morning about who would get taped first. If I'd had any doubts about whether pot was antiaggressive they disappeared. By the day before the next game a dozen Chargers had told me privately that they'd been clean for a week.

The speed problem was harder. We did persuade several younger players that they would make fewer errors and remember their assignments better if they stayed off the uppers. Better than a dozen of them went off the stuff. They worried about errors, and they were young enough to muster the natural energy of rage.

But veterans were a different story. Many had incorporated certain drugs into their life and work. Like millions of other men and women, they used stimulants, tranquilizers and sleeping medications in habits that are not easy to break. Intelligently controlled, maybe, but not eliminated. Some had been taking stimulants before games for as long as 10 years. Their bodies needed those agents to function in their jobs, so they used them 20 days a year, no more. Such veterans hated the pills and never popped them offseason. They were in no sense addicted.

"Purple Turnarounds." These were experienced, steady performers, not just hangers-on. And since the League had suddenly stopped teams from the hallowed practice of issuing uppers along with helmets and cleats, they had no source of legitimate stimulants. They were buying the street stuff.

They were desperate and would take anything, even their wives' diet pills. Some gave me their street pills for chemical analysis. Chromatography of these "black beauties" or "purple turnarounds" and other junk revealed as many as six or eight compounds. My talk could not convince this small group of men that they didn't need them. They knew better. Any time they stopped they got benched because they couldn't hit or move.

Some of these players were clearly in a medical bind. The best I could do was to put an occasional long-term user on a prescription that I knew was pure and then steadily reduce the dosage. It was not spectacular, not dramatic, but I knew it gave us the best chance to work with the problem that already existed. I was vulnerable to the wrath of the Commissioner, whose ex-FBI narc squad was already sneaking into player's lockers, but the players were in better health. I still believe that Rozelle would share my view if he could set aside the time to work closely with individual players.

Death in Their Blood. I hadn't had much success converting them by conditioning or autohypnosis or other natural tricks. But at least, if they required surgery, we could tell the anesthesiologist what was in the bloodstream. Unknown chemicals flooding through a player's arteries can suddenly boost blood pressure beyond the danger line and add substantially to the risk.

Reducing the danger to the players was a great comfort, but we were still trying to modify behavior when we did not control the real reinforcers. With juvenile drug offenders you can, with luck, set up a variety of success experiences. In the NFL there's only one reward: winning. Americans don't pay dollars to see losers; the owners know that, and League officials know that. So do the players. We were losing, and it was heartbreaking to watch. We out-toughed the opposition in one game, shutting off their running attack. Our new defense was working, the play was crisp and assertive. The players, I know, were clean. But two fluke pass plays lost the game and, it turned out, helped lose us the chance to stay clean.

One break, a timely reinforcer, might still have saved us. A win the next week would have rewarded the clean-up, and perhaps permitted the attention, and faith, we needed to apply the rest of our psychological weapons. But we lost, and the team slid into a vicious circle of negative performance. Booze and grass killed the pain of losing, and speed cranked them up for the blind, futile effort each weekend.

Losers Lie Down. Obviously I hadn't been able to do my client much good. But the case history went from sad to horrible. Our internal struggle had, from the beginning, been encumbered by the League's legal moves. Under pressure from a football hearing staged by Democratic Congressman Harley Staggers' subcommittee, the Commissioner's office had launched its own investigation into drugs. They hired a pharmacologist who was unfamiliar with the drugs of abuse and with football, and hired more security men who got their training with the FBI and whose personal choice for making life bearable was the bottle, not the pill. Perhaps unknown to the NFL, these private eyes transformed an atmosphere that was already depressive and futile into one of utter paranoia. Players reported being followed and having their clothes searched in the locker room. Tape recorders were used without warrants.

I knew that very few of the Chargers used anything but booze, marijuana, and game-day amphetamines. It is no secret that all three problems run through pro football. The League's own administrative action vis à vis drugs was a tacit admission of trouble. In innocence, I wondered why the investigations focused on the San Diego team.

The answer came through clearly at season's end. A team with a 2–1–11 record obviously is doing something silly, and our drug program sounded softheaded to outsiders. Amputation would not stir up the fans; they'd already disowned the losers. You could do it without an anesthetic; losers lie down and suffer as though they deserve it.

Me, the Pusher. After the 1973 Super Bowl the Commissioner's office summoned us to New York. We were to discuss, after the hurrah of the play-offs, certain "punitive measures" designed, they said, to resolve the Chargers' drug problems. In this morality play I was to be cast as the pusher, the source of drugs; in the language of the NFL, I had "contributed to the difficulties."

My problem was not one of ethics nor one of law. Against the background of my experience and knowledge, I was operating as a responsible psychiatric physician. Moreover, representatives from the State Board of Medical Examiners had been through my records and checked out the prescriptions. I discussed with them the clinical circumstances and demonstrated with data that we were making progress, especially with younger players. I explained why it is hard for players over 25, who have not known any other way of doing their Sunday work, to believe that anything else will do the job. Stimulants are an issue for every football player; he has to make a choice. After my report, I never heard from the Board of Medical Examiners again.

But at the Commissioner's office, punishment, public embarrassment, and meat-ax discipline were the order of the day. I cannot say I was surprised. I've seen these kinds of ineffectual, even damaging, efforts grow out of the urge to solve medical problems quickly and simply. Yet, the National Football League had, *and has,* other choices. I believe any of the following would help:

1. The NFL could institute random postgame urinalysis and disqualify a team if drugs were found; this is already being done in European soccer.

2. They could allow open, supervised prescription of stimulants, with limits governed by the responsible choices of involved physicians who understand the conditions of play.

3. They could modify the conditions of play and create a more humane "work environment" for these professionals, one that would not drive the finest veterans into the pillbox.

We were, I saw, naive to hope that any of these options would be tried. Instead, we got punitive measures and press conferences that I believe will not solve the real drug agony that rages now, silently as a plague, through the body of professional football. But the League and the public will have business as usual, and the players will continue to be the unintended victims of our own addiction to football beyond human limits.

We were at the very frontier of the ethics of the new psychopharmacology. If anger and murderous rage are necessary to do a job and one can't get to that state with any other techniques, is drug use acceptable? If a person can't control his irritability and temper, is it acceptable to take a tranquilizer before a critical meeting in order to function better, to maintain control? If a person is passive by nature and is no longer upwardly mobile in a corporation because of it, could he take a drug such as the monoamine oxidase inhibitors, that would make him more assertive on a long-term basis?

Amphetamines in football are but an early test of the general ethical problem we face in the years ahead. The coming cornucopia of precise medications with more specificity and fewer side effects will force these decisions upon us.

Your Sunday Entertainers. But I was foolish to hope to work out these issues in the crucible of the National Football League. The Commissioner came up with a dramatic visible resolution that both press and public bought as just: Svare got a year's probation and a $5,000 fine; had Eugene Klein, the owner, not threatened to sell the team, I think Svare would have been thrown out of football. I was informally banned from NFL activities. No other team suffered public disgrace at the NFL's hands.

I went back to my department and the research lab. A tougher coach took over the Chargers. And the pushers will continue to get rich on the big, desperate men who will buy and swallow dangerous, unknown chemicals this fall to be able to entertain you each Sunday afternoon and Monday night.

VIII EDUCATION

Education has always occupied a special place in the American myth. The public school system, particularly, has usually been hailed as a pillar of all that is best in the American way of life. It has provided — so the argument runs — an unparalleled avenue of social mobility, a breeding place for democratic values, and a training ground for the skills necessary in an advanced industrial society. For decades education has been seen as the remedy for almost every important social problem — unemployment, poverty, crime, and a dozen others.

The mounting criticism of American society generally in the 1960s has led to a revision of these claims. The new critique of American education began with the growing awareness during this period that many children — especially poor minority children — were learning little in the public schools. This sparked a number of critical studies of what actually went on in the classroom, particularly in the ghetto schools. More recently, the roots of our system of public education have been subjected to critical analysis by social historians. The result has been a growing body of evidence that the reality of the schools is and has been very different from the myth.

In the selection from *Death at an Early Age*, one of the most powerful studies of the repressive and dehumanizing forces at work in the classroom, Jonathan Kozol describes the almost obsessive concern with discipline and obedience pervading the Boston ghetto schoolroom where he taught.

What is the *source* of this stultifying emphasis on obedience and submission in the classroom? It is often assumed that this and other problems of the modern school system result from the schools' failure to live up to their historic goals. The next selection questions that explanation. As Paul Lauter and

Florence Howe put it, the schools have not "failed" but have been "horrifyingly successful": we have simply misunderstood the nature of their goals.

Lauter and Howe argue that the role of the schools has been shaped by the demands of the economy, as those demands have been interpreted by the wealthy and privileged. Historically, they argue, the purpose of the public school has *not* been to ensure social mobility, but to solidify the going system of social stratification by channeling lower class people into the most "suitable," that is, lower status, occupations. In the modern school system the primary device for achieving this purpose has been the tracking system, which stratifies students within the schools, both mirroring and perpetuating existing patterns of power and privilege. For Lauter and Howe, recent innovations such as "open admissions" policies are inherently limited, because they do not challenge the basic relationship between the schools and the class structure; hence, they cannot produce a system that would "permit children to develop according to their own needs."

The analysis by Lauter and Howe suggests that any major change in the nature and goals of the educational system is as likely to be strongly resisted in contemporary American society as it has been in the past. The rigidities and inequalities of the school system are not just reflections of the stupidity or mean-spiritedness of the people who run it; they are crucially important props that help maintain the larger inequalities of the social system as a whole.

Pamela Roby's discussion of the role of women in higher education illustrates this on a different level. Historically, women have entered higher education in large numbers only when the economic needs of the system as a whole, and/or the specific financial needs of the universities themselves, have been served by their presence. Such gains as women have made in higher education have reflected the imperatives of the labor market more than any commitment to women's equality. And changing the position of women in higher education, Roby argues, may require a more basic change in the economic organization of American society.

28. DEATH AT AN EARLY AGE

Jonathan Kozol

There is a booklet published by the Boston Public Schools and bearing the title "A Curriculum Guide in Character Education." This booklet was in the desk of my new classroom and so, as few things are explicitly stated to you and so much must be done by guessing within these poorly run schools, I made the guess that I was supposed to look at it and perhaps make use of it. I did look at it but I did not make use of it. I kept it, however, and studied it and I have it in front of me now.

The booklet, really, is little more than an anthology broken down according to the values which the Boston School Committee hopes to instill or inspire in a child. This is the list of character traits which the teacher is encouraged to develop in a child:

CHARACTER TRAITS TO BE DEVELOPED: OBEDIENCE TO DULY CONSTITUTED AUTHORITY . . . SELF-CONTROL . . . RESPONSIBILITY . . . GRATITUDE . . . KINDNESS . . . GOODWORKMANSHIP AND PERSEVERANCE . . . LOYALTY . . . TEAMWORK . . . HONESTY . . . FAIR PLAY.

Two of the things that seem most striking about this list are (1) the emphasis upon obedience characteristics and (2) the way in which the personality has been dissected and divided and the way in which consequently each "character trait" has been isolated and dwelt upon in the manner of a list of favorable characteristics in the eulogy at a funeral or in the citation of an honorary degree during a commencement ceremony. You look in vain through this list for anything that has to do with an original child or with an independent style. You also look in vain for any evaluation or assessment or conception of the human personality as a full or organic or continuously living and evolving firmament rather than as a filing cabinet of acceptable traits.

The section on obedience characteristics begins with the following verse: "We must do the thing we must/Before the thing we may;/We are unfit for any trust/Till we can and do obey." It goes on to list the forms that obedience can take and it recommends a list of "selected memory gems" having to do with compliance to authority. Some of them are good and some are by famous people, but all of them, coming at you this way, out of context, have a killing, dull effect. They come one after another, some good, some dumb, and leave you feeling very obedient:

Honor thy father and thy mother [is the first one]. He who knows how to obey will know how to command. . . . Obedience to God is the best evidence of sincere love for Him. . . . True obedience is true liberty. . . . The good American obeys the laws. . . . Help me to be faithful to my country, careful for its good, valiant for its defense, and obedient to its laws. . . . He who would command others must first learn to obey. . . . The first law that ever God gave to man was a law of obedience. . . . My son Hannibal will be a great general, because of all my soldiers he best knows how to obey. . . . Obedience sums up our entire duty. . . . The first great law is to obey. . . . Children, obey your parents in all things; for this is well pleasing to the Lord. . . . Wicked men obey from fear; good men from love. . . . We are born subjects and to obey God is perfect liberty. He that does this shall be free, safe, and happy. . . . Obedience is not truly performed by the body if the heart is dissatisfied. . . . Every day, in every way/It is our duty to obey./ "Every way" means prompt and willing,/Cheerfully, each task fulfilling./It means, too, best work achieving/Habits of obedience, weaving./To form a cable firm and strong/With links unbreakable and long;/To do a thing, at once, when told/A blessing, doth the act enfold./Obedience, first to God, we owe;/It should in all our actions show. . . . If you're told to do a thing,/And mean to do it really,/Never let it be by halves,/Do it fully, freely!/Do not make a poor excuse/Waiting, weak, unsteady;/All obedience worth the name/Must be prompt and ready.

Of all the quotations included in this list, I think there are only two which are deeply relevant to the case at hand: "Wicked men obey from fear; good men from love" — this comes from Aristotle. And: "Obedience is not truly performed by the body if the heart is dissatisfied," which comes from the Talmudic scholar Saadia. Both of these quotations are directly applicable to the exact problem exemplified by the kind of school system in which such a list could be seriously employed. If it is true, as Aristotle wrote, that wicked men obey from fear and good men from love, then where else is this more likely to become manifest than within these kinds of penitential schools? One thinks of the pathos of anxiety with which teachers and principals go about their duties, seldom out of respect for their superiors, which in so many cases is impossible, but out of an abject fear of being condemned or of being kicked out. I think of the art teacher confiding to me in an excited whisper: "Can you imagine that this principal honestly and truly can stand there and call herself an educator? It's the biggest laugh of the school year." The reading teacher, with equal vehemence, talking about my supervisor: "That man doesn't know as much about elementary education as the first-year substitutes do. You'll have to agree to whatever he says and then ignore it when he's gone." To these people whom they held in deeply justified contempt, both women paid ample lip service. If ever they were honest, I do not see how they could have avoided holding both themselves and each other in some portion of the same contempt.

Saadia's eloquent statement that "obedience is not truly performed by the body if the heart is dissatisfied" seems also appropriate to the Boston public schools. For the heart *is* dissatisfied here, and the obedience *is* perfunctory, and the whole concept of respect for unearned and undeserved authority is bitter and brittle and back-breaking to children, whether rich or poor, or black or white, within these kinds of schools. Only the authority of visible character demands respect. No other kind deserves it. No child in his heart, unless drugged by passivity, will pay obeisance to authority unless authority has earned it, and authority based upon political maneuvering and upon the ingestion and assimilation of platitudes is an authority which no person, white or Negro, adult or child, should respect. There is too much respect for authority in the Boston schools, and too little respect for the truth. If there were more of the latter, there would be less need of the former, and the atmosphere of the Boston schools would not have to be so nearly what it is today: the atmosphere of a crumbling dictatorship in time of martial law. The emphasis both in this one booklet and in the words of the school administration in general upon the need for dumb obedience belies its deepest fear.

Another section of the "Character Education" booklet has to do with self-control: "Teach the necessity for self-discipline by all people," the teacher is advised.

Guide the children through discussion to recognize the necessity of self-discipline. . . . Responsible, self-disciplined people are an asset to the community. . . . People in a community should live by principle, not by emotion. . . . Emergencies are met by disciplined people, e.g., pilots, drivers, teachers, pioneers, policemen, fire-fighters, doctors, nurses, American Red Cross workers, clergymen, astronauts. . . . Disciplined people make good neighbors. . . .

The teacher is next told to "select many examples of self-disciplined people and discuss events in their lives which exemplify self-control, e.g., Abraham Lincoln, Louis Pasteur, Robert Fulton, Thomas Edison, Charles Lindbergh, Robinson Crusoe, Daniel Boone, George R. Clarke, Helen Keller, Florence Nightingale, Clara Barton, Dwight D. Eisenhower, Dr. Tom Dooley, Dr. Albert Schweitzer."

The unit on "good workmanship and perseverance" puts forth another list of famous men, several of them the same ones as before. The list in this case is notable partly for the odd discrepancies between the statures of the different people who are involved and partly, simply, for the heavy and thudding and skull-hammering manner in which the whole thing is gotten across:

Discuss the perseverance and good workmanship of (1) Individuals whose inventions have made our way of life easier, e.g., Gutenberg, Watts, Whitney, Bell, Edison, Howe, Wright. (2) Individuals whose research has made it possible for us to be safer from disease, e.g., Curie, Roentgen, Lister, Pasteur, Salk, Sabin. (3) Individuals who have shown good workmanship in spite of physical handicaps, e.g., Demosthenes, R. L. Stevenson, Helen Keller, Stein-metz, Dr. Tom Dooley, President Roosevelt, President Kennedy, Mayor John F. Collins. (4) Individuals whose artistry has provided us with pleasure, e.g., a. Music — Chopin, Mozart, Schubert, Leonard Bernstein, Arthur Feidler [sic], etc. b. Authors — Dickens, Anderson, Longfellow, Alcott, Stevenson, etc. c. Artists — Raphael, Michelangelo, Millet, Grandma Moses. . . .

When I look at this list, I find myself wondering who on earth could ever have put it all together and I also wonder whether anyone really thinks that you are going to teach character, or anything, to children by rattling off a list of all the people in the world or in America or in Boston who have struggled to make good. "Like a postage stamp, a man's value depends on his ability to stick to anything until he gets there." This is quoted from someone by the name of Chamberlain. "Excellence is never granted to man, but is a reward of labor," is quoted from Reynolds. "Do the very best you can today and tomorrow you can do better," says some-one named M. Vanbee. Can teachers and children be expected to take this seriously? And who is it who bears responsibility for this soul-drowning dreariness and waste of hours? With material as bad as this, surely it is no wonder that the matter of motivation has become such an overriding factor in the considerations of those who administer these schools. It cannot be unexpected that motivation becomes the all-important obstacle when the material is so often a diet of banality and irrelevance which it is not worth the while of a child to learn or that of a teacher to teach.

This seems to be a central issue. For the problem of motivation is talked about endlessly in Boston, and the point has been made repeatedly in the writings of Miss Sullivan and others that the motivational difficulty has its origin in the children and in their backgrounds, rather than in the teachers or the schools. I think the opposite is true. But the predictability with which this wrong assertion has been restated suggests the nervous-ness which the school administration of this city must experience in regard to its own failure.

"How can we motivate these culturally deprived in-migrant minorities to learn?"

This is the form of the standard question. The blame, in almost all cases, is immediately placed upon the child's background and his family. Then, but only after it has divested itself of prior responsibility, does the school administration come forward to profess a willingness to do what it can. Miss Sullivan, for example, in putting forward the aims of the com-pensatory program designed for Negro children, presented such an atti-tude in the following words: "This endeavor," she said,

is a preventive program designed to catch undesirable situations in their incipiency, to improve children's attitudes toward school, to inspire standards of excellence which should be carried over into secondary education for all and

beyond for many. It is our hope through this program to raise the achievement of these pupils closer to their potentials which have for too long been
submerged by parental lack of values.

The last phrase is a defensive one. It suggests that the child be granted
full mercy, high pardon, and even a certain amount of compassion just so
long as it is made absolutely clear ahead of time that the heart of the
problem is the lack of values of his parents. I don't think that the Negro
parents lack values. I think the people who administer the Boston school
system do. To go a bit further, honestly, I do not understand what is implied by such a phrase as "the lack of values" of the culturally deprived. I
think that when we are faced with an expression of that kind, we have
to ask whose values we are talking about and "deprived" in the eyes of
whom? To say that Negroes in Boston are deprived of rights would be an
honest statement. It would also be honest to say that they are deprived of
good schools and that, along with this, they are deprived of a fair chance,
of democracy, of opportunity, and of all the things these words are supposed to mean. But to say that they are deprived culturally, in the face
of Boston's school superintendent, in the face of Mrs. Hicks, in the face of
the profound cynicism of the entire system, seems to me meaningless.
The phrase "cultural deprivation" has not met with a great deal of favor
among Negroes and is, as a consequence, going out of fashion quickly
with white liberals. Needless to say, it is still a fervent catch-cry in the
Boston schools.

Edgar Friedenberg has written recently that the education and assimilation of Negro people provide American society with one of its last
chances "to transfuse into itself a stream of people whose moral vision
has been — relatively, at least — preserved and sharpened by exclusion
from opportunities for self-betrayal as well as self-advancement." If people regret, as some must, the exclusion of Negroes from opportunities for
advancement, there is at least reason to be grateful for an equal exclusion
from opportunities for self-betrayal. Too many white people in Boston are
compromised, to the point of seeming almost impotent, because they have
been, not by others, but by themselves essentially betrayed. There is also
the problem of those who, having grown up in low status, are determined,
once their head is a little bit above water, to make the next generation of
unlucky people pay. One man at my school, the redneck teacher I have
quoted often, once said to me in his usual frankness that he had been
beaten all around and treated rough and whipped and so on by his parents or teachers or both when he had been a child. To him, this seemed
to clear the field for beating others around today. The attitude of many
older people in our school system has been consistent with this view:
"We had a hard time of it, so why shouldn't they?" This less than gentle
attitude is characteristic of a less than gentle city in which the overriding outlook of those who are moderately successful is too likely to be that

they have got theirs and the others can damn well wait a while before they get the same. Friedenberg has also written in a somewhat different context that former prisoners make bad jailers. A corollary to this is that former slum-residents make poor landlords. And former Irish boys beaten by Yankee schoolmasters may frequently make ungenerous teachers for little boys whose skins are black. The matter of where the real values lie seems to me to be the final important question. . . .

You can't, obviously, say things like this without bringing down professional resentment on your head. In a school system like Boston's, where there is so little inward credential for service, the outward credential counts for a great deal. For the lack of such credentials, therefore, any straightforward critic is apt to be condemned. Ushers take their usher uniforms seriously. In Boston, teachers take their degrees and accumulated credits seriously and administrators take their political positions as a palliation for their inward sense of empty space. Mechanical credentials make up for genuine ones in this system and it is precisely in this manner that fragile bureaucracies have often defended themselves and their areas of power from the dangers of real life. That same blunt redneck teacher at my school who spoke with so much honesty on most topics once made this remark to me while we were chatting:

They talk about the Negroes being culturally deprived. I'm the one who's been goddamn culturally deprived and I don't need anyone to tell me. I haven't learned a thing, read a thing that I wished I'd read or learned since the day I entered high school, and I've known it for years and I tried to hide it from myself and now I wish I could do something about it but I'm afraid it's just too late.

Few people in Boston have the openness to talk that way. The man who spoke these words will probably be a principal some day. I think he will probably be a much better principal than most, if for no other reason than that he knows so well what he is lacking. But how many other people in our city will ever allow themselves even that degree of insight? And how many of those others, who may have the superficial trappings and the polysyllables of "culture," will ever stop to think of some of the deeper and truer things that culture ought to be about?

29. HOW THE SCHOOL SYSTEM
IS RIGGED FOR FAILURE

Paul Lauter and Florence Howe

There has hardly been a time during the last 150 years when Americans were not being told that the schools were at a "turning point," "confronted with a crucial challenge," "entering an era of new importance." At the same time, they have forever been at the edge of failure. Indeed, one major enterprise of educators in every generation has been to analyze that failure and propose new remedies. In the 1840's, industrialization, urbanization, and immigration produced conflict and dislocation in most cities of the North. Educational innovators envisioned public high schools as the means for unifying and civilizing communities, as well as promoting economic growth and social mobility. According to Joseph White, fourth secretary of the Massachusetts Board of Education during this period, in the high schools,

The children of the rich and poor, of the honored and the unknown, meet together on common ground. Their pursuits, their aims and aspirations are one. No distinctions find place, but such as talent and industry and good conduct create. In the competitions, the defeats, and the successes of the schoolroom, they meet each other as they are to meet in the broader fields of life before them; they are taught to distinguish between the essential and true, and the fractious and false, in character and condition. . . . Thus a vast and mutual benefit is the result. Thus, and only thus, can the rising generation be best prepared for the duties and responsibilities of citizenship in a free commonwealth. No foundation will be laid in our social life for the brazen walls of caste; and our political life, which is but the outgrowth of the social, will pulsate in harmony with it, and so be kept true to the grand ideals of the fathers and founders of the republic.[1]

The aspirations of mid-nineteenth-century America are thus to be fulfilled in the schoolroom.

Similarly, Sputnik launched the demand, in the 1950's, for a new high-school curriculum to save the national honor and restore military superiority. Vice-Admiral Hyman Rickover and President James Bryant Conant of Harvard proposed more rigorous mathematics and science courses, better preparation of teachers, and special attention to the "gifted." Schools all over the country adopted the slogan "Quality Education."

During the 1960's, the focus of agitation shifted to the "disadvantaged" student, and the byword became "equality of educational opportunity." No major school system is now without some special project for the children of the poor. Nor has there been any shortage of federally sponsored programs: Head Start, Follow-through, Upward Bound, NDEA Institutes, Model Cities colloquia, Titles I–IV. During the single fiscal year ending June 1967, the federal government alone provided over one billion dollars, supposedly for educating poor children, under Title I of the Elementary and Secondary Education Act. Another $100 million was authorized under Title III for experimental and model programs, many of which could be directed to the problems of the "disadvantaged." Private foundations have invested very heavily in "educational innovation." And during the last year or more, dozens of books have offered new hopes and desires to straining educational bureaucracies and a public impatient to solve the continuing and deepening "crisis."

There are a few common threads in these diverse and sometimes contradictory efforts: that the schools play crucial roles in achieving transcendent national goals, and especially in breaking the "cycle" of ignorance, joblessness, and poverty; and that the educational system has, for the most part, failed to achieve these objectives. The goals and assumptions to which most writers on education, congressmen, and parents would subscribe have been stated, for example, by the Committee for Economic Development, a very influential organization of financial and corporate executives:

The well-being of individual citizens, the integrity of the nation's social institutions, the strength of the economy, and the long-term national security depend on the effectiveness of the schools. Unless schooling keeps pace with the large demands that will be made on it in the years ahead, the American people will not achieve their personal, community, and national goals. A free society must always depend on the capacity of its schools to provide the kind of education that produces rational, responsible, and effective citizens.[2]

If these are, indeed, the goals of our educational system, it has surely failed, especially in the urban ghetto. The statistics bear witness to the fact that schools in Harlem, Watts, the District of Columbia do not impart even basic skills to their pupils. Nearly 81 percent of sixth-grade Harlem pupils score below grade level in reading comprehension, 77.5 percent in word knowledge, 83.3 percent in arithmetic. Often these poor and black children are two or three years behind in achievement scores,[3] and in the years since Kenneth Clark publicized these statistics, the situation has not materially improved. But, of course, defective schools are not confined to the ghettos. In the Elementary and Secondary Education Act of 1965 the failures of the schools are noted, with somewhat more down-to-earth insights about the objectives of the educational system than those posited by the Committee for Economic Development:

A national problem . . . is reflected in draft rejection rates because of educational deficiencies. It is evidenced by the employment and manpower re-training problems aggravated by the fact that there are over eight million adults who have completed less than five years of school. It is seen in the 20 percent unemployment rate of our 18-to-24-year-olds.[4]

Surely, the proposers of the 1965 Act seem to be saying, if the schools fail to prepare men for the Army and for industry, they have failed altogether.

This litany over the failure of the schools is repeated in almost every new book on the subject. Mario Fantini and Gerald Weinstein, who have had much to do with shaping the Ford Foundation's broad program of educational support, cite Kenneth Clark and the ESEA in their *The Disadvantaged: Challenge to Education*. They add their own variations on the theme: the schools have not only failed the poor and the black, but they have not taught "adult maturity" or necessary skills to many children from comfortable middle-class families.

. . . it becomes all too clear that our education has been severely deficient in achieving its purpose, quantitatively and qualitatively. Yet education is the only institution upon which we, as a nation, can rely to provide us with a population which has a significant proportion of truly democratic, socially oriented, dedicated adults who will contribute to our country's welfare.[5]

Thus Fantini and Weinstein join their hopes to those of Joseph White a hundred years ago, to those of the Committee for Economic Development, to those of the Elementary and Secondary Education Act. And they devote their 455 pages to strategies for helping educators achieve these presumed — and traditional — objectives.

But are the schools "failures"? If they do not accomplish the goals which educators have laid out for them, it may well be that all they need — as the CED, Congress, and Fantini and Weinstein urge — is more money, more innovation, more machines, more specialization. It may also be, however, that the stated goals of American education are deceptive and irrelevant ones, that their grand rhetoric clouds the character and social objectives of the schools. A review of the alleged "failures" of the selective-service system — the uncertainty it has engendered, its unfairness, its apparently arbitrary and harebrained procedures — reveals features that have been built in because they are necessary to its function of channeling young men into what are thought to be socially desirable activities.[6] Looking at what the schools *do* rather than at what they should or might do may tell a similar story. What if the apparent "failures" of the American educational system have served necessary functions in American society? Perhaps the schools, like almost all other American institutions, have been very, indeed horrifyingly, successful.

Such a proposition may seem shocking, if not perverse, since Americans have traditionally believed in the virtues of schooling as much as in motherhood or a balanced budget. The black and Jewish communities in

New York City continue to quarrel bitterly about the control of education, yet they agree about the fundamental importance of keeping children in schools. Recently, however, observing conditions in Harlem, Kenneth Clark suggested that schools function in a manner precisely contrary to their acclaimed ideals:

. . . American public schools have become significant instruments in the blocking of economic mobility and in the intensification of class distinctions rather than fulfilling their historic function of facilitating such mobility.

In effect, the public schools have become captives of a middle class who have failed to use them to aid others also to move into the middle class — it might even be possible to interpret the role of the controlling middle class as that of using the public schools to block further mobility.[7]

Although Clark's analysis of the present situation is accurate, he accepts too readily the historical claims, rather than the performance, of American education.

Michael B. Katz has compared in some detail such historical claims with what the schools really accomplished. High schools in the nineteenth century were presented by their promoters as mechanisms for achieving social mobility and economic development, for democratizing society, for eliminating class distinctions, and for producing, as Fantini and Weinstein put it more than a century later, "truly democratic, socially oriented, dedicated adults who will contribute to our country's welfare." In fact, however, as Katz shows, the innovation called high schools achieved none of these goals. Few poor and working-class children actually attended, and before very long, those who did were channeled off into vocational programs "more suitable to their interests and capacities." The pressure for schools originated in response to economic growth, but, as Katz suggests, there is little evidence to demonstrate that continued industrial development depended in any sense on the expansion of education.

This is not to say that the public educational system had *no* functions. On the contrary, some of its achievements seem to have been inversely related to the claims made for it. For the middle-class children who made up the bulk of high-school students, schools helped to maintain their status and position in the community. Schools were an entree for boys into business (though they taught little of major importance to enterprise) and for girls into teaching. And teaching, as Katz says, "was undoubtedly the most attractive vocational goal for the middle-class girl who wanted to earn some money because all the other occupations populated by large numbers of females were manual, arduous, and decidedly lower-class."[8] The public high school also served middle-class parents, because "they could spread among the population at large the [fiscal] burden of educating their children."[9] Thus, far from pulling down "the brazen walls of caste," as Joseph White had asserted, the high schools reinforced them.

Though the schools did not function to the advantage of poor and working-class children, they did not ignore them. Katz quotes a contributor to the *Massachusetts Teacher* who in 1861 explained the value of education to business: "The habit of prompt action in the performance of the duty required of the boy, by the teacher at school, becomes in the man of business confirmed; thus system and order characterize the employment of the day laborer."[10] Katz quotes a Lowell manufacturer, one H. Bartlett, who insisted in 1841, that:

Workers with more education possessed "a higher and better state of morals, [were] more orderly and respectful in their deportment, and more ready to comply with the wholesome and necessary regulations of an establishment." Perhaps most important, "in times of agitation, on account of some change in regulations or wages, I have always looked to the most intelligent, best educated and the most moral for support." . . . The educated, in short, were seen as company men.[11]

In their conscious attempt to impose personal habits of restraint, self-control, diligence, promptness, and sobriety on their students, particularly those from "loose," "shiftless" (or "disadvantaged") backgrounds, schoolmen served the desires of business for a disciplined and acquiescent work force. In this sense, too, schools served the dominant interests of the middle-class community; and, not surprisingly, such businessmen and industrialists were among the major promoters of school reforms.

This history is important, for it contradicts the easy assumptions we have usually made about the uniform virtues of schooling. And it suggests that earlier "failings" in the educational system can better be understood as contradictions between the professed objectives of educators — their ideology — and the real social and economic forces to which the educational system was in fact responding. Such forces continue to operate: a recent Harris poll shows that 62 percent of parents questioned thought that in school "maintaining discipline is more important than student self-inquiry."[12] A *Life* reporter, commenting on the study, wrote that "the parents in the *Life* poll know exactly what *they* want from the schools: 'Teach the kids to understand our existing values,' they say; 'discipline them to conform.' . . . They think the schools should keep the children passive and disciplined, and provide them with the tools that lead to college and a job."[13] To what extent does our educational system today continue, not to "fail," but to succeed in serving these by now traditional objectives?

In 1927 many Americans were troubled about their society. Morals seemed to be disintegrating, crime increasing. Indeed, some felt there was a "legal bias in favor of the criminal." He "is petted and pampered and protected to a degree which makes the punishment of crime relatively rare." Educators were quick to rise to this social crisis. They urged their fellow Americans to look to the schools to train citizens not to "set themselves against the state." After all, there was "no other organized force which aims primarily at citizenship and at the same time represents the state." Schools could, moreover, satisfy the demands of industry for "the type of help that knows something, that has social graces arising from extended social experience" of the sort provided by high schools.

There was one problem, however: how to keep the children *in* school. Many dropped out because their main experience in the classroom was one of frustration. A new way of organizing schools had to be found that would not forever be confronting those most in need of schooling with failure, that might more fully "individualize" their instruction in order to prepare children more efficiently for the kinds of jobs they would get. This way was "ability grouping."

Ability grouping in the junior high school is to be defined as the classification of the pupils of the school into groups which, within reasonable limits, are homogeneous in ability to perform the kind of task which confronts those pupils in the classroom. It is not a social segregation. It is not a caste stratification. It is not an attempt to point out those who are worth while and those who are not. It is not a move to separate the leaders from the followers.[14]

Despite the best intentions of its promoters, ability grouping — or tracking, or streaming, as it is variously called — has unfortunately become all that they asserted it would not be. What it has *not* been is either a means of keeping children in school or of improving their performance while they attend.

In Washington, D.C., for example, where an elaborate track system reached far down into the elementary schools, 54 percent of the classes of 1965 and 1966 dropped out before graduation. The most extensive and careful study of ability grouping, moreover, concludes "that ability grouping, *per se,* produces no improvement in achievement for any ability level and, as an administrative device, has little merit."[15] The study indicates further that children may learn better in strongly heterogeneous groups. Arthur W. Foshay, who wrote the Foreword, suggests also that evidence from Sweden and England "raises the dark possibility that ability grouping functions . . . as selective deprivation."[16] Tracking may actually *prevent* children from learning, the study indicates, because "teachers generally underestimate the capability of pupils in lower-track classes, expect less of them, and consequently the pupils learn less."[17] None of this is surprising, since teachers generally concentrate on students who respond. But why, then, if tracking has not succeeded in keeping most kids in school and has succeeded in creating for those lower-tracked kids the "self-fulfilling prophecy" that they won't learn anything in school — why, then, has it persisted for more than forty years?

In the first place, tracking is to schools what channeling is to the draft. Its function is identical, namely, the control of manpower "in the national interest." In democratic societies like that of the United States, individuals are encouraged to believe that opportunities for social advancement are unlimited; such beliefs are part of the national myth, and also necessary to encourage young people to achieve and get ahead. Yet opportunities are, in fact, limited. Not everyone with the talent can, for example, become a scientist, industrial manager, engineer, or even a college professor; the economy has greater need for technologists, technicians, salesmen, white-collar workers, not to speak of men on production lines. It has been estimated that industry demands five semiprofessionals and technicians to enable every professional to function.[18]

There must be "valves" which can help to control the flow of manpower into the economy. "Tracking" is one of those important valves; it helps to ensure that the American work force is not "overeducated" (as has been the case, for example, in India, where there are far too few jobs "suitable" for college graduates). It also helps to ensure that unpopular industries, like the Army, or less prestigious occupations, like sanitation work, are supplied with manpower.

Indeed, sociologist Theodore Caplow has argued that:

. . . the principal device for the limitation of occupational choice is the education system. It does this in two ways: first, by forcing the student who embarks upon a long course of training to renounce other careers which also require extensive training; second, by excluding from training and eventually from the occupations themselves those students who lack either the intellectual qualities (such as intelligence, docility, aptitude) or the social characteristics (such as ethnic background, wealth, appropriate conduct, previous education) which happen to be required.[19]

Tracking is one of the educational system's major techniques for thrusting forward students with the necessary qualities of school-measured intelligence, docility, background, and the rest; and for channeling the others into "appropriate" slots. James Bryant Conant is explicit about this practice. "I submit," he writes in *Slums and Suburbs*, "that in a heavily urbanized and industrialized free society, the educational experiences of youth should fit their subsequent employment." Accomplishing this goal in cities is difficult, Conant continues, given the limitations of guidance personnel and parental indifference; therefore, "the system of rigid tracks may be the only workable solution to a mammoth guidance problem."[20]

The "valves" of ability grouping, some economists complain,[21] have become sticky, and have slowed economic growth by limiting the flow of students with middling talent and motivation, particularly those from lower-class backgrounds. In fact, however, from another point of view one might argue that the valves have been operating effectively to limit competition with the children of white, middle-class parents who, on the whole, have controlled the schools.[22] In New York City in 1967, for example, nonwhites, the vast majority of them poor, made up 40 percent of the high-school population; they constituted about 36 percent of students in the "academic" high schools and about 60 percent of those tracked into "vocational" high schools. In the Bronx High School of Science and in Brooklyn Tech, elite institutions for which students must qualify by examination, "nonwhites" totaled only 7 and 12 percent of the students respectively.

But the real effects of tracking can better be seen in the statistics of students in the academic high schools. A majority of blacks and Puerto Ricans fill lower tracks, which lead them — if they stay at all — to "general" rather than "academic" diplomas. Only 18 percent of academic high-school graduates were black or Puerto Rican (though they were, as we said, 36 percent of the academic student population); and only one-fifth of that 18 percent went on to college, as compared with 63 percent of whites who graduated. In other words, only 7 percent of the graduates of New York's academic high schools who went on to college were black or Puerto Rican. The rest, for the most part tracked into noncollege-preparatory programs, left school with what amounted to a ticket into the Army.[23]

The statistics for Washington, D.C., are even more striking, in part because figures are available on the basis of income as well as race and ethnic background. In the nation's capital, where, in 1966, 91 percent of the students were black, 84 percent of those black children were in schools *without any honors track*. In areas with a median income of $3,872 a year, 85 percent of the children were in a basic or general track, neither of them college-bound; while in areas where the income was $10,374 or better, only 8 percent of the children were in the general track, and in such areas there was *no basic track at all*. Theoretically, tracking ranks students according to their ability to achieve. Yet Washington's statistics suggest that the children of the poor have less than one-tenth of the ability of the children of the well-to-do — an obvious absurdity. Indeed, tracking in Washington was more than absurd: in 1967 Federal Judge J. Skelly Wright declared that the system unconstitutionally discriminated against poor and black children and ordered it abolished.[24] But although it has officially been disbanded in the District's schools, it lingers on subtly in placement and curriculum, and more openly in the way teachers teach.

If one studies the means by which students are selected into tracks, one discovers a further layer of discrimination against the children of the poor. It is on the basis of reading scores, IQ, and other standard achievement tests — as well as teachers' recommendations — that children are determined "slow" or "superior." Yet Herbert Kohl reports that he was able to help his students raise their reading scores from one to three years, within a period of months, simply by teaching them how to take tests. Middle-class children, Kohl points out, learn about tests early in their school careers; indeed, a "predominantly white school located less than a mile down Madison Avenue [from Kohl's Harlem school] even gave after-school voluntary classes in test preparation." But in the Harlem schools it was "against the rules" to provide copies of old tests so that teachers could help their pupils prepare for them; Kohl had to obtain such copies from friends who taught in white, middle-class schools, where back files were kept and made available.[25] Recent studies have suggested, moreover, that the content of "standardized" tests conforms to the experience and norms of white, middle-class children, thereby discriminating in still another manner against able children of poor or black parents.

Thus, just as the establishment of high schools in the nineteenth century promoted the interests of middle-class parents, so ability grouping has become an elaborate mechanism for ensuring those same interests. In this respect the track system has joined with "the ordinary operations of educational institutions," which, deliberate discrimination aside, by themselves tend to deny poor and working-class children equal opportunities for social mobility. Experienced teachers transfer out of schools in poor neighborhoods, seeking better-paying and less-exacting assignments.[26] Schools develop studied institutional defenses of secrecy and professional mystification against criticism or even inquiry by lower-class parents. But they are, of course, much more responsive to wealthier parents, who often control PTAs and school boards and whom, in any case, schoolteachers and administrators emulate.

Thus, as the sociologist Howard Becker has written, "The schools, organized in terms of one of the subcultures [that of the middle class] of a heterogeneous society, tend to operate in such a way that members of subordinate groups of differing culture do not get their fair share of educational opportunity, and thus of opportunity for social mobility."[27] Which is an elaborate way of saying that schools institutionalize and maintain privilege in America.

But statistics and abstractions may obscure the lives of children trapped in what has been called "programmed retardation." A group of New York City parents, whose children have been tracked into the special "600" schools for allegedly "difficult" children, has begun to prepare a suit to challenge the compulsory-attendance law. While the state has the right to make laws for the health, welfare, or safety of children, they claim, it has no right to subject children to a system that deprives and injures them. Their point is that tracking is not simply a neutral "valve" to control manpower flow, as our initial image might at first have suggested. Rather, tracking harms some children, depriving those we call "deprived," making them less competent, less able to reach, let alone to use, the instruments of power in U.S. society. In the light of tracking, schools become for such children not the means of democratization and liberation, but of oppression.

On the other hand, tracking is also one means of controlling middle-class students. The selective service's "channeling" system benefits the young man who can afford to go to college, and whose culture supports both higher education and avoiding the draft if he can. Channeling helps him, however, only so long as he lives up to the draft board's standards of behavior and work. Just as the threat of loss of deferment drives draft registrants into college or jobs in the "national interest," so the threat of losing privileged status within the school system is used to drive students to fulfill upper-track, college-bound requirements. In a school in which students are tracked from, say, "12–1" — the twelfth-grade class for college-bound students — down to "12–34" — the class for alleged unteachables — demotion not only would threaten a student's social position, but his entire future life. Having a child placed in a lower track is a stigma for a college-oriented family, as every principal faced with angry parents pushing to have their children in the "best" classes will testify. Moreover, entry into prestige colleges, or even into college at all, normally depends upon track and other measures of school status. Thus though the threat, like that of channeling in the past, has been largely unspoken, it continues to push students to behaving and achieving as required by the system.

These operations of tracking and channeling (and of racial segregation, for which tracking is often an administrative substitute)[28] help to explain why, contrary to popular American mythology, this society has more and more rapidly become stratified, structured by class. Increasingly, Americans follow the occupations of their fathers or, at any rate, enter occupations of roughly the same prestige and income.[29] Level of education — which must be distinguished both from what a student has learned and from how competent he might be — is a major determinant of what kind of job he can get.[30] The more education attained, on the whole, the better the job; and, of course, the more prestigious the college the better. There is a direct correlation between a student's social and economic class and the likelihood that he will enter *or* graduate from college. A recent study by the Carnegie Commission of Higher Education found that children from families whose income is above the national median have a chance of getting into college three times greater than that of children from families below the median. And only 7 percent of college students come from families in the bottom quarter of national income.[31] "The passage from school to college, in fact, seems to depend more upon socialization, life experience, and opportunity than upon intellective factors."[32]

The track system provides a formal basis for translating these class-based factors into academic criteria for separating students into different groups: those who drop out; those whose diplomas will not admit them to college, those who will be able to enter only two-year or junior colleges; and the lucky few in the honors classes who will go on to elite institutions and to graduate or professional schools. Thus while tracking may assure the "failure" of lower-class students, as a system it allows the schools to "succeed" in serving middle-class interests by preparing their children to fill the technological and professional needs of corporate society.

In several cities during the past few years, as the contradictions between systems of tracking and the rhetoric of social mobility have become especially apparent, some groups have begun to pressure for the abolition of tracking and others, in the meantime, for "open" admissions to colleges. It is clear enough to students and their parents that there are fewer jobs available for young men who have not completed high school or who have emerged from "basic" or other lower tracks. Jobs requiring no secondary education have decreased 25 percent in the past ten years; and white-collar workers, who made up 15 percent of the work force in 1900 and 28.5 percent in 1940, will make up about 48 percent in 1970. Schools with tracking systems have not been particularly responsive to a job market changed by automation and "upgrading" (an economist's term for saying that you now need more educational credentials to get the same level of job). Manpower specialists, often writing under the auspices of major foundations, have therefore called on school systems to change their practice so that their products will suit a modernizing industrial economy.[33] But of course, the pressure to maintain a system segregated by class has not abated.

The clash between those upholding tracking and those wishing to end it has taken particularly dramatic forms in several cities. In Washington, D.C., for example, tracking was a primary issue in the battle over former Superintendent Carl Hansen's job. In New York City, the issue of whom the schools will serve has been fought over "community control." Experiments designed to make schools more responsive to the needs of blacks and Puerto Ricans by giving them direct control over the education of their children through the creation of community school boards have been financed by the Ford Foundation and supported by politicians, including Mayor Lindsay and Governor Rockefeller, who have been sensitive to the changing needs of large industry as well as the demands of black voters.

In opposition to community-controlled decentralization, the New York Teachers' Union and much of the white, middle-class electorate correctly understand the demand for community control as a demand that the schools help the children of poor blacks and Puerto Ricans to compete with their own children instead of preventing them from doing so. Jewish teachers remember their battle against WASPs and Irish Catholics entrenched in the schools before them. Odd alliances between the Ford Foundation and the Ocean Hill-Brownsville local board, on the one hand, and the liberal Jewish and conservative Italian communities, on the other, as well as the bitterness of the struggle in New York City suggest how fundamental are the social and economic stakes at issue in the control of the schools.

This issue is also powerful and divisive for higher education. Encouraged by U.S. society to believe that young people can rise to the top, whatever their race or class, blacks, Chicanos, Puerto Ricans, and some working-class white students are beginning to press into colleges. Higher education in the United States has had to manage an elaborate and delicate technique for diverting many of these students from goals toward which they have been taught to aspire, but which a stratified society cannot allow them all to teach. "Cooling" them "out," the term openly used in higher education and now beginning to become as familiar to students as "channeling," means that certain students are deliberately and secretively discouraged from aspirations middle-class youth take for granted. Working-class students are tracked into second-class or "junior" colleges, "cooled out" and counseled into substitute curricula (a medical technician's program rather than a premedical course), or, if they get to a university, programmed for failure in large "required" courses.[34]

California's three-tiered system of higher education has provided a model for other states: the "top" eighth of high-school graduates may be admitted to the university system, the "top" third to the state colleges; the rest are relegated to what one writer has described as "those fancied-up super high schools, the local two-year 'community colleges.' "[35] Factors closely related to race and economic class — students' high-school track, grades, and College Board scores — determine placement into a particular level of higher education, though the fees students pay are relatively similar wherever they may go in the state.[36] Like tracking in high schools, state-subsidized higher education channels students into distinctly inequitable systems. In Maryland, for example, the average per pupil expenditure during fiscal year 1966 was $802 in community colleges, $1,221 in the state colleges, and $1,724 (excluding research funds) in the University of Maryland.[37]

Another significant index of discrimination is the relative teaching load of faculties: at the University of Maryland, an English professor teaches three courses, at state colleges four, and at community colleges five. Theoretically, at least, university students are taught by professors with better credentials, higher salaries, and lighter teaching loads than at state or community colleges. It is not surprising, therefore, as Todd Gitlin has pointed out, that from the university campuses come "high professionals and managers for the great corporations. At the bottom, the two-year junior colleges take on all comers, and process them into clerks, punch-card operators, foremen — the dregs of the white-collar labor force."[38]

But it is not only that the student attending a junior college will have far less public money spent on his education than the student attending Berkeley, Michigan, or the University of Maryland. It is rather that tracking at public colleges also benefits the children of the rich at the expense of the children of the poor. Patricia Cayo Sexton has stated the case: "In general the more money a student's parents make, the more money will be spent on his education, despite some efforts at public 'compensatory' expenditures for the disadvantaged."[39] In New York City, for example, tuition-free colleges with "'high standards' . . . have . . . subsidized many middle-income students and virtually excluded most impoverished ethnic groups." "Low college tuition," Mrs. Sexton writes, "offers few opportunities to lower-income students if entrance 'standards' are too high to hurdle."

Significantly, her statistics bear out the relationship between income and admission: at the University of Michigan, only 25 percent of the fathers of entering freshmen had less than a college education, only 4.8 percent less than a high-school diploma; consequently, only 1.8 percent of the students were from families with incomes under $4,000.[40] The circular process is obvious: just as the economic class of a student's family largely determines his admission to a particular college or university in the first place, so does his placement at that college determine his future. Indeed, money is destined![41] Given the process of "upgrading" jobs, one might find suitable the image of a squirrel in a circular cage: the faster he runs, the more firmly does he remain bound to his position. While the admission of working-class students to community colleges may seem to be serving their desire for upward mobility, in fact it may barely be keeping the lid on potentially explosive campuses.

Demonstrations throughout the nation during the spring of 1969 arose from students' increasing awareness that tracking, and its methods of cheating and controlling the poor, have been translated into new campus forms. Demands for "open admissions" of black and "third world" students, prominent first at San Francisco State College, attempt to strike at the heart of the tracking system by negating the streaming process of earlier school years. Students at San Francisco State, at City College in New York, and elsewhere, in lengthy strikes and demonstrations, have first paralyzed the institution, then divided it irrevocably on principles similar to those we have described with relation to high schools.

In the official catalogue of San Francisco State, a passage claims that the curriculum ought to satisfy "existing student interests" and "the technical and professional manpower requirements of the State."[42] But interests of students and those of manpower specialists often diverge fundamentally: they are obviously most divergent with respect to working-class students' aspirations for the alleged room at the top and industry's needs for a highly differentiated work force.

Can the track system survive this new and deeply outraged onslaught of college students? The "valves" of tracking in high school may be sticky, at once denying both reasonable opportunity to poor and black students and better-trained manpower to industry. But the demand for dividing the work force by some tracking mechanism remains. To be sure, it doesn't much matter, at least abstractly, to the corporation manager just *who* fills what slots — so long as young people are channeled and prepared to fill them. In this respect, the need for a class-based track system diminishes. But a particular John D. Executive — not to speak of Jack Salesman — wants to maintain *his* privilege for *his* kids. Thus the pressure to maintain the present social and class divisions has hardly diminished. Colleges are, on the one hand, pressed from below by poor, black, and radical students to end discriminatory admissions practices. On the other hand, they are pressed from above by politicians, trustees, and contributors to "maintain standards," not to "capitulate to the demands of demonstrators."[43] Implicitly, they are of course urged to maintain the present system of class and economic privilege embodied in those "standards."

In March 1969, Rutgers University agreed to an "open admissions" policy for disadvantaged students from the three cities in which its campuses are located. Almost at once, opposition to the program developed in the New Jersey legislature, partly because the plan would reduce the number of students eligible to enter the state university who were not from those lucky three cities. Similarly, an announcement by New York City's Board of Higher Education that it would attempt to implement an "open admissions policy by 1970 was greeted with opposition by key state legislators."[44]

More sensitive to the complexities of New York City's educational politics, a conservative Democratic candidate for mayor in 1969, Mario A. Procaccino, "hoped" that money could be found so that all city youths would have access to "free education," but warned "against any lowering of academic standards at the university." The New York City plan by no means envisaged an end to tracking. As initially presented, it pictured only 19 percent of graduating high-school seniors entering the senior colleges, some 26 percent going on to community colleges, and another 20 percent or more being channeled into "educational skills centers," where, presumably, they would be trained to fill vacancies in low-paying hospital, teaching-aid, and clerical positions.

The revised plan now being implemented considerably increased the proportion of high-school graduates entering senior colleges. But more ingeniously, it changed the standard of admission to the senior colleges from high-school grade-point average alone, adding as an alternative criterion a student's rank in his high-school class. Thus the student from ghetto schools, where grade-point averages are notoriously low, will be able to enter one of the senior colleges by finishing in the top half or so of his class.

The competition for places in the city's colleges will thus be increased even for middle-class students, since the compromise tries to placate white, middle-class advocates of "standards" by saying to them that their children can be admitted to a senior college if they maintain high standards. At the same time, the compromise attempts to placate ghetto residents by opening the senior colleges to more of their children — those, on the whole, perhaps, with middle-class aspirations. What the plan does, rather neatly, is to turn a threatening racial and ethnic crisis into a division of students by class; it is precisely such school-maintained divisions that Americans have in the past chosen not to contest.

New York City's response to the pressure for open admissions and an end to tracking seems a likely harbinger. It shifts part of the burden of tracking upward to "education beyond high school," now available for "all who want it," and held out as a carrot for disaffected minorities. The plan expands Upward Bound and SEEK programs to permit more individuals of "high potential but weak background" to flow into higher educational streams. In short, it places the valves higher in the educational system and lets them function a bit more freely. It gives the needs of the economy for a screened, differentiated, and controllable work force somewhat higher priority than the wishes of white middle-class parents that the schools perpetuate their privilege. But it by no means destroys the mechanisms by which schools have maintained class privilege. Now students will be separated — according to grades and class standing — into senior college, community college, and "other" categories.

Not surprisingly: for the systems of tracking are so closely tied to those who control American education and to the qualities of American schools that it is hard to imagine their replacement altogether — certainly not by a system which would permit children to develop according to their own needs and abilities.

REFERENCES

1. *The 28th Report of the Massachusetts Board of Education*, pp. 83–84. Quoted in Michael B. Katz, *The Irony of Early School Reform* (Cambridge, 1968), pp. 44–45.

2. "Innovation in Education: New Directions for the American School," a statement by the Research and Policy Committee, July 1968, pp. 9, 10.

3. Kenneth Clark, *Dark Ghetto* (New York, 1965), pp. 120–121.

4. *Elementary and Secondary Education Act of 1965*, Report #143, House of Representatives, 89th Congress.

5. Mario D. Fantini and Gerald Weinstein, *The Disadvantaged: Challenge to Education* (New York, 1968), pp. 172–173.

6. See our article in *NYR* (June 20, 1968) and Chapter 7 of our forthcoming book, *The Conspiracy of the Young*.

7. Kenneth Clark, in a paper for a conference sponsored by the U.S. Commission on Civil Rights in November 1967.

8. Katz, *op. cit.*, p. 91.

9. *Ibid.*, p. 92.

10. *Ibid.*, p. 87.

11. *Ibid.*, p. 88.

12. *Life*, 66 (May 16, 1969), p. 29.

13. Bayard Hooper, "The Task Is to Learn What Learning is For," *Life*, 66 (May 16, 1969), pp. 34, 39.

14. All quotations from Heber Hinds Ryan and Philpine Crecelius, *Ability Grouping in the Junior High School* (New York, 1927), pp. 1–10.

15. Miriam L. Goldberg et al., *The Effects of Ability Grouping* (New York, 1966), p. 163. "Differences in achievement growth over the two-grade span," the authors found, "did not support the common wisdom that narrowing the ability range or separating the extreme groups from the intermediate groups enables teachers to be more effective in raising the pupils' achievement level. . . . On the contrary, although the achievement differences among patterns of varying ability range were small, overall observed increments tended to favor the *broad range*" (p. 160).

See also Joseph Justman, "Ability Grouping — What Good Is It?" *The Urban Review*, 2 (February 1967), pp. 2–3: ". . . homogeneous grouping is not a panacea for educational ills. . . . Grouping by itself, without curricular modification as a concomitant, will not give rise to the desired outcome of improved pupil performance." Unfortunately, no one has shown, either, that grouping with "curricular modifications" would make real differences, or just what "curricular modifications" there might be that would not, for example, strait-jacket and limit "slow learners."

16. The *Times* of London reported August 12, 1966, on a set of samples being taken by the British Foundation for Educational Research: "Most of the existing research of streaming [tracking] has come to the conclusion that children get better results in unstreamed schools. One notable piece of work was that of Dr. J. C. Daniels (1961). . . . Dr. Daniels compared academic progress in two streamed and two unstreamed schools in detail. He reported that progress in reading, English, and arithmetic was more rapid for all children in unstreamed schools, but particularly for the weakest children. These findings have not yet been seriously challenged by later research. . . ."

Dr. J. W. B. Douglas examined the "school careers of 5,000 children in the Medical Research unit's permanent sample." He showed that "although children in higher streams all made good progress, the IQs of children in lower streams actually deteriorated during the later years of primary school. This deterioration was most marked in children of working-class background. Dr.

Douglas' general conclusion was that 'streaming by ability tends to reinforce the process of social selection.' The initial act of streaming was, in Dr. Douglas' view, heavily influenced by social and nonacademic factors."

17. Goldberg, *op. cit.*, p. 165. The study "reinforces the conclusion that what pupils learn is at least as much a function of what teachers teach and expect of them as it is a function of pupil attitudes, self-percepts, or, within limits, even tested intellectual ability" (p. 164). See in this regard, Robert A. Rosenthal, *Pygmalion in the Classroom* (Cambridge, 1968). Rosenthal relates the results of an experiment in which teachers were told that certain of their students were revealed through "tests" as having superior, though hidden, ability. Though the students were not, in fact, special, they began to perform better, apparently in response to teachers' special ministrations.

18. See, for example, Maryland Council for Higher Education, *Master Plan for Higher Education in Maryland* (Baltimore, 1968), Section 2, p. 36.

19. Theodore Caplow, *The Sociology of Work* (Minneapolis, 1954), p. 216.

20. *Slums and Suburbs* (New York: McGraw-Hill, 1961), pp. 40, 66. Conant's comments on tracking help to explain some of the mistrust felt by black communities for liberal educational reformers. He writes: "In short, my recommendation in both my senior-high report and my junior-high report still stands. In these subjects [English, social studies, mathematics, science — in short, in all the academic curriculum] there ought to be subject-by-subject grouping in three groups — fairly small top and bottom groups and a large middle group. Such an arrangement may well isolate Negroes in some schools in the bottom group, but surely there will be considerable mixing in the large middle group if not in the top group. Moreover, with an integrated staff and with frank discussions of the problem I should think a workable solution might be arrived at in good faith" (p. 64). What is one to say in the face of such naive optimism?

21. See, for example, John Vaizey and Michael Debeauvais, "Economic Aspects of Educational Development," in *Education, Economy, and Society*, ed. A. H. Halsey, Jean Floud, and C. H. Anderson (Glencoe, 1961), p. 43.

22. See, for example, Patricia Cayo Sexton, *Education and Income* (New York, 1962), pp. 228, 234.

23. These figures were obtained by Columbia University SDS from the records of the N.Y.C. Board of Education through the office of the Reverend Milton Galamison, then a member of the board.

24. The figures cited in this paragraph are contained in the briefs filed by the plaintiff in *Hobson vs. Hansen*, the case decided by Judge Wright. See our article on "The Washington School Mess," *NYR*, February 1, 1968.

Hansen's own description of Washington's track system, printed in the November 1960 *Atlantic Monthly*, is worth quoting at length.

Honors Level: ". . . To protect the quality of instruction, the honors curriculum is selective. A student is enrolled in this curriculum only if he has demonstrated ability to do superior work by his previous grades, by test scores, and by teacher judgment. . . ."

Regular College Preparatory: ". . . While the program is designed as preparatory for college, it offers excellent general background for able students not planning college careers. If I could be, or wanted to be, fully authoritarian on this point, I would require every capable pupil, college-bound or not, to choose this or the honors curriculum. The intellectual development most needed for general citizenship can best be obtained through study of the great and significant disciplines taught at a demanding and invigorating level. . . . Many capable students are underachieving, and maximum persuasion, short of authoritative controls, should be used to motivate them to move up to the more difficult but richer curriculums. . . ."

General Curriculum: ". . . cafeteria-type election of subjects with bargain-basement rummaging for good grades at reduced prices. . . ."

Basic Curriculum: ". . . This curriculum is for the academically delayed high-school student, as indicated by standardized test scores in reading and mathematics, academic grades, and teacher opinion. . . . Teacher opinion is of first importance. . . . The two objectives of the basic curriculum are to upgrade the academic achievement of retarded pupils and to provide education for those whose innate endowments, so far as they are reflected in performance, limit the range and difficulty of learning. . . ."

Small wonder passions in the black community ran rather high against the superintendent.

25. See Herbert Kohl, *36 Children* (New York, 1968), p. 178.

26. In forty schools in New York City with more than 90 percent black and Puerto Rican enrollment, for example, 46.8 percent of the teachers had three years of experience or less, whereas only a quarter of the teachers in similar schools with predominantly white enrollment were similarly inexperienced. In Washington, where the median income is under $4,000, about 46 percent of the teachers are "temporary" — that is, they cannot, for one reason or another, achieve permanent certification.

27. Howard S. Becker, "Schools and Systems of Stratification," *Education, Economy and Society, op. cit.,* p. 103. See also August Hollingshead's classic study, *Elmtown's Youth* (New York, 1949), which describes how schools give rewards to students based on their families' class position.

28. Because assignment to track reflects so closely class and racial factors, it is still not unusual to observe in theoretically "integrated" schools predominantly white "advanced" classes and predominantly (more often, all) black "slower" classes.

29. See, for example, J. W. Bennett and Melvin M. Tumin, *Social Life* (New York, 1949), p. 587. In his study, *Wealth and Power in America,* Gabriel Kolko shows that despite the New Deal and higher levels of government spending on welfare, there has been no change in basic distribution of income and wealth in the United States since 1910.

30. See, for example, Patricia Cayo Sexton, *The American School* (Englewood Cliffs, N.J., 1967), p. 51: "There is, in fact, an absence of evidence that the most able in performance of jobs or other real-life tasks are selected or produced by the standards set and training offered by higher education. Employers often hire from among the degree elite because of the prestige rather than the superior training or job-performance skill attached to a college degree."

31. See *Chronicle of Higher Education,* Dec. 9, 1968.

32. Bruce K. Ecklund, "Social Class and College Graduation: Some Misconceptions Corrected," *American Journal of Sociology,* 70 (July 1964), p. 36.

33. See, for example, John Vaizey and Michael Debeauvais, "Economic Aspects of Educational Development," *Education, Economy, and Society, op. cit.,* pp. 38–39, 43.

34. See, for example, Burton R. Clark, "The 'Cooling-Out' Function in Higher Education," *American Journal of Sociology,* LXV (May 1960): "In summary, the cooling-out process in higher education is one whereby systematic discrepancy between aspiration and avenue is covered over and stress for the individual and the system is minimized. The provision of readily available alternative achievements in itself is an important device for alleviating the stress consequent on failure and so preventing anomic and deviant behavior. The general result of cooling-out processes is that society can continue to encourage maximum effort without major disturbance from unfulfilled promises and expectations. . . .

"For an organization and its agents one dilemma of a cooling-out role is that it must be kept reasonably away from public scrutiny and not clearly perceived or understood by prospective clientele. Should it become obvious, the organization's ability to perform it would be impaired. If high-school seniors and their families were to define the junior college as a place which diverts college-bound students, a probable consequence would be a turning-away from the junior college and increased pressure for admission to the four-year colleges and universities that are otherwise protected to some degree. This would, of course, render superfluous the part now played by the junior college in the division of labor among the colleges."

35. Kingsley, Widmer, "Why Colleges Blew Up," *The Nation,* 208 (Feb. 24, 1969), p. 238.

36. Bowdoin College recently eliminated College Board scores as an entrance requirement. Richard M. Moll, the director of admissions, explained that "there is a widespread feeling and convincing evidence today that standardized aptitude and achievement tests cannot escape cultural bias and that they thereby work in favor of the more advantaged elements of our society, while handicapping others." *The Chronicle of Higher Education,* February 2, 1970, p. 1.

37. *Master Plan for Higher Education in Maryland,* Section 2, p. 19.

38. "On the Line at S. F. State," *Mayday* (now *Hard Times*), 18 (February 10–17, 1969).

39. *The American School,* p. 54.

40. *Ibid.,* p. 52.

41. Race is obviously also a factor of exclusion: even the most casual observation of campuses in Maryland bears out the same kind of racial divisions that Mrs. Sexton documents for other states. Indeed, so few blacks attend the university that it is under orders from the U.S. Office of Education to implement a plan for integration.

42. Todd Gitlin called this passage to our attention in his "On the Line at S.F. State."

43. See, for example, Leonard Buder, "On Open Admissions," *The New York Times,* July 11, 1969.

44. See "Open Admissions in City U. Opposed by Albany Chiefs," *The New York Times,* July 11, 1969.

30. WOMEN AND AMERICAN HIGHER EDUCATION

Pamela Roby

Equality of opportunity is the most frequent ideological justification given for inequality of conditions in capitalist societies. In America, the assertion that equal opportunity exists for all is generally defended on the grounds that education is open to all. When educational inequalities are recognized, it is assumed that they are being rapidly eliminated by the plethora of American demonstration projects, legislative actions, administrative guidelines, and court rulings aimed at assuring equal educational opportunity.

The history of higher education for women in the United States does not support these comfortable assumptions.[1] Rather, the available historical evidence suggests that:

1. inequality between the educational resources offered to men and women has not been significantly reduced and may have grown over the last century;

2. the relatively small number of higher-level degrees granted to women over the last hundred years, although earned through completion of the same examinations and other institutional requirements as those earned by men, have had less economic value in terms of income and other occupational benefits than degrees granted to men; furthermore, over the last two decades, as an increasing proportion of bachelor's degrees have been granted to women, the gap between the economic rewards to men and women who have completed the degree and have entered the labor force has grown;

3. the initial admittance of women to degree granting course work and the acceptance of increased numbers of women in institutions of higher education have been closely related to the economy's need for women workers with particular skills and to institutions' financial need for students; when these economic needs have declined, women have quickly been discouraged in more or less subtle ways from enrolling in and/or fulfilling degree requirements of institutions of higher education;

4. institutions of higher education which have enrolled and granted degrees to women have not and do not function in a pluralistic manner, but rather, with few exceptions, force women students and faculty members to either adopt a competitive, egocentric, entrepreneurial, and stereotypically masculine culture and its norms which mesh with needs of the larger economy, or to leave the institutions;

From *The Annals* of the American Academy of Political and Social Science, Volume 404, November 1972. Reprinted by permission.

5. the categorization and subsequent separation of women, blacks, and other minority groups and the less educated from men, elite whites, and the more educated buttresses the economy's unequal distribution of income and other rewards by providing an objective — although many would argue illogical — basis for the distribution of resources[2] and by tending to bar groups receiving fewer benefits and opportunities from communication with those receiving more, so that the less well-off are unlikely to have evidence to show or to even know that they are receiving an unequal share;[3]

6. because the inequitable educational and occupational treatment of women buttresses the economy's unequal distribution of resources in the manner described above, this inequitable treatment is unlikely to be rectified before general economic inequalities are eliminated or greatly reduced.

Given the limitations of space, support for these assertions which suggest an interrelationship between our economic and educational systems can be sketched only impressionistically. Furthermore, the assertions are confined to the U.S. economy and educational system. The educational systems of other capitalist nations vary greatly, and both the educational and economic systems of many so-called socialist nations have characteristics similar to our own. In addition, to say that education and the economy are interrelated is not to say that the nature of our educational system is unrelated to political, religious, or familial institutions. Nor do I wish to imply that women's own pressure to change educational institutions has been totally ignored, but rather that, as described below, it has been most often responded to when it has met needs of the economy or institutions of higher education. Still, some may reject the suggestion that a relationship exists between the economy and women's education as economic determinism. Such a rejection would be fairly simple at this stage in our study since, on the one hand, over the last several decades, both social scientists and educators have treated education narrowly, devoting little time to studying the interconnections between education and the economy or any other institution, and since, on the other hand, the actual relationship between economic and educational structures is most likely much subtler and more complex than simple theories of economic determinism would suggest.[4]

WOMEN'S HIGHER EDUCATION: THE LAST TWO HUNDRED YEARS

Two hundred years ago, during the Revolutionary War, Judith Murray, the daughter of a prosperous Massachusetts merchant and sea captain, wrote:

Is it upon mature consideration we adopt the idea that nature is partial in her distributions? Is it indeed a fact that she hath yielded to one half the human species so unquestionable a mental superiority? May we not trace the source [of this judgment that men are intellectually superior to women] in the difference of education and continued advantages? . . . [Is] it reasonable, that a candidate for immortality, for the joys of heaven, an intelligent being, . . . should at present be so degraded, as to be allowed no other ideas, than those which are suggested by the mechanism of a pudding, or the sewing of the seams of a garment?[5]

During colonial times and decades to follow, women, as Murray protested in the quote above, were considered intellectually inferior to men. Colleges established in the colonies prior to the Revolutionary War — Harvard (1636), William and Mary (1693), Yale (1701), Princeton (1746), Pennsylvania (1749), and Columbia (1754) — were limited to gentlemen, the sons of white Anglo-Saxon Protestant elite property holders, many of whom had been educated at Cambridge or Oxford. The colonies' college graduates often played active roles in colonial governments. Over half of Harvard's early graduates became ministers; others entered law and teaching, then a man's profession.

The sons and daughters of most colonial families did not need an institutionalized education to carry out their adult roles. Boys learned farming by helping their fathers farm. Girls learned from their mothers the skills of caring for a home; spinning; weaving; making lace, quilts, clothes, shoes, and candles; planting and tending crops; and caring for children and the sick. Daughters of the well-to-do learned from their mothers how to supervise servants and embroider, and from both parents how to read the Bible and occasionally how to write. Having, in most colonies, no right to property, no right to vote, no legal entity, women needed no formal education.[6]

Water Power, Women's Seminaries, and Normal Schools

Despite the vociferous voices of several male and female advocates of female education, seminaries for women were opened for only the well-to-do few during the fifty years following America's Declaration of Independence. Then the economy underwent a significant change. A surge in industrial production outside the home was made possible by the harnessing of water power to spin cotton. In 1814 the first power-driven loom was set up in Waltham, Massachusetts, and operated by Deborah Skinner.[7] Since most men were fully employed when the looms were invented, hundreds of women were encouraged to and did join Skinner as wage earners working fourteen-hour days in the young textile industry — in 1831, 80 percent of the workers in Massachusetts textile mills were women.

Women were also increasingly sought as teachers for the burgeoning common schools, which radical working men saw as a means to guarantee social and economic equality[8] and employers viewed as a means to achieve a disciplined, loyal labor force.[9] Hiring women was a logical way to meet the need for teachers not only because they had become accustomed to teaching their own and often neighbors' young children and because men were not available for the jobs, but because taxpayers wanted to pay the cheapest possible wages. Female teachers earned one-fourth to one-half the salary paid to men.[10] By 1850, two million school age children required two hundred thousand teachers, nearly 90 percent of whom were women.[11] Thus a pattern was begun which was to long characterize American labor force practices: women were hired to fill a new job when men were not available, and the job soon became too low-paying even for men who needed work to be able to take it.

Once thousands of women were hired as operatives and teachers, "women's place" could no longer be said to be confined solely to the home, and their need for formal education to equip them for their new duties was harder to deny. However, teaching, like factory work, was seen as a prelude to marriage rather than a life-long career for women. After marriage, the economy most needed women to perform myriad tasks within the nuclear family. Each day they "produced and groomed" the next generation of workers, a task covering most of their married lives.[12] Each evening they physically revived the nation's "productive" workers so that the following morning they could return to their jobs ready for a good day's work. As wives, they also soothed husbands' feelings brutalized by the increasingly alienated and regulated situation in which they had to labor each day — a task which, as Jessie Bernard has pointed out, supported and supports the status quo of industrial society by draining off energy and hatred which might otherwise be turned against the society as revolutionary anger.[13]

Some two-year women's seminaries were created specifically in response to the need for teachers; others, founded earlier, were begun in response to wealthy fathers' desires that their daughters reflect well on themselves and have the grace and social talents required to attract proper husbands. In both cases, the seminaries' teacher education programs reflected the belief that women would teach only a few years and then turn to their second, primary economic role of wife and mother. For example, the founders of Troy Female Seminary, established in 1825 and said by some to mark the beginning of higher education for women in the United States, viewed the "first object and mission" of the seminary as "teaching the broad sphere of women's duties and accomplishments"; training teachers was a secondary purpose.[14]

In the late 1820s and during the 1830s, state commissions in New York, Connecticut, and Massachusetts argued that the seminaries were not providing enough teachers and that a distinct institution was needed to qualify persons for this purpose. In 1839 the first state-supported normal training school was established in Lexington, Massachusetts. It was exclusively for women, but others, opened over the following decade in Massachusetts, Pennsylvania, Connecticut, Michigan, Maine, and New York, were for both sexes. Although far beneath the standards of Harvard, Yale, and other men's colleges, their course of study was rigorous, including composition; geometry; algebra; physiology; natural, intellectual, and moral philosophy; natural history; botany; political economy; bookkeeping; vocal music; and the art of teaching.[15]

The Civil War and Women's Admission to Bachelor's Degree Programs

At only ten institutions could women, like men, obtain a full four-year course leading to an A.B. degree prior to 1861 and the Civil War. In 1837, two hundred and one years after Harvard opened its doors to men, four women requested and were granted admission to Oberlin's regular college course. Hillsdale (in Michigan) and Antioch (in Ohio) admitted women when they opened in 1844 and 1853; and in 1855, four women along with eighty-five men entered the University of Iowa's collegiate department, giving that university the longest continuous record of coeducation — a few women enrolled in the University of Deseret, now the University of Utah, in 1851, but the following year its instruction was suspended for over a decade owing to lack of funds. In addition to the four coeducational institutions, six women's colleges — Oxford Female (Ohio), Illinois Conference Female, Ingham (New York), Mary Sharp (Tennessee), Elmira, and Vassar — offered women a chance to work toward bachelor's degrees.[16]

Despite political pressures and promises, other institutions of higher education refused to allow women to work toward A.B. degrees until financial pressures generated by the Civil War and declining male enrollments led them to do so during or immediately following the war. At the University of Wisconsin, for example, coeducation was debated during the fifties and a Regents' report declared:

> The entire success which has attended the common education of the sexes in the normal school and higher academies of the eastern states goes far toward settling the question [of coeducation] for the university. There is not wanting collegiate experience of some authority in the same direction . . . [and] the board deem it right to prepare to meet the wishes of those parents who desire university culture for their daughters by extending to all such the privileges of the institution. . . .[17]

But not until 1860 were women admitted to the University's normal school. By 1863, the war had so increased the attendance of women that their numbers actually exceeded those of men. In 1866, the University was reorganized so that all departments were officially open to men and women equally, a policy which the State Superintendent thoroughly approved since the "expense of carrying on the institution [would] be greatly lessened, if both sexes were generally to recite together."[18] By 1870, six other state universities — Kansas, Indiana, Minnesota, Missouri, Michigan, and California in addition to Iowa and Wisconsin — were open to women.[19]

Economy was the reason most often cited for coeducation's sudden success, according to Woody, the primary historian of women's higher education.[20] States needed to educate women so that they could teach in elementary and high schools, and the western states "were too poor to support two high grade educational institutions, one for men and one for women."[21] In New England, on the other hand, "the need for" coeducation was "not urgent because the liberality of founders and benefactors . . . provided in at least five women's colleges . . . an excellent education."[22]

In other cases, not poverty and the need for teachers, but financial donations secured coeducation for women. Women were not admitted to Cornell until Henry W. Sage gave a building and an endowment of $250 thousand for them.[23] When the University of Michigan faculty objected to the extra expense of a "two sex college," Michigan women raised $100 thousand and their younger sisters were admitted.[24] The admission of women to Johns Hopkins University Medical School in 1893 was assured by funds collected by women all over the United States, a $350 thousand gift by Mary E. Garrett and a $10 thousand gift by Marian Hovey, originally offered to Harvard to provide medical instruction for women "on equal terms with men."[25] And suffragist Susan B. Anthony is said to have nearly ruined her health raising money for the University of Rochester so that women might be admitted.[26]

Although by the early 1870s women could obtain B.A. degrees in eight state universities and approximately forty private coeducational colleges, only about eight hundred of the three thousand bachelor's degrees awarded to women in 1870 were granted by these institutions. The remainder were attained in "female institutions."[27] Debate raged in these female colleges as well as in their co-ed sister institutions during the sixties and early seventies, concerning the type of education women should receive. On one side, many feminists and professors — probably not wishing to have their own status lowered by teaching subjects unlike those taught in men's colleges — argued that women's schools should imitate men's in every particular. Others, including Durant, founder of Wellesley, believed that women's education should be as thorough as men's but not the same. He stressed "the importance of developing powers of thought and reason," but wanted "instruction in religion and health," and "regarded one hour of domestic work a day as an integral part of the educational program" — not a concession to the college's economy but an important contribution to the economy of future families and the society.[28] Smith — opened in 1875 — was the first women's college to provide a program of study almost identical with that of the prestigious male institutions.[29] Soon other women's colleges followed suit; and Bryn Mawr, opened in 1880, provided the unique feature for a women's college of a graduate school.

The Return to the Hearth:
Glamorized Domesticity

By the turn of the century women had proven they could perform academically as well as men without, as some had previously believed, being physically harmed or made infertile in the process. But no sooner had women proven their academic ability than old questions concerning whether women *should* cultivate their minds were raised with new forcefulness. The primary charge lodged against women's education was that it lowered the birth rate. Each new report that showed ever lower marriage and childbearing rates among Wellesley, Smith, and Vassar graduates renewed the panic of the white Anglo-Saxon Protestant elite who feared being overcome by the influx of Italian, Irish, and Jewish immigrants and therefore accepted as principle that well-to-do women should have as many children as possible.[30]

College-educated women also reacted against female education. Their attitudes developed out of their own plight as humans unfit for any social or economic role. Rigorous collegiate course work generally left them dissatisfied as homemakers, and unable to qualify as elementary or secondary school teachers,[31] still nearly the only profession open to women. William O'Neill has described their dilemma, "Suddenly they found themselves not merely alone, but alone in a society that had no use for them. Their liberal education did not prepare them to do anything in particular, and the stylized, carefully edited view of life it gave them bore little relation to the actual world."[32] Although many college graduates were frustrated by a sense that they should use their education in some way that society had not yet defined, most, as Adele Simmons has pointed out, were neither "ready to challenge the view that women's first goal in life was to marry and have children and that such a role excluded other possibilities," nor adventurous enough to embark on political action which was viewed as "inconsistent with the behavior expected of a college girl."[33] Even history's exceptional women were, for periods of their lives, anguished by feeling overcultured, out of place, and useless.

Jane Addams, who did not discover poverty until several years after receiving her B.A. from Rockford College (1881), recalled:

I gradually reached a conviction that the first generation of college women had taken their learning too quickly, had departed too suddenly from the active, emotional life led by their grandmothers and great-grandmothers; that the contemporary education of young women had developed too exclusively the power of acquiring knowledge and of merely receiving impressions; that somewhere in the process of "being educated" they had lost that simple and almost automatic response to the human appeal, . . . that they are so sheltered and pampered they have no chance even to make "the great refusal."[35]

While many questioned the advantages of higher education for women, faculty, administrators, and male students within coeducational institutions generally contented themselves with ridding their own hallowed halls of the second sex rather than opposing female education per se. Informally the men charged that the presence and superior scholarship of women in some subjects forced male students into unfair competition. One opponent of coeducation wrote, "Girls are better students than boys, surpassing them in the power of application and the will to learn. They read more, write more and have a wider range of ideas. . . ."[36] Others feared the feminization of campus culture. A Cornell professor is reported to have argued for separation of the sexes, saying:

It [separation of the sexes] is to be effected in a gentlemanly way, but effected it must be. The situation is due, perhaps, to the fact that the girls have a civilization and interests of their own and do not share in those of the boys. Their sports, views, and habits differ so that they have little in common. Enforced association under the circumstances is irksome. It is promised in regard to coeducation that it will "refine" the boys, but college boys want their fling and don't wish to be refined. They prefer congenial savagery.[37]

The four reasons, according to Woody, most often officially given for separating the sexes were: (1) women's rapid increase at the universities concerned; (2) their election of certain liberal arts courses to such an extent as to drive men from courses; (3) the objection of men students to the attendance of women; and (4) the need for a "peculiar education for woman that should have regard for her nature and vocation."[38] Underlying the first three of these reasons lay university officials' fear that women would drive male students away from their campuses and thereby decrease total enrollments and endowments. The fourth reason was both political and economic in nature. Many believed that women working outside the home interfered with their own personal interests; and the economy, in a period of peace, did not need large numbers of women in the labor force and could benefit from their assuming roles as homemakers and consumers. For all these reasons, in rapid succession Stanford, the University of Chicago — offered an endowment provided that women should be segregated — Wisconsin, Tufts, and Western Reserve moved women into separate classes or colleges, and Wesleyan completely closed its doors to women, not reopening them until 1970 when it found the number of applicants declining owing to boys' preference for co-ed schools![39]

Clerical Work and College Women

Whether or not student and faculty men reversed their attitudes concerning co-eds, between 1910 and 1930, the First World War and the increasing complexity of industrial production,[40] distribution, and sales promotion created a spiraling need for educated female white-collar workers; and university policies became more cordial toward women — see Table 1. Between 1910 and 1920 the percentage of women workers employed in white-collar jobs spurted 12.7 percent — from 26.1 to 38.8 percent — and the percentage of bachelor's degrees awarded to women jumped 11.5 percent — from 22.7 to 34.2 percent. During the next ten years, both the percentage of women workers employed in white-collar jobs and the portion of bachelor's degrees awarded to women increased by roughly half as much as during the 1910–20 decade — the former by 4.5 percent and the latter by 5.7 percent.

Clerical work accounted for most of the increased demand for female white-collar employees between 1910 and the Depression, and continued to do so through the sixties. Between the turn of the century and 1970, the proportion of female workers in clerical jobs increased from 4 to 34 percent. The growth in clerical jobs was vastly greater for women than that in any other occupational area. At the turn of the century, twice as many women were employed in professional jobs as in clerical jobs; but by 1970 well over twice as many women were employed in clerical as compared to professional positions — the proportion of female workers in professional and technical occupations grew slowly from 8 to 14 percent over the seventy years.

Similarly, the increase in the percentage of bachelor's degrees awarded to women was much greater over the seventy-year period than that in the percentage of doctor's degrees awarded to the "second sex" — the proportion of bachelor's degrees awarded to women rose from 19 to 43 percent, while the proportion of doctor's degrees awarded to them increased from 6 to 13 percent. Although the proportion of women workers employed in white-collar positions increased steadily over the seven decades, the percentage of bachelor's, master's, and doctor's degrees awarded to women

Table 1 Major Occupation of Employed Persons by Sex: 1900 to 1970

Major Occupation Group	1970	1960	1950	1940	1930	1920	1910	1900
			Both Sexes					
Total number[a]	78,626	66,681	58,999	51,742	48,686	42,206	37,291	29,030
Percent of total								
White-collar workers	48.3%	43.1%	36.6%	31.1%	29.4%	24.9%	21.3%	17.6%
Professional and technical workers	14.2	11.2	8.6	7.5	6.8	5.4	4.7	4.2
Managers, officials, and proprietors	10.5	10.6	8.7	7.3	7.4	6.6	6.6	5.8
Clerical workers	17.4	14.7	12.3	9.6	8.9	8.0	5.3	3.0
Salesworkers	6.2	6.6	6.9	6.7	6.3	4.9	4.7	4.5
Blue-collar workers	35.3	36.3	41.1	39.8	39.6	40.2	38.2	35.8
Craftsmen and foremen	12.9	12.8	14.1	12.0	12.8	13.0	11.6	10.5
Operatives	17.7	18.0	20.4	18.4	15.8	15.6	14.6	12.8
Nonfarm laborers	4.7	5.5	6.6	9.4	10.9	11.6	12.0	12.5
Service workers	12.4	12.5	10.5	11.7	9.8	7.8	9.5	9.0
Farmworkers	4.0	8.1	11.8	17.4	21.2	27.0	30.9	37.5

Female

Total number[a]	29,667	22,196	16,445	12,574	10,752	8,637	7,445	5,319
Percent of total								
White-collar workers	60.5%	54.6%	52.4%	44.9%	44.2%	38.8%	26.1%	17.8%
Professional and tech- nical workers	14.5	12.2	12.2	12.8	13.8	11.7	9.8	8.2
Managers, officials, and proprietors	4.5	5.0	4.3	3.3	2.7	2.2	2.0	1.5
Clerical workers	34.5	30.0	27.8	21.5	20.9	18.7	9.2	4.0
Salesworkers	7.0	7.6	8.6	7.4	6.8	6.3	5.1	4.3
Blue-collar workers	16.1	16.4	22.4	21.6	19.8	23.7	25.7	27.7
Craftsmen and foremen	1.1	1.0	1.5	1.1	1.0	1.2	1.4	1.4
Operatives	14.5	15.0	20.0	19.5	17.4	20.2	22.9	23.8
Nonfarm laborers	0.5	0.4	0.9	1.1	1.5	2.3	1.4	2.6
Service workers	21.7	24.7	21.5	29.4	27.5	23.9	32.4	35.5
Farmworkers	1.8	4.5	3.7	4.0	8.4	13.5	15.8	19.0

SOURCE: U.S. Bureau of the Census, *Historical Statistics of the United States, Colonial Times to 1957* (Washington, D.C.: U.S. Government Printing Office, 1960), p. 74; U.S. Bureau of the Census, *Statistical Abstract of the United States: 1971* (Washington, D.C.: U.S. GPO, 1972), p. 222.
[a] In thousands.

rose sporadically with great leaps and precipitous declines. . . . Seemingly, educational institutions' policies toward women reflected not only labor force needs for women, but institutional ones as well.

During the Depression and again during the Second World War, institutions of higher education experienced declining enrollments. At these times many men's colleges, which had long had local women who could not afford to leave home to attend college knocking on their doors, became coeducational; and coeducational institutions began to admit women to, and encourage them to take, previously male courses of study.[41] By the fall of 1942, in response to World War II, Rensselaer Polytechnic Institute admitted women, upsetting a 116-year tradition; Pennsylvania State College included "women for the first time among prospective war-industry workers" in the Department of Industrial Engineering; and New York University reported a "larger percentage of women among the undergraduate and graduate enrollees" than had before been the case and that they were "being trained to replace men in virtually all clerical, professional and technical fields."[42] The University of Wisconsin also admitted greater numbers of women than ever before in its history; and, as during the Civil War but never in peace time, more women than men were enrolled in the University's undergraduate schools and colleges.[43]

The Reaction Against Women's Higher Education

With the war's end and soldiers' return, journalists, economists, and educators, fearing a glutted labor market, admonished women to leave their wartime jobs, and glamorized domesticity and full-time motherhood as they never had before. By the 1950s, the age at which women married had dropped, and dreams of careers were replaced by dreams of babies. Husbands' new roles as managers, salesmen, and lawyers required much entertaining and seemingly a full-time "helpmate." Women's magazines, which during war years had dwelt heavily on means by which women might most quickly and efficiently prepare meals and care for their homes as well as on the advantages of child care centers, now encouraged women to become gourmet cooks, responsive to all the needs of their children, and expert consumers. The latter role, of course, helped prevent a much-feared postwar economic recession, as well as tied husbands ever tighter to what were often restrictive, repressive, exploitative jobs.

The percentage of university acceptances and bachelor's, master's, and doctor's degrees going to women, which had peaked during the war, plunged to levels well below those in 1930. Women students declined from 50 to 30 percent of the resident college enrollment between 1944 and 1950.[44] Educators who still had women in their classes were told that they

must help women understand that the homemaker's maternal role calls for knowledge and expertness as does any other occupational role. . . . Besides preparing women for this role, educators should attempt to elevate this role to the same esteem, if not glamor, that any male occupational role enjoys.[45]

With women marrying and becoming absorbed in child rearing at decidedly younger ages, employers happily faced in the fifties with economic expansion, had to seek older women whose children were grown to fill their need for clerical workers, teachers, and other traditionally female jobs. In 1955, for the first time on record, women aged forty-five to sixty-four had a higher labor force participation rate than those twenty-five to forty-four years of age. . . .

Economic Expansion: Women Urged Back to School and Work

The expansion continued into the sixties. Schools and colleges were flooded with baby-boom children. Clerical and sales jobs were also expanding. Then the War on Poverty, launched in 1964, created more — traditionally low-paying — jobs fitting women's skills; recreation leaders, social workers, nurses, teachers, and clerical workers were in short supply. With the Vietnam buildup, the official overall unemployment rate dropped below 4 percent in 1966 and remained there until 1970 — by 1971 the overall unemployment rate was up to 5.9 percent.[46] Higher percentages of women of every age joined the labor force than ever before in history — female labor force participation rates rose well above those of other war years; by 1970, exactly 50 percent of women aged nineteen to sixty-four were employed.

Warren Weaver, Vice President of the Alfred P. Sloan Foundation in 1960 urged, ". . . as the pressure for able personnel increases, we simply must create new and appropriate opportunities for women."[47] The percentage of bachelor's, master's, and doctor's degrees awarded to women began to increase, although the percentage of B.A. and M.A. degrees granted to women never climbed near to that of 1944; and the percentage of doctorates awarded to women, like the percentage of college and university faculty comprised by women, did not come near to the level of the 1920s and 1930s. . . . In recognition of the need to train or retrain women past their child-rearing years, special programs for continuing education for women were also founded.[48]

Women's increasing educational attainment did not lead, as one might expect, to decreased inequality between the incomes of women and men. In fact, quite the reverse occurred. The gap between the wages paid to full-time female and male workers increased.[49] This trend was not reversed, as one might again expect, when education was taken into account. The median income of female college graduates was 53 percent of that of men in 1950, 45 percent in 1960, and 44 percent in 1970 — see Table 2.

Alice Rossi has maintained that it was the increased employment of post-childrearing aged women and the discrimination that they experienced in the labor force that

provided the momentum leading to the establishment of the Kennedy Commission on the Status of Women and the formation of new women's rights organizations in the mid-1960s. So long as women worked mostly before marriage or after marriage only until a first pregnancy, . . . there were but feeble grounds for a significant movement among women, since their motivation for working was short-lived. Only among women who are relatively permanent members of the work force could daily experience force an awareness of economic inequities based on sex and a determination to do something about them.[50]

Rossi predicted that this fortunate circumstance would change:

. . . In the 1970's there will be a reversal in the demographic pattern. The birth rate is now on the decline, the age at marriage creeping upward, and the time interval between marriage and childbearing widening. In the 1970's there will be more young unmarried and childless married women seeking jobs, for they will be the baby-boom females grown to maturity. At the same time, graduate schools will be producing large numbers of young people with advanced degrees, who will face a very different job market from the one that young Ph.D.'s faced during the past twenty years.[51]

The impact of the demographic pattern described by Rossi was already felt in 1970, and then it was coupled with a shrinking economy and the government's slowing down the expansion of jobs in the public sector. On the front page of the *Wall Street Journal,* journalist Richard Martin bemoaned women's seeking jobs at a time of high unemployment:

The "liberation" of more and more women into the work force is giving the nation's rising unemployment rate an unwelcome boost.

With the economy slowing down and production declining, the number of available jobs has been shrinking steadily since the end of last year. But in the same period the size of the labor force has ballooned unexpectedly, and some economists blame the abnormal growth largely on a big jump in the proportion of women entering the work force. . . . The trend has been building for a long time, but the current influx of women couldn't be hitting the job market at a worse time, as far as many economists are concerned.[52]

Martin did concede that two overriding economic factors were responsible for the surge of females into the job market:

The rising cost of living is forcing more wives to work just to help maintain the family's standard of living. And the rising unemployment rate is forcing

Table 2 Income by Educational Attainment and Sex for Wage Earners Twenty-five Years Old and Over, United States, 1950, 1960, 1970

| | Median Income | | | | | | | | |
| | 1950 | | | 1960 | | | 1970 | | |
	Men	Women	Women as % of Men	Men	Women	Women as % of Men	Men	Women	Women as % of Men
Years of school completed									
High school, 4	$3,285	$1,584	48.2%	$5,441	$2,184	40.1%	$8,772	$3,400	38.7%
College, 1–3	3,522	1,660	47.1	5,978	2,408	40.3	9,879	3,722	37.7
College, 4	4,407	2,321	52.7	7,388	3,322	45.0	12,144	5,362	44.1
College, 5 or more				7,971	4,664	58.5	13,426	7,889	58.7
Total of all wage earners	2,699	1,089	40.3	4,618	1,535	33.2	7,891	2,595	32.9
	Median Education (Years of Schooling)								
All wage earners	9.0	9.6		10.4	10.8		12.2	12.2	

SOURCE: U.S. Bureau of the Census, *U.S. Census of Population, 1950*, vol. 4, Special Report, pt. 5, chap. B, "Education" (Washington, D.C.: U.S. GPO, 1953), Table 12, pp. 108, 112, Table 13, p. 128; U.S. Bureau of the Census, *U.S. Census of Population: 1960, Subject Reports*, "Educational Attainment," Final Report PC(2)–5B (Washington, D.C.: U.S. GPO, 1963), Table 6, p. 88, Table 7, p. 112; U.S. Bureau of the Census, *Current Population Reports*, Series P–60, no. 80, "Income in 1970 of Families and Persons in the United States" (Washington, D.C.: U.S. GPO, 1971), Table 49, pp. 102, 106. Statistics are available only for 1970 on income by educational attainment and sex for year-round full-time workers. In 1970, the mean income of year-round full-time female workers with five or more years of college was 55.3 percent of the income of the same category of male workers. The overall median income of full-time year-round female workers decreased from 63.9 percent of men's in 1955 to 60.8 percent in 1960 and 59.4 percent in 1970. Women's Bureau, U.S. Department of Labor, "Fact Sheet on the Earnings Gap," Washington, D.C., 1971, p. 1.

more of them to find jobs because their husbands are either already out of work or likely to be laid off if the economy slows further.[53]

In 1971, the overall unemployment rate among women rose to 6.9 percent, and a U.S. Office of Management and Budget report estimated that there were 2.4 million women who wanted jobs but were not actively seeking work.[54] Bertram Gross estimated that actually as many as 7.5 million women were eager and able to work full- or part-time, but were unable to find a job.[55] Not only higher unemployment, but recommendations to cut spending in institutions of higher education were triggered by the economy's doldrums. In spring 1972, the Carnegie Commission on Higher Education, headed by Clark Kerr, urged colleges and universities to reduce their current spending rate by 20 percent or about $10 billion a year.[56]

It is too early to know exactly what statistical effect this latest economic recession has had on the enrollment of women students and their completion of higher education. Although the recession comes at a time when women's organizations are pressing hard for greater educational opportunities for women, if past trends in the relationship between the economy and education have any predictive value, the growth or decline of inequalities between higher educational opportunities available to women and men will very much depend upon which has greater influence on educational policies: the need of institutions of higher education, faced with declining applications, for more students; or the labor force's slackening need for women, including many categories of professional women. . . .

REFERENCES

1. Elsewhere I have questioned whether education is an effective means of redistributing resources in the United States and have examined structural and internalized barriers to women in higher education. Compare S. M. Miller and Pamela Roby, "Education and Redistribution: The Limits of a Strategy," *Integrated Education* 6, no. 5 (September 1968); S. M. Miller and Pamela Roby, *The Future of Inequality* (New York: Basic Books, 1970); Pamela Roby, "Women in Higher Education: Structural and Internalized Obstacles," in Constantina Safilios-Rothschild, ed., *Toward a Sociology of Women* (Lexington, Mass.: Ginn-Blaisdell, 1972); and Pamela Roby, "Institutional Barriers to Women Students in Higher Education," in Alice Rossi and Anne Calderwood, eds., *Academic Women on the Move* (New York: Russell Sage Foundation, forthcoming). Also see Bowles's and Greer's analyses of how American public education has failed to reduce inequality and to promote immigrants in American society. Samuel Bowles, "Unequal Education and the Reproduction of the Hierarchical Division of Labor," in Richard C. Edwards, Michael Reich, and Thomas E. Weisskopf, eds., *The Capitalist System* (Englewood Cliffs, N.J.:

Prentice-Hall, 1972); Colin Greer, *The Great School Legend: A Revisionist Interpretation of American Public Education* (New York: Basic Books, 1972).

2. Compare Pamela Roby, "Inequality: A Trend Analysis," THE ANNALS 385 (September 1969), pp. 110–17.

3. Compare John Kenneth Galbraith, Edwin Kuh, and Lester C. Thurow, "The Galbraith Plan to Promote Minorities," *New York Times Magazine,* August 22, 1971.

4. The interconnections between the economy and the government have been shown by Kolko and others to be both very real and very complex. The relationship between the economy and education one would assume is no less complex. Gabriel Kolko, *Triumph of Conservatism* (Chicago: Quadrangle Books, 1963). Compare Martin J. Sklar, "Woodrow Wilson and the Political Economy of Modern United States Liberalism," in James Weinstein and David W. Eakins, eds., *For a New America: Essays in History and Politics* (New York: Random House, 1970); Frances Fox Piven and Richard Cloward, *Regulating the Poor: The Functions of Public Welfare* (New York: Random House, 1971); Anthony M. Platt, *The Child Savers, The Invention of Delinquency* (Chicago: University of Chicago Press, 1969).

5. Judith Murray's essay was not published until 1790, and then under her pen name, Constantia. Constantia, "The Equality of the Sexes," *Massachusetts Magazine* (March 1790), pp. 132–33, quoted in Eleanor Flexner, *Century of Struggle* (Cambridge, Mass.: Harvard University Press, 1959), p. 16.

6. Compare Leo Kanowitz, *Women and the Law: The Unfinished Revolution* (Albuquerque: University of New Mexico Press, 1969), pp. 40–41.

7. Flexner, *Century of Struggle*, p. 17.

8. Compare Murray Milner, Jr., *The Illusion of Equality: The Effect of Education on Opportunity, Inequality and Social Conflict* (San Francisco: Jossey-Bass, 1972), p. 25; and R. Welter, *Popular Education and Democratic Thought in America* (New York: Columbia University Press, 1962).

9. For example, in 1841, H. Bartlett, a Lowell manufacturer who supervised four hundred to nine hundred persons yearly, wrote, "I have never considered mere knowledge . . . as the only advantage derived from a good Common School education . . . in times of agitation, on account of some change in regulations or wages, I have always looked to the most intelligent, best educated and most moral for support. . . . [They are] more orderly and respectful in their deportment, and more ready to comply with the wholesome and necessary regulations of the establishment." H. Bartlett quoted in Michael B. Katz, *The Irony of Early School Reform: Educational Innovation in Mid-Nineteenth Century Massachusetts* (Boston: Beacon Press, 1970), p. 88.

10. Compare Thomas Woody, *A History of Women's Education in the United States* (1966; reprint ed., New York: Octagon Books, 1929), vol, 1, pp. 460–70, 483–505.

11. Ibid., p. 236.

12. Joan Mandle, "Women's Liberation: Humanizing Rather than Polarizing," THE ANNALS 397 (September 1971), p. 125. Compare Elizabeth F. Baker, *Technology and Woman's Work* (New York: Columbia University Press, 1964); Edith Abbott, *Women in Industry: A Study in American Economic History* (1910; reprint ed., New York: Arno, 1969); and Marilyn Power Gold-

berg, "The Economic Exploitation of Women," in Richard Edwards, Michael Reich, and Thomas Weisskopf, eds., *The Capitalist System* (Englewood Cliffs, N.J.: Prentice-Hall, 1972).

13. Jessie Bernard, *Women and the Public Interest* (New York: Aldine, 1971), p. 89.

14. Woody, *History of Women's Education*, vol. 1, pp. 344–46; vol. 2, pp. 192–93.

15. Woody, *History of Women's Education*, vol. 1, pp. 473–80.

16. Mabel Newcomer, *A Century of Higher Education for American Women* (New York: Harper and Brothers Publishers, 1959), pp. 10–12; Woody, *History of Women's Education*, vol. 2, pp. 137–382.

17. Woody, *History of Women's Education*, vol. 2, p. 239.

18. Ibid., p. 242.

19. Newcomer, *Century of Higher Education*, p. 14.

20. Woody, *History of Women's Education*, vol. 2, pp. 256–59.

21. Charles T. Van Hise, "Educational Tendencies in State Universities," *Educational Review* 34 (December 1907), p. 509.

22. James Bryce, *The American Commonwealth* (London: Macmillan and Company, 1889), vol. 2, p. 605.

23. Woody, *History of Women's Education*, vol. 2, p. 248.

24. Ibid., p. 259.

25. Ibid., p. 358.

26. Ibid., p. 259.

27. Newcomer, *Century of Higher Education*, p. 19.

28. Ibid., p. 56.

29. Woody, *History of Women's Education*, vol. 2, p. 182.

30. One report showed that from twenty-seven to thirty-six years after graduation, only slightly more than 55 percent of Vassar's early alumnae were married, and among this group the average number of children born was slightly more than two per married member. Of the next ten Vassar classes (1877–86), less than 51 percent were married from seventeen to twenty-six years after graduation; and the average number of children per married alumna was down to 1.5. Willystine Goodsell, *The Education of Women* (New York: Macmillan Company, 1923), p. 36. Compare Robert J. Sprague, "Education and Race Suicide," *Journal of Heredity* 6 (April 1915), p. 180.

31. Newcomer, *Century of Higher Education*, p. 89.

32. William O'Neill, *Everyone Was Brave* (Chicago: Quadrangle, 1969), p. 79.

33. Adele Simmons, "Education for What? The Response of Educational Structures to the Changing Roles of Women" (Paper presented at the Eastern Sociological Society Meeting, Boston, Mass., April 22, 1971) (Princeton University, Department of History, stencil), pp. 14–15.

34. Christopher Lasch, *The Social Thought of Jane Addams* (Indianapolis: The Bobbs-Merrill Company, 1965), p. 1.

35. Jane Addams, *Twenty Years At Hull House: With Autobiographical Notes* (New York: The Macmillan Company, 1910), pp. 71, 73.

36. Quoted in Woody, *History of Women's Education*, vol. 2, p. 282.

37. Quoted by Woody, *History of Women's Education*, vol. 2, p. 248, from *The School Journal*, vol. 74, p. 550.

38. Woody, *History of Women's Education*, vol. 2, p. 282.

39. Woody, *History of Women's Education*, vol. 2, pp. 272–95; 304–20; Simmons, "Education for What?" pp. 12–13.

40. Compare Irving Bernstein, *The Lean Years: The History of the American Worker 1920–1933* (Baltimore: Penguin Books, 1960), pp. 55–56.

41. Newcomer, *Century of Higher Education*, p. 38.

42. Editor, "Adjustments in Educational Programs for the Training of Women," *School and Society*, October 10, 1942, pp. 320–21; compare Ruth Strang, "Women's Education and Defense," *Educational Forum* 5 (May 1941).

43. E. B. Fred, "Women and Higher Education: With Special Reference to the University of Wisconsin," *The Journal of Experimental Education* 31, no. 2 (December 1962), p. 162.

44. W. W. Ludeman, "Declining Female College Attendance: Causes and Implications," *Educational Forum* 25 (May 1961), p. 505.

45. Aaron Lipman, "Educational Preparation for the Female Role," *Journal of Educational Sociology* 32 (September 1958), p. 43.

46. Generally a higher percentage of women than men have been looking for work. When the overall unemployment rate dropped to beneath 4 percent, the female unemployment rate fell to just under 5 percent; by 1971 the female rate was up to 6.9 percent, as compared with the 5.9 percent overall rate of unemployment. U.S. Department of Labor, *Employment and Earnings — July 1972* (Washington, D.C.: U.S. GPO, 1972), pp. 21–22.

47. Warren Weaver, "A Great Age for Science," *The American Assembly* (New York: Columbia University Press, 1960), p. 116, quoted in Fred, "Women and Higher Education," p. 160.

48. These included the Radcliffe Institute for Independent Study; the University of Minnesota Plan for the Continuing Education of Women; the Ford Foundation Program for the Re-Training in Mathematics of College Graduate Women, Rutgers University; the Sarah Lawrence Center for Continuing Education for Women; the Michigan State University Program for Women; the Barnard College Plan for Special Students; and the American Association of University Women Graduate Program of Continuing Education for Women. Fred, "Women and Higher Education," p. 160.

49. U.S. Bureau of the Census, *Current Population Reports*, P.–60 Series, annual issues.

50. Alice Rossi, "Women — Terms of Liberation," *Dissent* 17, no. 6 (November 1970), p. 534.

51. Ibid., p. 536.

52. Richard Martin, "Leaving the Home: More Women Seek Jobs, Contributing to Boost in Unemployment Rate," *Wall Street Journal*, June 29, 1970, p. 1.

53. Ibid.

54. Carol Mathews, "The Unemployed Women," *New York Post*, Financial Section, April 4, 1972, p. 67.

55. Bertram Gross quoted by Mathews, ibid.

56. Carnegie Commission on Higher Education, *The More Effective Use of Resources: An Imperative for Higher Education* (13th Interim Report) (New York: The Carnegie Commission, 1972) quoted in the *New York Times*, June 16, 1972, p. 17.

HEALTH CARE IX

One of the most dramatic and devastating inequalities in American society is the social stratification of health and illness — the absence of decent medical care for many (if not most) people, and the subjection of many groups — including minorities, women, and blue-collar workers — to living and working conditions that systematically undermine and destroy their health.

Similar inequalities in medical care exist in many societies, but the health record of the United States is more unequal than that of any other developed country. In fact, as a National Advisory Commission on Health Manpower put it in 1967, the health statistics of certain groups — the rural poor, urban ghetto-dwellers, migrant workers, and others — "occasionally resemble the health statistics of a developing country."[1] Moreover, the quality of health care available to the middle classes is erratic and in some ways diminishing. Behind all of this is the continuing American refusal to alter what remains essentially a market system of medical care.

One consequence of this is the lack of any systematic provision for public medical care in the United States. A few countries, among them England, the USSR, and New Zealand, have national health programs through which medical care is provided for all citizens as a matter of right. Several other countries have extensive programs of national health "insurance" covering everyone, or almost everyone: among them, Japan, Sweden, Norway, Australia, and Denmark. In one way or another, every highly industrialized nation in Western Europe (and many others) has a broad program of national medical care for the majority of the population. The effective-

ness of such programs in reducing disparities in health care
varies, of course, and should not be exaggerated. But in the
United States there is *no* national health program for the
population as a whole. Our only national health insurance is
that for the aged and pensioners. Special classes of persons are
eligible for governmental health care, including servicemen,
veterans, Indians, and a few others.

The inequity of American health care has several sources:
industries more concerned with profit than with the well-
being of workers; professional groups jealously guarding their
control over the distribution of medical services; and deeply
rooted ideologies stressing the beneficial role of competition
and private enterprise even in the area of human health. The
nature and dimensions of the crisis in health care are surveyed
in Barbara and John Ehrenreich's selection, "The American
Health Empire." Medical care in the United States is expensive, fragmented, and clothed in frightening mystification. Its
practicioners are increasingly unaccountable to the people
they serve, and they and the institutions they work in are rid-
den with racist and sexist conceptions of their clients and the
uses of medicine. Contrary to those who believe that the
medical crisis results from the fact that our health care system
is an unorganized "nonsystem," the Ehrenreichs argue that
medical care in the United States is in fact a very organized
enterprise — but organized toward generating profit rather
than toward providing decent health care.

The following selections illustrate this point more specifically. In "Getting Cancer on the Job," Larry Agran shows
how the growing epidemic of cancer among blue-collar
workers is fed by the systematic unconcern of American industries, which have been known to cover up evidence of unsafe
levels of cancer-causing chemicals produced by their own staff
physicians. Government response to the growth of industrial
cancer has been minimal at best; the regulatory agencies are
either too timid to take on the industries or are so understaffed
and poorly funded that they can barely make a dent on the
massive problem of industrial health.

The most extreme example of the domination of American
health care by the market mentality can be seen in the buying
and selling of human blood. In "The Gift of Blood," Richard
Titmuss shows how the treatment of blood as a marketable
commodity has made the crucial process of giving and receiving blood a dangerous and precarious business. Ultimately, the
question raised in Titmuss' chilling analysis is that of the

value placed on human life itself in a society dominated by commercial values.

REFERENCES

1. Report of the National Advisory Commission on Health Manpower, quoted in R. M. Titmuss, "Ethics and Economics of Medical Care," in *Commitment to Welfare* (New York: Pantheon, 1968), p. 268.

31. THE AMERICAN HEALTH EMPIRE: THE SYSTEM BEHIND THE CHAOS
Barbara and John Ehrenreich

The American health crisis became official in 1969. President Nixon announced it in a special message in July. Liberal academic observers of the health scene, from Harvard's John Knowles to Einstein College of Medicine's Martin Cherkasky, hastened to verify the existence of the crisis. Now the media is rushing in with details and documentation. *Time, Fortune, Business Week*, CBS, and NBC are on the medical scene, and finding it "chaotic," "archaic," and "unmanageable."

For the great majority of Americans, the "health care crisis" is not a TV show or a presidential address; it is an on-going crisis of survival. Every day three million Americans go out in search of medical care. Some find it; others do not. Some are helped by it; others are not. Another twenty million Americans probably ought to enter the daily search for medical help, but are not healthy enough, rich enough, or enterprising enough to try. The obstacles are enormous. Health care is scarce and expensive to begin with. It is dangerously fragmented, and usually offered in an atmosphere of mystery and unaccountability. For many, it is obtained only at the price of humiliation, dependence, or bodily insult. The stakes are high — health, life, beauty, sanity — and getting higher all the time. But the odds of winning are low and getting lower.

For the person in search of medical help, the illness or possibility of illness which prompted the search is quickly overshadowed by the difficulties of the medical experience itself:

From *The American Health Empire: Power, Profits and Politics* by Barbara and John Ehrenreich. Copyright © 1970 by Health Policy Advisory Center, Inc. Reprinted by permission of Random House, Inc.

PROBLEM ONE: FINDING A PLACE WHERE THE
APPROPRIATE CARE IS OFFERED AT A REASONABLE PRICE

For the poor and for many working-class people, this can be all but impossible. Not long ago it was commonly believed that sheer distance from
doctors or hospitals was a problem only in rural areas. But today's resident of slums, like Brooklyn's Bedford-Stuyvesant, or Chicago's south side,
is as effectively removed from health services as his relatives who stayed
behind in Mississippi. One region of Bedford-Stuyvesant contains only
one practicing physician for a population of one hundred thousand.
Milwaukee County Hospital, the sole source of medical care for tens of
thousands of poor and working-class people, is sixteen miles outside the
city, an hour and a half bus ride for many. A few years ago, a social
science graduate student was able to carry out her thesis work on rural
health problems in a densely populated Chicago slum.

After getting to the building or office where medical care is offered,
the next problem which affects both poor and middle-class people is paying for the care. Except at a diminishing number of charitable facilities,
health care is not free; it is a commodity which consumers purchase from
providers at unregulated, steadily increasing prices. Insurance plans like
Medicaid, Medicare, and Blue Cross help soften the blow for many, but
many other people are too rich for Medicaid, too poor for Blue Cross,
and too young for Medicare. A total of twenty-four million Americans
have no health insurance of any variety. Even for those who are insured,
costs remain a major problem: first there is the cost of the insurance itself, then there is the cost of all those services which are not covered by
insurance. 102 million Americans have no insurance coverage for visits to
the doctor, as opposed to hospital stays. They spend about ten dollars just
to see a doctor; more, if laboratory tests or specialists are needed. Otherwise, they wait for an illness to become serious enough to warrant hospitalization. Hardly anyone, of course, has insurance for such everyday
needs as dental care or prenatal care.

Supposing that one can afford the cost of the care itself, there remains
the problem of paying for the time spent getting it. Working people must
plan on losing a full work-day for a simple doctor's appointment, whether
with a private physician or at a hospital clinic. First, there is a long wait
to see the doctor. Middle-class people may enjoy comfortable chairs,
magazines, and even coffee, while waiting in their doctor's anteroom, but
they wait just the same. As busy private doctors try to squeeze more and
more customers into their day, their patients are finding that upwards of
an hour's wait is part of the price for a five- or ten-minute face-to-face
encounter with a harried physician.

Not all kinds of care are as available, or unavailable, as others. In a city studded with major hospitals the person with multiple bullet wounds or a rare and fatal blood disease stands a far better chance of making a successful medical "connection," than the person with stomach pains, or the parents of a feverish child. Hospitals, at all times, and physicians, after 7:00 P.M. (if they can be located) are geared to handling the dramatic and exotic cases which excite professional interest. The more mundane, or less obviously catastrophic, case can wait — and wait. For psychiatric problems, which are probably the nation's single greatest source of disability, there are almost no outpatient facilities, much less sympathetic attention when one finds them. Those of the mentally ill who venture forth in search of help are usually rewarded with imprisonment in a state institution, except for the few who are able to make the investment required for private psychiatric care. Even for the wealthy, borderline problems, like alcoholism and addiction, may as well be lived with — there are vanishingly few facilities of any kind to deal with them.

PROBLEM TWO: FINDING ONE'S WAY AMIDST THE MANY AVAILABLE TYPES OF MEDICAL CARE

Most of us know what buildings or other locations are possible sources of medical help. Many of us can even arrange to get to these buildings in a reasonable amount of time. But, having arrived at the right spot, the patient finds that his safari has just begun. He must now chop through the tangled morass of medical specialization. The only system to American health services, the patient discovers, is the system used in preparing the tables of contents of medical textbooks. Everything is arranged according to the various specialties and subspecialties doctors study, not according to the symptoms and problems which patients perceive.

The middle-class patient is relatively lucky. He has a private doctor who can serve as a kind of guide. After an initial examination, which may cost as little as five dollars or as much as fifty dollars, the patient's personal doctor sends him to visit a long list of his specialist colleagues — a hematologist, allergist, cardiologist, endocrinologist, and maybe a urologist. Each of these examines his organ of interest, collects twenty dollars and up, and passes the patient along to the next specialist in line. If the patient is lucky, his illness will be claimed by one of the specialists fairly early in the process. If he is not so lucky, none of them will claim it, or — worse yet — several of them will. Only the very wealthy patient can afford the expense of visiting and retaining two medical specialists.

The hospital clinic patient wanders about in the same jungle, but without a guide. The hospital may screen him for his ills and point him in the right direction, but, from then on, he's on his own. There's nobody to take overall responsibility for his illness. He can only hope that at some point in time and space, one of the many specialty clinics to which he has been sent (each at the cost of a day off from work) will coincide with his disease of the moment.

Just as exasperating as the fragmentation of medical care is the fragmentation of medical care financing. Seymour Thaler, a New York state senator from Queens, likes to tell the story of one of his constituents who came to Thaler's office, pulled out his wallet, and emptied out a stack of cards. "Here's my Medicaid card, my Medicare card, my Blue Cross supplementary card, my workmen's compensation card, and my union retirement health plan card." "So what are you complaining about?" Thaler asked. "I've got a stomach ache," the old man answered, "so what do I do?"

A family makes matters even more complicated and confusing. Grandparents have Medicare, children have Medicaid, the parents may have one or several union hospitalization insurance plans. No one is covered for everything, and no mother is sure just who is covered for what. If three members of the family came down with the same illness, they would more than likely end up seeing three different doctors, paying for it in three (or more) different ways, and staying in separate hospitals. In 1968, a New York father of six quit his job and applied for welfare, claiming he couldn't work and see to his children's health care. One child, diagnosed as retarded, had to be taken to and from a special school each day. All required dental care, which was free at a Health Department clinic on Manhattan's lower east side. For dental surgery, however, they went to a clinic a bus ride away, at Bellevue. The youngest children went to a neighborhood pediatrician who accepted Medicaid patients. An older child, with a rare metabolic defect, required weekly visits to a private hospital clinic a half hour's trip uptown. The father himself, the victim of a chronic back problem, qualified for care at a union health center on the west side. For him, family health maintenance was a full-time job, not, as it is for most parents, just a busy sideline.

Doctors like to tell us that fragmentation is the price of quality. We should be happy to be seeing a specialist, twice as happy to be seeing two of them, and fully gratified to have everyone in the family seeing a special one of his own. In many difficult cases, specialization does pay off. But evidence is accumulating that care which is targeted at a particular organ often completely misses the mark. Take the case of the Cleveland woman who had both a neurological disease and a damaged kidney. Since the neurologist had no time to chat, and since she assumed that doctors know a good deal more than their patients, she never mentioned her kidney to her neurologist. Over a period of time, her urologist noted a steady deterioration of her kidney problem. Only after the kidney had been removed did the urologist discover that his colleague, the neurologist, had been prescribing a drug which is known to put an extra strain on the kidney.

The patient may have only one problem — as far as his doctors are concerned — and still succumb to medical fragmentation. Recently, an elderly man with a heart condition was discharged from a prestigious private medical center, assured he was good for another decade or two. Four weeks later he died of heart failure. Cause? Overexertion. He lived on the fifth floor of a walk-up apartment — a detail which was obviously out of the purview of his team of hospital physicians, for all the time and technology they had brought to bear on his heart. Until human physiology adapts itself to the fragmentation of modern medical practice, it is up to the patient himself to integrate his medical problems, and to integrate them with the rest of his life.

PROBLEM THREE: FIGURING OUT WHAT THEY ARE DOING TO YOU

Many people are not satisfied to have found the correct doctor or clinic. They also want to know what is being done to their bodies, and why. For most, this is not just idle curiosity. If the patient has to pay all or some of the bill, he wants to know whether a cheaper treatment would be just as efficacious, or whether he should really be paying for something much fancier. The doctors' magazine *Medical Economics* tells the story of the family whose infant developed bronchopneumonia. The physician who visited the home judged from the furnishings that the family could not afford hospitalization. With little or no explanation, he prescribed an antibiotic and left. The baby died six hours later. The parents were enraged when they learned the diagnosis and realized that hospitalization might have helped. They wanted to know the risks, and make the decision themselves.

More commonly, the patients fear they will be overtreated, hence overbilled, for a medical problem. A twenty-five-year-old graduate student, a victim of hayfever, was told by an allergist at prestigious New York Hospital that his case would require several years of multiple, weekly, antiallergy injections. When he asked to know the probability that this treatment would actually cure his hayfever, the allergist told him, "I'm the doctor, not you, and if you don't want to trust my judgment you can find another doctor — or be sick forever for all I care!" Following this advice, the patient did, indeed, find a new doctor. And when the limitations of the treatment were explained to him, he decided the treatment was probably worth the trouble after all. The important thing is that *he* decided.

Some people, perhaps more trusting of doctors, never ask for an explanation until they have to in sheer self-defense. Residents of Manhattan's lower east side tell the story of the woman who was admitted to a ward at Bellevue for a stomach operation. The operation was scheduled for Thursday. On Wednesday a nurse told her she was to be operated on that day. The patient asked why the change. "Never mind," said the nurse, "give me your glasses." The patient could not see why she should give up her glasses, but finally handed them over at the nurse's insistence. Inside the operating room, the patient was surprised when she was not given general anesthesia. Although her English was poor, she noticed that the doctors were talking about eye cancer, and looking at her eyes. She sat up and said there was nothing wrong with her eyes — her stomach was the problem. She was pushed back on the operating table. With the strength of panic, she leapt up and ran into the hall. A security guard caught her, running sobbing down the hall in an operating gown. She was summarily placed in the psychiatric ward for a week's observation.

Even when confronted with what seems to be irrational therapy, most patients feel helpless to question or complain. A new folklore of medicine has emerged, rivaling that of the old witch doctors. Medical technology, from all that the patient has read in the newspapers, is as complex and mystifying as space technology. Physicians, from all he has seen on TV serials or heard thirdhand from other patients, are steely-nerved, omniscient, medical astronauts. The patient himself is usually sick-feeling, often undressed, a nameless observer in a process which he can never hope to understand. He has been schooled by all the news of medical "space shots" — heart transplants, renal dialysis, wonder drugs, nuclear therapy, etc. — to expect some small miracle in his own case — a magical new prescription drug or an operation. And miracles, by their very nature, are not explainable or understandable. Whether it's a "miracle detergent," a "miracle mouth wash," or a "miracle medical treatment," the customer can only pay the price and hope the product works.

PROBLEM FOUR: GETTING A HEARING IF THINGS DON'T GO RIGHT

Everything about the American medical system seems calculated to maintain the childlike, dependent, and depersonalized condition of the patient. It is bad enough that modern medical technology has been infused by its practitioners with all the mystery and unaccountability of primitive shamanism. What is worse is that the patient is given absolutely no means of judging what care he should get or evaluating what he has gotten. As one Washington, D.C. taxi driver put it, "When I buy a used car, I know it might be a gyp. But I go over it, test it, try to figure out if it's O.K. for the price. Then take last year when I got started getting some stomach problem. The doctor says I need an operation. How do I know I need an operation? But what can I do — I have an operation. Later I get the bill — $1700 — and Blue Cross left over $850 for me to pay. How should I know whether the operation should cost $50 or $1700? Now I think my stomach problem is coming back? Do I get my money back?"

Doctors and hospitals have turned patients into "consumers," but patients have none of the rights or protections which consumers of other goods and services expect. People in search of medical care cannot very easily do comparative shopping. When they're sick, they take help wherever they can get it. Besides, patients who switch doctors more than once are viewed by other doctors as possible neurotics. Health consumers know what they'd like — good health — but they have no way of knowing what this should entail in terms of services — a new diet, a prescription, or a thousand-dollar operation. Once they've received the service, the doctor, not their own perception, tells them whether it did any good. And if they suspect that the price was unduly high, the treatment unnecessarily complicated or drastic, there is no one to turn to — no Better Business Bureau or Department of Consumer Protection.

When something goes really wrong — a person is killed or maimed in the course of medical treatment — there is still no formal avenue of recourse for the patient or his survivors. Middle-class people, who know the ropes and have some money to spend, can embark on a long and costly malpractice suit, and win, at best, a cash compensation for the damage done. But this process, like everything else in a person's encounter with doctors and hospitals, is highly individualistic, and has no pay-off in terms of the general health and safety of the community. For the poor, there is usually no resource at all short of open resistance. A Manhattan man, infuriated by his wife's treatment in the emergency room of New York's Beth Israel Medical Center, beat up the intern on duty. Another man, whose child died inexplicably at a big city public hospital, solitarily pickets City Hall summer after summer.

PROBLEM FIVE: OVERCOMING THE BUILT-IN RACISM AND MALE CHAUVINISM OF DOCTORS AND HOSPITALS

In the ways that it irritates, exhausts, and occasionally injures patients, the American medical system is not egalitarian. Everything that is bad about American medicine is especially so for Americans who are not male or white. Blacks, and in some areas Indians, Puerto Ricans, or Mexicans, face unique problems of access to medical care, and not just because they are poor. Many hospitals in the south are still unofficially segregated, or at least highly selective. For instance, in towns outside of Orangeburg, South Carolina, blacks claim they are admitted to the hospital only on the recommendation of a (white) employer or other white "reference."

In the big cities of the north, health facilities are available on a more

equal footing to blacks, browns, and poor whites. But for the nonwhite
patient, the medical experience is more likely to be something he will not
look forward to repeating. The first thing he notices about the large
hospital — he is more likely to be at a hospital clinic than at a private
doctor's office — is that the doctors are almost uniformly white; the
nonskilled workers are almost entirely brown or black. Thus the nonwhite patient enters the hospital at the bottom end of its social scale,
quite aside from any personal racial prejudices the staff may harbor. And,
in medicine, these prejudices take a particularly insulting form. Black
and Puerto Rican patients complain again and again of literally being
"treated like animals" by everyone from the clerks to the M.D.'s. Since
blacks are assumed to be less sensitive than white patients, they get less
privacy. Since blacks are assumed to be more ignorant than whites, they
get less by way of explanation of what is happening to them. And since
they are assumed to be irresponsible and forgetful, they are more likely
to be given a drastic, one-shot treatment, instead of a prolonged regimen
of drugs, or a restricted diet.

Only a part of this medical racism is due to the racist attitudes of individual medical personnel. The rest is "institutional racism," a built-in
feature of the way medicine is learned and practiced in the United
States. As interns and residents, young doctors get their training by
practicing on the hospital ward and clinic patients — generally nonwhite.
Later they make their money by practicing for a paying clientele — generally white. White patients are "customers"; black patients are "teaching
material." White patients pay for care with their money; black patients
pay with their dignity and their comfort. Clinic patients at the hospital
affiliated with Columbia University's medical school recently learned
this distinction in a particularly painful way. They had complained that
anesthesia was never available in the dental clinic. Finally, a leak from
one of the dental interns showed that this was an official policy: the patient's pain is a good guide to the dentist-in-training — it teaches him not
to drill too deep. Anesthesia would deaden the pain and dull the intern's learning experience.

Hospitals' institutional racism clearly serves the needs of the medical
system, but it is also an instrument of the racist, repressive impulses of
the society at large. Black community organizations in New York have
charged hospitals with "genocidal" policies towards the black community.
Harlem residents tell of medical atrocities — cases where patients have unwittingly given their lives or their organs in the cause of medical research. A more common charge is that, to public hospital doctors, "the
birth control method of choice for black women is the hysterectomy."
Even some doctors admit that hysterectomies are often performed with
pretty slim justification in ghetto hospitals. (After all, they can't be expected to take a pill every day, can they? And one less black baby is one

less baby on welfare, isn't it?) If deaths from sloppy abortions run highest in the ghetto, it is partly because black women are afraid to go to the
hospital for an abortion or for treatment following a sloppy abortion,
fearing that an involuntary sterilization — all for "medical" reasons — will
be the likely result. Aside from their medical policies, ghetto hospitals
have a reputation as racist because they serve as police strongholds in
the community. In the emergency room, cops often outnumber doctors.
They interrogate the wounded — often before the doctor does, and pick
up any vagrants, police brutality victims, drunks or addicts who have mis-
takenly come in for help. In fact, during the 1964 riots in New York, the
police used Harlem Hospital as a launching pad for their pacification
measures.

Women are the other major group of Americans singled out for special
treatment by the medical system. Just as blacks face a medical hierarchy
dominated by whites, women entering a hospital or doctor's office encounter a hierarchy headed by men, with women as nurses and aides
playing subservient, hand-maid roles. And in the medical system, women
face all the male supremacist attitudes and superstitions that characterize American society in general — they are the victims of sexism, as
blacks are of racism. Women are assumed to be incapable of understanding complex technological explanations, so they are not given any.
Women are assumed to be emotional and "difficult," so they are often
classified as neurotic well before physical illness has been ruled out.
(Note how many tranquilizer ads in medical journals depict women,
rather than men, as likely customers.) And women are assumed to be
vain, so they are the special prey of the paramedical dieting, cosmetics,
and plastic surgery businesses.

Everyone who enters the medical system in search of care quickly finds
himself transformed into an object, a mass of organs and pathology.
Women have a special handicap — they start out as "objects." Physicians,
despite their supposed objectivity and clinical impersonality, share all
the sexual hangups of other American men. The sick person who enters
the gynecology clinic is the same sex as the sexual "object" who sells cars
in the magazine ads. What makes matters worse is that a high proportion
of routine medical care for women centers on the most superstitious and
fantasy-ridden aspect of female physiology — the reproductive system.
Women of all classes almost uniformly hate or fear their gynecologists.
The gynecologist plays a controlling role in that aspect of their lives
society values most, the sexual aspect — and he knows it. Middle-class
women find a man who is either patronizingly jolly, or cold and condescending. Poorer women, using clinics, are more likely to encounter
outright brutality and sadism. Of course, black women have it worst of
all. A shy teenager from a New York ghetto reports going to the clinic
for her first prenatal check-up, and being used as teaching material for

an entire class of young, male medical students learning to give pelvic examinations.

Doctors and hospitals treat pregnancy and childbirth, which are probably among the healthier things that women experience, as diseases — to be supervised by doctors and confined to hospitals. Women in other economically advanced countries, such as Holland, receive their prenatal care at home, from nurses, and, if all goes well, are delivered at home by trained midwives. (The Netherlands rank third lowest in infant mortality rate; the U.S. ranks fourteenth!) But for American women, pregnancy and childbirth are just another harrowing, expensive medical procedure. The doctor does it; the woman is essentially passive. Even in large cities, women often have to go from one obstetrician to another before they find one who approves of natural childbirth. Otherwise, childbirth is handled as if it were a surgical operation, even to the point of "scheduling" the event to suit the obstetrician's convenience through the use of possibly dangerous labor-inducing drugs.

Most people who have set out to look for medical care eventually have to conclude that there *is* no American medical system — at least there is no systematic way in America of getting medical help when you need it, without being financially ruined, humiliated, or injured in the process. What system there is — the three hundred thousand doctors, seven thousand hospitals and supporting insurance plans — was clearly not designed to deal with the sick. In fact the one thing you need most in order to qualify for care financially and to survive the process of obtaining it is *health*, plus, of course, a good deal of cunning and resourcefulness. The trouble is that it's almost impossible to stay healthy and strong enough to be able to tackle the medical system. Preventive health care (regular check-ups, chest X-rays, pap tests, etc.) is not a specialty or even an interest of the American medical system.

The price of this double bind — having to be healthy just to stay healthy — is not just consumer frustration and discomfort. The price is lives. The United States ranks fourteenth among the nations of the world in infant mortality, which means that approximately 33,000 American babies under one year old die unnecessarily every year. (Our infant mortality statistics are not, as often asserted, so high because they are "spoiled" by the death rates for blacks. The statistics for white America alone compare unfavorably to those for countries such as Sweden, the Netherlands, Norway, etc.) Mothers also stand a better chance of dying in the United States, where the maternal mortality rate ranks twelfth among the world's nations. The average American man lives five years less than the Swedish man, and his life expectancy is shorter than for males in seventeen other nations. Many American men never live out their already relatively short lifetime, since the chance of dying between ages forty and fifty is twice as high for an American as it is for a Scandinavian. What is perhaps most alarming about these statistics is that they are, in a relative sense, getting worse. The statistics improve a little each year, but at a rate far slower than that for other advanced countries. Gradually, the United States is slipping behind most of the European nations, and even some non-European nations, in its ability to keep its citizens alive. These are the symptoms; unhealthy statistics, soaring costs and mounting consumer frustration over the quality and even the quantity of medical care. Practically everyone but the A.M.A. agrees that something is drastically wrong. The roster of public figures actively concerned about the health care crisis is beginning to read like *Who's Who in America:* Labor leaders Walter Reuther of the Auto Workers and Harold Gibbons of the Teamsters, businessmen like General James Gavin of Arthur D. Little, Inc., politicians like New York's Mayor John Lindsay and Cleveland's Mayor Carl Stokes, doctors like Michael DeBakey of Baylor College of Medicine, and civil rights leaders like Mrs. Martin Luther King, Jr. and Whitney Young, Jr. With the help of eminent medical economists like Harvard's Rashi Fein and Princeton's Ann Somers, these liberal leaders have come up with a common diagnosis of the problem: the medical care system is in a state of near-chaos. There is no one to blame — medical care is simply adrift, with the winds rising in all directions. In the words of the official pamphlet of the Committee for National Health Insurance (a coalition of one hundred well-known liberals): "The fact is that we do not have a health care system at all. We have a 'nonsystem.'" According to this diagnosis, the health care industry is, in the words of the January, 1970, *Fortune* magazine, a "cottage industry." It is dominated by small, inefficient and uncoordinated enterprises (private doctors, small hospitals, and nursing homes), which add up to a fragmented and wasteful whole — a nonsystem.

Proponents of the nonsystem theory trace the problem to the fact that health care, as a commodity, does not obey the orderly, businesslike laws of economics. With a commodity like bacon, demand reflects people's desire to eat bacon and ability to pay for bacon. Since the supply gracefully adjusts itself to demand, things never get out of hand — there is a *system* of bacon production and sales. No such invisible hand of economic law operates in the health market. First, people buy medical care when they have to, not when they want to or can afford to. Then, when he does go to purchase care, the consumer is not the one who decides what and how much to buy — the doctor or hospital does. In other words, in the medical market place, it is the supplier who controls the demand. Finally, medical care suppliers have none of the usual economic incentives to lower their prices or rationalize their services. Most hospitals receive a large part of their income on a cost-plus basis from insurance organizations, and couldn't care less about cost or efficiency. Doctors do not compete on the basis of price. In fact, given the shortage of doctors (which is maintained by the doctors themselves through the A.M.A.'s prevention of medical school expansion), they don't have to compete at all.

Solutions offered by the liberal viewers of the medical nonsystem are all along the lines of putting the health industry on a more "rational," i.e., businesslike basis. First, the consumer should not have to fish in his pocket each time the need for care arises; he should have some sort of all-purpose medical credit card. With some form of National Health Insurance, all consumers, rich or poor, would have the same amount of medical credit, paid for by the government, by the consumer, or both through payroll taxes. . . . Second, the delivery of health services must be made more efficient. Just as supermarkets are more efficient than corner groceries, and shopping centers are more efficient than isolated super-markets, the medical system ought to be more efficient if it were bigger and more integrated at all levels. Doctors should be encouraged to come together into group practices, and group practices, hospitals and medical schools should be gradually knitted together into coordinated regional medical care systems. Since they are the centers of medical technology, the medical schools should be the centers and leaders of these regional systems — regulating quality in the "outposts," training professional and paraprofessional personnel, and planning to meet changing needs. . . .

There is only one thing wrong with this analysis of the health care crisis: it's based on a false assumption. The medical reformers have assumed, understandably enough, that the function of the American health industry is to provide adequate health care to the American people. From this it is easy enough to conclude that there is no American health *system*. But this is like assuming that the function of the TV networks is to give comprehensive, penetrating, and meaningful information to the viewers — a premise which would quickly lead us to believe that the networks have fallen into wild disorganization and confusion. Like the mass media, the American medical industry has many items on its agenda other than service to the consumers. Analyzed in terms of all of its functions, the medical industry emerges as a coherent, highly organized system. One particular function — patient care — may be getting slighted, and there may be some problems in other areas as well, but it remains a *system*, and can only be analyzed as such.

The most obvious function of the American medical system, other than patient care, is profit-making. When it comes to making money, the health industry is an extraordinarily well-organized and efficient machine. The most profitable small business around is the private practice of medicine, with aggregate profits running into the billions. The most profitable big business in America is the manufacture and sale of drugs. Rivaling the drug industry for Wall Street attention is the burgeoning hospital supply and equipment industry, with products ranging from chicken soup to catheters and heart-lung machines. The fledgling nursing home (for profit) industry was a speculator's dream in 1968 and 1969, and even the stolid insurance companies gross over ten billion dollars a year in health insurance premiums. In fact, the health business is so profitable that even the "nonprofit" hospitals make profits. All that "nonprofit" means is that the hospital's profit, i.e., the difference between its income and its expenditures, is not distributed to shareholders. These nonprofits are used to finance the expansion of medical empires – to buy real estate, stocks, plush new buildings, and expensively salaried professional employees. The medical system may not be doing too well at fighting disease, but, as any broker will testify, it's one of the healthiest businesses around.

Next in the medical system's list of priorities is research. Again, if this undertaking is measured in terms of its dividends for patient care, it comes out looking pretty unsystematic and disorganized. Although the vast federal appropriations for biomedical research are primarily motivated by the hope of improving health care, only a small fraction (much smaller than need be) of the work done in the name of medical research leaks out to the general public as improved medical care. But medical research has a *raison d'être* wholly independent of the delivery of health services, as an indispensable part of the nation's giant research and development enterprise. Since the Second World War, the United States has developed a vast machinery for R.&D. in all areas – physics, electronics, aerospace as well as biomedical sciences – financed largely by the government and carried out in universities and private industry. It has generated military and aerospace technology, and all the many little innovations which fuel the expansion of private industry.

For the purposes of this growing R.&D. effort, the medical system is important because it happens to be the place where R.&D. in general comes into contact with human material. Medical research is the link. The nation's major biomedical research institutes are affiliated to hospitals to a significant extent because they require human material to carry out their own, usually abstract, investigations. For instance, a sophisticated (and possible patentable) technique for investigating protein structure was recently developed through the use of the blood of several dozen victims of a rare and fatal bone marrow disease. Even the research carried out inside hospitals has implications for the entire R.&D. enterprise. Investigations of the pulmonary disorders of patients in Harlem Hospital may provide insights for designing space suits, or it may contribute to the technology of aerosol dissemination of nerve gas. Or, of course, it may simply lead to yet another investigation.

Human bodies are not all that the medical care system offers up to R.&D. The sociological and psychological research carried out in hospitals and ghetto health centers may have pay-offs in the form of new counterinsurgency techniques for use at home and abroad. And who knows what sinister – or benignly academic – ends are met by the routine neurological and drug research carried out on the nation's millions of mental hospital inmates?

Finally, an important function of the medical care system is the reproduction of its key personnel – physicians. Here, again, there seems to be no system if patient care is the ultimate goal. The medical schools graduate each year just a few more doctors than are needed to replace the ones who retire, and far too few doctors to keep up with the growth of population. Of those who graduate, a growing proportion go straight into academic government, or industrial biomedical research, and never see a patient. The rest, according to some dissatisfied medical students, aren't trained to take care of patients anyway – having been educated chiefly in academic medicine (a mixture of basic sciences and "interesting" pathology). But all this is not as irrational as it seems. The limited size of medical school classes has been maintained through the diligent, and entirely systematic, efforts of the A.M.A. Too many – or even enough – doctors would mean lower profits for those already in practice. And the research orientation of medical education simply reflects the medical schools' own consuming preoccupation with research.

Profits, research and teaching, then, are independent functions of the medical system, not just adjuncts to patient care. But they do not go on along separate tracks, removed from patient care. Patients are the indispensable ingredient of medical profit-making, research, and education. In order that the medical industry serve these functions, patient care must be twisted to meet the needs of these other "medical" enterprises.

Different groups of patients serve the ends of profit-making, research and education in different ways. The rich, of course, do much to keep medical care profitable. They can afford luxury, so, for them, the medical system produces a luxury commodity – the most painstaking, supertechnological treatment possible; special cosmetic care to preserve youth, or to add or subtract fatty tissue; even sumptuous private hospital rooms with carpeting and a selection of wines at meals. The poor, on the other hand, serve chiefly to subsidize medical research and education – with their bodies. City and county hospitals and the wards and clinics of private hospitals provide free care for the poor, who, in turn, provide their bodies for young doctors to practice on and for researchers to experiment with. The lucky poor patient with a rare or interesting disease may qualify for someone's research project, and end up receiving the technically most advanced care. But most of the poor are no more interesting than they are profitable, and receive minimal, low-quality care from bored young interns.

The majority of Americans have enough money to buy their way out of being used for research, but not enough to buy luxury care. Medical care for the middle class is, like any other commodity, aimed at a mass market: the profits are based on volume, not on high quality. The rich man may have his steak dinners catered to him individually; the middle-class consumer waits for his hamburger in the check-out line at the A&P. Similarly, the middle-class patient waits in crowded waiting rooms, receives five minutes of brusque, impersonal attention from a doctor who is quicker to farm him out to a specialist than to take the time to treat him himself, and finally is charged all that the market will bear. Preventive care is out of the question: it is neither very profitable nor interesting to the modern, science-oriented M.D.

The crisis experienced by the poor and middle-class consumer of health care can be traced directly to the fact that patient care is not the only, or even the primary, aim of the medical care system. But what has turned the consumer's private nightmare into a great public debate about the health care crisis is that the other functions of the system are also in trouble. Profit-making, research, and education are all increasingly suffering from financial shortage on the one hand and institutional inadequacies on the other. The solutions offered by the growing chorus of medical reformers are, in large measure, aimed at salvaging profits, research, and education as much as they are aimed at improving patient care. They are simple survival measures, aimed at preserving and strengthening the medical system as it now operates.

No one, so far, has seen through the proposed reforms. Union and management groups, who have moved into the forefront of the medical reform movement, seem happy to go along with the prescription that the medical system is writing for itself. The alternative — to marshall all the force of public power to take medical care out of the arena of private enterprise and recreate it as a public system, a community service, is rarely mentioned, and never considered seriously. To do this would be to challenge some of the underlying tenets of the American free enterprise system. If physicians were to become community employees, if the drug companies were to be nationalized — then why not expropriate the oil and coal industries, or the automobile industry? There is an even more direct antipathy to nationalizing the health industry: a host of industries, including the aerospace industry, the electronic industry, the chemical industry, and the insurance industry, all have a direct stake in the profitability of the medical care system. (And a much larger sector of American industry stands to profit from the human technology spun off by the medical research enterprise.) Of course, the argument never takes this form. Both business and unions assert, in their public pronouncements, that only a private enterprise system is capable of managing medical services in an efficient, nonbureaucratic, and flexible manner. (The obvious extrapolation, that all medical services, including voluntary and city hospitals, would be in better shape if run as profit-making enterprises, is already being advanced by a few of the more visionary medical reformers.)

For all these reasons, business and unions (and, as a result, government) are not interested in restructuring the medical care system in ways contrary to those already put forth by the doctors, hospitals, and medical industry companies. Their only remaining choice is to go along with the reforms which have been proposed, in the hope that lower costs, and possibly even more effective care, will somehow fall out as by-products.

For the health care consumer, this is a slim hope. What he is up against now, what he will be up against even after the best-intentioned reform measures, is a system in which health care is itself only a by-product, secondary to the priorities of profits, research, and training. The danger is that, when all the current reforms are said and done, the system as a whole will be tighter, more efficient, and harder to crack, while health services, from the consumer's point of view, will be no less chaotic and inadequate. Health care will remain a commodity, to be purchased at great effort and expense, and not a right to be freely exercised.

But there are already the beginnings of a consumer rebellion against the reformer-managers of the medical care system. . . . The demand is to turn the medical system upside down, putting human care on top, placing research and education at its service, and putting profit-making aside. Ultimately, the growing movement of health care consumers does not want to "consume" health care at all, on any terms. They want to take it — because they have to have it — even if this means creating a wholly new American health care system.

32. GETTING CANCER ON THE JOB

Larry Agran

In April 1973, Joseph Fitman's doctor told him he had lung cancer. A few days later, he underwent a radical left pneumonectomy — the removal of his left lung. Recovery from the surgery was very slow, difficult and imperfect. At 63, after more than four decades of industrial labor, Joe Fitman was finished as a productive worker.

Now, two years after his cancer operation, Fitman is alive but not well. He sees his life in narrowly measured terms:

I can't do too much. Mostly I just watch TV or walk to the patio and sit down. I tried to work, but I just can't, 'cause I'm fightin' so many things. If I

From *Nation*, April 12, 1975. Reprinted by permission of *Nation*.

do too much, I wind up goin' to the hospital, an emergency. I get the feelin' like if you ran around the block, stopped, sat down—you'd be takin' deep breaths. Well that's my problem. I get spells where my air was bein' shut off and I feel I'm not gettin' oxygen, and I found myself strugglin' for some air.

Statistically, Joe Fitman's case is one of more than 600,000 new cancer cases in the United States in 1973. But upon analysis, it becomes evident that his cancer was not an inexplicable, unpredictable occurrence. His work history suggests a classic case of job-caused cancer. Fitman toiled for a quarter-century as a hot metalworker, first in a Pennsylvania tin mill and after that as a blacksmith in a steel mill. Long-time metalworkers who are exposed to iron oxides and a host of metallic dusts and fumes develop lung cancer at rates significantly higher than the general population. Later on, in 1958, Fitman went to work for Douglas Aircraft in Long Beach, Calif. His job was to operate a bench saw, cutting fiberglass. While he wore goggles to shield his eyes, he did not wear a respirator; unwittingly, he was inhaling millions of tiny fiberglass particles, now suspected to be a cancer-causing agent. After he was laid off at Douglas in 1961, Fitman took a job, his last one, with a Southern California plastics firm. There, daily for twelve years he handled and breathed a variety of recognized carcinogens, including asbestos, carbon black and vinyl chloride. It is impossible to say which of these agents was chiefly responsible for his malignancy, but it is reasonable to conclude that it originated with one or more of them.[1]

In 1973, more than 353,000 Americans died from cancer, up by almost 7,000 from the 1972 death toll. More than a decade ago, a World Health Organization committee of cancer experts concluded that a majority of human cancers could well be attributed to known environmental carcinogens. Since then, U.S. and international authorities have estimated that 80 per cent of human cancers, perhaps even 90 per cent, are environmentally induced: that is, they result from exposures to certain cancer-causing substances in the air, water and soil — at work, in the community, or in the home. To those who study such things, it is apparent that the vast majority of these environmentally induced cancers derive from direct and indirect exposure to industrial carcinogens.

In 1942, Dr. Wilhelm C. Hueper, then a research pathologist, wrote a monumental text, *Occupational Tumors and Allied Diseases*. Drawing upon studies of selected worker populations both here and abroad, Hueper convincingly established the relationship between occupational contact with certain chemicals, metals and minerals and a subsequent high incidence of cancer. In the book, he urged adoption of comprehensive preventive measures to minimize the cancer hazards faced by the industrial workforce. His words had little effect.

From the late 1940s through the 1950s, evidence mounted to support Hueper's theory. Still, despite the persuasive body of evidence, public health authorities remained, for the most part, unmoved. By this time, Hueper had become chief of the National Cancer Institute's Environmental Cancer Section and an embattled pioneer in the field of occupational cancer. In 1964, at the age of 70, he was co-author of a second massive text, *Chemical Carcinogenesis and Cancers.* There, Hueper wrote ominously of an impending "epidemic in slow motion." He noted that human cancer ordinarily does not appear until ten, twenty, or even thirty years after exposure to a carcinogen. With this long latent period in mind, he warned that the unbridled proliferation of cancer-causing substances which accompanied the frenetic industrialization after 1940 would, in time, produce a terrible cancer epidemic in the United States. It now appears that a continuing policy of national neglect is, with the passage of time, proving Hueper right.

Rubber workers, routinely exposed to multiple cancer-causing substances, are dying of cancer of the stomach, cancer of the prostate and of leukemia and other cancers of the blood-and-lymph-forming tissues at rates ranging from 50 to 300 per cent greater than in the general population.

Steelworkers, particularly the thousands who handle coal as it is transferred to coke ovens for combustion and distillation, fall victim to lung cancer at excessive rates. Those who labor atop the hot coke ovens are most vulnerable to the carcinogenic coal-tar emissions and experience a lung cancer rate seven times as great as would normally be expected.

Asbestos workers, including those who mill the mineral and those who must use it regularly in construction work and elsewhere, die from lung cancer at a rate more than seven times that of comparable control groups. Mesothelioma, a fatal malignancy which attacks the lining of the lungs and abdominal organs, used to be an extremely rare form of cancer. But it has become relatively commonplace among asbestos workers, even those with short-term occupational exposures.

Workers who produce dyestuffs, using benzidine and other so-called aromatic amines, have evidenced notoriously high rates of bladder cancer.

Miners of uranium, iron ore, nickel, chromium and other industrial metals succumb to a wide range of occupationally related cancers. In the case of uranium miners, the lung cancer rate is extraordinary, accounting for upward of 50 per cent of all deaths among these workers.

An estimated 2 million workers, among them dry cleaners, painters, printers and rubber and petroleum workers, are exposed to the solvent benzene, a known leukemia-producing agent.

Another 1.5 million laborers, among them insecticide workers, farm workers and copper and lead smelter workers, are exposed to inorganic arsenic, a carcinogen which causes high rates of lung cancer and lymphatic cancer.

Machinists, chemical workers, woodworkers, roofers — and many more

— join an ever expanding list of workers who hold jobs posing special cancer risks of one kind or another.

These developments, and others, indicate that we are in the grip of an emerging national epidemic of blue-collar cancer. Yet for decades, federal and state health agencies have treated occupational cancer as a relatively inconsequential issue. A partial explanation for this neglect might be attributed to the widely held but thoroughly misguided expectation of a universal cancer "cure," a dramatic breakthrough which would obviate the need for expensive preventive policies. But a more probable explanation is the tendency of key public health officials, frequently acting with industry spokesmen, to play down the question of occupational cancer, lest it "frighten" workers and possibly impair production.

Even today, federal policy in the area of occupational cancer is only a notch or two above the do-nothing policies of the 1940s, 1950s and 1960s. In 1970, hope rose temporarily among health-conscious reformers when Congress passed the Occupational Safety and Health Act, an ambitious measure establishing a federal framework for the adoption and enforcement of nationwide occupational health standards to assure that "no employee will suffer diminished health, functional capacity, or life expectancy as a result of his work experience." Sponsors of the legislation had reason to believe that the Department of Labor's Occupational Safety and Health Administration (OSHA), an agency created to administer the act, would give top priority to setting the toughest possible standards for protection against job-caused cancer.

No such luck. Throughout 1971, OSHA adopted no new federal standards. This was no ordinary case of bureaucratic sloth. As we now know, in June of 1972 George C. Guenther, then head of OSHA, sent a confidential memo to higher-ups in the Department of Labor, assuring these administration loyalists that, prior to Election Day, "no highly controversial standards will be proposed by OSHA." Eager to enlist the agency in the Nixon re-election drive, he stressed the attractiveness of a management-oriented OSHA as a "sales point for fund raising."

True to his word, Guenther did not offend management when OSHA finally adopted its first cancer-related work standard, a standard for asbestos exposure. Studies dating back to the 1930s had established airborne asbestos fibers to be a dangerous carcinogen, but the recent work of Dr. Irving Selikoff at the Mount Sinai Medical Center in New York brought out the shocking extent of the damage. About 18 per cent of Americans die of cancer; among asbestos insulation workers, Selikoff found, the toll approaches 50 per cent. Twenty per cent of all long-term asbestos workers die of lung cancer. Another 5 per cent die from the previously rare cancer, mesothelioma. Stomach and colon cancer accounts for still more of the excess cancer deaths.

Armed with this data, Selikoff and labor officials urged upon OSHA the only prudent course when dealing with a carcinogen of such demonstrated potency: adoption of a standard which allows "no detectable level" of exposure. For its part, the industry proposed a standard which would permit the prevailing death-dealing asbestos exposure levels to continue. In the end, OSHA adopted a standard which fell between the two proposals, cutting maximum exposure levels in half. OSHA thus ignored a fundamental principle of cancer prevention policy: there is no "safe level" for exposure to a cancer-causing agent. While lowering the level of exposure can ordinarily be expected to lower the incidence, anything short of a "zero tolerance level" carries the strong likelihood of excessive cancer deaths.

Quite obviously OSHA officials were attempting to balance competing interests by striking a compromise with their new asbestos standard, but the compromise is so weak in content that it will have only marginal effect on cancer rates among asbestos workers. Accordingly, it will certainly lead to still thousands more of needless cancer deaths among the several hundred thousand asbestos workers in the United States.

In early 1974, the Occupational Safety and Health Administration passed up an extraordinary opportunity to get a firm hold on the entire problem of workplace carcinogens. The Oil, Chemical, and Atomic Workers Union and the Washington-based Health Research Group filed a petition with OSHA requesting that exposure levels for ten recognized workplace carcinogens be set at "zero tolerance." Even more important, the petition included a request that OSHA adopt a precedent-setting permit system whereby carcinogens would be barred in industrial processes unless a firm had sought and received a government-issued use permit. In that way, a manufacturer could not legally use specified carcinogens until OSHA had surveyed the work environment and certified it to be exposure-proof.

OSHA did adopt fairly rigorous standards for the ten cancer-causing substances, and for another four substances. But it rejected the all-important permit proposal, on the dubious ground that initiation of such a system was beyond the scope of its statutory authority. For the first time, an industry producing or using certain carcinogens would have been required to make a convincing showing that: (1) the substance was essential to its operations; (2) there were no appropriate substitutes of lesser danger; and (3) all necessary steps were being taken to safeguard employees against any exposure whatever. OSHA determined this was too much to ask.

Without a permit system, OSHA will need a veritable army to enforce even the limited number of carcinogen standards adopted to date. No such army exists. There are at present 800 federal occupational health and safety compliance officers. And, of these, fewer than 100 are technically qualified industrial hygienists. Charged with monitoring all of the abuses of the workplace — among them, noise, heat and the use of toxic but non-carcinogenic chemicals — this staff cannot pretend to police effectively the country's plants and factories.

Joe Fitman was a helpless victim of this kind of lax enforcement effort, particularly during his last twelve years as a worker when he was employed by a Southern California plastics outfit. It was with some bitterness that he described the squalid conditions of his labor:

> In a way I knew the materials I was workin' with was dangerous, but when you're up in age like me — your age is against you. You've got a house payment. You've got five kids around the table.
>
> I feel sorry for the fellas that are tryin' to hold their jobs in that place because only I know, due to my experience, how dangerous that place is to work. From my point of view, that place is filthy up there. And I just wonder, throughout this country, if the rest of the places are like that.

The Occupational Safety and Health Act took effect on April 28, 1971. But Joe Fitman couldn't remember any inspections ever taking place, either before or after that date.

A second federal agency intimately involved with the occupational cancer issue is the National Institute for Occupational Safety and Health (NIOSH). It is the research agency responsible for conducting studies and recommending workplace standards to OSHA. But while OSHA is part of the Department of Labor, NIOSH is within the Department of Health, Education, and Welfare. It was set up as a worker-oriented health protection agency and the caliber of its work has been in keeping with that purpose. Thanks to a staff of aggressive young technicians, there has never been any real problem with the quality of NIOSH's work, but there has always been a problem with the quantity. The institute is starved for funds and for personnel. Its entire 1974–75 budget for occupational cancer was a puny $1.8 million. To conduct a single study on the effects that a suspect carcinogen has had on the death rates of a defined population of workers costs $250,000 and occupies six people for at least a year. Since the equivalent of only twenty-eight full-time staff positions are devoted to these occupational cancer studies, it is obvious that only a handful of studies can be completed each year. As a result, the backlog of both recognized and suspect carcinogens not yet studied by NIOSH grows ever larger: commercial talc, mineral wool, antimony, wood dust, phosphoric acid, benzidine — there are scores of urgent studies left undone for lack of resources.

Though a relatively small proportion of chemicals induce cancers, nevertheless hundreds of commercially important compounds are known to be cancer-causing, or at least are highly suspect. And the industrial process feeds hundreds of new substances into industrial and commercial channels each year. Only the foolhardy would assume them all to be non-carcinogenic.

In years past, the cancer-causing properties of new compounds were generally not discovered until at least two or three decades after their adoption by industry. The method of discovery was a crude kind of human experimentation: counting the number of cancer victims among the dead workers to see if any abnormal trends could be detected. That was how vinyl chloride was spotted.

Vinyl chloride was first produced commercially in this country in 1939. It is an organic chemical, a gas at normal air temperature and pressure. Chemical plants convert this gas into a hard granular resin, called polyvinyl chloride, which has become the base for a cornucopia of solid and flexible plastics: food wrappings, bottles, vinyl tiles, phonograph records, water pipes, toys, car upholstery, tubing and thousands of other commonly used plastic products. The country now produces more than 7 *billion* pounds of polyvinyl chloride a year. Some 300,000 workers are involved in the chain of production — from the synthesis of the gas to the manufacture of the resin to the fabrication of the plastics. They work with vinyl chloride in its principal cancer-causing forms, and they have borne the brunt of this latest occupational peril.

Raymond P. Gettelfinger, Jr. began to work with vinyl chloride in 1954, when at the age of 22 he hired on at the B.F. Goodrich plant in Louisville. His job included operating the giant vat-like reactors used to transform the gas into resin. Gettelfinger recalls that the sweet smell of vinyl chloride was always thick in the air, but that it was worst when he and his colleagues had to climb down into the reactors and spend as many as four hours at a time cleaning and scraping the residue of the resin off the walls.

You have a residue build-up on the wall of your reactor and in some cases you have a water residue in the bottom. When I went to work there, that was the job of the helper—to get in and take the residue off the wall, which we done with scrapers. And if there was any left on the bottom . . . you'd pick it out with your hands—bare hands or leather gloves and your hands were wet. . . . When I began we wore nothing for protection. All we done was took an exhaust hose and stuck it in there and sucked the vinyl chloride out and we got in. . . .

Now, vinyl chloride has a characteristic that if there should be a mixture near the bottom of the vessel or reactor you were in, your feet would start feeling cold if there was much in there. Then you would know it was time to get out and see what is wrong. That, is the early years when I worked there, that was your first warning sign. . . . We didn't even—it wasn't in the safety regulations when I began working there to keep your exhaust hose in the reactor with you all the time.

It was in the mid-1960s, more than ten years after Gettelfinger joined Goodrich, that some of the workers there began to worry about the effect of vinyl chloride on their health. According to Gettelfinger:

We just got to noticing that there was just a few too many of us young men — the men working in the company, we were young men — they were losing two many guys. As we sat and ate and had our breaks, we just got to thinking that maybe there might be a little too much — too many of us guys getting out of this world too young.

It wasn't until January 1974, that the company publicly acknowledged similar fears. Dr. John L. Creech, a Louisville surgeon who is also the plant physician at Goodrich, was alert enough to notice that three Goodrich workers had died of angiosarcoma of the liver, an extremely rare form of cancer that attacks the blood vessels of the liver. Some months earlier, industry representatives had received in secret the results of animal studies commissioned by European plastics manufacturers. They showed that rats breathing air with vinyl chloride concentrations as low as 250 ppm — 250 parts per million — developed a variety of cancers, including angiosarcomas of the liver. Then, in June 1974, it was found that angiosarcomas could be induced in rats with exposures of only 50 ppm. Yet for years workers had been breathing air with vinyl chloride concentrations ranging as high as 8,000 ppm.

After what was apparently an industry attempt to withhold the animal cancer findings from NIOSH during the last six months of 1973, in January 1974, Goodrich announced the cause of the three deaths that Dr. Creech had noticed. Once the story was out, the body count began in earnest. From the beginning, interest centered primarily on victims of angiosarcoma. This type of liver tumor had previously been so rare that there were thought to be fewer than thirty cases a year in the United States. Yet, so far, at the Louisville plant alone nine workers are reported to have the disease. In other U.S. plants, another dozen victims have been found, with new cases turning up almost monthly. All but two are now dead. One of the victims was Raymond Gettelfinger; age 43, the father of six. He died on March 11.

Since a latent period of ten to thirty years is typical for this and other human cancers, it is apparent that we are now seeing just the onset of this particular outbreak of occupational cancer. Reduced exposure levels were adopted last fall by OSHA (exposures as high as 25 ppm are still permitted), but the malignant cells are already loose in the bodies of countless vinyl chloride workers, and it seems likely that during the next twenty years the liver cancer toll will climb into the hundreds. Moreover, while the victims of angiosarcoma have received the major share of public concern, the even more tragic fact is that vinyl chloride also produces less exotic cancers at alarmingly excessive rates: cancers of the lung and respiratory system at more than one and one-half times the normal expectancy, lymphoma and leukemia at nearly twice normal and brain cancer at five and one-half times normal.

Of course the industry could have done more than it did to prevent this suffering. But more important, public policy should have required more. The animal studies on vinyl chloride which were completed in Europe in 1973 should have been done in 1939, before plastics became a multibillion-dollar industry in which workers are the unwitting subjects of a vast on-the-job experiment in human carcinogenesis.

In response to the vinyl chloride disaster, and to similar but less publicized cancer episodes over the years, the new Congress will almost certainly adopt a proposed Toxic Substances Control Act. This legislation would establish machinery to require the animal testing of specified chemical compounds for their toxic and carcinogenic properties. But which compounds would be subject to testing is not all that clear. Apparently, the Congress intends to vest enormous discretionary authority with the director of the Environmental Protection Agency. Under pending proposals, the director could require the testing of any substance which he or she "has reason to believe may pose an unreasonable threat to human health or the environment."

If the Toxic Substances Control Act had been in effect ten years ago, would the government have ordered testing of vinyl chloride? Maybe yes, maybe no; at the time the evidence did not necessarily compel such a course. That is why it would be preferable if the Congress adopted a Toxic Substances Control Act which required — perhaps over a ten-year span — that *all* industrially and commercially significant substances be tested for their carcinogenicity and other destructive effects. It would be an enormous undertaking, but one more than matched by the need to gain firm control over the industrial environment. Are there other vinyl chlorides lurking out there? Certainly. Perhaps less dramatic in impact, but certainly. The tens of thousands of substances now in use make it certain that in the years ahead more workplace disasters will be uncovered.

There is yet another dimension to the menace of job-caused cancer: occupational carcinogens frequently do not remain within the factory gates. Certain of them, such as asbestos fibers, pose a distinct take-home risk. Family members are inadvertently exposed when work clothes covered with millions of tiny fibers are brought home to be hung or washed. This kind of incidental exposure has already produced a number of documented cases of the ever fatal mesothelioma. And X-rays of the families of asbestos workers have revealed excessive rates of the lung abnormalities common to the workers themselves.

Nor are the relatives of workers the only members of the community who face such hazards. Many plants producing or using carcinogens pose exceptional risks to those who live nearby. In the case of asbestos, both South African and U.S. studies have related a high incidence of "neighborhood cases" of mesothelioma to exposure to fibers airborne from nearby production sites. In the case of vinyl chloride, even at this early point victims of angiosarcoma of the liver have been reported among citizens who have never worked with the substance but who have lived for some time near a vinyl chloride plant. The neighborhood victims of vinyl chloride-induced lung cancer can never be identified with any measure of certainty. Statistically, they are lost in a national swamp of 80,000 annual lung cancer deaths. Last year, plastics producers discharged more than 200 million pounds of vinyl chloride into the air. Nevertheless, according to Environmental Protection Agency officials — the EPA monitors emissions beyond the factory gates — it will be another year before the agency adopts standards to limit community exposures to vinyl chloride.

Vinyl chloride and asbestos are only tiny aspects of the community cancer question. A study of Los Angeles County cancer rates recently reported a markedly higher incidence of lung cancer among residents in the heavily industrialized south-central area. The study attributed the excess lung cancers to particularly high levels of benzo(a)pyrene, a carcinogen that is probably formed of effluents from the petroleum and chemical industries concentrated in the area. Years earlier, a similar study on Staten Island, New York disclosed that unusually high lung cancer rates in certain areas were related to wind conditions and the resultant exposure to airborne industrial carcinogens.

The indirect effect of occupational carcinogens was brought home again recently when elevated cancer rates in New Orleans and several other cities were attributed to water supplies contaminated with industrial carcinogens. Biostatisticians are only now beginning to consider the question of miscarriages among the wives of male workers exposed to carcinogens. The phenomenon was first noted among the wives of anesthesiologists who were regularly exposed to the gases present in an operating room. Now, among the wives of vinyl chloride workers, early evidence indicates a striking increase in the rates of both miscarriages and stillbirths.

In a related and highly disturbing development, two Canadian investigators surveyed the records of several hundred children who died of malignant diseases. Upon checking the occupations of their fathers at their time of birth, the investigators found that a disproportionately high number held jobs that exposed them to recognized cancer-causing agents: for example, service-station attendants, painters, dyers and cleaners working with solvents. The possibility of take-home exposure in this study looms large, since the developing cells of the fetus are known to be particularly vulnerable to carcinogens that cross the placental barrier. A second possibility, more frightening still, is that the workplace carcinogens have damaged the father's sperm cells, initiating a "carcinogenetic defect" which is then transmitted at conception, producing a child who subsequently develops cancer as a youngster.

If this society is to come to terms with the multiple horrors of occupational cancer, it must begin by discarding the distracting notion of a universal and imminent cancer "cure." Despite the more than $500 million per year spent on cancer research, there is no reason to believe that a major breakthrough is at hand. There will be no quick fix for occupational cancers, or for any other environmentally induced cancers. It is equally important that we discard the fatalistic notion that "everything causes cancer." While many widely used industrial and commercial substances are carcinogenic, the vast majority — both at the workplace and elsewhere — are in this respect harmless. The real task is to identify the agents that are carcinogens and then enforce the strictest measures to prevent human exposure to them.

If this Congress were to adopt a tough Toxic Substances Control Act, requiring the prior testing of all commercially and industrially significant substances, it would be taking an important step toward isolating workplace carcinogens much earlier than is now the case. But, if it is to be more than a gesture, the Congress must back that kind of legislation with major appropriations to the Environmental Protection Agency which will administer its provisions. Furthermore, the Congress should see to it that the chemical testing program within the National Cancer Institute is accelerated with significantly larger appropriations. Currently, the Chemical Carcinogenesis Program receives only 6 per cent of the National Cancer Institute's funds, despite the evidence that cancers are largely the result of chemical exposures.

Beyond the animal testing programs, there is the question of on-site worker studies carried out by NIOSH. Its present $1.8 million budget for occupational cancer studies is disgracefully inadequate. Just to keep from being overwhelmed by a backlog of undone studies, NIOSH needs another $10 million earmarked for occupational cancer.

The situation is perhaps most discouraging with respect to the Occupational Safety and Health Administration, the Department of Labor's standards-setting and enforcement agency. In the area of occupational carcinogens, and in other areas as well, OSHA has been a bitter disappointment during its four-year history. Perhaps by way of Congressional mandate, the agency can be compelled to adopt a use-permit system to assure the most stringent and effective controls over occupational carcinogens. Its snail-paced operations indicate that OSHA lacks the money, manpower and single-minded determination to carry out its mission on behalf of American workers. Congress can remedy the first two problems; the third will probably have to await a new administration.

When he wrote *Occupational Tumors and Allied Diseases* in 1942, Dr. Hueper began with a chapter dealing with what he called "the new artificial environment." He observed that the great medical advances of the late 19th century and the first half of the 20th century came with an understanding of the biologically destructive effects of bacteria, viruses and other microorganisms. Similarly, he argued, the great challenge for the second half of the 20th century was to recognize the cancer-causing effects of many chemicals and other substances which have been introduced at the workplace in burgeoning numbers as part of the industrial age. It was a vital message, one that has been largely ignored for thirty-three years.

REFERENCE

1. Joe Fitman died on March 30.

33. THE GIFT OF BLOOD

Richard Titmuss

Blood transfusion represents one of the greatest therapeutic instruments in the hands of contemporary physicians. It has made possible the saving of life on a scale undreamt of several decades ago, and for conditions that were long considered hopeless. Moreover, the demand for blood increases yearly in every Western country as physicians adopt more radical surgical techniques entailing the loss of massive amounts of blood, and as new uses are found for blood, both in the saving of life and in the prevention of disease and disability.

All these scientific and technical developments in the field of blood transfusion have not only produced new and as yet unsolved problems for the biological and medical sciences, they have also set in train social, economic, and ethical consequences that present society with issues of profound importance. It is part of the purpose of this essay to explore these consequences.

BLOOD-BANKING IN AMERICA

It is difficult to assemble information about the total activities of all blood-banking systems in the United States. It has been estimated that there were in 1966–68 some 9,000 central, regional, and local blood banks in the United States concerned with the collection of blood from donors. Some (for example, hospital blood banks) will also be concerned with processing, cross-matching, and transfusion; some have the function of producing and preparing blood components; some operate solely as collectors, distributors, and suppliers of whole blood; and some provide a comprehensive community service.

This diversity of single and multipurpose agencies may be classified in terms of five distinct types of blood banks:

1. Fifty-five independent but cooperating American Red Cross Regional Blood Centers based on 1,700 participating local chapters and accounting, according to rough estimates in 1967, for about 40 percent of total blood supplies in the United States.

2. Some 6,000 individual hospital blood banks, which perform a great variety of services and are estimated to be responsible for about 20 to 30 percent of total blood supplies.

3. About 100 nonprofit organizations known as community blood banks, which generally aim to ensure an adequate blood supply for the communities in which they are situated. These agencies also perform various services, some simply acting as collectors and distributors to hospitals, others having a wide range of functions. The community banks were thought in 1966 to account for about 15 to 20 percent of total blood supplies.

4. An unknown number of independent profit-making commercial blood banks, which generally obtain their blood supplies from paid donors, process it, and sell it to hospitals at a profit. These banks were believed in the early 1960's to account for some 10 to 15 percent of total blood supplies. As we shall see, however, more recent estimates arrive at substantially higher figures. Indeed there seems to be no doubt that in recent years the percentage of blood supplied by these commercial agencies has been increasing, partly at the expense of voluntary programs.

5. An unknown number of commercial blood banks directly operated by pharmaceutical firms which rely heavily on a newly developed method of drawing blood, plasmapheresis. In nontechnical terms, this means that after the donor has given a pint of blood, the red cells are separated from

the plasma (the liquid part of blood as distinguished from the suspended elements) and injected back into the donor. For the donor, the process takes less than an hour. Provided that the strictest medical standards are observed, and that the donor is in excellent health and eats a nutritious high-protein diet, it is claimed by some authorities that one individual can make several donations a week. Other authorities believe, however, that it is too soon to be certain that plasmapheresis may not involve serious long-term hazards for the donors.

Plasmapheresis of donors is used by these blood banks to obtain plasma, plasma protein components, and platelets, for all of which there has been an immensely increasing demand. Various estimates in 1968 suggested that pharmaceutical firms were paying for 1 to 1.5 million donations a year, yielding, with "double bleed" sessions, approximately 2 million units. A number of firms operate their own plasmapheresis centers; others obtain their supplies from "independent blood contractors." Some regular donors are, in effect, "semisalaried" and paid $150 to $200 a month for a specified number of donations; some are long-term prisoners.

As the blood-transfusion services of the United States become increasingly dependent on the paid or professional donor, it is important that we have some sense of the social characteristics of those who sell their blood. A survey we conducted in 1968 was in part designed to produce some evidence on this matter. In all, I received statistics from a large number of commercial banks (some operated by pharmaceutical firms) accounting for some 366,000 units of blood. While very few appear to maintain detailed records on their sources of supply with respect to age, sex, marital status, and other characteristics, many provided summary accounts. It would seem that most paid donors (apart from those in prisons, in the armed forces, or university students) fall into three categories:

1. Professional donors — registered donors who contribute regularly and who are paid on a fee basis or are semisalaried (this category figures largely in the plasmapheresis programs).
2. Call-in donors — individuals (perhaps with less common blood groups) who are on a register of some kind and who respond to a call for blood on payment of a fee of $5 to $15 or more.
3. Walk-in donors — who may be attracted by advertisements, who are paid $5 or more a pint depending on local circumstances, such as the extent of the shortage of blood and other market considerations.

Many commercial blood banks, often open (at least in New York) from 7:30 in the morning to midnight, are better placed to attract walk-in donors because their "store fronts" are located in Negro and ghetto areas. In 1966, according to one journalistic report, voluntary and private hospitals bought 100,000 pints of "Skid Row blood from New York City's 31 pay-for-blood stores." The hospitals paid $35 a pint or more for the blood. A typical journalistic account which appeared in 1963 described the scene at one of these blood banks:

A bleary-eyed, vacant-faced man shuffles up to a building in an industrial part of town, checks the address with a scrap of paper in his shaking hand, and walks inside. In a bleak third-floor office, he joins a number of other men, many derelicts like himself. One by one they are summoned to a desk where an attendant asks a few quick questions and directs them to an inner room.

This is not a flophouse. It is not an employment agency or a social service bureau for weary, homeless men. This is a blood donor center.

Similar accounts have appeared since 1963 of conditions in commercial blood banks in Chicago, Seattle, Georgia, Cleveland, Boston, Miami, Detroit, Cincinnati, Los Angeles, San Francisco, Washington, Baltimore, Philadelphia, New Jersey, Kansas City, and many other places in addition to New York.

Most of these accounts, however, are not the products of keen-eyed journalists but of physicians concerned about the problem of serum hepatitis. We will discuss this problem in a moment. Meanwhile, we conclude that, despite all the statistical inadequacies in the data on blood-transfusion services in America, the trend appears to be markedly in the direction of the increasing commercialization of blood and donor relationships. Concomitantly, we find that proportionately more blood is being supplied by the poor, the unskilled, the unemployed, Negroes and other low-income groups and, with the rise of plasmapheresis, a new class is emerging of an exploited human population of high blood yielders. Redistribution in terms of "the gift of blood and blood products" from the poor to the rich appears to be one of the dominant effects of the American blood-banking systems.

TRUTH, TRUST, AND HEPATITIS

To the recipient the use of human blood for medical purposes can be more lethal than many drugs. The transfusion and use of whole blood and certain blood products carries with it the risk of transmitting disease, particularly serum hepatitis, malaria, syphilis, and brucellosis. Not only are there risks in infected blood and plasma but there are also risks in the use of contaminated needles and apparatus in the collection and transfusion processes.

In the United States and other modern societies the most dangerous of these hazards is serum hepatitis. It is becoming a major public-health problem throughout the world. No scientific means have yet been found to detect in the laboratory the causative agents of hepatitis in the blood before it is used for a transfusion or for conversion into various blood products. The quantity of infected blood that can transmit hepatitis may be as little as one-millionth of a milliliter. The absence of a scientific check on quality and safety means that the subsequent biological condition of those who receive blood constitutes the ultimate test of whether the virus was present in the donation; in effect, therefore, the patient is the laboratory for testing the quality of the gift of blood.

But few — if any — patients know that their bodies perform this role. They do not ask and in most cases are in no condition to ask: Will this blood cause hepatitis? Who supplied it? In what circumstances? What safeguards were employed to ensure as far as humanly possible that this blood is not going to harm or kill me? Even if such questions were asked, it has to be recognized that they could not be satisfactorily answered by those administering transfusions or blood products.

In these situations of consumer ignorance and uncertainty, as in many others in the field of medical care, the patient has to trust the medical profession and the organized system of medical care. He has no alternative but to trust. If, subsequently, he develops hepatitis and it is clinically diagnosed as such (which in many instances it is difficult to do), it is still virtually impossible in most cases to establish a causal relationship and to connect the infection or the ill health to the blood transfusion or the blood product. Many complex factors are involved in these difficulties of diagnosing, identifying, and naming the causal agent(s), one being the long incubation period in serum hepatitis — possibly up to six months.

Not only, therefore, has the patient no alternative to trust when receiving blood but, subsequently, and apart from a very small proportion of obvious cases of infection where causal attribution can be established, he can have no redress. He is not only unknowingly the laboratory test of "goodness," he and his family must bear the biological, social, and economic costs of infected blood and misplaced trust in terms of physical incapacity, loss of earnings and career prospects, the effects on family life, and other unquantifiable factors. These costs may be mitigated, but they may never be entirely eliminated. In many cases, the costs are irreversible.

For these and many other reasons those responsible for blood-transfusion services have stressed the great importance of maintaining the most rigorous standards in the selection of donors. The state of health, the health history, and the social habits of the donor become crucial because the laboratory cannot identify the virus. Again, however, there are definite limits to the clinical assessment of "health"; no single test or battery of liver-function tests has yet been devised which will reliably distinguish carriers of the virus from "normal" subjects.

A great deal depends, therefore, on the truthfulness of the donor in the processes of medical examination, history-taking, and selection. Just as the recipient of blood has to trust the doctor, so the doctor has, within limits, to trust the giver. Those responsible for making medical decisions and administering blood have to act in certain circumstances on the assumption that donors have been truthful. In situations of total ignorance and total helplessness this is one social right the patient has — the right to truthfulness. Essentially, this is because he can exercise no preferences, and because one man's untruthfulness can reduce another man's welfare.

In different blood-donation systems, therefore, we are led to ask: What particular set of conditions and arrangements permits and encourages maximum truthfulness on the part of donors? To what extent can honesty be maximized? Can this objective be pursued regardless of the donor's motives for giving blood? What principles should the medical profession, in the interests of patients and of the profession, consider as fundamental in the organization and operation of blood-donor programs?

Is the Gift a Good One?

Martin L. Gross has summarized the evidence on the risks of hepatitis:

Hepatitis is the most widespread transfusion danger for the hospital patient, the result of contaminated blood. Its exact toll is elusive, but the *Journal of the American Medical Association* has editorially indicated that the hepatitis transfusion problem is significant and considerably more prevalent than previously thought. "It has been reliably shown" (ran the editorial), "that an essential therapeutic measure, blood transfusion, causes death in approximately one of every 150 transfusions in persons over 40 years of age as a result of serum hepatitis. Since this is the age group to which most blood transfusions are given, and since many hundreds are given daily, such a high fatality rate becomes a problem."

Key area studies — in Chicago, New Jersey, Philadelphia, Los Angeles, and Baltimore — which have carefully followed up transfused patients are discouraging. The hepatitis scourge, they show, strikes about one in 25 to 50 patients, with sizable death rates of up to 20 percent of those stricken. "It appears that the incidence of hepatitis after blood transfusion is greater than prior estimates have indicated," states Dr. John R. Senior, a Philadelphia researcher. Dr. Garrott Allen of Chicago has reported hepatitis danger so extensive that it surprised the most inured of the profession: 3.6 percent of all transfused hospital patients later contracted the disease (the risk rises with the number of units transfused). Judging from these samples, there may be 75,000 cases of hepatitis yearly, with almost 10,000 deaths.

More optimistic statistics have been garnered in Boston by Tufts University School of Medicine researchers with a hopeful transfusion rationale for the future. A 12-year study of the nine Boston teaching hospitals has produced only 171 patients rehospitalized for posttransfusion hepatitis, 12 percent of whom died. Since their total study represents about 5 percent of the nation's one-year blood use, we might thus expect 3,500 cases nationally. The actual toll of blood-transfusion hepatitis is possibly between the extremes of the Boston and Chicago studies.

DONORS AND DISEASE

Over the past decade many studies in different parts of the United States have incriminated the paid donor (and blood obtained from commercial blood banks) as the major source of infection. The most recently reported of these studies was conducted by Dr. Paul Schmidt and his colleagues at the National Institutes of Health, Bethesda.

This was a controlled prospective study (unlike many previous retrospective ones) of two groups of patients 21 years and older who were undergoing cardiac surgery at the National Institutes of Health hospital. There were no significant differences between the groups with respect to age, sex, type of heart disease, type of operation, and severity of preoperative symptoms. One group received 94 percent of their blood from one or both of two commercial blood sources employing paid donors (in the Mississippi Valley area and an East Coast port city). The second group received 97 percent of their blood from voluntary donors in the Washington area. The average number of units of blood transfused per patient was 18.5 in the commercial group and slightly more (19.6) in the voluntary group.

In the commercial group, the total hepatitis attack rate was 53 percent; in the voluntary group, nil. This study suggests not only that there is an extremely high attack rate among cardiac surgery cases (average age 47) transfused with paid blood in the United States but also that an immense number of cases of infection are at present undetected. Because the number of patients involved was small (a total of 68), surveillance of the hepatitis risk is being continued and expanded on a nationwide basis. Further studies are also under way to eliminate the possibility of a geographic factor (because some of the paid blood was obtained from the Mississippi Valley area).

Nor is the problem of serum hepatitis confined to the use of whole blood. There is a serious risk in the use of whole pooled plasma and certain blood products, the production of which has been, as we saw, greatly aided by the use of plasmapheresis programs. It has been argued, however, that, compared with the hepatitis risks involved in the use of walk-in, irregular, skid-row donor types, more regular selected, longer-term plasmapheresis donors have a lower carrier rate. But a great deal depends here — as it does with all donors — on two factors: the precise nature of external quality and safety controls exercised by some scientific supervisory agency (even though there are limits to effective screening) and, second, the degree of *continued* truthfulness among paid donors.

As to the controls, it has been repeatedly shown in the United States that the official public-health standards designed to ensure the continued safety, purity, and potency of biological products are only minimal standards and in many cases are either inapplicable, inadequate, or ineffective (partly because of the inherent difficulties of continually inspecting and checking all procedures at blood banks). "Under the standards set by the National Institutes of Health, an ancient physician, a nurse, and a former bartender can theoretically combine their resources to form a blood bank. They can draw most of their blood from skid-row donors at the minimum fee and sell their blood to hospitals that seek the lowest bidder and are not concerned with the scientific aspects of blood banking." Moreover, the great expansion during 1968–69 in chains of profit-making hospitals (newly built hospitals as well as voluntary hospitals bought by some 33 nationwide investor-owned companies) is likely to increase the risks as more blood is purchased from commercial banks. Altruistic donors can hardly be expected to give their blood to profit-making hospitals.

With regard to the issue of truthfulness, again it has been repeatedly shown that paid donors — and especially poor donors badly in need of money — are, on average and compared with voluntary donors, relatives, and friends, more reluctant and less likely to reveal a full medical history and to provide information about recent contacts with infectious disease, recent inoculations, and about their diets, drinking, and drug habits that would disqualify them as donors.

PRISONERS OF COMMERCE

The hazards involved in the commercial blood-transfusion system, both to the American people and internationally, were made more explicit in 1969 by reports on the activities of Southern Food and Drug Research and its associated corporations. These corporations, operating in three states, acted as "intermediate contractors" to some 37 major American pharmaceutical firms, a number of which have large international markets. Their main role, as commercial enterprises, was to supply plasma, hyperimmune immunoglobulin, and other products and to carry out clinical trials on human beings of proposed new pharmaceutical products. The supply of hyperimmune immunoglobulin (used for therapeutic purposes in connection with mumps, whooping cough, tetanus, and small-pox) involved vaccinating donors to build up the antibodies in the plasma. The technique mainly used was plasmapheresis.

With the assistance of prison physicians (some of whom were re-munerated by these corporations) extensive use was made of prisoners (who were paid for taking pills, vaccinations, and supplying plasma) from 1962 to 1969. In all, these corporations are said to have conducted be-tween 25 and 50 percent of the initial drug tests (or first-phase tests usu-ally carried out on healthy subjects) annually undertaken in the United States.

A series of investigations and inquiries into the activities of these cor-porations reported:

1. Potentially fatal new compounds have been tested on prisoners with little or no direct medical observation of the results.

2. Prisoners failed to swallow pills, failed to report serious reactions to those they did swallow, and failed to receive careful laboratory tests.

3. Control records for validation purposes were totally inadequate, plasmapheresis rooms were "sloppy," and gross contamination of the rooms containing donors' plasma was evident.

4. One prisoner on plasmapheresis received back another man's red cells and was seriously damaged for life.

5. Another prisoner, injected with a whooping cough vaccine, died.

6. Large outbreaks of hepatitis occurred at various prisons, involving over 1,000 prisoners of whom at least six died.

7. It is alleged that several agencies of the Department of Health, Edu-cation and Welfare knew for years about the activities and standards of these corporations and did not curtail or stop them.

8. Many internationally known pharmaceutical firms knew of the stan-dards of medical supervision, laboratory and quality control being exer-cised by these corporations. No concerted or collective action was taken to stop using these intermediaries. Some firms remained the biggest con-sumers of Southern Food and Drug Research and its associated corpora-tions. Those who were still using these facilities in 1969 are reported to have defended the validity of the data provided.

This is only a brief summary of an immense amount of documentation available in the United States. We have not included here much material raising ethical and political issues similar to those made explicit in the Nuremberg Code.

This case — or series of cases — is relevant in a number of ways to the problems raised here: the issues of donor "truthfulness," theories of social costs in relation to blood and blood products, and questions of safety, purity, and potency.

In private market terms, we see that "untruthfulness" was maximized at many points in the system, from the prisoners themselves to officials employed by the pharmaceutical firms. The social costs involved extend far beyond the areas of cost-benefit analysis conventionally studied by economists and statisticians. They embrace the prisoners and their families (many of whom were Negroes), the prison system itself, the medical profession, the pharmaceutical industry in the United States, and the consumers of these products not only in the United States but in many countries of the world.

At least one conclusion can be drawn at this point. Governmental systems of licensing, inspection, and quality validation appear to be helpless to control private markets in blood and blood products. Their ineffectiveness has contributed in recent years to the phenomenon in the United States of numerous legal suits based on negligence, implied warranty, and various food and drug acts. What is involved, of course, is the question whether blood transfusion is a commercial transaction or a professional service.

. . . If blood as a living human tissue is increasingly bought and sold as an article of commerce and profit accrues from such transactions, then it follows that the laws of commerce must, in the end, prevail. What this trend holds in store for the future of medicine in the United States as legally it is increasingly treated as a trade and as the doctrine of charitable immunity disappears into the mists of history is not a matter for this particular study. To consider all such legal ramifications would eventually lead us away from law and into the broader issues of medical ethics, the purpose of medicine, and, ultimately, the value of human life.

Nevertheless, the choice of blood as an illustration and case study was no idle academic thought; it was deliberate. Short of examining humankind itself and the institution of slavery — of men and women as market commodities — blood as a living tissue may now constitute in Western societies one of the ultimate tests of where the "social" begins and the "economic" ends. If blood is considered in theory, in law, and is treated in practice as a trading commodity, then ultimately human hearts, kidneys, eyes, and other organs of the body may also come to be treated as commodities to be bought and sold in the marketplace.

Profitable competition for blood "is a healthy thing," it is argued by some in the United States. It improves services, increases supplies of blood, and is the answer to a "shiftless, socialistic approach." If competition for blood were eliminated, it is warned, it would "be the entering wedge for the destruction of our entire antimonopoly structure" and would threaten the interests of "great pharmaceutical companies."

Is medical care — analyzed in its many component parts, such as blood-transfusion services — a consumption good indistinguishable from other goods and services in the private economic market? What are the consequences, national and international, of treating human blood as a commercial commodity? If blood is morally sanctioned as something to be bought and sold, what ultimately is the justification for not promoting individualistic private markets in all other component areas of medical care, social work skills, the use of patients and clients for professional training, and other "social service" institutions and processes?

X   SOCIAL SERVICES

A major theme in the ideology of American capitalism is that people should not get "something for nothing." Human welfare is seen as dependent on individual effort. The idea that society as a whole should have responsibility for the welfare of its members is downplayed or rejected altogether. There are exceptions to this, of course: large corporations that run into financial trouble are not hesitant to ask for massive amounts of support from the rest of us in the form of government subsidies. But for most people, such basic human needs as food, shelter, and the care of children are things that we have to acquire on our own, if we can. For those who can't afford them at all, government programs do exist to provide basic social services — but they are provided skimpily, inhumanely, and usually only in amounts that are sufficient to keep people from open rebellion, but insufficient for decent living. And in times of economic crisis, our meager social services are among the first casualties of governmental belt-tightening.

The welfare system offers a classic example of this. Its ideology comes to us from the repressive and Puritanical mentality of seventeenth century England. A central theme from the beginning has been the division of the poor into the categories of "deserving" and "undeserving" — the former including the aged and disabled, the latter comprising those who were presumably physically able, but "unwilling," to work: "study beggars." Most of our current programs for the poor tend to treat them as "undeserving." In these programs, benefits are contingent on "good" behavior, and are accompanied by a host of special provisions and restrictions applying only to those "on welfare." In return for granting some support, the welfare system assumes the authority to demand of the poor behavior that is not demanded of anyone else. In this way a "dual system of law" has developed: one law for the poor, another for everyone else.

If, as many people have argued, this system is cruel and unjust, why has it persisted? In "The Relief of Welfare," Frances Fox Piven and Richard A. Cloward analyze the functions that public welfare has historically performed for European and American economies. According to them, the welfare system exists to regulate the labor force in capitalist societies. The puny and demeaning levels of assistance and the tendency to throw people off the welfare rolls for "immoral" behavior are means of enforcing low-wage work during times when labor is needed; but under conditions of massive unemployment, the welfare rolls are expanded in order to forestall disorder. Thus, the persistence of a degrading welfare apparatus, for Piven and Cloward, is linked to the most fundamental requirements of an essentially unstable economic system. As long as we are unwilling to provide decent and decently paid work there must be a system to enforce work by making nonwork degrading and painful.

The development of child care in the United States has been shaped by similar principles. Day care, in fact, has been traditionally regarded in this country as primarily a welfare problem — something to be provided only to "problem" families who can't otherwise take care of their children. As Rosalyn Baxandall notes, child care is viewed as the responsibility of the individual nuclear family (especially the mother), an attitude that ignores the fact that millions of mothers of very young children must work full time. A real commitment to the welfare of children, Baxandall argues, would mean the creation of free, parent-controlled day care for all who wanted it.

The same attitudes show up again at the other end of the life cycle. In America, as the selection from *Time* points out, aging has become a painful and demeaning process for many people. As in the case of child care, there is no public commitment to providing a comfortable and meaningful life for the aged. Dealing with old age is considered a private problem. Those with enough means may be able to afford good housing and medical care, but for most growing old means segregation in "nursing homes" — which may be shockingly inadequate or worse — or isolation in private poverty.

The privatization of what should be a social responsibility

can also be seen in the case of American housing. As Cushing Dolbeare shows, the United States, in recent years, has actually been moving farther and farther away from accepting public responsibility for providing shelter. Millions of Americans live in housing that is dilapidated, unsafe, or lacking in basic facilities. For millions of others, decent housing represents a crushing financial burden. Government's approach to the housing problem has been passive, subordinated to the interests of the large real estate and financial institutions that now shape the housing situation in this country. According to Dolbeare, the housing mess won't begin to be solved until housing is seen as a basic social right, rather than as a "private commodity best supplied by the private market."

34. THE RELIEF OF WELFARE

*Frances Fox Piven
and Richard A. Cloward*

Aid to Families with Dependent Children (AFDC) is our major relief program. It has lately become the source of a major public controversy, owing to a large and precipitous expansion of the rolls. Between 1950 and 1960, only 110,000 families were added to the rolls, yielding a rise of 17 percent. In the 1960's, however, the rolls exploded, rising by more than 225 percent. At the beginning of the decade, 745,000 families were receiving aid; by 1970, some 2,500,000 families were on the rolls. Still, this is not the first, the largest or the longest relief explosion. Since the inauguration of relief in Western Europe three centuries ago, the rolls have risen and fallen in response to economic and political forces. An examination of these forces should help to illuminate the meaning of the current explosion, as well as the meaning of current proposals for reform.

Relief arrangements, we will argue, are ancillary to economic arrangements. Their chief function is to regulate labor, and they do that in two general ways. First, when mass unemployment leads to outbreaks of turmoil, relief programs are ordinarily initiated or expanded to absorb and

From *Regulating the Poor* by Frances Fox Piven and Richard A. Cloward. Copyright © 1971 by Frances Fox Piven and Richard A. Cloward. Reprinted by permission of Pantheon Books, a Division of Random House, Inc.

control enough of the unemployed to restore order; then, as turbulence subsides, the relief system contracts, expelling those who are needed to populate the labor market. Relief also performs a labor-regulating function in this shrunken state, however. Some of the aged, the disabled, and others who are of no use as workers are left on the relief rolls, and their treatment is so degrading and punitive as to instill in the laboring masses a fear of the fate that awaits them should they relax into beggary and pauperism. To demean and punish those who do not work is to exalt by contrast even the meanest labor at the meanest wages. These regulative functions of relief are made necessary by several strains toward instability inherent in capitalist economics.

LABOR AND MARKET INCENTIVES

All human societies compel most of their members to work, to produce the goods and services that sustain the community. All societies also define the work their members must do and the conditions under which they must do it. Sometimes the authority to compel and define is fixed in tradition, sometimes in the bureaucratic agencies of a central government. Capitalism, however, relies primarily upon the mechanisms of a market — the promise of financial rewards or penalties — to motivate men and women to work and to hold them to their occupational tasks.

But the development of capitalism has been marked by periods of cataclysmic change in the market, the main sources being depression and rapid modernization. Depressions mean that the regulatory structure of the market simply collapses; with no demand for labor, there are no monetary rewards to guide and enforce work. By contrast, during periods of rapid modernization — whether the replacement of handicraft by machines, the relocation of factories in relation to new sources of power or new outlets for distribution, or the demise of family subsistence farming as large-scale commercial agriculture spreads — portions of the laboring population may be rendered obsolete or at least temporarily maladjusted. Market incentives do not collapse; they are simply not sufficient to compel people to abandon one way of working and living in favor of another.

In principle, of course, people dislocated by modernization become part of a labor supply to be drawn upon by a changing and expanding labor market. As history shows, however, people do not adapt so readily to drastically altered methods of work and to the new and alien patterns of social life dictated by that work. They may resist leaving their traditional communities and the only life they know. Bred to labor under the discipline of sun and season, however severe that discipline may be, they may resist the discipline of factory and machine, which, though it may be no more severe, may seem so because it is alien. The process of human adjustment to such economic changes has ordinarily entailed a generation of mass unemployment, distress, and disorganization.

Now, if human beings were invariably given to enduring these travails with equanimity, there would be no governmental relief systems at all. But often they do not, and for reasons that are not difficult to see. The regulation of civil behavior in all societies is intimately dependent on stable occupational arrangements. So long as people are fixed in their work roles, their activities and outlooks are also fixed; they do what they must and think what they must. Each behavior and attitude is shaped by the reward of a good harvest or the penalty of a bad one, by the factory paycheck or the danger of losing it. But mass unemployment breaks that bond, loosening people from the main institution by which they are regulated and controlled.

Moreover, mass unemployment that persists for any length of time diminishes the capacity of other institutions to bind and constrain people. Occupational behaviors and outlooks underpin a way of life and determine familial, communal, and cultural patterns. When large numbers of people are suddenly barred from their traditional occupations, the entire network of social control is weakened. There is no harvest or paycheck to enforce work and the sentiments that uphold work; without work, people cannot conform to familial and communal roles; and if the dislocation is widespread, the legitimacy of the social order itself may come to be questioned. The result is usually civil disorder — crime, mass protests, riots — a disorder that may even threaten to overturn existing social and economic arrangements. It is then that relief programs are initiated or expanded.

Western relief systems originated in the mass disturbances that erupted during the long transition from feudalism to capitalism beginning in the sixteenth century. As a result of the declining death rates in the previous century, the population of Europe grew rapidly; as the population grew, so did transiency and beggary. Moreover, distress resulting from population changes, agricultural and other natural disasters, which had characterized life throughout the Middle Ages, was now exacerbated by the vagaries of an evolving market economy, and outbreaks of turbulence among the poor were frequent. To deal with these threats to civil order, many localities legislated severe penalties against vagrancy. Even before the sixteenth century, the magistrates of Basel had defined twenty-five different categories of beggars, together with appropriate punishments for each. But penalties alone did not always deter begging, especially when economic distress was severe and the numbers affected were large. Consequently, some localities began to augment punishment with provisions for the relief of the vagrant poor.

CIVIL DISORDER AND RELIEF

A French town that initiated such an arrangement early in the sixteenth century was Lyons, which was troubled both by a rapidly growing population and by the economic instability associated with the transition to capitalism. By 1500 Lyons' population had already begun to increase. During the decades that followed, the town became a prosperous commercial and manufacturing center — the home of the European money market and of expanding new trades in textiles, printing, and metalworking. As it thrived it attracted people, not only from the surrounding countryside, but even from Italy, Flanders, and Germany. All told, the population of Lyons probably doubled between 1500 and 1540.

All this was very well as long as the newcomers could be absorbed by industry. But not all were, with the result that the town came to be plagued by beggars and vagrants. Moreover, prosperity was not continuous: some trades were seasonal and others were periodically troubled by foreign competition. With each economic downturn, large numbers of unemployed workers took to the streets to plead for charity, cluttering the very doorsteps of the better-off classes. Lyons was most vulnerable during periods of bad harvest, when famine not only drove up the cost of bread for urban artisans and journeymen but brought hordes of peasants into the city, where they sometimes paraded through the streets to exhibit their misfortune. In 1529 food riots erupted, with thousands of Lyonnais looting granaries and the homes of the wealthy; in 1530, artisans and journeymen armed themselves and marched through the streets; in 1531, mobs of starving peasants literally overran the town.

Such charity as had previously been given in Lyons was primarily the responsibility of the church or of those of the more prosperous who sought to purchase their salvation through almsgiving. But this method of caring for the needy obviously stimulated rather than discouraged begging and created a public nuisance to the better-off citizens (one account of the times describes famished peasants so gorging themselves as to die on the very doorsteps where they were fed). Moreover, to leave charity to church and citizen meant that few got aid, and those not necessarily according to their need. The result was that mass disorders periodically erupted.

The increase in disorder led the rulers of Lyons to conclude that the giving of charity should no longer be governed by private whim. In 1534, churchmen, notables, and merchants joined together to establish a centralized administration for disbursing aid. All charitable donations were consolidated under a central body, the "Aumone-Generale," whose responsibility was to "nourish the poor forever." A list of the needy was established by a house-to-house survey, and tickets for bread and money were issued according to fixed standards. Indeed, most of the features of modern welfare — from criteria to discriminate the worthy poor from the unworthy, to strict procedures for surveillance of recipients as well as measures for their rehabilitation — were present in Lyons' new relief administration. By the 1550's, about 10 percent of the town's population was receiving relief.

Within two years of the establishment of relief in Lyons, King Francis I ordered each parish in France to register its poor and to provide for the "impotent" out of a fund of contributions. Elsewhere in Europe, other townships began to devise similar systems to deal with the vagrants and mobs cast up by famine, rapid population growth, and the transition from feudalism to capitalism.

England also felt these disturbances, and just as it pioneered in developing an intensively capitalist economy, so it was at the forefront in developing nationwide, public relief arrangements. During the closing years of the fifteenth century, the emergence of the wool industry in England began to transform agricultural life. As sheep raising became more profitable, much land was converted from tillage to pasturage, and large numbers of peasants were displaced by an emerging entrepreneurial gentry which either bought their land or cheated them out of it. The result was great tumult among the peasantry, as the Webbs were to note:

When the sense of oppression became overwhelming, the popular feeling manifested itself in widespread organized tumults, disturbances, and insurrections, from Wat Tyler's rebellion of 1381, and Jack Cade's march on London of 1460, to the Pilgrimage of Grace in 1536, and Kett's Norfolk rising of 1549 — all of them successfully put down, but sometimes not without great struggle, by the forces which the government could command.

Early in the sixteenth century, the national government moved to try to forestall such disorders. In 1528 the Privy Council, anticipating a fall in foreign sales as a result of the war in Flanders, tried to induce the cloth manufacturers of Suffolk to retain their employees. In 1534, a law passed under Henry VIII attempted to limit the number of sheep in any one holding in order to inhibit the displacement of farmers and agricultural laborers and thus forestall potential disorders. Beginning in the 1550's the Privy Council attempted to regulate the price of grain in poor harvests. But the entrepreneurs of the new market economy were not so readily curbed, so that during this period another method of dealing with labor disorders was evolved.

Early in the sixteenth century, the national government moved to replace parish arrangements for charity with a nationwide system of relief. In 1531, an act of Parliament decreed that local officials search out and register those of the destitute deemed to be impotent and give them a document authorizing begging. As for those who sought alms without authorization, the penalty was public whipping till the blood ran.

Thereafter, other arrangements for relief were rapidly instituted. An act passed in 1536, during the reign of Henry VIII, required local parishes to take care of their destitute and to establish a procedure for the collection and administration of donations for that purpose by local officials. (In the same year Henry VIII began to expropriate monasteries, helping to assure secular control of charity.) With these developments, the penalties for beggary were made more severe, including an elaborate schedule of branding, enslavement, and execution for repeated offenders. Even so, by 1572 beggary was said to have reached alarming proportions, and in that year local responsibility for relief was more fully spelled out by the famous Elizabethan Poor Laws, which established a local tax, known as the poor rate, as the means for financing the care of paupers and required that justices of the peace serve as the overseers of the poor.

After each period of activity, the parish relief machinery tended to lapse into disuse, until bad harvests or depression in manufacturing led again to widespread unemployment and misery, to new outbreaks of disorder, and then to a resuscitation and expansion of relief arrangements. The most illuminating of these episodes, because it bears so much similarity to the present-day relief explosion in the United States, was the expansion of relief during the massive agricultural dislocations of the late eighteenth century.

Most of the English agricultural population had lost its landholdings long before the eighteenth century. In place of the subsistence farming found elsewhere in Europe, a three-tier system of landowners, tenant farmers, and agricultural workers had evolved in England. The vast majority of the people were a landless proletariat, hiring out by the year to tenant farmers. The margin of their subsistence, however, was provided by common and waste lands, on which they gathered kindling, grazed animals, and hunted game to supplement their meager wages. Moreover, the use of the commons was part of the English villager's birthright, his sense of place and pride. It was the disruption of these arrangements and the ensuing disorder that led to the new expansion of relief.

By the middle of the eighteenth century, an increasing population, advancing urbanization, and the growth of manufacturing had greatly expanded markets for agricultural products, mainly for cereals to feed the urban population and for wool to supply the cloth manufacturers. These new markets, together with the introduction of new agricultural methods (such as cross-harrowing), led to large-scale changes in agriculture. To take advantage of rising prices and new techniques, big landowners moved to expand their holdings still further by buying up small farms and, armed with parliamentary Bills of Enclosure, by usurping the common and waste lands which had enabled many small cottagers to survive. Although this process began much earlier, it accelerated rapidly after 1750; by 1850, well over six million acres of common land — or about one-quarter of the total arable acreage — had been consolidated into private holdings and turned primarily to grain production. For great numbers of agricultural workers, enclosure meant no land on which to grow subsistence crops to feed their families, no grazing land to produce wool for home spinning and weaving, no fuel to heat their cottages, and new restrictions against hunting. It meant, in short, the loss of a major source of subsistence for the poor.

New markets also stimulated a more businesslike approach to farming. Landowners demanded the maximum rent from tenant farmers, and tenant farmers in turn began to deal with their laborers in terms of cash calculations. Specifically, this meant a shift from a master–servant relationship to an employer–employee relationship, but on the harshest terms. Where laborers had previously worked by the year and frequently lived with the farmer, they were now hired for only as long as they were needed and were then left to fend for themselves. Pressures toward short-term hiring also resulted from the large-scale cultivation of grain crops for market, which called for a seasonal labor force, as opposed to mixed subsistence farming, which required year-round laborers. The use of cash rather than produce as the medium of payment for work, a rapidly spreading practice, encouraged partly by the long-term inflation of grain prices, added to the laborer's hardships. Finally the rapid increase in rural population at a time when the growth of woolen manufacturing continued to provide an incentive to convert land from tillage to pasturage produced a large labor surplus, leaving agricultural workers with no leverage in bargaining for wages with their tenant-farmer employers. The result was widespread unemployment and terrible hardship.

None of these changes took place without resistance from small farmers and laborers who, while they had known hardship before, were now being forced out of a way of life and even out of their villages. Some rioted when Bills of Enclosure were posted; some petitioned the Parliament for their repeal. And when hardship was made more acute by a succession of poor harvests in the 1790's, there were widespread food riots.

Indeed, throughout the late eighteenth and early nineteenth centuries, the English countryside was periodically beseiged by turbulent masses of the displaced rural poor and the towns were racked by Luddism, radicalism, trade-unionism and Chartism, even while the ruling classes worried about what the French Revolution might augur for England. A solution to disorder was needed, and that solution turned out to be relief. The poor-relief system — first created in the sixteenth century to control the earlier disturbances caused by population growth and the commercialization of agriculture — now rapidly became a major institution of English life. Between 1760 and 1784, taxes for relief — the poor rate — rose by 60 percent; they doubled by 1801, and rose by 60 percent more in the next decade. By 1818, the poor rate was over six times as high as it had been in 1760. Hobsbaum estimates that up to the 1850's, upwards of 10 percent of the English population were paupers. The relief system, in short, was expanded in order to absorb and regulate the masses of discontented people uprooted from agriculture but not yet incorporated into industry.

Relief arrangements evolved more slowly in the United States, and the first major relief crisis did not occur until the Great Depression. The inauguration of massive relief-giving was not simply a response to widespread economic distress, for millions had remained unemployed for several years without obtaining aid. What finally led the national government to proffer aid was the great surge of political disorder that followed the economic catastrophe, a disorder which eventually led to the convulsive voting shifts of 1932. After the election, the federal government abandoned its posture of aloofness toward the unemployed. Within a matter of months, billions of dollars were flowing to localities, and the relief rolls skyrocketed. By 1935, upwards of 20 million people were on the dole.

The contemporary relief explosion, which began in the early 1960's, has its roots in agricultural modernization. No one would disagree that the rural economy of America, especially in the South, has undergone a profound transformation in recent decades. In 1945, there was one tractor per farm; in 1964 there were two. Mechanization and other technological developments, in turn, stimulated the enlargement of farm holdings. Between 1959 and 1961, one million farms disappeared; the three million remaining farms averaged 377 acres in size — 30 percent larger than the average farm ten years earlier. The chief and most obvious effect of these changes was to lessen the need for agricultural labor. In the years between 1950 and 1965 alone, a Presidential Commission on Rural Poverty was to discover, "New machines and new methods increased farm output in the United States by 45 percent, and reduced farm employment by 45 percent." A mere 4 percent of the American labor force now works the land, signaling an extraordinary displacement of people, with accompanying upheaval and suffering. The best summary measure of this dislocation is probably the volume of migration to the cities; over 20 million people, more than four million of them black, left the land after 1940.

Nor were all these poor absorbed into the urban economic system. Blacks were especially vulnerable to unemployment. At the close of the Korean War, the national nonwhite unemployment rate leaped from 4.5 percent in 1953 to 9.9 percent in 1954. By 1958, it had reached 12.6 percent, and it fluctuated between 10 and 13 percent until the escalation of the war in Vietnam after 1964.

These figures pertain only to people unemployed and looking for work.

They do not include the sporadically unemployed or those employed at extremely low wages. Combining such additional measures with the official unemployment measure produces a subemployment index. This index was first used in 1966 — well after the economic downturns that characterized the years between the end of the Korean War and the escalation of the war in Vietnam. Were subemployment data available for the "Eisenhower recession" years, especially in the slum ghettos of the larger central cities, they would surely show much higher rates than prevailed in 1966. In any event, the figures for 1966 revealed a nonwhite subemployment rate of 21.6 percent compared with a white rate of 7.6 percent.

However, despite the spread of economic deprivation, whether on the land or in the cities, the relief system did not respond. In the entire decade between 1950 and 1960, the national AFDC caseload rose by only 17 percent. Many of the main urban targets of migration showed equally little change: the rolls in New York City moved up by 16 percent, and in Los Angeles by 14 percent. In the South, the rolls did not rise at all.

But in the 1960's, disorder among the black poor erupted on a wide scale, and the welfare rolls erupted as well. The welfare explosion occurred during several years of the greatest domestic disorder since the 1930's — perhaps the greatest in our history. It was concurrent with the turmoil produced by the civil-rights struggle, with widespread and destructive rioting in the cities, and with the formation of a militant grass-roots movement of the poor dedicated to combatting welfare restrictions. Not least, the welfare rise was also concurrent with the enactment of a series of ghetto-placating federal programs (such as the antipoverty program) which, among other things, hired thousands of poor people, social workers, and lawyers who, it subsequently turned out, greatly stimulated people to apply for relief and helped them obtain it. And the welfare explosion, although an urban phenomenon generally, was greatest in just that handful of large metropolitan counties where the political turmoil of the mid- and late 1960's was the most acute.

The magnitude of the welfare rise is worth noting. The national AFDC caseload rose by more than 225 percent in the 1960's. In New York City, the rise was more than 300 percent; the same was so in Los Angeles. Even in the South, where there had been no rise at all in the 1950's, the rolls rose by more than 60 percent. And most significant of all, the bulk of the increase took place after 1965 — that is, after disorder reached a crescendo. More than 80 percent of the national rise in the 1960's occurred in the last five years of the decade. In other words, the welfare rolls expanded, today as at earlier times, only in response to civil disorder.

While muting the more disruptive outbreaks of civil disorder (such as rioting), the mere giving of relief does nothing to reverse the disintegration of lower-class life produced by economic change, a disintegration which leads to rising disorder and rising relief rolls in the first place. Indeed, greatly liberalized relief-giving can further weaken work and family norms. To restore order in a more fundamental sense the society must create the means to reassert its authority. Because the market is unable to control men's behavior, a surrogate system of social control must be evolved, at least for a time. Moreover, if the surrogate system is to be consistent with normally dominant patterns, it must restore people to work roles. Thus even though obsolete or unneeded workers are temporarily given direct relief, they are eventually succored only on condition that they work. As these adjustments are made, the functions of relief arrangements may be said to be shifting from regulating disorder to regulating labor.

RESTORING ORDER BY RESTORING WORK

The arrangements, both historical and contemporary, through which relief recipients have been made to work vary, but broadly speaking, there are two main ways: work is provided under public auspices, whether in the recipient's home, in a labor yard, in a workhouse, or on a public-works project; or work is provided in the private market, whether by contracting or indenturing the poor to private employers, or through subsidies designed to induce employers to hire paupers. And although a relief system may at any time use both of these methods of enforcing work, one or the other usually becomes predominant, depending on the economic conditions that first gave rise to disorder.

Publicly subsidized work tends to be used during business depressions, when the demand for labor in the private market collapses. Conversely, arrangements to channel paupers into the labor market are more likely to be used when rapid changes in markets or technology render a segment of the labor supply temporarily maladapted. In the first case, the relief system augments a shrunken labor market; in the other, its policies and procedures are shaped to overcome the poor fit between labor demand and supply.

Public work is as old as public relief. The municipal relief systems initiated on the Continent in the first quarter of the sixteenth century often included some form of public works. In England, the same statute of 1572 that established taxation as the method for financing poor relief charged the overseers of the poor with putting vagrants to work. Shortly afterwards, in 1576, local officials were directed to acquire a supply of raw goods — wool, hemp, iron — which was to be delivered to the needy for processing in their homes, their dole to be fixed according to "the desert of the work."

The favored method of enforcing work throughout most of the history of relief was the workhouse. In 1723, an act of Parliament permitted the local parishes to establish workhouses and to refuse aid to those poor who would not enter; within ten years, there were said to be about fifty workhouses in the environs of London alone.

The destitute have also sometimes been paid to work in the general community or in their own homes. This method of enforcing work evolved in England during the bitter depression of 1840–1841. As unemployment mounted, the poor in some of the larger cities protested against having to leave their communities to enter workhouses in order to obtain relief, and in any case, in some places the workhouses were already full. As a result, various public spaces were designated as "labor yards" to which the unemployed could come by the day to pick oakum, cut wood, and break stone, for which they were paid in food and clothing. The method was used periodically throughout the second half of the nineteenth century; at times of severe distress, very large numbers of the able-bodied were supported in this way.

The first massive use of public work under relief auspices in the United States occurred during the 1930's when millions of the unemployed were subsidized through the Works Progress Administration. The initial response of the Roosevelt administration was to appropriate billions for direct-relief payments. But no one liked direct relief — not the President who called for it, the Congress that legislated it, the administrators who operated it, the people who received it. Direct relief was viewed as a temporary expedient, a way of maintaining a person's body, but not his dignity; a way of keeping the populace from shattering in despair, discontent, and disorder, at least for a while, but not of renewing their pride, of bringing back a way of life. For their way of life had been anchored in the discipline of work, and so that discipline had to be restored. The remedy was to abolish direct relief and put the unemployed to work on subsidized projects. These reforms were soon instituted — and with dramatic results. For a brief time, the federal government became the employer of millions of people (although millions of others remained unemployed).

Quite different methods of enforcing work are used when the demand for labor is steady but maladaptions in the labor supply, caused by changes in methods of production, result in unemployment. In such circumstances, relief agencies ordinarily channel paupers directly into the private market. For example, the rapid expansion of English manufacturing during the late eighteenth and early nineteenth centuries produced a commensurately expanded need for factory operatives. But it was no easy matter to get them. Men who had been agricultural laborers, independent craftsmen, or workers in domestic industries (i.e., piecework manufacturing in the home) resisted the new discipline. Between 1778

and 1830, there were repeated revolts by laborers in which local tradesmen and farmers often participated. The revolts failed, of course; the
new industry moved forward inexorably, taking the more dependent and
tractable under its command, with the aid of the relief system.

The burgeoning English textile industry solved its labor problems during the latter part of the eighteenth century by using parish children,
some only four or five years old, as factory operatives. Manufacturers
negotiated regular bargains with the parish authorities, ordering lots of
fifty or more children from the poorhouses. Parish children were an ideal
labor source for new manufacturers. The young paupers could be shipped
to remote factories, located to take advantage of the streams from which
power could be drawn. (With the shift from water power to steam in the
nineteenth century, factories began to locate in towns where they could
employ local children; with that change, the system of child labor became a system of "free" child labor.) The children were also preferred
for their docility and for their light touch at the looms. Moreover, pauper-
children could be had for a bit of food and a bed, and they provided a
very stable labor supply, for they were held fast at their labors by inden-
tures, usually until they were twenty-one.

Sometimes the relief system subsidizes the employment of paupers —
especially when their market value is very low — as when the magistrates
of Lyons provided subsidies to manufacturers who employed pauper
children. In rural England during the late eighteenth century, as more
and more of the population was being displaced by the commercialization
of agriculture, this method was used on a very large scale. To be sure, a
demand for labor was developing in the new manufacturing establishments that would in time absorb many of the uprooted rural poor. But
this did not happen all at once: rural displacement and industrial expansion did not proceed at the same pace or in the same areas, and in any case
the drastic shift from rural village to factory system took time. During the
long interval before people forced off the land were absorbed into manufacturing, many remained in the countryside as virtual vagrants; others
migrated to the towns, where they crowded into hovels and cellars, subject to the vicissitudes of rapidly rising and falling markets, their ranks
continually enlarged by new rural refugees.

These conditions were not the result of a collapse in the market. Indeed, grain prices rose during the second half of the eighteenth century,
and they rose spectacularly during the Revolutionary and Napoleonic
wars. Rather, it was the expanding market for agricultural produce which,
by stimulating enclosure and business-minded farming methods, led to
unemployment and destitution. Meanwhile, population growth, which
meant a surplus of laborers, left the workers little opportunity to resist
the destruction of their traditional way of life — except by crime, riots,

and incendiarism. To cope with these disturbances, relief expanded, but in such a way as to absorb and discipline laborers by supporting the faltering labor market with subsidies.

The subsidy system is widely credited to the sheriff and magistrates of Berkshire, who, in a meeting at Speenhamland in 1795, decided on a scheme by which the Poor Law authorities would supplement the wages of underemployed and underpaid agricultural workers according to a published scale. It was a time when exceptional scarcity of food led to riots all over England, sometimes suppressed only by calling out the troops. With this "double panic of famine and revolution," the subsidy scheme spread, especially in counties where large amounts of acreage had been enclosed.

The local parishes implemented the work subsidy system in different ways. Under the "roundsman" arrangement, the parish overseers sent any man who applied for aid from house to house to get work. If he found work, the employer was obliged to feed him and pay a small sum (6 d) per day, with the parish adding another small sum (4 d). Elsewhere, the parish authorities contracted directly with farmers to have paupers work for a given price, with the parish paying the combined wage and relief subsidy directly to the pauper. In still other places, parish authorities parceled out the unemployed to farmers, who were obliged to pay a set rate or make up the difference in higher taxes. Everywhere, however, the main principle was the same: an underemployed and turbulent populace was being pacified with public allowances, but these allowances were used to restore order by enforcing work, at very low wage levels. Relief, in short, served as a support for a disturbed labor market and as a discipline for a disturbed rural society. As the historians J. L. Hammond and Barbara Hammond were to say, "The meshes of the Poor Law were spread over the entire labor system."

The English Speenhamland plan, while it enjoys a certain notoriety, is by no means unique. The most recent example of a scheme for subsidizing paupers in private employ is the reorganization of American public welfare proposed in the summer of 1969 by President Richard Nixon; the general parallel with the events surrounding Speenhamland is striking. The United States relief rolls expanded in the 1960's to absorb a laboring population made superfluous by agricultural modernization in the South, a population that became turbulent in the wake of forced migration to the cities. As the relief rolls grew to deal with these disturbances, pressure for "reforms" also mounted. Key features of the reform proposals included a national minimum allowance of $1,600 per year for a family of four, coupled with an elaborate system of penalties and incentives to force families to work. In effect, the proposal was intended to support and strengthen a disturbed low-wage labor market by providing what was called in nineteenth-century England a "rate in aid of wages."

Enforcing Low-Wage Work During Periods of Stability

Even in the absence of cataclysmic change, market incentives may be insufficient to compel all people at all times to do the particular work required of them. Incentives may be too meager and erratic, or people may
not be sufficiently socialized to respond to them properly. To be sure, the
productivity of a fully developed capitalist economy would allow for
wages and profits sufficient to entice most of the population to work; and
in a fully developed capitalist society, most people would also be reared
to want what the market holds out to them. They would expect, even
sanctify, the rewards of the marketplace and acquiesce in its vagaries.

But no fully developed capitalist society exists. (Even today in the
United States, the most advanced capitalist country, certain regions and
population groups — such as southern tenant farmers — remain on the
periphery of the wage market and are only partially socialized to the
ethos of the market.) Capitalism evolved slowly and spread slowly. During most of this evolution, the market provided meager rewards for most
workers, and none at all for some. There are still many for whom this is
so. And during most of this evolution, large sectors of the laboring classes
were not fully socialized to the market ethos. The relief system, we contend, has made an important contribution toward overcoming these per-
sisting weaknesses in the capacity of the market to direct and control
men.

Once an economic convulsion subsides and civil order is restored, relief
systems are not ordinarily abandoned. The rolls are reduced, to be sure,
but the shell of the system usually remains, ostensibly to provide aid to
the aged, the disabled, and such other unfortunates who are of no use as
workers. However, the manner in which these "impotents" have always
been treated, in the United States and elsewhere, suggests a purpose
quite different from the remediation of their destitution. These residual
persons have ordinarily been degraded for lacking economic value, relegated to the foul quarters of the workhouse, with its strict penal regimen
and its starvation diet. Once stability was restored, such institutions were
typically proclaimed the sole source of aid, and for a reason bearing
directly on enforcing work.

Conditions in the workhouse were intended to ensure that no one with
any conceivable alternatives would seek public aid. Nor can there be any
doubt of that intent. Consider this statement by the Poor Law Commissioners in 1834, for example:

Into such a house none will enter voluntarily; work, confinement, and discipline will deter the indolent and vicious; and nothing but extreme necessity
will induce any to accept the comfort which must be obtained by the surrender
of their free agency, and the sacrifice of their accustomed habits and gratifica--

tions. *Thus the parish officer, being furnished an unerring test of the necessity of applicants, is relieved from his painful and difficult responsibility: while all have the gratification of knowing that while the necessitous are abundantly relieved, the funds of charity are not wasted by idleness and fraud.*

The method worked. Periods of relief expansion were generally followed by "reform" campaigns to abolish all "outdoor" aid and restrict relief to those who entered the workhouse — as in England in 1722, 1834, and 1871 and in the United States in the 1880's and 1890's — and these campaigns usually resulted in a sharp reduction in the number of applicants seeking aid.

The harsh treatment of those who had no alternative except to fall back upon the parish and accept "the offer of the House" terrorized the impoverished masses in another way as well. It made pariahs of those who could not support themselves; they served as an object lesson, a means of celebrating the virtues of work by the terrible example of their agony. That, too, was a matter of deliberate intent. The workhouse was designed to spur men to contrive ways of supporting themselves by their own industry, to offer themselves to any employer on any terms, rather than suffer the degraded status of pauper.

All of this was evident in the contraction of relief which occurred in the United States at the close of the Great Depression. As political stability returned, emergency relief and work relief programs were reduced and eventually abolished, with many of those cut off being forced into a labor market still glutted with the unemployed. Meanwhile, the Social Security Act had been passed. Widely hailed as a major reform, this measure created our present-day welfare system, with its categorical provisions for the aged, the blind, and families with dependent children (as well as, in 1950, the disabled).

The enactment of this "reform" signaled a turn toward the work-enforcing function of relief arrangements. This became especially evident after World War II during the period of greatly accelerated agricultural modernization. Millions were unemployed in agriculture; millions of others migrated to the cities, where unemployment in the late 1950's reached extremely high levels. But few families were given assistance. By 1960, only 745,000 families had been admitted to the AFDC rolls. That was to change in the 1960's, as we have already noted, but only in response to the most unprecedented disorder in our history.

That families without jobs or income failed to secure relief during the late 1940's and the 1950's was in part a consequence of restrictive statutes and policies — the exclusion of able-bodied males and, in many places, of so-called employable mothers, together with residence laws, relative responsibility provisions, and the like. But it was also — perhaps mainly — a consequence of the persistence of age-old rituals of degradation. AFDC mothers were forced to answer questions about their sexual behavior ("When did you last menstruate?"), open their closets to inspection ("Whose pants are those?"), and permit their children to be interrogated ("Do any men visit your mother?"). Unannounced raids, usually after midnight and without benefit of warrant, in which a recipient's home is searched for signs of "immoral" activities, have also been part of life on AFDC. In Oakland, California, a public-welfare caseworker, Bennie Parish, refused to take part in a raid in January 1962 and was dismissed for insubordination. When he sued for reinstatement, the state argued successfully in the lower courts that people taking public assistance waive certain constitutional rights, among them the right to privacy. (The court's position had at least the weight of long tradition, for the withdrawal of civil rights is an old feature of public relief. In England, for example, relief recipients were denied the franchise until 1918, and as late as 1934 the constitutions of fourteen American states deprived recipients of the right to vote or hold office.)

The main target of these rituals is not the recipient, who ordinarily is not of much use as a worker, but the able-bodied poor who remain in the labor market. It is for these people that the spectacle of the degraded pauper is intended. For example, scandals exposing welfare "fraud" have diffuse effects, for they reach a wide public — including the people who might otherwise apply for aid but who are deterred because of the invidious connotations of being on welfare. Such a scandal occurred in the District of Columbia in 1961, with the result that half of all AFDC mothers were declared to be ineligible for relief, most of them for allegedly "consorting with men." In the several years immediately before the attack, about 6,500 District of Columbia families had applied for aid annually; during the attack, the figure dropped to 4,400 and it did not rise for more than five years — long after that particular scandal had itself subsided.

In sum, market values and market incentives are weakest at the bottom of the social order. To buttress weak market controls and ensure the availability of marginal labor, an outcast class — the dependent poor — is created by the relief system. This class, whose members are of no productive use, is not treated with indifference, but with contempt. Its degradation at the hands of relief officials serves to celebrate the virtue of all work and deters actual or potential workers from seeking aid.

The Current Call for Reform

From our perspective, a relief explosion is a reform just because a large number of unemployed or underemployed people obtain aid. But from the perspective of most people, a relief explosion is viewed as a "crisis."

The contemporary relief explosion in the United States, following a period of unparalleled turbulence in the cities, has thus resulted in a clamor for reform. Similar episodes in the past suggest that pressure for reform signals a shift in emphasis between the major functions of relief arrangements — a shift from regulating disorder to regulating labor.

Pressure for reform stems in part from the fiscal burden imposed on localities when the relief rolls expand. An obvious remedy is for the federal government to simply assume a greater share of the costs, if not the entire cost (at this writing, Congress appears likely to enact such fiscal reform).

However, the much more fundamental problem with which relief reform seeks to cope is the erosion of the work role and the deterioration of the male-headed family. In principle, these problems could be dealt with by economic policies leading to full employment at decent wages, but there is little political support for that approach. Instead, the historic approach to relief explosions is being invoked, which is to restore work through the relief system. Various proposals have been advanced: some would force recipients to report regularly to employment offices; others would provide a system of wage subsidies conditional on the recipient's taking on a job at any wage (including those below the federal minimum wage); still others would inaugurate a straightforward program of public-works projects.

We are opposed to any type of reform intended to promote work through the relief system rather than through the reform of economic policies. When similar relief reforms were introduced in the past, they presaged the eventual expulsion of large numbers of people from the rolls, leaving them to fend for themselves in a labor market where there was too little work and thus subjecting them once again to severe economic exploitation. The reason that this happens is more than a little ironic.

The irony is this: when relief is used to enforce work, it tends to stabilize lower-class occupational, familial, and communal life (unlike direct relief, which merely mutes the worst outbreaks of discontent). By doing so, it diminishes the proclivities toward disruptive behavior which give rise to the expansion of relief in the first place. Once order is restored in this far more profound sense, relief-giving can be virtually abolished as it has been so often in the past. And there is always pressure to abolish large-scale work relief, for it strains against the market ethos and interferes with the untrammeled operation of the marketplace. The point is not just that when a relief concession is offered up, peace and order reign; it is, rather, that when peace and order reign, the relief concession is withdrawn.

The restoration of work through the relief system, in other words, makes possible the eventual return to the most restrictive phase in the cycle of relief-giving. What begins as a great expansion of direct relief, and then turns into some form of work relief, ends finally with a sharp contraction of the rolls. Advocates of relief reform may argue that their reforms will be long-lasting, that the restrictive phase in the cycle will not be reached, but past experience suggests otherwise.

Therefore, in the absence of economic reforms leading to full employment at decent wages, we take the position that the explosion of the rolls is the true relief reform, that it should be defended, and that it should be expanded. Even now, hundreds of thousands of impoverished families remain who are eligible for assistance but who receive no aid at all.

35. WHO SHALL CARE FOR OUR CHILDREN? THE HISTORY AND DEVELOPMENT OF DAY CARE IN THE UNITED STATES

Rosalyn F. Baxandall

Given America's expressed concern for the well-being of children and the shocking extent of childhood poverty, it is all the more ironical that of all groups among the poor it is children who have been most neglected and most shabbily treated by current social policies.[1] Recently, however, there has been a growing concern for the welfare of children. Many child-care programs are under debate or in the early stages of development. Thus it is important that we should analyze various policies and programs to determine if possible which will be most beneficial over the long haul. Such an analysis, limited to the problem of day care, will be undertaken here with an eye to proposals for an effective and meaningful day-care policy.[2]

In planning a child-care policy for today it is extremely important to examine the programs of yesterday. Much of present day-care policy stems from the idea that the nuclear family ought to be a self-sufficient unit, performing according to its structure a series of economic, educative, protective, recreational, sexual, and biological functions.[3] Moreover, it is considered that a natural division of labor occurs within this family

From *Women: A Feminist Perspective,* edited by Jo Freeman. Reprinted by permission of the author.

unit, with nurturance allotted to the mother and breadwinning to the father. Provision for early child-care is seen then as a private matter — to be carried out by the nuclear family, and specifically the mother. Yet not so long ago, and not only in rural areas, child-rearing was shared among members of two or more generations, by mothers-in-law and grand-mothers, often living under the same roof or nearby, and was not the sole province of the young children's mothers. The situation today is of course much different. Most families live in single-generational units, and usually at some distance from relatives.

At the same time that child-rearing has become chiefly the responsibil-ity of the single-family unit, a tendency toward family breakups has developed. According to 1969 figures, one marriage in three results in divorce.[4] Of public resources allocated to child-welfare services, 70 per-cent now goes to foster care.[5] Moreover, more than 11.6 million mothers work; and of these more than 4 million have children under six years of age.[6] Even among those whose children are old enough to be in school, few can be home as early as their children. Where the single-family unit no longer exists as a unit, or is overburdened in one way or another, some other solution must be found. Communal living, a return to ex-tended families, and various forms of day care are among the most frequently mentioned solutions, but only the last will concern us here.

HISTORICAL PERSPECTIVES

The first infant school in the United States seems to have been organized by Robert Owen in New Lanark, Pennsylvania, in the 1830's, after Owen had visited Pestalozzi's infant nursery (modelled on Rousseau's) in Swit-zerland.[7] Owen's school was, however, a utopian experiment that did not inspire many imitators. The next nursery was opened in 1854 in New York City: the Nursery for Children of the Poor. It was followed by the Vir-ginia Nursery (1872) and the Bethany Day (1887), also in New York.[8] These nurseries provided philanthropic assistance, at first to children of Civil War widows, and later to children who were left during the day by their mothers of immigrant origin while they worked in factories or in domestic service. The care was custodial; wealthy women performed it. The purpose was described as being to "feed the starving, clothe the naked, enlighten the soul."[9]

Parallel with the growth of the day nurseries was the rise of the kindergarten movement that took its inspiration from Friedrich Froebel. German liberals brought Froebel's thought to the United States after 1848. Froebel stressed the freeing of little children from harsh discipline and fear, and he sought to encourage children's natural development through creative play, nature study, art, and music.[10] Many settlements adopted kindergarten programs. Elizabeth Peabody House in Boston began as a combination settlement and kindergarten. At Hull House in Chicago, the settlement activist Mary McDowell taught kindergarten. Many neighborhood kindergartens established in Boston in the 1840's and 1880's became settlements in the 1890's.

On the whole, the kindergarten tradition with its stress on education for the normal child led to the establishment of private nursery schools for the well-to-do. In marked contrast, the day nurseries originated in a welfare tradition that emphasized care and protection for the neglected child and family. Of course, the separation of emphasis was by no means rigid. Day care benefitted greatly from improvements in medicine, hygiene, nutrition, and knowledge of child development. Nevertheless, two distinct traditions developed in the field of child care outside the home in this country. This distinction survives today.

In 1896 a National Federation of Day Nurseries was organized to work for high standards. In 1905 physicians began to inspect day-care facilities and examine the children who used the centers. A new concern for research and experimentation in the area of educational aids for the under-privileged followed from the establishment of special teacher-training schools at Bank Street in New York, Merrill Palmer in Detroit, and else-where. These schools, with their emphasis on teacher training, marked the entrance of professionals into the field. Most of these professionals, however, have gone to nurseries and kindergartens rather than into day-care centers. The teachers in day care belong to a *welfare* union, and they are not nearly so well paid as regular teachers who belong to a *teachers'* union.

In 1919 the day nursery was first included in the National Conference of Social Work. By the 1930's, social-work concepts, emphasizing the value of the day nursery in uplifting family life, were particularly being stressed in the day nurseries sponsored by social agencies. For example, Sophie Van S. Theis found "all child caring agencies, irrespective of the particular type of service which they give . . . have come to think in recent years of casework as an essential part of a good child care pro-gram."[11] She goes on to say that traditionally, by charter and by history, the day nursery is a social agency. This social-work legacy — not, of course, a part of nursery-school education — led to further emphasis on day care as a welfare service for the unfortunate, deprived, and malad-justed and to further separation between the two traditions.

The major impetus for day-care development in the United States has been furnished by depression and war. Federally financed nursery schools were established in the 1930's — the greatest era of growth for day care — under the Federal Emergency Relief Administration (FERA), later known as the Works Progress Administration (WPA). The primary pur-pose of federal action in 1933 was to create employment for needy teachers, nutritionists, clerical workers, cooks, and janitors, all part of a larger program to counteract massive unemployment.[12] The WPA spent large sums of public funds on group programs for children aged two to five from welfare-recipient families, and on staff training and parent education. Outstanding people from the child-development field were enlisted for the extensive training programs, which included brief, intensive teacher-training courses to supply immediate staff needs.[13]

WPA day care was conceived primarily as a residual welfare service. The WPA nursery school, by contrast, was identified as an educational service. Nutrition and health services were likewise stressed. Most of the nurseries (except those in New York City) were located in Board of Education facilities and were staffed by jobless school teachers. (In New York City in 1938, of fourteen WPA nurseries only one was located in a public school; the rest were set up in settlements and other social agencies and even in vacant lots, churches, cellars, stores. These were staffed by recreation directors, nurses, and teachers.) By and large the WPA nurseries were kept open ten to twelve hours a day six days a week. By 1937, 40,000 American children were being provided with what most professionals today still consider high standards of care and education.

In October of 1942 the Federal government notified WPA nurseries that they were no longer needed as a source of employment. Therefore, relief-status children need not be served, although children of working mothers might be cared for, so that these mothers could supply the war industries with much-needed woman-power. Also, there were fewer and fewer unemployed teachers to staff the centers; on the contrary, teacher-shortages were beginning to appear.

In 1941 when World War II began, thousands of women entered industrial production to replace the men who had to leave for the armed forces. The demand for women workers was so great that single and childless women alone could not fill it.[14] Women with young children could not work without child care. Consequently in 1941 Congress passed, in a record two weeks, the Community Facilities Act, usually referred to as the Lanham Act. This Act made federal funds available to states on a fifty-fifty matching basis for the expansion of day-care centers and nursery schools in defense areas. These funds could also be used to convert WPA facilities into wartime nurseries. The Children's Bureau was responsible for the development and extension of day-care centers, whereas the United States Office of Education under the aegis of local school boards handled nursery-school operations. Again the separation of approaches, with the more well-to-do children getting education and the poorer children receiving therapeutic services. The Children's Bureau proved quite ambivalent about the idea of women at work; it felt that in the long run a mother's absence would be destructive to the family and to basic American values. Most social-work leaders joined the Children's

Bureau in the concern that publicly funded nurseries might sanction the employment of women.[15] However, widespread popular acceptance of these day-care centers is indicated by the fact that by July of 1945 the Children's Bureau was responsible for 3,100 day-care centers serving 130,000 children,[16] and about 1,600,000 children were receiving care financed largely by federal funds.[17] Every state except New Mexico had some day-care centers. California supported the most: 392 nurseries.

The purpose of these nurseries was first to relieve unemployment and later to encourage the employment of mothers. When the Second World War ended, and women were no longer wanted in the factories, Congress withdrew the Lanham Act funds for day care. Without funds, most of the nurseries had to close. In Chicago there were 23 wartime centers; in 1968 there were none in the entire state of Illinois. In Detroit during the war there were 80 centers, but by 1957, just three remained. In California, where there was a continued demand for women workers in the electronic and aircraft industries, the Lanham Act funds were not withdrawn, and in fact continue to this day on a "temporary" basis, administered through the State Department of Labor.

New York City has a special history. The Lanham Act did not apply to this city because it was not designated a "war-impact" area. However with the threat of withdrawal of funds to the WPA nurseries, active groups of parents and professionals and labor union representatives sent hundreds of petitions, and publicly pressured Mayor LaGuardia not only to keep open existing city-supported nurseries but also to expand the program. The campaign was successful, and day care survived in New York City.

The 1962 Public Welfare amendments to the Social Security Act mark the first time that day care was included in a federal program that was not part of an emergency or wartime measure. However, the major thrust of these amendments was to be in the direction of rehabilitative social services. Day care was provided to protect children whose parents were unable to provide adequate parental supervision for their children. More money ($800,000) was made available for day-care services under the 1962 amendments, but the sum was still far from adequate. The funds were allotted on a matching basis to the states, and it was up to each state to decide whether, and if so how, to launch or extend a day-care program for children.[18] Unfortunately, the poorest, most conservative states with the greatest need generally make the least provision for child care.

The passage of the Economic Opportunity Act in 1964 was another major step in the history of day care. Project Headstart, as an arm of the Office of Economic Opportunity (OEO), directed specific attention to programs for children. Here again, the program was made available only through the states, and the emphasis was on giving poor, deprived children a "head start" rather than on developing day care as a fundamental development service for all. At least 90 percent of the children in Head-start programs must be from families whose income falls below the poverty line, defined as $4,000 for a family of four.[19]

THE NEED

More mothers are working outside the home now than ever before. In the 1940's only 9 percent of all mothers with children under eighteen worked for wages. In 1968, 38 percent of mothers with minor children worked, including 29 percent with children under six and 21 percent with children under three. The labor-participation rate of mothers has increased two times faster than the participation rate of all women, and the labor-participation rate has increased even more rapidly for mothers of pre-school-age children than it has for mothers of school-age children. More women (60 percent) work when the husband has absented himself from the family household, than when the husband is present (30 percent). Among mothers of children under six, a greater proportion of non-white women (42 percent) than white women (25 percent) work for wages.[20]

Day-care facilities have not increased commensurately with the increase in employment of mothers. Licensed public and voluntary day-care centers now care for only one-sixth the number of children cared for at the end of World War II.[21] The gap between availability and need has widened over a period of thirty years. Only in the last few years has the trend been reversed and that, only to a slight degree.[22]

What are the child-care arrangements for these children of working mothers? Forty-six percent of them were cared for in their own homes; 15 percent were cared for by the father; 21 percent by a relative; and 9 percent by a non-relative. Nearly 8 percent looked after themselves; and 4 percent of these were under six, undoubtedly an underestimate, as most women would hesitate to admit that they have no other alternative. Only 2 percent of the children were cared for in group care, whether day-care nurseries or after-school programs.[23]

How many parents would use day care if it were available? The figures are of course impossible to provide. An indication of need is that in New York City in 1970 there were 8,000 children on the waiting list for day-care centers operated by the Department of Social Services. No official waiting lists exist or are available from Central Head Start, but many Head Start centers in 1970 recorded waiting lists as long as the lists of those currently enrolled.[24] Many women are known to be unable to take jobs because there is no day care for their children. The Labor Department made a study of underemployment and unemployment in ten high-poverty areas. They found that one out of every five residents who was not in the labor force but who desired a regular job, gave as the principal reason for not looking for work an inability to arrange child care.[25]

Families who can afford to pay for day care do not have enough nursery facilities, either. For one thing, the suburban areas where many of them live have health and zoning laws precluding establishment of nursery schools in many residential areas.[26] At private nurseries in 1970, competition for admission was record-high, with applications outnumbering vacancies by as much as 150 to one.[27]

ATTITUDES TOWARD DAY CARE

Since there seems clearly to be a desperate need for day care, why is the need unmet? Part of the reason is that day care has been stigmatized by its welfare origins. It is thought of as something needed by the problem family. The Ladies' Home Journal carried a series on day care from June through November of 1967. One conclusion of this series was that "the concept of day care has not been more widely accepted because it was being presented as something solely for the poor and not for every mother."[28] Day care is often equated with maternal deprivation and emotional problems. Mr. Charles Tobin, secretary of the New York State Welfare Conference, said, "The child who needs day care has a family problem which makes it impossible for his parents to fulfill their parental responsibilities without supplementary help."[29]

Psychiatrists and social workers with their stress on the early mother-child relationship have certainly contributed to the negative attitude toward day care. No one has ever bothered to explore the importance of the paternal relationship, or other alternatives to the maternal nexus. As Barbara Wooten, a British sociologist, wrote: "But so long as the study of the role of the father continues to be so much neglected as compared with that of the mother, no opinion on the subject [the emphasis on the young child's need for its mother] can be regarded as more than purely speculative."[30] In the Soviet Union, where group child care from infancy onward is provided for all children as a right, Bronfenbrenner found that not only were the children better socialized, but there was greater companionship between parents and children, and Soviet parents spent even more time with their children than did American parents.[31]

Studies show that there are no detrimental effects on the child if the mother makes an effort to spend an hour or two a day with the child when she is home. Another study illustrates that if a mother enjoys her job, a child benefits from the mother's working. There seems no reason, then, to equate day care with maternal deprivation.[32]

A general prejudice against women's working has also prevented the development of adequate child care facilities outside the home in the United States. A recent study that originated in the Child Welfare League found that the average opinionmaker in the community, including the educator and the social worker, does not believe women should work. If they do work, they are working for frivolous reasons and therefore might better take care of their own children.[33] Another kind of negative attitude toward working women is exemplified by Samuel Nocella, International Vice President of the Amalgamated Clothing Workers, who says: "We have looked upon the presence of women in industry a little cynically because years ago we felt that the only way we could solve the problem of unemployment was for women to stay home so that men could have jobs."[34]

The attitude toward women's employment has often been tied in with the general mythology, or conventional wisdom, regarding a nurturing role for women. Part of this myth holds that only the biological mother can effectively "mother," and that a child will obviously therefore be harmed by the mother's absence in a work situation. The welfare mother has been the brunt, then, of contradictory attitudes: on the one hand she is urged to get off the tax rolls and into the job market; on the other hand she is mindful of the approval to be had from staying home to care for her children. Studies show that there is, on the whole, no higher rate of delinquency among the children of working mothers, nor is there evidence that either the husband-wife or the child-parent relationship is impaired.[35] Maternal employment has not been shown to have other harmful consequences for children, either.[36] In general, the impact of a mother's employment upon her child or children varies with the adequacy of the substitute arrangement, or the mother-child relationship prior to the separation for work, and with the mother's motivation to work and the gratification she receives from her employment.[37] In fact, "group care . . . has positive features. Often those in charge of children's groups are better trained, more patient, and objective in dealing with children than the mothers. A child can be allowed greater freedom to run, climb, and throw in a nursery school than in a home full of breakable objects."[38] "There has been some speculation that greater variety of stimulation provided by several close mother figures may be intellectually stimulating and promote flexibility."[39] Day care in various experiments and full-scale programs in the Soviet Union, East Germany, Czechoslovakia, Hungary, Israel, Greece, and France seems to have benefitted children.[40]

Since day care has never been studied from a feminist perspective, there have been few studies on the importance of day care *for the mother*. However, anyone who has been a mother knows that mothers need some kind of break from routine, some breathing spell, and some time for recreation, socializing, and creative pursuits — impossible on any meaningful scale without day care of some kind. In fact, most mothers are better mothers when they have some satisfying independent life of their own.[41] Mothers should not be forced to place their children in day care centers, but the option should always be present.

Part of the reason why professionals in the child-care field oppose women's working and group care for children of working mothers is that these professionals equate maternal separation, even for a few hours a day, with maternal deprivation. They seem to think that maternal separation for any reason and in any manner has to have traumatic, deleterious effects on young children.[42] This misunderstanding comes out of the Bowlby, Spitz, Roudinesco, and Goldfarb studies showing that children who lived in impersonal institutions and were totally bereft, not only of maternal care but also of adequate maternal substitution, developed irreversible psychopathic or autistic characteristics. But these studies have little bearing on the situation of the child of a working mother generally considered; and they probably have little relevance even to questions of maternal deprivation. Barbara Wooten has questioned the scientific validity of these maternal-deprivation studies, inasmuch as they tended to use only disturbed children in institutions as a sample, never following the subjects into later experiences, whereas their clinical observations and statistics altered with time.[43] Regrettably, these studies are still respected in professional psychological and educational circles. It is true generally that scientific evaluations of the effects of day care on mothers and children are colored by cultural norms. And in a society where one must be considered abnormal in order to qualify for the day-care center, how is the evaluation of such services to be contemplated along guidelines that might with accuracy be termed scientific?

PERSPECTIVES AND PROBLEMS

Day care can be viewed as a benefit in kind, as opposed to a cash benefit. Benefits in kind are preferred when a quality service is too expensive to be purchased on an individual basis.[44] In 1970 it was estimated that decent day care cost $1,600 per year per child.[45] Together with large sums of money, complex administrative and technological and educational skills are required if the demand for adequate day care is to be met. Individual families cannot be expected to meet these expensive, complex demands themselves. Even if they could, there is a view of society whereby the well-being of children is too important a priority to be left to individual family discretion; childhood and education are societal rather than individual functions, since they ensure the continuity and survival of the society as a whole.

Day care, then, should be seen as a universal entitlement, like public education, rather than as it is now perceived, as a means-tested provision on the order of welfare. Means tests are not efficient as a way of concentrating help on those in need.[46] Means tests usually degrade and stigmatize and therefore only reinforce the conditions they are intended to alleviate and widen the inequity gap they purport to diminish.[47] In a society such as ours, which sets great emphasis on monetary reward and success, an admission of poverty and failure can prove so detrimental that it outweighs the reward it brings.[48] Many liberal-minded people believe that those who could pay for day care should do so on a sliding scale. However, because of the lingering welfare associations of day care, I feel the only way to make day care available without stigma must be to treat it as an unconditionally free public utility.

One of the problems with benefits in kind, however, is that they are often employed as mechanisms for social control.[49] Day care has in the past been used in this way. At present, day care is made available only on condition that women on welfare become enrolled in Special Work Incentive Programs (WIN) and Concentrated Employment Programs (CEPS). The proposed Nixon Family Assistance Plan (FAP) would likewise combine day care with work.

In FAP plans, the welfare recipients would be provided vouchers enabling them to purchase day care from government or private profit-making centers. This would constitute a windfall for private, franchised centers that would exist for profit rather than owing to any special evinced vocation for child care. Such centers would naturally seek to cut corners to increase their profits. The existing ones generally are over-crowded, with inadequate equipment and untrained part-time personnel. They are geared not toward child development but rather toward the readiest means to give parents the impression that their children are happy. They also seek to inveigle the parents into purchasing the products made by the day-care franchisers.[50]

The only way to prevent this balance-sheet-dominated kind of day care is to be insistent about having genuine parental control. With this, certain criteria and health and education standards should be maintained in day care. Unlike the present Code enforcement, such standards and criteria should not militate against experiment and innovation. Different communities should be able to develop varying centers to meet their needs. For example: in an area where many parents are employed at night, the day-care center should be open 24 hours a day. In contrast, where parents sought care for half-days only, this too should be made possible, and with due budgetary benefit.

Day care has begun to be a factor in labor-market planning. Recently the AVCO Corporation of Dorchester, Massachusetts, Bell Telephone, Whirlpool, and the Rochester Clothing Company have commenced to use day care as a fringe benefit to attract and attach women workers to relatively poorly paid jobs.[51] This is a genuine benefit and may take the place

of another $100 or more a month in salary. Moreover, insofar as it suc-
ceeds in reducing turnover, it may be taken up by other industries. However, since many of the women in most need of the program would find it
difficult to get another job, clearly the plan can also be used to control
workers. Women are also less apt to engage in action that threatens the
firm: organizing strikes, picketing, etc., when the threat is not only loss
of a job, but loss of day care.

Day care should be financed by the federal government. This should
be done from general tax revenue, rather than from any wage-related tax.
Wage-related taxes are often employed to psychologically reinforce a
relationship between participation in the labor force and receipt of a
benefit.[52] And taxes applied from the general tax revenues are on the
whole considered to be of universal benefit. It is true the cost of universal
day care stands to be enormous — perhaps as much as 6 to 10 billion dollars annually. The issue, however, is not in fact one of economic feasibility. In the world's wealthiest country the issue is rather one of priorities
and readiness. Day-care services might best be administered under a
special Early Childhood Agency rather than be distributed among the
existing (bureaucratic, outmoded, but entrenched) education or welfare
systems. It would probably prove simpler to innovate, and to go directly
to the task with a new agency structured for it. Early childhood education is a special field, with educational, health, nutritional, developmental, and behavioral components.

Another question often raised when universal day care is proposed is
that of work incentive. Will the widespread availability of day care encourage women to engage in economically productive labor? And if so,
with what consequences? Already we have explored the social and
psychological consequences, and found no necessarily detrimental results,
but rather the possibility of beneficial results both for the mother and for
the child. As to economic consequences, these might include an even
stronger influx of women into the labor market, adding to the unemployment problem. Yet with a growing unemployment among men to match
the institutionalized unemployment (housewifery) among women, there
might be more incentive for a rethinking of the entire question of the
duration and constitution of the work week. Part-time work for all might
prove to be a partial solution to unemployment and to family needs alike,
especially if men are encouraged to share in housekeeping. Also, it might
be argued that day care could in the short run reduce the public assistance rolls, as it would leave welfare mothers free to work. It is estimated that in New York City alone, 250,000 women on welfare would be
employable if day-care centers and job training were provided.[53]

At present, the absence of day care operates as a work disincentive.
The cost of babysitters and nurseries, transportation, work clothing, and
lunches often makes it financially unfeasible for women to work, espe-

cially those with low pay. Work-related expenses plus taxes are estimated to take 50 percent of a mother's paycheck.[54]

In the past a combination of voluntary and publicly sponsored day care has been controlled by boards of directors, the welfare apparatus, or the tendencies of the labor market, and shaped to respond to the welfare and therapeutic needs of special families and the labor-productive sector. Yet day care is a unique and invaluable service. It is not interchangeable with other institutions for the structuring of human resources. Obstacles to universal day care seem to consist of its origin in welfare arrangements; negative attitudes on the subject of working women; the psychiatric social-work emphasis on the mother's role in early childhood; the tradition of a single dominant maternal role; the confusion between separation and deprivation; the association of day care with communism;[55] and a general emphasis in our modern psychological and educational theory on individual as opposed to group or contextual development and achievement.[56]

It is time for Americans to face the present realities — the breakdown of the nuclear family, the transformation of women's roles, the new awareness of human (child and parental) needs. It is accordingly time to reorient day-care policy to correspond to this changed reality. This in turn must call forth federally funded, community-controlled, universal day care, under a distinct administration for early childhood purposes.

References

1. Eveline Burns, "Childhood Poverty and the Children's Allowance," in Eveline Burns, ed., *Children's Allowances and the Economic Welfare of Children* (New York: Citizens' Committee for Children, 1968), p. 3.

2. *New York Times,* Dec. 19 and 29, 1970; Jan. 11, 1971.

3. Alva Myrdal, *Nation and Family* (Cambridge, Mass.: M.I.T. Press, 1941), pp. 3–5.

4. *Statistical Abstracts of the United States,* 1970, Department of Commerce, Bureau of the Census, 91st edition, p. 47.

5. Eveline Burns, "The Government's Role in Child and Family Welfare," in *The Nation's Children,* vol. 3, *Problems and Prospects,* ed., Eli Ginzberg (New York: Columbia University Press, 1960), p. 161.

6. *New York Times,* Nov. 30, 1970, p. 1.

7. Ethel Beer, *The Day Nursery* (New York: E. P. Dutton & Co., 1930).

8. Bernice Fleiss, "The Relationship of the Mayor's Committee on Wartime Care of Children to Day Care in New York City," doctoral thesis (Education), New York University, 1962; and Mary Bogue and Mary Moran, "Day Nurseries" in *Social Work Yearbook,* vol. 1 (1929), pp. 118–19.

9. Child Welfare League of America, "A Historical Sketch of the Day Nursery Movement," New York, 1940 (typescript in Child Welfare League of America Library).

10. Allen F. Davis, *Spearheads for Reform: The Social Settlements and The Progressive Movement, 1890–1914* (New York: Oxford University Press, 1967), pp. 43–46.

11. Fleiss, *op. cit.*, who quotes from Sophie Van S. Theis, *The Importance of Casework in the Day Nursery* (New York: National Federation of Day Nurseries, 1935), p. 1.

12. Anna Mayer, *Day Care as a Social Instrument, A Policy Paper*, Columbia University School of Social Work, Jan. 1965, p. 24.

13. Fleiss, *op. cit.* Most of my material on the 1930's comes from the Fleiss thesis, and from Gussack Anne LeWine and R. Alice McCabe, *The Public Voluntary Agency-Sponsored Day-Care Program for Children in New York City*, an Administrative Study prepared for the Subcommittee on Day Care of the Committee on Family and Child Welfare, Community Service Society, Dept. of Public Affairs, July 1965.

14. Valerie Oppenheimer, *The Female Labor Force in The United States: Demographic and Economic Factors Governing Its Growth and Changing Composition* (Berkeley: University of California Press, 1970).

15. Mayer, *op. cit.*, p. 27.

16. Fleiss, *op. cit.*, p. 82, who quotes Alice Dashiell, "Trends in Day Care," *The Child*, 2 (Sept. 1946): 56.

17. Mayer, *op. cit.*, p. 27.

18. Katherine Oettinger, "Day Care Today: A Foundation for Progress," in *Report of a Consultation on Working Women and Day-Care Needs* (Wash., D.C.: United States Department of Labor), June 1, 1967 (hereafter, *Report*); Title I, Section 102B, of the Social Security Act as amended in 1962.

19. *Children Are Waiting* (Washington, D.C.: Human Resources Administration, Task Force on Early Childhood Development, July 1970; pamphlet), Appendix A, p. 2.

20. *1969 Handbook of Women Workers*, Women's Bureau Bulletin 294, pp. 40–43.

21. Florence Ruderman, *Child Care and Working Mothers: A Study of Arrangements Made for Daytime Care of Children*, Child Welfare League of America, 1968, p. 10.

22. Mary Keyserling, "Working Mothers and Their Children: The Urgent Need for Day-Care Services," in *Report*, see footnote 20, p. 3.

23. Seth Low and Pearl Spindler, *Child-Care Arrangements of Working Mothers in the United States*, Children's Bureau and Women's Bureau, 1968, pp. 15–16 (based on a study done in 1965).

24. *Children Are Waiting*, p. 8.

25. Keyserling, *op. cit.*, pp. 5–6.

26. *Ibid.*, p. 6.

27. Martin Tolchin, "Nursery Schools Arouse Rivalry," *New York Times*, Feb. 17, 1964.

28. Keyserling, *op. cit.*, p. 8.

29. *Guides to State Welfare Agencies for the Development of Day-Care Services*, (Washington, D.C.: United States Dept. of Health, Education and Welfare, Children's Bureau, Welfare Administration, 1963).

30. Barbara Wooton, *Social Science and Social Pathology* (New York: Macmillan, 1959), p. 144.

31. Urie Bronfenbrenner, *Two Worlds of Childhood: U.S. and U.S.S.R.* (New York: Russell Sage Foundation, 1970).

32. F. Ivan Nye and Lois Wladis Hoffman, eds., *The Employed Mother in America* (Chicago: Rand McNally, 1963).

33. Joseph Reid, "Legislation for Day Care," in *Report*, p. 35.

34. "Innovative Approaches—a Panel," *Ibid.*, p. 55.

35. Rose A. John, "Child Development and the Part-Time Mother," *Children* (Nov.–Dec. 1959): 213–18; and Leon Yarrow, "Conceptualizing the Early Environment," in Laura L. Dittman, ed., *Early Child Care: The New Perspectives* (New York: Atherton, 1968), pp. 15–27.

36. Bettye Caldwell and Julius Richmond, "Programmed Day Care for the Very Young Child—A Preliminary Report," *Child Welfare*, 44 (Mar. 1965): 134–42; and Stig Sjolin, "Care of Well Children in Day-Care Centers," *Care of Children in Day Care Centers* (Geneva: World Health Organization, 1964), p. 22.

37. Milton Willner, "Day Care, a Reassessment," *Child Welfare*, 44 (Mar. 1967): 126–27.

38. Eleanor Maccoby, "Children and Working Mothers," *Children*, 5–6 (1958–59): 86.

39. Yarrow, *op. cit.*, pp. 22–23.

40. Dale Meers and Allen Marans, "Group Care of Infants in Other Countries," in Dittman, *op. cit.*, pp. 234–82.

41. Willner, *op. cit.*, p. 129.

42. Julius Richmond, "Twenty Percent of the Nation," *Spotlight on Day Care: Proceedings of the National Conference on Day-Care Services*, May 13–15, 1965 (Washington, D.C.: United States Department of Health, Education, and Welfare), p. 45.

43. Wooton, *op. cit.*, pp. 146, 151, 153.

44. Gerald Holden, "A Consideration of Benefits in Kind for Children," *Children's Allowances and the Economic Welfare of Children* (New York: Citizens' Committee for Children, 1968), pp. 150–42.

45. *New York Times*, Nov. 30, 1970, p. 51.

46. David Bull, "Action for Welfare Rights," in *The Fifth Social Service: Nine Fabian Essays* (London: Fabian Society, May 1970; pamphlet), p. 148.

47. Peter Townsend, Introduction, "Does Selectivity Mean a Nation Divided," *Social Services for All: Eleven Fabian Essays* (London: Fabian Society, Sept. 1968), pp. 1–6.

48. Brian Abel Smith, Conclusion, "The Need for Social Planning," *Ibid.*, p. 114.

49. Holden, *op. cit.*, p. 151 and Myrdal, *op. cit.*, p. 150.

50. Joseph Featherstone, "The Day-Care Problem: Kentucky Fried Chicken," *The New Republic*, Sept. 12, 1970, pp. 12–16; and Ann Cook and Herbert Mack, "Business Education, the Discovery Center Hustle," *Social Policy*, Sept.–Oct. 1970, pp. 3–11; *New York Times*, Dec. 27, 1969. For example, if Creative Playthings (a toy corporation) runs a day-care center they will try to convince the parents of the children that certain Creative Playthings toys are needed for the children's educational development.

51. *New York Times,* Jan. 21, 1970, pp. 59 and 65, and Oct. 29, 1970.

52. Shlakman, *op. cit.,* p. 28.

53. *New York Times,* Dec. 15 and 29, 1970.

54. Nadine Brozan, "To Many Working Mothers, a Job Is Almost a Losing Proposition," *New York Times,* Jan. 5, 1971, p. 30.

55. Mayer, *op. cit.,* p. 129, who is quoting Raymond J. Gallagher, Secretary of the National Conference of Catholic Charities, in testimony on Public Welfare Amendments of 1962, Bill No. 10032, *Congressional Record,* 87th Congress, 2d Sess., pp. 578–80.

56. Rochelle Paul Wortis, "Child-Rearing and Women's Liberation," paper delivered at Women's Weekend, Ruskin College, Oxford University, February 28, 1970; pamphlet, p. 1.

36. NEW OUTLOOK FOR THE AGED

Time Magazine

Throughout history the aged have occupied a precarious position in society. Some primitive peoples like the Eskimos and other nomads respected the elderly but left them to die when they could no longer care for themselves. Natives of some South Seas islands paddled away from their families — to death — when age overtook them. Nor is the idea of abandoning the elderly unique to primitive societies. Marya Mannes' 1968 novel *They* postulated a world in which everyone over 50 was herded into public institutions and eventually liquidated. A 1966 Rand Corporation study concluded that if the U.S. survived a nuclear war it would be "better off without old and feeble" citizens, and suggested that no provisions be made to care for the surviving elderly.

The U.S. has clearly not taken such advice. Most Americans, whether moved by religion or common decency, still try to follow the Fifth Commandment and "honor" their parents. But despite their concern, and frequently the anguish that marks their hard decisions about the elderly, the position of the aged in the U.S. has grown parlous. A couple of decades ago, most Americans who reached 65, the admittedly arbitrary age for retirement, could look forward to spending their last years in peace and security, respected and cared for by their families and friends. No longer. For an increasing number of Americans, the years after 65 are a time of growing uncertainty and isolation as, cut off from family, beset by illness and impoverished by inflation, they struggle not to enjoy the rest that they have earned but simply to survive.

Their problem is a pervasive, urgent one, both for the old and for their children. America as a society has yet to develop a practical, human policy for dealing with the woes of old age in a modern world. For those elderly Americans who can still manage — both physically and financially — life goes on much as it always has. But for those who cannot manage, the end of life, or at least of life as most people would want to live it, can be an agony. About a million, or 5%, of the nation's elderly already live in nursing homes, too many of which are grim warrens for the unwanted. Tragically, the population of the nursing homes is growing. But so, too, is the public's concern over the plight of the old. Americans have yet to come up with the answers, but more and more are at least asking themselves the question that most must face sooner or later: What do we do with our parents?

There is no easy, single answer. In an earlier time, when most Americans lived on farms, the relatively few who reached old age simply stayed at home, inevitably working less and less but expecting and getting as their rightful due more and more care from their families. Industrialization, urbanization and the automobile have ended that. Most Americans no longer live on farms or in closely knit family groups. Ever more mobile, Americans by the tens of millions do not stay rooted in one place all their lives but pull up stakes, move and move again. Of those who hold on in the old home town, few live out their lives in one house. Married couples rarely stay with parents any more; even young singles are encouraged to strike out on their own. Those who leave frequently lose contact with their parents because of distance or because they are too busy to bother with the old folks, and may even be embarrassed by them. Says Anthropologist Margaret Mead, 73, and a grandmother: "The modern family, in its present form, is not equipped to care for old persons."

The problem is that there are more old people than ever to care for. In 1900 only 3.1 million, or one out of every 25 Americans, were over 65. Now 21.8 million, or one out of every ten, fall into this category. The reason for the rise is twofold. Modern medicine has cut infant mortality rates and increased the average life expectancy from 47 years in 1900 to 71.3 today. Since 1957 the U.S. birth rate has dropped (*Time*, Sept. 16), increasing the ratio of elderly to young people. If present population trends continue, those over 65 and those under 15 should each account for 20% of the population by the year 2000.

Except for numbers, the two groups have little in common. For one thing, a disproportionate number of the American aged are women, who outnumber men by a ratio of 143 to 100. The reasons are obvious. Women tend to outlive men by an average of seven years; they also tend to marry men several years older than themselves, a fact that accounts for the high proportion of widows among elderly women. Nor is this the only difference between the young and the old. A significant number of today's elderly are, according to University of Chicago Professor Bernice Neugarten, "disporportionately disadvantaged." Many are foreign born, uneducated and unskilled. Far from all the aged are infirm, but 38% do suffer from some kind of chronic condition that limits their activities. Of these, fully half have serious problems and 5%, or one out of every 20, are homebound. About a third of all aged Americans are also plagued by poverty. Despite pensions, savings and Social Security, which will disburse $72 billion to 33.5 million recipients this year, fully 4.75 million of the nation's aged exist on less than $2,000 a year — well below the Federal Government's poverty line.

Depending on what they can afford and the extent to which they can take care of themselves or count on their families for help, the aged live in a wide variety of arrangements. For most, the accommodations are reassuringly familiar. More than two-thirds of America's elderly remain in the communities that they have known for most of their lives — and in the same homes. Most like the security of the familiar. For many, however, the decision not to pull up roots is economic as well as emotional: nearly 70% of older people own their own homes, humble as they may be. For owners, housing costs — utilities, taxes (often reduced for those over 65) and repairs — have long been relatively low. Now all of those costs are climbing sharply.

Not surprisingly, lots of elderly homeowners live in rural areas (many of them in Kansas, where nearly 12% of the population is over 65, and Nebraska, where the elderly make up as much as 23% of the population of Boyd and Saline counties). Many remain in small towns where they can live cheaply, with good houses going for as little as $10,000. Others settle in out-of-the-way places that are crime-free and friendly. Most have a simpler reason: to them, these hamlets are home.

In Swift Creek Township, near Raleigh, N.C., doctors urged Oscar Maynard, 67, to go to a nursing home after he suffered a stroke several months ago. Maynard refused, saying: "I'll be on my own, and I'll go where I want to go." Where Maynard wanted to go was to the simple brick home that he shares with his wife Essie, 63, on 25 acres of land. Says Maynard: "I'd rather be here than anyplace else in the world."

Many of the elderly with more money prefer plusher living. An estimated 500,000 have bought or leased property in the "adult" or "retirement" communities that have mushroomed round the country, primarily in Florida and the Southwest, where the weather is warm and the cost of living relatively low. Most of these "villages," "cities" and "worlds" follow the lead of Arizona's Sun City (pop. 34,000) and exclude younger people; no one under 50 can buy or lease property there. Some residents like the segregation-practiced in the gerontopolises, but the majority are more interested in the amenities. A number of communities boast well-designed cottages or apartments and programs of social activities, such as dancing and crafts; many have swimming pools and offer residents free bus rides to and from shopping centers and entertainment; some even have golf courses. Miami's Park West community bars dogs, for example, and puts a three-week limit on visits by children. Warner Moore, 64, a retired General Motors executive, and his wife Elizabeth, 65, consider Park West an ideal place to live. It may be, for those who can afford it. The cost of a one-bedroom condominium in Park West begins at $27,000, a similar home in Sun City costs $28,000 and one in New York's handsome Heritage Hills $41,500.

Thousands can afford this expensive *apartheid;* thousands more can bear the costs of living in pleasant apartments in high-rise buildings in New York, Miami or Chicago. But millions of elderly Americans, the majority of them women and widowed, have to make do more modestly. Ella Larson, 73, a retired nurse in Santa Monica, Calif., finds apartment living increasingly expensive. She gets $107.80 a month from Social Security, which goes for food. An additional $147 from old-age assistance pays her rent and utilities, which leaves her almost nothing for clothes and entertainment. Mrs. Larson worries constantly that her rent will go even higher. "I feel very insecure," she says. "I never know if the landlady is going to raise my rent again or tell me they're going to tear the place down to build one of those new apartment buildings. Then we'd all be homeless."

Some elderly Americans cannot afford even the smallest apartment. For them, what passes for independence is a clammy rented room and a hot plate. An estimated 2,000 oldsters cling to life in $15-a-week furnished rooms in Boston's shabby South End. A few others find homes in peeling, decrepit residential hotels like the once elegant Miami resort where Mrs. David Yates, 90, gets a suite of rooms, maid service and two meals a day (no lunch) for $500 a month. People who cannot afford even this much may sometimes find a plain but safe haven in public housing projects specially designed for the elderly, which offer low-rent living to those who are physically, if not financially, able to go it alone. Chicago shelters 9,250 aged tenants at 41 special sites, including the huge Britton I. Budd complex near Lake Front Park. There Martin Smith, 82, pays $55 a month for an apartment that he feels is better than his daughter's $195-a-month place, and complains only about his arthritis.

For some, old age means giving up solitary independence and moving in with their children. Sometimes that works out well. Edna Segar, 74, who plays the piano in a Culver City, Calif., senior citizens' dance band, finds the arrangement fine. So do her son Donald, 54, and his wife

Frances, 59. Says Donald: "You wouldn't throw your kids out, so you don't throw your parents out when they need you."

For others, caring for parents is a serious problem. Many urban Americans simply do not have the room to house an elderly father or mother, especially in New York and other cities where an extra room means paying an enormous increase in rent or buying a larger home than they can afford. Others claim that the presence of a parent in the home strains marital relations and puts tremendous pressures on children. Still others just cannot take the tension involved in caring for senile parents.

Many families also cannot handle the physical aspects of aging. The Jury family, of Clarks Summit, Pa., watched helplessly as "Grandpa" Frank Tugend faded. The Jurys kept the retired coal miner with them, bearing with him as he became confused and forgetful, cleaning up after him as he lost control of his bodily functions. In his lucid moments, the proud 81-year-old Tugend knew what was happening to him. One day he took out his false teeth and refused to eat any more. He had decided to die, and no one — not his doctor, nor his family — could do anything to change that. His children and grandchildren cared for him with anguished tenderness until death claimed him three weeks later.

Few children have the devoted patience or endurance of Tugend's family. Each year more and more of them face the problem of deciding what to do when aged parents need more care than they can — or are willing to — give. In some cases, the answer is obvious: put them in a nursing home. The decision is often devastating for parents and children alike, and has ripped many families apart. Whatever happens, guilt hangs in the air like a sulfurous, corrosive fog. Even children who keep their parents at home generally feel remorse about what Paul Kirschner of the University of Southern California calls the "battered senior syndrome," which involves caring for aged parents but excluding them from many family activities. Those who place their parents in nursing homes often feel a still heavier burden of guilt for "abandoning" the old folks.

In many cases, what they have done, for whatever reason, amounts to abandonment. Mary Adelaide Mendelson, of Cleveland, a former community-planning consultant, has spent ten years studying institutions for the aged. Last year, in a book titled *Tender Loving Greed,* she concluded that U.S. nursing homes are a national scandal. She writes: "There is widespread neglect of patients in nursing homes across the country and evidence that owners are making excessive profits at the expense of patients."

This does not mean that all of the country's 23,000 nursing homes are bad. A number of them scattered throughout the country are, by any standards, excellent. Others provide their patients with at least good, competent care. They come in all sizes, under highly diverse sponsorship.

Members of Southern California's Japanese community need have no qualms about placing their parents in Los Angeles' Keiro (which translates as Home for Respected Elders), a 184-bed facility that bespeaks the Oriental tradition that old age should be a time of ease. Keiro's appeal ranges from chaste Japanese décor to good food served from a gleaming stainless-steel kitchen. The home also has a largely bilingual staff that is genuinely interested in the welfare of its patients, and a program that includes everything from physical rehabilitation to concerts on traditional Japanese instruments.

Nor need children feel guilty about putting their parents in some of the smaller, less shiny but equally good homes round the country. Associated with the Christian Missionary Alliance, the Alliance Residence in Minneapolis is a nondescript three-story building minus any lush lobby or manicured grounds. But what it lacks in gilding, it more than makes up for in concern for its patients. Alliance's 100 occupants are in the care of seven nurses and 25 nurse's aides, who work in three shifts so that the home will be staffed round the clock. Most of Alliance's patients are not only healthy but happy. Elvira Axeen, 82, still goes out every Wednesday to make coffee for her Bible group. "I'm going to be busy as long as I can do it," says she. So are others. "As long as you can complain and be up and around, you're young," says 91-year-old Mrs. Ellen Wicklander as she stitches on a quilt.

The best nursing homes deprive their patients of some independence. The worst deprive them of far more: their resources, rights and, ultimately, their humanity. They are killer institutions. An investigation still under way in New York has dug out evidence of widespread abuse and exploitation of nursing-home patients. Inspectors who have made surprise visits to homes have found in the worst of them incontinent patients wallowing in their own filth, patients shot full of tranquilizers to keep them bovinely docile, others whose requests for help went unanswered and still others who were unfed or given the wrong foods and medication. They have also found many patients – like those at the now closed Towers Nursing Home in New York City – who were unwilling to complain for fear that they would be punished later by the attendants.

The crimes against the weak are not confined to New York. Authorities in Illinois are investigating not only suspected fraud but also the deaths of seven patients in a home in Rockford. California officials have turned up even more disturbing evidence. Los Angeles County investigators reported that a paralyzed woman at the Torrance Medical Convalescent Center, a 212-bed nursing home in Torrance, Calif., died after a nurse tried to feed her orally rather than through a stomach tube, then dismissed her gasping and flailing as an attempt to burn off "excess energy." The victim was not the only patient to die at Torrance, whose license to operate is being challenged. One patient died when he apparently leaped from a second-story window. "He probably jumped because of the conditions inside," said one angry health official.

A few of these substandard homes are public institutions. The majority, however, are private. The reason for the ratio is money — public money, ironically, appropriated to give aid and comfort to the indigent aged. In 1966 the Federal Government began to pay for nursing-home care through Medicaid, a federal-state program that last year spent $4.4 billion of its $12.7 billion budget on the elderly. The sudden gush of cash set loose a nursing-home boom as many entrepreneurs, many of them interested only in the bottom line, rushed into the business.

It is not difficult to understand how the homes make money. Medicaid pays them from $8.50 to $49.10 per patient per day, but many homes spend far less on care for their patients. Most save money on staffing, hiring only a handful of professionals and then filling their rosters with unskilled, often careless attendants, who are paid rock-bottom minimum wages. Some proprietary homes save by spending next to nothing on their buildings, which may not only be dirty and stink but may also be unsafe. Also, many nursing-home operators save on food. One owner admitted to investigators that he was feeding his patients for 54¢ a day, less than the county jail spent on its prisoners. Given such practices, it is not surprising that some private nursing homes yield an annual return of more than 40% on money invested. Unblinkingly, nursing-home operators defend themselves as performing a necessary service. "The public does not really want to accept the fact that taking care of a sick old person is not a pleasure," says Max Lewko, administrator of New York's Mayflower Nursing Home. "If some of these people had their mother at home for four weeks, they would appreciate what we are doing."

That begs the question. Regardless of their condition, the elderly deserve to be treated like human beings. Fortunately, action to guarantee such treatment has already begun. A special commission in New York has submitted an eleven-bill package that would include unannounced inspections of nursing homes, establish a stiff schedule of fines for violations of state standards and give the state the right to sue nursing homes that failed to provide proper care. The Minnesota state legislature has tightened up certification procedures and passed laws requiring close monitoring of nursing-home operations. Massachusetts authorities have shut down eight substandard homes and plan to close three more unless they are sold to someone who will run them properly.

Congress is also acting. Senator Frank Moss, chairman of a Senate subcommittee on long-term care, has introduced 48 bills that would, among other things, require 24-hr. attendance of a registered nurse, offer financial incentives to nursing-home operators by allowing higher payments for better care, and provide for full disclosure of the identities of all individuals involved in a nursing home's operation.

The enactment of pending legislation — indeed, even the enforcement of existing state and federal regulations — would go a long way toward ending the dehumanization and exploitation of those who can no longer care for themselves. But improving nursing homes will not help 95% of America's elderly. What will help them and those who will one day join their ranks is a realization that the U.S. suffers from what Dr. Robert Butler of Washington, D.C., calls "ageism" — or prejudice against the elderly — and a determination to end this cruel form of discrimination. "The tragedy of old age is not that each of us must grow old and die," writes Butler in his newly published book *Why Survive?* (Harper & Row; $15), "but that the process of doing so has been made unnecessarily and at times excruciatingly painful, humiliating, debilitating and isolating through insensitivity, ignorance and poverty."

But, says Butler, much of this pain and humiliation can be eliminated. He and his fellow gerontologists urge those who want to help their parents — and other elderly — to help overhaul old policies and develop some new ones, particularly with regard to:

Retirement. Most people assume that to be old is to be finished or "over the hill," and at least half of all American workers are now employed by companies that have institutionalized this assumption by forcing their employees to retire at age 65, if not earlier. The effects of this involuntary idleness can be traumatic. "One day they have life, the next day nothing," says Margaret Mead of unwilling retirees. "One reason women live longer than men is that they can continue to do something they are used to doing, whereas men are abruptly cut off — whether they are admirals or shopkeepers."

Most companies claim that mandatory retirement is necessary to maintain efficiency, preserve profits and clear the way for younger employees. But gerontologists find the arguments unfair. There is no evidence that an individual's efficiency or creativity declines dramatically once he passes his 65th birthday; indeed, many people — from scientists to craftsmen to musicians[1] — have done their best work during their declining years. Nor can it be assumed that most elderly Americans are too feeble to support themselves. At least half of those now over 65 are physically capable of doing a day's work. Mandatory retirement is, in fact, now under challenge. A former civil servant has filed suit to set aside the Federal Government's retirement policies. The American Medical Association has allied itself with him, insisting in a friend-of-the-court brief that there is no evidence that older workers are any less efficient than younger ones.

Income. It is pure romanticism, say most gerontologists, to assume that prudent people can provide adequately for their old age. Inflation in the 1970s can erode the value of the most liberal of pensions and shrink the worth of even the fattest savings accounts. Nor does Social Security, upon which most elderly Americans depend for at least a third of their income, enable most to live with any measure of financial security or comfort. A 65-year-old couple entering the plan this year and entitled to the maximum benefits, which they have paid for in taxes, draws only $474 a month. That inches them above the poverty line but hardly enables them to live beyond the bare-bones level. Besides, the average couple receives only $310 a month.

To alleviate the financial plight of the elderly, experts recommend placing a reasonable floor, pegged to the actual cost of living, under retirement incomes, either by increasing Social Security benefits or supplementing them from other state or federal funds. They also recommend reforms in both Government and private pension systems, to assure that all workers who contribute to a pension plan will derive at least some benefits from it.

Medical Care. Most medical plans are designed to care for the elderly once they become ill. Gerontologists believe that the emphasis should be on preventing illness and preserving health and keeping the aged in the community.

To accomplish this, New York's Montefiore Hospital 28 years ago inaugurated home care for the elderly with regular visits to the homebound by doctors, physical therapists and social workers. Since then, about 100 other hospitals across the country have set up similar programs. Three years ago, Montefiore branched out with an after-care program, under which stroke, arthritis and cancer patients were brought to the hospital for follow-up treatments that doctors hope will eliminate the need for institutional care. Two years ago, the hospital helped set up a day-hospital program. It offers custodial care to those who have no one at home to watch over them during the day.

Dr. Isadore Rossman, who directs the Montefiore programs, hopes that the success of these pilot projects and the acceptance of others like them round the country will lead to the passage of legislation to create and buttress alternatives to institutional care. Such programs would prove an unexpected bargain. Montefiore's home-care costs about $12 a day, or a maximum of $4,380 a year. Even with an elderly person's rent and food bills — averaging at least $2,400 a year — added on, this makes staying out of a nursing home far cheaper than going in. The average cost of a modern New York nursing home is up to $42 a day, or a whopping $15,000 a year.

Attitudes Toward Aging. Americans, says Butler, take an unhealthy and often unrealistic attitude toward aging, assuming that old people have no further contributions to make to society and should be excluded from it. Many of the elderly share this view, occasionally attempting to conceal evidence of their advancing years and withdrawing from an active life. Butler and others believe that attitudes must change if the aged are ever to be treated fairly in the U.S. They urge society to recognize the basic rights of old people to independence and security. Gerontologists also urge society to make better use of the elderly, drawing on their experience and talents and giving them a greater voice in matters that concern them. It is ridiculous, they agree, to have panels of 35-year-olds determining the wishes of and setting policy for the aged when the aged are better equipped to do the job.

Improvements in these areas are on the way. Congress has moved — albeit not very far — to tap the reservoir of talents the elderly have accumulated during their lives. It has approved $45 million for a variety of projects, including the Foster Grandparent Program, which pays oldsters for supervising dependents and neglected youngsters; $17.5 million for the Retired Senior Volunteer Program (RSVP), which pays out-of-pocket expenses to 100,000 involved in such community activities as entertaining the handicapped and visiting homebound patients; and a skimpy $400,000 for the Senior Corps of Retired Executives (SCORE), which reimburses some 4,500 retired executives for expenses incurred while counseling small businesses and community organizations.

Other programs are under way. One feeds the elderly, who often stretch their skintight budgets by subsisting on peanut butter sandwiches or skipping meals entirely. The nutrition section of the 1965 Older Americans Act, funded for $125 million this year, now provides 220,000 seniors with a hot meal a day through local nutrition centers or "Meals on Wheels" vans that deliver hot food right to the doors of the homebound aged.

More encouraging are the programs to keep the elderly in the community and out of institutions. Chicago, which set up the nation's first municipal office for the aged in 1956, sponsors some 600 senior citizens' clubs, where they can meet to talk out their problems and organize to get things done. It also operates some 62 nutrition centers, where an estimated 3,800 come for a low-cost hot meal and some companionship.

At present, these programs reach and benefit only a handful of the nation's elderly. But the prospects for their expansion and for the development of other new approaches toward aging are brightening. One reason for this improved outlook is the growing recognition by most Americans that the country has a lot of catching up to do in its treatment of the aged and the new desire to change what more and more agree is an intolerable situation.

This urge to change things has been inspired in large part by the realization that other countries have done so much more than the U.S. in caring for the elderly. Sweden, Denmark and Norway have used part of the mountain of taxes collected from their citizens (as high as 50% of most salaries in Sweden) to ease many of the burdens of aging. In Sweden, city governments run housing developments where the aged can live close to transportation and recreational activities. Denmark, with a population of 5 million, houses many of its more than 600,000 elderly in subsidized houses or apartments and helps those who want to remain in their own homes by providing them with day helpers and meals. Those who need nursing homes find them a considerable cut above most of their American counterparts: with their excellent design, many look like modern hotels.

Another force behind the new impetus for change is the growing political power and militancy of the elderly themselves. Many groups — blacks, young people, women — have realized how much political muscle their numbers provide and organized in recent years to demand and get attention and help from federal, state and local officials. The aged are following their lead. No longer content to pass their days playing checkers or weaving potholders at senior citizens' centers, a growing number of elderly Americans are banding together to make their wishes known. Several thousand of them have joined a five-year-old group known informally as the Gray Panthers, whose leader, a retired Philadelphia social worker named Maggie Kuhn, 69, is dedicated to altering U.S. attitudes toward the aged. The Panthers have agitated for better housing and medical care and more employment opportunities for the elderly. "Most organizations tried to adjust old people to the system," says Miss Kuhn, "and we want none of that. The system is what needs changing."

WHERE TO GET HELP

Americans over 65 face a bewildering set of problems as they try to adjust to old age, retirement, and often, financial shortage. Federal, state and local governments offer a wide variety of programs to help out. Among them:

Financial Assistance. Almost every American over 65 and many over 62 can apply for Social Security through some 1,300 local Social Security offices, which are listed under "U.S. Government" in telephone directories. Those not eligible for railroad retirement, civil service or veterans' pensions probably qualify for state-administered Supplemental Security Income (SSI). SSI information is available through local welfare or social service agencies.

Health Care. Anyone eligible for Social Security benefits also qualifies for Medicare, which is financed through Social Security and covers most of the cost of any hospitalization that may be needed by those who are eligible. The medical portion of the program, which costs beneficiaries $6.70 a month, covers doctors' bills. Anyone who is eligible for welfare or old-age assistance is also eligible for Medicaid, which covers doctors' and some hospital services, as well as nursing-home care. Local welfare departments administer the program.

Nutrition. The Federal Government has earmarked $125 million for nutrition programs for the elderly. These funds enable hundreds of communities to serve the aged one hot meal daily five days a week, mainly at communal eating places, but also at the homes of those unable to get out. Food stamps, worth more than their purchase price, can help stretch tight food budgets. Information on eligibility for the stamps and other nutritional aid is available from local commissions on the elderly and from welfare offices or agricultural extension services.

Housing. The National Council on the Aging in Washington, D.C., publishes a directory of special housing for the elderly. Other information on publicly sponsored low- and moderate-income housing, tax relief and rent grants is usually available from local housing authorities, tax collectors or agencies for the aged.

Legal Services. Old people in need of legal services to protect their rights to housing, Social Security or medical benefits, safeguard their assets and guard against exploitation by the unscrupulous, can usually obtain them through local legal-aid societies, which provide free or low-cost legal guidance. More specialized help is available from the National Council of Senior Citizens, which has its headquarters in Washington, and local Gray Panthers' organizations.

REFERENCE

1. Giuseppe Verdi produced his great opera, the joyously exuberant *Falstaff*, at age 80; Justice Oliver Wendell Holmes Jr. crafted some of his most powerful opinions in his tenth decade.

37. THE HOUSING STALEMATE

Cushing Dolbeare

Ironically, while as a society we have moved from accepting public responsibility for education — accomplished a century ago — to greater acceptance of public responsibility for health and nourishment, we are simultaneously moving away from accepting public responsibility for providing shelter.

At the root of the failure of our housing programs — and they have failed in scope and scale — is a failure of will and commitment. When we decided, for better or worse, to reach the moon during the 1960s, we were not detained by cost or the problems that had to be solved in the process. We succeeded. Similarly, we can decide to solve our housing problems, and we can make the necessary commitments of public responsibility, resources, and energy. But we will do this only by developing a concept of the necessary role and responsibility of government, and an active concern with the rights of all citizens to decent shelter.

The situation is dismal. Millions of American families live in shelter that is unsafe, unsanitary, or lacks basic facilities. A substantial portion of these families are paying more than they can afford for such housing — 35, 40, or 50 percent of incomes that are well below the poverty level. Additional millions of households are living in housing that meets minimum standards of physical adequacy but costs far more than they can afford — again, 30, 40, 50 percent of their incomes or more. New housing, with few exceptions, is priced beyond the reach of all but the most affluent 20 percent of Americans. The availability of money to finance new housing, either for builder or consumer, is at the mercy of large financial institutions and federal manipulations of monetary policy to control inflation. There are no effective mechanisms providing for the construction, financing, or maintenance of housing in vast sections of the country: in rural areas, with few exceptions, and in inner-city areas.

The governmental support systems for housing, at federal, state, and local levels, have one thing in common: they are passive rather than active. While there have been mortgage-insurance programs, interest-subsidy programs, loan-and-grant programs, even direct-subsidy programs for housing authorities — none of them operate independently of outside, nonfederal initiative. They have another common element: the initiative comes not from the consumer but from the producer. Thus housing is neither in the hands of government, except negatively — to

From *Dissent*, vol. 21, no. 4, fall 1974. Reprinted by permission of the author and publisher.

prevent various "undesirable" things — nor in the hands of consumers. It is in the hands of producers, predominantly speculative builders.

As zoning restrictions, building code, subdivision requirements, and other suburban constraints have artificially forced up the price of housing by requiring builders to construct single-family houses on fairly large lots, builders increasingly support federal-subsidy programs. Most housing consumers have been priced out of the market, and more by local governments and governmental practices than by the builders. This has a variety of causes. Builders operate largely in suburban areas, where there is a presumptive market, available land and financing mechanism. Builders tend not to operate in the inner cities or in rural areas. Yet, suburban communities are no longer expansionist — if they ever were. A longtime truism has it that the last person to move into a suburban community wants to remain just that: the last person to move in. Thus the availability of land zoned for moderate-density housing is the result of interaction between community people who don't want it, and builders, often with strong political influence, who do.

One obvious answer to the problem of rising suburban costs — building either in inner cities or in rural areas — seems beyond the capacity of our present institutions. Much rhetoric has been directed at the need to revitalize our inner cities but little of it at concrete, responsive programs. Rural areas have been spared both the rhetoric and, except for the Farmer's Home drops in the bucket, the programs.

Has Public Housing Failed?

The words "public housing" almost invariably conjure up a vision of high-rise, high-density, often atrociously designed projects — poorly maintained, strewn with rubble and trash, with hallways and elevators reeking of urine. One enters, if at all, fearing for life or limb. Within the past year, pictures of the dynamiting of one such project in St. Louis have engraved this image dramatically on our minds. Public housing? Clearly a failure — a solution to slums perhaps worse than the original disease. So goes the new wisdom.

Public housing's image has been determined by the large number of projects constructed in big cities during the 1950s and 1960s, mostly on cleared sites. The combination of our laws of eminent domain and federal-subsidy constraints forced public housing authorities into building high-density buildings in order to absorb the inflated site costs of compensating slumlords for the income stream they had been receiving from their former "investments."

The reality, however, is that four-fifths of all public housing units are in low-rise buildings: garden apartments or single-family homes. Many are in small projects, well integrated into the life of their neighborhoods. Less than 30 percent of all public housing is in cities of a half-million people or more: a comparable number of units is in communities with less than 25,000 people. For the past five years, except for housing specifically designed for the elderly, public housing outside of New York City has been almost exclusively low-rise: the days of new monster, high-rise public housing projects are over.

For over three decades, beginning in 1937, the public housing subsidy covered *only* the interest and amortization of 40-year bonds floated on the private market to finance site acquisition for construction; operating costs — and usually part of the amortization, too were covered by tenant rents. During the depression, war, and immediate postwar years, public housing was occupied primarily by working people and their families. The very poor were largely excluded, rental income was steady, and the subsidy mechanism worked.

A shift in occupancy patterns began in the 1950s, the product of improving economic opportunities, the widespread availability of new FHA housing for white families with steady incomes, and the mandate of public housing to provide shelter for people displaced by slum clearance. Public housing was increasingly occupied by very poor families, often receiving most or all of their income from public assistance. Rental income dropped and this, combined with rising operating costs and the absence of operating subsidies, led to declining quality of management and maintenance. Welfare families were discriminated against in a variety of ways.

During the last decade, public housing development activities have been transformed! Renewal subsidies became available to reduce site costs, permitting sensible development. Housing authorities were enabled to buy or lease existing housing, either in usable condition or for rehabilitation. Small projects of less than 100 units became feasible. Options to permit and encourage home ownership were introduced. Housing authority boards, previously confined to "providers," became open to tenant membership. Many housing authorities became less paternalistic and more genuinely responsive to tenant needs and concerns.

The failures of public housing are real, and should not be minimized. Basically, however, they are failures to reach far enough in the direction of government support and responsibility. Public housing needs to be both expanded and reformed. It should be expanded through legislation guaranteeing both development and operating subsidies and mandating sufficient production, acquisition, or rehabilitation to provide shelter for all low-income families needing it. It should be reformed through provisions for greater tenant rights and participation, and through elimination of local vetoes over project location.

Public housing is critical because, given our present panoply of housing institutions, only public housing authorities are capable, under *public* control, of providing for low- and moderate-income families what private developers and financing institutions provide for the affluent.

It is easy to slip into oversimplification — to speak of "the housing problem." But "the housing problem" only means that shelter in this country is inadequate. "The Housing Problem" indeed is an amalgam of many different problems, each problem affecting a particular segment of the population and affecting that segment differently. There is little perceived common ground, say, between the problems of the occupant of a rural shack and those of the tenant in a city tenement.

Low-income housing victims perceive one set of problems. Reformers, often, see another. Owners and builders see a third. Finally, governments, depending on their level and orientation, see a fourth set. There have been, over the years, a number of efforts to unite the perceptions of reformers, builders, and government. *Too often the perceptions of the victims have been left out.* As almost everyone has a personal housing problem, our citizens find it difficult to sympathize with others who have different problems, and to support programs of no immediate personal benefit.

There is a variety of perspectives.

Affluent people see the housing problem in terms of too much growth, rising taxes and, perhaps, if they are living in cities, changing neighborhoods and declining services. With the new awareness of the energy crisis, relationship to community facilities, including public transportation, will be of growing importance.

Middle-income people face all these problems and more: taxes and maintenance-and-repair costs are rising more rapidly than incomes. So is the cost of new housing, which is often unavailable at hoped-for prices or in hoped-for locations.

Moderate-income people find no new housing available and the existing market tight, with little choice of location. Even when suitable housing can be found, financing is difficult. Down payments have to be substantial, and interest costs over the life of the mortgage are at least double the nominal cost of the house.

Landlords increasingly find rental housing an unprofitable investment or, at best, less profitable than other investments. Tenants — in the eyes of most landlords — are troublesome and careless. They are likely to complain, even occasionally to withhold rent. Tenants often do not recognize the cost squeeze that rising prices have put on landlords or the fact that many landlords see themselves locked into unattractive investments. The landlord's solution: condominiums — transfer the ownership and the attendant problems of maintenance to the tenants.

Tenants, on the other hand, are confronted by unfair and often technically illegal leases, under which they waive rights established by law. Maintenance lags behind need. For families with children, little choice is available. Minority families and families on welfare have even less choice. Rents are high for value received.

Old people, too, have their special problems. If they are owners, frequently the houses are an increasing burden: larger than they need, with maintenance costs and property taxes placing a growing burden on their budgets, while income is meager. U.S. owners 65 years old or over spend an average of 8 percent of their income on real estate taxes alone. Those with incomes below $2,000 spend an average of 16 percent of their income for real estate taxes. Yet, very likely, their houses are their major economic assets, with secure alternatives unavailable.

Young people, who are just setting up their households, have another set of problems. If they live in rural areas, neither decent housing nor decent jobs are likely to be available. In suburban communities, housing for sale is beyond their means, and rental housing is often excluded under zoning laws or, if available, is exorbitant. Current rental costs are so high that it is difficult to make the necessary savings for a down payment. There has been much rhetoric on the housing problem of low-income and minority people. It will not be elaborated here, except to note that it is often understated rather than exaggerated.

Overarching these components of the broader housing problem is the fact that efforts to confront housing problems seem to bring out the worst characteristics of American politics and economics. The bundle of prejudices commonly known as the Protestant Ethic operates to reduce the role of government and extol the virtues of private enterprise and individual intiative. Housing programs operate in an atmosphere of pervasive racism and prejudice against poor people. In part, this is because efforts to meet housing needs often appear to threaten our citizens' few components of security in this insecure society. Often, the purchase of their home is the largest single investment of their lives. Commonly, this is a debt difficult to pay at the outset and, with rising taxes and repair costs, often growing increasingly onerous. Added to the concern for the safety of this investment, there now is a growing concern for safety, both in the home and in the community. These fears have been translated into effective political power, at both the local and national levels. Locally, they have prevented the introduction of subsidized housing or even of moderate-density zoning. At the federal level, they have made political support of broad-scale housing programs seem hazardous at best and suicidal at worst.

In 1934 the federal government set out to build housing for low-income people, partly to provide shelter, but more to provide jobs. A federal district court ruling that this was beyond the scope of federal authority has

never since been appealed or challenged. Instead, federal housing programs have since been designed to work either through or with active
consent of local governments. Thus, public housing authorities were
created by local governments and authorized to construct housing units
— but, in practice if not in law, only in the numbers and locations approved by those governments. We have poorly located, high-density,
high-rise public housing in many urban areas, not because planners and
administrators were incompetent, but because they were allowed no other
choice. Rural and suburban areas, by and large, had no public housing.

But was public housing in fact public? For 30 years, local housing authorities were composed of builders, realtors, and bankers, with an occasional
minister or other reformer thrown in — but they never included a low-
income person or a tenant. They were authorized to construct and operate
housing projects. This they did by contracting wtih local private architects and builders, financing the projects through bonds bought by private
investors. True, there was public subsidy by the federal government and
public management by the local housing authority — but *public housing,*
in the sense that we have public roads, *has never existed,* and it has been
equally resisted by governments, reformers, and private enterprise.

   Programs designed to benefit poor people have had little appeal in this
country. During the depression, when poverty was a majority fear though
not quite a majority problem, there was a brief period of support for
low-income programs. But since the end of World War II, in a time of
prevailing middle-class prosperity, it has been tacitly assumed that poverty in this country was a social disease, curable by a combination of
individual effort and public supportive services. The notion that it is
society's responsibility to provide a basic level of income and the necessities of life has by and large been advanced timorously or apologetically,
not as a self-evident truth. We have defined "reality" not in terms of the
nature and extent of social problems but rather in terms of the constraints
that bear upon their solutions.

   After a generation of effort to expand the public housing program has
resulted, at best, in only nominal progress, reformers have shifted their
approach from advocacy of additional measures to aid the poor to efforts
to create significant vested interests capable of providing an expanded
level of support for housing programs. Quantitatively, this new approach
was enormously successful. The four years following the Housing Act of
1968 produced more subsidized units for moderate-income families than
four decades of public housing efforts have produced for low-income
families. Moreover, the most effective lobby for subsidized housing on
Capitol Hill is now the National Association of Home Builders. The traditional supporters of public housing, represented most visibly by the National Housing Conference, have been largely reduced to haggling among

themselves over whether they should continue to serve very-low-income people, or whether the route to housing salvation is through an economic mix — which translates in practice into eviction of the very poor (and therefore "undesirable") in favor of the less poor and upwardly mobile (or "desirable") tenants. The voices of consumers and their friends — tenants, rural people, and a scattering of others — are either silent or effectively drowned out.

Federal housing programs have evolved along two rather separate axes. The first, and older, is represented by programs with broad standards of eligibility, available as a matter of right to all eligible people. Relationships are established directly between the federal government and the consumer. These programs are designed for predominantly middle-income and affluent people. They include income tax deductions for local property taxes, mortgage interest, and depreciation; the tax-free features of housing authority bonds; FHA and VA mortgage insurance, particularly on new construction; and savings deposits in member institutions of the home-loan banking system. It could be argued that the housing component of public-assistance payments should be included in this category. In contrast to the foregoing programs, however, the constituency is low-income, eligibility is far from an established right, and payments differ from state to state.

The other major axis of housing programs has consisted of the housing subsidies designed for low- or moderate-income families. Here, housing assistance has been regarded as a privilege rather than a right. The programs have operated through intermediary institutions — state and local governments, nonprofit or limited-dividend development corporations or housing authorities, builders, bankers, and investors. While the scope and cost of these programs are far smaller, these are the programs that have generated the discussions, evaluations, freezes, and charges of high costs, waste, inequity, or maladministration.

The true cost of federal housing subsidies, counting everything, is massive. But the major housing subsidies do not appear in the federal budget and are seldom accounted for. They are provided through the tax system: deductibility for home owners of mortgage interest and local property taxes and, for investors, accelerated depreciation on rental housing and tax-free bonds issued by local housing authorities. While only crude estimates are available, it seems clear that *housing subsidies for households with incomes above $20,000 are at least four times as great as housing subsidies for families with incomes below $3,000.* [See Table 1.] Perhaps only in agriculture do we have a comparable picture of federal subsidies for the rich while the poor are ignored or systematically deprived of their rights.

If the inequities of our present total housing programs were to be

Table 1   Housing Subsidies — Total — By Income Circa 1970

Annual Income	Est. Subsidy	Number of Households, 1970	Average Subsidy per Household
$0–$2,999	$ 641 million	1,493 million	$56
$3,000–$5,999	$1,113 million	10,939 million	$102
$6,000–$9,999	$1,949 million	15,821 million	$123
$10,000 +	$4,510 million	25,192 million	$179

demonstrated, and if there is genuine understanding of the nature and extent of our housing needs and the inadequacy of current public and private institutions to meet them — then we might, conceivably, achieve a successful housing program.

Consider the analogy of health care. Until the adoption of medicare and medicaid, government spending for health services, primarily veterans benefits at the federal level and other hospital and medical care at the state and local level, were one-quarter of all health expenditures. Since medicare and medicaid were adopted, not only have total health-care expenditures risen sharply, but the public share has risen to almost 40 percent. The expansion of effective demand, financed through medicare and medicaid, has led to recognition of a crisis in health care. In 1950 total health expenditures were $12 billion, which was 4.6 percent of the gross national product. Public expenditures accounted for 25 percent of this total or roughly $3 billion. In 1970, by contrast, total health expenditures were $68 billion, 7 percent of the gross national product, and the public share was 37 percent, or $25 billion. This increase was prompted by two important decisions: to provide health services to elderly people, regardless of income, and to low-income people, regardless of age. The crisis generated by these programs is not new: there always has been a need for health care. The crisis resulted when those needing health care were given hope of access to it. Existing health delivery systems were not equipped to respond adequately, and are now being reevaluated.

In housing, we may now be at the premedicare stage of health programs. That is, we have a limited number of programs, inadequately serving selected groups of people, and a delivery system that is incapable of responding to a sudden surge of effective demand.

We need a whole new approach to housing: one that deals with all legitimate housing problems — whether of young, old, black, white, rich, poor, urban, suburban, or rural. *We need to see decent housing as a right and its provision as a public responsibility.* We need to design new institutions and delivery systems that are genuinely responsive and controlled by their consumers. Finally, we need a commitment of government financial support, initiative, and action to bring all this about.

The policy statement contained in the Housing Act of 1949 set the goal of "a decent home and a suitable living environment for every American family." Two essentials, at least, need to be added: freedom of housing choice and ability to pay.

The Housing Act of 1968 put some concrete figures on the first half of the 1949 goal: "the decent home." It set a target of 26 million new or rehabilitated units to be added during a decade; 6 million of these — the number of existing substandard units to be replaced — were to be subsidized. This 26-million-unit target ignores the factors of suitable living environment, freedom of choice, and ability to pay. Thus it grossly understates the crudest measurements of housing needs.

For many, control over their housing is at least as important as the adequacy of the shelter itself. Home ownership is as important as a symbol of self-determination as it is as a financial arrangement. Indeed, the distinctions between rented or purchased housing are becoming increasingly blurred. There is not a great deal of difference between a rental unit, a condominium, a cooperative, and a house being bought on a lease-purchase contract or a 40-year mortgage. The type of structure — location and age and whether it is a single- or multi-family unit — is probably at least as important as tenure.

Therefore, self-determination and consumer or resident control over housing must be an important part of any major housing program. By now experience has taught us that supportive services are a key component of home ownership programs, at least for marginal-income people. Our housing problems will not be met by half measures, or half-hearted proposals. While public housing, in the words of Anthony Henry of the national tenant movement, is "a roaring success compared to what the private market provides," it has not secured the loyalty of its residents; nor does public housing provide a rallying point for those wishing to deal with housing problems. Our other direct housing programs have even less appeal. While their faults are not as great as current HUD and other criticism implies, they are cumbersome, costly, inadequate in scope, and totally unable to meet our housing needs of low-income people.

Fair play is important to most people. Most people not only resent being pushed around themselves, they are not happy seeing others pushed around. The notion of a total housing subsidy system, framed so that the subsidy rises as income goes up, is so egregiously unjust that it is intolerable. The current indignation over minimum rents in public housing is a tempest in a teapot compared to this inequity. And the cost to the federal government is far higher.

The Housing Act of 1968, which resulted in a five-fold increase in the production of subsidized housing, was not alone the product of an awakened and aggressive lobbying effort by housing producers. It was also the product, in part at least, of two searching examinations — one by the Douglas Commission and the other by the Kaiser Committee — of the nature and extent of our housing problems and, perhaps not least, the dawning recognition that prior to 1968 the federal government was, tax expenditures aside, as likely to make a profit on its housing programs as to spend money on them. Even those most insulated from the realities of American life could recognize that we could not solve our housing problems without spending some money.

No one, yet, has the prescription for adequate housing programs. Interestingly, however, there has been a recent revival of interest in public housing as the mechanism for either major or incremental improvement. Public housing has never really been tried in this country. In order to try it now, it would be appropriate to provide for public financing, production, and operation of housing, at least for those who cannot afford decent private housing. It would be appropriate for the federal government to exercise its powers to override the objections of local governments to providing poor people with access to decent housing. It would be appropriate to spend perhaps 10 percent of our gross national product for providing decent shelter.

Two ingredients seem essential for real progress. We must lay to rest the myth that housing is a private commodity best supplied by the private market. And those with housing problems must stop seeing themselves as being in the grip of unfortunate circumstances; they must come to see that, in reality, they are being deprived of what should be a basic right in an enlightened society.

CRIMINAL JUSTICE XI

The criminal-justice system is a manifestation of the coercive power of the state. Such power often seems to generate sacred and awe-filled interpretations of its nature and meaning. In fact, however, the criminal-justice system is more politicized than traditional social science and jurisprudential interpretations would suggest. Such interpretations obscure the vested bureaucratic interests — police, judicial, and correctional officials — who maintain lobbying groups in state legislatures; and the variety of economic, religious, and other interest groups who benefit from the power of the state to impose coercive sanctions. Moreover, legal officials exercise wide discretion in enforcing the law. The criminal law offers a flexible, not a rigid, mandate, and flexibility always introduces the political preferences of government officials and their constituencies.

No set of four selections can successfully illustrate all the facets of discretion in criminal justice. Those included here cut across a broad spectrum. The Knapp Commission report on police corruption in New York is first of all — although it may not seem so — a report about the problems of using the criminal law to prohibit activities for which there is a widespread and profitable market, and which many people — police included — may not consider immoral. The illegal gambling establishments in New York thus provide the main economic base for police corruption. The decision to make gambling legal or illegal is a legislative decision, but it is carried out by police who, in other circumstances, may legitimately exercise broad discretion. A fundamental question for a democratic society is how to prevent legitimate police discretion from escalating into corruption.

Corruption is not the only outcome of abuse of police discretion. During the 1960s and into the 1970s, as America became a society of fear and anger, increasingly organized into protesting groups, the police emerged as a prominent and powerful instrument of social control. There was rebelliousness and rioting in the black communities; the police were employed to bring "order." There were demonstrations against the Vietnam War; the police were used to keep the demonstrators in line. The campuses erupted in protest against the war, against racism, against the underlying assumptions and life-styles of the cold-war establishment; the police were brought in to quiet the campuses. Crime in the streets became a central political issue; the police came to enjoy greater legal authority and a larger claim on national resources.

This was true not only at the local level, but at the national as well. As police came to be viewed as the primary instrument of internal security, the United States developed an increasingly well-funded and widespread political intelligence apparatus that was, and continues to be, largely unaccountable to the public or its elected representatives. Frank Donner's selection provides a comprehensive discussion of the political intelligence apparatus. If anything, post-Watergate disclosures have shown this analysis not only to be accurate, but perhaps understated.

Another instance of discretion in criminal justice is to be found in the area of white-collar crime. The discussion by Mark Green et al. of crimes by corporations and their executives suggests that governmental authorities often bend over backwards to protect wealthy corporate criminals. There is leniency in bringing prosecutions, in accepting guilty pleas, in judicial sentencing, and, when imprisonment occurs, in assignment to prison.

The imprisonment of wealthy corporate officials is, statistically, a rarity. Most prisoners are nonwhite and from poverty backgrounds. Yet, theories of incarceration derive from the experience and psychology of persons from a totally different background. In the early nineteenth century, reformers of the day, notably Quakers, developed the idea of the penitentiary, where prisoners could rehabilitate their character through prayer and reflection.

The history of prisons is the history of supposed reforms that actually increased the power of prison authorities. Jessica Mitford's selection offers a biting analysis of perhaps the ultimate in criminal justice discretion, the indeterminate sentence. The indeterminate sentence was originally adopted in California presumably as a way of offering "individual treatment" to convicted offenders. In fact, it turns out to offer less in the way of individualized treatment than uncertainty and anxiety, and an instrument for managing prisoners conduct in prison. Mitford calls for abolition of the indeterminate sentence and, like the other authors in this chapter, suggests that the criminal justice system is too often characterized by arbitrary, sometimes unlimited, power of officials. Thus, for criminal justice to be achieved, the balance in the system needs to be moved from official power and discretion to official accountability.

38. POLICE CORRUPTION IN NEW YORK

Knapp Commission

THE EXTENT OF POLICE CORRUPTION

We found corruption to be widespread. It took various forms depending upon the activity involved, appearing at its most sophisticated among plainclothesmen assigned to enforcing gambling laws. In the five plainclothes divisions where our investigations were concentrated we found a strikingly standardized pattern of corruption. Plainclothesmen, participating in what is known in police parlance as a "pad," collected regular biweekly or monthly payments amounting to as much as $3,500 from each of the gambling establishments in the area under their jurisdiction, and divided the take in equal shares. The monthly share per man (called the "nut") ranged from $300 to $400 in midtown Manhattan to $1,500 in Harlem. When supervisors were involved they received a share and a half. A newly assigned plainclothesman was not entitled to his share for about two months, while he was checked out for reliability, but the earnings lost by the delay were made up to him in the form of two months' severance pay when he left the division.

Evidence before us led us to the conclusion that the same pattern existed in the remaining divisions which we did not investigate in depth.

From a report by the Commission to Investigate Allegations of Police Corruption in New York City, Whitman Knapp, Chairman, August 3, 1972.

This conclusion was confirmed by events occurring before and after the period of our investigation. Prior to the Commission's existence, exposures by former plainclothesman Frank Serpico had led to indictments or departmental charges against nineteen plainclothesmen in a Bronx division for involvement in a pad where the nut was $800. After our public hearings had been completed, an investigation conducted by the Kings County District Attorney and the Department's Internal Affairs Division — which investigation neither the Commission nor its staff had even known about — resulted in indictments and charges against thirty-seven Brooklyn plainclothesmen who had participated in a pad with a nut of $1,200. The manner of operation of the pad involved in each of these situations was in every detail identical to that described at the Commission hearings, and in each almost every plainclothesman in the division, including supervisory lieutenants, was implicated.

Corruption in narcotics enforcement lacked the organization of the gambling pads, but individual payments — known as "scores" — were commonly received and could be staggering in amount. Our investigation, a concurrent probe by the State Investigation Commission, and prosecutions by federal and local authorities all revealed a pattern whereby corrupt officers customarily collected scores in substantial amounts from narcotics violators. These scores were either kept by the individual officer or shared with a partner and, perhaps, a superior officer. They ranged from minor shakedowns to payments of many thousands of dollars, the largest narcotics payoff uncovered in our investigation having been $80,000. According to information developed by the SIC and in recent federal investigations, the size of this score was by no means unique.

Corruption among detectives assigned to general investigative duties also took the form of shakedowns of individual targets of opportunity. Although these scores were not in the huge amounts found in narcotics, they not infrequently came to several thousand dollars.

Uniformed patrolmen assigned to street duties were not found to receive money on nearly so grand or organized a scale, but the large number of small payments they received present an equally serious if less dramatic problem. Uniformed patrolmen, particularly those assigned to radio patrol cars, participated in gambling pads more modest in size than those received by plainclothes units and received regular payments from construction sites, bars, grocery stores, and other business establishments. These payments were usually made on a regular basis to sector car patrolmen and on a haphazard basis to others. While individual payments to uniformed men were small, mostly under $20, they were often so numerous as to add substantially to a patrolman's income. Other less regular payments to uniformed patrolmen included those made by after-hours bars, bottle clubs, tow trucks, motorists, cab drivers, parking lots, prostitutes, and defendants wanting to fix their cases in court. Another practice found to be widespread was the payment of gratuities by policemen to other policemen to expedite normal police procedures or to gain favorable assignments.

Sergeants and lieutenants who were so inclined participated in the same kind of corruption as the men they supervised. In addition, some sergeants had their own pads from which patrolmen were excluded.

Although the Commission was unable to develop hard evidence establishing that officers above the rank of lieutenant received payoffs, considerable circumstantial evidence and some testimony so indicated. Most often when a superior officer is corrupt, he uses a patrolman as his "bagman" who collects for him and keeps a percentage of the take. Because the bagman may keep the money for himself, although he claims to be collecting for his superior, it is extremely difficult to determine with any accuracy when the superior actually is involved.

Of course, not all policemen are corrupt. If we are to exclude such petty infractions as free meals, an appreciable number do not engage in any corrupt activities. Yet, with extremely rare exceptions, even those who themselves engage in no corrupt activities are involved in corruption in the sense that they take no steps to prevent what they know or suspect to be going on about them.

It must be made clear that — in a little over a year with a staff having as few as two and never more than twelve field investigators — we did not examine every precinct in the Department. Our conclusion that corruption is widespread throughout the Department is based on the fact that information supplied to us by hundreds of sources within and without the Department was consistently borne out by specific observations made in areas we were able to investigate in detail.

THE NATURE AND SIGNIFICANCE OF POLICE CORRUPTION

Corruption, although widespread, is by no means uniform in degree. Corrupt policemen have been described as falling into two basic categories: "meat-eaters" and "grass-eaters." As the names might suggest, the meat-eaters are those policemen who, like Patrolman William Phillips who testified at our hearings, aggressively misuse their police powers for personal gain. The grass-eaters simply accept the payoffs that the happenstances of police work throw their way. Although the meat-eaters get the huge payoffs that make the headlines, they represent a small percentage of all corrupt policemen. The truth is, the vast majority of policemen on the take don't deal in huge amounts of graft.

And yet, grass-eaters are the heart of the problem. Their great numbers tend to make corruption "respectable." They also tend to encourage the code of silence that brands anyone who exposes corruption a traitor. At the time our investigation began, any policeman violating the code did so at his peril. The result was described in our interim report: "The rookie who comes into the Department is faced with the situation where it is easier for him to become corrupt than to remain honest."

More importantly, although meat-eaters can and have been individually induced to make their peace with society, the grass-eaters may be more easily reformed. We believe that, given proper leadership and support, many police who have slipped into corruption would exchange their illicit income for the satisfaction of belonging to a corruption-free Department in which they could take genuine pride.

The problem of corruption is neither new, nor confined to the police. Reports of prior investigations into police corruption, testimony taken by the Commission, and opinions of informed persons both within and without the Department make it abundantly clear that police corruption has been a problem for many years. Investigations have occurred on the average of once in twenty years since before the turn of the century, and yet conditions exposed by one investigation seem substantially unchanged when the next one makes its report. This doesn't mean that the police have a monopoly on corruption. On the contrary, in every area where police corruption exists it is paralleled by corruption in other agencies of government, in industry and labor, and in the professions.

Our own mandate was limited solely to the police. There are sound reasons for such a special concern with police corruption. The police have a unique place in our society. The policeman is expected to "uphold the law" and "keep the peace." He is charged with everything from traffic control to riot control. He is expected to protect our lives and our property. As a result, society gives him special powers and prerogatives, which include the right and obligation to bear arms, along with the authority to take away our liberty by arresting us.

Symbolically, his role is even greater. For most people, the policeman is the law. To them, the law is administered by the patrolman on the beat and the captain in the station house. Little wonder that the public becomes aroused and alarmed when the police are charged with corruption or are shown to be corrupt.

Departmental Attitudes Toward Police Corruption

Although this special concern is justified, public preoccupation with police corruption as opposed to corruption in other agencies of government inevitably seems unfair to the policeman. He believes that he is unjustly blamed for the results of corruption in other parts of the criminal-justice system. This sense of unfairness intensifies the sense of isolation and hostility to which the nature of police work inevitably gives rise.

Feelings of isolation and hostility are experienced by policemen not just in New York, but everywhere. To understand these feelings one must appreciate an important characteristic of any metropolitan police department, namely an extremely intense group loyalty. When properly understood, this group loyalty can be used in the fight against corruption. If misunderstood or ignored, it can undermine anticorruption activities.

Pressures that give rise to this group loyalty include the danger to which policemen are constantly exposed and the hostility they encounter from society at large. Everyone agrees that a policeman's life is a dangerous one, and that his safety, not to mention his life, can depend on his ability to rely on a fellow officer in a moment of crisis. It is less generally realized that the policeman works in a sea of hostility. This is true, not only in high crime areas, but throughout the City. Nobody, whether a burglar or a Sunday motorist, likes to have his activities interfered with. As a result, most citizens, at one time or another, regard the police with varying degrees of hostility. The policeman feels, and naturally often returns, this hostility.

Two principal characteristics emerge from this group loyalty: suspicion and hostility directed at any outside interference with the Department, and an intense desire to be proud of the Department. This mixture of hostility and pride has created what the Commission has found to be the most serious roadblock to a rational attack upon police corruption: a stubborn refusal at all levels of the Department to acknowledge that a serious problem exists.

The interaction of stubbornness, hostility, and pride has given rise to the so-called "rotten-apple" theory. According to this theory, which bordered on official Department doctrine, any policeman found to be corrupt must promptly be denounced as a rotten apple in an otherwise clean barrel. It must never be admitted that his individual corruption may be symptomatic of underlying disease.

This doctrine was bottomed on two basic premises: First, the morale of the Department requires that there be no official recognition of corruption, even though practically all members of the Department know it is in truth extensive; second, the Department's public image and effectiveness require official denial of this truth.

The rotten-apple doctrine has in many ways been a basic obstacle to meaningful reform. To begin with, it reinforced and gave respectability to the code of silence. The official view that the Department's image and morale forbade public disclosure of the extent of corruption inhibited any officer who wished to disclose corruption and justified any who preferred to remain silent. The doctrine also made difficult, if not impossible, any meaningful attempt at managerial reform. A high command unwilling to acknowledge that the problem of corruption is extensive cannot very well argue that drastic changes are necessary to deal with that problem. Thus neither the Mayor's Office nor the Police Department took adequate steps to see that such changes were made when the need for them was indicated by the charges made by Officers Frank Serpico and David Durk in 1968. This was demonstrated in the Commission's second set of public hearings in December 1971.

Finally, the doctrine made impossible the use of one of the most effective techniques for dealing with any entrenched criminal activity, namely persuading a participant to help provide evidence against his partners in crime. If a corrupt policeman is merely an isolated rotten apple, no reason can be given for not exposing him the minute he is discovered. If, on the other hand, it is acknowledged that a corrupt officer is only one part of an apparatus of corruption, common sense dictates that every effort should be made to enlist the offender's aid in providing the evidence to destroy the apparatus.

THE COMMISSION'S ACTIONS

The Commission examined and rejected the premises upon which the rotten-apple doctrine rested. We concluded that there was no justification for fearing that public acknowledgment of the extent of corruption would damage the image and effectiveness of the Department. We are convinced that instead of damaging its image a realistic attitude toward corruption could only enhance the Department's credibility. The conditions described in the Commission's public hearings came as no surprise to the large numbers of City residents who had experienced them for years. If, then, the Department makes it a point to acknowledge corrupt conditions the public already knows to exist, it can hardly damage its image. On the contrary, it can only promote confidence in the Department's good-faith desire to deal with those conditions.

The Commission looked at the question of morale in much the same way. We did not — and do not — believe that the morale of the average policeman is enhanced by a commanding officer who insists on denying facts that the policeman knows to be true. We believed — and continue to believe — that such false denials can only undercut the policeman's confidence in his commander. If a policeman listens to his commander solemnly deny the existence of an obvious corrupt situation, the policeman can draw only one of two conclusions: either the commander is hopelessly naive or he is content to let the corruption continue.

Once we had rejected the premises of the rotten-apple doctrine, the Commission determined to employ one of the techniques that adherence to the doctrine had made impossible, namely to persuade formerly corrupt police officers to work with us in providing evidence of continuing corruption.

The mere decision to use the technique did not automatically produce a body of officers able and eager to assist us in this manner. Indeed, knowledgeable persons assured us that the code of silence was so strong that we would never find a corrupt officer who could be persuaded to assist in exposing corruption. We ultimately did persuade four officers, including Detective Robert L. Leuci and Patrolmen William Phillips, Edward Droge and Alfonso Jannotta to undertake undercover work. Of these, all but Detective Leuci did so under the compulsion of having been caught by Commission investigators. Patrolmen Phillips and Droge testified at public hearings held in October 1971. Patrolman Jannotta was unavailable due to illness at the time of the hearings. The information disclosed by Detective Leuci was so vital that we did not, since our time was limited, feel justified in keeping it to ourselves. Leuci and the Commission staff members who had debriefed him and worked with him on his initial undercover operations were turned over to the federal government for the long-term investigation which was required. Leuci's work as a federal undercover agent is now resulting in the series of important narcotics-related indictments being obtained by United States Attorney Whitney North Seymour, Jr.

Success in persuading these officers to assist in the investigation was a first step in demonstrating that the rotten-apple doctrine was invalid. Patrolman Phillips' three days of testimony about systematic corruption in various parts of the Department, corroborated by tape-recorded conversations with many police officers and others, was in itself enough to make the doctrine seem untenable. Patrolman Droge described how departmental pressures gradually converted an idealistic rookie into an increasingly bold finder of bribes and payoffs. Former Patrolman Waverly Logan, who volunteered to testify about corruption in which he had been involved, corroborated Droge's testimony and went on to tell about policemen in Harlem who received monthly as much as $3,000 each in narcotics graft. Patrolman Logan also introduced the Commission to two addicts who were willing to work with us in obtaining evidence to corroborate these assertions. The Commission's work with these addicts produced movies and recorded conversations of policemen selling narcotics. Some of the narcotics were paid for with merchandise the policemen believed to be stolen. Captain Daniel McGowan, a police officer of unquestioned integrity and experienced in anticorruption work, testified that the picture of corruption presented by Patrolmen Phillips, Droge, and Logan was an accurate one. In addition, there was testimony from, among others, a Harlem gambler, Commission agents describing their investigations, and witnesses in the business community revealing corrupt police dealings with the hotel and construction industries. Recorded conversations and movies documented instances of police corruption, including gambling and narcotics payoffs, fixing court cases, and shaking down a tow-truck operator. The cumulative effect of these two weeks of testimony made it not only unrealistic but absurd for anyone thereafter to adhere to the rotten-apple doctrine, either publicly or privately.

The doctrine did not die easily. Institutional pressures within the Department seemed to force the high command to continue giving lip service to the doctrine even when speaking out against corruption. Commissioner Murphy in his early statements about corruption regularly included a pointed statement indicating that the corruption in the Department was limited to a few officers. On one occasion he went so far as to imply that there were no more than about 300 corrupt police officers in the entire Department. After Patrolman Phillips had completed two of his three days of testimony at our public hearings, Commissioner Murphy found it necessary to discount his testimony of widespread corruption, referring to him as a "rogue cop."

However, one week later, after Phillips had completed his testimony and had been followed by Patrolmen Logan and Droge and others, the Department, speaking through First Deputy Commissioner William H. T. Smith, forthrightly rejected the rotten-apple doctrine by name. Smith defined it as standing for the proposition that "police departments are essentially free of corruption except for the presence of a few corrupt officers who have managed to slip into police service and also into key assignments such as gambling investigations, despite rigorously applied screening procedures designed to keep them out." He said that traditional police strategy had been to react defensively whenever a scandal arose by "promising to crack down on graft, to go after the 'rogue cops,' to get rid of 'rotten apples.'" Smith said the Department now rejected this approach "not just on principle, but because as a way of controlling corruption it had utterly failed." He acknowledged that the result of adherence to the theory had been a breakdown in public confidence: ". . . they [the public] are sick of 'bobbing for rotten apples' in the police barrel. They want an entirely new barrel that will never again become contaminated."

Changing Departmental Attitudes

The public hearings, in addition to helping bring about official abandonment of the rotten-apple doctrine, have had dramatic effect on the way members of the Department discuss corruption. This change was graphically described shortly after our hearings by former Assistant Chief Inspector Sidney C. Cooper in colorful language: "Not very long ago we talked about corruption with all the enthusiasm of a group of little old ladies talking about venereal disease. Now there is a little more open discussion about combatting graft as if it were a public health problem." In short, the first barrier to a realistic look at corruption has been overcome: the problem has been officially, and unofficially, acknowledged.

Some time after the public hearings were over, it was revealed that Detective Leuci had been doing undercover work for the federal government for over a year and a half, and that he had been doing it with both the knowledge and protection of the Department's high command. News also began to spread throughout the Department that other formerly corrupt policemen were doing undercover work for the Department's Internal Affairs Division and for at least one district attorney's office. These revelations had considerable impact, both direct and indirect, upon attitudes toward corruption within the Department.

To put the direct impact in proper perspective, it should be pointed out that any criminal activity, within a police department or elsewhere, cannot thrive unless all of its participants are able to maintain confidence in each other. Patrolman Phillips' testimony made this very clear. In testifying about his own corrupt activities, he described how he could, by making a few telephone calls within five or ten minutes, "check out" the reliability of any other officer whose assistance he might require in a corrupt enterprise. By way of illustration, he described instances where he had been similarly checked out while doing undercover work for the Commission. This ability to check out, and rely upon, an officer with whom one has had no previous contact rested on the assumption — unchallenged before the advent of our Commission — that no police officer who had once become involved in corruption could ever be persuaded to disclose the corruption of others. The actions of Detective Leuci and Patrolmen Phillips and Droge and of others as yet unnamed who are presently working undercover have undermined this assumption.

Even more important was the indirect effect produced by general knowledge that the undercover activities of these formerly corrupt policemen had been known to — and protected by — the Department's high command. Traditionally, the rank and file have shown a deep cynicism, well justified by history, concerning pronouncements of new police commissioners. They carefully examine the new commissioner's every word and action, searching for "messages": Does he mean business? Can he stand up against institutional pressures?

The initial lack of clarity in Commissioner Murphy's statements on the rotten-apple theory and his "rogue cop" reaction to the first widely publicized defiance of the code of silence was interpreted by some as suggesting a lack of commitment to total war on corruption. However, the Department's final repudiation of the doctrine, and the general knowledge that the Department was using and protecting policemen who had agreed to do undercover work, gave reassurance to the doubters.

In short, we believe that the Department's recent reactions to the Commission's activities have promoted realistic self-criticism within the Department. This spirit of self-criticism is an encouraging sign. For one thing, it is becoming less unusual for police officers to report evidence of police corruption. If this tendency continues, the day may be approaching when the rookie coming into the Department will not be pressured toward corruption, but can count on finding support for his desire to remain honest.

The present situation is quite like that existing at the close of previous investigations. A considerable momentum for reform has been generated, but not enough time has elapsed to reverse attitudes that have been solidifying for many years in the minds of both the public and the police.

After previous investigations, the momentum was allowed to evaporate.

The question now is: Will history repeat itself? Or does society finally realize that police corruption is a problem that must be dealt with and not just talked about once every twenty years?

Both immediate and long-term actions are mandatory. The reforms already initiated within the Department must be completed and expanded; there must be changes, both legislative and administrative, to curb pressures toward police corruption and to facilitate its control; and the momentum generated by the events before and during the life of this Commission must be maintained.

39. THE THEORY AND PRACTICE OF AMERICAN POLITICAL INTELLIGENCE

Frank Donner

I

The twentieth century has been marked by a succession of different forms of restraint on political expression: criminal-anarchy statutes, sedition laws, deportations, congressional antisubversive probes, loyalty oaths, enforced registration. These and related measures still survive. But in recent years new, more formidable ways of responding to political and social movements on the left have emerged. The most important of these

Reprinted with permission from *The New York Review of Books,* April 22, 1971. Copyright © 1971 by Nyrev, Inc. Footnotes appearing in the original have been deleted.

is the system of political intelligence, which is rapidly coalescing into a national network.

Despite the efforts of intelligence officials to keep intelligence operations secret, reliable information about our intelligence system is steadily accumulating. We now have a clearer picture of the methods and targets of political surveillance. As a result, we can no longer seriously doubt that the main purpose of such activity is political control of dissent or that the frequently advanced justifications of law enforcement or national security are often no more than a "cover."

On March 21, 1971, a group calling itself the Citizens' Commission to Investigate the FBI mailed or delivered to a congressman and senator as well as to the *Washington Post*, the *New York Times*, and the *Los Angeles Times* a packet containing fourteen documents, selected from over 1,000 stolen from a small FBI office in Media, Pennsylvania, a suburb of Philadelphia. The fourteen documents, all of them of recent date and undisputed authenticity, show that the FBI concentrates much of its investigative effort on college dissenters and black student groups. According to a memorandum from J. Edgar Hoover such groups "pose a definite threat to the Nation's stability and security," a conclusion that he has not been able to support and that both the *Washington Post* and the *New York Times* have challenged.

When conducting surveillance of a Swarthmore College philosophy professor regarded as a "radical," the FBI enlisted the assistance of the local police and postmaster, as well as a campus security officer and switchboard operator. In one of the documents, the FBI agent in charge of the Philadelphia bureau instructs his agents at Media that more interviews are

. . . in order . . . for plenty of reasons, chief of which are it will enhance the paranoia endemic in these circles and will further serve to get the point across that there is an FBI agent behind every mailbox. In addition, some will be overcome by the overwhelming personalities of the contacting agent and will volunteer to tell all—perhaps on a continuing basis.

Dramatic disclosures of this sort as well as the recent Senate hearings on Army intelligence will undoubtedly help to cure the surviving skepticism about these practices. Until fairly recently even the targets of surveillance were reluctant to credit the existence of police activities which violate the most deeply held premises of their society. But political surveillance has become so obtrusive and its targets so numerous that it can no longer be easily ignored or justified. A sharper awareness of intelligence has, in turn, opened up new sources of data about a field which I have been researching since the McCarthy era.

Of course dossiers, informers, and infiltrators are hardly new. But since the early sixties, when attorneys general in the South formed a rudimentary intelligence network in order to curb the integrationist activities of students, political surveillance and associated practices have spread throughout the nation.

Surveillance has expanded largely because of the scale and militance of the protest movements that erupted in the sixties. Policy-makers and officers of intelligence agencies were then faced with the need to identify and control new actors on a new political stage — no easy matter in view of the anarchic radical milieu, characterized by highly mobile and anonymous young people, who tend to be hostile to formal organization and leadership. The social remoteness of new radicals concentrated in "tribal," self-contained groups made it all the more difficult to identify them.

Most of the existing intelligence agencies at that time were no more effective than other institutions in our society. Their techniques were as outmoded as their notions of subversion dominated by an old Left composed of "Communists," "fellow travelers," and "fronts." Intelligence files were choked with millions of dossiers of aging or dead radicals. At the same time, new gadgetry — miniaturization, audioelectronics, infrared-lens cameras, computers, and data banks — gave intelligence possibilities undreamed of by the most zealous practitioners of the repressive arts of the nineteenth century.

According to the herald of the "technetronic" society, Zbigniew Brzezinski, new developments in technology will make it "possible to assert almost continuous surveillance over every citizen and maintain up-to-date files, containing even personal information about the . . . behavior of the citizen, in addition to the more customary data." Full access to critical data, he adds, will give the undercover agent and the roving political spy greater flexibility in planning and executing countermeasures.

II

Twenty federal agencies are engaged in intelligence activities. The most important are:

the FBI, with an estimated 2,000 agents on political investigative assignments in charge of thousands of undercover informers

the Army, which concededly had at one time 1,200 agents in the field, together with a huge staff operating a dossier bank of 25 million "personalities"

the CIA

the Internal Revenue Service (for several weeks in 1970 its agents requested access to the circulation records of public libraries in a number of cities in order to learn the names of borrowers of books on explosives and other "militant and subversive" subjects, a practice which it defended as "just a continual building of information") the Intelligence Division of the Post Office

the Secret Service (where names of 50,000 "persons of interest" are on file)

the Customs Bureau of the Treasury Department

the Civil Service Commission (15 million names of "subversive activity" suspects)

the Immigration and Naturalization Service

the Navy, Air Force, Coast Guard

the Passport Division of the State Department

the Department of Justice Community Relations Service, which feeds information into its computerized Inter-Divisional Intelligence and Information Unit

civil-rights and poverty projects sponsored by the Department of Health, Education and Welfare and the Office of Economic Opportunity. The executive department agencies cooperate with and are supplemented by the congressional antisubversive committees.

Intelligence operations are also flourishing in states and counties. A typical state intelligence agency is the Massachusetts Division of Subversive Activities, which conducts investigations in response to complaints by private citizens and acts as a central repository for information about subversion. The Division's Annual Report for 1969 is revealing:

A file is kept of peace groups, civil rightists, and other such groups where, due to their enthusiasm, they might have a tendency to adopt or show a policy of advocating the commission of acts of force or violence to deny other persons their rights under the Constitution. These files are kept updated by communications with the Federal Bureau of Investigation, the House Internal Security Committee, subversive activities units in other states, and decisions of the United States Supreme Court.

The files in this Division have grown to such an extent that the Federal Bureau of Investigation, Immigration and Naturalization Service, Department of Defense, U.S. Army Intelligence, Federal Civil Service Commission, Treasury Department, several department of the Commonwealth, Industrial Plants and Educational Insitutions now clear with this Division on security checks.

Requests for investigations, or assistance in investigations, received from various police departments, Federal Bureau of Investigation, House Committee on Un-American Activities and the Subversive Activities Control Board, complied with such requests [sic].

Members of the Division attended demonstrations conducted in the area by various groups. Note was made of the leaders and organizations participating, occasionally photographs were taken, the persons identified, and a file was made.

The Division is continuing to compile and tabulate a check on new organizations in the civil-rights area so as to be sure of any inclinations toward communist-front activities or the infiltration into these organizations of known communists or communist sympathizers.

During the yast year, as a result of the increased activity of the communist and subversive groups in racial demonstrations throughout the country, this Division has kept a watch on these developments so as to note any trend toward that end in Massachusetts.

During the past year, this Division continued to submit information relative to subversive organizations and individuals to several local police departments who are in the process, or have started, intelligence units within their respective departments.

Sometimes state intelligence agencies operate under concealed or obscure auspices. For example, the Ohio Highway Patrol runs an intelligence unit which claims to have recruited student informers on every campus in the state. According to the head of the unit, "We have actually had informers who are members of the board of trustees [sic] of various dissident groups." State intelligence units are also at work in several universities in Maryland and Illinois.

Urban intelligence units ("red squads") have multiplied greatly and are becoming a standard tool in local police practice. Increasingly powerful, they operate under a variety of names (Anti-Subversive Squad, Intelligence Unit, Civil Disobedience Unit); in some cases they use a "Human Relations" or "Community Relations" cover, which is considered an efficient means of penetrating the ghetto.

Black communities swarm with urban intelligence agents and informers, as do university and peace groups; invitations to young people to defect or to sell information at high prices are becoming routine. Young college graduates — black and white — are offered "career opportunities" in urban intelligence; courses in intelligence and surveillance are being taught to municipal police units and campus security police.

In fact, the campus constabulary is spreading throughout the country's higher-education community. Its functions are expanding to include clandestine intelligence activities such as undercover work and wiretapping and are meshed with the work of other intelligence agencies. We get a glimpse of this new collaboration in one of the recent Media documents, dated November 13, 1970.

On 11/12/70 MR. HENRY PEIRSOL, Security Officer, Swarthmore College, Swarthmore, Pa., advised that DANIEL BENNETT is a Professor of Philosophy at that School and in charge of the Philosophy Department. He has been there about three years having previously taught at University of Mass. MRS. BENNETT is not employed and there are two small children in the family ages about 8 to 12 years.

The BENNETTs reside in a semi-detached house located near PEIRSOL's residence although he does not have any social contact with them. PEIRSOL has noted that there does not appear to be anyone other than the BENNETTs residing at their home but that numerous college students visit there frequently. BENNETT drives a two tone blue, VW station wagon, bearing Penna. license

5V0245. There are no other cars in the family and no other cars normally parked in their driveway.

PEIRSOL was funished [*sic*] with the wanted flyers on the subjects and he stated he would remain alert in his neighborhood for their possible appearance. Also he will alert his sources at the college for any information about the subjects particularly any information that subjects might be in contact with the BENNETTS.

(Those who are familiar with the quality of FBI reporting will not be surprised to learn that some of this report is not true. As Professor Bennett has pointed out, he is unacquainted with the subject of the "wanted flyers," has one child not two, and owns two cars not one.)

Many of the red squads run by city police are growing so fast that they are hard put to find enough agents. The permanent intelligence staffs are frequently augmented by detectives and plainclothesmen — as Chicago's regular intelligence unit was doubled for the SDS convention in 1969. There are also many informer recruits and trainees who report to intelligence units but are not counted as employees or officers. The official membership of Detroit's intelligence unit, which was formed in 1961, grew by 1968 to seventy members. In 1968, Boston had forty agents, New York had at least sixty-eight on its intelligence staff (ninety as of 1970) and fifty-five more line agents planted undercover; Chicago had more than 500, Houston fourteen. The Los Angeles Police Department doubled its Intelligence Division personnel from eighty-four in 1969 to 167 in 1970.

Intelligence is not a wholly public function. Political surveillance has been routinely practiced by private detectives since the nineteenth century, when objections to a political police force left the Pinkerton and Burns agencies free to engage in these activities without official competition. Today the private agencies are an important channel for political intelligence. Often they recruit employees with access to official files from government intelligence agencies and sell such information to private industry.

Local and national intelligence agencies are beginning to coalesce into an "intelligence community." For example, the young demonstrators who came to Chicago in 1968 encountered red-squad operatives from their home towns. The overheated reports of these visiting local agents led Mayor Daley's office to conclude that a plot to assassinate Johnson had been hatched. The urban agents cooperated with their federal counterparts, as well as with the Army and Navy secret operatives at the Chicago demonstrations. During the subsequent conspiracy trial no fewer than thirty of about forty substantive prosecution witnesses were police agents or infiltrators associated with governmental surveillance at various levels.

The FBI plays a central role in coordinating the intelligence system; it exchanges information with other agencies, performs investigative work for intelligence groups with limited jurisdiction, and trains intelligence agents for service in other agencies. Its intelligence techniques and political standards serve as a model for local operations. It compiles albums of photographs and files of activists which are transmitted to agencies throughout the United States.

Congressional antisubversive committees have also expanded their intelligence activities beyond the passive compilation of dossiers available only to government investigative personnel. They now provide a forum for local intelligence agencies, publish dossiers, mug shots, and other photographs of subjects obtained by surveillance and supplied by police witnesses. They also independently engage in intelligence activities.

III

The changing role of the police in carrying out surveillance was described a few years ago by Inspector Harry Fox of the Philadelphia police. In his Senate testimony, he said:

Police now have become "watchdogs" and "observers" of vocal, subversive, and revolutionary-minded people. This function has been institutionalized in Philadelphia in a "civil-disobedience unit" composed of selected and highly trained plainclothesmen. They cover all meetings, rallies, lectures, marches, sit-ins, laydowns, fasts, vigils, or any other type of demonstration that has ominous overtones. . . .

These officers know by sight the hard-core men and women who lead and inspire demonstrations. They know their associates, family ties, techniques, and affiliations with organizations leaning toward Communism both on and off the Attorney General's list. They see them day in and day out recruiting, planning, carrying signs, and verbally assaulting the principles of democracy.

Yes, the police role has become one of . . . surveillance, taking photographs, identifying participants, and making records of the events. On this basis, local police are able to piece together this jigsaw puzzle and see the widespread activity of the hard-core demonstrators and instigators.

This account naturally omits the harassing and "guerrilla warfare" aspects of police tactics. To the policeman, public protest is an unwelcome disruption of the tranquility which he regards as natural and proper. His response to antiwar activities is particularly hostile because he sees himself as a beleaguered defender of "patriotic" values, which he tends to protect by abusing his power, harassing demonstrators, and intimidating suspects. His resentment and anger are provoked in the same way by the nonconformity and personal style of many young people, who are now

the principal targets of heavy surveillance and who are constantly subjected to detention and arrest on flimsy charges.

Protest activities have inevitably served to draw the police into politics
and to expand their intelligence functions. Especially ominous is the
widening use of photographic surveillance by intelligence units. Police
in communities throughout the country systematically photograph demonstrations, parades, confrontations, vigils, rallies, presentations of petitions
to congressmen and senators, and related activities. The photographers
attached to the Philadelphia intelligence unit, for example, cover more
than a thousand demonstrations a year. Any "incident" considered "controversial" is a predictable subject for the police photographer. Protest
demonstrations against the Vietnam war are automatically considered
"controversial," but not those in favor. In the South, photographing integrationist protesters is given top priority.

Subjects are often photographed from as close as three to five feet.
Sometimes police photographers openly ridicule the demonstrators. Children who accompany their parents are photographed as are casual bystanders and nonparticipants. To convery and conceal photographic
equipment, panel trucks are sometimes used, occasionally camouflaged
to look like the equipment of a television station (referred to by veteran
surveillance subjects as "WFBI"). Surveillance photographers acquire
spurious press credentials; bona-fide cameramen often moonlight as
police or FBI informers. Supplementary photographic data are occasionally obtained from cooperating newspaper and television stations.

Photographs are sometimes covertly taken by unobtrusive plainclothesmen when a "respectable" group is involved — for example, parents
picketing a school. Usually, however, policemen, sometimes in uniform,
do not bother to conceal their activities: they either man the cameras
themselves or direct their aides by pointing out individuals or groups to
be photographed. The deterrent effect of open photography is not lost on
the police but is justified on the ground, among others, that it "cools" the
"subversive agitator" and prevents potential lawlessness.

Photographs of individuals not already known to the police are submitted to informers and undercover agents for identification. Sometimes
tentative identifications are verified by automobile license numbers which
the police systematically collect at meetings and rallies and in front of
the houses of "known militants." Then they ask other agencies, urban,
state, and federal, to help to identify the subjects.

Once the individual is identified, his name is entered in an index. The
local intelligence unit then sets out to obtain information about the subject — solely on the basis of his or her attendance at a single "controversial" event — from other intelligence sources, state and federal. In
addition, the contents of the file are passed on, as Captain Drake, Commander of the Intelligence Division of the New Orleans Police Depart-

ment, has explained, to "every conceivable authority that might have an interest in causing any prosecution or further investigation of these persons. . . ."

IV

Photography describes the subject. But other techniques must also be used to obtain political data. These include interrogation of associates, employers, landlords, etc., collection of data about financial resources, bank deposits and withdrawals, and about the subject's background. Where meetings are held publicly, whether indoors or out, the speeches are monitored by portable tape recorders, a practice which is common in large cities but which also is growing in smaller communities, especially in college towns.

Wiretapping and electronic bugging are also common, in spite of judicial restraints on their use. Local police specialists use these devices not only for their own purposes but also on behalf of the FBI. The 1968 Crime Control Law has authorized electronic eavesdropping in certain criminal cases; twelve states have passed similar legislation, while six others are now considering it. A variety of electronic devices is now being offered by commercial supply houses to state and local police departments to implement this legislation. Once they become available for even limited purposes, it is extremely unlikely that they will not be used for political surveillance as well.

Still, personal surveillance is necessary in those areas where technology cannot — at present anyway — replace human beings. Thus infiltration of dissident groups by informers remains a common procedure. Ironically, the Warren Court's limitations on wiretapping and bugging have themselves led to a heavier reliance on informers as a substitute. Moreover, these limitations encourage the use of informers because they can supply "probable cause" of a crime and so justify a wiretap order.

Informers are indispensable to political intelligence systems. Electronic eavesdropping and wiretapping are ill-suited to the slow pace, confusion, ambiguity, and factionalism of the dissenting political activities that are the targets of intelligence. Besides, wiretaps can be circumvented once the subject becomes aware of them. Indeed, nothing can quite take the place of the classic tool of intelligence, the informer. But in addition to the moral stigma attached to informing in Western culture, informers have always been regarded anyway as unreliable and treacherous observers, reporters, and witnesses. Most of them become informers for money. Their income, tenure, and future usefulness depend on their capacity to produce material useful to the police. Others are "hooked" because of previous involvements with the law, or are recruited for ideological reasons — either as police plants or as defectors.

Both the pressures and the inducements, along with the sense of guilt that requires the betrayer to find some justification for his betrayal, tend to produce tained information. All too frequently it is inaccurate, highly selective, and based on sinister and unwarranted inferences. Where a literal version of a target's utterances would seem innocent, the informer will insist on stressing the connotations; conversely, where the language is figurative or metaphysical the informer reports it as literally intended. Most important of all, he seizes on the transient fantasies of the powerless — rhetoric and images not intended to be acted upon — and transforms them into conspiracies whose purpose and commitment are wholly alien to their volatile and ambiguous context.

It need only be added that the hazards inherent in the testimony of political informers are especially great in conspiracy cases. The vague, inchoate character of the conspiracy charge and the atmosphere of plotting and hidden guilt which accompanies it make it a perfect foil for the undercover agent who surfaces on the witness stand, a hero returned from the dark wood.

The informer is not only a reporter or an observer, but also an actor or participant, and he frequently transforms what might otherwise be idle talk or prophecy into action. Professor Zachariah Chafee, Jr., once remarked, "The spy often passes over an almost imperceptible boundary into the *agent provocateur*." The purpose of such provocations, as Allen Dulles wrote in *The Craft of Intelligence*, is to "provide the pretext for arresting any or all of [the group's] members. Since the agent report[s] to the police exactly when and where the action is going to take place, the police [have] no problems."

There are powerful reasons for viewing provocation as the handmaiden of infiltration, even when it is not part of a planned intelligence strategy. A merely passive, "cool" infiltrator-observer cannot hope to play more than a lowly "Jimmy Higgins" role in the target group, if he gains entry at all. In order to enhance his usefulness he must penetrate planning circles by becoming highly active. Moreover, the pressure to produce results in the form of concrete evidence of illegal activity often drives the infiltrator into provocative acts, regardless of the official cautionary advice which he may be given when he receives his assignment. Such advice is routinely conveyed by the agent's "handler" for the record, as a defense against a possible charge of entrapment.

Convincing evidence of provocation has emerged in a number of recent cases. But the motives of the *agent provocateur* are frequently complex and difficult to reconstruct from the materials available. The most common *provocateur* is simply a professional police agent who coldly engineers a single provocative act designed to "set up" leaders for roundup and arrest.

Another type (of which Tommy the Traveler is an example) is the ultrarightist who becomes a spy in order to destroy the target group. He is often driven to act out his paranoid fantasies with bombs and guns when his delusions about the group's sinister goals fail to conform to reality.

On the other hand, as the FBI student informer William T. Divale has disclosed in his recently published confessions, *I Lived Inside the Campus Revolution,* a planted informer may come to share the values of his victims, with the result that his newly acquired convictions carry him far beyond the call of duty — a form of conversion characteristic of infiltrators of black and youth groups. The infiltrator's secret knowledge that he alone in the group is immune from accountability for his acts dissolves all restraints on his zeal. He does, of course, take the risk of exposure and punitive reprisal, but this possibility itself encourages him to disarm suspicion by acting as a supermilitant. This almost schizoid quality of the behavior of informers seems inherent in political surveillance and has recurred throughout its history.

Many student informers who have surfaced or recanted have been revealed as operating for two intelligence agencies at the same time — usually a local and a federal one. Several informers commonly penetrate a single organization; indeed this is prescribed as sound intelligence practice, because each surveillance report can cross-check the others. Attempts to recruit young leftists as police spies have also recently become common: For example in the fall of 1969, young volunteers for the New Mobilization Committee to End the War in Vietnam were solicited to become informers by FBI agents. "Will you work for us?" they were asked as they entered the elevator on their way to the Committee's office. The FBI has recently acquired official jurisdiction on college campuses, which will result in even more extensive subsidy of student informers.

As the FBI Media documents make clear, Bureau agents now have formal authority from Washington to recruit informers as young as eighteen, including those attending two-year junior and community colleges. This authorization of September 1970 made official a practice which long preceded the issuance of the directive but was consistently denied for public-relations reasons. In fact, J. Edgar Hoover repeated this denial as recently as February of this year.

Moreover, local police — especially in university communities — have lately been given special funds to hire secret informers. For this purpose at least one state, Wisconsin, has made available the sum of $10,000.

V

In the past the police agencies (whether federal or local) preferred to act as the informer's "handler," "controller," or "contact." Police officers themselves only rarely resorted to impersonation, dissembling loyalties, the fabrication of false cover identities — techniques made familiar by foreign intelligence practice and regarded as abhorrent to our traditions. It was one thing to hire an agent as an independent contractor to do the dirty work of political snooping, but quite another for a public servant to do it himself.

Today, however, the police themselves often go underground. In New Orleans an intelligence division officer gained access to the Black Panther headquarters by impersonating a priest. At least six agents of New York's Special Service Division infiltrated the Black Panthers, and appeared as witnesses in their current trial.

Three members of Chicago's intelligence unit infiltrated the Chicago Peace Council. One of them, in order to enhance his credibility, exposed another to Council leaders as a policeman. According to Karl Meyer, the Council's chairman, "At our meetings they invariably took the most militant positions, trying to provoke the movement from its nonviolent force to the wildest kind of ventures." "They were," he concluded, "about our most active members." The Peace Council became suspicious of possible spies when it and other Chicago groups — the Latin American Defense Organization, Women Strike for Peace, the Fellowship of Reconciliation — suffered a number of burglaries of files and records. (Office machines and small amounts of money were also stolen but subsequently returned.)

Agents of the Chicago intelligence unit are scattered throughout Illinois, and sometimes do not report to their superiors for days or even months. Their real identities are concealed even from their colleagues. Their methods include disguises, wiretapping, and the creation of elaborate "covers," such as dummy businesses. In numerous cities, including San Diego, Houston, Oakland, Los Angeles, New Orleans, and Columbus, the agent-informer is becoming a familiar phenomenon. We are moving toward the classic European model of political infiltration, in which the planted police agent lives a double life for years if necessary, clandestinely reporting to his superiors. This kind of intelligence requires skill and training; so one should not be surprised to see the emergence of schools of instruction in the deceptive arts, similar to those run by the CIA for indoctrination in foreign intelligence and guerrilla activity.

VI

At an ever-increasing rate the activities of antiwar, anti-Establishment, civil rights, black militant, student, and youth groups are being recorded and compiled. Lists and dossiers are coded, computerized, stored, and made accessible to all branches of the intelligence network. Here is how Lt. George Fencl, head of Philadelphia's civil disobedience unit, describes its filing system:

We've been acquainted with quite a number of people throughout the years we've been handling demonstrations. We have made a record of every demonstration that we've handled in the city of Philadelphia and reduced this to writing, first by report and then taking out the names of persons connected with the different movements.

We have some 18,000 names and we've made what we call an alphabetical file. We make a 5x8 card on each demonstrator that we know the name and so forth that we handle. This card shows such information as the name, address, picture if possible, and a little rundown on the person . . . which group he pickets with and so forth.

Also on the back of the card, we show the different demonstrations, the date, time and location, and the groups that the person picketed with. We have some 600 different organizations that we've encountered in the Philadelphia area.

This new intelligence system concentrates more on compiling names than on the content of speeches or other activities. For example, a report submitted to the Detroit Criminal Investigation Bureau by two undercover agents reads as follows:

At 8:00 P.M. on Thursday, November 11, 1965, the WEST CENTRAL ORGANIZATION held a special meeting which was comprised primarily of executives, delegates, and clergy. The meeting was called for a briefing by MR. SAUL ALINSKY of the INDUSTRIAL AREAS FOUNDATION, Chicago, Illinois, who was in the Detroit area on November 10 and 11, 1965. Thirty-seven persons attended this meeting.

The following persons were identified as being in attendance at the above meeting, identification being made by surveilling officers as well as by Confidential Informant 059. [A list of twenty-one names follows.]

The following vehicles were observed parked in the immediate vicinity of 3535 Grand River, occupants entering same. [There follows a list of eleven automobiles together with the names and addresses of eleven individuals who are presumably the title registrants.]

There is nothing in the report which suggests the reason for the surveillance or what took place at the meeting.

Experience with other official record systems suggests that it is only a matter of time before the intelligence now being collected by thousands of federal and local agencies will be codified and made accessible on a broad scale. Indeed, we are not far away from a computerized nationwide system of transmittal and storage.

VII

While the recent bombings and the hunt for fugitives have supplied justification for some surveillance practices, the emerging system as a whole is oriented toward the future and is justified as preventive: the security of the nation against future overthrow is said to require the present frenzy of surveillance. In cases where such an argument makes no sense, surveillance is justified on grounds that it is necessary to prevent local violence and disorder in the future.

Political intelligence indiscriminately sweeps into its net the mild dissenters along with those drawn to violence; when the national security is at stake, so the argument runs, it is folly to take risks. The quarry is pursued long before expressions or associations of radicals are likely to incubate into violent or revolutionary acts. The fear of waiting "until it is too late" conditions the intelligence mind to suspect all forms of dissent as signs of potential "subversion."

Thus peaceful, moderate, lawful organizations — from the NAACP to the Fellowship of Reconciliation — become intelligence targets on the theory that they are linked to communism or subversion. This lack of selectivity, a familiar phenomenon to students of intelligence, has now been abundantly documented by the Senate testimony of former Army Intelligence agents and the recent Media documents.

To equate dissent with subversion, as intelligence officials do, is to deny that the demand for change is based on real social, economic, or political conditions. A familiar example of this assumption is the almost paranoid obsession with the "agitator." Intelligence proceeds on the assumption that most people are reasonably contented but are incited or misled by an "agitator," a figure who typically comes from "outside" to stir up trouble. The task is to track down this sinister individual and bring him to account; all will then be well again.

Since the agitator is elusive and clever, one never knows who he will turn out to be or where he will show his hand. Indeed, the striking characteristic of the agitator, according to the rhetoric and testimony of the intelligence people, is not his views nor his actions but his persistence. A subject who keeps coming to meetings or rallies or is repeatedly involved in "incidents" is soon marked as an agitator (more sophisticated terms: "militant," "activist," sometimes preceded by "hard core").

The outside agitator is a descendent of the "foreign agitator" or the "agent of a foreign power," as he came to be called. The thesis that domestic radicals are either tools or dupes of foreign manipulation provides intelligence agencies with their most effective way of exploiting popular fears, one which is also cherished by legislators. All movements on the left — and especially groups such as the Panthers — have come under attack as agents for foreign powers.

Such ideological stereotypes give intelligence a powerful bias against movements of protest from the center leftward. To be sure, a handful of ultrarightist groups such as the Klan and the Minutemen are also under surveillance, but for political intelligence, the presumption of innocence is largely confined to the defenders of the status quo. For individuals and groups committed to social or political protest, the presumption is re-

versed: Peaceful, nonviolent activity must be constantly scrutinized because it may turn out to be a vital clue to a vast subversive conspiracy.

VIII

While intelligence is developing new clandestine activities, it is also becoming highly visible. American political activity is plagued by an intelligence "presence" which demoralizes, intimidates, and frightens many of
its targets — and is intended to do so. And it is not merely a "presence."
A variety of sanctions are improvised to punish politically objectionable
subjects. These include "information management" (such as inclusion on
the "ten most wanted" list), press leaks, harassment, prosecution on drug
charges, legislative inquisition, physical violence, the vandalizing of cars,
blacklisting, the refusal to give police protection when needed, illegal
searches and raids on pretexts.

One prevailing assumption of intelligence officers is that "subversion"
is financed and supported by respectable "front" institutions (churches,
foundations, and universities, for example) and individuals (such as lawyers). Special pressures are brought by intelligence agencies to cut off
such suspected subsidies — for example, J. Edgar Hoover's attacks on
white contributors to Black Panther defense funds and the listing by the
House Internal Security Committe of honoraria paid to liberal and radical
campus speakers.

Intelligence is thus becoming an end in itself, rather than an investigative means — a transformation all too clearly reflected in the encouragement of FBI agents to confront subjects in order to "enhance" their
"paranoia," as one of the Media documents states. But its claim to be conducting a neverending investigation into some future unspecified threat
to the national security is consistently used to legitimize its expansion.
Few want to shackle the police in their hunt for wrongdoers, especially
those who threaten the safety of the Republic. Why should one question
a "mere" investigation, even if tons of constitutional ore may have to be
excavated in order to find a single subversive nugget?

IX

What are the standards that intelligence agencies must follow for select-
ing subjects of surveillance, for the techniques they use or the data they
develop? In fact, there are no effective standards, and there are no effective authorities in this country to insist on such standards. Every surveillance unit claims its own authority to deal with "subversion" or "subversive
activities," terms which mean whatever the agency wants them to mean.

The head of the Chicago intelligence unit, Lt. Joseph Healy, summed up the matter when he testified at the conspiracy trial that his squad maintained surveillance over "any organization that could create problems for the city or the country." That Army Intelligence took the same view is shown by recent disclosures that it was snooping into a virtually unlimited range of civilian activity.

In most cases, the jurisdiction to engage in political-intelligence activities is wholly improvised. This is true not merely of many local agencies but the FBI itself. The authority the FBI claims it has to stalk nonconformists can be justified neither by its law-enforcement powers nor by its domestic spy-catching jurisdiction. The latter, in fact, is based on an obscure 1939 directive which J. Edgar Hoover has interpreted as conferring upon the FBI the power, in his words, "to identify individuals working against the United States, determine their objectives and nullify their effectiveness." Who are these "individuals?" Those whose activities involve "subversion and related internal security problems."

The unlimited scope of their jurisdiction and their virtual autonomy encourage intelligence institutions to consolidate and expand. Intelligence thus constantly enlarges its operations by exaggerating the numbers, power, and intentions of the subversive enemy.

Ironically, this exaggeration is further stimulated by the need to develop some plausible political and constitutional justification for violating democratic rights. Intelligence not only continually expands the boundaries of subversion in its operations, but inevitably generates a stream of fear-mongering propaganda in its evaluation of intelligence data. A troubled period such as the present intensifies this process: the number of surveillance subjects increases greatly as the intelligence agencies circulate propaganda dramatizing their life-and-death struggle with subversion.

X

The link between drug use and political radicalism has also served to expand the scope of political surveillance. In the past, narcotics law enforcement and the policing of political crimes have drawn on similar surveillance techniques. This was so because both involve conduct to which the parties consent and both frequently leave little proof that any crime was committed. Today the "nark" and undercover intelligence operatives are frequently in pursuit of the same prey. The same agents sometimes function in both areas and political militancy is a common cover for the "nark," especially on college campuses.

Similarly, students under surveillance for drug use are frequently selected for their political nonconformity, a link manifest in the background of both the Kent State and Hobart College cases, as well as in the conviction of Dr. Leslie Fiedler of the State University of New York at Buffalo for maintaining premises where marijuana was used. The pot bust has become a punitive sanction against political dissent and the threat of prosecution is a favorite method of "hooking" student informers. Lee Otis Johnson, former head of Houston's Student Non-Violent Coordinating Committee, is now serving a thirty-year jail term for the sale of a single marijuana cigarette to a Houston undercover policeman.

XI

Many young radicals are finding ways of evading undercover surveillance of their political activities. Intelligence inevitably generates counter-measures ("security"), driving its targets into protective secrecy and sometimes underground even though they are usually engaged in legal protest. Such furtiveness is then cited as further proof of subversion and conspiracy ("What have they got to hide?") and reinforces the justifica-tion for surveillance.

Radicals in the past few years have tried to protect themselves by rigorously checking the backgrounds of possible infiltrators, isolating a suspected agent or feeding him bogus information, giving him test assign-ments, banning the use of drugs, cars, and private phones, and forming affinity groups. The radicals themselves sometimes use disguises and false names. The ultimate response to intelligence is counterintelligence, including the penetration of intelligence institutions to thwart their effec-tiveness. Some groups are beginning to boast about their double agents, counterspies, and pipelines to police sources. One Berkeley police officer has already complained (and not very convincingly): "I'm afraid they do a better job spying on us than we do on them."

The pilferage and circulation of the Media FBI documents seem to suggest an escalation in counterintelligence tactics. The group responsible for the action has already announced, as a follow-up measure, a planned exposure of a "first group" of FBI informers whose names appear in as yet unreleased stolen documents. This listing of a "first group" is presumably to be followed by publication of lists of others.

Such a tactic will not only create a painful dilemma for present Phil-adelphia-area informers but may vastly complicate the FBI's problems in future recruitment. Because political spies are the keystone of the entire federal political-intelligence system, the FBI goes to extraordinary lengths to shield their identities and stresses these protective practices as an in-ducement for recruits. A breach in the FBI security system may well scare off potential informers not only in the Philadelphia area, but every-where — Who knows where the Citizens' Commission will strike next?

The increased risk is bound to boost the price of the informers' services. At the very least, it will "enhance" among the hunters the same "paranoia" now "endemic" among the hunted.

XII

Our political-intelligence apparatus has begun to exert a dangerous influence on the exercise of political power. The attempt by the Los Angeles Chamber of Commerce to use intelligence data to discredit and destroy a group of Los Angeles poverty agencies is a dramatic example of a spreading phenomenon. A candidate for public office learns that he has been made an intelligence target by orders of his opponent, the incumbent. A lawyer for a victim of police brutality is threatened with being disbarred as a "subversive" because of leaks in the police department's intelligence files.

Mayor Alioto of San Francisco discovers that unevaluated intelligence files compiled by federal and urban agencies, full of smears and unverified rumors, are opened up to the press for an article which threatens his political ruin. A check of the California Un-American Activities Committee files discloses dossiers on many legislators, including the Senate president, with notations reflecting intensive surveillance. A courageous Chicago newsman, Ron Dorfman, who has vigorously attacked intelligence practices in that city, is confronted with a detailed dossier on himself in a session with the Illinois Crime Commission.

It is chilling enough to learn that in this country literally millions of people are systematically suffering invasions of privacy, and, what is worse, are forced to exercise their rights of free expression and assembly under the fear of surveillance. But when a secret political police begins to play an important role in political decisions and campaigns, the democratic process is in grave danger.

Nor is there much comfort in the notion that our current intelligence mania is only a transient response to a particular emergency. History — and for that matter the annals of J. Edgar Hoover's FBI — painfully teaches that once a political-intelligence system takes root, it is almost impossible to eradicate it. Fear and blackmail ensure its autonomy and self-perpetuation. How many of us can be expected to challenge a system which has such power to do injury to its critics?

Americans will now have to answer the question whether the risks that we face — and some of them are real enough — outweigh the danger of a national secret police. One can hardly question the right of the government to inform itself of potential crimes and acts of violence. The resort to bombing as a political tactic obviously creates a justification for intelligence to forestall such practices. But the evolving intelligence system I have been describing clearly exceeds these limited ends. Before it is too late we must take a cold look at our entire political-intelligence system: not to determine whether one aspect or another is repressive — whether, for example, it is possible to keep a dossier confidential — but to decide whether internal political intelligence as an institution, divorced from law enforcement, is consistent with the way we have agreed to govern ourselves and to live politically.

Eighteen cases have now been filed throughout the country, with American Civil Liberties Union support, to challenge various surveillance and filing practices by police agencies as violating constitutional rights of free expression, assembly, privacy, and the protection against unreasonable search and seizure. The constitutional issues imbedded in these cases will undoubtedly be presented ultimately to the Supreme Court. These challenges are important if for no other reason than that they will drag undercover surveillance out of the shadows.

But the political-intelligence system cannot be controlled by piecemeal attacks in the courts. If our past experience is a guide, even successful litigation may leave unchecked the particular abuses involved by limiting surveillance in ways that are readily ignored or circumvented by a bureaucracy which is a law unto itself.

Political intelligence is both a symbol of a dying politics and the means of keeping it alive through powerful myths and constraints. A truly effective attack on the evils of intelligence cannot be mounted apart from the political process. A legislative investigation, more sharply focused and more searching than Senator Ervin's investigation, is vital in order to scour this area as thoroughly as Senator LaFollette's investigation scoured labor espionage in the thirties. Such a probe could develop a fuller understanding of political intelligence and might lay the basis for dismantling a system which, if it is allowed to grow, may choke all possibility of real change in this country. But it is illusory to talk of an effective investigative and statutory attack on the powerful intelligence system at present. The elimination of the evils of political surveillance and dossiers is yet another reason why we need a new politics.

40. CRIMINAL LAW AND CORPORATE DISORDER

*Mark J. Green, Beverly C. Moore,
and Bruce Wasserstein*

Home-improvement and auto-repair frauds, supermarket underweighting and mislabeling, embezzlement and securities thefts, tax evasion and price-fixing — all comprise the world of the white-collar criminal. Coined and defined by sociologist Edwin Sutherland in the 1940s, white-collar crime is crime committed by businessmen, government offiials, and professionals in their occupational roles. Rather than triggering visions of Richard Speck or Danny Escobedo, the culprits look like us, which is partly why the concept is difficult for many to digest. For example, white-collar crime never made it into Richard Nixon's "law and order" campaign. But Lyndon Johnson, to his credit, recognized it in 1967. Addressing Congress on the occasion of the release of his Commission on Law Enforcement and the Administration of Justice, he announced that "the economic cost of white-collar crime . . . dwarfs that of all crimes of violence."

This assessment should hardly be surprising. Millions of dollars are involved in antitrust crime, government kickbacks, and securities frauds, but how many million-dollar bank robberies are there? Still, white-collar crime is largely ignored by a populace conditioned to imagine a rapist or rioter when the word "crime" is uttered. Especially difficult to establish is the fact of *corporate antitrust crime,* a subcategory of white-collar crime which involves premeditated business practice. Having shucked off its robber-baron image of 75 years ago — "You don't suppose you can run a railroad in accordance with the statutes, do you?" Arthur Vanderbilt had said — the corporate community today commands respect as concerned, hard-working, and law-abiding "pillars of the community." Business statesmen populate urban task forces, churches, and charitable boards; they initiate job training for minorities and decry pollution with the rest of us.

Yet how are we to distinguish between the pillars and pillagers of the community? For the reality of antitrust crime can be as hidden as a card-up-the-sleeve. After relieving Colonel Vanderbilt of much money by business chicane some decades back, businessman Daniel Drew vowed that he would never again defraud a powerful victim. Instead Drew declared that henceforth he would confine himself to those consumers scattered throughout the community, those who could neither recognize their plight, organize, nor fight back. This vow, anecdotally, explains both the prevalence and invisibility of corporate economic crime. When one person is robbed face to face, the injustice and indignity are obvious. But when millions are deceived in a complex economic structure, when pinpointing blame is difficult if not impossible, when crime grows so impersonal that it becomes "technical" — then we lose our perception of the criminal act.

The moral and legal content of an act, however, should not depend on our distance from the victim. The plotter of a kidnapping who stays in his retreat is as guilty as he who commits the actual act. So too with businessmen who knowingly raise prices or divide markets to pocket extra income at the expense of everyone else. The impact of the scheme is the thing — *e.g.*, a kidnapping or price-hike — not how complex the perpetrators can make it.

When recognized for what it is, corporate crime is more costly in both economic and social terms than street crime. The street criminal dents over pocketbooks and security. The business criminal, however, sabotages our body politic, social ideals, and economic structure. For, unlike his street equivalent, he violates our trust and, consequently, inspires mistrust. If nothing else, the street robber usually robs from necessity and promises us nothing. The suite robber robs from want, after taking us into respectable confidence. "If the word 'subversive' refers to efforts to make fundamental changes in a social system," Edwin Sutherland once noted, "the business leaders are the most subversive influence in the United States."

It has been said that one can tell how civilized a society is by the way it treats its criminal defendants. Such a sentiment, no doubt, envisioned a street criminal in the defendant's chair. The adage, for different reasons, is equally applicable when corporate defendants are on trial. For once institutionalized favoritism affects law enforcement, once the wealthy are treated differently because they are considered a different class of citizens, a cornerstone of our system — equal justice under law — is yanked out from under the legal edifice. It is a situation engendering cynicism and disrespect in those less able to fend. "The law," muttered a Blackstone Ranger recently. "When last you hear of a millionaire going to the electric chair? When last you hear of the president of one of those big old corporations going to jail for fixing prices or selling people rotten meat or even for income-tax evasion? When you hear anything like that?"

BUSINESS ETHICS

Not very often, although the old-style businessmen in the Upton Sinclair and Ida Tarbell critiques have not entirely disappeared. In 1949 Edwin

Sutherland published his now classic *White Collar Crime,* a study of crime committed by "persons of respectability and high social status," for whom "a violation of the legal code is not necessarily a violation of the business code." Sutherland found such crime and attitudes prevalent. He considered 60% of the 70 corporations he studied in depth "habitual criminals" — i.e., those having four convictions or more, with most of them coming in the 10 years before his study. Slightly over 97% of the corporations were "recidivists," with at least two convictions. He went on to conclude that "practically all large corporations engage in illegal restraint of trade, and . . . from half to three-fourths of them engage in such practices so continuously that they may properly be called 'habitual criminals.'"

This view of business ethics was reaffirmed by a 1961 *Harvard Business Review* survey. Seventeen hundred executive readers, 34% of the magazine's 5,000 circulation, replied to the questionnaire. About four out of seven respondents to one question believed that businessmen "would violate a code of ethics whenever they thought they could avoid detection." One-half of the respondents agreed that "the American business executive tends to ignore the great ethical laws as they apply immediately to his work. He is preoccupied chiefly with gain." And when asked, "In your industry are there any [accepted business] practices which you regard as unethical?" four-fifths responded affirmatively. That same year a corporate executive convicted of an antitrust violation told the *Wall Street Journal* in an interview, "One of the problems of business is what is normal practice, not what is the law. If it is normal practice, it's ethical — not legal, but ethical." Finally, the Businessmen's Questionnaire sent by the Study Group asked recipients if they agreed with a statement by a GE executive that price-fixing is illegal but *not* immoral: Over a quarter agreed. "At Carthage," Greek historian Polybius noted two millennia ago, "nothing which results in profits is regarded as disgraceful."

While the corporate sector is far from ethically pure, the precise amount of criminal antitrust activity is difficult to gauge. One empirical fact is that some five to 25 criminal antitrust indictments are filed each year, but that tells little. Educated speculation must substitute for prevalency studies, which have never been attempted.

First, many consider industrial collaboration to be the inevitable result of competitive capitalism. One businessman testifying before the FTC candidly confessed the prevailing situation:

When two businessmen get together, whether it is a chain institute meeting or a bible class meeting, if they happen to belong to the same industry, just as soon as the prayers have been said, they start talking about the conditions in the industry, and it is bound definitely to gravitate, that talk, to the price structure in the industry. What else is there to talk about?

After the electrical manufacturers were convicted, the president of Allen

Bradley, Inc., one of those involved, said: "No one attending the gatherings was so stupid he didn't know the meetings were in violation of the law. But it is the only way business can be run. It is free enterprise."

The encouragement at trade-association meetings for all to raise their prices, camouflaged in speeches on poor profit margins of all the members, is legion. And many firms oxymoronically believe, as did the Allen Bradley president, that price-setting is essentially to competition: In 1959 the Antitrust Division actually got a letter from a group of businessmen who had gotten together to set prices and who wanted to know what action could be taken against a participating member who was not living up to the agreement! A book entitled *Profitable Oil Jobbing*, written for petroleum marketers, unabashedly notes that:

> The jobber who is engaged in community affairs will have opportunities to become better acquainted with his competitiors. Such friendly contacts can help avoid bitter misunderstandings. A disastrous price war can be avoided by friendly competitors who are willing to discus a situation instead of taking angry reprisals for real or fancied wrongs.

Finally, in utter naiveté, one trade association wrote to its members: "We are advised by our attorneys that it is all right for us to set uniform prices as long as we don't put the agreement in writing."

The vast scale of the electrical-manufacturing conspiracy of 1961, involving nearly every firm in that industry, startled many complacent antitrust watchers who had intoned that price-fixing was nonexistent, even unnecessary, in an oligopolistic industry. One defendant in the case commented, "Conspiracy is just as much 'a way of life' in other fields as it was in electrical equipment." When businessmen were asked in our questionnaire if they agreed with this assertion, 46.8% of the replies from the 500 top industrialists agreed, while a huge 70.5% of the second-500-firm respondents agreed. Due to the increased number of informers and co-conspirators who came forward to the Antitrust Division, spurred on by the publicity over the electrical case, First Assistant Bob Wright reasoned that price-fixing was far more frequent than government enforcers had imagined. The only scholarly attempt to estimate the extent of price-fixing concluded — based on the electrical-manufacturing situation, an analysis of state and federal enforcement, and scrutiny of TNEC (Temporary National Economic Committee, 1940) records — that "it is apparent that price-fixing is quite prevalent in American business."

Federal enforcement each year attacks only a small number of antitrust criminal activities. The pattern and consistency of violations, when combined with the inadequate budget of the Antitrust Division, has led two well-placed observers 20 years apart to come to identical conclusions: Attorney General Tom Clark said in 1949 that "the effectiveness of the enforcement of the antitrust laws is sort of like an iceberg . . . about 96% under water"; and in 1970 Harold Kohn, a noted plaintiff's antitrust counsel, told a Senate subcommittee that, based on the number of violations which are discovered, "I would suspect what we unearth is like the tip of the iceberg and the rest is below the surface."

Although the number of cases prosecuted each year is actually small — averaging 25 a year from 1960 to 1964, and 11 a year from 1965 to 1970 — the total number of industries involved in criminal antitrust acts in the past 30 years is quite large. Nearly every conceivable industry has been affected, from milk and bread to heavy electrical equipment, from lobster fishing, shrimping, and the cranberry and chrysanthemum industries to steel sheets and plumbing fixtures. This large volume, plus the fact that the industries implicated are in no significant way unlike many others, suggest that their illegal acts are practiced elsewhere — without detection.

The business community takes umbrage at such estimates. They often see antitrust as antibusiness (one-half of the respondents to the Businessmen's Questionnaire did) and are dismayed by laws which make some of their clan out to be criminals. John T. Cahill, well-known Wall Street lawyer, protested in 1952 against the bringing of *any* criminal cases, giving as one reason that they aided Communist propaganda. More recently the president of Morton Salt told a business group what many of their ilk feel: that all businessmen should band together to support any of their number accused of an antitrust violation, and that any successful defense of an antitrust suit is a victory for business as a whole. The general complaints of businessmen against criminal antitrust suits follow:

1. "The law is so complex that an innocent businessman could be indicted." This canard is contradicted by actual enforcement. Cases are filed only against clearly established violations (the so-called *per se* cases like price-fixing, market divisions, and boycotts), and only against individuals who broke the law knowingly. Furthermore, one suspects that a large reason for the very high percentage of no-contest pleas in criminal cases is that the defendants were caught and knew it.

2. "There is no moral wrongdoing to justify criminal sanctions." When labor leaders violate the trust of their union members by appropriating funds, all would agree that a criminal and immoral breach has occurred. Breach of consumer trust, by corporations who appropriate additional profits by means of price-fixing, is equally blameworthy. The nature of the crime is complex, the harm vast but diffuse, and the victim not readily apparent. But the damage is real, often involving millions and billions of dollars transferred from consumer pocketbooks into corporate coffers. And, regardless of the collar color of the perpetrator, antitrust violations do involve "moral turpitude." Lee Loevinger, during his term of office, expressed this view well:

It should now be clear that a deliberate or conscious violation of the antitrust laws is not a mere personal peccadillo or economic eccentricity, but a serious offense against society which is as immoral as any other act that injures many in order to profit a few. Conspiracy to violate the antitrust laws is economic racketeering which gains no respectability by virtue of the fact that the loot is secured by stealth rather than by force.

3. "The defendants are not criminals but respected citizens." So were Bobby Baker and Billy Sol Estes, until caught. To the extent that many businessmen and much of the public holds this view, the Justice Department and the media have failed to communicate the pervasiveness and impact of corporate crime. Justice Department press releases luridly describe names and individual charges against organized-crime defendants — but not against antitrust indictees; and there is often lavish pretrial publicity in the political-dissident cases — but not in antitrust cases. Coverage of white-collar crime is constantly underplayed by the media as compared to the street crimes — murder, rape, drugs, and demonstrations — which dramatically grab the headlines. For example, in 1961 the *New Republic* discovered that of 22 large newspapers surveyed the day after the 29 electrical-conspiracy defendants had pleaded *nolo contendere* or guilty, only four put the story on their front pages, four had one column of type on it in the inside pages, 10 had less than a column on the inside, and four well-known newspapers entirely failed to cover the story — the *Boston Globe,* the *New York Daily News,* the *Christian Science Monitor,* and the *Kansas City Times. Newsweek* gave it six inches of space, *Time* four inches, and *U.S. News and World Report* gave it none at all. Five days later, after sentencing had occurred and seven executives were sent to jail, 20 newspapers, with one-fifth of all the newspaper circulation in the United States, were surveyed: 45% kept the sentencing off the front page, and, according to a comment in the *Yale Law Journal,* "None of the newspapers emphasized that the corporations were actually guilty of committing crimes." Why the muted coverage? Sutherland once answered that the media is an industry too. "Public opinion in regard to pickpockets would not be well organized," he said, "if most of the information regarding this crime came to the public directly from the pickpockets themselves."

4. "The spectacle of a trial is severely damaging to a defendant, even if later acquitted." However true, it is an ancillary cost of all criminal enforcement. The only way to avoid it is not to indict anyone, or guarantee that only the guilty are indicted — which is the purpose of a trial. Yet even the extent of this complaint is slim: in the past two decades fully 88% of those indicted were convicted.

While many corporations complain about antitrust laws and/or criminally violate them, many others (there is some overlap) institute intrafirm programs aimed at wiping out antitrust illegality. According to the replies from our Businessmen's Questionnaire, for example, 43 of 51 firms listed in *Fortune*'s top 500 had such programs, and 30 of 56 in the second

500 did. Effective programs can include the following: a written statement of corporate antitrust policy; pamphlets explaining the operations of, and importance of, the antitrust laws; warnings about the legal consequences and firm disciplinary measures to be taken if a violator is found out; a procedure for contacting the firm's legal-counsel section if a question should arise concerning certain practices; and workshops and seminars. Unfortunately, some programs include document destruction — the burning of old and unnecessary files which might contain evidence of some antitrust indiscretion.

Even more unfortunately, such programs often exist without any behavioral effect. General Electric had Policy Directive 20.5 since 1946, forbidding illegal antitrust activities through all levels of the corporate hierarchy. Thus, either the directive was flagrantly disobeyed or it was never meant to be followed. After the convictions in 1961, the *Wall Street Journal* noted that "the violations were known and condoned at the highest echelons of the companies, or else the top officials were not acquainted with important aspects of their business."

CASE STUDIES

Based on Richard Posner's statistics, of the 1,551 separate cases brought by the Antitrust Division between 1890 and 1969, 694 have been criminal cases, 45% of the total. The trend has been toward fewer criminal prosecutions in recent times: in 1940–49, 58% of the cases were criminal; in 1950–59, 48% were criminal; and in 1960–69, 31% were criminal. In fiscal 1970, Richard McLaren and John Mitchell filed a total of five criminal cases, a mere 9% of the 59 total cases brought. Of the criminal cases filed and disposed of from 1890 to 1969, 57% have been settled by acceptance of a *nolo contendere* (no-contest) plea, 21% by a guilty plea or conviction, and 22% by acquittals and dismissals. Adding the first two statistics, there has been a 78% conviction rate in all criminal antitrust cases brought in the 80 years of antitrust history. While the number of criminal cases brought has recently decreased, the conviction percentage has gone up: from 78% in the 1940s, to 89% in the 1950s and 88% in the 1960s.

Although the absolute level of criminal enforcement is dwindling, and although the extent of punishment, as discussed later, is feeble, there have been some significant criminal cases in the last decade. Three of the more notorious cases follow.

Electrical Equipment Manufacturing Cases

The conspiracy began sometime in the mid-1940s, when various electrical manufacturers met at the annual meeting of the National Electrical

Manufacturers' Association. These meetings traced back to the New Deal–OPA days, "but instead of discussing pricing under government controls," noted one commentator, "the conspirators turned to fixing prices among themselves." By the 1950s there were some 19 little cartels fixing prices and allocating markets in numerous products, from $2 insulators to multimillion-dollar turbine generators. Nearly every firm in the industry participated at one time or another, with General Electric and Westinghouse being the most prominent conspirators. During the period of the conspiracy, some $7 billion of equipment sales were implicated.

Meetings to coordinate the conspiracy took place in a variety of obscure bars and expensive hotels on the Eastern Seaboard.[1] Many of the conspirators aped the intelligence establishment by their clandestine techniques: they would never list their employer when registering at hotels; they would never breakfast with another conspirator; only pay phones would be used; all communications would be sent in plain envelopes to home addresses, to avoid unreliable secretaries; and they would never tell their lawyers anything. When someone in the GE organization would worry about Chairman Ralph Cordiner's Directive 20.5, which strongly forbade antitrust violations, "They would be told it doesn't apply now," said one conspirator; "we understood this was what the company wanted us to do." One GE executive later explained that "the boys could resist everything but temptation."

The conspiracies were of two types — open bids and sealed bids. Open bids were sales to the private sector, accounting for $55–$60 million per year. They were based on classic price-fixing, with frequent meetings (35 in 1959 alone) to set the price. Sealed bids involved the submission of bids for jobs to public agencies, which the member firms divided up among themselves according to what they called the "phase of the moon system." All the companies would submit very high bids; but one firm, chosen in advance by a schedule based on the lunar cycle, would submit a slightly lower bid and obtain the commission. When each firm's "phase" arrived, it reaped the illegal returns. The spoils were divided according to a strict formula: in switchgears, for example, involving $650 million in sales during 1951–58, GE got 45%, Westinghouse 35%, Allis-Chalmers 10%.

The result of these machinations was grossly inflated prices. Generator prices rose 50% from 1951 to 1959, while wholesale prices on all commodities rose only 5%. The Senate Small Business Committee later asserted that Westinghouse had bilked the Navy by a 900% overcharge on certain gear assemblies, and that GE had charged 446% too much on another contract.

The Antitrust Division first became interested in the situation when the TVA complained to Senator Estes Kefauver about the frequent submission of identical bids by American companies. Although the Division had investigated various aspects of the electrical-equipment industry in 1949–50 and again in 1952–53 without any results, they convened a grand jury in Philadelphia on the suspect pricing patterns. A general probe to the I-T-C Circuit Breaker Company firm arrived at the desk of Nye Spencer, a local sales manager and, as it turned out, secretary for the switchgear conspiracy. Spencer, incredibly, had kept memoranda of the meetings to train his assistant. When the subpoena arrived, he turned over all the incriminating evidence rather than multiply his crimes by document destruction. Then, in late 1959, Paul Hartig of GE, a lower-level executive, admitted his role in the insulator price-fix to the grand jury. His testimony implicated Ray Smith, a GE vice president, in the far bigger transformer cartel. After Smith was fired by GE, he fingered William Ginn, his boss and head of GE's turbine division. With these two leads, the case clicked open like a safe.

Indictments began to be handed down in February, 1960, and by the end of the summer 19 corporations and 45 executives had been charged with price-fixing, bid-rigging, and market-splitting. Many observers, despite the magnitude of the crime, expected the court to accept no-contest pleas from the defendants, but Division Chief Robert Bicks and Attorney General Rogers made unique appeals to ward it off. Bicks personally went to Philadelphia to oppose acceptance of the no-contest pleas and Rogers sent a letter to the judge arguing that enforcement would suffer if guilty pleas were not demanded. Judge J. Cullen Ganey agreed. Division and defendant lawyers then negotiated a settlement: of the 20 total indictments (involving multiple defendants), defendants would plead guilty in seven cases while they could plead no contest in the remaining 13 cases.

On February 6, 1961, sentencing began. Judge Ganey's review of the case chilled the courtroom:

> This is a shocking indictment of a vast section of our economy, for what is really at stake here is the survival of the kind of economy under which America has grown to greatness, the free enterprise system. The conduct of the corporate and individual defendants alike . . . flagrantly rocked the image of [this] economic system . . . and destroyed the model which we offer today as a free world alternative to state control and eventual dictatorship.

First to step forward was John H. Chiles, 57, a vice president and division manager of Westinghouse, a senior warden of St. John's Episcopal Church in Sharon, Pennsylvania, vice president of his United Fund drive, and "the benefactor of charities for crippled children and cancer victims," according to his lawyer. Judge Ganey sentenced him to 30 days in the Montgomery County Jail. Despite attorney protestations against sending their clients to jail with the likes of embezzlers and thieves, Judge Ganey sentenced six more individuals to 30-day jail terms. Twenty others received suspended sentences. In all, $1,954,000 in fines was assessed. GE paid out $437,500, Westinghouse $372,500, while the individual defendants were fined only $1,000 to $12,500 apiece. It was the first time in the 70-year history of the Sherman Act that officials of "big business" had been sent to prison.

The indicted had been convicted. Yet what of the top management of the corporations, like GE's Cordiner? In court, GE counsel Gerhard Gesell stressed that the case involved derelictions of individuals, not of the company. The next defense lawyer, however, in pleading for clemency for his individual client, said the defendant "only followed long-established company policy by getting together with supposed competitors, to arrange their business." He added that "there is such a thing as business compulsion, as corporate coercion. . . . There is such a thing as atmosphere, there is such a thing as knowing acquiescence in a situation." Judge Ganey affirmed this assessment:

> In a broader sense, [the companies] bear a grave responsibility of the present situation, for one would be most naive indeed to believe that these violations of the law, so long persisted in, affecting so large a segment of industry and, finally, involving so many millions upon millions of dollars, were facts unknown to those responsible for the conduct of the organization.

It was about this time — December 10, 1960, exactly — that the National Association of Manufacturers proclaimed Ralph Cordiner its man of the year.

The Quinine Cartel

The basic facts of this international cartel were broken open by the Senate Antitrust Subcommittee in 1967 after it had managed to obtain secret minutes of 17 meetings held by the conspirators. The product involved was quinidine, a chemical derivative of quinine. The Subcommittee estimated that it was used by a quarter-million people in this country, most by the elderly in order to maintain normal heart rhythm. Therefore, when the retail price of quinidine jumped 300 to 600% in 1964–65, it was cause for alarm.

The cartel traces back to an 1892 agreement between Dutch and German quinine processors. By 1913 the European quinine manufacturers and the producers of Javanese bark (from which quinine comes) had divided the world markets among themselves. Fifteen years later the international and American conspirators were indicted for antitrust transgressions, which had a complete lockhold on world quinine. The case was settled by a companion consent decree, which, as it turned out, did little to arrest the cartel's activities.

It became reactivated in 1959–62 when the 17 meetings were held by the conspirators in Paris, London, Hamburg, and Brussels. According to John Blair in the Subcommittee report, the cartelists "entered into a series of restrictive agreements designed to control prices, distribution, and production in every aspect of the quinine industry," with a key objective being "the elimination of competition among the various producers in securing the U.S. stockpile." The stockpile was 13.8 million ounces of quinine which the United States declared as surplus in 1955 and which the General Services Administration (GSA) planned to dispose of to private firms. Between 1958 and 1962 secret negotiations occurred among the GSA, the State Department, and the Dutch Embassy, with the last acting for the cartel. The Dutch Embassy asked for the entire quantity, and the State Department was not averse because, according to the GSA Administrator at the meetings, "[it] has indicated that it would strenuously oppose domestic sales of the stockpile as this would seriously disturb relations with the Netherlands and with the Government of the Republic of Indonesia."

As a result of the complicity of GSA and State, the cartel was able to corner about 90% of the surplus quinine — despite the fact that the Small Business Administration and the Comptroller General had committed GSA to sell half the surplus to small business. The result: Nedchem, the Dutch firm acting for the conspiracy, bought the quinine for 21¢ per ounce, although the GSA listed its book value as 63¢; by the end of 1964 the cartel was reselling the 21¢ quinine at more than $2 per ounce; by the end of 1966 it was more than $3. After obtaining the quinine for the cartel, Nedchem then double-crossed its co-conspirators and dissolved the cartel which it had created. This Dutch firm shared its world monopoly only with a German firm, leaving the French and British members of the cartel with no quinine and without legal redress, for one cannot enforce an illegal agreement.

"Where does the blame lie?" asked Senator Hart, who ran the hearings which uncovered this evidence. "Principally," he said, "in the operations of an international cartel, with the Dutch firm in the driver's seat . . . [and] in the State Department, [which] rendered valuable assistance to the cartel."

Plumbing Fixtures

"A trail of deceit, blackmail, and stupidity led some of them to jail," read the sub-headline to the *Fortune* magazine article on this most recent and momentous price-fixing conspiracy. It involved 15 manufacturers of plumbing fixtures, from the 76-employee Georgia Sanitary Pottery firm to American Standard, with more than $1 billion sales a year. In all, bathtubs, sinks, and toilets worth more than $1 billion were affected by the illegal activity. The plumbing-fixture industry had actually been fixing prices since the 1920s, with two major interruptions. A 1940 case against some of their members shattered the organization, and a slumping market for housing construction in the late 1950s led to a break-up of the cartel. As one conspirator later confided in an interview of the Study Group, "From 1957 to 1961 was the only period that you had what you could call really American-style competition. . . . That was the only time that there was any significant improvement in the product and product methods."

In late 1961 the industry reverted to its mood of cooperation. The first meeting was held a mere six months after the seven electrical executives had earned their convict status. Metings occurred under the auspices of the Plumbing Fixtures Manufacturing Association (PFMA); after the legitimate business had been dispatched, the conspiracy reconvened at rump sessions. The first meetings in 1961 and 1962 were held without the bigger firms in attendance. *Fortune* described their caper:

> The conspirators were like members of Alcoholics Anonymous, Pope [a conspirator] remarked. They had to meet repeatedly to "reassure" themselves. As the meeting broke up, Oscar Gerber warned the others not to allow incriminating memoranda to creep into their files, and Stan Backner cautioned a colleague not to throw votes in the wastebasket. They departed in a jovial mood.

By late 1962 the major companies, which produced both the high-quality enamel and lower-quality china fixtures, had joined in. There were two rapid and profitable results: prices on enameled cast-iron bathtubs increased 7%; then the united industry convinced the Bureau of Standards in the Commerce Department to change its "bathtub standard" so that only the more expensive acid-resistant enamel tubs, not regular enamel tubs, could be produced. This action, successful in July, 1963, reduced consumer choice and compelled purchase of the high-priced model, thereby making the conspiracy easier to manage and the illegal profits even more lucrative.

William Kramer, the executive secretary of PFMA, was centrally involved in uncovering the conspiracy. Kramer bugged some of the conspirators' meetings for self-serving purposes. When the PFMA threatened to fire and expose Kramer, he in turn threatened to release his tapes. Having failed to browbeat him, the Association tried to bribe him with a 10-year $50,000-per-year contract if he would keep quiet. Kramer instead resigned his position and left the country.

Meanwhile the IRS was investigating him and came to his former office to locate canceled salary checks. As they were leaving, Stan Backner, the new executive secretary and an active conspiracy member, made a friendly gesture. "By the way," he said, pointing to Kramer's old desk, "I'm throwing out a bunch of Kramer's stuff. Want to take a look at it?"

They did and, to Backner's dismay, found three of Kramer's secret tape recordings. With these as leads, the Justice Department empaneled a grand jury. Kramer, tired of lamming and hopeful of official leniency, sent in 16 more tapes and surrendered. In the summer of 1966 the grand jury returned 18 indictments.

All entered guilty pleas except for three corporations — American Standard, Borg-Warner, and Kohler Company — and three individuals, who pleaded not guilty and who went on trial in 1969. The jury found all guilty. The three convicted individuals and five other individual defendants who had pleaded no contest served jail sentences up to 30 days. Fines totaling $752,500 were paid by the firms, with five of them paying the $50,000 maximum.

From this partial list of antitrust criminality, conclusions of general applicability emerge. In each, the ethic of the unfettered marketplace quashed all notions of legal and public respectability. The everyday consumer was cheated. He paid more for such necessities as bathroom fixtures, electrical bills, and medical supplies. All involved government complicity prior to government crackdown: price paternalism in the OPA led to price-fixing in the electrical industry; the State Department and GSA willfully aided the Dutch quinine cartel; and the Bureau of Standards formalized the plumbing price-fix by its helpful bathtub standard. . . .

"Competition has survived," Walter Lippmann has commented, "only where men have been unable to abolish it." In these cases at least, especially the electrical and plumbing cases, those who were guilty did suffer. Some actually went to jail and all paid fines. In this respect these studies were misleading, for the overwhelmingly frequent situation is that antitrust violators do not go to jail, do pass go, and do collect $200 — even when found guilty.

COSTS/BENEFITS — CRIME PAYS

Any system based on deterrence intends that when a potential transgressor contemplates a crime, the risk of getting caught and the punishment when caught will outweigh in his mind any anticipated benefits if not caught. If this balance is close or if the benefits exceed the costs, the deterrent is a failure. The system of antitrust sanctions is such a failure. The possible profits so outweigh the possible penalties that widespread noncompliance is inevitable.

The possible benefits are obvious: excessive profits. "According to the various empirical studies conducted in this area," writes one antitrust analyst, "[price-fixing] inflates prices by some 25% or more above the noncollusive or competitive level." More spectacularly, as noted in the cases above, overcharges of 900% and 446% in the electrical cases and up to 600% in the quinine case were reported. In the recent antibiotic conspiracy . . . it was revealed that in 1953–61, the time covered by the indictment, the manufacturing cost of 100 capsules of 250-milligram dosages of tetracycline was about $1.52. The price to druggists, however, was $30.60, and the retail price was $51. Thus, there was a 3,350% mark-up on these medical necessities. A decade later, in 1971, post-conspiracy, the comparable amount of tetracycline was selling for about $5. Every time a consumer purchased a 100-capsule bottle, he paid about $46 extra to the druggist and producer because of an illegal conspiracy. In every illegal conspiracy such computations can be made, as corporations steal money from consumers.

Assuming what Justice Holmes termed the "bad man" theory of law, that there are individuals who scheme to break the law if it benefits them, what are the countervailing costs which could dissuade such business crime? There are four basic sanctions — imprisonment, criminal fines, treble damages, and loss of good will. Yet undermining the impact of *all* these sanctions are the no-contest (or *nolo contendere*) plea and the general judicial antipathy to antitrust.

By a no-contest plea a defendant admits without trial that he committed the alleged offense. Theoretically, it can subject the defendant to the same fines and sentences as if he had pleaded guilty. In fact, judges sentence far more leniently after a *nolo* plea than after a guilty plea or guilty conviction, and the press and public tend to treat a defendant entering a *nolo* plea as having technically violated the law, but not seriously. Most significantly, a *nolo* plea counts as a "consent decree" under Section 5(a) of the Clayton Act, which says that "consent judgments or decrees entered before any testimony has been taken" are not *prima facie* evidence in later civil proceedings. If later plaintiffs seeking damages from the defendants could refer to an earlier admission of criminal guilt by defendants as proof that they are liable for provable damages, the plaintiffs' case would be greatly benefited. This can be done with a guilty plea or an adjudication of guilty, but *not a* no-contest plea. This freedom from later liability is a key motive for the frequency with which defendants plead no contest. "Its value to defendants is incalculable," concludes a *Yale Law Journal* article on the subject.

In the history of the antitrust laws, 73% of all convictions have been via *nolo contendere*. (In the past decade it has been 79%.) Judges usually overrule government objections to disposing of a criminal case by such a mild rebuke. Between fiscal 1960 and fiscal 1970, courts accepted *nolo* pleas in 95% of the cases where the government opposed it. . . .

Even more subversive of antitrust enforcement than the judicial preference for *nolo contendere* pleas is the frequent judicial hostility toward any antitrust prosecution. District Court Judge Leon Yankwich undoubtedly reflected the views of many others on the bench when he said in one private antitrust case, "Antitrust laws are a part of America's romantic dream, which can never be realized in modern economics and [can never] actually maintain competition in a modern industrial system."

The district court of Los Angeles, where many antitrust cases are heard, is among the nation's worst in this regard. Judge Charles Carr has greeted Antitrust Division attorneys as they enter the courtroom with a "Well, here come the drop-dead guys from Washington" — which, we're told, refers to his opinion that government lawyers act like big shots. The late Chief Judge Thurmond Clarke in the same district viewed antitrust crime with equanimity. The 1963 *United Fruit* indictment charged that firm and two of its officials with successfully monopolizing the importation of bananas into the Western states. *Nolo* pleas were accepted by Judge Clarke, who then fined United Fruit and the two individual defendants — who had reaped millions of dollars of illegal profits for years due to their criminal scheme — a grand total of $4,000. . . .

While the frequency of no-contest pleas and antagonistic judges reduces the deterrent potential of the four basic sanctions, each one is already perforated with exceptions and non-enforcement.

Imprisonment

The likelihood of a white-collar antitrust criminal spending time in prison is near nil. Even in the 1940s, when a record number of criminal cases were filed, there was not one case where a defendant was actually incarcerated. Since 1890, 461 individual defendants have been sentenced to prison. Most were labor racketeers or mixed violence with a labor or management scheme. In all but 26 criminal cases between 1890 and 1969, according to Richard Posner, the sentences were immediately suspended. Of these remaining 26, only *three* involved pure price-fixing by businessmen. The first prison sentence ever actually served for pure price-fixing by businessmen (*i.e.*, without the involvement of labor or violence) occurred in 1959. From fiscal 1960 to fiscal 1970 there have been only two cases, out of 188 criminal cases brought (counting all the electrical-equipment cases as one), where some business defendants have served jail sentences of from one to 60 days: the electrical-equipment cases and the plumbing-fixtures case.

The reasons for the absence of prison terms are multiple. The Antitrust Division often reserves jail recommendations for big cases, and then gets them in neither the big nor the small since judges are unimpressed that sentences were not requested in earlier, smaller cases. The Division also prefers indicting corporations rather than individuals because (a) it is easier to prove institutional guilt than personal guilt, and because (b) juries are often loath to sentence a white-collar defendant to prison. Alan Dershowitz, professor of law at Harvard, taking note of the prior point, wrote that "because the corporation is a term on a very high level of abstraction, it frequently tends to conceal the real actors in a given situation."

Point (b) is obvious to Division trial attorneys. It is difficult to convince 12 jurors that a mass of economic data, interspersed by some conduct by the defendants, equals criminal guilt beyond a reasonable doubt. Yet even when the evidence is strong, a form of jury nullification can occur where the jurors realize that a well-dressed, white, wealthy, articulate father of three might actually go to jail with unkempt, nonwhite, poor, uneducated street criminals. At times, when a jury has been told that a corporation can only act through its agents, and that if the individual agents are innocent the corporation cannot be guilty, the jury has *still* acquitted the individuals and convicted the corporations. Such *non sequiturs* lead some courts to rue, "We cannot understand how the jury could have acquitted all of the individual defendants. As a matter of logic, reconciliation . . . is impossible"; and, "How an intelligent jury could have acquitted any of the defendants we cannot conceive."

If juries have difficulty convicting respectable businessmen, judges are overtly deferential. Judge George Hart of the United States District Court in Washington, D.C., like many of his colleagues, does not require indicted defendants in antitrust cases to be fingerprinted and photographed as other criminal defendants would be. (Why? Are the rich somehow different? "Yes. They have money," said Ernest Hemingway.) When judges were asked, "Why do so few convicted Sherman Act violators ever serve jail sentences?" in the Judges' Questionnaire, some of the typical replies were: "Recidivism is unlikely," "Violators are *not* hardened criminals," "Defendants are victims of economic forces," and "Not clear in corporate case that guilty ones are in court."[2] In the defendant's chair a judge sees someone who looks as he does, who may belong to the same country-club milieu, or who, at the very least, is the kind of client he represented in his former law practice. This simpatico style has implications beyond the defendant. One interviewee told us that "it is best to find the judge's friend or law partner to defend an antitrust client — which we have done."

Leniency toward corporate criminality contrasts with the often sadistic sentences imposed on street criminals. A year after seven electrical manufacturers were sent to jail for 30 days apiece, a man in Asbury Park, New Jersey, stole a $2.98 pair of sunglasses and a $1 box of soap and was sent to jail for four months. A George Jackson was sent to prison for 10 years to life for stealing $70 from a gas station, his third minor offense; and in Dallas one Joseph Sills received a 1,000-year sentence for robbing

$73.10. Many states send young students, who are marijuana first of-
fenders, to jail for five to 10 years. But the *total* amount of time spent in
jail by all businessmen who have violated the antitrust laws is a little
under two years. Yet the electrical conspiracy alone robbed the public
more than all other robberies and thefts in 1961 combined. This timidity
toward antitrust violators is understood well by the violators themselves,
for "recidivism" is not a word monopolized by preventive-detention advocates. Richard Posner found that at least 46 of 320 corporations convicted of a criminal violation between 1964 and 1968 had been previously
convicted. But repeaters were punished no more severely than new defendants in the same case.

When prison sentences are imposed, they require an unusual combination of circumstances. As in the electrical and plumbing-fixtures cases,
defendants may go to jail if their actions are flagrant, willful, affect substantial commerce on a national scale, and involve businessmen sneaking
around hotel rooms conversing in code. Even then it took personal pleas
from an Assistant Attorney General and an Attorney General, as well as
the happy coincidence of a strict, intelligent judge, to send the electrical
executives to prison. . . .

Criminal Fines

From 1890 to 1955 the maximum Sherman Act fine was $5,000 per viola-
tion; in 1955 it was increased to $50,000 per violation. It should be im-
mediately apparent that both maxima are dwarfed by the average $48
million profit of the 500 top industrial firms in 1969. Yet however inconsequential they are as compared to the size of the defendants, the *actual*
fines levied are usually far below the maximum possible. Between 1946
and 1953, for example, the average Sherman Act fine was $2,600. The
tenfold increase in possible penalties in 1955 did little to concern corporate boardrooms: between 1955 and 1965 corporate fines averaged
$13,420 and individual fines $3,365.

From 1955 to 1962 the maximum fine was never imposed on an individual and was assessed against corporations in only four of the more than
130 Sherman Act cases where fines were imposed. (The frequency increased somewhat between July, 1966, and December, 1969, when nine
criminal cases out of 44 had defendants who suffered the $50,000 fine.)
But even in the very serious electrical cases the maximum $50,000 fine
was imposed only one out of 159 total sentences. The average corporate
fines per count in these cases was $16,500, although the commerce
affected totaled some $7 billion (or an overcharge of approximately $840
million based on a modest 12% estimated inflated price); on one occasion
the fine was one ten-millionth of the net profit aggregated during the
period of the indictment. While some court-imposed fines achieve com-

pensation and others create deterrence, antitrust fines have the distinction of doing neither. . . .

Treble-Damage Suits

Such actions under Section 4 of the Clayton Act could be a great deterrent to price-fixing. The theory is that any person who can prove damages from the illegal conspiracy can then recover three times his damages from the corporate defendant. The multifold return was intended to spur such private suits, which would both penalize the violator and indemnify the victim.

Again, neither goal has been attained. "Judicial reluctance to ease the path of treble-damage plaintiffs," Victor Kramer has written, "demonstrates that our courts are not prepared to emphasize the role of punishment in antitrust law enforcement." For a number of reasons — the high rate of no-contest pleas, the difficulty of proving actual damage, the inhibitions of many harmed companies to sue a brother firm, and procedural obstacles — private treble-damage suits have never realized their potential and have not created a serious deterrence to antitrust crime. . . . A recent *Yale Law Journal* article concluded that "in the overwhelming majority of all cases in which the government convinced a court that a violation of the antitrust laws had been committed, the convicted corporation paid nothing to private claimants in the form of damages or settlement."

Until 1970, even if a successful suit was brought against a price-fixing corporation, the pain was cushioned by the Internal Revenue Service. Revenue Ruling 64–224 in 1964 upheld the policy that treble-damage payments are tax deductible from income as an "ordinary and necessary [business] expense." Put another way, the ruling says: If you have to pay money for corporate criminality, the government in effect will subsidize one-half of the penalty, since corporations are taxed at 52% of net profits. (This deduction is only for treble damages, not the Sherman Act fines, which are far lower than damage payments.). . . .

Goodwill

A potentially powerful deterrent occurs when a corporation's goodwill is damaged by an antitrust conviction. "Who steals my purse steals trash," protested Iago, "but he that filches from me my good name . . . makes me poor indeed." So it is with corporations, who do not mind paying minor sums out of their coffers but do mind if their reputation is dimmed in consumers' minds. The disinterest of the news media, which underplay or ignore corporate crime, eases the burden of this informal stigma. And, as already stressed, "nolo" does not ring in people's minds as does "guilty." At times, however, business firms and law firms still contort to maintain the fiction that a *nolo* plea, while legally an admission of guilt, really concedes nothing at all, or even that a guilty plea doesn't mean quite that. Former Attorney General Herbert Brownell represented Westinghouse during the 1961 courtroom proceedings. Upon pleading his client guilty to seven counts, he had the pluck to assert that Westinghouse "does not admit the allegations of any of these indictments, but is simply changing its pleas for the purpose of promptly disposing of pending litigation."

In sum, the network of sanctions which aim to deter antitrust criminality do not outweigh the possible benefits to the violator. The meager fines imposed and even treble-damage payments become merely costs of doing business. This is the conclusion, among others, of H. N. McMenimen, Jr., consultant-analyst to the Law Department of the City of New York. He conducted a study for the City of New York, which is a huge purchaser of various commodities, to see if existing penalties discouraged antitrust violators. He found they did not, with one key element being the "interest-free borrowing" which indirectly occurs when one firm uses another's money (via an antitrust violation) for a long period of time. Based on six case studies, with some involving firms who had their damage payments trebled, McMenimen concluded:

> Indictment by a federal grand jury, punishment inflicted through criminal action, the payment of trebled damages resulting from civil trials, all legal costs incurred in the process, *none of these nor any combination of them succeeds today in denying the price fixer a profit realization at least double a normal level.* [Emphasis supplied.]

This view is corroborated by other interested authorities. Robert F. Lanzillotti and Joel Dirlam argued that for the rational businessman interested in profit maximization, "antitrust involvement may even mean a sizable profit factor and reliable revenue stabilizer." W. Bruce Erickson of the University of Minnesota conducted a careful study of the possible profitability of price-fixing based on four factors: the likelihood of getting caught; the proportion of sales involved in the treble-damage litigation; the length of time between discovery of the violation and the payment of damages; and the relationship between profits derived by the violator and the judge's or jury's evaluation of single damages. Even assuming that *all* antitrust violations are detected, Erickson concluded that "the typical violation may be profitable." When, more realistically, the probability of detection is assumed to be 50% or far less, "in all cases . . . antitrust violations are profitable, even after the possibility of treble damage payments is considered. . . . [T]he profitability of violations in high-return industries is impressive."

The electrical-equipment and tetracycline cases, where the settlements to purchasers were among the largest in antitrust history, support these three studies. Manufacturers of electrical equipment paid out approximately $500 million to their overcharged victims; these were basically single damages or less, since all the private cases except four were settlements, not court-imposed treble damages. But a member of the GE antitrust-settlement unit told the Study Group that his firm overcharged customers by at least 12%. Based on the $7 billion of commerce affected, as charged by the criminal complaint (which covers only some of the years of the conspiracies), he estimated that excess profits due to the price-fixes were at least $840 million. An estimated $300 million-plus profit was therefore shared by all the defendants — even *after* damage payments and assessed fines. As a second example, drug houses selling certain broad-spectrum antibiotics have paid out about $29 million to individual consumers in settlement of private litigation. Using conservative estimates, Paul Scanlon, an attorney for some of the plaintiffs, estimates that a $630 million overcharge, not $29 million, was retained in the years at issue, 1954–61. Again, as always, collusion was highly profitable.

REFERENCES

1. In 1957 a major meeting, apportioning the TVA 500,000-kilowatt contract to GE, occurred at the Barclay Hotel in New York. Three years later this hotel suavely advertised itself in *The New York Times:* "Antitrust-corporation secrets are best discussed in the privacy of an executive suite at the Barclay."

2. In 1959 four manufacturers of garden tools were sent to jail for 90 days each. On the way to begin serving his sentence, one defendant shot and killed himself. The well-publicized incident cooled any inclination judges did retain toward prison sentences.

41. KIND AND USUAL PUNISHMENT
IN CALIFORNIA

Jessica Mitford

The California prison empire, largest in the world with a population of 28,400 convicted felons, of whom roughly 45 percent are nonwhite, is widely regarded by many as a model of advanced, humane penology. (I am speaking here not of the city and county jails, universally recognized as hellish places, but of the state penitentiaries for felons serving long sentences.) It has incorporated as its stated policy reforms fought for over the decades: rehabilitation, as opposed to punishment; classification of prisoners based on their performance in prison; a chance for every offender to return to the community as soon as he is ready. Its policies and practices are studied and often emulated in other states.

Dr. Karl Menninger, in *The Crime of Punishment*, lavishes unstinted praise on it:

The California correctional system . . . has been far out in the lead among the states, with excellent programs of work, education, vocational training, medical services, group counseling, and other rehabilitative activities. A notable feature is the combination of diagnosis, evaluation, treatment, and classification. . . . This constitutes a systematic effort along scientific principles to ascertain from collected case-history data and from firsthand examination just what the assets and liabilities of the floundering individual are.

Observers closer to the California prison scene — criminologists, legislative researchers, sociologists, lawyers — who look past the rhetoric of reform into the realities of prison life, disagree profoundly with these observations. Dr. Bernard L. Diamond, professor of criminology and of law and clinical professor of psychiatry at the University of California, told me: "In 'good' prisons, like those in California, physical degradation is replaced by psychological degradation. I call these 'pastel' prisons; they look good, shiny, sanitary. Inmates will tell you thousands of ways in which they are psychologically degraded." And prisoners and parolees, who are the supposed beneficiaries of the new, enlightened penology in this best of all possible correctional worlds, denounce it as bureaucratic window-dressing designed to impress the public, behind which their lot has, if anything, deteriorated.

In the course of writing this piece I have met with criminologists, prison administrators, ex-convicts, legislators, lawyers. I have dipped into the voluminous prison literature, much of it, alas, as forbidding as the jailhouse itself, couched in the mind-glazing language of sociology: ". . . the prison as a formal or complex organization, a large-scale, multi-group organization characterized by a task orientation, functional specialization, and role-reciprocity," as one writer puts it. I have learned the latest terminology, which no doubt makes everything just a little bit nicer for the convicted felon: prison/*correctional facility*, prisoner/*inmate*, guard/*correctional officer*, initial lockup/*Reception and Guidance Center*, solitary confinement/*adjustment center*, or better yet, *meditation cell*. I have been warned by prison officials not to believe what convicts will tell you, and by convicts not to believe their keepers.

How to find a focus in this arcane world, with its complex of juvenile detention homes, city and county jails, federal and state penitentiaries? My inquiry is directed not to the excesses but to the norm, the state of prisoners' rights in a reform prison setting, specifically that of California's state prisons for men.

California pioneered in the adoption of the indeterminate sentence for felony offenders. Under this system the legislature sets the minimum and maximum term for each offense (for example, burglary, second degree, one to fifteen years; robbery, five years to life; sale of marijuana, five years to life), and the judge, instead of sentencing the defendant to a specific term, simply remands him to the state prison "for the term prescribed by law."

As conceived by its advocates among the early reformers, the indeterminate sentence is integral to rehabilitation. The idea was to grant an earlier discharge than would be possible under a determinate sentence to those prisoners who demonstrate by their behavior a readiness to return to the community. The sentencing power would be removed from a possibly prejudiced trial judge and placed in the hands of skilled experts in human behavior. These experts would look at the man rather than his crime, take into account all the circumstances, and make a prognosis for his rehabilitation via the aforementioned "excellent programs of work, education, vocational training."

But there is another side to this coin. To prison administrators, the indeterminate sentence is a potent instrument for inmate control. "The Corrections people never lost sight of its punitive advantages; in fact, they seized on it as the best control measure ever handed to them," a sociologist told me.

It's a hell of a lot more effective for maintaining discipline than the whip. In effect, the message to the prisoners is: "Keep this joint running smoothly and we'll let you out earlier." Conversely, they can keep the really "dangerous" criminal in almost indefinitely. Yet, who is to decide which is the "dangerous" man? This category is elastic enough to embrace political nonconformists, inmate leaders of ethnic groups, prison troublemakers. From the vindictive guard who sets out to build a record against some individual, to the parole board, the indeterminate sentence grants Corrections the power to play God with the lives of inmates.

While the indeterminate sentence implies a policy of early release for the rehabilitated offender, it is also a means of assuring much longer sentences for the troublesome element than would normally be imposed by judges; the theme that judges do not give long enough sentences, that under the determinate sentence system miscreants are let out too soon, recurs in the writings of nineteenth-century penologists. The indeterminate sentence reassures the public on both counts: by promising a benevolent prison system wherein criminals will be dealt with as fairly as their fallen state deserves, and by offering the assurance that only those who are thoroughly "safe" will be loosed on the community.

In California, sentencing and paroling of male convicts is entrusted to a nine-member Adult Authority, according to its published literature "composed of persons who have demonstrated skills, abilities, and leadership in many fields."

Its members are appointed by the governor for four-year terms. The composition of the present board is not easily squared with its self-appraisal. It is, with the lone exception of a retired dentist, drawn from the ranks of law enforcement and Corrections: former policemen, prosecutors, FBI and prison personnel. This board wields total, arbitrary, despotic power over the destinies and liberties of California's state prison population, not only while they are in custody but also after they have been released on parole.

Under cover of the indeterminate sentence, the median term served by California's "felony first releases" had by 1968 risen to thirty-six months, highest in the nation and probably the world. Without exception, prisoners in jurisdictions that have adopted the indeterminate sentence serve more time month-for-month than those in jurisdictions where the judge sets the maximum term of imprisonment and the parole board has to operate within that maximum.

At a meeting of ex-convicts, I asked what they conceived to be the major grievances of the California prison population. There was near unanimity: surprisingly, the wretched physical conditions of prison life are by no means their major concern. The food, they said, is generally lousy. Medical treatment amounts to criminal neglect in many instances. Overcrowding, which leads to every sort of problem from aggravated homosexual assaults and inmate fights to filthy living conditions, is endemic in most of the "correctional facilities." The highly touted vocational training is a fraud; in San Quentin there are 350 places in the trade programs for a population of over 3,500 (you have to be on a waiting list for eighteen months or more to get in), and even in the minimum-security conservation camps there is little opportunity to learn skills that will be useful on the outside.

But these features of prison existence, disheartening, degrading, and dangerous though they are, pale in importance, say the former convicts, beside the total arbitrariness of the bureaucracy that rules every aspect of their existence. One former inmate summed it up: "Don't give us steak and eggs; get rid of the Adult Authority! Don't put in a shiny modern hospital; free us from the tyranny of the indeterminate sentence!"

The convicts see themselves trapped in a vise between, as one put it, "the punitive nineteenth-century guard and the 1984 headshrinker." Most prison authorities still regard "protection of the public" and "deterrence" (meaning lockup and punishment) as the primary functions of the penal system, the traditional rigors and privations of which the prisoner must endure. Overlaid on these are the modern "therapy" and "treatment" goals. The offender must not only pay his debt to society in the old-fashioned way of "doing his time," but in addition he must prove that the modern treatment method has worked, that he is cured, rehabilitated, and ready for parole.

In an essay about English prisons written shortly after World War I (which could have been written yesterday about American reform prisons, so pertinent is its application to these), George Bernard Shaw points out the fundamental incompatibilities of the proclaimed goals of prison officialdom. Reformation, he says, is "a false excuse for wickedness . . . if you are to punish a man you must injure him. If you are to reform him, you must improve him. And men are not improved by injuries. . . . We are told that the reformation of the criminal is kept constantly in view; yet the destruction of the prisoner's self-respect by systematic humiliation is deliberately ordered and practiced."

Implementation of these conflicting goals is what modern prison life is all about.

In the opinion of many sociologists, the "combination of diagnosis, evaluation, treatment, and classification" so highly rated by Dr. Karl Menninger is in fact the Catch-22 of modern prison life, "a grand hypocrisy in which custodial concerns, administrative exigencies, and punishment are all disguised as treatment," as John Irwin puts it in *The Felon*. According to a California legislative committee report, most inmates look upon treatment programs as "phony"; "Seventy percent of inmates polled answered 'yes' to the question, 'Do you believe that therapy and treatment are games?'"

To decline to play, however, can be dangerous indeed. The prisoner who refuses to submit to therapy will find himself labeled "defiant," "hostile," "uncooperative," and the classification committee will act accordingly by confining him in a maximum-security prison — not, of course, as punishment, but as the next logical step in his treatment. If he continues in his "defiance," the parole board will hear about it, and he will end up serving twice the sentence normally imposed for his offense. Little wonder that the legislative committee concluded, "Most cons know how to walk that walk, talk that talk, and give the counselor what he wants to hear."

An ex-convict described the therapy program to me as "vicious, attritional. The whole point of the psychological diagnosis is to get the prisoner to go for the fact he's 'sick,' yet the statement he's sick deprives him of his integrity as a person. Most prisoners I know would rather be thought bad than mad. They say society may have a right to punish them, but not a hunting license to remold them in its own sick image."

Thomas S. Szasz, M.D., a specialist in the interrelationship of law and psychiatry, concurs:

Most of the legal and social applications of psychiatry, undertaken in the name of psychiatric liberalism, are actually instances of despotism. The thesis that the criminal is a sick individual in need of treatment — which is promoted today as if it were a recent psychiatric discovery — is false. Indeed it is hardly more than a refurbishing, with new terms, of the main ideas and techniques of the inquisitorial process . . . [the deviant] is first discredited as a self-responsible human being, and then subjected to humiliating punishment defined and disguised as treatment.

As summed up by Caleb Foote, a law professor at the University of California: "The alleged rehabilitation goal in a prison setting is to some extent a smoke screen to satisfy an ambivalent public, which sometimes feels guilt at merely punishing, and is primarily a managerial device to make it easier to manipulate prisoners in ways that minimize administrative problems."

As for the lockup and punishment aspects of prison, the view from the top is benign. California Corrections Department publicity stresses "more than just warehousing these individuals, humane conditions, rehabilitative efforts. . . ." Ray Procunier, director of Corrections, told me that the department's aim is to treat prisoners as human beings: "Prisoners are people in trouble — what can we do to help repair their lives? We're trying to create a climate in which a man can learn to make his own choices, in which he can grow."

Yet the on-the-job attitude of keeper to kept is perhaps more accurately reflected in San Quentin's confidential "orientation booklet" for new prison employees and part-time personnel (such as college instructors) who may have occasional contact with the prisoners. It reads like instructions for entering a cage of wild animals: "Remember, CUSTODY is always first in order of importance." "Constant vigilance is the price of efficient custody." "Always imply that you expect the correct attitude." "Be constantly on the look-out for contraband, especially weapons of any kind." "Never show the slightest uncertainty as to the course of your action. You must be a leader in the strongest sense of the word; must know and show your authority." "Do not fraternize with any inmate or group of inmates. *It could cost you your job.*" (Emphasis in the original.)

Corrections Department policy regarding inmate discipline, as stated in the director's rules, is "to develop in the inmate self-reliance, self-control, self-respect, self-discipline," and "the ability and desire to conform to accepted standards for individual and community life in a free society." Discipline shall be administered, says the rule book, "in such a way as to conserve human values and dignity and to bring about desirable changes in attitude."

Attainment of these goals is the task of a three-member hearing committee consisting of the associate warden and two other officers, before whom the prisoner accused of breaking the rules is brought. The hearing lasts typically from two to ten minutes. The prisoner is not permitted to confront or cross-examine his accuser, or to call witnesses in his defense, nor may his lawyer be present.

Given the nature of this proceeding, a guilty verdict would appear inevitable. I asked a recent graduate of the California prison system whether, in fact, there would ever be a finding of not guilty by the disciplinary committee. His answer: "No, they wouldn't do that because it would mean taking the word of a convict over that of a guard. But if they really do believe you are innocent, they'll find you guilty and let you off with a reprimand." Punishment for disciplinary infractions may range from loss of privilege (mail, visitors, and so forth) to twenty-nine days of confinement in the "Adjustment Center" (formerly known as "solitary" and recently described by a San Francisco *Examiner* reporter as "a species of human zoo").

The punishment does not end with these privations. His record blotted, the prisoner who falls afoul of the committee will be moved out of the category of "normal" prisoner, and hence will serve more than the sentence normally imposed for his crime.

Jurisdiction of the prison disciplinary committee extends not only to the infractions of the prison *rules* but to *crimes* such as theft, assault, murder. While these are as a matter of policy reported to the district attorney, he seldom prosecutes — why should he?, the reasoning goes. The accused is already serving a prison sentence. Under the indeterminate-sentence law he can be locked up almost indefinitely by the simple expedient of referring the case to the Adult Authority, which will readily accommodate and reset his sentence at the maximum.

What if the prisoner accused of a felony maintains he is innocent and demands a court trial with all of the procedural safeguards — right to counsel, right to cross-examine his accusers and to call witnesses in his defense? I pursued this question with James Park, associate warden at San Quentin, and with Ray Procunier.

"He hasn't a right to a trial," said Mr. Park. "We find him guilty or not guilty administratively."

"But, how can you be sure he is guilty, if no witnesses are called and no evidence given?"

"That's simple; we know who did it from the other inmates," explained Mr. Park with the weary patience of one who has suffered through these questions before. "If several reliable inmates point to this guy, or refuse to clear him, we know he's guilty. We don't have the type of case we could take to court: it would be too dangerous for our inmate-informers to have to testify. You middle-class due-processors don't understand; it's an administrative matter, not judicial."

And Mr. Procunier: "We have to deal with communities within communities. We must decide where the inmate is to be housed. He stabs somebody — we can't prove it, but we know he did it. The truth of these things is pretty obvious in an enclosed institution. We don't have the arresting officer at the hearing because we don't want to get involved in an adversary sort of argument."

The crucial moment in the prisoner's life is his hearing before the Adult Authority, which will determine whether or not to set his sentence, whether or not to grant a parole date. If he is serving five years to life, he is legally eligible for parole after twenty months, one third of the minimum term. His first hearing will be eighteen months after he enters prison, and he will come before the board annually thereafter until it is ready to fix an "individualized" maximum term short of life and set a date for his release on parole.

The Adult Authority is under no legal obligation to set the sentence, and in practice it does not do so until it is ready to grant parole. By keeping the prisoner in perpetual suspense, never knowing from year to year what portion of his one-to-twenty or five-to-life sentence he will serve, the Adult Authority maintains maximum control over him for the entire period of his incarceration.

Assisted by a number of full-time case-hearing representatives, the Adult Authority makes the circuit of the prisons, splitting up into teams of two, to conduct the prisoner interviews. A prison staff member is present to brief the panel on the inmate's record, to make notes on his "attitude" during the hearing and comments made about him by the panel members after he has left, and to record the panel's decision.

Presumably to ensure a decision uninfluenced by the possible bias of prison authorities, the staff worker is not permitted to make recommendations to the panel. But since he is charged with reporting the institution's evaluation of the prisoner, the outcome is generally predetermined by his presentation.

There are no written guidelines for the conduct of the hearing, and if parole is denied, the prisoner is not entitled to know the reason. No transcript is made of the hearing. The prisoner's family, his counsel, and the press are excluded.

Compared with the prison disciplinary committee, the Adult Authority claims it is lavish in the time it accords to the convicts who come before it: according to its literature, the average is a little less than seventeen minutes per prisoner. At that, the panel does not give him its undivided attention. While one panel member conducts the interview, the other is reading the file on the next case.

From one who has been through it several times, I learned something about the interview from where the prisoner sits. Nasty, short, and sometimes brutish, he found it. "Seventeen minutes may be the mathematical average," he said. "In my experience, five to seven minutes is more like it."

The panel bases its decision largely on the contents of the prisoner's central file folder, a formidable pile of paper work containing everything the authorities know, or think they know, about him: probation officer's report, comments of trial judge and district attorney, psychiatric evaluation, reports by guards of disciplinary infractions. While guards are encouraged to familiarize themselves with the contents of the folder, neither the prisoner nor his lawyer is permitted to see it. The rationale: it contains "confidential psychiatric material" — a curious distortion of the privileged doctor-patient relationship, which is supposedly for the patient's benefit and subject to waiver by him. In prison, the privilege is waived not for the "patient" or his counsel, but for policing agencies and the FBI, who are permitted full access to everything concerning him.

Adult Authority policy is to rotate the panels, so that the man whose parole is denied year after year will confront a different duo each time. Nostrums for his rehabilitation vary, depending on the idiosyncracies of the individual panel members. "Panel Member A may be hipped on religion, and tell the prisoner to go to church every week," said my informant.

But fifty-two Sundays later, he comes before Panel Member Y, whose bag is Alcoholics Anonymous, and even if the prisoner doesn't happen to have a drinking problem, he'll be told, "Attend the AA for a year and then we'll see about a parole date." This can go on indefinitely, as long as they haven't set his sentence. If he shows his true feelings and says, "You're arbitrary and unjust," they will say he's not ready for parole. If he says he has benefited enormously from the rehabilitation programs, they may put him down as a smoothie and deny parole anyway. The prisoner is totally in the dark; he has no way of knowing on what they base their decision. Is it any wonder that when he eventually comes out he's bitter and full of revenge?

The Adult Authority's official orientation bulletin states, "The offense for which a man is committed is only one of the factors that the Adult Authority considers when making a decision." Other factors may be (and often are) alleged crimes for which the prisoner was arrested but never brought to trial, or crimes for which he was tried in a court of law and acquitted. The indeterminate-sentence law gives the Adult Authority the power to inflict any punishment it deems fit for these unproved crimes, its decision often based on hearsay in the form of letters from prosecutors or police agencies.

Inevitably, a politically appointed lay board such as the Adult Authority is bound to be influenced by changing public attitudes toward crime. Yet another "factor the Adult Authority considers" is newspaper publicity given to certain categories of crime. The luckless prisoner serving time for robbery whose parole hearing comes in the wake of a particular sensational, violent armed robbery that has made the front pages will find himself caught in the same spotlight, although in his own case no violence was alleged. Robbery having suddenly become the crime of the week, the prisoner is punished accordingly — not for his own offense, but for the one currently in the headlines — and his parole is denied.

I have tried to sketch those routine procedures of the California prison system that most closely affect the everyday lives of the majority of inmates. But it should not be inferred that psychological manipulation by prison personnel and the Adult Authority is the only means of coercion to which the convicts are subjected. In the background lurks the ever-present threat of physical brutality. Last year alone newspapers reported a number of abuses: a black inmate of San Quentin tear-gassed to death in his cell by guards; an experimental "fright drug" that produces terrifying sensations of suffocation and drowning administered by psychiatrists to unruly prisoners at Vacaville; three unarmed black convicts at Soledad shot to death in the exercise yard by a white guard stationed on a gun tower. The tip of the iceberg? Probably. Other allegations of mistreatment, smuggled out by inmates, are currently under investigation by lawyers and public officials, but most instances of brutality go unreported by victims or inmate witnesses for fear of reprisal.

The foregoing would seem to bear out the comment of a criminologist whom I consulted early in my inquiry. "Prisoners' rights?" he said. "That's an easy assignment; just turn in a sheaf of blank papers. They *haven't* any rights." Nevertheless, there are portents of change from three directions: the legislature, the courts, and the prisoner himself, whose muffled protests are at last beginning to be heard beyond the prison fastness. And the assumptions on which the prison system rests are being challenged from all sorts of quarters, not only by convicts and their supporters on the outside, but by some prison administrators, criminologists, and elements of government.

In a study entitled *The Effect of Criminal Sanctions,* the California State Assembly Committee on Criminal Procedure flatly declares that the prisons are meeting *none* of their proclaimed goals. They do not protect the public, because most crimes are unreported, unprosecuted, and "the great majority of criminals are in the community, not in prison." Long prison terms not only do not deter, they have the opposite effect; numerous studies show that the longer a man stays in prison, the more likely he is to return to crime when released. Ergo, "rehabilitation" is a delusion; in fact, the committee points out that "what is often neglected in official statements is not that prison fails to rehabilitate but the *active* nature of the destruction that occurs in prison." The Adult Authority, the committee found, "operates without a clear and rationally justified policy," is "legally and scientifically unequipped" for its responsibilities. "As a result, California general parole policy, reflecting emotion, not facts, has become increasingly conservative, punitive, and expensive."

Bills recently introduced in the California state legislature would for the first time establish due process in Adult Authority procedures in sentence-setting and paroling of prisoners, provide for court hearings in parole revocation cases, curb the powers of the Adult Authority, and change its composition (one bill would include an ex-convict in its membership).

There are signs that the traditional "hands-off" policy adopted by the courts in matters of prison administration is giving way. Heretofore the courts have generally refused to hear cases which challenge the conduct of prison administrators on the theory that judicial interference "would be prejudicial to the proper administration of discipline." Since the prisons are run for a benevolent purpose and are staffed with experts in the art of rehabilitation, the courts have reasoned, procedural restraints would be inappropriate. Thus in effect the courts have delegated the final word on acceptable prison practices to the guard on duty, and have been saying to the prisoner: "Once the jailhouse door has clanged behind you, there *is* no further law. You have no legal redress."

In the last few years there has been a marked increase in the number of lawsuits challenging traditional discretionary powers of prison personnel, and the interest in this litigation is reflected in a spate of law-review articles on the subject. The courts are being bombarded with writs by "prison lawyers," inmates who write their own. (In the heads-I-win-tails-you-lose prison setting this even presents certain advantages to the administration: while writ-writing and the study it involves can serve as a tranquilizer for the convict who undertakes it, it also enables the authorities to identify him as a malcontent and deal with him accordingly.) Few prisoner writs are successful. Yet their very volume exerts some pressure on the courts.

A more promising route to legal redress for the convicts may be at hand. The ranks of lawyers willing to undertake the difficult and unremunerative task of representing convicts are being fast augmented by a mutation of the genus lawyer emerging from the law schools. Top in his class or editor of his law review, he turns a deaf ear to the siren call of Wall Street law firms with their $15,000 starting salary and promise of future millions. Instead he batters at the doors of the impecunious civil-liberties firms, or works in a neighborhood OEO office, or happily starves in a legal-services commune.

His work brings him into daily contact with delinquents, "deviants," lawbreakers. Having successfully challenged arbitrary administrative power in the vast public-welfare domain, where because of recent court decisions the clichés of "grant" and "privilege" are giving way to new legal concepts of "entitlement," he is ready to champion the rights of prisoners, which he sees as inextricably linked with the rights of students, draftees, the mentally ill — all subject to the arbitrary rule of administrative despotism.

"We must mount a careful, concerted legal attack on the unconstitutionality of prisons," one of these told me.

The total discretion of prison authorities is the real issue. The composition of the Adult Authority isn't important — even if it *wasn't* loaded with cops, the prisoners wouldn't be better off. What's needed is a tool, a mechanism, a vehicle to review the deprivation of prisoners' rights within the closed prison world. Until we get that, even legislation won't help. If a bill were passed tomorrow granting all conceivable rights, as long as the courts say they won't go into the prison, the prisoner in reality has no rights, no way of enforcing the law.

When the courts do venture behind prison walls, they are aghast at the things that they see. In 1966 a U.S. district court, noting that this was the first inquiry of its kind into the procedures and practices of a state penal institution, made a firsthand investigation of maximum-security cells (described in Corrections handouts as "special units for problem inmates") in California's Soledad prison. The court declared that prison authorities had "abandoned elemental concepts of decency by permitting conditions to prevail of a shocking and debased nature," and ordered them to restore "the primal rules of a civilized community." Yet four years later, in 1970, a committee of black legislators investigated charges that black inmates of the self-same "special units" under jurisdiction of the self-same warden were targets of unbridled racism and brutality on the part of guards. The legislators concluded, "If even a small fraction of the reports received are accurate, the inmates' charges amount to a strong indictment of the prison's employees on all levels as cruel, vindictive, dangerous men."

In 1970, some landmark decisions were handed down signifying a new willingness on the part of some courts to intervene on behalf of prisoners. To cite two examples:

In a class action case brought by a number of Arkansas inmates, an Arkansas district court found that "confinement itself within a given institution" where conditions are "so bad as to be shocking to the conscience of reasonably civilized people" may amount to cruel and unusual punishment. The court declared that the Arkansas penitentiary system as it exists today is unconstitutional, and ordered authorities to "make a prompt and reasonable start toward eliminating the conditions that have caused the court to condemn the system. . . . The lives, safety, and health of human beings, to say nothing of their dignity, are at stake. . . . The start must be prompt and the prosecution must be vigorous."

In New York (whose prison system has been rated second only to

California's for its humane, enlightened policies) a district court reached some conclusions which, if they stand up on appeal, would call into question existing disciplinary practices in every penal institution in the country: "The prisoner carries with him to prison his right to procedural due process which applies to charges for which he may receive punitive segregation or any other punishment for which earned good time credit may be revoked . . . prisoners do not lose all of their rights under the Constitution when sentenced to prison." Finding that the inmate plaintiff was subjected to punitive segregation without due process for more than one year under "conditions which violate present standards of decency," the court awarded him damages against the prison authorities of $13,020.

Largely owing to the activities of prisoners themselves, the prison is fast becoming Topic A in the media. As manifestations of rising militancy in the black population — from southern sit-ins to northern ghetto riots — focused public attention on black demands in the sixties, so the current wave of prison disturbances (itself a spillover of black militancy) is forcing the public, the legislature, and the judiciary to turn unwilling eyes in the direction of that long-neglected secret world.

In the early sixties Black Muslim groups in the prisons forced an opening wedge. Regarded as prime troublemakers by the authorities, they nevertheless won important court decisions affirming their right to practice their religion behind bars. Today, prison administrators look back to those days with a certain nostalgia; Mr. Park told me he now considers the Muslims to be quite a constructive influence, especially compared with Panther groups, which are forming in all the facilities.

Convicts and their keepers alike agree that traditional prisoners' grievances are undergoing fundamental change. They ascribe various reasons for this:

1. Radical and revolutionary ideologies are seeping into the prisons. In spite of administrative vigilance, inmates manage to come by copies of the underground press, the works of Ché Guevara, Frantz Fanon, Mao Tse-tung. (This is a two-way street: the writings of prisoners are suddenly in great demand by publishers. Following the spectacular success of *Soul on Ice, Soledad Brother, An Eye for an Eye,* literary agents are scouting the prisons for convict talent.)

2. A new and more sophisticated type of offender is entering the prison system: the civil disobedient, the collegiate narcotics user, the black or brown militant. Racial antagonisms, traditionally fostered by guards as a convenient method of divide and rule, are beginning to break down. In late 1970, prison rebels in San Quentin, Soledad, and Folsom for the first time united across color lines, establishing black/white/brown committees to press their demands. There is a growing alliance between these prisoners and political activisits on the outside.

3. Whereas formerly prisoners tended to regard themselves as unfortunates whose accident of birth at the bottom of the heap was largely responsible for their plight, today many are questioning the validity of the heap. Search the tomes and scholarly articles on penology, and you will find therein the thesis (or bromide) that the prisons, once filled with the poor, the Irish, the Italian, are today filled with the poor, the black, the Chicano.

4. Increasing numbers of prisoners are beginning to look upon the whole criminal-justice system, with the penitentiary at the end of it, as an instrument of class and race oppression. The screening process begins with the policeman on the beat: the young car thief from a "nice home" will be returned to his family with a warning; for the identical crime the ghetto boy will be arrested and imprisoned in the juvenile detention home. Once in the toils of the system, he must submit or suffer the consequences. The nonconformist, the protester, the man who demands his constitutional rights, may never get out. "When is a person considered rehabilitated?" said a convict. "The official view is that one whose head is sufficiently bowed, who appears quiet and industrious, who no longer presents a threat to the white middle-class ethic of his captors, is 're-formed' and ready for parole."

In an essay addressed to prison and law-enforcement administrators, the associate warden of San Quentin examines "some characteristics of the new rebellion" as evidenced in the 1968 riots at San Quentin: "The age-old dissatisfactions of the convict were translated into a well-planned and sophisticated attack on state laws and policies, the operations of the paroling agency, the limitations on legal rights of parolees, the indeterminate sentence, and other issues far removed from the usual minor food grievances." He notes that "the intake of young inmates in the next few years will include many who have been exposed to the concepts of social revolution," and counsels administrators to read books on revolutionary techniques, as these "have been studied by many inmates and may be useful in understanding the thinking of inmate leaders."

His conclusion: participation of outside dissidents in prison turmoil is becoming an increasing problem for administrators, therefore "advance planning with local law-enforcement agencies regarding crowd control and the closing of access roads would be prudent."

My conclusion: the immediate opening up of vast new access roads not only would be prudent but is of imperative urgency. Prisons are traditionally secret places, hermetically sealed off from public and judicial scrutiny. The investigator is blocked at every turn, as I soon discovered in the course of this inquiry: my request to sit in on the Adult Authority hearings was officially turned down on the ground that "the presence of additional persons tends to distract the prisoners," and the warden of Soledad opined it would be "unwise" for me to visit his special units for problem inmates in view of the pending Soledad Brothers trial. True, I could have gone on one of the San Quentin guided tours for approved citizens, but after reading this instruction to prisoners in the Department of Corrections rule book, I didn't bother: "When visitors are present do not try to attract attention or talk with a visitor." Prisoners, it seems, like good children, should be seen and not heard.

I believe the first essential step is to penetrate the closed doors behind which the authorities, from prison administrator to parole board, operate. The new access roads should be broad enough to accommodate the courts, legislators, the media, political activists who are spearheading demands for fundamental change — and that amorphous entity, the public, which bears ultimate responsibility.